Monty Waldin

BIODYNAMIC
GARDENING

Senior Editor Helen Fewster
Senior Art Editor Sonia Moore
Senior Designer Alison Gardner
Design Assistant Amy Keast
Jacket Designer Sonia Moore
DK Picture Library Claire Cordier
Senior Producer Ché Creasey
Pre-production Producer Andy Hilliard
Managing Editor Penny Warren

Publisher Mary Ling
Art Director Jane Bull

Biodynamic Shoot Consultant Briony Young
Lead Photographer Will Heap

First published in Great Britain in 2015 by
Dorling Kindersley Limited
80 Strand, London, WC2R 0RL
A Penguin Random House Company

2 4 6 8 10 9 7 5 3 1

001–259425–March/2015

A CIP catalogue record of this book is available
from the British Library.

ISBN 978-1-4093-6938-7
Printed and bound in China by Hung Hing.

A WORLD OF IDEAS:
SEE ALL THERE IS TO KNOW

www.dk.com

DK CHILDREN'S ILLUSTRATED ENCYCLOPEDIA

SPECIAL EDITION

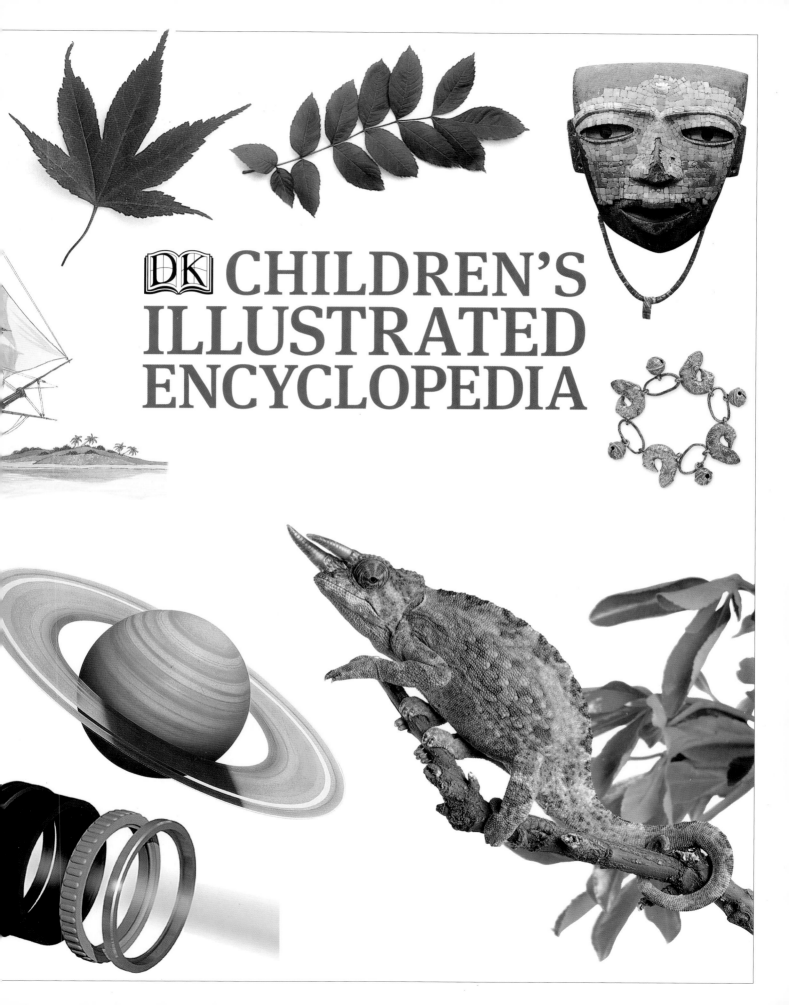

DK CHILDREN'S ILLUSTRATED ENCYCLOPEDIA

DK

LONDON, NEW YORK,
MELBOURNE, MUNICH, AND DELHI

SPECIAL EDITION 2010

Editors Suchismita Banerjee, Alicia Ingty, Ashwin Khurana
Designer Romi Chakraborty
Senior Art Editor Sheila Collins
Project Editor Jenny Finch
Managing Editor Linda Esposito
Managing Art Editors Jim Green, Diane Thistlethwaite
Category Publisher Laura Buller
Picture Researchers Myriam Megharbi, Karen VanRoss
DK Picture Library Martin Copeland
Senior Cartographic Editor Simon Mumford
Production Controller Angela Graef
Production Editors Balwant Singh, Marc Staples
Jacket Designer Natalie Godwin
Jacket Editor Matilda Gollon
Jacket Manager Sophia Tampakopoulos

FIRST EDITION 1991

Senior Editor Ann Kramer
Senior Art Editor Miranda Kennedy
Editors Christiane Gunzi, Susan McKeever,
Richard Platt, Clifford Rosney
Art Editors Muffy Dodson, Debra Lee,
Christian Sévigny, Val Wright

First published in Great Britain in 1991
This special edition published in 2010 by
Dorling Kindersley Limited,
80 Strand, London WC2R 0RL
Reprinted 1991, 1992 (twice), 1993
Reprinted with revisions 1992
Second edition 1993
Third edition 1995
Fourth edition 1996, reprinted 1997
1998, 1999
Fifth edition 2000
Sixth edition 2006
Special edition 2010

ISBN: 978-1-40356-232-0

Hi-res workflow proofed by Colourscan, Singapore
Printed and bound by Hung Hing, China

Discover more at
www.dk.com

Contents

HOW TO USE
THE WEBSITE 6

A

Africa 7-10
Africa, history of 11-12
Aircraft 13-14
Alphabets 15
Anglo-Saxons 16-17
Animals 18-19
Antarctica 20-21
Architecture 22-23
Arctic 24-25
Asia 26-29
Asia, history of 30-31
Assyrians 32
Astronauts and
space travel 33
Astronomy 34-35
Atlantic Ocean 36-37
Atmosphere 38
Atoms and molecules 39
Australia 40-43
Australia, history of 44-45
Aztecs 46

B

Babylonians 47
Big Bang 48
Birds 49-50
Black Death 51
Brain and nerves 52
Britain, Ancient 53
British Empire 54-55
Bronze Age 56
Byzantine Empire 57

C

Cameras 58
Canada 59-60
Caribbean 61-62
Cars 63-64
Castles 65-66
Celts 67
Central America 68-69
China 70-73
Climates 74
Cold War 75
Colour 76
Columbus, Christopher 77
Communism 78
Computers 79-80
Conservation and
endangered species 81-82
Continents 83
Crusades 84

D

Deep-sea wildlife 85-86
Democracy 87
Desert wildlife 88-89
Dickens, Charles 90
Digestion 91
Dinosaurs 92-93
Disease 94

E

Ears 95
Earth 96-97
Earthquakes 98
Ecology and food webs 99-100
Egypt, Ancient 101-102
Electricity 103-104
Electronics 105

Elizabeth I 106
Emigration and immigration 107
Energy 108
Engines 109-110
England 111
English Civil War 112
Europe 113-116
European Union 117
Europe, history of 118-119
Evolution 120-121
Explorers 122-123
Eyes 124

F · G

Farming 125
Films 126-127
Fire of London 128
Fish 129-130
Flowers and herbs 131-132
Force and motion 133
Forest wildlife 134-135
Fossils 136
French Revolution 137
Fruits and seeds 138-139
Genetics 140-141
Government and politics 142-144
Grassland wildlife 145-146
Gravity 147
Greece, Ancient 148-149
Gunpowder Plot 150

H · I

Heart and blood 151
Henry VIII 152
Hibernation 153
Horses, zebras, and asses 154-155
Human body 156-157
Human rights 158
Hundred Years War 159

Incas 160
Indian Ocean 161-162
Industrial Revolution 163-164
Information technology 165-166
Insects 167-168
Internet 169
Ireland 170-171
Iron Age 172

L

Lake and river wildlife 173-174
Languages 175
Law 176-177
Leonardo da Vinci 178
Light 179-180
Lions, tigers, and other
big cats 181-182
Literature 183-184
Lizards 185-186
Lungs and breathing 187

M

Machines 188-189
Magnetism 190
Mammals 191-192
Marsh and swamp wildlife 193
Maya 194
Medicine 195
Medicine, history of 196-197
Medieval Europe 198-199
Metals 200
Mexico 201-202
Microscopes 203
Money 204
Mongol Empire 205
Monkeys and apes 206-207
Moon 208
Mountains 209
Mountain wildlife 210
Muscles and movement 211
Mushrooms 212
Music 213-214
Musical instruments 215-216

N · O

Napoleon Bonaparte 217
New Zealand 218-219
Normans 220
North America 221-224
Northern Ireland 225
Nuclear energy 226
Numbers 227

Oceans and seas 228-229
Ocean wildlife 230-231
Olympic Games 232
Ottoman Empire 233
Oxygen 234

P

Pacific Ocean 235-236
Painters 237-238
Peasants Revolt 239
Persians, Ancient 240
Phoenicians 241
Pilgrims 242
Pirates 243
Planets 244-245
Plants 246-247
Polar wildlife 248-249
Pollution 250-251
Prehistoric life 252-253
Prehistoric peoples 254

R

Rain and snow 255
Reformation 256
Religions 257-258
Renaissance 259-260
Reproduction 261-262
Reptiles 263-264
Rivers 265
Robots 266
Rocks and minerals 267-268
Roman Empire 269-270

S

Satellites 271
Science 272
Science, history of 273-274
Scotland 275
Seashore wildlife 276-277

Shakespeare, William 278
Sharks and rays 279
Ships and boats 280-281
Skeletons 282-283
Slavery 284-285
Snakes 286
Sound 287
South America 288-291
South America, history of 292-293
Soviet Union, history of 294-295
Space flight 296-297
Spiders and scorpions 298
Stars 299-300
Stone Age 301
Storms 302
Stuarts 303
Sumerians 304
Sun 305

T

Technology 306-307
Teeth 308
Telephones 309
Telescopes 310
Television 311-312
Time 313
Trade and industry 314-315
Trains 316-317
Trees 318-319
Tudors 320

U · V · W

United Kingdom 321-324
United Kingdom, history of
325-326
United Kingdom, regional
history of 327-328
United Nations 329
United States of America 330-332
United States, history of 333-334
Universe 335

Victorians 336-337
Vietnam War 338
Vikings 339
Volcanoes 340

Wales 341
Water 342-343
Weather 344-345
Whales and dolphins 346-347
Wind 348
Women's rights 349
Wonders of the ancient world 350
World War I 351-352
World War II 353-354

X · Z

X-rays 355
Zoos 356

INDEX 357-362

ACKNOWLEDGEMENTS 363-364

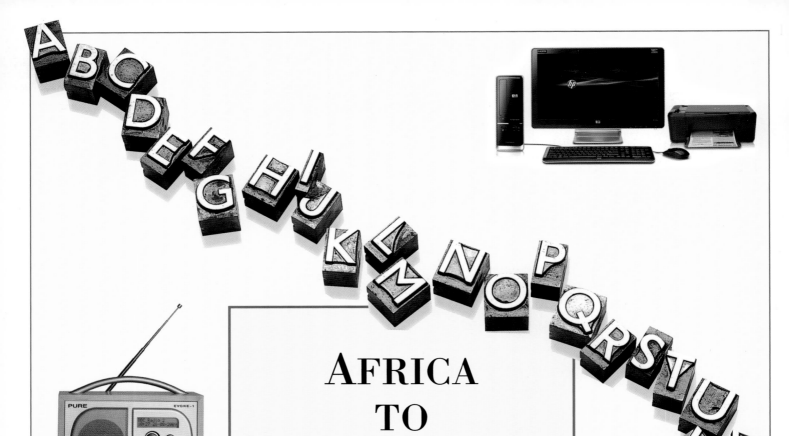

AFRICA
TO
ZOOS

HOW TO USE THE WEBSITE

1. Enter the website address
www.children.dkonline.com
2. Find the keyword at the top of the
page above the entry heading.
3. Enter the keyword.
4. Click on the chosen link.
5. Go back to the book for your
next chosen subject.
6. Enter a new keyword.

HAPPY SURFING!

AFRICA

FEW REGIONS OF THE WORLD are as varied as Africa. On this vast continent there are 53 independent nations and many times this number of peoples and ancient cultures. There are mountains, valleys, plains, and swamps on a scale not seen elsewhere. The northern coast is rich and fertile; below it lies the dry Sahara Desert. South of the Sahara, lush rainforest grows. Most of southern and eastern Africa is savanna, a form of dry plain dotted with trees and bushes. The nations of Africa are generally poor, though some, such as Nigeria, have rich natural resources. Many governments are unstable, and rebellions and civil wars are common. There are few large cities; most are near the coast. The rest of the continent is open countryside where people follow traditional lifestyles.

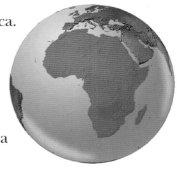

Africa is roughly triangular in shape. The Atlantic Ocean lies to the west and the Indian Ocean to the east. In the northwest only a few kilometres of sea separate the African continent from Europe.

SCHOOLS
Schools in African towns and cities are much like schools anywhere in the world. Sometimes, however, pupils must walk many kilometres from their homes to the schoolhouse.

The Tuareg peoples, who inhabit the Sahara, are pastoralists.

The Ashanti peoples of West Africa are mainly farmers.

The tall Masai of Kenya herd cattle on the open plains.

PEOPLE
In the African countryside many people live in tribal villages. Some, such as the Kikuyu of East Africa, are descended from tribes that have lived in the same place for many centuries. Others are recent immigrants from other parts of Africa or from other continents. Borders between countries take little account of these varied cultures. People of one culture may live in two different countries, and in one nation may be found more than a dozen different tribal groupings.

Few pygmies are taller than 1.25 m (4 ft). They live in the dense Congo rainforest.

The towers of mosques dominate Cairo's skyline.

The Bushmen roam the deserts of southern Africa and gather wild food from the harsh environment.

KILIMANJARO
The tallest and most beautiful mountain in Africa is Kilimanjaro, in Tanzania. Its highest peak, which rises 5,895 m (19,340 ft), is an extinct volcano. Although the mountain is only a few kilometres from the equator, the top is always covered in snow. A footpath leads to the top, which can be reached in three days from the nearest road. Many people live on the lower slopes, where they farm tropical fruit.

CAIRO
Cairo is the capital city of Egypt and the largest city in Africa, with a population of nearly 17 million. It sits on the River Nile near the head of the river's delta. The older part of the city contains narrow, winding streets. The new city has wider streets and many modern office buildings and flats. The people of Cairo are mostly Egyptian, although some come from all over North Africa, as well as from Europe and the Middle East.

SAHARA DESERT

The Sahara is the largest desert in the world and covers nearly one third of Africa. In recent years the desert has spread, destroying farmland and causing famine. In some areas irrigation has stopped the spread of the desert, but long-term irrigation can make the soil salty and infertile. Temperatures have been known to exceed 50°C (120°F) in this inhospitable environment.

MEDICINE AND HEALING

When seeking a cure for sickness, some Africans consult Western-style doctors. Others consult a traditional healer (above). Healers are respected members of a community, with vast knowledge of local herbs and plants and the ways in which they can be used as medicines. To identify the source of an illness, the healer might contact good or evil spirits by going into a trance. Treatment may include animal sacrifice.

In West Africa, drumming is a highly developed art. People once used drum beats to pass on messages.

MUSIC AND CULTURE

Africa has a rich and varied culture. North Africa shares the Islamic traditions of the Middle East, producing beautiful mosques and palaces. West African music has a strong rhythm, and there are many interesting dances from this region. The area is also home to a flourishing wood-carving industry. Eastern and southern Africa have become famous for beautiful beadwork and colourful festive costumes.

WAR AND FAMINE

Civil wars and famines are common in Africa. Many are caused by political disagreements, and some are the result of tribal conflicts. In Chad a civil war lasting many years was fought between the desert Tuaregs, backed by Libya, and the farmers of the wetter areas. In Rwanda and Burundi fighting between the Tutsi and Hutu tribes led to thousands of deaths. Other misery is caused by famine. Traditionally, most people grew enough food each year to last until the next harvest. However, African countries increasingly produce export crops and rely on imported food. If food distribution breaks down or drought ruins crops, thousands of people may starve.

RURAL LIFE

Although African cities have been growing fast, most Africans still live in the countryside. They grow their own food and only rarely have a surplus to sell or exchange for other goods. Many tribes have farmed the same land for generations, living in villages with all of their relatives. Sometimes the young men go to live in cities for a few years to earn money in mines or factories. Then they return to the village to marry and settle down. The types of crops grown vary widely. Yams, cassava, and bananas are produced in the lush tropical regions; farmers in drier areas concentrate on cattle and corn.

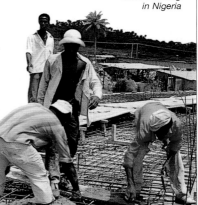

Road building in Nigeria

DEVELOPMENT

Poor infrastructure, including unreliable roads, railways, and electricity supplies, holds back the economic growth of many African nations. Most countries rely on loans from Western governments and international banks to pay for their development programmes.

Find out more

AFRICA, HISTORY OF
CONTINENTS
DESERT WILDLIFE
GRASSLAND WILDLIFE
HUMAN RIGHTS

POLITICAL AFRICA

Independent African states, with few exceptions, are territorially identical to the colonies they replaced. Until the 1960s, most of Africa was controlled by European countries as part of their overseas empires. By the late 1980s, nearly every country had gained its independence. In many cases, hasty attempts were made to set up European-style governments. Leaders often became dictators, or the army seized power. However, in recent years, there has been a shift towards multi-party democracy.

ALGERIA
Area: 2,381,740 sq km
(919,590 sq miles)
Population: 34,178,000
Capital: Algiers

ANGOLA
Area: 1,246,700 sq km
(481,551 sq miles)
Population: 12,799,000
Capital: Luanda

BENIN
Area: 112,620 sq km
(43,480 sq miles)
Population: 8,791,000
Capital: Porto-Novo

BOTSWANA
Area: 600,370 sq km
(231,804 sq miles)
Population: 1,991,000
Capital: Gaborone

BURKINA
Area: 274,200 sq km
(105,870 sq miles)
Population: 15,746,000
Capital: Ouagadougou

BURUNDI
Area: 27,830 sq km
(10,750 sq miles)
Population: 8,988,000
Capital: Bujumbura

CAMEROON
Area: 475,440 sq km
(183,570 sq miles)
Population: 18,879,000
Capital: Yaoundé

CAPE VERDE
Area: 4,033 sq km
(1,557 sq miles)
Population: 429,000
Capital: Praia

CENTRAL AFRICAN REPUBLIC
Area: 622,984 sq km
(240,535 sq miles)
Population: 4,511,000
Capital: Bangui

CHAD
Area: 1,284,000 sq km
(495,752 sq miles)
Population: 10,329,000
Capital: N'Djamena

COMOROS
Area: 2,170 sq km
(838 sq miles)
Population: 752,000
Capital: Moroni

CONGO
Area: 342,000 sq km
(132,040 sq miles)
Population: 4,013,000
Capital: Brazzaville

DEMOCRATIC REPUBLIC OF THE CONGO
Area: 2,345,410 sq km
(905,563 sq miles)
Population: 68,693,000
Capital: Kinshasa

DJIBOUTI
Area: 23,200 sq km
(8,958 sq miles)
Population: 516,000
Capital: Djibouti

EGYPT
Area: 1,001,450 sq km
(386,660 sq miles)
Population: 83,083,000
Capital: Cairo

EQUATORIAL GUINEA
Area: 28,050 sq km
(10,830 sq miles)
Population: 633,000
Capital: Malabo

ERITREA
Area: 117,600 sq km
(45,406 sq miles)
Population: 5,647,000
Capital: Asmara

ETHIOPIA
Area: 1,104,300 sq km
(426,373 sq miles)
Population: 85,237,000
Capital: Addis Ababa

GABON
Area: 267,670 sq km
(103,347 sq miles)
Population: 1,515,000
Capital: Libreville

GAMBIA
Area: 11,300 sq km
(4,363 sq miles)
Population: 1,783,000
Capital: Banjul

GHANA
Area: 239,460 sq km
(92,456 sq miles)
Population: 23,832,000
Capital: Accra

GUINEA
Area: 245,860 sq km
(94,926 sq miles)
Population: 10,058,000
Capital: Conakry

GUINEA-BISSAU
Area: 36,120 sq km
(13,940 sq miles)
Population: 1,534,000
Capital: Bissau

IVORY COAST
Area: 322,463 sq km
(124,503 sq miles)
Population: 20,617,000
Capital: Yamoussoukro

KENYA
Area: 582,650 sq km
(224,962 sq miles)
Population: 39,003,000
Capital: Nairobi

LESOTHO
Area: 30,350 sq km
(11,718 sq miles)
Population: 2,131,000
Capital: Maseru

LIBERIA
Area: 111,370 sq km
(43,000 sq miles)
Population: 3,442,000
Capital: Monrovia

LIBYA
Area: 1,759,540 sq km
(679,358 sq miles)
Population: 6,310,000
Capital: Tripoli

MADAGASCAR
Area: 587,040 sq km
(226,660 sq miles)
Population: 20,654,000
Capital: Antananarivo

MALAWI
Area: 118,480 sq km
(45,745 sq miles)
Population: 14,269,000
Capital: Lilongwe

MALI
Area: 1,240,190 sq km
(478,837 sq miles)
Population: 12,667,000
Capital: Bamako

MAURITANIA
Area: 1,030,700 sq km
(397,955 sq miles)
Population: 3,129,000
Capital: Nouakchott

MAURITIUS
Area: 2,040 sq km
(7172 sq miles)
Population: 1,284,000
Capital: Port Louis

MOROCCO
Area: 446,550 sq km
(172,414 sq miles)
Population: 34,859,000
Capital: Rabat

MOZAMBIQUE
Area: 801,590 sq km
(309,493 sq miles)
Population: 21,669,278
Capital: Maputo

NAMIBIA
Area: 824,290 sq km
(318,260 sq miles)
Population: 2,109,000
Capital: Windhoek

NIGER
Area: 1,267,000 sq km
(489,188 sq miles)
Population: 15,306,000
Capital: Niamey

NIGERIA
Area: 923,770 sq km
(356,668 sq miles)
Population: 149,229,000
Capital: Abuja

RWANDA
Area: 26,340 sq km
(10,170 sq miles)
Population: 10,473,000
Capital: Kigali

SÃO TOMÉ AND PRÍNCIPE
Area: 1,001 sq km
(386 sq miles)
Population: 213,000
Capital: São Tomé

SENEGAL
Area: 196,720 sq km
(75,950 sq miles)
Population: 13,712,000
Capital: Dakar

SEYCHELLES
Area: 455 sq km
(176 sq miles)
Population: 87,000
Capital: Victoria

SIERRA LEONE
Area: 71,740 sq km
(27,699 sq miles)
Population: 6,440,000
Capital: Freetown

SOMALIA
Area: 637,660 sq km
(246,200 sq miles)
Population: 9,832,000
Capital: Mogadishu

SOUTH AFRICA
Area: 1,221,040 sq km
(471,443 sq miles)
Population: 49,052,000
Capital: Pretoria/Tshwane

SUDAN
Area: 2,505,815 sq km
(967,493 sq miles)
Population: 41,088,000
Capital: Khartoum

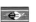
SWAZILAND
Area: 17,360 sq km
(6,703 sq miles)
Population: 1,124,000
Capital: Mbabane

TANZANIA
Area: 945,090 sq km
(364,900 sq miles)
Population: 41,049,000
Capital: Dodoma

TOGO
Area: 56,790 sq km
(21,927 sq miles)
Population: 6,020,000
Capital: Lomé

TUNISIA
Area: 163,610 sq km
(63,170 sq miles)
Population: 10,486,000
Capital: Tunis

UGANDA
Area: 236,040 sq km
(91,136 sq miles)
Population: 32,370,000
Capital: Kampala

ZAMBIA
Area: 752,614 sq km
(290,586 sq miles)
Population: 11,863,000
Capital: Lusaka

ZIMBABWE
Area: 390,580 sq km
(150,800 sq miles)
Population: 11,393,000
Capital: Harare

| Volcano | Mountain | Ancient monument | Capital city | Large city/town | Small city/town |

STATISTICS
Area: 30,065,385 sq km
(11,608,310 sq miles)
Population:
946,968,000
**Number of
independent countries:**
53
Highest point:
Kilimanjaro (Tanzania)
5,895 m (19,340 ft)
Longest river: Nile,
6,695 km (4,160 miles)
Largest lake: Lake
Victoria: 69,484 sq km
(26,828 sq miles)
Main occupation:
Agriculture

MINING
Africans have been mining and processing minerals, including iron ore, copper, and gold, for more than two thousand years. Gold mined in the forest country of western Africa was carried across the Sahara by African traders and exported to Europe and Asia. During the colonial period mining was intensified. Today, South Africa, Zimbabwe, Zambia, and Democratic Republic of Congo possess heavily industrialized mining areas. These areas have yielded minerals such as gold, diamond, copper, and uranium.

Large-scale drilling equipment (above) is used in the gold mining industry.

Dogon dancers (right) from Mali perform a funeral dance.

MASKS AND DANCE
Masked dance is performed in many communities in west and central Africa and plays an important part in social events. Once inside the costume, the person takes on the character represented by the mask. Often parts of the body are exaggerated with padding or pieces of wood (left). The dance steps, songs, and sounds complete the costume and energetically represent both the spirit world and the world of humans.

CAPE VERDE
The independent republic of the Cape Verde islands lies 620 km (385 miles) off the coast of Senegal, in the Atlantic Ocean. The islands have a population of 429,000, but almost twice this number of Cape Verdeans live abroad.

HORN OF AFRICA
Because of its shape, the easternmost point of the African continent is called the Horn of Africa. It is one of the poorest regions on Earth, with few natural resources. Droughts and civil wars have killed thousands of people and made many more homeless.

SAO TOME AND PRINCIPE
The volcanic islands of São Tomé and Príncipe form a republic with a population of 213,000. São Tomé, the larger island, lies just north of the equator.

GAME PARKS AND CONSERVATION
The animal life of Africa is rich and varied. However in the last century, numerous animal and plant species have been lost forever. As the land has been turned into farms and industrial sites, many animals have been driven from their habitats. Their numbers have also been severely reduced by hunters. To protect animals from extermination, several African governments have set aside large game reserves where hunting is prohibited.

SCALE BAR
0   400   800   km
0   400   800 miles

HISTORY OF
AFRICA

FOR MUCH OF ITS HISTORY, Africa has been hidden from outsiders' eyes. The Sahara Desert cuts off communication from north to south for all but the hardiest traveller. The peoples of Africa have therefore developed largely by themselves. By about 2600 BCE, rich and powerful empires such as Ancient Egypt had arisen. The empires have disappeared, but they left behind buildings and other clues to their existence. Other African peoples left records of their history in songs that have been passed down from parent to child through countless generations. Europeans remained ignorant of this rich history until, during the 1400s, they explored the west coast. Soon they were shipping thousands of Africans to Europe and the Americas as slaves, a "trade" that destroyed many traditional societies. During the late 1800s, Europeans penetrated the interior of Africa and, within 20 years, had carved up the continent between them. Almost all of Africa remained under European control until the 1950s, when the colonies began to gain their independence. Today, the peoples of Africa are free of foreign control.

Ivory traders

Bantu speakers originated here and spread to striped area.

Africa

BANTUS
Most of the peoples of southern Africa are related to the Bantus, who originated in the western part of the continent between 3000 and 2000 BCE. They had reached southern Africa by 400 CE.

GREAT ZIMBABWE

The stone city of Great Zimbabwe was a major religious, political, and trading centre in southern Africa between the 11th and 14th centuries. It grew rich on the proceeds of herding cattle and mining gold, copper, and iron. The peoples of Great Zimbabwe exported their produce to the coastal port of Sofala in what is now Mozambique, and then up the coast of Africa to Arabia.

Men armed with spears and shields guarded the city's walls.

Thatched buildings

City's walls were made from huge granite slabs.

Cattle herder

Great enclosure at Great Zimbabwe

BENIN
The West African kingdom of Benin reached the height of its power between the 14th and 17th centuries. Its people traded ivory, pepper, palm oil, and slaves with the Portuguese. They also excelled in casting realistic figures in bronze. On the left is a Benin bronze mask.

SOAPSTONE BIRDS
Soapstone carvings of local birds on columns stood in an enclosure outside Great Zimbabwe. One of these birds has been the national symbol of Zimbabwe since the country gained its independence in 1980.

ON THE SWOOP!

SCRAMBLE FOR AFRICA

Until the 1880s, European conquest in Africa was restricted to the coastal regions and the main river valleys. But European powers wanted overseas colonies (settlements). Throughout the 1880s and 1890s, European nations competed for land in Africa. By 1900, almost all of Africa was in European hands. The only independent states left were the ancient kingdom of Ethiopia in the east, and the free slave state of Liberia in the west. The cartoon (left) shows Germany as a bird "swooping" onto Africa.

ZULU WARS
Some African peoples managed to resist the Europeans for a time. After 1838, the Zulus of southern Africa fought first the Boers (Dutch settlers) and then the British. In 1879, however, Britain finally defeated the Zulus. In 1887, Zululand became a British colony. Above is a picture of the British trying to break through Zulu lines.

INDEPENDENCE
The coming of independence to much of Africa after 1956 did not always bring peace or prosperity to the new nations. Many were weakened by famines and droughts or torn apart by civil wars. Few have managed to maintain civilian governments without periods of military dictatorships. In 1964 Malawi (formerly Nyasaland) became Africa's 35th independent state. Above is the celebration scene.

APARTHEID

In 1948 the National Party came to power in South Africa. Years of segregation, known as apartheid, followed. This policy gave white people power but denied black people many rights, including the vote. In 1990 the African National Congress (ANC), a banned black nationalist movement led by Nelson Mandela, was legalized, and the apartheid laws began to be dismantled. In 1994, the first-ever free elections were held.

ORGANIZATION
OF AFRICAN UNITY
Despite the many political differences that exist between the individual African states, they all share problems of poverty, poor health, and lack of schools. In 1963, the Organization of African Unity (OAU) was founded to co-ordinate policies to solve these problems. It was replaced in 2002 by the African Union (AU). Above are two members of the OAU medical unit treating civil war victims.

NELSON MANDELA
In 1994, Nelson Mandela (left), a leader of the ANC, became the President of South Africa.

**AFRICA
700-1200**
Kingdom of Ghana in West Africa grows rich on cross-Saharan trade with the Arabs.

c. 800-1800 Kanem-Bornu kingdom.

1200s Trading cities flourish on east coast.

1235-1500 Kingdom of Mali.

1300-1600 Kingdom of Benin.

1300s Great Zimbabwe flourishes.

1350-1591 Kingdom of Songhai.

1500-1800s Europeans take Africans as slaves to America.

1838-79 Zulus fight against Boers and British.

1880s Europeans take almost total control of Africa.

1957-75 Most of Africa independent.

1990 Namibia independent.

Find out more

AFRICA
EGYPT, ANCIENT
EUROPE, HISTORY OF
PREHISTORIC PEOPLES
SLAVERY

AIRCRAFT

LESS THAN 100 YEARS AGO, even the fastest ship took more than a week to cross the Atlantic Ocean. Today, most jet airliners (large passenger planes) can make this 4,800-km (3,000-mile) journey in less than seven hours. Aircraft are the fastest way to travel because they can soar straight over obstacles such as mountains and oceans. Powerful jet engines enable the fastest combat aircraft to reach speeds in excess of 2,400 km/h (1,500 mph) – more than twice as fast as sound. Even ordinary jet airliners fly at more than 850 km/h (530 mph). Modern aircraft are packed with advanced technology to help them fly safely and economically at great speed. Sophisticated electronic control and navigation systems keep the aeroplane on course. Computer-designed wings help cut fuel costs. And airframes (aircraft bodies) are made of metal alloys and plastic composites that are lightweight and strong.

FLIGHT DECK
The captain and crew control the aircraft from the flight deck. In the past, the flight deck of an aeroplane was a mass of dials and switches. New jet airliners are packed with electronics, and computer screens have replaced the dials. Other new features include computer-controlled autopilot systems that enable the plane to take off and land when bad weather obscures the pilot's vision.

JET AIRLINER
Like all jet airliners, the *Boeing 747-400* flies high above the clouds to avoid bad weather. Its airtight cabin is pressurized – supplied with air at a suitable pressure. This protects passengers and crew from the drop in air pressure and lack of oxygen at high altitudes.

The undercarriage (landing wheels) folds up inside the aeroplane during flight to reduce drag (air resistance).

The Boeing 747-400 airliner can carry 412 people and fly non-stop for more than 13,600 km (8,470 miles). Seats are arranged on two decks.

The aircraft's radar shows the crew the weather conditions up to 320 km (200 miles) ahead so that they can avoid storms.

FLYING AN AEROPLANE
Every aeroplane has three main controls: the throttle to control speed; rudder pedals for turning the plane's nose to the left or right (yawing); and a control column that tilts the aircraft to either side (rolling), or up and down (pitching). The pilot usually operates all three to guide the plane through the air.

To roll, the pilot moves the control column to the left or right, which raises the ailerons on one wing and lowers them on the other.

Aileron

Elevator

To pitch up or down, the pilot pushes or pulls on the control column, raising or lowering the elevators on the tail wing.

To yaw left or right, the pilot's feet swivel the rudder bar, turning the upright rudder on the tail of the aeroplane.

Rudder

Like a bicycle going around a curve, an aircraft has to bank into a turn. To do this, the pilot uses the control column and the rudder pedals together so that the aircraft rolls and yaws at the same time.

AEROPLANES
Aeroplanes are powered aircraft that have wings. The word aircraft describes all flying machines including helicopters, gliders, hang gliders, and aeroplanes. Most large airliners and combat aeroplanes have jet engines enabling them to fly fast and high. But jets are expensive and use a lot of fuel, so many smaller planes are driven by propeller, just like the first aeroplanes.

OBSERVATION PLANES
Specially designed aircraft give a clear view of everything from traffic jams to diseased crops.

JET AIRCRAFT
Each year billions of people make long journeys in jet airliners and smaller business jets. These aircraft are powered by a type of jet engine called a turbofan. Turbofans are powerful and relatively quiet.

SEAPLANES
Aircraft are ideal for getting in and out of remote places. Seaplanes have floats instead of landing wheels to land and take off on water.

CONCORDE
This airliner, in service from 1976 to 2003, was supersonic, which means that it flew faster than sound. It cruised at more than twice the speed of sound, crossing the Atlantic Ocean in less than four hours.

Space for passengers' hand luggage is available in compartments above the seats.

Baggage is carried in an unpressurized hold beneath the passengers.

The fuselage, or aircraft body, is made of special lightweight aluminium alloys and plastic composites.

Interior surfaces made of fire-resistant materials

If necessary, seats can be removed or rearranged to give more space.

Every part of the airframe is rigorously tested to ensure that it can withstand the stresses of flying fast and high.

The tail fin and wings of a jet aircraft are swept back to reduce air resistance in flight.

Pilot uses the rudder, ailerons, and elevators to control the aeroplane.

Elevators on the tail plane swivel to control the up-and-down tilt of the aircraft.

CONTROL SURFACES
Nearly all aeroplanes have a rudder and hinged surfaces in the wings and tail fins that swivel to steer the plane. In older aircraft the pilot operates the flaps mechanically via cables. In modern planes the control surfaces often work electronically, with the aid of a computer. This system is called fly-by-wire. A new system, called fly-by-light, uses fibre optic cables instead of wires.

Air rushing over and under the aircraft wings produces an upward force called lift.

Hinged surfaces that tilt the aeroplane from one side to the other are called ailerons.

Angled winglets provide extra lift which helps to lower fuel costs.

WINGS
Aeroplanes can fly because air streaming past lifts their wings. A wing, or airfoil, is always curved upwards, so that air rushing over the top is forced to speed up and stretch out, making pressure drop. Beneath the wing, air travels more slowly and pressure builds up. So, in effect, the wing is sucked from above and pushed from below.

Jet airliners have special landing flaps. These swivel down to give extra lift as the aeroplane flies slowly just before landing. While the aeroplane flies at cruising speed, the pilot retracts (draws in) the landing flaps to reduce drag.

Four powerful turbofan jet engines push the plane through the air.

FAMOUS AVIATORS
The early days of flying inspired many brave feats. In 1919, for instance, British fliers John Alcock and Arthur Whitten Brown made the first non-stop flight across the Atlantic in a plane with an open cockpit. Eight years later, in 1927, American aviator Charles Lindbergh made the crossing entirely alone, a feat repeated by American Amelia Earhart in 1932. In 1930, English aviator Amy Johnson (right) flew solo from England to Australia.

HISTORY OF FLIGHT
During the late 1840s, the English inventor Sir George Cayley built a glider that could carry a person when it was towed into the air. Soon, many would-be aviators were trying to take off in flying machines powered first by steam engines and later by petrol engines. But it was not until early in the 20th century that the American Wright brothers made the first successful powered flight.

OTTO LILIENTHAL
In the 1890s, German engineer Otto Lilienthal took to the air in a kind of hang glider. This was the first flight in which the pilot controlled the aircraft.

WRIGHT BROTHERS
Orville and Wilbur Wright's *Flyer* made the world's first controlled, powered flight at Kitty Hawk, North Carolina, United States on 17 December 1903. Although the flight lasted only 12 seconds, the age of the aircraft had begun.

SOUND BARRIER
Many people once believed that aeroplanes could never fly faster than the speed of sound. But on 14 October 1947, American pilot Chuck Yeager proved them wrong when he broke the sound barrier in the rocket-powered *Bell X-1*.

Find out more
ENERGY
ENGINES
MACHINES
METALS
SCIENCE, HISTORY OF
SPACE FLIGHT
TECHNOLOGY

ALPHABETS

WHEN PEOPLE FIRST BEGAN TO WRITE, they did not use an alphabet. Instead, they drew small pictures to represent the objects they were writing about. This is called picture writing, and it was very slow because there was a different picture for every word. An alphabet does not contain pictures. Instead, it is a collection of letters or symbols which represent sounds. Each sound is just part of one word. Joining the letters together forms a whole word. The human voice can make about 35 different sounds in speech. So alphabets need at most 35 letters to write any word, and most alphabets manage with fewer. The Phoenicians, who lived about 3,000 years ago in the Middle Eastern country now called Syria, developed the first modern alphabet. The ancient Greeks adapted the Phoenician alphabet, and later the Romans improved it. The Roman alphabet is now used widely throughout the world.

Ancient Romans used certain letters for numbers. For example, C is 100.

abcdefghi jklmnopqr stuvwxyz

CAPITAL AND SMALL LETTERS
The first Roman alphabet had only capital letters. Small letters started to appear after the 8th century. In English, capital letters are used at the beginning of a sentence, and for the first letter of a name. Capital letters are also used when words are abbreviated, or shortened, to their first letters, such as UN for United Nations.

.,;?!éäêç

SYMBOLS AND ACCENTS
In addition to letters, writers use punctuation marks such as a full stop to show where a sentence ends. Some languages, such as French, also use accents – marks which show how to speak the word. The sloping acute accent over the *e* in *café* makes it sound like the *a* in *day*.

ROMAN ALPHABET
The alphabet used in English and other European languages is based on the Roman alphabet, which had 23 letters. This alphabet is also used in some Southeast Asian languages, such as Vietnamese and Indonesian.

In every alphabet, letters have a special order that does not change. Dictionaries, phone books, and many other books are arranged in alphabetical order so that it is easy to find a word or a name.

In traditional printing, raised lead letters are used to print the words on paper.

The Romans did not have the letter W. For J they used I, and for U they used V.

АБВГДЕЁЖЗИЙКЛМНОПРСТУФХЦЧШЩЪЬЫІЭЮЯ
Cyrillic (Russian)

ΑΒΓΔΕΖΗΘΙΚΛΜΝΞΟΠΡΣΤΥΦΧΨΩ
Greek

अ आ इ ई उ ऊ ए ऐ ओ औ ऋ क ख ग घ ङ च छ ज झ ञ ट ठ ड ढ ण त थ
द ध न प फ ब भ म य र ल व श ष स ह क्ष त्र ज्ञ श्र
Hindi (India)

MODERN ALPHABETS
The Roman alphabet is only one of the world's alphabets. Many other languages use different symbols to represent similar sounds, and the words may be written and read quite differently from the Roman alphabet. Japanese readers start on the right side of the page and read to the left, or start at the top and read down the page.

ROSETTA STONE
The ancient Egyptians used a system of picture writing called hieroglyphics. The meaning of this writing was forgotten 1,600 years ago, so nobody was able to read Egyptian documents until 1799 when some French soldiers made a remarkable discovery. Near Alexandria, Egypt, they found a stone with an inscription on it. The words were carved in hieroglyphics and in Greek. Using their knowledge of Greek, scholars were able to discover what the hieroglyphics meant.

CUNEIFORM
More than 5,000 years ago in Mesopotamia (now part of Iraq, Syria, Turkey, and Iran) a form of writing called cuneiform developed. It started off as picture writing, but later letters began to represent sounds. The Mesopotamians did not have paper; instead they wrote on damp clay using wedge-shaped pens. Cuneiform means "wedge-shaped".

CHINESE PICTOGRAMS
The earliest Chinese writing used pictograms (picture signs) standing for objects or ideas. Chinese writing still has no signs for sounds.

Bird

Horse

Tree

Sun

Find out more
BABYLONIANS
BRONZE AGE
EGYPT, ANCIENT
LANGUAGES
NUMBERS
PHOENICIANS

ANGLO-SAXONS

TRADITION HAS IT THAT AROUND 449 CE King Vortigern of Britain was finding it hard to fight off the invading Picts and Scots. So he invited the Saxons (a Germanic tribe) to come and help him. They quarrelled with the British and were later joined by other Germanic groups – the Angles and Jutes – who came together to form a single people (the Anglo-Saxons), and established a series of kingdoms. By 600 CE, they had driven out the native British and taken over most of the country. Eventually there were seven main kingdoms, and these in turn became three. These kingdoms were known as *Engla land*, or *Angle land*, which is where the name England comes from. Anglo-Saxon rule lasted about 500 years, until 1066. During that time, Anglo-Saxon kings fought many battles and made alliances with the Vikings and Danes. Christianity was brought to England. The greatest Anglo-Saxon king was Alfred.

Wooden building, with thatched roof

ANGLO-SAXON OCCUPATION
By the end of the 9th century, Anglo-Saxon England was divided into Wessex, Mercia, and Northumbria.

ANGLO-SAXONS

c. 449 Angles, Saxons, and Jutes come to Britain.

597 Ethelbert, King of Kent, becomes a Christian.

802-39 King Egbert rules Wessex; unites Anglo-Saxon kingdoms.

830s Vikings invade.

871-899 Alfred reigns; beats Danes at Edington in 878.

978-1016 Ethelred II the Unready pays money to Vikings to keep the peace.

1016 Danish king Canute takes the English throne.

1042 Edward the Confessor becomes king.

1066 William of Normandy conquers England.

A minstrel entertains people in the mead hall.

BATTLE OF MALDON
In 991 CE, the men of Essex, led by Brihtnoth, fought a battle at Maldon, Essex, against 5,000 Vikings, led by Olaf Tryggvason. The Vikings won. They became more powerful, and, by 1016, England had a Danish king. All we know about the battle comes from *The Battle of Maldon*, a poem from the 10th or 11th century.

Ash spear and shield

MEAD HALL
Daily life in an Anglo-Saxon village centred around the mead hall. This was a large building where people came to meet and feast. Travelling minstrels would sing or recite long story poems to entertain the people while they drank. The mead hall belonged to the local *eorl*, or lord.

CANUTE
In 1016, the Danes finally overthrew the Anglo-Saxons and took the English throne. The Danish prince Canute, or Cnut (994-1035 CE), became King of England. He was popular, ruled wisely, passed laws to restore order and kept up Anglo-Saxon customs. In 1018 he became King of Denmark, and in 1028 took over the Norwegian throne. For a short time England and Scandinavia formed an empire.

Canute

EDWARD THE CONFESSOR
A descendant of Alfred the Great, Edward the Confessor (1002-66), founded Westminster Abbey, and was made a saint in 1161. He was not a strong king, and allowed his Norman advisors to rule for him. Edward had no children, and after his death there was a squabble for the throne. William of Normandy claimed that Edward had promised it to him. Edward's brother-in-law, Harold, said the throne was rightly his. Harold was crowned in 1066.

BEOWULF

The most important piece of literature in the Anglo-Saxon language is *Beowulf* – a very long, epic (heroic) poem. It tells the story of the noble warrior Beowulf (his name means Bee Wolf) who fights the monster Grendel and Grendel's even more terrifying mother, who were threatening the people of the Danish King Hrothgar. It was written in the 700s CE, but the author is unknown.

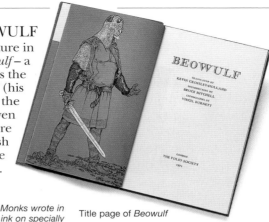

Title page of *Beowulf*

Anglo-Saxon Chronicle

Monks wrote in ink on specially prepared parchment.

MONKS

Books and manuscripts were produced by monks. They had to copy each book by hand, and so books were very precious. The monks worked in a special room in the monastery called a scriptorium. One monk prepared the parchment, a second copied in the words, and a third illustrated the manuscript (text). Books were written in Latin and Anglo-Saxon.

Illustrations and decorative initials added to the text

ANGLO-SAXON CHRONICLE

Started by the Saxon King Alfred the Great, the Anglo-Saxon Chronicle was a kind of early newspaper. It recorded events in England, gave accounts of wars and battles, and included works translated from Latin. Alfred undertook many translations himself. The Chronicle continued until 1154, and is a very important source of information about the history and language of the Anglo-Saxon people.

Coloured inks made from plants and minerals.

Sompting Church

THE VENERABLE BEDE

Known as "The Father of English History", Bede, or Baeda (673?-735 CE) was a monk and teacher who lived and worked in a monastery in Jarrow, north-eastern England. He wrote many books on the Bible and scientific subjects. Bede's most famous work is *The Ecclesiastical History of the English Nation*, finished in 731 CE.

SUTTON HOO

In 1939, archaeologists unearthed buried treasure at Sutton Hoo in Suffolk, England. They found 11 burial mounds containing Anglo-Saxon coins, weapons, bowls, and ornaments dating from between 650 and 670 CE. The site was probably a memorial to a great king.

Iron helmet trimmed with bronze and silver

CHURCH BUILDING

Most of the Anglo-Saxon buildings that can still be seen today are churches. This is because they were built from stone rather than wood. Sompting Church is in West Sussex but most surviving Anglo-Saxon churches are in East Anglia.

Find out more
MEDIEVAL EUROPE
NORMANS
RELIGIONS
UNITED KINGDOM, HISTORY OF
VIKINGS

ANIMALS

THE ANIMAL KINGDOM is one of the largest groups of living things; scientists believe that there are up to 30 million species. Animals range from tiny, simple creatures that look like blobs of jelly, to gigantic blue whales. The huge animal kingdom is divided into many groups. A lion, for example, belongs to the order Carnivora because it eats meat. It also belongs to the class of placental mammals. All mammals are vertebrates (animals with backbones) and belong to a group known as chordates. An animal is a living creature that feeds, moves, and breeds. During its life cycle, an animal is born, grows, matures, reproduces, and eventually dies. It ingests (takes in) food to build and develop its body. Food provides the animal with the energy to move around. Some types of animal do not move at all; the adult sponge, for example, spends its life anchored to a rock. All kinds of animals from dinosaurs to dodos have become extinct; many others, including elephants and tigers, may soon disappear if their habitat is destroyed and if they continue to be killed recklessly for their hides and bones.

FROG
Like all animals, the common green frog is aware of its surroundings and able to move, feed, and reproduce. Frogs belong to the class of animals called amphibians. All amphibians spend part of their lives in or near water.

INTERNAL SKELETONS
The animal world can be divided into vertebrate animals and invertebrate animals. Vertebrates have an internal skeleton with a vertebral column or backbone. In most cases, this is made of bone. Some sea-dwelling vertebrates, such as sharks, have a backbone made of tough, rubbery gristle called cartilage.

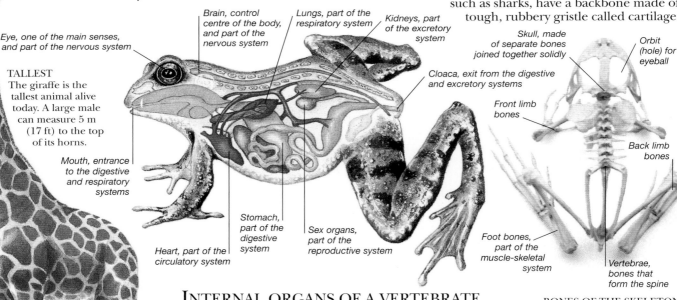

TALLEST
The giraffe is the tallest animal alive today. A large male can measure 5 m (17 ft) to the top of its horns.

Eye, one of the main senses, and part of the nervous system

Mouth, entrance to the digestive and respiratory systems

Brain, control centre of the body, and part of the nervous system

Lungs, part of the respiratory system

Kidneys, part of the excretory system

Cloaca, exit from the digestive and excretory systems

Heart, part of the circulatory system

Stomach, part of the digestive system

Sex organs, part of the reproductive system

Skull, made of separate bones joined together solidly

Orbit (hole) for eyeball

Front limb bones

Back limb bones

Foot bones, part of the muscle-skeletal system

Vertebrae, bones that form the spine

INTERNAL ORGANS OF A VERTEBRATE
Inside an animal, such as the frog above, are many different parts called organs. Organs are all shapes and sizes. Each one has a job to do. Several organs are grouped together to form a body system, such as the digestive system, the circulatory system, and the reproductive system. The nervous system and the hormonal system control and co-ordinate all the internal systems.

BONES OF THE SKELETON
The skeletons of vertebrate animals are similar in design, but each differs in certain details through adaptation to the way the animal lives. A frog, for example, has long, strong back legs for leaping. All vertebrates have a skull that contains the brain and the main sense organs. Most vertebrates also have two pairs of limbs. Some bones, such as the skull bones, are fixed firmly together; others are linked by flexible joints, as in the limbs.

SMALLEST
The smallest organisms are single-celled creatures called protozoa – so tiny they can hardly be seen by the human eye. The tiniest mammals are the bumblebee bat and Savi's pygmy shrew. This pygmy shrew measures only 6 cm (2.3 in) including its tail.

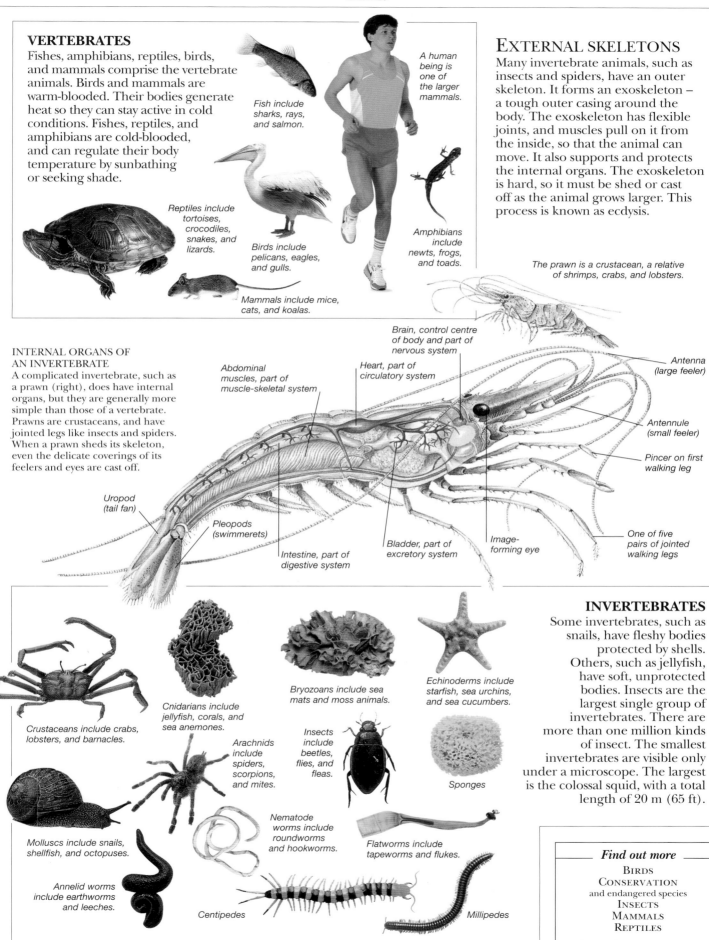

VERTEBRATES

Fishes, amphibians, reptiles, birds, and mammals comprise the vertebrate animals. Birds and mammals are warm-blooded. Their bodies generate heat so they can stay active in cold conditions. Fishes, reptiles, and amphibians are cold-blooded, and can regulate their body temperature by sunbathing or seeking shade.

Fish include sharks, rays, and salmon.

A human being is one of the larger mammals.

Reptiles include tortoises, crocodiles, snakes, and lizards.

Birds include pelicans, eagles, and gulls.

Amphibians include newts, frogs, and toads.

Mammals include mice, cats, and koalas.

EXTERNAL SKELETONS

Many invertebrate animals, such as insects and spiders, have an outer skeleton. It forms an exoskeleton – a tough outer casing around the body. The exoskeleton has flexible joints, and muscles pull on it from the inside, so that the animal can move. It also supports and protects the internal organs. The exoskeleton is hard, so it must be shed or cast off as the animal grows larger. This process is known as ecdysis.

The prawn is a crustacean, a relative of shrimps, crabs, and lobsters.

INTERNAL ORGANS OF AN INVERTEBRATE

A complicated invertebrate, such as a prawn (right), does have internal organs, but they are generally more simple than those of a vertebrate. Prawns are crustaceans, and have jointed legs like insects and spiders. When a prawn sheds its skeleton, even the delicate coverings of its feelers and eyes are cast off.

Brain, control centre of body and part of nervous system

Heart, part of circulatory system

Abdominal muscles, part of muscle-skeletal system

Antenna (large feeler)

Antennule (small feeler)

Pincer on first walking leg

Uropod (tail fan)

Pleopods (swimmerets)

Intestine, part of digestive system

Bladder, part of excretory system

Image-forming eye

One of five pairs of jointed walking legs

INVERTEBRATES

Some invertebrates, such as snails, have fleshy bodies protected by shells. Others, such as jellyfish, have soft, unprotected bodies. Insects are the largest single group of invertebrates. There are more than one million kinds of insect. The smallest invertebrates are visible only under a microscope. The largest is the colossal squid, with a total length of 20 m (65 ft).

Cnidarians include jellyfish, corals, and sea anemones.

Bryozoans include sea mats and moss animals.

Echinoderms include starfish, sea urchins, and sea cucumbers.

Crustaceans include crabs, lobsters, and barnacles.

Arachnids include spiders, scorpions, and mites.

Insects include beetles, flies, and fleas.

Sponges

Molluscs include snails, shellfish, and octopuses.

Nematode worms include roundworms and hookworms.

Flatworms include tapeworms and flukes.

Annelid worms include earthworms and leeches.

Centipedes

Millipedes

Find out more
BIRDS
CONSERVATION
and endangered species
INSECTS
MAMMALS
REPTILES

ANTARCTICA

STRETCHING ACROSS AN AREA greater than the United States, the continent of Antarctica sits beneath a huge sheet of ice up to 2 km (1.2 miles) thick. Antarctica is centred on the South Pole and is surrounded by the ice-covered Southern Ocean. Powerful winds create a storm belt around the continent, bringing fog and severe blizzards. It is the coldest and windiest place on earth. Even during the short summers the temperature barely climbs above freezing, and the sea ice only partly melts. In winter, temperatures can plummet to -80°C (-112°F). Few animals and plants can survive on land, but the surrounding seas teem with fish and mammals. Due to its harsh climate, there are no permanent residents on Antarctica. The only people on the continent are tourists, and scientists and staff working in research stations. These few people have brought waste and pollution to the region. Other environmental concerns include overfishing, the depletion of the ozone layer above the region, and the effects of global warming, which has led to the melting of ice in some coastal areas.

Situated at the southernmost point of the world, Antarctica covers an area of about 14 million sq km (5.5 million sq miles). The nearest land masses are South America and New Zealand. The highest point is Vinson Massif, which rises to 4,897 m (16,067 ft).

Radio transmitters allow scientists to track the movements of penguins.

ANTARCTIC TEMPERATURES

2°C (28°F) Sea water freezes. On the Antarctic coast, summer temperatures are only a degree or so warmer than this.

-25°C (-13°F) Steel crystallizes and becomes brittle.

-40°C (-40°F) Synthetic rubber becomes brittle, and exposed flesh freezes rapidly.

-89°C (-128.6°F) Lowest temperature ever recorded, at Vostok Research Station, Antarctica, 1983.

SCIENTIFIC RESEARCH

There are 40 permanent, and as many as 100 temporary, research stations in Antarctica devoted to scientific projects for 15 different nations. Teams of scientists study the wildlife and monitor the ice for changes in the Earth's atmosphere. Antarctic-based research has resulted in a number of scientific breakthroughs, including the discovery of a hole in the ozone layer above the continent.

TOURISM

Cruise liners have been bringing tourists to the Antarctic region since the 1950s. In 1983, Chileans began to fly to King George Island where an 80-bed hotel has been built for holiday-makers. Antarctica receives several thousand tourists each year. Visitors come to see the dramatic landscape and unique wildlife, such as King penguins.

Platinum

Iron

Gold

MINERAL WEALTH
Antarctica has deposits of minerals, such as gold, copper, uranium, and nickel. However, extracting them may damage the fragile polar environment.

Find out more
CONTINENTS
OCEANS AND SEAS
POLAR WILDLIFE
RAIN AND SNOW
WIND

Volcano | Mountain | Ancient monument | Capital city | Large city/town | Small city/town | Research Station

STATISTICS
Area: 14,000,000 sq km (5,405,430 sq miles)
Population: No permanent residents
Capital: None
Languages: English, Spanish, French, Norwegian, Chinese, Polish, Russian, German, Japanese
Religions: Not applicable
Currency: None
Main occupation: Scientific research
Main exports: None
Main imports: None

WHALE PROTECTION
Large-scale whale hunting in Antarctic seas began in the 20th century. The whale population soon fell and in 1948 the International Whaling Commission was set up to monitor the diminishing numbers. Following an international agreement in 1994, a whale sanctuary was created to protect whale feeding grounds from overfishing.

FOREIGN TERRITORIES
Various nations, including Australia, France, New Zealand, Norway, Argentina, Chile, and the UK claimed territory in Antarctica when it was first discovered in the 19th century. However, these claims have been suspended under the 1959 Antarctic Treaty which came into force in 1961. Under the treaty, the continent can be used only for peaceful purposes. Stations may be set up for scientific research but military bases are forbidden.

FROZEN SEAS
During the cold winter months, the seas surrounding Antarctica freeze, almost doubling the size of the continent.

ANTARCTIC ICE
Icebergs barricade more than 90 per cent of the Antarctic coastline. The continent contains over 80 per cent of the world's fresh water in the form of ice.

LAMBERT GLACIER
The Lambert Glacier is the world's largest series of glaciers. It is 80 km (50 miles) wide at the coast and reaches more than 300 km (186 miles) inland.

TRANSANTARCTIC MOUNTAINS
The Transantarctic Mountains run across the continent, splitting it into Greater and Lesser Antarctica.

PETER I ISLAND (to Norway)

ROSS ICE SHELF
Ice shelves are permanent floating ice sheets that are attached to land and are constantly fed by glaciers. The Ross Ice Shelf is 183–914 m (600–3,000 ft) thick and about 966 km (600 miles) long.

SOUTHERN OCEAN

Drake Passage
Scotia Sea
South Orkney Islands
South Shetland Islands
King George Island
Weddell Sea
Antarctic Peninsula
Palmer Land
Alexander Island
Bellingshausen Sea
Coats Land
Queen Maud Land
Berkner Island
Ronne Ice Shelf
Enderby Land
Kemp Land
Lambert Glacier
Cape Darnley
Mackenzie Bay
Prydz Bay
East ANTARCTICA
Princess Elizabeth Land
Davis Sea
Ellsworth Land
Vinson Massif 4897m
South Pole +
Amundsen-Scott (US)
West Antarctica
Transantarctic Mountains
South Geomagnetic Pole +
Vostok (Russian Federation)
Shackleton Ice Shelf
Amundsen Sea
Marie Byrd Land
Mount Sidley 4181m
Ross Ice Shelf
Roosevelt Island
Mount Erebus 3794m
Victoria Land
Wilkes Land
Cape Poinsett
Ross Sea
Limit of summer pack ice (December)
Oates Land
George V Land
Cape Adare
SOUTHERN OCEAN
Limit of winter pack ice (June)

N
W E
S

SCALE BAR
0   500   1000   km
0   500   1000   miles

ARCHITECTURE

MOST OF OUR BUILDINGS have been planned by architects. The word architect is Greek for "builder" or "craftsworker" and architects aim to design and construct buildings that are attractive, functional, and comfortable. Architecture means designing a building; it also refers to the building style. Styles of architecture have changed over the centuries and differ from culture to culture, so architecture can tell us a lot about people. The Ancient Greeks, for example, produced simple, balanced buildings that showed their disciplined approach to life. Architects are artists who create buildings. But unlike other artists, they must sell their ideas before they are able to produce their buildings.

Built around 200 BCE, this Indian stupa, or dome, was originally a mound covering a site sacred to Buddha or a relic of his.

In 447 BCE, the Greek architects Ictinus and Callicrates designed the Parthenon, a temple to the goddess Athena, in Athens, Greece. With its graceful columns, it is a perfect example of classical architecture.

CLASSICAL ARCHITECTURE
The Ancient Greeks and Romans developed a style that we call classical architecture. Most Greek buildings consisted of columns to support the roof. The types of columns varied according to the particular classical "order" (style) that was used. Everything was simple and perfectly even. The Romans, who came after the Greeks, developed the arch, dome, and vault.

Elegantly curving skyward in several tiers, pagodas were built as shrines to Buddha. On the right is the pagoda of Yakushi-ji Temple, Japan. Each element in the building's design originally had a religious meaning.

Milan Cathedral in Italy (right) is an example of late Gothic architecture.

GOTHIC ARCHITECTURE
With their multitudes of pointed arches, finely carved stonework, and intricate windows, Gothic buildings are the opposite of simple classical ones. The Gothic style of architecture began in western Europe in the 12th century. It was used mainly in building cathedrals and churches. Although most Gothic buildings were huge, their thin walls, pointed arches, and large areas of stained-glass windows made them seem light and delicate.

Following the client's brief, the architect presents a drawing (below) to the client to show how the finished building will look.

FRANK LLOYD WRIGHT
American architect Frank Lloyd Wright (1869-1959) influenced many other architects. He tried to blend buildings into their natural surroundings and create a feeling of space, with few walls, so that rooms could "flow" into one another. At Bear Run, Pennsylvania, he built Falling Water, a house over a waterfall.

ARCHITECTS
If you wanted to build a house, you would approach an architect, giving clear and precise details of what you required (a brief). An architect must know from a client what the building is to be used for, how many people will use it, and how much money is available. A good architect will make sure that the new design fits in with existing buildings around it, and is built from suitable material. The architect then presents drawings and plans to the client. When the plans are approved, work on the building can begin.

| Doric column | Ionic column | Corinthian column | Barrel vault | Groin vault | Rib vault | Dome |

EXTRAORDINARY ARCHITECTURE

Some architects design weird and wonderful buildings which really stand out from the rest. In 1965, a new town was built outside Paris, France, called Marne-la-Vallée. It has many extraordinary buildings, designed by various adventurous architects. The apartment complex, left, is like a monument that people can live in. Two circular buildings face each other across a central courtyard. It was designed by a Spaniard named Manolo Nunez-Yanowsky.

Jean Louis Charles Garnier was the architect of the Paris Opera House (built 1861-75). It is neo-baroque – a 19th-century revival of the baroque style.

The American Chrysler Building, a New York City skyscraper, was completed in 1929.

Designed by the British architect Richard Rogers, the Lloyds office building in London, England, has all its services, such as plumbing, on the outside. This means they can be easily replaced.

BAROQUE ARCHITECTURE

During the 1500s in Rome, architects wanted to break the classical rules of simplicity and evenness and build more exciting, dramatic buildings. So they added domes, clusters of statues, and ornate decoration and carving to their buildings. This style, known as baroque, spread from Italy to other parts of Europe. Many churches and grand palaces were built in the baroque style.

The architect draws up detailed plans of the inside of the building to show how the space will be used.

Working drawings contain exact measurements, materials, and structures, down to the tiniest detail.

The builder works from working drawings (above) when constructing the building.

CONTEMPORARY ARCHITECTURE

Glass, steel, and concrete are the building materials of today's architecture. There is little decoration, because a building's purpose is considered more important than its shape or form. The "international" style – glass and concrete suspended on a steel framework – is seen almost everywhere in the world.

Pediment

Gothic arch

Romanesque arch

Cornice

Find out more
CASTLES
INDUSTRIAL REVOLUTION
RENAISSANCE
WONDERS
of the ancient world

ARCTIC

The Arctic Ocean centres on the North Pole, the northern extremity of the Earth's axis. Three of the world's largest rivers, the Ob, Yenisey, and Lena, flow into the cold waters of the Arctic Ocean. The Arctic regions consist of Alaska, Canada, Greenland and northern Siberia.

THE SMALLEST OF THE world's oceans, the Arctic centres on the North Pole. Between the months of December and May, most of the Arctic Ocean is covered by polar sea ice, up to 30 m (98 ft) thick. The ocean is surrounded by the Arctic regions, where much of the ground is permanently frozen to depths of 460–600 m (1,500–2,000 ft). During the long, cold winters in the far north, much of the land is subject to periods of total darkness. This is because of the low angle of the Sun in relation to the ground. Beneath the rocks of the Arctic regions lie rich reserves of iron, nickel, copper, zinc, and oil. Severe weather conditions have made it hard to exploit these resources. But global warming is thinning the sea ice and opening up new areas of land. Arctic countries now want to claim areas of the sea bed.

ICE-BREAKING

Although half of the Arctic Ocean is covered by ice in winter, special ships called ice-breakers can still sail through the ice. During particularly harsh winters, ice can become so dense in harbours and ports that it freezes right down to the sea bed, marooning ships for months at a time. Ice-breakers are designed to crush the ice with their steel hulls, opening up a lane that other ships can pass through. The Russian atomic-powered *Arcticka* is the world's most powerful ice-breaker. It can cut through ice that is 2.1 m (7 ft) thick at 11 km/h (7 mph).

Teams of hardy husky dogs were traditionally used to pull sleds across the frozen ground.

ARCTIC SETTLERS

The Arctic is one of the world's most sparsely populated regions. Today, some 120,000 Inuit (Eskimo) peoples live in Greenland, Alaska, and Canada. Over the past 3,000 years they have adapted to their ice-bound conditions, hunting with kayaks (canoes) and harpoons, and existing on a diet of caribou, seal, whale meat, and fish. They lived in houses made of frozen snow (igloos) or semi-underground stone pit-houses. Today, snowmobiles (above) have replaced sleds, and rifles are used for hunting.

COAL MINING
The Norwegian island of Spitsbergen, in the Arctic Ocean, has very extensive coal deposits. Its coal-mining towns are isolated and are desolate places. The sea-route to mainland Norway, some 1,000 km (620 miles) away, is frozen for four months of the year. Many Inuit have moved to towns such as these to work in the coal mines.

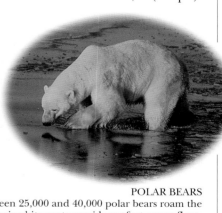

POLAR BEARS
Between 25,000 and 40,000 polar bears roam the Arctic. Their white coats provide perfect camouflage, and a 10-cm (4-in) layer of body fat keeps them warm. Bears gorge on seals from April to July – they can survive for eight months without food. They can swim as far as 150 km (93 miles) in search of prey.

Find out more
CLIMATES
OCEANS AND SEAS
OCEAN WILDLIFE
POLAR WILDLIFE
RAIN AND SNOW

STATISTICS

GREENLAND
Area:
2,166,086 sq km
(836,330 sq miles)
Status: Self-governing
territory of Denmark
Claimed: 1380
Population: 57,600
Capital: Nuuk

JAN MAYEN
Area:
377 sq km (146 sq miles)
Status: Norwegian
dependency
Claimed: 1929
Population: None
Capital: None

SVALBARD
Area:
61,020 sq km
(23,560 sq miles)
Status: Norwegian
dependency
Claimed: 1920
Population: 2,200
Capital: Longyearbyen

Halibut

ARCTIC FISH
Large quantities of cod, haddock,
and halibut are found in the
Arctic Ocean. Arctic catches
are mainly processed in Greenland.

GREENLAND
Greenland, the world's largest
island, is a self-governing
territory of Denmark. The
interior of Greenland is covered
by an enormous ice-sheet, which
rises to a height of 3,000 m
(10,000 ft). The coastline is
deeply indented with fjords.

GIANT ICEBERGS

Icebergs are frozen lumps of freshwater ice
that have broken off a glacier. Most Arctic
icebergs have broken off the coastal
glaciers of Greenland, Baffin Island, and
Ellesmere Island. Each year, about 375
icebergs flow into the the North Atlantic
where they are extremely dangerous to
shipping. Icebergs can vary from the size
of a grand piano to a ten-storey building,
45 m (147 ft) high. They are moved by
winds and currents, and melt and break
up within two years of entering the ocean.

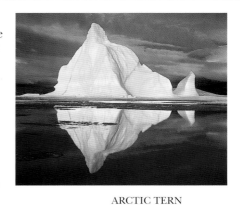

NORTHERN LIGHTS
The northern lights
(*aurora borealis*) occur
when highly charged
particles from the sun
collide with particles in
the Earth's atmosphere.
These glowing streaks
of light are brightest
at the North Pole.

ARCTIC TERN
The arctic tern (left)
breeds in the southern
Arctic and winters
in the Antarctic,
the longest annual
migration of any bird.

ARCTIC OCEAN
The Arctic Ocean is
characterized by a wide
continental shelf and
deep basin around
the North Pole.

PRUDHOE BAY
Rich reserves of oil are
found in Alaska's Prudhoe
Bay. A 1,280-km
(795-mile) long
pipeline transports
oil from Prudhoe
Bay to the
ice-free port
of Valdez.

SCALE BAR
0   250   500   km
0   250   500   miles

ASIA

The Ural Mountains form the border between the continents of Asia and Europe. Asia is separated from Africa by the Red Sea. The Bering Strait, only 88 km (55 miles) wide, marks the gap between Asia and North America. Australia lies to the southeast.

THE LARGEST OF THE SEVEN CONTINENTS, Asia occupies one-third of the world's total land area. Much of the continent is uninhabited. The inhospitable north is a cold land of tundra. Parched deserts and towering mountains take up large areas of the central region. Yet Asia is the home of well over half of the world's population, most of whom live around the outer rim. China alone has more than 1,300 million people, and India has more than 1,000 million. Altogether, Asia contains 48 nations, and many times this number of peoples, languages, and cultures. It has five main zones. In the north is the Russian Federation. Part of this is in Europe, but the vast eastern region, from the Ural Mountains to the Pacific Ocean, is in Asia. The Pacific coast, which includes China, Korea, and Japan, is known as the Far East. To the south of this lie the warmer, more humid countries of Southeast Asia. India and Pakistan are the principal countries of the Indian subcontinent in south Asia. One of the world's first civilizations began here, in the Indus Valley. Bordered by the Mediterranean and Arabian seas, the Middle East lies to the west where Europe, Asia, and Africa meet.

MIDDLE EAST
The hot, dry lands of the Middle East occupy the southwest corner of Asia. Almost the entire Arabian peninsula, between the Red Sea and The Gulf, is desert. To the north, in Iraq and Syria, lie the fertile valleys of the rivers Tigris and Euphrates. Most of the people of the Middle East are Arabs, and speak Arabic.

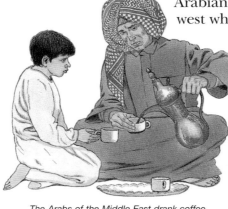

The Arabs of the Middle East drank coffee long before it reached other countries.

Siberian scientists looking for minerals in north Asia have to work in subzero temperatures, and the cold can freeze their breath.

SIBERIA
The northern coast of Asia is fringed by the Arctic Ocean. The sea here is frozen for most of the year. A layer of the land, called permafrost, is also always frozen. This area is part of the vast region of the Russian Federation called Siberia. Despite the cold, Russian people live and work in Siberia because the region is rich in timber, coal, oil, and natural gas.

ANCIENT TRADE ROUTES
Even 2,000 years ago, there was trade between the Far East and Europe. Traders carried silk, spices, gems, and pottery. They followed overland routes across India and Pakistan, past the Karakoram mountains (above). These trade routes were known as the Silk Road; they are still used today.

TROPICAL RAIN FORESTS
The warm, damp climate of much of Southeast Asia provides the perfect conditions for tropical rain forests, which thrive in countries such as Burma (Myanmar) and Malaysia. The forests are the habitat for a huge variety of wildlife, and are home to tribes of people whose way of life has not changed for centuries. But because many of the forest trees are beautiful hardwoods, the logging industry is now cutting down the forests at an alarming rate to harvest the valuable timber.

Sunlight breaks through the dense foliage of the rain forest only where rivers have cut trails through the trees.

PROSPERITY

Some Asian countries, such as Japan and Singapore, are among the world's most prosperous nations. The discovery of oil in a number of other countries, such as Saudi Arabia in the Middle East, and Brunei in Southeast Asia, has made them very wealthy.

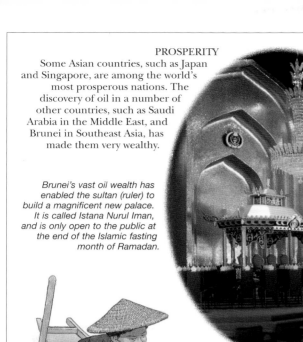

Brunei's vast oil wealth has enabled the sultan (ruler) to build a magnificent new palace. It is called Istana Nurul Iman, and is only open to the public at the end of the Islamic fasting month of Ramadan.

"Floating markets" are a common sight on the busy waterways of the Far East.

Vanilla vines grow well in the warm climate of Indonesia, and women harvest the pods by hand.

FAR EAST

East Asia is often called the Far East. In the 19th century, European traders and travellers used this name to distinguish east Asia from the Middle East. The Far East includes China, Japan, and Korea.

KOREA

The Korean peninsula juts out from northern China towards Japan. The two Korean nations were at war between 1950 and 1953. They have lived in constant mistrust of each other since the war ended, but are now trying to mend the divisions between them. South Korea has a booming economy and is heavily supported by the United States. North Korea is Communist and poorer. The climate favours rice growing, with warm summers and icy winters.

Construction work is a common sight in South Korea, as new offices and factories are built for the country's expanding industries.

SOUTHEAST ASIA

Many different people live in the warm, tropical southeastern corner of Asia. There are ten independent countries in the region. Some of them – Burma (Myanmar), Laos, Thailand, Cambodia (or Kampuchea), and Vietnam – are on the mainland attached to the rest of Asia. Further south lie Brunei, Malaysia, and the tiny island nation of Singapore. Indonesia stretches across the foot of the region. It is a scattered nation of more than 13,500 islands. The islands of the Philippines are to the east. Although some of these countries are very poor, Southeast Asia as a whole has one of the most rapidly developing economies in the world.

Hundreds of different languages are spoken in the Indian subcontinent, but Indian schools teach pupils to read and write Hindi, which is the country's official language.

INDIAN SUBCONTINENT

The triangular landmass of south Asia extends south from the Himalaya Mountains to the warm waters of the Indian Ocean. This region is also known as the Indian subcontinent. It includes not only India but also Pakistan, Nepal, Bangladesh, and Bhutan. At the very southern tip of India lies the island nation of Sri Lanka.

The port of Shanghai lies at the mouth of the River Yangtze.

RIVER YANGTZE

The Yangtze (or Chang Jiang), the world's third-longest river, flows 6,380 km (3,964 miles) through the middle of China, from its source in Tibet to the sea at Shanghai. In 1997, the first stage was completed on the Three Gorges Dam, China's largest construction project since the building of the Great Wall.

Find out more
ASIA, HISTORY OF
BRONZE AGE
CHINA
CONTINENTS
LANGUAGES
RELIGIONS

ASIA

Asia is the world's largest continent. It is a region of contrasts: both in its landscape, and peoples. The break up of the Soviet Union produced five new central Asian republics. The countries in the south are mainly Muslim, but are divided by religious differences and conflicts.

AFGHANISTAN
Area: 647,500 sq km
(250,001 sq miles)
Population: 33,610,000
Capital: Kābul

ARMENIA
Area: 29,800 sq km
(11,506 sq miles)
Population: 2,967,000
Capital: Yerevan

AZERBAIJAN
Area: 86,600 sq km
(33,436 sq miles)
Population: 8,239,000
Capital: Baku

BAHRAIN
Area: 665 sq km
(257 sq miles)
Population: 728,000
Capital: Manama

BANGLADESH
Area: 143,998 sq km
(55,598 sq miles)
Population: 156,051,000
Capital: Dhaka

BHUTAN
Area: 47,000 sq km
(18,147 sq miles)
Population: 691,000
Capital: Thimphu

BRUNEI
Area: 5,770 sq km
(2,228 sq miles)
Population: 389,000
Capital: Bandar Seri Begawan

BURMA
Area: 678,500 sq km
(261,970 sq miles)
Population: 48,138,000
Capital: Rangoon

CAMBODIA
Area: 181,040 sq km
(69,000 sq miles)
Population: 14,494,000
Capital: Phnom Penh

CHINA
Area: 9,396,960 sq km
(3,628,166 sq miles)
Population: 1,338,613,000
Capital: Beijing

CYPRUS
Area: 9,251 sq km
(3,572 sq miles)
Population: 797,000
Capital: Nicosia

EAST TIMOR
Area: 15,007 sq km
(5,794 sq miles)
Population: 1,132,000
Capital: Dili

GEORGIA
Area: 69,700 sq km
(26,911 sq miles)
Population: 4,616,000
Capital: Tbilisi

INDIA
Area: 3,287,590 sq km
(1,269,338 sq miles)
Population: 1,166,079,000
Capital: New Delhi

INDONESIA
Area: 1,904,570 sq km
(735,555 sq miles)
Population: 240,272,000
Capital: Jakarta

IRAN
Area: 1,648,000 sq km
(636,293 sq miles)
Population: 66,429,000
Capital: Tehran

IRAQ
Area: 437,072 sq km
(168,754 sq miles)
Population: 28,946,000
Capital: Baghdad

ISRAEL
Area: 20,700 sq km
(7,992 sq miles)
Population: 7,234,000
Capital: Jerusalem

JAPAN
Area: 377,800 sq km
(145,869 sq miles)
Population: 127,079,000
Capital: Tokyo

JORDAN
Area: 92,300 sq km
(35,637 sq miles)
Population: 6,343,000
Capital: Amman

KAZAKHSTAN
Area: 2,717,300 sq km
(1,049,150 sq miles)
Population: 15,400,000
Capital: Astana

NORTH KOREA
Area: 120,540 sq km
(46,540 sq miles)
Population: 22,665,000
Capital: Pyongyang

SOUTH KOREA
Area: 98,480 sq km
(38,023 sq miles)
Population: 48,510,000
Capital: Seoul

KUWAIT
Area: 17,820 sq km
(6,880 sq miles)
Population: 2,691,000
Capital: Kuwait City

KYRGYZSTAN
Area: 198,500 sq km
(76,640 sq miles)
Population: 5,432,000
Capital: Bishkek

LAOS
Area: 236,800 sq km
(91,428 sq miles)
Population: 6,835,000
Capital: Vientiane

LEBANON
Area: 10,400 sq km
(4,015 sq miles)
Population: 4,017,000
Capital: Beirut

MALAYSIA
Area: 329,750 sq km
(127,317 sq miles)
Population: 25,716,000
Capital: Kuala Lumpur

MALDIVES
Area: 300 sq km
(116 sq miles)
Population: 396,000
Capital: Male'

MONGOLIA
Area: 1,565,000 sq km
(604,247 sq miles)
Population: 3,041,000
Capital: Ulan Bator

NEPAL
Area: 147,181 sq km
(56,827 sq miles)
Population: 28,563,000
Capital: Kathmandu

OMAN
Area: 212,460 sq km
(82,030 sq miles)
Population: 3,418,000
Capital: Muscat

PAKISTAN
Area: 796,100 sq km
(307,374 sq miles)
Population: 176,243,000
Capital: Islamabad

PHILIPPINES
Area: 300,000 sq km
(115,831 sq miles)
Population: 97,977,000
Capital: Manila

QATAR
Area: 11,586 sq km
(4,473 sq miles)
Population: 833,000
Capital: Doha

RUSSIAN FED.
Area: 17,075,400 sq km
(6,592,800 sq miles)
Population: 140,041,000
Capital: Moscow

SINGAPORE
Area: 697 sq km
(239 sq miles)
Population: 4,658,000
Capital: Singapore City

SRI LANKA
Area: 65,610 sq km
(25,332 sq miles)
Population: 21,325,000
Capital: Colombo

SYRIA
Area: 185,180 sq km
(71,500 sq miles)
Population: 20,178,000
Capital: Damascus

TAIWAN
Area: 36,179 sq km
(13,969 sq miles)
Population: 22,974,000
Capital: Taipei

TAJIKISTAN
Area: 143,100 sq km
(55,251 sq miles)
Population: 7,349,000
Capital: Dushanbe

THAILAND
Area: 514,000 sq km
(198,457 sq miles)
Population: 65,905,000
Capital: Bangkok

TURKEY
Area: 780,580 sq km
(301,384 sq miles)
Population: 76,806,000
Capital: Ankara

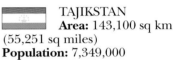
TURKMENISTAN
Area: 488,100 sq km
(188,455 sq miles)
Population: 4,885,000
Capital: Ashgabat

U. A. E.
Area: 83,600 sq km
(32,278 sq miles)
Population: 4,798,000
Capital: Abu Dhabi

UZBEKISTAN
Area: 447,400 sq km
(172,741 sq miles)
Population: 27,606,000
Capital: Tashkent

VIETNAM
Area: 329,560 sq km
(127,243 sq miles)
Population: 86,968,000
Capital: Hanoi

YEMEN
Area: 527,970 sq km
(203,849 sq miles)
Population: 23,823,000
Capital: Sana

STATISTICS
Area: 46,519,416 sq km
(17,961,247 sq miles)
Population:
3,152,429,000
Highest point: Mount
Everest (Nepal)
8,850 m (29,029 ft)
Longest river: Yangtze
(China) 6,380 km
(3,964 miles)
Largest lake: Caspian
Sea 371,000 sq km
(143,205 sq miles)

Volcano · Mountain · Ancient monument · Capital city · Large city/town · Small city/town

MOUNT EVEREST
The Himalayan mountain range runs along the China-Nepal border southeast from the Pamir mountains. It is a group of rugged peaks and valleys, sometimes described as the "roof of the world". The highest point in the Himalayas is Mount Everest (right) – the world's highest mountain.

SCALE BAR
0   500   1000   km
0   500   1000   miles

URAL MOUNTAINS
The Ural Mountains form a natural border between Asia and Europe.

KURILE ISLANDS
The Kurile Islands are part of the Russian Federation, but Japan claims the southernmost islands in this chain as part of its own territory.

SEOUL
Modern office blocks crowd together in Seoul, the capital city of South Korea, but a few ancient buildings still survive. The South Gate (below) was built at the end of the 14th century as part of a wall that once surrounded the city. Today, Seoul is spreading far beyond its original boundaries as rapid industrial growth creates a need for more offices, factories, and homes.

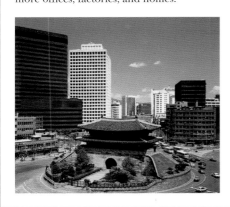

EAST TIMOR
In 1975 Indonesia invaded the Portuguese colony of East Timor, the eastern part of the island of Timor. The following year the region was made a province of Indonesia. In a UN-monitored referendum in 1999, voters rejected Indonesian rule and in 2002 East Timor became an independent state.

JAVA
Rice terraces (right) provide the staple food for Indonesia. These fields are on the island of Java, which has only seven per cent of Indonesia's land area but is the home of some 60 per cent of the country's people.

29

HISTORY OF
ASIA

THE VAST CONTINENT OF ASIA is home to the oldest civilizations and religions in the world. Because Asia contains many virtually impassable deserts and mountain ranges, individual countries developed separately from each other. However, links between these countries sprang up as merchants travelled along the Silk Road, Indian kings invaded neighbouring countries, Buddhist monks crossed the Himalayas, and Arab traders sailed across the Indian Ocean. As a result, the great Hindu, Buddhist, and Islamic religions spread across the continent. For much of the last 500 years, Europe controlled large parts of Asia, but since 1945 Asian countries have gained their independence. Many of them are now world-class economies.

EARLY CIVILIZATIONS

Asia's extreme land forms, such as the towering peaks of the Himalayas, which separate India from China, meant that early Asian cultures had little contact with each other, or the rest of the world. As a result, the first great Asian civilizations, such as the Indus Valley civilization in the Indian subcontinent, and the Shang Dynasty in China, developed very different and distinct cultures.

Bactrian (two-humped) camel pottery made in China.

HINDUISM

Hinduism began in the ancient civilizations of the Indus Valley, in India, around 2500 BCE. Over the centuries, the religion spread across India to Sri Lanka and the islands of Southeast Asia. Hinduism is the oldest religion in the world still practised today, and provides a thread linking together all of India's history.

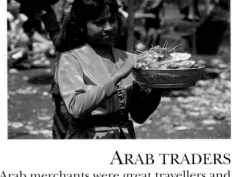

ARAB TRADERS

Arab merchants were great travellers and adventurers, crossing deserts and oceans in search of new markets in which to buy and sell their goods. On their journeys, they converted local people to their Islamic religion, founded by Muhammad in Arabia in the early 600s. As a result, Islam spread across Asia as far as the southeastern islands.

SILK ROAD

The Silk Road was an important trading route that stretched across Asia from Loyang, China's capital, in the east to the Mediterranean Sea in the west. It was called the Silk Road because of the Chinese silk that was traded along its length. The road was not continuous, but was made up of a series of well-marked routes connecting major towns. Here merchants bought and sold their goods, creating a link between Asia and Europe.

Buddhist monks shave their heads and wear saffron-coloured robes.

BUDDHIST MONKS

Siddhartha Gautama, the founder of Buddhism, was born in India c. 563 BCE. By his death c. 483 BCE, his teaching had spread throughout India. From about 100 CE, Buddhist monks took Buddhism across the Himalayas to China, and along the Silk Road into central Asia. Today, most of the world's Buddhists live in Asia.

MONGOLS

The Mongols were fierce warriors who lived as nomads on the steppes, or grasslands, of central Asia. In the 1200s they created an empire that stretched from China into eastern Europe. Their power declined in the 1300s, but in 1369 one of their leaders, Tamerlane the Great, became ruler of central Asia. He built many fine mosques in his capital, Samarkand.

EUROPEAN DOMINATION

In 1498, Portuguese explorer Vasco da Gama sailed to India around the southern tip of Africa. He was the first European to reach Asia by sea. Other Europeans followed, and over the next 400 years, Europeans dominated much of Asia, first as traders and merchants, then as conquerors and colonizers. Only Persia (present-day Iran), Afghanistan, Thailand, and Japan remained free from European control.

Portuguese colonial house in Macau

WORLD WAR II

During World War II (1939-45), the Japanese invaded China and much of Southeast Asia in order to create an empire. Some welcomed the Japanese invaders, because they threw out the European colonial masters and gave the people a greater degree of independence. After Japan's defeat in 1945, Britain, France, the Netherlands, and the USA returned to take control of their former colonies.

COMMUNIST ASIA

In 1949, the Communist Party finally gained power in China after years of civil war. Communists also took control in North Korea, Mongolia, North Vietnam, Cambodia, and Laos. The Communist governments of these countries improved people's living standards, but failed to match the economic success of Japan and other Asian countries.

The Red Guard, followers of Chinese Communist leader Mao Zedong

Chinese students bearing a portrait of Mao Zedong (1893-1976)

Chinese demonstrate their revolutionary fervour in 1967

ASIA

c. 2,500 BCE Hinduism is founded in India.

c. 563-c. 483 BCE Life of Buddha.

500s BCE The Silk Road is established.

250 BCE Buddhism spreads to Sri Lanka and Southeast Asia.

100 CE Monks take Buddhism to China and into central Asia.

850-1200 Chola kings of India take Hinduism to Sri Lanka and into Southeast Asia.

1279 Mongol Empire under Kublai Khan reaches greatest extent.

1369 Tamerlane the Great creates a new Mongol Empire in the city of Samarkand.

1498 Vasco da Gama sails to India.

1600 British merchants establish an East India Company in order to trade with India.

1619 Dutch begin to control the East Indies.

1757 British take over Bengal and expand their rule in India.

1850s French begin to control Southeast Asia.

1937 Japanese troops invade China.

1941-45 World War II rages in eastern Asia and the Pacific.

1947-48 British rule in India comes to an end.

1949 Indonesia becomes independent.

1999 Portuguese hand Macau back to China.

INDEPENDENCE

Following World War II, the European countries began to grant their Asian colonies independence. India became independent from Britain in 1947-48, and Indonesia gained its independence from the Netherlands in 1949. The last colony – the Portuguese territory of Macau – was handed back to China in 1999.

TIGER ECONOMIES

Japan and other countries began rebuilding their economies after World War II. They concentrated on heavy industries such as car manufacturing and shipbuilding, and on hi-tech industries such as computing and electronics. Today Japan is the world's second biggest economy, while Taiwan, South Korea, Singapore, and China have become industrial powerhouses.

Find out more

ASIA
CHINA
COMMUNISM
TRADE AND INDUSTRY
VIETNAM WAR
WORLD WAR II

ASSYRIANS

ABOUT 3,000 YEARS AGO, a mighty empire rose to power in the Middle East where Iraq is today. This was the Assyrian Empire. It lasted for more than 300 years and spread all over the surrounding area from the River Nile to Mesopotamia. Under King Shalmaneser I (1273-1244 BCE) the Assyrians conquered Babylon and many other independent states, and eventually united the region into one empire. With an enormous army, armoured horses, fast two-wheeled chariots, and huge battering rams, the Assyrians were highly skilled, successful fighters, ruthless in battle. The Assyrian Empire grew quickly with a series of warlike kings, including Ashurbanipal II and Sennacherib. Great wealth and excellent trading links enabled the Assyrians to rebuild the cities of Nimrud and Nineveh (which became the capital), and to create a new city at Khorsabad. Assyria was a rich, well-organized society, but by the 7th century B.C. the empire had grown too large to protect itself well. In about 612 BCE, the Babylonian and Mede peoples destroyed Nineveh, and the Assyrian Empire collapsed.

WARRIORS
The Assyrians were famed and feared for their strength in battle and for torturing their victims. They developed the chariot and fought with swords, shields, slings, and bows.

ASSYRIAN EMPIRE
In the 7th century BCE the Assyrian Empire reached its greatest extent. It stretched down to the Persian Gulf in the south and the Mediterranean coast in the west, and included Babylon.

Men armed with spears and swords accompanied the king on lion hunts.

LION HUNT
Hunting and killing lions was a favourite pastime of the Assyrian kings. Lions represented the wild strength of nature. It was considered a noble challenge to seek them out and kill them, although captive lions were also hunted. Only the king was allowed to kill a lion.

ROYAL LIFE
Stone reliefs tell us much about the lives of the Assyrian royalty. This relief sculpture shows King Ashurbanipal II (669-621 BCE) drinking wine in his garden with his queen. It looks like a quiet, domestic scene, but on another section of this sculpture there is a head hanging from a tree. It is the head of Teumann, the king of the Elamites, whose defeat the king and queen are celebrating.

WINGED BULLS
Massive stone sculptures (right) of winged bulls were placed on each side of important doors and gateways.

Winged bulls have a human head, wings, and fish-like scales, suggesting that they represent a combination of all the best qualities of animals and people.

Assyrian slaves had to drag the massive sculptures to the palace.

___
Find out more
BABYLONIANS
PERSIANS, ANCIENT
___

ASTRONAUTS
AND SPACE TRAVEL

The astronaut wears a special undergarment with tubes that water flows through, keeping the astronaut's body cool.

The different parts of the suit, such as the gloves and helmet, are locked in position.

ON 12 APRIL 1961, the world watched in wonder as Yuri Gagarin of Russia blasted off from Earth aboard a huge rocket and entered space. He was the first cosmonaut, the Russian word for astronaut, a person trained to work in space. Eight years later, Neil Armstrong walked on the Moon and became the first human being to step onto another world away from our planet. Since then, a few hundred other astronauts, both men and women, have voyaged into space. Astronauts have jobs to do during their missions. They help with the construction of the International Space Station and perform scientific experiments under the weightless conditions of space. Today, astronauts are preparing for the next major landmarks in space exploration – to go back to the Moon and then perhaps to Mars.

Pressure helmet

Visor

Cap

Communications headset

Water inlet and outlet

There is no air in space to carry sound waves, so astronauts communicate by radio.

Main tanks provide oxygen for the astronaut to breathe.

Communications input socket

Reserve oxygen tanks provide emergency oxygen supply.

Oxygen inlets and outlets

Wrist clamp

Control panel allows the astronaut to adjust the temperature and oxygen flow in the suit.

Battery provides power for spacesuit systems.

Urine transfer collection

Extra vehicular glove

Integrated thermal micrometeoroid garment

Cosmonaut Salizhan S. Shapirov installing navigation and communication equipment outside the International Space Station.

Urine-collection device worn by the astronaut is like a big nappy.

Layers of different plastics make the suit strong yet flexible.

Strap-on fastener

Lunar overshoe

SPACESUIT

Space is a perilous place for a human being. There is no air to breathe, and without a spacesuit for protection, an astronaut would explode. This is because the human body is built to function under the constant pressure of the Earth's atmosphere, which is not present in space.

WEIGHTLESSNESS

We have weight because of the pull of the Earth's gravity. In space, gravity holds the astronauts and their spacecraft in orbit around the Earth. But there is no force holding the astronauts to their spaceship, so they float around inside it. This is called weightlessness.

On some spacecraft, astronauts sleep in sleeping bags fixed to the cabin walls.

Food and drinks come in special packs that do not spill. There is an oven to heat food.

Special exercise machines help the astronauts keep fit.

TRAINING
People have to undergo long training programmes to become astronauts. They also must be very fit. These cosmonauts are practising working under weightless conditions using a life-size model of a *Salyut* spacecraft inside a huge water tank.

LIVING IN SPACE
While on board a spacecraft, astronauts consume the same kind of food and drink as they do on Earth. There is usually no bath or shower; astronauts wash with damp pieces of cloth instead. Regular exercise is essential, because living in weightless conditions can weaken bones and muscles.

Find out more
GRAVITY
MOON
SOVIET UNION, HISTORY OF
SPACE FLIGHT

ASTRONOMY

THERE ARE AMAZING SIGHTS to be seen in the heavens – other worlds different from our own, great glowing clouds of gas where stars are born and immense explosions in which stars end their lives. Astronomers are scientists who study all the objects in the universe, such as planets, moons, comets, stars, and galaxies. Astronomy is an ancient science. The early Arabs and Greeks looked up to the sky and tried to understand the moons, stars, and planets. However, most of these objects were too distant for early astronomers to see in any detail. It was only after the invention of the telescope in the 17th century that people really began to learn about the universe. Today, astronomy makes use of a vast array of equipment to explore space. Astronomers use ground-based telescopes of many kinds, launch spacecraft that visit the other planets in the solar system, and send up satellites to study the universe from high above the Earth's surface.

OBSERVATORY
Astronomers study space from observatories (above) that are often at the top of a mountain where there is a clear view of the sky. This photograph took several hours to make. The stars trace circles because the rotation of the Earth makes them appear to move across the sky.

Fine guidance sensors lock onto bright stars, to ensure that the telescope is steady and the images are not blurred.

High-gain antenna receives commands from Earth, and returns Hubble pictures as TV signals.

Sunshade protects the telescope at launch, and helps to prevent bright sunlight from spoiling images.

Secondary mirror is supported within the telescope tube.

Reaction wheels point Hubble at stars and other targets in space.

Space Telescope Imaging Spectrograph breaks up light into its constituent wavelengths.

Handrail for astronauts

Magnetometer senses Hubble's movements through the Earth's magnetic field.

Light is reflected from the main mirror to the secondary, and then to the cameras and other detectors behind the main mirror.

Cosmic Origins Spectograph (hidden from view) analyses ultraviolet light.

Computers coordinate all the on-board systems.

Wide Field Camera (WFC3) is the main camera for visible light.

Main (primary) mirror, 2.4 m (7.8 ft) in diameter, collects and focuses light.

Second high-gain antenna

Solar arrays provide power by converting sunlight into electricity.

Advanced Camera for Surveys is very sensitive, but has a more restricted view than the WF/PC.

Near-Infrared Camera and Multi-Object Spectrometer contains three infrared detectors.

SPACE TELESCOPE
The optical telescope is one of the main tools of an astronomer. Most astronomical optical, infrared, and ultraviolet telescopes focus light from distant stars using a large curved mirror instead of lenses. This is because it is not possible to construct a lens big enough, and even if it were, a lens would produce distorted images. Launched in 1990, the Hubble Space Telescope is an optical telescope that orbits high above the Earth in order to avoid the blurring effect produced by the Earth's atmosphere.

RECEIVING DATA ON EARTH
All signals to and from the Hubble Space Telescope pass through NASA's Goddard Space Flight Center, Maryland, USA. Here, engineers constantly monitor the spacecraft's health. Hubble astronomers work at the Space Telescope Science Institute, and control the telescope's observing schedule. Astronomers from far-off countries use Hubble through remote control. An astronomer (right) receives a Hubble image of the Tarantula nebula (a group of stars).

EXPLORING THE UNIVERSE

Stars and other objects in the universe produce streams of tiny particles and many kinds of waves, such as radio waves. Except for light, these waves and particles are all invisible, but astronomers can study them to provide information about the universe. The atmosphere blocks many of the rays, so detectors are mounted on satellites that orbit above the Earth's atmosphere.

INFRARED RAYS

Objects in space can also send out infrared (heat) rays. Satellites and ground-based telescopes pick up these rays. They can reveal the centres of galaxies, and gas clouds called nebulae (right), where stars are forming.

ULTRAVIOLET RAYS

Stars that are much hotter than our Sun give out far more ultraviolet radiation than visible light. This ultraviolet image of a spiral galaxy was taken from a space observatory to help astronomers understand when and where new stars have formed.

X-RAYS

Special satellites carry detectors that pick up x-rays. These satellites have discovered black holes, which give out x-rays as they suck in gases from nearby stars. This is an x-ray image of a supernova, which is an exploding star.

GAMMA RAYS

Some satellites detect gamma rays, which are waves of very high energy. Gamma rays come from many objects, including pulsars, which are the remains of exploded stars. This is a gamma ray map of our own galaxy.

VISIBLE LIGHT

Telescopes on the ground and on satellites detect the light rays that come from planets, comets, stars, and galaxies. The Earth's atmosphere distorts light rays, making pictures slightly fuzzy. However, new computer-controlled telescopes are able to reduce this distortion.

Radio image of a quasar. A quasar is a kind of powerful galaxy with a very bright centre.

RADAR SIGNALS

Astronomers produce radar maps of planets and moons by bouncing radio waves off their surfaces. The radar map of Venus (left) was recorded by the *Pioneer Venus* spacecraft of the United States. The map is colour-coded to represent plains and mountains on the planet's surface.

RADIO WAVES

Many bodies produce their own radio waves, which are picked up by the large dishes of radio telescopes. Objects called pulsars, quasars, and radio galaxies were discovered in this way.

A supernova remnant as seen through an optical telescope.

An array of sensitive light detectors pick up flashes of light produced when neutrinos enter the tank.

NEUTRINOS

Tiny particles called neutrinos come from stars. Most neutrinos pass right through the Earth, but special detectors lying deep underground can detect a few of them. By studying neutrinos, astronomers can find out about the Sun and exploding stars.

SKYWATCHERS OF THE PAST

In the third century BCE, the Greek scientist Aristarchus suggested that the Earth and planets move around the Sun. The telescope, first used to observe the heavens by Italian scientist Galileo, proved this to be true and led to many other discoveries. In the 1920s, the astronomer Edwin Hubble found that stars exist in huge groups called galaxies and that the universe is expanding in size.

The ancient observatory at Jaipur, India, contains stone structures that astronomers built to measure the positions of the Sun, Moon, planets, and stars.

Neutrino detectors consist of large tanks of water, in which flashes of light occur as the neutrinos pass through.

Find out more

BIG BANG
MOON
PLANETS
SATELLITES
SPACE FLIGHT
STARS
SUN
TELESCOPES
UNIVERSE

ATLANTIC OCEAN

THE UNDERWATER LANDSCAPE of the Atlantic is dominated by the mid-Atlantic ridge, the world's longest mountain chain. Some of the ridge's peaks rise above sea level as volcanic islands, such as Iceland and the Azores. The deepest part of the Atlantic, the Puerto Rico Trench, plunges to 9,200 m (30,185 ft) below sea level. The Atlantic Ocean is rich in oil and natural gas. In recent years, offshore oil reserves have been exploited in the Gulf of Mexico, the Niger Delta and the North Sea. Sand, gravel and shell deposits are also mined by the USA and UK for use in the construction industry. The Atlantic is the most productive and heavily utilized fishing ground in the world, providing millions of tonnes a year. The Atlantic Ocean has been crossed by shipping routes for many centuries. It is still heavily used for sea-borne trade, especially the bulk transport of raw materials, such as oil, grain, and iron, to industrial centres.

SUBTROPICAL SCILLIES
The Gulf Stream is a warm ocean current that flows up the east coast of North America, and then across to western Europe, driven by north-easterly trade winds. These winds carry moisture and warmth from the ocean to the land. In England's Scilly Islands, subtropical plants flourish in winter because of the impact of the current.

The Atlantic Ocean is bounded by the Americas in the west, and by Europe and Africa in the east. Along the mid-Atlantic ridge, a long submarine mountain chain, high volcanic peaks pierce the water's surface as islands.

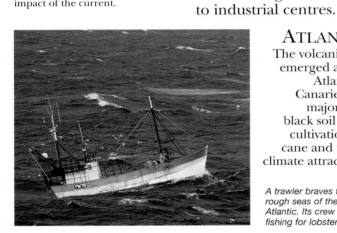

ATLANTIC TOURISM
The volcanic islands which have emerged along the ocean's mid-Atlantic ridge, especially the Canaries, Azores and Madeira, are major tourist attractions. The fertile black soil of the Canaries is ideal for the cultivation of bananas, tomatoes, sugar cane and tobacco. The mild sub-tropical climate attracts winter visitors from Europe.

A trawler braves the rough seas of the Atlantic. Its crew are fishing for lobster.

SUBMARINE ACTIVITY
During the Cold War, from the 1950s to the 1980s, the Atlantic Ocean was patrolled by both the US and Russian navies. Since the 1990s, US and Russian scientists are sharing advances in submarine technology – developed for defence purposes – to survey, map, and analyze the unexplored world beneath the Atlantic.

ATLANTIC FISHING
The Atlantic Ocean, a productive fishing ground for centuries, contains over half the world's total stock of fish. In the North, cod, haddock, mackerel, and lobster are the main catch, while the South Atlantic catch is dominated by hake, tuna, and pilchard. Freezer trawlers, that can catch and process a tonne or more of fish in just an hour, are in danger of over-fishing the Atlantic. Countries claim exclusive rights to zones extending 370 km (200 nautical miles) from their coastlines to conserve fish stocks.

NAVIGATION
Compasses are vital in cross-ocean navigation. The compass needle points to magnetic north, in the Canadian Arctic.

ICELANDIC HEATING
Iceland was formed by volcanic action along a fault line in the Earth's crust, 65 million years ago. Iceland still has over 100 volcanoes, many still active. The vast natural heat reserves beneath Iceland's icy surface, are being harnessed to provide hot water and heating for much of the population.

Plumes of steam rise from a geothermal power station (left). Iceland has the most solfataras (volcanic vents) and hot springs in the world. The intense heat deep underground creates bubbling hot springs and mud pools.

Find out more
FISH
OCEANS AND SEAS
SHIPS AND BOATS
VOLCANOES
WIND

OVERSEAS TERRITORIES AND DEPENDENCIES

ASCENSION
Area: 90 sq km (35 sq miles)
Status: British dependent territory of St Helena
Claimed: 1673
Population: 1,200
Capital: Jamestown (St Helena)

BERMUDA
Area: 53 sq km (20.5 sq miles)
Status: British Crown colony
Claimed: 1612
Population: 68,000
Capital: Hamilton

BOUVET ISLAND
Area: 49 sq km (19 sq miles)
Status: Norwegian dependency
Claimed: 1928
Population: None
Capital: None

FAEROE ISLANDS
Area: 1,399 sq km (540 sq miles)
Status: Self-governing territory of Denmark
Claimed: 1380
Population: 48,000
Capital: Tórshavn

FALKLAND ISLANDS
Area: 12,173 sq km (4,699 sq miles)
Status: British dependent colony
Claimed: 1832
Population: 3,100
Capital: Stanley

SAINT HELENA
Area: 122 sq km (47 sq miles)
Status: British dependent territory
Claimed: 1673
Population: 7,600
Capital: Jamestown

TRISTAN DA CUNHA
Area: 98 sq km (38 sq miles)
Status: British dependent territory of St Helena
Claimed: 1612
Population: 300
Capital: Jamestown (St Helena)

SOUTH GEORGIA & THE SOUTH SANDWICH ISLANDS
Area: 3,903 sq km (1,507 sq miles)
Status: British dependent territory
Claimed: 1775
Population: No permanent residents
Capital: None

ATLANTIC YACHT RACING
Cross-ocean racing began in 1866, with a race from Connecticut, USA, to Cowes in the Isle of Wight, which took 13 days. Single-handed ocean races became popular in the 1960s.

BERMUDA TRIANGLE
The Bermuda Triangle lies between Bermuda, Florida, and Puerto Rico. Many ships, submarines, and aeroplanes have disappeared in its waters. In 1872 a deserted sailing ship, the *Mary Celeste*, was found drifting across the Atlantic – its ten crew members were never located.

SCALE BAR

INDEPENDENT STATES

CAPE VERDE
Area: 4,030 sq km (1,556 sq miles)
Population: 429,000
Capital: Praia

ICELAND
Area: 103,000 sq km (39,770 sq miles)
Population: 307,000
Capital: Reykjavík

ATMOSPHERE

There is no definite upper limit to the atmosphere. The final layer before outer space is called the exosphere; it contains hardly any air at all.

A layer of very thin air called the thermosphere extends from about 80 to 480 km (50 to 300 miles) above the ground. It contains the ionosphere – layers of electrically charged particles, from which radio waves can be bounced around the world.

The mesosphere extends from 50 to 80 km (30 to 50 miles) above the Earth. If meteors fall into this layer, they burn up, causing shooting stars.

Under the mesosphere lies the stratosphere. It extends from 11 to 50 km (7 to 30 miles) up. The stratosphere is a calm region. Airliners fly here to avoid the winds and weather lower down.

Although it is the narrowest layer, the troposphere contains most of the gas in the atmosphere. It reaches about 11 km (7 miles) above the ground, but this varies around the globe and from season to season. Most weather occurs in the troposphere.

WITHOUT THE ATMOSPHERE, it would be impossible to live on Earth. The atmosphere forms a layer, like a blanket around the Earth, protecting us from dangerous rays from the Sun and from the cold of outer space. It contains the air that we breathe, together with water vapour and tiny pieces of dust. Air contains the gases oxygen, carbon dioxide, and nitrogen, which are necessary for life; water vapour forms the clouds that bring rain. The atmosphere is held by the pull of the Earth's gravity and spreads out to about 2,000 km (1,250 miles) above the Earth. Three quarters of the air in the atmosphere lies beneath 10,700 m (35,000 ft) because the air gets thinner higher up. The air at the top of Mount Everest is only one third as thick as it is at sea level. That is why mountain climbers carry an air supply and why high-flying aircraft are sealed and have air pumped into them.

LAYERS OF THE ATMOSPHERE

The Earth's atmosphere is divided into several layers. The main layers, from the bottom upwards, are called the troposphere, the stratosphere, the mesosphere, the thermosphere, and the exosphere.

OZONE LAYER

Within the stratosphere, there is a thin layer of the gas ozone. Ozone is a form of oxygen that absorbs ultraviolet rays from the sun. Without the ozone layer, these rays would reach the ground and kill all living creatures. Pollution and the use of certain chemicals are destroying the ozone layer.

Compared to the size of the Earth, the atmosphere forms a very narrow band – approximately equivalent to the skin around an orange.

SKY AND SUNSET

When light travels through the atmosphere, it hits gas molecules and tiny particles such as pollen and dust. This causes the light to scatter, or bounce off, in all directions. Some colours are scattered more than others.

OTHER ATMOSPHERES

Other planets' atmospheres are very different from Earth's. Neptune (above) is surrounded by a thick layer of hydrogen and helium. A small amount of methane gas in this atmosphere makes Neptune look blue.

BLUE SKY
The atmosphere scatters mainly blue light; this is why the sky looks blue. The other colours of light are scattered much less than blue so that they come to Earth directly. This causes the area of sky around the Sun to look yellow.

SUNSET AND SUNRISE
At sunset and sunrise, when the Sun is below the horizon, the light travels through much more of the atmosphere before we see it. The blue light is scattered so much that it is absorbed, or soaked up, by the atmosphere. Only red light reaches us, so the sky looks red.

Find out more
CLIMATES
OXYGEN
PLANETS
SUN
WEATHER

ATOMS AND MOLECULES

A drop of water contains about 1,000 million billion molecules.

LOOK AROUND YOU. There are countless millions of different substances, from metals and plastics to people and plants. All of these are made from about 100 different kinds of "building blocks" joined together in different ways. These building blocks are tiny particles called atoms. Atoms are so small that even the tiniest speck of dust contains more than a million billion atoms. Some substances, such as iron, are made of just one kind of atom; other substances, such as water, contain molecules – atoms joined together in groups. Such molecules may be very simple or very complex. Each water molecule contains two hydrogen atoms and one oxygen atom; plastics are made of molecules which often contain millions of atoms. An atom itelf is made up of a dense centre called a nucleus. Particles that carry electricity, called electrons, move around the nucleus. Scientists have discovered how to split the nucleus, releasing enormous energy which is used in nuclear power stations and nuclear bombs.

A molecule of water contains three atoms – two hydrogen atoms and one oxygen atom.

Protons and neutrons are made up of quarks.

Electrons whiz around the nucleus. An atom of oxygen has eight electrons.

There is a lot of empty space in an atom. If the nucleus were the size of a tennis ball, the nearest electron would be 1 km (about half a mile) away.

The nucleus of an oxygen atom has eight protons and eight neutrons. The nucleus is held together by powerful forces.

PROTONS AND NEUTRONS
The nucleus of an atom contains particles called protons and neutrons. These contain even smaller particles called quarks. Protons carry electricity. However, they carry a different kind of electricity from electrons. They have a "positive charge", whereas electrons have a "negative charge". Neutrons have no electric charge.

DISCOVERING THE ATOM
About 2,400 years ago, the Greek philosopher Democritus believed that everything was made up of tiny particles. It was not until 1808 that English scientist John Dalton proved that atoms exist. Around 1909, New Zealand scientist Ernest Rutherford (below) discovered the nucleus.

IMMORTAL ATOMS
The particles that make up atoms never disappear but are constantly journeying through the universe as part of different substances. All these particles originated with the formation of the universe around 13,700 million years ago. The atoms that make everything on Earth were formed from these particles in stars, which then exploded like the crab nebula (above).

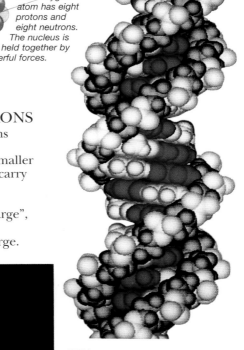

DNA
All plants and animals contain molecules of DNA (deoxyribonucleic acid). DNA carries the blueprint for life: coded information in DNA molecules determines the characteristics of each living thing and its offspring. A DNA molecule consists of millions of atoms arranged in a twisted spiral shape.

Find out more
GENETICS
OXYGEN
SCIENCE
SCIENCE, HISTORY OF

AUSTRALIA

LOCATED BETWEEN THE INDIAN AND PACIFIC OCEANS, Australia is a continent, and the sixth largest country in the world. It is a land of varied landscapes, including tropical rainforests, vast deserts, snow-capped mountains, rolling tracts of pastoral land, and magnificent beaches. The country boasts a great number of natural features, the most famous of which are the Great Barrier Reef and Uluru (Ayers Rock). Australians have an outdoor lifestyle and enjoy a high standard of living. Almost 90 per cent of the country's 21.2 million people live in the fertile strip of land on the east and southeast coast. Many of them live in Melbourne and Sydney, Australia's two largest cities, and in the nation's capital, Canberra. Today few people live in the dry Australian interior known as the Outback. The original inhabitants of Australia, the Aborigines, learned to survive in the harsh conditions there. However, only a small number of the 517,000 Aboriginal population live a traditional life in the Outback today. Other Australians are descendants of settlers from Britain, continental Europe and Southeast Asia.

Australia lies southeast of Asia, with the Pacific Ocean to the east and the Indian Ocean to the west. It is the only country that is also a continent. Together with several nearby islands, Australia covers a total area of 7.61 million sq km (2.94 million sq miles).

SURFING

Surfing is a favourite Australian sport. Surfing carnivals are held regularly in many towns. Polynesian people invented the sport hundreds of years ago; recently it has expanded to include windsurfing, trick surfing, and long-distance surfing. Surfers often travel vast distances to reach a beach with the best waves of the day.

At a surfing carnival lifeguards give demonstrations of lifesaving. Surfing competitions are hotly contested and often draw many spectators.

During the celebrations of Australia's 200th anniversary, ocean-going sailing ships gathered in Sydney's famous harbour.

SYDNEY

Sydney is the oldest and largest city in Australia. Sydney was founded in 1788 as a British prison colony with about 1,000 prisoners and their guards; today it is home to more than 4 million people. The city stands around Port Jackson, a huge natural bay spanned by Sydney Harbour Bridge. Sydney is a busy industrial centre and tourist resort.

BEACH CULTURE

The majority of Australians live in towns and cities along the coast. Therefore the beach is the most popular venue for leisure pursuits. Australia's climate is ideal for beach activities such as surfing, swimming, sailing and beach volleyball. Mild winter temperatures mean that these sports can be enjoyed all year round.

Australia's currency is the Australian dollar. On one side the coins feature a portrait of the Queen of England, who is the head of state.

FILMMAKING

The Australian film industry produces a number of important films each year. Some, such as *Picnic at Hanging Rock* (1975), which tells of the mysterious disappearance of a group of Australian schoolgirls, have received international acclaim.

TASMANIA

The island of Tasmania lies off the southeast coast of Australia and is a state in itself, with a population of nearly half a million. The island has a cooler, damper climate than the rest of the country and is famous for its fruit, vegetables, and sheep. Tin, silver, and other products are mined. Much of western Tasmania is unpopulated and covered in dense forest where native wildlife, such as the Tasmanian devil, below, survive in large numbers.

GREAT DIVIDING RANGE

Running along the eastern coast of the continent from Cape York to Ballarat is a 3,700 km (2,300 mile) mountain chain called the Great Dividing Range. The tallest mountain is Kosciuszko, at 2,228 m (7,310 ft). Other peaks are much lower. The mountains divide the fertile coastal plains from the dry interior. The steep hills were once a major barrier to travel; even today only a few roads and railways cross from east to west.

The Three Sisters formation in New South Wales belongs to the Great Dividing Range.

Outback ranchers ride motorbikes or horses to round up cattle and sheep.

OUTBACK

Very few people live in Australia's interior, called the Outback. However, sheep and cattle are farmed on the dry land. Some ranches, called stations, cover hundreds of square kilometres. Because of the great distances, Outback Australians live isolated lives and communicate by radio.

Ancient rock and bark paintings show that Aboriginal culture flourished nearly 40,000 years before European settlers arrived.

ULURU (AYERS ROCK)

One of the most impressive natural sights in Australia is Uluru (formerly known as Ayers Rock). This huge mass of sandstone stands in the middle of a wide, flat desert and is 335 m (1,142 ft) high. Although it lies hundreds of kilometres from the nearest town, Uluru is a major tourist attraction with its own hotel. The rock is particularly beautiful at sunset, when it seems to change colour.

STRIP MINING

Australia has huge mineral wealth, and mining is an important industry. The country produces one third of the world's uranium, which is essential for nuclear power. In recent years iron ore has been excavated in large strip mines where giant digging machines remove entire hills.

PERTH

Founded in 1829, Perth (below) is the state capital of Western Australia and its financial and commercial heart. Most Australian people live in cities, and the population of Perth reflects the European ancestry of a large percentage of today's Australians.

CANBERRA

Canberra, the capital city of Australia, is situated in the Australian Capital Territory (A.C.T.), an area of 2,360 sq km (911 sq miles) completely surrounded by the state of New South Wales. The capital was designed as a city of parks and gardens by American landscape architect, Walter Burley Griffin. Construction of the city began in 1913. Canberra is a political and educational centre rather than a commercial or industrial town.

Hay Street mall (left) is a pedestrian shopping precinct located in Perth's central business district.

ADELAIDE

Adelaide (right) is the capital and chief port of South Australia. A well-planned city, it was designed in a grid pattern by Colonel William Light, the first surveyor-general of South Australia. The city is bordered by 6.9 sq km (2.7 sq miles) of parkland, and was named after Queen Adelaide, wife of King William IV of England.

MELBOURNE

The capital city of Victoria and the second largest city in Australia, Melbourne (below) displays a dramatic mixture of old and new. Melbourne was founded in 1835 by an Australian farmer, John Batman. Nearly 20 years later, gold was discovered in Victoria and Melbourne's population climbed sharply. Today, Melbourne is a leading seaport, and the commercial and industrial centre of Victoria.

BRISBANE

The state capital of Queensland and its largest city, Brisbane (right) is a bustling seaport lying above the mouth of the Brisbane river at Moreton Bay. In this way, it is similar to Australia's other state capitals, all of which were founded near rivers close to ocean harbours. Like other state capitals, Brisbane too is the commercial centre of its state, with its main business district situated near the waterfront.

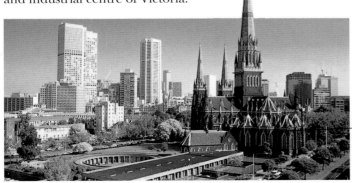

St Paul's Cathedral stands proudly amid modern architecture in Melbourne. The building was designed by William Butterfield in the 1880s in a Gothic style.

Find out more

ARCHITECTURE
AUSTRALIA, HISTORY OF
CONTINENTS
FARMING
OCEANS AND SEAS

Volcano   Mountain   Ancient monument   Capital city   Large city/town   Small city/town

STATISTICS
Area: 7,686,850 sq km (2,967,893 sq miles)
Population: 21,282,000
Capital: Canberra
Languages: English, Greek, Vietnamese, Aboriginal languages
Religions: Roman Catholic, Anglican, United Church, non-religious
Currency: Australian dollar
Main occupations: Agriculture, mining, animal husbandry
Main exports: Lager, wine, coal, iron ore, gold, bauxite, copper
Main imports: Vehicles, manufactured goods

DESERT
Few people live in Australia's huge interior, which is covered mainly by desert. The four largest deserts are the Simpson, Gibson, Great Sandy, and Great Victoria deserts. Most are vast areas of swirling sand that drifts into giant sand dunes.

GREAT BARRIER REEF
Coral reefs are created by the build-up of the skeletons of tiny marine creatures called polyps. Coral cannot grow above water, or below 30 m (100 ft) in cool waters. The Great Barrier Reef has been formed over 600,000 years by the upward growth of coral, triggered by a general rise in sea-level during this period. Located off the coast of Queensland, the Reef stretches from Bundaberg to the tip of Cape York.

The Great Barrier Reef is teeming with over 2,000 species of fish and numerous types of coral. The various life forms inhabiting the waters display a wonderful variety of colours.

DRY LAKES
Many of Australia's vast desert "lakes" contain no water. Lake Eyre, in South Australia, for example, fills with water rarely and was completely dry for a century until 1950.

NULLARBOR PLAIN
The Nullarbor Plain was given its name because it is completely treeless: in the Latin language, null means nothing, and arbor, tree.

SCALE BAR
0   200   400   km
0   200   400   miles

43

HISTORY OF
AUSTRALIA

c. 40,000 BCE First Aborigines arrive in Australia from Asia.

1770 Captain Cook sails into Botany Bay and claims Australia for Britain.

1788 British convicts arrive.

1901 Australia becomes an independent dominion within the British Empire.

1915 Australian troops fight at Gallipoli in World War I.

1945-65 Australia pays fares for poor Europeans to settle in Australia.

As RECENTLY AS 1600, the only people who knew about Australia were the Aboriginal peoples who had lived there for more than 40,000 years. The rest of the world had no idea that the continent existed. In 1606, the Dutch explorer William Jansz landed in northern Australia. Although he did not know it, he was the first European to see the country. Further exploration of the coastline by Dutch and British explorers revealed that Australia was an island. In 1770, the British captain James Cook claimed the east coast of Australia for Britain and named it New South Wales. The British sent convicts to their new colony, forming the basis of Sydney, today the country's largest city. Throughout the 19th century, the population of Australia grew as more convicts arrived, followed by free immigrants. For many of them life was tough, but the British colony grew richer when gold was discovered in 1851. Farming also became established. In 1901, Australia became an independent commonwealth, although it remained close to Britain for many years and Australian troops fought in both world wars on the side of Britain. More recently, Australia has branched away from Britain and set up links with other countries.

ABORIGINES
The first Aboriginal peoples probably arrived in Australia from the islands of Southeast Asia about 40,000 years ago. In 1770, there were about 300,000 Aborigines in Australia.

Convict ships in the bay

Chopping wood to make timber huts

The convicts carried supplies onto the shore.

At first, the convicts (prisoners) were miserable and hungry.

The first British settlement in Australia was at Port Jackson in Sydney Harbour, next to the location of the present-day Sydney Opera House.

BOTANY BAY
In 1770, the English explorer James Cook dropped anchor in Botany Bay, south of what is now the city of Sydney. In 1788, the first 750 British settlers arrived in Australia. These people were convicts – guarded by 250 soldiers – who had been transported abroad to relieve the overcrowded British prisons. They lived in a prison camp set up on the shores of Sydney Harbour. The colonists came close to starvation, but gradually their lives improved. The tents they lived in were replaced by brick and timber huts, and eventually the colony began to prosper. In 1868, the transportation of convicts ended, leaving more than 160,000 convicts living in Australia.

EXPLORATION

The first explorers of Australia mapped out the coastline but left the interior largely untouched. In 1606, the Dutch navigator William Jansz briefly visited northeastern Australia. Between 1829 and 1830, the English explorer Charles Sturt explored the rivers in the south but failed to find the inland sea that many people assumed existed in the centre of Australia. Between 1839 and 1840, Edward Eyre, from England, discovered the vast, dry salt lakes in South Australia before walking along its southern coast. In 1860 and 1861, the Irishman Robert O'Hara Burke and Englishman William Wills became the first people to cross Australia from south to north. In 1862 John McDouall Stuart succeeded in crossing the continent from South Australia and returning alive.

- Burke and Wills
- Sturt
- Eyre
- Cook
- Jansz

Alice Springs
Perth
Brisbane
Sydney
Adelaide
Melbourne

Map showing the routes of the different explorers of Australia

BURKE AND WILLS

In 1860 and 1861, Burke and Wills succeeded in crossing Australia from south to north. However, they both died of starvation on the return journey south.

GOLD RUSH

Gold was discovered in 1851 in New South Wales and Victoria. Thousands of prospectors rushed from all over the world, including China, to make their fortunes in Australia. The national population rose from 400,000 in 1850 to 1,100,000 by 1860. Conditions were tough for the gold miners, and in 1854 a group of miners at Eureka Stockade at Ballarat, near Melbourne, refused to pay the licence fee required to mine for gold. The government sent in troops; 24 miners and six soldiers were killed in the battle that followed.

The Aborigines were amazed to see the crowds of white people landing in their territory.

OVERCOMING ABORIGINES

During the 19th century, the European settlers disrupted the Aboriginal way of life. Many Aboriginal languages and customs died out as their land was taken. Children were taken away from their parents to be educated in the European way. As a result, the Aborigine population fell from 300,000 in 1770 to about 60,000 by 1900.

IMMIGRATION

In 1880, there were only two million people on the vast Australian continent. A century later, almost 15 million people lived there. Most had come to Australia from Britain, Italy, and Greece. In a deliberate attempt to boost the population after 1945, the Australian government offered to pay part of the passage for poor Europeans. About two million people took advantage of the scheme, which ended in 1965, with one million coming from Britain alone. Asians and other non-white peoples were denied entry until the 1960s. Many children travelled on their own. The group of immigrants (left) are on their way to a farm school in Western Australia from Waterloo Station, London, England.

URANIUM MINING

Australia is rich in minerals, like uranium, the raw material used to fuel nuclear power stations and produce nuclear bombs. Although uranium mining increased dramatically during the 1970s, many Australians opposed it because of the dangers of radiation from uranium. In addition, many of the uranium deposits lie within Aboriginal tribal lands. Protests have therefore regularly occurred to prevent the exploitation of this dangerous mineral.

Find out more
AUSTRALIA
EMIGRATION AND IMMIGRATION
INDIAN OCEAN
NUCLEAR ENERGY
PACIFIC OCEAN

AZTECS

MORE THAN SEVEN HUNDRED YEARS AGO a civilization was born in what is now Mexico. The Aztecs, founders of this civilization, were the last native American rulers of Mexico. They were a wandering tribe who arrived in the Mexican valley during the 13th century. The Olmecs and Toltecs had already established civilizations in this area, and influenced the Aztecs. Over the next 200 years the Aztecs set up a mighty empire of some 12 million people. The Aztecs believed that the world would come to an end unless they sacrificed people to their sun god, Huitzilopochtli. They built pyramids and temples where they sacrificed prisoners from the cities they had conquered. In 1519 Spanish conquistadors (adventurers) arrived in Mexico and defeated the Aztecs. Moctezuma II, last of the Aztec emperors, was killed by his own people, and the Aztec empire collapsed.

Victim being sacrificed on top of the temple.

Preaching priest

Aztec pyramid with temple at top

The bodies of sacrificed victims were thrown to the ground.

Causeway

Temple precinct at Tenochtitlán

TENOCHTITLÁN

The Aztec capital, called Tenochtitlán, was a "floating city", built in Lake Texcoco, on one natural and many artificial islands. To reach the mainland, the Aztecs built causeways (raised roads) and canals between the islands. Today Mexico City stands on the site.

AZTEC ARTISTS
The Aztecs made beautiful jewellery using gold, turquoise, pearls, shells, and feathers. They also used other valuable stones, such as obsidian and jade.

HUMAN SACRIFICES
Aztec priests used knives with stone blades to kill up to 1,000 people each week, offering the hearts to their sun god, Huitzilopochtli.

TRIBUTES
The Aztecs became very rich by collecting tributes (payments) from conquered tribes. Cloth, maize (a type of corn), pottery, and luxury goods were brought to Tenochtitlán from the conquered cities by porters, and exchanged in four huge markets. Officials made lists of all the tributes in picture writing. The Aztecs declared war on any tribe that refused to pay tribute.

Ceremonial jade mask

Find out more
MEXICO
SOUTH AMERICA
SOUTH AMERICA, HISTORY OF

BABYLONIANS

CYLINDER SEAL
The Babylonians wrote using cylinder seals. These seals were often made of semiprecious stone and were very delicately carved. To sign or stamp a document, a person rolled a cylinder seal over damp clay. This seal shows clearly the god Shamash, the goddess Ishtar (with wings), and the god, Ea.

ONE OF THE FIRST CIVILIZATIONS developed about 6,000 years ago in the Middle East, between the Tigris and Euphrates rivers. This region was known as Mesopotamia, meaning "land between rivers". The land was fertile, and farming methods were highly refined. The people were among the first to develop a system of writing, use the wheel, and build cities. One of these cities was Babylon, founded before 2500 BCE. It became the capital city of Babylonia (now part of Iraq). Babylon was an important trading centre. It was also a religious centre and the site of many splendid temples. Its people were strong and prosperous under the great king Hammurabi, who united the different areas into one empire. Babylon became even more magnificent later, under King Nebuchadnezzar II. In 538 BCE, the Persian king Cyrus the Great conquered Babylon; Alexander the Great conquered it again in 331 BCE. The city was then ruled by the Parthians and the Persian Sassanid dynasty until the 7th century CE, but by then had lost its importance and fallen into ruins.

Ziggurat

Ishtar Gate was named after the goddess Ishtar. The gate has been reconstructed and today it stands in the Berlin Museum, Germany.

BABYLONIAN EMPIRE
Babylon was one of several important cities in Mesopotamia. For about 2,000 years, its fortunes rose and fell. At its height, under King Hammurabi, and later King Nebuchadnezzar II, the Babylonian empire controlled the entire southern area of Mesopotamia.

BABYLON
The city of Babylon was rebuilt many times before its final destruction. It reached the height of its glory in about 600 BCE. It was an impressive city, with massive walls and elaborate religious buildings, including a pyramid-like ziggurat. Babylon also had a fabulous Hanging Garden – one of the Seven Wonders of the Ancient World.

RUINS OF BABYLON
About 90 km (55 miles) south of Baghdad, Iraq, lie the ruins of ancient Babylon. Although the ruins are sparse, it is still possible to see where the palaces and ziggurat once stood. During the 19th century, archeologists excavated the site. Today, various parts of the ancient city wall have been rebuilt, as shown above.

HAMMURABI
Under King Hammurabi (1792-1750 BCE), Babylon gained control of a large part of Mesopotamia. Hammurabi is famous for the laws he introduced, which are carved on a stela, or pillar, of stone. The stone shows a portrait of Hammurabi standing before Shamash, the god of justice. Beneath this are the laws of Babylon, carved in cuneiform (wedge-shaped) writing. They deal with all aspects of life and show that Babylon was a sophisticated civilization.

NEBUCHADNEZZAR
Nebuchadnezzar II (605-562 BCE) was one of the most famous kings of Babylonia. Among other conquests, he captured Jerusalem and forced thousands of its people into exile in Babylonian territory. This story is told in the Bible, in the Book of Daniel. Nebuchadnezzar is said to have gone mad at the end of his reign, as shown in this picture of Nebuchadnezzar by the English artist William Blake (1757-1827).

Find out more
ALPHABETS
ASSYRIANS
PHOENICIANS
WONDERS
of the ancient world

BIG BANG

The Big Bang, 13.7 billion years ago

NEARLY FOURTEEN BILLION YEARS AGO, the universe exploded out of virtually nothing. The first scientist to propose this astonishing theory, now known as the Big Bang, was George Lemaître (1894-1966). His idea was supported by the work of Edwin Hubble (1889-1953), which showed that the universe is expanding. If this is so, the entire cosmos must have originated from a single point of explosion. But what was that single point? Scientists call it a "singularity" – a tiny, infinitely dense dot that once contained all the matter of the universe. Such a thing is impossible to imagine, and even astronomers do not really understand it. Yet within a few minutes of the Big Bang, the single point would have been converted into an immense, expanding cloud of gas. Over millions of years this became the galaxies, stars, and planets of the universe.

FRED HOYLE
It was astronomer Fred Hoyle (1915-2001) who suggested the term "Big Bang", as a joke. He believed the universe had no beginning and no end.

Galaxies started to form 500 million years after the Big Bang.

Stars formed in spinning clouds of dust and gas.

RED SHIFT
The light from some stars looks redder than it should. This is due to the Doppler Effect, and shows that these stars are moving away from us. Distant galaxies also look redder but because the whole of space is expanding their lightwaves are stretched when they reach us. This is called red shift.

The solar system formed, 4.6 billion years ago.

Stretched wave, light redder

Star

Wavelength and colour unchanged

The Earth

Star

Compressed waves, light bluer

Star

If a star is moving away, its light waves are stretched out and shift towards the red end of the spectrum.

If a star is staying in the same position relative to Earth, then the wavelengths of light emitted remain unchanged.

If a star is moving towards the Earth, light waves are compressed and shift to the blue end of the spectrum.

First life forms appeared on Earth, 3.8 billion years ago.

As the ambulance moves away, the siren's sound waves stretch, increasing their wavelength and lowering their pitch.

CHAIN OF EVENTS
Scientists believe that the universe was created in an explosive event called the Big Bang. At the instant of creation, matter was concentrated in an infinitely small, dense dot called a singularity. This then began to expand and cool, allowing the conversion of energy into particles. After thousands of years, these particles joined to make atoms of hydrogen and helium that would eventually form galaxies and stars.

DOPPLER EFFECT
Christian Doppler (1803-53) showed that sound waves are compressed if the source is moving towards your ear, and stretched if it is moving away. This alters the pitch of the sound you hear. The same principle applies to light waves arriving from distant stars.

The sound waves of an ambulance siren are compressed as it comes nearer, reducing their wavelength and raising their pitch.

Find out more
ASTRONOMY
PLANETS
STARS
UNIVERSE

BIRDS

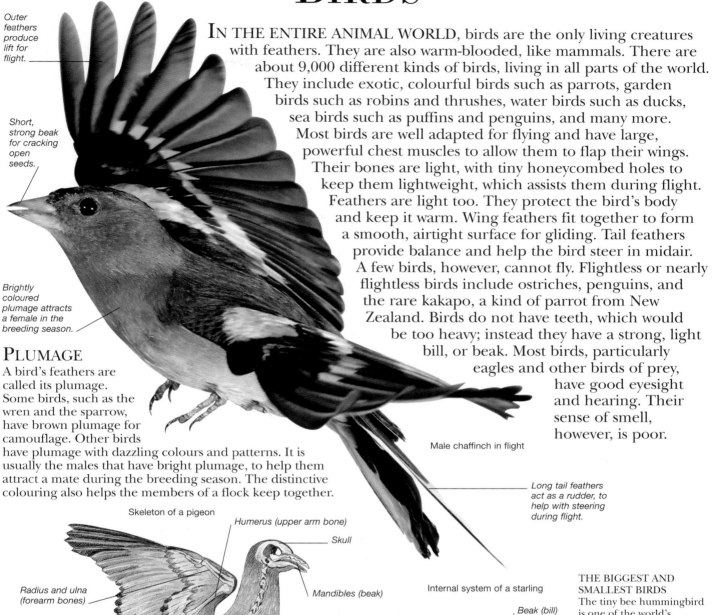

IN THE ENTIRE ANIMAL WORLD, birds are the only living creatures with feathers. They are also warm-blooded, like mammals. There are about 9,000 different kinds of birds, living in all parts of the world. They include exotic, colourful birds such as parrots, garden birds such as robins and thrushes, water birds such as ducks, sea birds such as puffins and penguins, and many more. Most birds are well adapted for flying and have large, powerful chest muscles to allow them to flap their wings. Their bones are light, with tiny honeycombed holes to keep them lightweight, which assists them during flight. Feathers are light too. They protect the bird's body and keep it warm. Wing feathers fit together to form a smooth, airtight surface for gliding. Tail feathers provide balance and help the bird steer in midair. A few birds, however, cannot fly. Flightless or nearly flightless birds include ostriches, penguins, and the rare kakapo, a kind of parrot from New Zealand. Birds do not have teeth, which would be too heavy; instead they have a strong, light bill, or beak. Most birds, particularly eagles and other birds of prey, have good eyesight and hearing. Their sense of smell, however, is poor.

Outer feathers produce lift for flight.

Short, strong beak for cracking open seeds.

Brightly coloured plumage attracts a female in the breeding season.

Male chaffinch in flight

Long tail feathers act as a rudder, to help with steering during flight.

PLUMAGE

A bird's feathers are called its plumage. Some birds, such as the wren and the sparrow, have brown plumage for camouflage. Other birds have plumage with dazzling colours and patterns. It is usually the males that have bright plumage, to help them attract a mate during the breeding season. The distinctive colouring also helps the members of a flock keep together.

Skeleton of a pigeon

Humerus (upper arm bone)

Skull

Radius and ulna (forearm bones)

Spine (backbone)

Mandibles (beak)

Keel on breast bone

Ribs

Sternum (breast bone)

Femur (thigh bone)

Pelvis (hip bone)

Pygostyle (tail bone)

Tibia (shin bone)

Tarsus (ankle bone)

Internal system of a starling

Beak (bill)

Lungs

Gullet

Kidney

Crop

Heart

Liver

Gizzard

Cloaca

Intestine

THE BIGGEST AND SMALLEST BIRDS
The tiny bee hummingbird is one of the world's smallest birds. It measures about 5 cm (2 in) from beak to tail, and is so light that 17 bee hummingbirds would weigh only 28 gm (1 oz). The ostrich, which is more than 2.5 m (8 ft) tall, is the world's largest bird, but it cannot fly at all.

This ostrich head looks huge in comparison to a tiny bee hummingbird.

A bee hummingbird is so small that it can fit in the palm of your hand.

BIRD BONES

Most of the bones in a bird's skeleton are hollow, to save body weight. Wings are controlled by powerful muscles attached to the keel, which is a ridge along the edge of the breastbone.

INSIDE A BIRD

Most of a bird's body is taken up by the muscles, heart, lungs, and digestive system. Birds have two stomachs, as in the starling shown here. The first stomach, the crop, stores food; the second, the gizzard, grinds the food to a pulp.

BEAKS AND BILLS

The beak is also called the bill. It is the bird's tool for all kinds of jobs. Bills are made of a hard substance called keratin, and are used for feeding, preening (trimming the edges of feathers), making a nest, and fighting off predators. The shape of the bill shows what sort of food the bird eats. Hooked bills are good for tearing flesh.

Curlew feeding

CURLEW BILL
A long, thin bill for probing into seashore mud to find worms and shellfish.

GULL BILL
An all-around shape for probing, cutting and tearing food, and holding slippery fish.

PARROT BILL
The hooked tip is for grasping and tearing up soft fruit. The strong base cracks open seeds and pips.

MACAW BILL
The huge, heavy macaw's bill breaks up nuts and seeds. Many macaws and other parrots are becoming rare because the tropical rain forests in which they live are being destroyed.

Wing feather of a macaw

Rachis (stiff shaft)

Barbs

Flat part of feather, called the vane

Quill or base of feather, embedded in skin

Blue tit egg

Hard, chalky eggshell

Baby bird

Food store of yolk

FEATHERS

Tiny hummingbirds have less than 1,000 feathers; swans have more than 25,000. Feathers are made mainly of keratin, which is also found in human hair and nails. Feathers have a central shaft, or rachis. On each side of the shaft, hooks called barbs lock together like a zip to make a flat part called the vane. Flight feathers make a smooth wing surface; down feathers keep the bird warm.

Soft, downy parrot feather

Peacock feathers

Colourful patches on feathers, known as "eyes", are used for the breeding display.

NESTS AND EGGS

Birds do not give birth to babies the way that mammals do. Instead, they lay eggs with hard shells, then sit on them to keep them warm. The baby bird develops inside the shell, nourished by the yolk. After a few weeks the bird pecks its way out of the shell. Some birds, such as flamingos, build big nests for their eggs. Others, such as guillemots, do not make nests, but lay eggs on a cliff edge. Some cuckoos lay eggs in another bird's nest and abandon them, leaving the owner of the nest to raise the young.

Day-old blue tit nestlings

NESTLINGS
Most newly hatched birds are helpless, for they have no feathers and cannot see. They stay in the nest to be fed and protected by one or both parents until their feathers grow. A parent bird may make dozens of trips back to the nest each day, bringing food for the chicks.

BIRD BEHAVIOUR

During the day, birds are busy looking after their young, communicating with other birds, eating, and preening. Bird behaviour such as migrating in winter or pecking at food is instinctive, so it does not have to be learned. Some birds, such as the tawny frogmouth of Australia, feed at night, but during the day the frogmouth sits very still, looking like a tree stump.

BREEDING DISPLAY
During the breeding season, the male blue bird of paradise hangs upside down in a tree, showing off his feathers to attract a female. The males of some kinds of birds, such as the grouse, fight over a patch of ground called a lek. Without a territory, no females will come to mate.

Blue bird of paradise

Eyelids still joined together

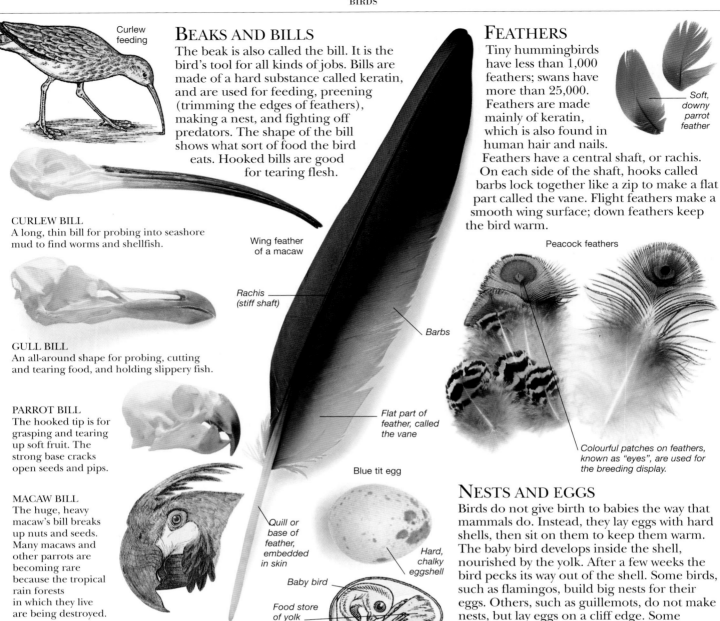

Find out more
ANIMALS
CONSERVATION
and endangered species
ECOLOGY AND FOOD WEBS
FOREST WILDLIFE
LAKE AND RIVER WILDLIFE
SEASHORE WILDLIFE
ZOOS

BLACK DEATH

Map showing how the plague spread in waves across Europe

1350

1348

1347

THE MEDITERRANEAN ISLAND OF SICILY was a terrifying place in 1347. Everywhere people were dying of a mysterious disease. Those who caught it usually had violent stomach cramps and boils under their arms. Dark patches covered their bodies, and death followed within three days. The disease became known as the Black Death because of the dark patches; today we know it was bubonic plague. It spread into Italy and France. By the end of 1348 millions had died – about one third of the population of Europe. There was panic as the Black Death advanced. People avoided each other, fearful that they might catch the plague. Many townspeople fled into the countryside carrying the disease with them. There was a shortage of food because there were fewer people to farm the land. Fields were filled with rotting animal bodies.

SPREAD OF PLAGUE
The Black Death began in Asia. It spread through Turkey, then arrived on ships at Sicily in October 1347, and reached Britain near the end of 1348. The plague reappeared every few years until the early 18th century; outbreaks were even reported in the early 19th century.

15th-century illumination

THE BLACK DEATH
Death came to rich and poor alike. Some, thinking the plague was a punishment from God, whipped themselves and prayed to be saved.

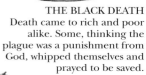

Large plague grave where victims were buried

CROSS OF DEATH
Crosses were painted on the doors of plague-ridden houses. Criminals and volunteers put the dead bodies on carts and buried them in large graves.

BUBONIC PLAGUE

Fleas living on black rats carried the bubonic plague. The fleas passed on the disease when they bit people. A more infectious form of the plague – pneumonic plague – was spread by coughing.

TREATMENT OF PLAGUE

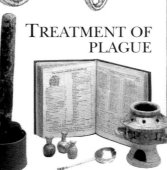

Doctors used herbs or cut open people's veins to let out "bad" blood. But these methods failed. Many people refused to go near sufferers, even sick members of their own family.

PEASANTS REVOLT
The Black Death killed so many people that there was a shortage of workers. The survivors demanded higher wages and organized revolts in France and England against high taxes and strict, out-of-date laws.

Find out more
DISEASE
MEDIEVAL EUROPE
PEASANTS REVOLT

BRAIN AND NERVES

THE BRAIN AND OTHER PARTS of the nervous system – the spinal cord and nerves – are made from billions of interconnected nerve cells called neurons that transmit millions of high-speed nerve signals, or impulses, every second. When signals reach the brain, it processes them and sends out instructions to the body. The spinal cord that runs from the brain down the back, relays signals between spinal nerves and the brain, and also controls many reflexes. Cable-like nerves contain bundles of neurons: sensory neurons carry signals from receptors in the skin and sense organs to the spinal cord and brain, enabling us to sense and respond to our surroundings; motor neurons carry signals from the brain and spinal cord to muscles, telling them to move the body in a smooth, co-ordinated fashion.

SLEEP
When we sleep, the body rests but the brain is still working, controlling our breathing and heartbeat. We remember some of our night thoughts as dreams.

CEREBRAL HEMISPHERES
The largest parts of the brain are the two folded cerebral hemispheres. Our thoughts are based in these hemispheres. The outer layer of the brain is called the cerebral cortex. It is rich in nerve cell bodies. The inner layer is called the white matter. It consists mainly of nerve fibres. If the two hemispheres were spread out, they would cover an area the size of a pillowcase.

White matter

Skull

Meninges are membranes which surround and cushion the brain within the skull.

Hypothalamus has overall control of the internal organs and is linked to the pituitary gland and hormonal system.

Pituitary gland

Cerebellum processes and coordinates signals going out to muscles from hemispheres.

Spinal cord

Brain stem

Area involved with consciousness, creativity, and personality

Area associated with touch

Area that controls the muscles which make body movements

Area that controls vision

Area that controls hearing, smell, and taste

Area associated with coordination and balance

Area that controls breathing and blood pressure

Nerve fibre (axon)

Neuron cell body

Cerebral cortex

White matter

NERVE REFLEX
When you prick your finger, sensory neurons carry signals to the spinal cord. Here they pass through relay neurons and then straight back along motor neurons to the muscles. This is called a reflex – an automatic reaction that we make without thinking.

Brain

Spinal cord

Thorn touches skin.

Sensory neuron carries nerve signals to the spinal cord from pain receptors in the skin.

Muscles pull arm away.

Signals pass along arm through sensory neuron

Pain receptor in hand

Relay neuron in spinal cord

Motor neuron carries signals to muscles in upper arm.

NERVE CELLS
Each neuron has a main cell body with fine spidery connections called dendrites, and a long, wirelike fibre called the axon. The dendrites and axon connect the neuron to thousands of other neurons, creating millions of pathways for nerve signals.

Find out more
HEART AND BLOOD
HUMAN BODY
MUSCLES AND MOVEMENT

ANCIENT
BRITAIN

THE TERM ANCIENT BRITAIN describes the period of British history from about 3500 BCE until the Romans invaded in 43 CE Prehistoric people had lived in Britain for many thousands of years before this, but evidence shows that real changes began during the Neolithic, or New Stone Age, when early people in Britain, like those elsewhere, learned to make pottery, and to grow their own food by farming. They were also the first people in Britain to leave behind large-scale monuments, which they built with simple stone tools. They, and the people of the Bronze and Iron Ages, who included the Celts, are known as Ancient Britons. They lived in a harsh environment, but developed stunning art, and became skilled warriors.

SKARA BRAE
Britain's best-preserved prehistoric village is Skara Brae, Orkney. Skara Brae dates back to the Stone Age, around 5,000 years ago. There were very few trees on Orkney, so the people built their houses out of stone. They even used stone to make the furniture – including beds and cupboards – which still survives.

STONEHENGE
Europe's greatest prehistoric monument is Stonehenge, a massive stone circle used for religious ceremonies, which stands on Salisbury Plain, England. Stonehenge was built in stages between 2950 and 2500 BCE. Its gigantic stones are called sarsens. These came from about 30 km (18.6 miles) away. No one knows how the Ancient Britons moved them to Stonehenge.

Each sarsen was about 9 m (29.5 ft) tall (6 m/19.7 ft above ground), and weighed some 40 tonnes.

Tops of sarsen stones had dimples, which fitted into holes on lintels.

Ancient Britons may have dragged stones on sleds or rollers.

Builders may have used poles as levers to raise the huge lintel stones.

This sarsen formed part of an inner arrangement of stones.

Builders used levers and ropes to haul a stone into position.

Mold cape

METALWORKING
Britain's metalworkers became highly skilled. In about 2500 BCE, they found out how to use copper and gold. Soon after, they were working in bronze, and discovered iron c. 800 BCE. They continued to use gold, making beautiful objects such this finely worked cape which was buried in a warrior's grave at Mold, North Wales.

MAIDEN CASTLE
This hill fort in Dorset, England is big enough to contain a sizeable village. It was built in the 6th century BCE, and enlarged some 200 years later. Its Iron Age inhabitants protected themselves with huge ditches, throwing up the earth to make ridges.

WOAD
Ancient Britons decorated their bodies with a blue dye made from the woad plant. They made the dye by mixing up a paste of woad leaves and water, and rolling this into a ball. When the ball dried, the paste on the inside turned blue. The Ancient Britons probably wore the dye to make themselves look fearsome in battle.

Woad leaves provide a rich blue dye.

Woad plant

Find out more
BRONZE AGE
CELTS
ROMAN EMPIRE
STONE AGE
UNITED KINGDOM, HISTORY OF

BRITISH EMPIRE

THE LARGEST EMPIRE THE WORLD has ever seen – the British Empire – began in the 1600s as merchants set up trading colonies on the east coast of America. More colonies were established in the Caribbean, India, and, after 1770, Australia, Oceania, and Africa. By 1920, the British Empire had reached its greatest extent. It grew through military conquest and the need for British industry to acquire raw materials. A vast civil service held it together. But such a large empire was too big to last, and by the end of the 20th century almost every colony had received its independence.

Surrounding fence kept out enemies and any dangerous wildlife.

JAMESTOWN

In 1607, Britain set up its first permanent overseas colony at Jamestown, Virginia, on the east coast of North America. The settlement was named after King James I, and consisted of log cabins surrounded by a protective wooden fence.

Settlers built cabins of wood from local forest.

Women looked after the animals and helped to harvest the crops.

CAPTURING CANADA
In the early 1600s, the French established colonies along the St Lawrence River in Canada. The British set up the Hudson's Bay Company in 1670 to trade furs and other goods with Inuits from the north of Canada. This caused tension between the British and French in the region. In 1759, the British army, under General Wolfe, captured Quebec, the capital of French Canada. The British defeated the French army, and took control of the whole of Canada.

THE RAJ
In 1600, English merchants set up the East India Company. It soon controlled large parts of India. Following the Indian Mutiny of 1857, the British government took over. By 1886, Britain controlled the whole Indian subcontinent. For the Victorians, India was the "jewel in the crown", and British rule was known as the "Raj" after the Hindu word meaning "reign".

THE INDIAN MUTINY
In 1857, a mutiny broke out among Indian troops, who feared they might be converted to Christianity, and suspected their gun cartridges were greased with pig fat (offensive to Muslims), or cow fat (offensive to Hindus). The British put down the mutiny, and took steps to reform the Indian government and army.

IMPERIAL TRADE
During the 18th and 19th centuries, the Empire helped Britain become the world's major industrial power. The Empire supplied Britain with raw materials, notably cotton, tea, rubber, and minerals. In return, Britain exported manufactured goods to all parts of the Empire. To support this trade, Britain acquired ports, including Malta and the Falkland Islands.

AUSTRALIA
The first colonists in Australia were British convicts sent out from 1788 to serve their sentences. Later arrivals included Irish people fleeing famine, and others seeking a new life in the wide open spaces of Australia. The discovery of gold in 1851 caused a rush of prospectors, leading to great social and economic change. In 1901, the six separate colonies in Australia were joined together as a single country.

IMPERIAL DREAM

Thousands of British men and a few women went to serve abroad. Some, such as Cecil Rhodes (1853-1902), made their fortunes in the empire, and believed British rule was the most advanced form of government the world had seen. Rhodes did much to enlarge the empire in Africa. He dreamed of a railway from Cairo to Cape Town passing entirely through British territory.

MISSIONARIES

As the empire expanded, British Christian missionaries set out to convert the local people. They set up schools and hospitals, and did much to bind the different parts of the empire together through Christianity and the British way of life. One of the most famous missionaries was Scotsman David Livingstone. In 1841 he arrived in Cape Town; by the time of his death in 1873, he had explored most of Africa.

WORLD WAR I

In 1914, war broke out between Britain and Germany. World War I involved 2.8 million troops from all over the empire. Indian troops fought on the Western Front. Australian and New Zealand (ANZAC) troops fought at Gallipoli, and African forces overran German colonies in Africa.

Canada

Great Britain

ATLANTIC OCEAN

PACIFIC OCEAN

India

PACIFIC OCEAN

New Zealand

South Africa

Australia

Britain and its overseas possessions

EXTENT OF EMPIRE

The British Empire reached its greatest extent in the years after the end of World War I in 1918, when former German and Turkish possessions were added to it. King George V (1865-1936) of Britain ruled over an empire that contained 410 million people – one in five of the world's population. It spread over 29,500,000 sq km (11,400,000 sq miles), and touched every continent.

DECOLONIZATION

The first countries to gain independence were the white dominions of Canada (1867), Australia (1901), and New Zealand (1907). Non-white countries followed. The Indian subcontinent became independent in 1947-48; Ghana and Malaya left the empire in 1957. Decolonization (withdrawal from the empire) continued through the 20th century, sometimes violently. By 2009, Britain governed 14 overseas territories, mostly small islands.

COMMONWEALTH

In 1931, more than 50 newly independent British colonies joined what is known as the British Commonwealth. The British queen, Elizabeth II, is its head, even though most members are republics or have their own monarchs. Commonwealth leaders meet once every two years to discuss matters such as trade.

THE BRITISH EMPIRE

1497 John Cabot claims Newfoundland for England.

1600 East India Company established.

1607 Jamestown founded.

1620s Caribbean island colonies established.

1763 Britain gains Canada under Treaty of Paris.

1783 Britain loses US colonies.

1788-1867 British convicts are transported to Australia to serve their sentences there.

1814 Britain acquires its first African colony in the Cape.

1867 Canada becomes the first dominion in the British Empire.

1876 Queen Victoria is created Empress of India.

1886 Britain takes control of India.

1901-10 Australia, New Zealand, and South Africa become British dominions.

1920s Empire at its greatest extent.

1931 Statute of Westminster recognizes full independence of the dominions.

1947 India and Pakistan become independent.

1997 Britain returns Hong Kong to China.

Find out more

EMIGRATION AND IMMIGRATION
UNITED KINGDOM
UNITED KINGDOM, HISTORY OF
VICTORIANS
WORLD WAR I

BRONZE AGE

MESOPOTAMIA
One of the earliest Bronze Age civilizations began in Mesopotamia, a plain lying between the Tigris and Euphrates rivers. Its fertile land was farmed by the Sumerians, Assyrians, and Akkadians.

THE BRONZE AGE refers to a period of time during which the predominant metal employed by a culture was bronze. It usually succeeds the Stone Age and the Copper Age and is followed by the Iron Age. The Bronze Age spans c. 3500 to 1000 BCE, but its onset occurred at different times in different parts of the world. During this period, civilizations sprang up in Egypt, Mesopotamia, the Hwang Ho Valley in China, on the Aegean Islands of the Mediterranean, and in the Indus Valley. People learnt to grow crops and domesticate animals, so they no longer needed to move to find food. This allowed communities more time to learn how to use metals. Bronze was formed by melting copper and tin together and was found to be harder and longer lasting than other metals. It was used to make weapons and ornaments, sometimes by pouring hot molten bronze into moulds, for example to make metal pins, or by being heated and beaten into shape. Metalworkers also used gold and copper for luxury items such as jewellery.

BRONZE AGE

3500 BCE Beginning of the Bronze Age in the Middle East. First cities built in Mesopotamia, and people begin to use bronze.

3250 BCE First picture writing develops in Mesopotamia.

3000 BCE The wheel appears in Mesopotamia, and the plough is first used in China.

2800 BCE Rise of Bronze Age culture of the Indus Valley, an agriculturally based civilization in India.

2650 BCE Start of great pyramid building era in parts of Egypt.

2500 BCE Use of bronze spreads across Europe. First stage of Stonehenge built in England.

2100 BCE Sumerian city of Ur reaches the height of its power.

c. 1600 BCE Bronze Age begins in China. Manufacture of magnificent bronze ceremonial vessels.

c. 1200 BCE Rise of the Assyrian empire.

1000 BCE Iron begins to replace bronze as the main metal used.

AEGEAN CIVILIZATIONS

The rise of the Aegean civilizations coincided with the start of bronzeworking in the region. Several important cultures arose during the Aegean Bronze Age (c. 3000 to 1100 BCE): chiefly the Cycladic, Minoan, and Mycenaean cultures. People became highly skilled in architecture, painting, and other crafts. Metalworkers used bronze to make weapons, such as this Mycenaean dagger blade (right) and tools for everyday use such as axes, adzes, and tweezers. People were often buried with a variety of valuable bronze weapons, household utensils, or ornaments. The Aegean people produced bronze objects in great quantity.

THE MYCENAEANS
The city of Mycenae was ruled by the legendary king Agamemnon, and when this gold funeral mask (shown right) was found, it was believed to have belonged to him. Mycenae was famous for its grand palace, walled fortress, and the beehive-shaped tombs where kings were buried. The Mycenaeans were wealthy and powerful, and dominated the Aegean region from 1450 BCE onwards.

SHANG DYNASTY
The Bronze Age coincided with the rise of the Shang dynasty (c. 1600 to 1046 BCE), which was located in the Hwang Ho Valley in China. Its Bronze Age lasted from 1500 to 1000 BCE. Shang techniques for metalworking and writing spread throughout the area. Most bronze vessels (such as the ritual water vessel shown below) were made for use in religious ceremonies. Bronze was also used to make weapons and chariot fittings for soldiers of the great Shang armies.

WRITING AND THE WHEEL

The earliest form of writing, called cuneiform, emerged during the Bronze Age. It was invented by the Sumerians, who also made the first wheels. Wheels were used on wagons and war chariots, and to make pottery. The chariot shown left is from the city of Ur and is being pulled into battle by wild asses.

Find out more
ASSYRIANS
BABYLONIANS
CELTS
GREECE, ANCIENT
PREHISTORIC PEOPLES
SUMERIANS

BYZANTINE EMPIRE

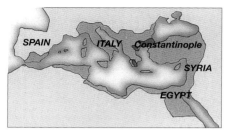

BYZANTINE EMPIRE
In 565 CE, the Byzantine Empire stretched from Spain in the west to Syria in the east. By 1350, the empire had shrunk to a fragment of its former area.

IN 330 CE THE ROMAN EMPEROR CONSTANTINE built a new city on the site of the old Greek town of Byzantium. It was called Constantinople (now Istanbul) after him, and it became the capital of the eastern part of the Roman Empire. As the western provinces of the Empire were overrun by the Germanic tribespeople, the eastern half remained prosperous, and Constantinople became the main political centre of the Roman Empire. When the Western Empire collapsed in the late 5th century, the Eastern Empire (which became known as the Byzantine Empire) survived and even expanded. Christianity became the state religion, and Constantinople became a Christian centre. Artists and scholars from all over Europe and the Middle East came there to study. Under Emperor Justinian I, the Byzantine Empire regained much of the territory of the old Roman Empire. Trade, art, and architecture thrived. But the empire suffered many attacks. By 642 Muslim Arabs had overrun Byzantine territories in North Africa and the Middle East. Gradually the empire lost its lands in Asia Minor (Turkey) and southeast Europe. In 1453 the Ottomans captured Constantinople, and the Byzantine Empire ended.

Central dome measures 31 m (100 ft) across.

Marble floors

HAGIA SOPHIA
Justinian I (483-565) built Hagia Sophia (Church of Holy Wisdom) in the centre of Constantinople. It was the largest Christian church in the Eastern world and was intended to provide a spiritual centre for the Byzantine Empire. After 1453, the church became a mosque (Muslim house of worship). Today the Hagia Sophia is a museum.

BYZANTINE EMPIRE

395 Roman Empire splits into East and West, with Constantinople as the capital of the Eastern Empire.

476 The Western Roman Empire collapses.

527-65 During the reign of Justinian I, the Byzantine Empire reconquers much of the old Roman Empire.

635-42 Byzantine Empire loses control of the Middle East and North Africa to the Arabs.

1071 Byzantine Empire loses Asia Minor to the Turks. Calls in help from Europe.

1354 Ottoman Turks gain a foothold in Europe and begin to encircle Constantinople.

1453 Constantinople falls to the Ottoman Turks; the Byzantine Empire comes to an end.

CONSTANTINE THE GREAT
In 314, Constantine the Great (288-337) became Roman emperor. At that time Christianity was forbidden, but in about 312, Constantine himself had been converted, some say by the sight of a cross in the sky. Christianity became the official religion of the Byzantine Empire, and within a century the traditional pagan temples were largely abandoned.

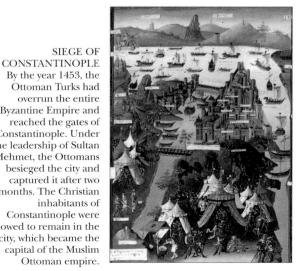

SIEGE OF CONSTANTINOPLE
By the year 1453, the Ottoman Turks had overrun the entire Byzantine Empire and reached the gates of Constantinople. Under the leadership of Sultan Mehmet, the Ottomans besieged the city and captured it after two months. The Christian inhabitants of Constantinople were allowed to remain in the city, which became the capital of the Muslim Ottoman empire.

Find out more
OTTOMAN EMPIRE
RELIGIONS
ROMAN EMPIRE

CAMERAS

ALTHOUGH THE FIRST PHOTOGRAPH was taken only about 180 years ago, cameras are much, much older. Hundreds of years ago, the Chinese found that light entering a dark room through a pinhole would project a fuzzy image of the world outside onto the opposite wall. Many years later, in 1500 in Europe, a room like this was called a camera obscura, which is Latin for "darkened room". In the 17th century some artists drew sketches with the aid of a camera obscura which had a lens instead of a pinhole to make the image sharper and brighter. The discovery of chemicals that darkened when exposed to light finally made it possible to fix the image permanently – on paper, on glass plates, or on film. Today, digital cameras use light-sensitive electronic sensors instead of film. Sophisticated electronic technology in most cameras ensures that each picture gets the right amount of light (autoexposure) and is perfectly sharp (autofocus). But all cameras still work on the same basic principle as the camera obscura of old.

Screen allows users to check pictures instantly.

Removable memory card stores images.

Autofocus system ensures sharp image.

Filter used to enhance image and protect lens.

Sensor is made of millions of pixels. Each measures brightness and colour of one tiny part of the image.

Light travels from subject to lens.

Circuit processes output from sensor into digital form, so it can be viewed, deleted, or stored.

SINGLE-LENS REFLEX CAMERA
The single-lens reflex (SLR) camera (above) may use either film or a digital sensor. It is popular with photographers for its versatility, and because the viewfinder shows exactly the same view that the camera will record. The lens can be interchanged with others to give a wide view or to magnify the subject.

KINDS OF CAMERAS
There are many different types of cameras, including film, digital, compact, single-lens reflex, disposable, instant-picture, and large-format cameras. However, film usage has dropped so dramatically that many manufacturers have stopped making it. Today, tiny digital cameras are also built into most mobile phone handsets.

DIGITAL CAMERA
A digital camera captures images electronically rather than on standard film and stores them on removable memory cards. Images can then be transferred to a computer and printed out or sent over the Internet.

Photos stored on the camera's memory card can be viewed on the LCD (liquid crystal display).

DIGITAL PHOTO PRINTERS
Some digital cameras can be connected directly to printers in order to print out photos, and many printers have slots for memory cards to be inserted. This makes transferring images to a computer unnecessary.

POLAROID CAMERA
The Polaroid "instant-picture" camera took just 90 seconds to process a picture. Today, however, they have been replaced by instant digital techniques, like portable printers.

MOVIE CAMERAS
The movement we see in the cinema is an illusion. A movie (cinema) film is really a series of still pictures projected on to the screen in such quick succession that they seem to merge into one another. If the subject is in a slightly different place in each picture it looks as if it is moving. Most movie cameras take 24 pictures, or frames, every second, on a very long strip of film wound steadily through the camera. The film stops while each picture is taken, then advances quickly, ready for the next picture.

LARGE-FORMAT CAMERA
In early cameras, the lens was focused by moving a bellows – a concertina-like cloth tunnel – in and out. Many photographers still use large-format bellows cameras for high-quality studio work.

Find out more

FILMS
LIGHT
TECHNOLOGY
TELESCOPES
TELEVISION

CANADA

THE SECOND LARGEST COUNTRY in the world is also one of the emptiest. Much of Canada is virtually uninhabited The northern part of the country is very cold and covered with snow and ice for much of the year. Few people live among the high Rocky Mountains in the west. Even in the huge wheat-growing plains in the centre there are few people. The majority of Canada's 33.5 million inhabitants live in the southeast, close to the border with the United States. Most Canadians speak English, but for some, particularly those in the province of Québec, French is the first language. This is because they are descendants of the French who settled in Canada in the 16th century. The languages of the native North American and Inuit inhabitants are rarely heard today. Much of Canada's trade is with its neighbour, the United States. However, Canada has close links with many European, Asian, and African nations.

Canada occupies the northern half of North America, stretching from the Pacific to the Atlantic oceans. Part of the country lies within the Arctic Circle. At 6,416 km (3,987 miles) the Canadian-US border is the world's longest continuous frontier between two nations.

TORONTO

More than five million people live in the city of Toronto. It is Canada's business centre and capital of the province of Ontario. Toronto has many skyscrapers, including the 553 m (1,815 ft) high Canadian National Tower.

Maple syrup is obtained by cutting into the maple tree and directing the flow of its sap into a collecting vessel.

SPORTS AND LEISURE

Winter sports such as skiing, skating, and ice hockey are popular in Canada because winters are long and there is plenty of snow and ice. Modern ice hockey was invented in Canada in the 1870s and is now played nearly everywhere in the world. During the summer, sailing, canoeing, and field hockey are also popular.

Ice hockey is the Canadian national sport. The country produces some of the best players in the world.

ROCKY MOUNTAINS

Western Canada is dominated by the Rocky Mountains, which stretch from the United States border in the south to Alaska in the north. The mountains are covered in trees and are a haven for bears and other wildlife.

LAW AND ORDER

The nickname of the Royal Canadian Mounted Police – the national police force – is the Mounties. They boast that they "always get their man".

NATURAL RESOURCES

Canada is rich in minerals such as zinc and iron ore and has huge reserves of oil, coal, and natural gas. Just off Canada's east coast lies the Grand Banks, one of the world's richest fishing areas. Waters within 320 km (200 miles) of Canada's coastline are reserved for Canadian fishermen only. The vast forests that grow across the country are a major source of timber. The country's exports are mainly sent south to the United States; the two countries have formed a free-trade zone with Mexico, which means that most exports or imports among them are not taxed.

▲	△	🏛	✦	●	●
Volcano	Mountain	Ancient monument	Capital city	Large city/ town	Small city/ town

STATISTICS
Area: 9,976,140 sq km (3,851,788 sq miles)
Population: 33,487,000
Capital: Ottawa
Languages: English, French, Chinese, Italian, German, Ukrainian, Portuguese, Inuktitut, Cree
Religions: Roman Catholic, Protestant
Currency: Canadian dollar
Main occupations: Manufacturing, mining, forestry, service sector, engineering
Main exports: Forest products, car parts, wheat, zinc, uranium, nickel, telecommunications equipment, aluminium oil, natural gas
Main imports: Cars, chemicals, machinery

THE PRAIRIES
The provinces of Manitoba, Saskatchewan, and Alberta are known as the prairie provinces. Grain thrives in the rich soil of the prairies, making the region the agricultural backbone of Canada. After the grain is cut, it is stored in huge grain elevators (left) and then sent by rail to cities or ports. Railways were the key to the development of farming on the prairies.

Grain elevators (right) are located beside this railroad on the prairies in Canada.

LOGGING
Timber is of great economic importance to Canada and over one-third of the country is covered by dense forest. Timber products, including pulp, newsprint, and building timber, account for 15 per cent of Canada's total exports. Québec, Ontario, and British Columbia are the major timber-producing provinces. Hardwoods from the forests of Québec and Ontario are ideal for making furniture, while wood from British Columbia provides sawn timber and plywood.

Until recently, there were no controls on logging in Canada. As a result, vast areas of trees, such as the one pictured above, were wiped out.

GREAT BEAR LAKE
With an area of 31,800 sq km (12,275 sq miles), the Great Bear Lake is the largest lake in Canada.

MAGNETIC NORTH
The magnetic North Pole is situated in northern Canada, hundreds of kilometres from the true North Pole. Close to magnetic north, compasses are useless for navigation.

BAFFIN BAY
In the summer months, open sea separates the islands of northern Canada. However, in winter, pack ice fills the channels between the islands.

CANADIAN SHIELD
The Canadian Shield, a huge U-shaped arc of ancient rock, covers more than half of Canada and includes most of Greenland, and parts of the USA.

SCALE BAR

0	250	500	750	km

0	250	500	750 miles

Find out more
MOUNTAINS
NORTH AMERICA
TRADE AND INDUSTRY

CARIBBEAN

STRUNG OUT LIKE a rope of pearls, there is a long row of tropical islands curving for more than 3,200 km (2,000 miles) between Mexico and Venezuela. Together they are usually called the Caribbean islands, sometimes the West Indies. Some are tiny, uninhabited rocks or coral reefs; others are much larger islands with thriving populations. On Martinique for instance, about 400,000 people live around the wooded slopes of several volcanoes which tower hundreds of metres above the sea. There are 13 countries and 12 other territories in the Caribbean. Cuba, with a population of more than 13 million people, is the biggest nation. Although each country has its own distinctive culture, many have connections with other countries. These links are left over from the 18th and 19th centuries, when the whole region was colonized by European kingdoms. The ruling nations brought African slaves to the Caribbean to harvest sugar cane. Today, descendants of these slaves make up a large proportion of the population.

The Caribbean Sea is about 1,943,000 sq km (750,193 sq miles) in area. It is enclosed on three sides by Central America, South America, and the Caribbean Islands.

TOURISM
The Caribbean islands are very beautiful, with lush trees, colourful birds, long sandy beaches, and months of sunshine. The region attracts tourists from all over the world. This has created many new jobs, particularly in the towns. Tourism is now the main source of income for several islands.

CRICKET
Cricket is a reminder of the Caribbean's colonial past. It is played, and passionately supported, in many of the former British colonies. For international test matches, the Caribbean islands join forces and compete as the West Indies. The West Indies were victorious in the cricket World Cup in 1975 and 1979.

Brian Lara (right) plays cricket for the West Indies. With 400 runs, he holds the world record for the highest test match score.

AGRICULTURE
More than half the people of the Caribbean earn a living from agriculture. Many work for a landowner, producing crops such as sugar and coffee. They may also rent or own a small plot of land. On this land they grow food to feed their families or to sell in local markets.

BASTILLE DAY
The islands of Guadeloupe and Martinique are part of France and the people have strong links with this country. They speak the French language, use French currency for money, fly the French flag, and celebrate French holidays such as Bastille Day. Other Caribbean islands have close political and financial links with Britain, the Netherlands, or the United States.

ARCHITECTURE
Brilliant colours enhance the traditional shapes of Caribbean architecture. Similarly, Caribbean music, literature, art, and food are a unique mixture of European and African culture.

__Find out more__
CENTRAL AMERICA
COLUMBUS, CHRISTOPHER
PIRATES
SLAVERY

Legend: Volcano · Mountain · Ancient monument · Capital city · Large city/town · Small city/town

ANGUILLA
Area: 102 sq km (39 sq miles)
Status: British dependent territory
Claimed: 1650
Population: 14,400
Capital: The Valley

ANTIGUA AND BARBUDA
Area: 442 sq km (170 sq miles)
Population: 85,600
Capital: St. John's

ARUBA
Area: 193 sq km (75 sq miles)
Status: Dutch autonomous region
Claimed: 1643
Population: 103,000
Capital: Oranjestad

BAHAMAS
Area: 13,935 sq km (5,380 sq miles)
Population: 309,100
Capital: Nassau

BARBADOS
Area: 431 sq km (166 sq miles)
Population: 284,600
Capital: Bridgetown

CAYMAN ISLANDS
Area: 259 sq km (100 sq miles)
Status: British dependent territory
Claimed: 1670
Population: 49,000
Capital: George Town

CUBA
Area: 114,524 sq km (44,218 sq miles)
Population: 11,452,000
Capital: Havana

DOMINICA
Area: 751 sq km (290 sq miles)
Population: 72,600
Capital: Roseau

DOMINICAN REPUBLIC
Area: 48,442 sq km (18,704 sq miles)
Population: 9,650,000
Capital: Santo Domingo

GRENADA
Area: 344 sq km (133 sq miles)
Population: 90,700
Capital: Saint George's

GUADELOUPE
Area: 1,779 sq km (687 sq miles)
Status: French overseas department
Claimed: 1635
Population: 440,000
Capital: Basse-Terre

HAITI
Area: 27,750 sq km (10,714 sq miles)
Population: 8,300,000
Capital: Port-au-Prince

JAMAICA
Area: 10,991 sq km (4,244 sq miles)
Population: 2,700,000
Capital: Kingston

MARTINIQUE
Area: 1,101 sq km (425 sq miles)
Status: French overseas department
Claimed: 1635
Population: 393,000
Capital: Fort-de-France

MONTSERRAT
Area: 101 sq km (38 sq miles)
Status: British dependent territory
Claimed: 1632
Population: 9,000
Capital: Plymouth

NETHERLANDS ANTILLES
Area: 960 sq km (371 sq miles)
Status: Dutch autonomous region
Claimed: 1816
Population: 221,000
Capital: Willemstad

PUERTO RICO
Area: 8,897 sq km (3,435 sq miles)
Status: US commonwealth territory
Claimed: 1898
Population: 3,971,000
Capital: San Juan

ST. KITTS AND NEVIS
Area: 261 sq km (101 sq miles)
Population: 40,100
Capital: Basseterre

ST. LUCIA
Area: 616 sq km (238 sq miles)
Population: 160,300
Capital: Castries

ST. VINCENT AND THE GRENADINES
Area: 388 sq km (150 sq miles)
Population: 104,600
Capital: Kingstown

TRINIDAD AND TOBAGO
Area: 5,128 sq km (1,980 sq miles)
Population: 1,230,000
Capital: Port-of-Spain

TURKS AND CAICOS ISLANDS
Area: 430 sq km (166 sq miles)
Status: British dependent territory
Claimed: 1766
Population: 22,900
Capital: Cockburn Town

VIRGIN ISLANDS
Area: 352 sq km (136 sq miles)
Status: US unincorporated territory
Claimed: 1917
Population: 109,800
Capital: Charlotte Amalie

VIRGIN ISLANDS, BRITISH
Area: 153 sq km (59 sq miles)
Status: British dependent territory
Claimed: 1672
Population: 24,400
Capital: Road Town

ISLAND GROUPS
The larger islands of the Caribbean between Cuba and Puerto Rico are often called the Greater Antilles, to distinguish them from the Lesser Antilles to the east. The small islands from the Virgin Islands to Dominica are sometimes called the Leeward Islands; and the islands to the south (Martinique to Grenada), the Windward Islands.

SCALE BAR 0 200 400 km / 0 200 400 miles

CARS

IF YOU COULD line up all the world's cars end to end, they would form a traffic jam stretching all the way to the moon; and the line is getting longer, because a new car is made every second. Most cars are family cars, used for trips to school, work, and shops, to see friends and take holidays. But there are also a number of special-purpose cars, including taxis, sports cars, and police patrol cars.

Petrol or diesel engines power modern cars, just as they did the first cars of the 19th century. But the cars of today are very different from cars even 30 years ago. The latest cars have low, sleek shapes that are attractive and also reduce drag, or air resistance. Other features include powerful brakes for stopping quickly and electronic engine control systems that allow cars to travel faster and use less fuel.

HOW A CAR WORKS

In most cars, the engine is at the front and drives the back or front wheels (or all four wheels) through a series of shafts and gears. There are usually four or five different gears; they alter the speed at which the engine turns the wheels. In low gear, the wheels turn slowly and produce extra force for starting and climbing hills. In high gear, the wheels turn fast for travelling at speed.

A car radiator is full of water. A pump keeps water flowing around the engine to keep it cool. As the car moves forward, cold air rushes through the radiator, cooling the water before its next circuit around the engine.

Tread, or grooves on the tyres, improve traction (grip) in the rain.

The steering wheel turns the steering gear via a long shaft.

This car has a manual gearbox, which means the driver uses the gear lever to change gear. In some cars, gear changes are automatic.

Turning the steering wheel inside the car turns a system of gears that point the front wheels towards the left or right.

Suspension springs and shock absorbers soften a bumpy ride for the passengers and keep the wheels firmly on the ground as the car travels over uneven surfaces.

Pressing on the brake pedal pushes a special liquid down tubes, which in turn push on pistons at each wheel. These pistons squeeze the brake pads against steel discs or drums attached to the wheels, slowing down the wheels and stopping the car.

ANTI-POLLUTION DEVICE
Waste gases from the engine of a car are highly toxic (poisonous). To keep them under control some cars have special filters, called catalytic converters, fitted to the exhaust system. These filters remove poisonous gases.

TYPES OF CARS

Cars have numerous uses, and there are many different kinds of cars available to suit almost any task. Most family cars combine a large interior with speed and fuel economy. However, for other, more specialized vehicles, speed, luxury, or power may be the most important design feature.

SPORTS CAR
With its large engine, sleek design, and usually seating for only two people, a sports car is designed purely for speed. Some can travel at about 300 km/h (200 mph).

CRASH PROTECTION
The driver and passengers are cocooned in a strong steel cage to protect them in a crash. But the rest of the car is designed to crumple easily and absorb some of the impact. Wearing seat belts can protect car passengers from injury in a crash.

LUXURY CAR
Large, carefully crafted cars such as the world-famous Rolls-Royce are among the most beautiful and expensive automobiles in the world.

OFF-ROAD VEHICLE
Rugged vehicles built specially for driving across country have powerful engines, four-wheel drive, and heavy ridged tyres for extra grip.

HISTORY OF THE CAR

People laughed at the first rickety "horseless carriages" of the 1880s. But rapid technical progress soon made it clear that cars were here to stay. In 1903, cars could already reach speeds of more than 110 km/h (70 mph). But they were expensive and often broke down. Since then cars have become steadily cheaper and more reliable. Now they are everyday transport for millions of people throughout the world.

NICOLAS CUGNOT

The first road vehicles were powered by steam. In 1769, Nicolas Cugnot, a French soldier, built a steam carriage for dragging cannon. It travelled about 5 km/h (3 mph) and had to stop about every 10 minutes to build up steam.

DAIMLER AND BENZ

In the 1880s, German engineers Karl Benz and Gottlieb Daimler worked independently to produce the first petrol engine. In 1885, Karl Benz built his flimsy motorized tricycle (left), the first petrol-powered car.

PANHARD AND LEVASSOR

In the 1890s, two Frenchmen, René Panhard and Emile Levassor, built the first car with the engine in the front, the arrangement found in most cars to this day.

The production line for the Ford Model T

FORD MODEL T

Early cars were handmade and cost so much money that only the rich could afford them. In 1908, Henry Ford opened a factory to produce large numbers of the Model T (above). This was the first car cheap enough to be purchased by more people.

Rear airfoil

Wide tyres, called slicks, are smooth to minimize rolling resistance, but wide to give a good grip on the track.

The lightweight body is carefully shaped to keep drag to a minimum.

Powerful disc brakes can slow the car from 300 km/h to 65 km/h (200 mph to 40 mph) in less than three seconds.

The frame is made of ultra-light carbon-fibre composites.

A computer continually adjusts the suspension to make sure the wheels do not bounce up from the track.

Aerofoils at the front and back work like upside-down aeroplane wings. Air rushing over them pushes the car firmly onto the track, which improves traction.

NEW DESIGNS

Prototypes (test models) of new cars are packed with electronics and computers that can do anything from parking the car automatically to steering the car automatically. Many parts of these cars are made of plastics and other new materials; some new engine designs contain ceramic components instead of metal ones.

RACING CAR

Grand Prix racing cars are designed for speed alone, so they are built very differently from road cars. They have big, powerful eight-cylinder engines made of special light materials. This allows them to reach top speeds of up to 400 km/h (250 mph). Their ultra-low shape allows them to slice through the air easily so they can travel as fast as possible. Indeed, the driver has to lie almost flat to fit in.

Find out more

ENERGY
ENGINES
MACHINES
METALS
POLLUTION
SCIENCE, history of
TECHNOLOGY

CASTLES

THE MASSIVE WALLS AND TOWERS of a castle were designed to make it impossible for enemy soldiers to destroy it. Inside was a whole world in miniature – lords and ladies, government officials, soldiers, servants, animals, gardens, treasure stores, and dungeons where prisoners could be tortured. The best site for a castle was on a hill surrounded by water. If there were no natural features, the builders made an artificial hill or dug a deep ditch and filled it with water to make a moat. A well-built castle with a good military commander in charge could withstand an enemy siege for many months. Most castles were built between the 9th century and the 16th century, when many countries were almost constantly at war. Early castles were small and made of wood; the later stone buildings housed town-sized populations; many are still standing today. The invention of gunpowder at the end of the 13th century made castles hard to defend. As times grew more peaceful, kings and lords moved into comfortable country houses.

LOOPHOLES
Archers fired through loopholes – narrow slits in the walls which were wider on the inside to make aiming easier. The inner walls were often higher than the outer walls, so archers could fire at the attackers over the heads of their own soldiers.

Siege engines had to be tall enough for attackers to fire down on castle soldiers.

Sandbags protected the attacking archers.

Towers which stuck out from the walls gave archers a clear view of the attackers trying to climb the walls.

Even if the attackers built a bridge across a moat, they could be stopped by boiling water or hot sand dropped on them from above.

DEFENDING A CASTLE
During a siege, attackers tried to climb over the walls, smash them down with siege engines, or starve out the inhabitants. The defenders used archers with bows and arrows to keep attackers away from the walls. If the archers failed, soldiers pushed the attackers' scaling ladders away with poles and poured tubs full of boiling water or hot sand onto the enemy below. Deep moats or solid rock foundations stopped the attackers from digging under the walls. In peacetime, the knights and soldiers of the castle trained for war by jousting and playing war games in elaborate tournaments.

Attackers used a battering ram to break down drawbridge.

Deep moats surrounded castle walls.

HOW CASTLES DEVELOPED

International wars, especially the Crusades in the Middle East, led to bigger armies, more powerful weapons, and stronger, more sophisticated defences. These wars speeded up castle building.

Bailey

Motte

MOTTE AND BAILEY
Early castles were built as a motte (hill) and bailey (court). They were made of wood and burned easily.

NORMAN CASTLE
The Normans built many stone castles such as this one (above) at Dover, England, between the 11th and 13th centuries.

ROUND TOWERS
Later castles had round towers. Rocks bounced off the curved surface and did less damage.

"Fairy tale" turret

SPANISH CASTLE
Some castles, such as the Alcázar in Segovia, Spain, became magnificent royal palaces.

The kitchen was usually in a separate outhouse, because it kept catching fire.

The lord and lady's bedchamber was richly furnished.

Spiral staircases were designed so swordsmen could fight on them if necessary.

Doves lived in the dovecote and were killed for food.

The storerooms were in the basement of the castle. Sacks could be pulled up to the next floor by a pulley.

The keep

THE KEEP
At the heart of the castle stood the keep, a thick-walled stone tower several storeys high. This was the last refuge in a siege, but in peacetime it was also home to the lord's family and followers. The entrance to the keep was always on the first floor, through the guardroom. Above this was a great hall for feasting, and sometimes sleeping. The lord's own rooms were on the top floor.

Bees were kept to provide honey, and herbs were grown for medicinal purposes.

Prisoners were kept in chains in the dungeons.

DAILY LIFE
A castle was like a small community. As well as the baron and baroness, their family, servants, and soldiers, the castle housed dozens of craftsworkers who kept the buildings and equipment in good repair. Food was brought in from the surrounding countryside or grown in the castle garden.

Find out more
ARCHITECTURE
CRUSADES
MEDIEVAL EUROPE
NORMANS

CELTS

TWO THOUSAND YEARS AGO, much of western Europe was inhabited by a fierce, proud, artistic people known as the Celts. They were skilled warriors, farmers, and metalworkers. For several hundred years their art and culture dominated northwest Europe. All Celts shared a similar way of life, but they were not a single group of people. They included many different tribes such as the Atrebates of southern Britain and the Parisii of northern France. Most Celts lived in villages or hill forts, some of which developed into small towns. But the Celts never formed a unified nation. Between 300 BCE and 100 CE they were absorbed into the Roman Empire. Today Celtic-speaking people can still be found in parts of Britain, Ireland, and France.

BOUDICCA
In 61 CE, Boudicca (or Boadicea), queen of the Iceni, a Celtic tribe in Britain, led a massive revolt against oppression by the Romans. The Britons, however, were no match for the well-organized Romans, and the revolt was suppressed.

THE HOME
Celtic families lived together in one large hut. Some huts were made of stone; others of wattle and daub – wood-framed huts covered in clay to make a hard wall. Thatch was often used to keep the rain out. An iron cauldron hung over a fire for cooking meat or boiling water. Bread was cooked in a domed clay oven. Members of the family wove cloth, worked as farmers, or made pots.

Livestock were kept for food and dairy produce.

Huts were covered in clay and thatch to protect them from bad weather.

Woven wooden frame of hut

The Celts wove their own cloth on looms.

DRUIDS
Druids, a very important group in Celtic society, were priests who led religious ceremonies, acted as judges and advisers, and were responsible for teaching the sons of chiefs. Druidism involved the worship of many gods. Oak trees and mistletoe were also sacred to Druids.

METALWORKING
The Celts worked with many different metals including iron, bronze, copper, gold, and silver. Farm tools, weapons, shields, chariots, and helmets were made from metal, and many were beautifully decorated with distinctive plants and animals, as shown on the border around this page.

The spread of Celtic occupation in Europe

Early Celts

6th-5th centuries BCE

4th century BCE

CELTIC LANDS
The earliest Celts lived in central Europe, in what is now southern Germany. By about 500 BCE Celts had spread out to cover much of Europe, from Ireland to the Black Sea.

Find out more
BRITAIN, ANCIENT
IRON AGE

CENTRAL AMERICA

LIKE LINKS IN A CHAIN, the seven Central American countries seem to tie together the continents of North and South America. The climate is hot and steamy; trees, plants, and jungle animals thrive around the marshy coasts and on the high mountains. More than 2,500 years ago Native Americans made Central America their home. Some of the people who live there today are direct descendants of these early inhabitants. Many are *mestizos*: people with both Native American and European ancestors. European people first came to Central America in about 1500, and the Spanish empire ruled the area for more than three centuries. By 1823, many of the countries had gained independence, but this did not bring peace and prosperity to their people. Most Central Americans are still very poor and have no land. There are too few jobs and not enough food. Governments in the region have been unable to solve these problems, and wars and revolutions are common.

Central America forms an isthmus, or narrow land bridge, from Mexico in the north to Colombia in the south.

There are many active volcanoes in Central America. The largest is Tajumulco in Guatemala.

The soil in the valleys is very fertile.

Jungle covers the eastern coastal plain and many mountains.

MAYAS

Between 250 and 900 CE Native American people called Mayas lived in Central America, where they created a vast empire. They built great cities at Palenque and Tikal (in present-day Mexico and Guatemala) and constructed huge stone temples and palaces in the shape of pyramids. To feed the people in the cities, the Mayas became skilled at cultivating food. They used ingenious farming methods to grow plentiful crops on the small areas of suitable land.

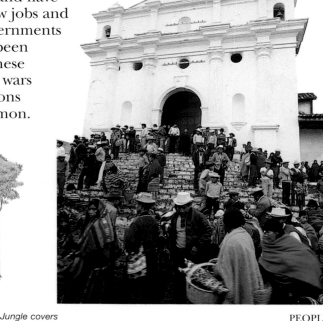

PEOPLE

More than 42 million people live in Central America, mostly in the countryside and in small towns. The biggest city is Guatemala City, which has a population of over 2 million. Most people speak either Spanish or one of the local Native American languages. In Belize, many people speak English. Many Central Americans are Christians, and the Roman Catholic Church is an important influence in everyday life and culture.

Bananas grown in Honduras are eaten all over the world.

Nicaragua was an important cotton producer until civil war disrupted farming.

In Panama sugar is extracted from sugar cane, which grows rapidly in the hot, humid climate.

EDUCATION

Civil wars and other armed conflicts have disrupted normal life in Central America. One result is that many people are illiterate. However, in Nicaragua there is a major campaign to teach people to read.

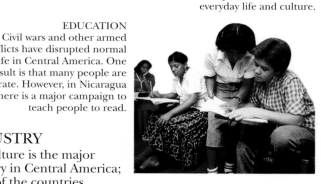

INDUSTRY

Agriculture is the major industry in Central America; many of the countries depend on one main crop for their income. Both Belize and El Salvador also make textiles and light industrial products. Guatemala produces oil for export.

Belize processes grapefruit and exports juice.

Coffee is Guatemala's most important export.

Find out more

AZTECS
CARIBBEAN
MAYA
MEXICO

Volcano Mountain Ancient monument Capital city Large city/town Small city/town

STATISTICS
Area: 523,160 sq km (201,993 sq miles)
Population: 42,068,000
Number of independent countries: 7

PANAMA CANAL
The Panama Canal is a great international waterway connecting the Atlantic and Pacific Oceans. It is more than 80 km (50 miles) long and up to 150 m (500 ft) wide, with a minimum depth of 12 m (39 ft). Over 13,000 ships from all over the world pass through the canal's locks each year. Most of their cargo travels to and from the United States.

MEXICO

BELIZE
San Ignacio
Flores
Belize City
BELMOPAN

GUATEMALA
Volcán Tacaná 4093m
Huehuetenango
Quezaltenango
Puerto Barrios
Cobán
Zacapa
GUATEMALA CITY
Escuintla
Santa Ana

Gulf of Honduras
Bay Islands
Puerto Cortés
San Pedro Sula
La Ceiba
Aguán
Caribbean Sea
Laguna de Caratasca

HONDURAS
Comayagua
Santa Rosa de Copán
Juticalpa
Coco
Patuca
TEGUCIGALPA

SAN SALVADOR
San Miguel
EL SALVADOR
Choluteca
Gulf of Fonseca

NICARAGUA
Jinotega
Esteli
Matagalpa
Chinandega
León
Lake Managua
MANAGUA
Juigalpa
Lake Nicaragua
Volcán Concepción 1610m
Rivas
Bluefields
Corn Islands
Mosquito Coast
Wawa
Cayos Miskitos

San Juan
Liberia
Golfo de Papagayo

Puntarenas
Alajuela
Volcán Barva 2906m
SAN JOSÉ
Cartago
Limón
Cordillera Talamanca

COSTA RICA
Península de Nicoya
Volcán Barú 3475m
David
Península de Osa
Santiago
Chitré
Chiriquí Gulf
Península de Azuero
Mosquito Gulf
Lake Gatún
Colón
Panama Canal
PANAMA CITY
Pearl Islands
Gulf of Panama
PANAMA
Gulf of Darien
COLOMBIA

PACIFIC COASTAL STRIP
Half the population of Central America lives on the western slopes, which are higher and drier than the lowlands that border the Caribbean coast. Most people in the west work as farmers, producing coffee, bananas, sugar cane, and cotton.

SCALE BAR
0   100   200   km
0   100   200   miles

PACIFIC OCEAN

BELIZE
Area: 22,960 sq km (8,865 sq miles)
Population: 308,000
Capital: Belmopan
Currency: Belizean dollar

COSTA RICA
Area: 51,100 sq km (19,730 sq miles)
Population: 4,254,000
Capital: San José
Currency: Colón

HONDURAS
Area: 112,090 sq km (43,278 sq miles)
Population: 7,793,000
Capital: Tegucigalpa
Currency: Lempira

EL SALVADOR
Area: 21,040 sq km (8,124 sq miles)
Population: 7,185,000
Capital: San Salvador
Currency: US dollar

NICARAGUA
Area: 130,000 sq km (50,193 sq miles)
Population: 5,891,000
Capital: Managua
Currency: Córdoba

GUATEMALA
Area: 108,890 sq km (42,043 sq miles)
Population: 13,277,000
Capital: Guatemala City
Currency: Quetzal

PANAMA
Area: 77,080 sq km (29,761 sq miles)
Population: 3,360,000
Capital: Panama City
Currency: Balboa

COSTA RICA
More than half of Costa Rica's people live on a broad, fertile plateau surrounded by volcanic ranges (above). Small farms dot the area; coffee, corn, rice, and sugar are grown on the hillsides. Unlike other Central American countries, Costa Rica enjoys political stability.

CHINA

China is the fourth-largest country in the world. It is situated in eastern Asia. The Russian Federation and Mongolia lie to its north, and Southeast Asia and the Indian subcontinent to its south and west. The East China Sea is to its east.

TO DESCRIBE CHINA you need to use enormous numbers. The country is vast, covering more than 9.3 million sq km (3.6 million sq miles). China's written history stretches back 3,500 years – longer than any other nation's. 1,338 million people live there, and one-fifth of the world's population is Chinese. In such a large country, there are many variations, including four major language families. The land, too, is tremendously varied. The east and southeast, where most people live, is green and fertile. Other parts of the country are barren deserts of sand and rock. Organizing and feeding the huge and varied Chinese population is a mammoth task. Since 1949 China has been ruled by a Communist government that has tried to provide adequate food, education, and health care to every part of the nation. During the late 1970s, Communist party moderates embraced economic reforms that lifted government controls and encouraged private enterprise. Consequently, China became the world's third-largest economy in the mid 1990s. China's human rights record, however, is still criticized because of political oppression at home and in Tibet.

TRANSPORTATION
The bicycle is a common method of transport in China, although private cars are becoming more common.

Chinese farmers make use of every suitable piece of land, carving steps or terraces in the hillsides to grow rice and other crops.

Rice is grown in flooded fields called paddies.

Tiananmen Square, Beijing

BEIJING
The capital city of China is Beijing, formerly Peking. Modern Beijing spreads out around the older central area. To the north and west are houses and Beijing University. The industrial area is to the east of the centre. At the heart lies Tiananmen (Gate of Heavenly Peace) Square. Here parades and celebrations take place on national holidays. In 1989, the government forcibly disbanded a pro-democracy student demonstration here, killing thousands.

AGRICULTURE AND LAND USE
Most Chinese people are crowded together in just 15 per cent of the total land area, mainly in river valleys in the east. Three in ten live in huge cities; the rest live in the countryside. There they grow rice and wheat and raise pigs and other livestock. Much of the rest of the country is mountainous and wild. The Takla Makan Desert in the west is dry and cold, and few people live there.

NEW YEAR
China's most important festival is the celebration of New Year. Each year is named after an animal and people celebrate with colourful processions. Tangerines with leaves are the lucky fruits of the New Year. Odd numbers are unlucky so people always give presents of tangerines in pairs.

FAMILY LIFE
The family is the most important institution in Chinese life. Children respect their parents and look after them in their old age. China's population is growing, and the government now rewards parents who limit their families to just one child. This policy works well in the cities, but in farming communities, people need large families to labour in the fields.

HAN CHINESE

China has a large number of ethnic groups. The Han Chinese people make up about 90 per cent of the total population. Their ancestors may have come east from Turkestan, which is now partly in western China and partly in Central Asia and Afghanistan. However, it is possible that Han Chinese people descended from Mongolian tribes who moved south.

PANDAS

The giant panda lives only in the mountainous forests of southwestern China. It feeds almost exclusively off bamboo. The woody grass is low in nutrients, so pandas must eat about 38kg (84 lb) of it every day to survive. The panda is classified as an endangered species, and fewer than 1,600 remain in the wild today. They live in areas of forest set aside as nature reserves by the Chinese government.

LHASA

Monasteries in Lhasa, capital of Tibet, are reminders that the city was once the centre of Lamaism (Tibetan Buddhism). The religion is an important part of Tibetan life, and at one time one-sixth of all Tibetan men were monks. The head of the religion, the Dalai Lama, was also the ruler of the country. However, in 1950 Communist China invaded Tibet, and has ruled the region ever since.

INDUSTRIAL TAIWAN

Boasting a highly educated and ambitious workforce, Taiwan is one of Asia's wealthiest economies. The country produces about 10 per cent of the world's computers, and is the world's leading television producer. It also specializes in shoe-manufacturing. Taiwan's mineral industry is not a significant earner as mineral resources are relatively modest.

SHANGHAI

The largest city in China, Shanghai (right), is one of the world's biggest seaports. For centuries China was closed to the west, but in 1842 the Treaty of Nanking, between China and Britain, opened the port to western trade. Since then Shanghai has been the leading commercial and industrial centre in China. Today, about half of China's foreign business passes through the city.

The spectacular Potala Palace (left), in Lhasa, was built in the 17th century.

To Western eyes in the Middle Ages, the Chinese junk (left) seemed an ungainly figure. However, the junk is still widely used today, thus proving its seaworthiness.

JUNK

The junk is an ocean-going sailing vessel of ancient unknown origin. By the Middle Ages, Chinese junks had sailed to the waters of Indonesia and India. The junk carries up to five sails consisting of panels of linen or matting flattened by bamboo strips. Each sail can be spread or closed at a pull, like a venetian blind. A massive rudder, which steers the boat, takes the place of a keel or a centreboard, and keeps the boat from tipping over or drifting with the wind. The hull is partitioned by solid bulkheads, which add greatly to the boat's strength.

Most Chinese people work in agriculture. However, over 10 per cent of China's 750 million-strong workforce is employed in industries such as textiles (left) and electronics.

MEDICINE
Medicine in China is a mixture of East and West. Modern surgical and drug techniques are borrowed from Europe and the United States. However, doctors still use traditional cures that have been popular for thousands of years, including herbs and other natural remedies. To relieve pain, Chinese doctors sometimes use acupuncture, a technique in which fine needles are inserted into specially-chosen parts of the body. "Barefoot doctors", or locally-trained healers, keep people healthy in the countryside with natural remedies.

Acupuncture charts show the positions of meridians, or lines of energy, where the acupuncturist inserts needles.

A Chinese apothecary, or chemist, makes use of a wide range of natural plant and animal cures.

INDUSTRY
Chinese factories have been modernized since 1949, but in comparison with the factories of Japan or the United States, some are still old-fashioned. However, China's economy has grown rapidly since the 1980s. It has set up industries in partnership with foreign companies and encouraged private enterprise. By 2009, it was the world's largest economy after the United States and Japan.

FOOD
Rice is one of the main ingredients of Chinese food, as are noodles and many vegetables. Dried foods, soya beans, fish, and meat are also used in Chinese cooking, which varies considerably in the different regions of China.

The Chinese eat with chopsticks. They hold both sticks in one hand, and pinch the tips together to pick up food.

Buddhist monks in Tibet, southwest China, spend much time studying and writing.

CHINESE LANGUAGE
Mandarin, the main language of China, is spoken in all but the southeast coastal areas. Within each language there are many dialects, or regional variations. Although each vocabulary is different, all the variations are written in the same script.

The Beijing Opera performs traditional and new works, mainly with political themes.

Chinese writing consists of thousands of symbols, each one representing a different word or idea.

HONG KONG AND MACAO
At midnight on 29-30 July, 1997, Hong Kong (above) returned to Chinese sovereignty after it had been a British colony for 157 years. Two years later, Hong Kong's neighbour, Macao, ceased to be a Portuguese colony. It officially came under Chinese rule at midnight on 19-20 December, 1999.

CULTURE
China has a rich and ancient culture: paintings found in some Chinese tombs are more than 6,000 years old. Today, artistic traditions continue in the form of folk dancing and music; films, opera, and theatre are all very popular. Artists are encouraged to produce works that depict the achievements of the Chinese people.

Find out more
ASIA
COMMUNISM
EXPLORERS
MONGOL EMPIRE
TRADE AND INDUSTRY

Volcano | Mountain | Ancient monument | Capital city | Large city/town | Small city/town

STATISTICS
Area: 9,597,960 sq km (3,705,793 sq miles)
Population: 1,338,613,000
Capital: Beijing
Languages: Mandarin, Wu, Cantonese, Hsiang, Min, Hakka, Kan
Religions: Non-religious (59%), traditional beliefs, Buddhism, Muslim
Currency: Yuan
Main occupation: Agriculture
Main exports: Chemicals, agricultural produce, titanium, coal
Main imports: Machinery, grain, iron

TEA
The origin of the use of tea as a beverage is unknown. However, the earliest reference to tea is in China, in the late 3rd century CE. It is believed that tea cultivation began in the interior of China, gradually extending down the Yangtze river valley to the coastal provinces. Today, many blends of teas are available in specialist tea shops such as this one in Beijing (right).

SCALE BAR

MOUNT EVEREST
Mount Everest, on the border between China and Nepal, is the highest mountain in the world. The Tibetan name for the mountain is Chomolungma, which means "Goddess Mother of the World".

AFGHANISTAN (claimed by India)

Aksai Chin (administered by China, claimed by India)

Demchok/Demqog (administered by China, claimed by India)

Arunachal Pradesh (much of Arunachal Pradesh claimed by China)

TAIWAN
The island republic of Taiwan lies 130 km (80 miles) off the southeast coast of mainland China. Part of China for many years, Taiwan has been isolated from the mainland since 1949, when the nationalist government of China fled to the island after it was overthrown by the communists. Few nations recognize Taiwan as a separate country.

TAIWAN
Area: 35,980 sq km (13,892 sq miles)
Population: 22,974,000
Capital: Taipei
Language: Chinese
Religions: Buddhism, Taoism, Christianity
Currency: Taiwan dollar

73

CLIMATES

SOME PARTS OF THE WORLD, such as the tropical rain forests of South America, are hot and damp throughout the year. Other regions, such as the Arctic, have long, freezing winters. Conditions such as these are known as the climate of an area. Climate is not the same as weather. Weather can change within minutes; climate describes a region's weather conditions over a long period of time. Every region has its own climate. This depends on how near it is to the equator, which governs how much heat it gets from the Sun. Landscape also influences climate; high mountain regions, such as the Himalayas, are cooler than nearby low-lying places. The ocean can prevent a coastal region from getting very hot or very cold, while the weather in the centre of a continent is more extreme. The climate of a region affects landscape and life – clothing, crops, and housing. But climate can change. Today, climatologists, people who study climates, believe that the world's climate is gradually warming up.

THE FREEZING ANTARCTIC
Only hardy creatures, such as penguins, can survive amid the ice and snow of the Antarctic.

The cool forest climate exists only in the northern half of the world.

The treeless landscape of the polar regions is called the tundra.

POLAR CLIMATE
It is cold all year, and ice and snow always cover the ground. No crops grow, and the few people who live there hunt animals for food.

In temperate climates, trees shed their leaves in winter.

TROPICAL CLIMATE
It is hot all year round in tropical regions, and torrents of rain fall often every afternoon. Rain forest covers much of the land. In regions where wet and dry seasons occur, tropical grasslands grow.

The Sahara is the largest desert in the world.

WORLD CLIMATES
The different climates of the world run in broad zones around the Earth on either side of the equator. They range from hot and rainy climates at the equator to cold climates at the poles. There are five main climatic zones, each of which is shown on this map by a different colour.

DESERT CLIMATE
In the dry, barren deserts, cold, clear nights usually follow burning-hot days. However, high mountain deserts may have cold, dry winters.

TEMPERATE CLIMATE
Warm summers and cool winters feature in warm temperate climates. Rain may fall all year, or the summer can be dry and sunny, as in Mediterranean regions.

COOL FOREST CLIMATE
Summers are cool and short, and winters are long and cold. Pines and other conifers grow in huge forests which cover much of the land.

Away from the equator, the Sun's rays are spread over a wide area.

GREENHOUSE EFFECT
The atmosphere works like a greenhouse, trapping the Sun's heat and warming the Earth. Pollution in the air traps more heat, making the Earth warmer. Unless pollution is reduced, the Earth's climate could be upset.

Sun's rays / Escaping heat / Trapped heat

CLIMATIC CHANGES
Great climatic changes, such as ice ages, come and go during thousands of years. But severe changes in climate can also occur suddenly or within a few years. Dust from volcanic eruptions can obscure the Sun, making a climate cooler. Changes in winds can cause rainfall to shift from a region, bringing drought. Human activities, such as pollution, also affect climate greatly.

SAHARA DESERT
The Tuareg nomads are one of the few peoples that live in the punishing climate of the Sahara Desert, coping with the searing heat of the day and the freezing temperatures at night.

SUN AND CLIMATE
The Sun's rays warm the equator directly from above, making the tropics hot. Away from the equator, the Sun's rays are less direct, making climates cooler.

Find out more
ATMOSPHERE
EARTH
RAIN AND SNOW
WEATHER
WIND

COLD WAR

WHEN WORLD WAR II ENDED in 1945, Europe was in ruins. The United States, and what was then the Soviet Union, had emerged as the world's two most powerful countries or "superpowers". By 1949, two new power blocs of countries had formed. The Eastern bloc, led by the Soviet Union, was Communist; the Western bloc, headed by the United States, was Capitalist. Over the next 40 years the two superpowers opposed each other in what became known as the Cold War. Each bloc attempted to become the most powerful by building up stocks of weapons. The Cold War was a time of great tension but during the late 1980s the rivalry eased. Both sides began to disarm, and in 1991 the Soviet Union broke up, bringing the Cold War to an end.

POTSDAM
In 1945, British Prime Minister Winston Churchill, US President Harry Truman, and Premier Joseph Stalin of the Soviet Union (left to right) met at Potsdam, Germany, to decide the future of the Western world. But serious disagreements arose because Stalin was not prepared to release the countries of Eastern Europe from Communist control. This greatly worried the Western leaders.

THE IRON CURTAIN
As soon as World War II ended, Stalin shut the borders of Eastern Europe. Winston Churchill declared that "an iron curtain has descended across the continent" of Europe. The Communists seized control of the countries behind the imaginary Iron Curtain. These countries became Soviet satellites – nations controlled by the Soviet Union. Yugoslavia broke away in 1948; Albania also rejected Soviet control in 1960.

Soviet Union
West Germany
East Germany
Czechoslovakia
Albania

The NATO symbol

NATO
In 1949, the United States and several European countries formed the North Atlantic Treaty Organization (NATO). A military organization, its aim was to prevent a Soviet invasion of Europe. In response to this the Soviet Union formed an alliance of Communist states called the Warsaw Pact.

BERLIN AIRLIFT
In 1945, Britain, France, the United States, and the Soviet Union divided Berlin between them. In 1948, Stalin blocked all traffic to West Berlin. But in the Berlin airlift, the Western allies flew in supplies, and Stalin lifted the blockade.

INF TREATY
From the 1960s onwards, relations between the two superpowers improved. In 1987, US President Ronald Reagan and Soviet General Secretary Mikhail Gorbachev signed the Soviet-American Intermediate-Range Nuclear Forces (INF) Treaty. The INF treaty cut down on the number of nuclear weapons and was a major breakthrough in the Cold War.

KOREAN WAR
In 1950, Communist North Korea, equipped with Soviet weapons, invaded South Korea. The United States led a United Nations force to drive the Communists out. When the United Nations troops invaded North Korea, China sent soldiers to fight them. It was the first time the United States had fought a "hot war" against Communism.

Find out more
COMMUNISM
EUROPEAN UNION
SOVIET UNION, HISTORY OF
UNITED NATIONS
VIETNAM WAR
WORLD WAR II

COLOUR

A WORLD WITHOUT COLOUR would be a dull place. It would also be difficult to live in. Imagine how hard it would be to tell if traffic lights meant stop or go if there were no red or green. Nature has colour signals too: the bright colours of a tree frog warn other animals that it is poisonous, and the beautiful colours of a flower attract bees to its nectar. Not every creature sees colours in the same way; some animals, such as guinea pigs and squirrels, are colour blind and cannot distinguish between different colours at all. Colour is really the way our eyes interpret different kinds of light. Light is made up of tiny, invisible waves, and each wave has a particular size or wavelength. Each coloured light is composed of different wavelengths, which our eyes are able to detect. White light, such as light from the Sun, is actually a combination of light of all the colours of the rainbow.

Indigo
Violet
Blue
Green
Yellow
Orange
Red

PRISM
A triangular chunk of glass, called a prism, separates all the colours in white light. When light goes through a prism, it is refracted, or bent, because glass slows it down. But every colour goes through at a different speed, and is bent to a different degree. So the colours spread out when they leave the prism.

SPECTRUM
When a prism splits white light into colours, they always come out in the same order, with red at one end and violet at the other. This is called the spectrum. When sunlight is refracted by raindrops, a rainbow is produced which contains all the colours of the spectrum.

Mixing any two primary colours produces secondary colours.

MIXING COLOURS
Red, green, and blue are called the primary colours of light. This is because you can mix red, green, and blue light in different proportions to make any colour in the spectrum. In printing there is a different set of primary colours: cyan (green-blue), magenta (blue-red), and yellow. These too can be mixed to give any colour except white.

PAINT PRIMARIES
Red, yellow and blue are the primary colours of paints. Mixing them together in the correct amounts gives black.

LIGHT PRIMARIES
When the three primary colours of light are mixed together in the correct proportions they make white. During rock concerts and theatre performances, lighting technicians produce a wide range of colours on the stage by mixing different coloured spotlights.

COLOURED OBJECTS
Objects look coloured because of the way they reflect the light that hits them. When white light falls on any surface, some colours are absorbed, or taken in, and some bounce off. When we look at the surface, we see only the colours that bounce off. It is this coloured light that produces the colour we perceive the object to be.

RED SHOES
When daylight hits a pair of red shoes, they look red because they reflect only red light and absorb all the other colours.

BLACK SHOES?
In blue light, red shoes look black because all the blue light is absorbed, and no light is reflected.

Find out more
EYES
LIGHT
PAINTERS
RAIN AND SNOW
TELEVISION

CHRISTOPHER
COLUMBUS

IN 1492 THREE SMALL SAILING SHIPS named the *Niña,* the *Pinta,* and the *Santa Maria* left Spain on a daring voyage. Their aim was to find a new sea route to Asia in search of spices and gold. In command was Christopher Columbus, an Italian sailor from Genoa. Unlike other explorers of the time, who were sailing east, Columbus believed that if he sailed west he would reach India and its luxuries within a few months. The Spanish were eager to profit from trade with India and the rest of Asia, and Columbus persuaded Queen Isabella of Spain to pay for his expedition. He set sail on 3 August and two months later sighted land which he believed was Asia. In fact, Columbus had arrived in the Caribbean Islands. He did not realize what he had found, but his journey paved the way for later European settlement in the Americas.

Landed on
San Salvador
12 October 1492.

Cuba

Hispaniola

Began homeward voyage
16 January 1493.

THE FIRST VOYAGE
Columbus's voyage to the Caribbean lasted four months. He made three more voyages, reaching Central America on his final voyage.

PTOLEMY'S WORLD MAP
The map used by Columbus had been produced by the ancient Greek mapmaker Ptolemy in the 2nd century. The world it showed did not include the continents of North and South America, Australia, or the Pacific.

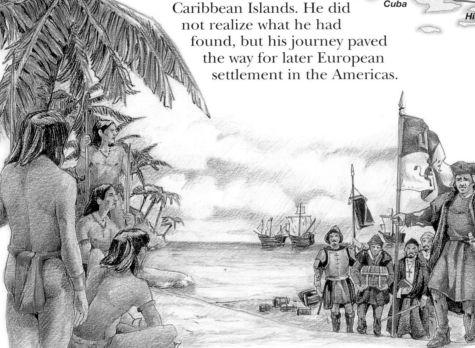

EXPLORING THE CARIBBEAN
When Columbus arrived in the Caribbean he was welcomed by the Carib and Arawak people. Native Americans became known as Indians because the early explorers thought they were in India.

Captain's cabin held navigation equipment and a chest to store treasure captured on the voyage.

Food and other supplies were stored here.

Bowsprit was a spar, or horizontal mast, supporting triangular sails.

THE CREW
The *Santa Maria* carried a crew of 40. The main risk of a long voyage was running out of food and fresh water.

THE *SANTA MARIA*
Columbus's flagship was a slow, clumsy, wooden cargo ship, no larger than a modern fishing trawler. The ship relied on wind power, and conditions on board were cramped and difficult.

Spare canvas for mending sails.

Off-duty sailors slept wherever there was space.

Find out more
CARIBBEAN
EXPLORERS
SHIPS AND BOATS

COMMUNISM

AFTER 1917, A NEW WORD came into popular use – Communism. For it was then that Russia set up the world's first Communist government. By 1950, nearly one-third of the world's population lived under Communist rule. The word communism comes from the Latin word *communis,* meaning " belonging to all". More than 2,000 years ago, the Greek writer, Plato, put forward the earliest ideas that resembled Communism in his book *The Republic.* Much later, Vladimir Lenin (1870-1924), the Russian revolutionary developed modern Communism from the writings of the German philosopher Karl Marx. Unlike Capitalists, who believe in private ownership, Communists believe that the state should own a country's wealth and industry, and wealth should be shared according to need. In Communist countries, the Communist party controls every aspect of daily life.

During the 20th century, Communism was a major political force. But people in Communist countries resented economic hardship and their lack of freedom. From the late 1980s, various countries, including the former Soviet Union, rejected Communist rule.

CHAINS AROUND THE WORLD
"The workers have nothing to lose . . . but their chains. They have a world to gain," wrote Marx in his *Communist Manifesto.* On this magazine cover, a worker strikes down "chains" that bind the world.

KARL MARX

Communism is based on the ideas of Karl Marx (1818-83). His major work, *Das Kapital,* became the Communist "bible". He believed that all history is a struggle between the rich rulers and the poor workers, and that the workers will eventually overthrow their rulers in a revolution. Marx died in exile in London, England.

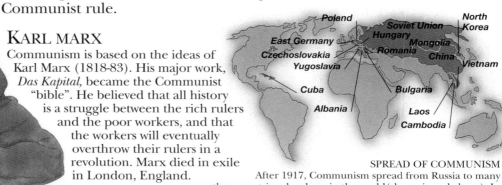

SPREAD OF COMMUNISM
After 1917, Communism spread from Russia to many other countries elsewhere in the world(shown in red above). In Eastern Europe and North Korea, Communist governments were installed by the Soviet army. In China and Southeast Asia, local armed Communist groups took power after fighting long wars.

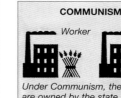

CAPITALISM

Owner Worker

Under Capitalism, a few companies own the factories. Workers are paid wages but do not always share the profits.

COMMUNISM

Worker Worker

Under Communism, the factories are owned by the state. The state sets wage levels for workers, and uses profits for other investments.

CHINA
In 1949, China became a Communist state under Mao Zedong (1893-1976). China has the largest Communist party in the world, with 70 million members. Since the 1970s China's rulers have gradually abandoned Communist economic policies, encouraging private enterprise to create economic growth. But the party has kept a tight grip on power. It encourages people to take part in group sports, such as tai chi (left).

FIDEL CASTRO
In 1959, Fidel Castro (left), a Cuban lawyer, led a revolution against Cuba's dictator, President Batista. Castro became head of government, and Cuba became a Communist state. Castro seized all American property and promised freedom to the Cuban people. In the 1960s, Castro encouraged and supported Communist movements throughout Central and South America.

Find out more
CHINA
COLD WAR
DEMOCRACY
EUROPE, HISTORY OF
SOUTH AMERICA, HISTORY OF
SOVIET UNION, HISTORY OF

COMPUTERS

Accurate weather forecasting, safe air travel, reliable medical technology – in today's world we take these things for granted, but they would be impossible without computers. Although a computer cannot "think" for itself like a person, it works like an electronic brain, doing tasks and interpreting data (information) very quickly. The computer in an air-traffic control system, for instance, can keep track of hundreds of aircraft at the same time and indicates which routes they should follow to avoid collisions. A personal computer can be used for a variety of tasks from word processing to searching the Internet and sending email. A computer consists of thousands of tiny electronic circuits. Before a computer can work, it must be given a set of instructions, called a program (or software), which tells the mechanical and electronic components inside the computer how to carry out a particular job. Additional components, such as a memory card or an internal modem, can be slotted into the computer as required.

HIDDEN COMPUTERS
People usually think of computers as having a screen and a keyboard, but this is not always the case. Many devices, such as washing machines, cars, and cameras, contain tiny computers that are specially programmed to control their function.

PERSONAL COMPUTERS
Many homes, schools, and offices use personal computers – small computers designed for use by one person. A personal computer, such as the laptop shown here, consists of four basic units: a keyboard, to type in information; a memory, to store information and programs; a processing unit, to carry out the instructions contained in the program; and a monitor, for displaying the results of the computer's work.

DATA STORAGE
The hard disc, shown below, is where all the computer's programs and data are stored permanently. Electronic memory chips, however, store data being used by the working computer. This data disappears when the power is switched off.

The monitor displays data.

PROCESSOR
The central processing unit (CPU) is a microchip that does calculations and other similar tasks.

The trackpad controls the cursor on the screen.

The DVD/CD Drive reads and writes removable discs that can store millions of pages of data.

When you press the keys on a keyboard it feeds information into the computer. Letters or numbers appear on screen, or the computer performs a function.

A range of sockets provides connections to external drives. Printers, MP3 players, and flash discs can be plugged into various ports.

PLUG-IN CARD
This device provides high-speed wireless access using Wi-Fi technology. This allows the laptop to connect to the Internet without plugging a cable into a telephone socket.

HOW COMPUTERS WORK

A computer converts everything it handles, such as letters of the alphabet, into numbers. The numbers are stored in the computer in the form of electronic signals in which "on" stands for 1 and "off" stands for 0. All numbers, letters, and pictures are represented by sequences of 1s and 0s. This is called binary code. The computer does all its different tasks, such as inserting a word into a sentence, by doing rapid calculations with these numbers. Once it has finished its job, the computer changes the numbers into words and pictures that we can understand.

All computers contain a set of microchips (left). Inside a microchip are millions of tiny electronic parts that store and process electronic signals.

SOFTWARE

The programs that make a computer perform different tasks are called software. A computer can perform many different jobs simply by using different software programs, from computer games and word processing packages to painting programs and scientific applications that do complex calculations.

Processor, memory, and hard drive are inside tower unit.

DVD/CD Drive reads and writes data onto discs.

Monitor displays information. Speakers are built in to the computer.

HARDWARE

Computer machinery is called hardware. There are many different kinds of hardware: personal computers, small portable computers, and large mainframe computers on which many people can work simultaneously. Hardware also includes components such as monitors, printers, and other computer equipment (below).

USB connectors enable memory sticks, cameras, and other hardware to connect to the computer.

Keyboard

Mouse

Printer produces paper copy of images or data from computer.

Scanner built into printer can turn images from photos or books into data usable by the computer.

HISTORY OF COMPUTERS

In 1834, English inventor Charles Babbage designed the first programmable mechanical computer. However, he could not make the machine as it was too complex for the technology of his day. The first electronic computer, ENIAC, was built in the US in 1946. During the 1980s, transistors and microchips enabled computers to become smaller and more powerful. Easy-to-use software programs such as those developed by Microsoft (below) encouraged the spread of computers in people's homes. In the 1990s, web browsers opened the Internet to private individuals.

In 1975, American Bill Gates (1955-) founded the Microsoft company. By the late 1990s, Microsoft was supplying more than half the world's software.

Bluetooth

Wi-Fi

Router connected to Internet or local network

Mobile phone

NEW TECHNOLOGY

Computers are becoming increasingly portable and versatile. Wireless or "Wi-Fi" technology means they can connect to the Internet via radio signals, and the similar "Bluetooth" enables them to communicate without cables over short distances with pocket computers, mobile phones, and even printers, keyboards, and mice.

Using wireless connections, a laptop computer can be used to send e-mails or surf the Internet from almost anywhere.

Handheld or "pocket" computers can send and receive e-mails, be used as mobile phones, and let you work on files from your desktop computer.

Find out more
ELECTRONICS
INFORMATION TECHNOLOGY
MACHINES
ROBOTS
TECHNOLOGY

CONSERVATION
AND ENDANGERED SPECIES

ANIMALS AND PLANTS ARE DYING OUT at a greater rate today than ever before. Living things have become extinct throughout the Earth's history – often due to dramatic changes in the climate – but today, humans are posing a greater threat. Thousands of animals and plants are endangered (in danger of extinction) because we cut down forests and drain wetlands to farm or build on the land where they live. We change the environment so much that animals and plants cannot survive. This is called habitat loss. Another great threat is hunting. People hunt animals for their fur, hide, horns, and meat, and sometimes simply because they consider animals a nuisance. Pollution is yet another serious threat, damaging many oceans, rivers, and forests. Conservation is the management and protection of wildlife and its habitats. It includes sheltering and trying to save wild animals and plants from destruction by humans. People are more aware of these threats to wildlife than ever before, and there are conservation organizations in many parts of the world. They work to protect endangered creatures by setting aside areas in the wild where animals and plants can live in safety.

GREENPEACE
International organizations such as Greenpeace work in various ways to save endangered polar wildlife, particularly whales and seals. Here, a Greenpeace worker is spraying a seal pup with harmless red dye so that seal hunters will not want to kill the pup for its beautiful fur.

PYGMY HOG
There may be only about 100 pygmy hogs left on Earth following the destruction of their grassland home in the Himalayan foothills of Assam, India.

SIAMESE CROCODILE
Many crocodiles and alligators have been killed for their skins, to be made into leather bags, shoes, and belts. Today, about 20 members of the crocodile family are in danger of extinction, including the Siamese crocodile and the Orinoco crocodile.

CACTUS
The Mexican neogomesia cactus and dozens of other cacti are very rare because plant collectors have taken them from the wild.

Neogomesia cactus

Siamese crocodile

GALAPAGOS TORTOISE
This huge reptile has suffered from the rats, dogs, goats, and other animals that people have taken to the Galapagos Islands, in the East Pacific Ocean. It is now a protected species.

SLIPPER ORCHID
Many orchids are in danger because collectors bring them away from the wild. Drury's slipper orchid has almost disappeared from its natural region in India, and may soon be extinct.

CONSERVING NATURE
Conservation involves studying wild places, identifying the animals and plants that live there, and observing what happens to them. The International Union for the Conservation of Nature and Natural Resources (IUCN) collects scientific data and works on conservation in many countries, together with organizations such as the United Nations Environment Programme (UNEP).

RED-KNEED TARANTULA
The red-kneed tarantula from Mexico (left) is rare because many people keep exotic spiders as pets. This tarantula is not a true tarantula but a member of the bird-eating spider group.

GIANT WETA CRICKET
There are many kinds of weta crickets in New Zealand. Fossils have been found that are more than 180 million years old. Today, several species of weta cricket are in danger of extinction, including the giant weta cricket shown here.

JAPANESE GIANT SALAMANDER
The Japanese giant salamander, shown left, is the world's largest amphibian, growing to more than 1.5 m (5 ft) long. Today it is protected, and is very rare to find.

GREY BAT
Many kinds of bats are threatened because of the loss of their forest homes to farmland, and because of the increasing use of insecticides on the food they eat. The American grey bat shown right is endangered.

AFRICAN VIOLET
The African violet is a well-known houseplant, but it has almost disappeared from its natural habitat – tropical mountain forests in Tanzania, Africa.

SPADEFOOT TOAD
There are many kinds of spadefoot toad. The Italian spadefoot toad shown here is particularly endangered.

81

MONK SEAL
Nature reserves have been set up for the Mediterranean monk seal so that it is not disturbed by tourists on the coasts where it breeds.

GOLDEN LION TAMARIN
Clearing forests for timber and farmland endangers the lives of many monkeys. Many tamarins and marmosets have been killed in South America, because people mistakenly believed that they spread the diseases malaria and yellow fever.

VICTORIA'S BIRDWING BUTTERFLY
The Victoria's birdwing butterfly was first collected by scientists in 1855, when they shot it with guns. Today this butterfly and many other kinds of butterflies are endangered because collectors kill them.

DODO
The dodo was a flightless bird that lived on islands in the Indian Ocean. All dodos were extinct by about 1800.

JACKASS PENGUIN
This flightless sea bird is also called the black-footed penguin. Its numbers have decreased in South Africa because of water pollution and because fishing boats catch the fish the penguin eats.

SUMATRAN RHINOCEROS
Rhinoceroses are in great danger of extinction, but poachers (illegal hunters) still kill them and sell their horns. The horns are carved into dagger handles or powdered into traditional Chinese medicine. There are only a few hundred Sumatran rhinoceroses left, in Sumatra and mainland Southeast Asia.

CAPTIVE BREEDING
One way to help an endangered species recover its numbers is by breeding it in captivity. Experts capture a few animals from the wild, raise them carefully, and encourage them to breed in captivity. Later, they release, or reintroduce, the offspring into a suitable area. The notornis is a flightless bird that scientists believed to be extinct until it was rediscovered in 1948. Eggs from its nests are hatched in an incubator, and the chicks are kept warm with tiny electric blankets. They are fed by someone wearing a puppet-like glove that resembles the parent bird.

Notornis

HABITAT LOSS
Tropical rain forests are being destroyed at an alarming rate. Trees are burned or sold for timber, and the land is farmed or used for roads and buildings. Scientists believe that many rain forests contain kinds of animals and plants that we have never seen. For every plant or creature that is threatened or extinct, there may be 100 that we do not know about.

CONTROLLING TRADE
Some animals and plants are taken from the wild for their skins and other products. Elephants are killed for their ivory tusks. Colourful flowers are made into pulp to make dyes. The Convention on International Trade in Endangered Species (CITES) has lists of hundreds of species, or kinds, of plants and animals. Selling or exporting these animals or their products without a special licence is illegal. All whales, dolphins, and porpoises are on this list; so are all monkeys, apes, and lemurs.

SNAKE SKIN
The brightly coloured objects shown above were once the skins of snakes and lizards. The skins are dyed different colours, then made into all sorts of leather goods, including bags and shoes.

SNOW LEOPARD
The snow leopard lives high in the mountains of the Himalayas and Central Asia. In winter its fur becomes thicker to keep out the bitter cold. In the past, the snow leopard's winter coat was much prized by fur traders. Today, the snow leopard and many other big cats are protected by the CITES agreement, but they are still hunted illegally in some remote areas.

Find out more
ANIMALS
ECOLOGY AND FOOD WEBS
FOREST WILDLIFE
PLANTS
POLLUTION
WATER

CONTINENTS

ALMOST A THIRD OF THE SURFACE of the Earth is land. There are seven vast pieces of land, called continents, which make up most of this area. The rest consists of islands which are much smaller land masses completely surrounded by water. The seven continents are crowded into almost one half of the globe; the huge Pacific Ocean occupies most of the other half. The largest continent is Asia, which has an area of more than 44 million sq km (17 million sq miles).

Most scientists now agree that, about 200 million years ago, the continents were joined together in one huge land mass. Over millions of years they drifted around and changed shape, and they are still moving today. The continents lie on vast pieces of solid rock, called plates, which collide and move against one another. These movements cause volcanoes and earthquakes, push up mountains, and create huge trenches in the Earth's crust.

3 THE WORLD TODAY
The Americas have moved away from the other continents and joined together, and India has joined Asia. Australia and Antarctica have drifted apart.

The continents are made of many smaller pieces of land which have been pushed together.

1 PANGAEA
The continents were joined in one supercontinent, called Pangaea, which began to break apart about 200 million years ago.

2 BREAK-UP
About 135 million years ago, Pangaea split up into two areas – Gondwanaland and Laurasia.

CONTINENTAL DRIFT
A glance at the globe shows that the eastern sides of North and South America and the western sides of Europe and Africa follow a similar line. In 1912, Alfred Wegener, a German meteorologist, suggested that the continents once fitted together like pieces of a jigsaw. This huge piece of land then broke up, and the continents drifted apart.

PLATE TECTONICS
The continents and oceans lie on top of several huge plates of rock about 100 km (60 miles) deep. These plates float on the hot, semi-molten rock in the mantle underneath. Heat from the Earth's interior makes the plates move, carrying the continents with them. Mountains and undersea ridges, deep trenches, and huge valleys form at the edges of the plates as they move and collide.

MOVING PLATES
The plates move about 2.5 cm (1 in) every year – about as fast as your fingernails grow. The Atlantic Ocean is widening at this speed as the Americas drift apart from Europe and Africa.

Molten rock from Nazca plate forces its way up, forming volcanoes along edge of continent.

Nazca plate moves under South American plate, forming trench in ocean floor.

Hot rock rises from below, pushing the American and African plates apart and forming an undersea ridge.

SAN ANDREAS FAULT
The San Andreas fault in the United States is at the border between two plates. They slide against one another, causing severe earthquakes.

Find out more
EARTH
EARTHQUAKES
MOUNTAINS
OCEANS AND SEAS
SCIENCE
VOLCANOES

CRUSADES

NINE CENTURIES AGO the Pope appealed to Christians to recapture the holy city of Jerusalem from the Turkish Muslims who had seized it. Thousands of European Christians – knights, princes, pilgrims, and peasants – responded to the call and set out on a long warring pilgrimage, called a crusade, from western Europe to Palestine (now Israel). Four years later, after battles, starvation, and disease, the surviving crusaders captured the city of Jerusalem. The crusaders set up a Christian kingdom on the shores of Palestine that lasted nearly a century. But in 1187, Saladin recaptured Jerusalem. At least seven more crusades set out. None were successful, but relations between Christians and Muslim worlds were long poisoned by the memory of the Crusades.

THE CHILDREN'S CRUSADE
In 1212, a tragic crusade occurred when thousands of Christian children set off on foot from Europe to Jerusalem. Most starved to death, or were sold into slavery.

Richard I sailed from London.

Philip of France set off from Vezelay.

● **Vezelay**

● **Regensburg**

● **Verona**

Constantinople ●

The Third Crusade made Richard I popular in his own time and earned him the nickname "the Lionheart".

Krak des Chevaliers was the strongest crusader castle.

● **Acre**

Crusader ship

THE THIRD CRUSADE
King Richard I of England (ruled 1189-99) took part in the Third Crusade with the king of France and the Holy Roman Emperor. King Richard I captured the port of Acre, but was caught and held for ransom on his return journey. Ultimately, they failed to take Jerusalem on this crusade, but did make a truce with Saladin allowing Christian pilgrims to enter the city.

ACRE BESIEGED
Huge wooden siege towers helped the crusaders attack the city of Acre. The defenders threw spears, hot sand, and boiling water on them.

SULTAN SALADIN
Leader of the Muslim forces, Saladin (1137-93) was a great commander. As sultan of Egypt and Syria, he made Egypt one of the most powerful regions in the Middle East.

THE CRUSADES

1096 First Crusade (also known as the People's Crusade) sets off. Many peasants die on the way, though knights survive.

1097 Crusaders arrive in Constantinople (now Istanbul).

1098 French and Norman armies capture Antioch.

1099 Crusaders capture Jerusalem. Divide coastal land into four kingdoms.

1147-49 Second Crusade attacks Muslims in Spain, Portugal, and Asia Minor.

1187 Saladin conquers Jerusalem and most of Palestine.

1189 Third Crusade sets off led by the kings of England and France and Frederick I, the Holy Roman Emperor. Frederick dies on the way.

1191-92 Crusaders capture Acre but return to Europe.

1202-04 Fourth Crusade sets off. Crusaders capture Constantinople and steal treasure.

1217 Fifth Crusade sets off. Crusaders capture Damietta, Egypt, but return it and make a truce.

1228-29 Sixth Crusade. Emperor Frederick II makes a 10-year truce.

1248-54 Seventh Crusade. Louis IX of France captures Damietta but is forced to return it.

1270 Eighth Crusade. Louis IX dies. This final crusade returns to Europe.

JOURNEY TO JERUSALEM
The journey from Europe to the Holy Land was long and dangerous, and many of the crusaders died on the way. Those who went back to Europe from Palestine took silks and spices with them, as well as Islamic learning such as mathematics and astronomy.

Find out more
CASTLES
EUROPE, HISTORY OF

DEEP-SEA WILDLIFE

THE DEPTHS OF THE SEA form the largest wildlife habitat on Earth. In waters below about 1,000 m (3,000 ft) no plants can grow because there is no sunlight. Yet here, in the vast blackness, many extraordinary creatures live. These animals are found nowhere else. They have adapted to survive where the water pressure is up to 1,000 times that at the surface. Some deep-sea fish feed on the bodies and remains of plants and animals that sink down from the water above. Some other fish have enormous mouths and long, back-curved teeth for grabbing and swallowing anything that swims by. These fish have huge stomachs which stretch to hold prey that is even bigger than themselves. On the deep-sea floor, sea anemones, worms, sea cucumbers, brittlestars, crabs, prawns, and other shellfish sieve the mud searching for tiny particles of food. Many kinds of deep-sea squid, shrimps, and jellyfish are also found here.

Lateral line organs along sides of body sense water currents made by prey.

Mouth gapes open to give the best chance of catching small fish and other prey.

LANTERN FISH
The lantern fish lives in the dim water hundreds of metres below the surface. With its large eyes it watches for predators as it eats tiny floating plants and animals. Scientists are not sure why the spots along its body glow – perhaps to help the fish recognize other lantern fish, see food, or confuse enemies.

This map shows the deep-sea areas of the world.

Deep-sea areas

North America

Asia

Africa

South America

Australia

GULPER EEL
Some kinds of gulper eel grow to more than 2 m (6.5 ft) in length. Gulper eels look as if they consist of a mouth and a tail, unless they have fed well, when the stomach bulges hugely. Like many deep-sea fishes, gulper eels are often black or dark brown. The gulper eel shown above is about 60 cm (24 in) long and has tiny teeth. It feeds on small prey, simply by swimming along with its mouth open.

Flexible spine on back

VIPERFISH
The viperfish is only 30 cm (12 in) long, but it is a fearsome hunter. It floats with the spine on the dorsal (back) fin held over its head. The tip of the spine glows, attracting curious fish. The viperfish stabs its victim with its long lower fangs, then swallows it, using its curved teeth to prevent the victim from escaping.

Light organs run along the sides of the body.

Thin body and long fins typical of the eel group

BIOLUMINESCENCE
Hundreds of deep-sea fish glow in the dark, including anglerfish, lantern fish, and slickheads. They make their own light by a process called bioluminescence. The light is produced by a chemical reaction in parts of the body called photophores; it may be a general glow or a pattern of spots. The lights may be bright (as a signal from a fish looking for a mate), or they may be a pale glow, for camouflage in the dull light.

The lure may be shaped like a blob, tassel, flap, or fringe, depending on the species.

ANGLERFISH
Dozens of different anglerfish patrol the ocean depths. They are similar to their relatives, the shallow-water anglerfish, in the way they fish for food. They use a long, flexible spine on their back as a fishing rod. A glowing lure on the end of the spine acts as bait.

CONSERVATION

Unlike other wildlife areas, such as the rain forests, the deep sea is not in great danger from habitat loss or pollution. However, harmful polluting chemicals have been found at great depths. Fishing boats have also overfished many shallow seas and are now fishing in deeper waters. Deep-sea fish such as these orange roughie fish (right) may soon be in danger because of overfishing.

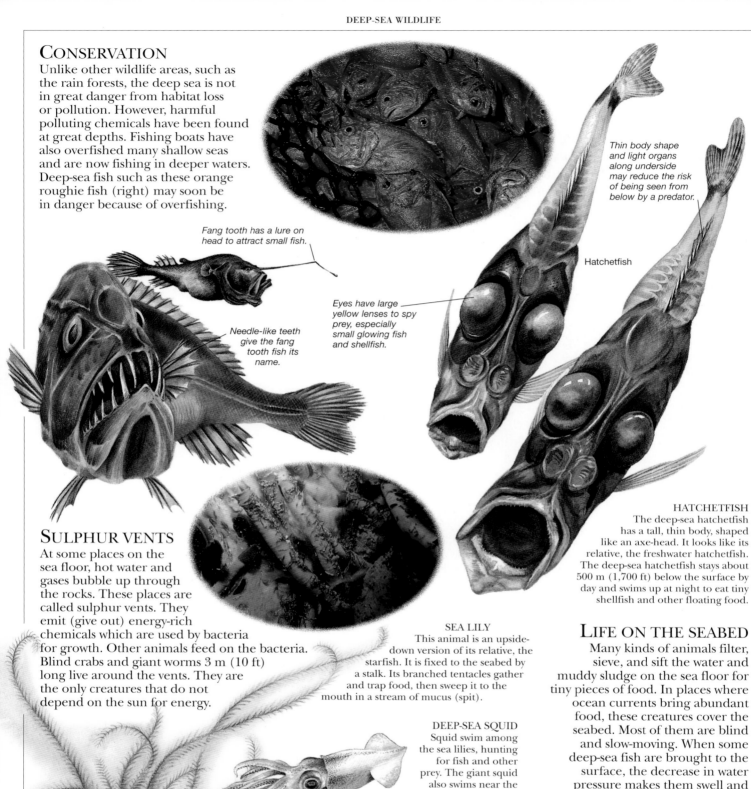

Fang tooth has a lure on head to attract small fish.

Needle-like teeth give the fang tooth fish its name.

Eyes have large yellow lenses to spy prey, especially small glowing fish and shellfish.

Thin body shape and light organs along underside may reduce the risk of being seen from below by a predator.

Hatchetfish

SULPHUR VENTS

At some places on the sea floor, hot water and gases bubble up through the rocks. These places are called sulphur vents. They emit (give out) energy-rich chemicals which are used by bacteria for growth. Other animals feed on the bacteria. Blind crabs and giant worms 3 m (10 ft) long live around the vents. They are the only creatures that do not depend on the sun for energy.

HATCHETFISH
The deep-sea hatchetfish has a tall, thin body, shaped like an axe-head. It looks like its relative, the freshwater hatchetfish. The deep-sea hatchetfish stays about 500 m (1,700 ft) below the surface by day and swims up at night to eat tiny shellfish and other floating food.

SEA LILY
This animal is an upside-down version of its relative, the starfish. It is fixed to the seabed by a stalk. Its branched tentacles gather and trap food, then sweep it to the mouth in a stream of mucus (spit).

DEEP-SEA SQUID
Squid swim among the sea lilies, hunting for fish and other prey. The giant squid also swims near the sea bottom.

SEA CUCUMBER
The cylindrical-shaped sea cucumber is an animal, and a relative of the starfish. It has a frill of tentacles at one end, around the mouth. These tentacles sweep up bits of food from the muddy floor as the sea cucumber moves along on its many tubed feet.

Sea cucumber

LIFE ON THE SEABED
Many kinds of animals filter, sieve, and sift the water and muddy sludge on the sea floor for tiny pieces of food. In places where ocean currents bring abundant food, these creatures cover the seabed. Most of them are blind and slow-moving. When some deep-sea fish are brought to the surface, the decrease in water pressure makes them swell and burst. Scientists study them with special remote-control submersibles which can carry cameras as deep as 6,000 m (20,000 ft).

Sea lily

Find out more
ANIMALS
ATMOSPHERE
FISH
OCEANS AND SEAS
OCEAN WILDLIFE
SEASHORE WILDLIFE

DEMOCRACY

THE WORD DEMOCRACY COMES FROM the ancient Greek words *demos*, which means "people", and *kratia*, which means "power". Democracy means "rule by the people". Within a democracy, all adults have the right to play a part in the government of their country. In most democracies, all persons over the age of 18 can elect a member of parliament to represent them in the national government; and a councillor – their representative in local government. Occasionally they vote about an issue in a referendum. Twenty-five hundred years ago the people of Athens, Greece, practised a form of democracy. Men met in one place to decide on laws for their community. Today, most democracy is representative. Because there are usually too many people in a country to be involved in making every decision, the people elect representatives to make decisions on their behalf.

BALLOT BOX
When people vote in an election, they mark their votes on a piece of paper which they then drop into a ballot box. Their vote is secret, because no one can tell who marked each piece of paper. Today, electronic voting booths are replacing ballot boxes.

A French journal shows political parties campaigning for votes in the United States, 1908.

REPRESENTATIVE DEMOCRACY
Representative democracy means that citizens vote for certain people to represent them. People form political parties and citizens vote for their favoured party in elections. The different parties compete with each other for votes in election campaigns. Getting the right to vote (suffrage) has been a dedicated struggle for both men and women. Today, adult men and women in most countries can vote.

Indians queue to cast their vote at polling booths around the country.

MAJORITY RULE
Democracy means government by the people, but one group of people might want to do one thing and another group something completely different. In that case, the view of the majority (the larger group of people) rules. This could lead to the views of the minority being ignored, so many democratic countries and organizations have a constitution (a set of rules) that safeguards the rights of individuals and minorities. A few countries still do not have a democracy and are ruled by just one person, usually called a "dictator".

Pro-democracy demonstrators in former Czechoslovakia light candles at a vigil.

VOTING
India is the biggest representative democracy in the world: more than 600 million people are able to vote. In the general election of 2004, close to 400 million people went to the polling stations to vote for their representatives in the national parliament. When so many people vote, it can take several days for all the votes to be counted.

Minority vote

Majority vote

EASTERN EUROPE
From 1989, people in Communist Eastern Europe demanded democratic governments. They felt they did not have enough say in how their countries were run. In 1990, what was then Czechoslovakia became the first of many Eastern European Communist countries to declare themselves a real democracy.

Find out more
COMMUNISM
GOVERNMENT AND POLITICS
GREECE, ANCIENT
LAW

DESERT WILDLIFE

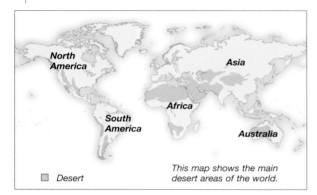

North America
Asia
Africa
South America
Australia

☐ Desert

This map shows the main desert areas of the world.

THE VAST, DRY EXPANSE OF A DESERT may look uninhabited, but all kinds of plants and animals survive in these sandy regions – including insects, reptiles, mammals, and fish. Deserts are the driest places on Earth; some have less than 10 cm (4 in) of rainfall each year. Desert animals have adapted to the lack of water in various ways. Camels, for example, can survive for a long time without drinking. Other animals find enough water in the plants and insects they eat, so they never have to drink at all. Plants such as baobab trees have deep-growing roots to search for water underground.

Other problems for desert wildlife are the extremes of temperature and the lack of shelter. Some deserts are scorching hot; others are freezing cold. Desert mammals have thick fur to keep out heat as well as cold. Many find shelter from the Sun and icy winds by digging burrows. In hot deserts, animals stay in their burrows by day and hunt at night when the temperature is lower.

MONGOOSE
These adaptable mammals hunt by day for all kinds of small animals, including bees, spiders, scorpions, mice, and snakes. A mongoose has extremely quick reactions, so it can easily dodge an enemy such as a snake. The mongoose then leaps onto the snake and kills it with one bite.

TAWNY EAGLE
The tawny eagle survives well in desert conditions. Its incredible eyesight enables it to spot a rabbit or lizard thousands of metres away. When it sees prey, the tawny eagle dives at great speed and grabs the victim in its powerful talons.

COBRA
The hooded cobra kills small mammals, frogs, and lizards by biting them with its deadly fangs full of venom (poison). When this snake is in danger, it rears up its head and spreads out the ribs in the loose skin of its neck to form a hood. The hood makes the cobra look bigger and more threatening.

COLD DESERTS
It is often bitterly cold at night and during the winter in deserts such as the Gobi Desert in Asia. This is partly because the Gobi is very high – about 1,000 m (3,500 ft) above sea level. Day temperatures rise as high as 50°C (122°F), then fall to -40°C (-40°F). For some creatures, a burrow is the only place that provides warmth. Some animals, such as the mongoose, dig their own burrow; others, such as snakes, take over an empty burrow or kill and eat the occupier.

LONG-EARED HEDGEHOG
The long-eared hedgehog shown here has large ears which give off excess warmth to keep the animal cool. Prickly spines protect it from predators. During the day, the long-eared hedgehog stays in its burrow; at night it hunts for insects and worms.

Long-eared hedgehog

Many lizards prowl across the dry sand, flicking their tongues in and out to taste the air. This monitor lizard eats eggs belonging to birds and other reptiles.

JERBOA
Many small mammals live in the desert, including various kinds of mice, gerbils, and jerboas. With its long back legs, the northern jerboa shown here can leap away from danger, keeping its large toes spread out to prevent it from sinking in the soft sand. Jerboas feed on seeds and other plant matter.

Northern jerboa

CONSERVATION
Desert wildlife is vulnerable due to habitat loss and over hunting. Irrigation has led to some desert areas being turned into farm land for growing cereals, fruit, and other crops, and this destroys the delicate balance between the natural plant life and the animals that live on them.

DORCAS GAZELLE
Dorcas gazelles are found across northern Africa, the Middle East, and India. They are an endangered species because they are being forced out of their natural habitat by farm animals and crops.

DATE PALM
The date palm tree has many different uses. The nourishing date fruit is food for people and animals, the stringy bark and wood are made into matting and ropes, and the leaves are fashioned into roofs and sunshades.

Dorcas gazelle

CACTUS
The cactus stores water in its swollen stem. Sharp prickles protect it from plant-eating animals. The cactus shown here is called the prickly pear cactus. The fruit is edible.

HOT DESERTS
The Sahara in Africa is the world's largest and hottest desert. At midday in the Sahara, the scorching sand is so hot that it can burn through skin in seconds. The temperature in the shade soars to more than 55°C (130°F). Few animals are active. Yet as the Sun sets and the air and sand cool, many creatures emerge from under rocks and out of burrows. Dew falls at night, providing the plants and animals with much-needed moisture.

ROADRUNNER
The roadrunner can fly, but it usually races along the ground and runs into the undergrowth if it is disturbed. Roadrunners live in deserts and dry, open country in North America, feeding on all kinds of small animals, including grasshoppers and snakes, eggs, and certain fruits.

ADDAX
This large grazing antelope from the Sahara never drinks – it obtains enough water from its food. Like other sandy desert dwellers, the addax's feet splay out widely to spread the animal's weight and keep it from sinking in the sand. The addax's horns have spiral ridges. The horns are used for defence and in contests for control of the herd.

SIDEWINDER
A row of S-shaped marks in the sand at daybreak is a sign that a sidewinder snake passed during the night, probably on the trail of a mouse or a rat. This snake's wavelike way of moving means that only two small parts of its body touch the ground at any time, giving a better grip on the shifting sand.

NAKED MOLE RAT
This hairless rat is virtually blind and lives in underground tunnels in groups called colonies. The colonies are organized in a similar way to an ant's nest, with one queen who gives birth to all the young. Naked mole rats feed only on tubers which they find in the soil.

YUCCA MOTH AND YUCCA PLANT
The yucca is a desert lily. It has pale, scented flowers which attract the tiny female yucca moth. The moth climbs into the flower and gathers pollen, then flies to another yucca. Here the yucca moth lays its egg in the flower's ovary (egg-bearing part), and transfers pollen. As the yucca's fruit ripens, the moth caterpillar feeds on it. The yucca moth and the yucca flower could not exist without each other.

PINK FAIRY ARMADILLO
Measuring only 15 cm (6 in) long, the pink fairy armadillo lives in the deserts of South America. It leaves its tunnel at nightfall to dig up ants, worms, and other food.

Find out more
ANIMALS
CLIMATES
CONSERVATION
and endangered species
INSECTS
REPTILES
SNAKES

CHARLES
DICKENS

IN 1836, A YOUNG ENGLISH JOURNALIST published his first novel. The book was called *Pickwick Papers*, and its unknown writer, Charles Dickens, quickly became famous. Pickwick was followed by many other novels, and made Dickens one of the best-loved of English writers. His books appealed to children and adults alike. They dealt with all levels of society, and included scenes of both touching emotion and hilarious comedy. As a journalist, Dickens was also good at tackling the important social problems of the time. In all his books, he brought to life poverty, bad schools, injustice, crime, and the poor working conditions in England's factories. His sympathy for the deprived, together with his entertaining stories, mean that his books are still very popular today. Many are made into films and television series.

1812 Born in Portsmouth, England.

1824 Goes to work in blacking warehouse.

1836-37 *Pickwick Papers* appears, first in instalments, then as a complete book.

1837-38 *Oliver Twist.*

1838-39 *Nicholas Nickleby.*

1852-53 *Bleak House.*

1855-57 *Little Dorrit.*

1860-61 *Great Expectations.*

1867-68 Reading tour in United States.

1870 Dies.

BLACKING FACTORY
When Dickens was 12 years old, his father was put in prison for debt. Charles had to go to work for a company that sold blacking – black polish that people used on shoes and iron fireplaces. He never forgot the poor conditions in the blacking factory, and his memories helped to make his descriptions of poverty both realistic and moving.

GREAT EXPECTATIONS
One of Dickens's most popular books, *Great Expectations* tells the story of Pip, a young boy who grows up expecting to become rich. In the end he learns to accept poverty and his poor friends.

DICKENS THE WRITER
In the 19th century, novels often came out in instalments, and this was the way Dickens usually worked. He liked to end episodes on a cliff-hanger, or dramatic scene, which kept his readers interested. Dickens edited a series of weekly magazines, including *Household Words*, in which his books appeared. He also wrote articles about current issues.

OLIVER TWIST
This much-loved novel tells the story of the orphan Oliver, who is brought up in a workhouse. In its most famous scene, he angers the workhouse staff by asking for more food. The novel has been adapted for film and television, and was made into a musical.

Dickens enjoyed performing, and played all the characters in public readings of his works.

PUBLIC READINGS
Towards the end of his life, Dickens gave a series of public readings. He adapted his books specially for performing, and went on a series of reading tours, including one to the United States. The tours were hugely successful, but exhausted Dickens and made him ill.

Find out more
LANGUAGES
LITERATURE
VICTORIANS

DIGESTION

HUMANS NEED FOOD TO SUPPLY ENERGY and to grow and repair itself. Food contains water and five vital nutrients – proteins, carbohydrates, fats, vitamins, and minerals. For food to be useful, the body has to break it down, or digest it, and to release simple, usable nutrients. The digestive system consists of a long tube called the alimentary canal which runs from the mouth to the anus. Each part does a particular job. The stomach is like a bag where chewed food is mixed with acids and digestive juices. The small intestine pushes the food along by a squeezing action called peristalsis. The tiny particles of digested food pass easily through the walls of the small intestine and into the bloodstream, to be used by the body. The large intestine digests and absorbs water from the food and turns the waste products into semi-solid lumps called faeces.

Teeth chew, crunch, and grind food into a pulp.

Tongue tastes different flavours.

Salivary glands produce a watery liquid to mix with food and help with swallowing.

Oesophagus pushes swallowed food down through the chest, behind the windpipe and heart, into the stomach.

Liver

Stomach is where muscles crush food into a pulp and mix it with digestive juices.

Small intestine absorbs digested food into the body.

Large intestine absorbs water from undigested pieces of food.

Rectum is the last part of the large intestine.

EATING FOOD
When you swallow food, it enters your throat. A flap called the epiglottis folds over the entrance to the windpipe so that food goes into the oesophagus and not into the trachea, where it could cause choking.

LIVER
The liver is the body's "chemical factory". It receives digested nutrients, such as glucose (sugar), from the small intestine, and either stores them, converts them, or dispatches them to another part of the body.

SMALL INTESTINE
The small intestine is coiled into the lower part of the body. It is very long, measuring about 6 m (20 ft) in length. Its lining has many folds and ridges, so that it can absorb nutrients efficiently.

Pancreas produces digestive juices.

LARGE INTESTINE
The large intestine is much shorter than the small intestine, but three times as wide, measuring up to 7 cm (2.5 in) in width.

Anus is where waste products leave the body as faeces.

DIGESTION
Digestion begins in the mouth, as teeth crush the food. Watery saliva moistens the food and makes it easy to chew and swallow. The muscular walls of the stomach churn food into a soup-like liquid that is released in spurts into the small intestine. This is where most digestion takes place and where simple nutrients are absorbed through the lining of the small intestine into the bloodstream.

STOMACH
This bag is lined with a thick layer of slimy mucus. Tiny glands in the lining produce strong digestive juices, which contain substances such as enzymes and acids.

TONGUE
The surface of the muscular tongue is covered by tiny bumps called papillae. Some house taste buds that detect five basic tastes in foods: sweet, salty, sour, bitter, and umami (a savoury taste). Before tastes can be detected by taste buds, they have to dissolve in saliva.

Papillae are tiny bumps on the tongue.

VILLI
Each fold of the lining of the small intestine has thousands of microscopic finger-shaped projections called villi. The villi allow the small intestine to absorb more nutrients.

ENZYMES
Digestive juices contain proteins called enzymes, which break down food into simple substances the body can absorb.

Find out more
GENETICS
HUMAN BODY
LUNGS AND BREATHING
MUSCLES AND MOVEMENT

DINOSAURS

WE HAVE KNOWN ABOUT DINOSAURS for only 150 years or so, but these great creatures roamed the Earth for 160 million years – long before humans appeared. Scientists first learned about dinosaurs in the 1820s, when they discovered the fossilized bones of unknown creatures. Today, these fossils show us where dinosaurs lived, what they looked like, and what they ate. Dinosaurs were reptiles and lived on land. Their name means "terrible lizard", and like lizards, many of them had tough, scaly skin. There were hundreds of different kinds of dinosaurs, divided into two main groups. The Ornithischians (bird-hipped dinosaurs), such as *Protoceratops*, had hipbones similar to birds; the Saurischians (lizard-hipped dinosaurs), such as *Diplodocus*, had hipbones similar to lizards. Not all dinosaurs were giants – *Compsognathus* was the size of a chicken and *Heterodontosaurus* was the size of a large dog. Some dinosaurs, such as *Tyrannosaurus rex*, were carnivores (meat eaters); others, such as *Stegosaurus*, were herbivores (plant eaters). About 65 million years ago, dinosaurs and the swimming and flying reptiles that lived at the same time died out. The reason for this is still uncertain.

REPTILES
Dinosaurs were reptiles, like crocodiles, alligators, and the lizard shown above. Like other reptiles, dinosaurs had scaly skin, and laid eggs. Unlike lizards and other reptiles, dinosaurs had long legs, so they could move faster on land.

When dinosaurs lived on the land, flying reptiles called pterosaurs flew in the air, and reptiles called ichthyosaurs and plesiosaurs swam in the sea.

Criorhynchus was a fishing pterosaur – it swept low over the seas and caught fish in its beak.

A lizard-type pelvis

Tyrannosaurus rex belonged to the group of lizard-hipped dinosaurs called Saurischians.

Tyrannosaurus had tiny hands which did not reach its mouth. We do not know what the hands were used for.

Carnivorous dinosaurs often had large, strong claws for grabbing their prey. The claw shown here belonged to Baryonyx, which is nicknamed "Claws".

TYRANNOSAURUS REX

The gigantic *Tyrannosaurus* was one of the largest carnivorous (meat-eating) dinosaurs. Scientists first discovered its fossils in North America. *Tyrannosaurus* measured 14 m (46 ft) in length and stood almost 6 m (20 ft) high. Its massive teeth were more than 15 cm (6 in) long. *Tyrannosaurus* weighed almost 7 tonnes (7 tons), so it was probably too heavy to run and hunt other dinosaurs. *Tyrannosaurus* fed on small creatures and dead dinosaurs.

GORGOSAURUS
Carnivorous dinosaurs, such as the *Gorgosaurus*, had huge teeth and powerful jaw muscles for a strong bite. Not all dinosaur teeth were this large, however; some were as small as human teeth.

Jaw bone of a *Gorgosaurus*

DIPLODOCUS

The largest dinosaurs, including *Diplodocus*, belonged to the group of plant eaters called sauropods. At 27 m (88 ft) in length, *Diplodocus* was one of the longest dinosaurs. Its long, thin tail made up most of its length. With its slim body, it probably weighed only about 9 tonnes (9 tons).

Protoceratops *was about 2 m (6 ft) long. It probably snipped at plants with its beak-like mouth.*

Diplodocus *was a herbivore; all its teeth were at the front of its mouth for nibbling at tough leaves.*

PROTOCERATOPS

Scientists discovered fossils of *Protoceratops* in the Gobi Desert, Mongolia, in the 1920s. The bones of adults and young were found, together with fossilized eggs. About 80 million years ago, this area was a nesting site for many families of *Protoceratops*.

BREEDING

The fossils of *Protoceratops* show that the female scooped out a shallow hole in the sand and laid the eggs in a circular pattern. Scientists found many nests near each other, which shows that these dinosaurs bred in colonies, or groups, in the same way as some birds do today.

TYPES OF DINOSAURS

Dinosaurs varied greatly in size and shape, and they did not all live at the same time. Some lived 200 million years ago; others lived 70 million years ago. This chart gives the sizes of some dinosaurs in comparison to the size of a 10-year-old child.

m.y.a. = million years ago

Coelophysis
210 m.y.a.

Diplodocus
140 m.y.a.

Iguanodon
120 m.y.a.

Ornithosuchus
210 m.y.a.

Triceratops
65 m.y.a.

Protoceratops
80 m.y.a.

Comp-
sognathus
140 m.y.a.

Baryonyx
120 m.y.a.

Euplocephalus
75 m.y.a.

Tyrannosaurus
70 m.y.a.

Scientists have been able to reconstruct some dinosaur species, such as this Tuojiangosaurus.

THE END OF THE DINOSAURS

There are many ideas about the end of the dinosaurs. Some people believe they died out because a giant meteorite crashed into the Earth, throwing up a dust cloud and blotting out the sun. Without sunlight, the plants and the dinosaurs that fed on them could not survive.

BARYONYX

In 1983, the fossilized claw and bones of a dinosaur were found in Surrey, England. This dinosaur is named *Baryonyx*. Fossilized scales of fish were found in this dinosaur's stomach, so it was probably a fish eater and may have used its claws to catch fish.

IGUANODON

Iguanodon was a herbivore. As an adult it was about 10 m (33 ft) long, with small hooves on its hands and feet. Some scientists believe that *Iguanodon* lived in herds because, in some areas of Europe, they have found many fossilized skeletons of *Iguanodon* together in one place.

Iguanodon *had versatile hands – the three middle fingers acted like hooves, the little finger could grasp food, and the spiked thumb was a fearsome weapon.*

A bird-type pelvis

Iguanodon *belonged to the bird-hipped group of dinosaurs called Ornithischians.*

Heavy tail balanced the rest of Iguanodon's *body.*

Find out more

EVOLUTION
FOSSILS
PREHISTORIC LIFE
PREHISTORIC PEOPLES

EARTH

A LARGE BALL OF ROCK spinning through space is our home in the universe. This is the Earth, one of eight major planets that circle around the Sun. The Earth is the only place we know of that supports life. It has liquid water and a protective atmosphere, both of which are essential for life. And of all the planets in the solar system, the Earth is at just the right distance from the Sun to be neither too hot nor too cold. Land makes up less than a third of the surface of the Earth; more than two thirds is the water in the oceans. The Earth's interior consists of layers of rock that surround a core made of iron and nickel.

The processes that support life on Earth are in a natural balance. However, many people are worried that pollution, human over-population, and misuse of resources may destroy this balance and make the Earth unsafe for plants and animals.

EARTH IN SPACE
When astronauts first saw the Earth from space, they were enthralled by the beauty of our blue planet. This picture shows the Earth over the Moon's horizon.

ATMOSPHERE
A layer of air called the atmosphere surrounds the Earth. It is roughly 2,000 km (1,250 miles) deep and contains mainly the gases nitrogen and oxygen. The atmosphere shields the Earth from harmful ultraviolet rays coming from the Sun and prevents the Earth from becoming too hot or too cold.

OCEANS
The oceans are large water-filled hollows in the Earth's crust. Their average depth is 3.5 km (2.2 miles).

MANTLE
Under the crust is the mantle, a layer of rock about 2,900 km (1,800 miles) thick. The temperature rises to 3,700°C (6,700°F) at the base of the mantle, but high pressure there keeps the rock solid.

OUTER CORE
The core of the Earth consists of two layers – the outer core and the inner core. The outer core is about 2,000 km (1,240 miles) thick and is made of liquid iron. Its temperature is approximately 2,200°C (4,000°F).

INNER CORE
A ball of solid iron and nickel about 2,740 km (1,712 miles) across lies at the center of the Earth. The temperature at the centre is about 4,500°C (8,100°F).

Clouds containing tiny drops of water float low in the atmosphere, carrying water from the seas and land which falls as rain.

Atmosphere

CRUST
The top layer of rock at the surface of the Earth is called the crust. It is up to 70 km (44 miles) deep beneath the continents, but as little as 6 km (4 miles) deep under the oceans. The temperature at the bottom of the crust is about 1,050°C (1,900°F).

Crust

Mantle

Outer core

Inner core

The Earth is made of layers of air, water, iron, nickel, and rock around a core of iron and nickel.

LIQUID ROCK
The interior of the Earth is very hot, heated by radioactive decay of the rocks inside the Earth. The temperature is so high that some rock inside the Earth is molten. This liquid rock rises to the surface at volcanoes, where it is called lava.

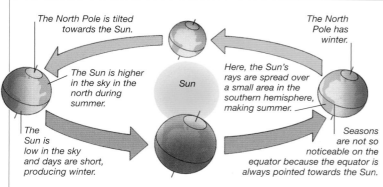

The North Pole is tilted towards the Sun.

The North Pole has winter.

The Sun is higher in the sky in the north during summer.

Sun

Here, the Sun's rays are spread over a small area in the southern hemisphere, making summer.

The Sun is low in the sky and days are short, producing winter.

Seasons are not so noticeable on the equator because the equator is always pointed towards the Sun.

SEASONS
Seasons change as the Earth moves around the Sun. The Earth's axis is not at right angles to its orbit but tilted over by 23.5°. This makes the Poles point toward or away from the Sun at different times of the year.

EARTH FACTS

Diameter at equator	12,756 km (7,926 miles)
Diameter at poles	12,714 km (7,900 miles)
Circumference at equator	40,075 km (24,901 miles)
Land area	29.2% of Earth's surface
Ocean area	70.8% of Earth's surface
Mass	6,000 billion billion tonnes (5,900 billion billion tons)
Time for one spin	23 hours 56 minutes 4 seconds
Time to orbit Sun	365 days 6 hours 9 minutes 9 seconds
Distance from Sun	150 million km (93 million miles)

The Earth spins around its axis, which passes through the North and South Poles. It also orbits the Sun at the same time.

1 A large clump inside a cloud of gas and dust contracted (shrank) to form the Sun about 4,4540 million years ago. A disk of gas and dust formed around the young Sun. Small particles stuck together and grew into chunks of rock and ice. Chunks came together to form planets.

2 The Earth may have taken about 100 million years to grow into a ball of rock. The new planet became hot as the rock particles crashed into one another. The surface was molten, and the young Earth glowed red-hot.

FORMATION OF THE EARTH
Scientists have calculated that the Earth is nearly 4,600 million years old. Some Moon rocks and meteorites (pieces of rock that fall to Earth from space) are the same age, which suggests that the whole solar system formed at the same time. The Sun, Earth, and the other planets were formed from a huge cloud of gas and dust in space.

3 Radioactivity in the rocks caused more heat, and the whole planet melted. Molten iron then sank to the centre of the Earth to form its core. Lighter rocks floated above the iron, and about 4,500 million years ago the surface cooled to form the crust. Volcanoes erupted and poured out gases, which formed the atmosphere, and water vapour, which condensed (changed into liquid) to fill the world's oceans.

GEOTHERMAL ENERGY
The heat from the interior of the Earth provides a source of safe, clean energy called geothermal energy. Hot rocks lie close to the surface in Iceland, Italy, and other parts of the world. The rocks heat underground water and often make it boil into steam. Wells dug down to these rocks bring up the steam and hot water, which are used to generate electricity and heat buildings.

Water that filled the oceans may have also come from comets that collided with the young Earth.

THEORIES OF THE EARTH
People once believed that the Earth was flat. About 2,500 years ago, the Greeks found out that the Earth is round. Aristarchus, a Greek scientist, suggested in about 260 BCE that the Earth moves around the Sun. It was not until 1543 that Polish astronomer Nicolaus Copernicus (1473-1543; right) reasserted this idea. New theories are still evolving. For instance, one idea called the Gaia theory suggests that the whole planet behaves as a living organism.

4 Tiny living things began to grow at least 3,500 million years ago. Some produced oxygen, which began to build up in the atmosphere about 2,300 million years ago. The continents broke up and slowly moved into their present-day positions. They are still moving slowly today, a process called continental drift.

Find out more
ATMOSPHERE
CLIMATES
CONTINENTS
MOUNTAINS
OCEANS AND SEAS
PLANETS
ROCKS AND MINERALS
UNIVERSE

EARTHQUAKES

ONCE EVERY 30 SECONDS, somewhere in the world, the Earth shakes slightly. These earth tremors are strong enough to be felt, but cause no damage. However, every few months a major earthquake occurs. The land shakes so violently that roads break up, forming huge cracks, and buildings and bridges collapse, causing many deaths. Earthquakes are caused by the movements of huge plates of rock in the Earth's crust. They occur in places that lie on the boundaries where these plates meet, such as the San Andreas fault which runs 435 km (270 miles) through central California. In some cases, scientists can tell in advance that an earthquake is likely to occur. In 1974, for example, scientists predicted an earthquake in China, saving thousands of lives. But earthquake prediction is not always accurate. In 1989, a major earthquake struck San Francisco, United States, without warning, killing 67 people.

INSTANT CHAOS
Destruction can be so swift and sudden that people have no time to escape. Falling masonry crushes cars and blocks roads.

CAUSES OF EARTHQUAKES
The Earth's crust consists of several vast plates of solid rock. These plates move very slowly and sometimes slide past each other. Most severe earthquakes occur where the plates meet. Sometimes the edges of the plates grip each other and cannot move, so pressure builds up. Suddenly the plates slip and lurch past each other, making the land shake violently.

The rocks suddenly slip along the fault; a movement of a few metres is enough to cause a severe earthquake.

FAULT
A deep crack, or fault, marks the boundary of two plates.

The earthquake is usually strongest at the epicentre, the point on the Earth's surface directly above the focus.

The place within the Earth where an earthquake occurs is the focus.

Rocks grip along the fault.

RICHTER SCALE
The severity of an earthquake is measured on the Richter scale, which runs from 0 to 9. An earthquake reaching 8 on the scale can flatten a city. The Richter scale measures the movement of the ground, rather than the damage an earthquake causes, which varies from place to place.

TSUNAMIS
Earthquakes that occur on the sea floor often produce a wave called a tsunami, which races towards the shore. The wave is not very high mid-ocean, but it begins to rise as it nears the coast, sometimes growing to about 75 m (250 ft) high. The tsunami smashes onto the shore, destroying buildings and carrying boats far inland. Tsunamis, which are often wrongly called tidal waves, are also caused by volcanic eruptions.

An earthquake in the Indian Ocean on December 26, 2004, caused tsunamis that devastated the coasts of parts of South East Asia, India, and Africa. It was one of the worst natural disasters of recent times.

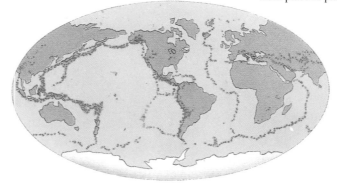

EARTHQUAKE BELTS
Earthquakes occur only in certain parts of the world. This map shows the world's earthquake belts, which also extend through the oceans. Most severe earthquakes happen near boundaries between plates in the Earth's crust, so the belts follow the edges of the plates.

SEISMOLOGY
Sensitive equipment can pick up vibrations far from an earthquake. This is because the sudden slip of rocks produces shock waves which move through the Earth. The study of earthquakes and the shock waves they cause is called seismology.

Find out more
CONTINENTS
EARTH
SCIENCE
VOLCANOES

ECOLOGY AND FOOD WEBS

WE CAN LOOK AT NATURE in the same way that we look at a complicated machine, to see how all the parts fit together. Every living thing has its place in nature, and ecology is the study of how things live in relation to their surroundings. It is a relatively new science and is of great importance today. It helps us understand how plants and animals depend on each other and their surroundings in order to survive. Ecology also helps us work towards saving animals and plants from extinction and solving the problems caused by pollution. Plants and animals can be divided into different groups, depending on their ecological function. Plants capture the Sun's light energy and use it to produce new growth, so they are called producers; animals consume (eat) plants and other animals, so they are called consumers. All the plants and animals that live in one area and feed off each other make up a community. The relationships between the plants and animals in a community is called a food web; energy passes through the community via these food webs.

ECOSYSTEM

A community and its surroundings, including the soil, air, climate, and the other communities around it, make up an ecosystem. The Earth can be seen as one giant ecosystem spinning through space. It recycles its raw materials, such as leaves and other plant matter, and is powered by energy from the Sun.

The European kingfisher has little to fear. Its brightly coloured plumage warns predators that it is foul-tasting. The kingfisher is well named – it is extremely skilful at fishing.

FOOD CHAINS AND FOOD WEBS

A plant uses the Sun's energy to grow. A herbivore (plant eater) eats the plant. A carnivore (meat eater) or an omnivore (plant and meat eater) then eats the herbivore. This series of events is called a food chain.

A frog forms a link between two different food webs – the pond and the meadow food webs.

During spring, the frog is part of the pond food web. In autumn, it moves onto land and becomes involved in the meadow food web.

Pond food web

Meadow food web

The fox is a top carnivore in the meadow food chain.

CARNIVORE
The adult frog is carnivorous; it catches flies and other small creatures.

OMNIVORE
Many small fish are omnivores, feeding on whatever they can find – from water weeds to tiny animals such as tadpoles.

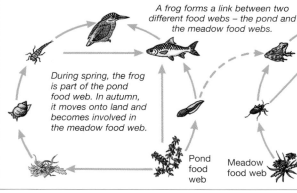

Plants form the beginning of the food chain in a pond, as they do on land.

DETRITIVORE
Certain types of worms and snails are called detritivores because they eat detritus, or rotting matter, at the bottom of a pond or river. They help recycle the materials and energy in dead and dying plants and animals.

HERBIVORE
As a young tadpole, the frog is a herbivore, eating water weeds.

KINGFISHER

Some carnivores are called top carnivores because they have almost no predators. Their usual fate is to die of sickness, injury, or old age, at which time they become food for scavengers. The European kingfisher shown here eats a wide variety of food, including small fish such as minnows and sticklebacks, water snails and beetles, dragonfly larvae, tadpoles, and small frogs. The kingfisher is therefore at the top of a complex food web.

HABITAT

A habitat is a place where a certain animal or plant usually lives. There are several characteristic habitats, such as oak forests, mangrove swamps, and chalk cliffs. A habitat often has one or a few main plants, such as the pampas grass which grows in the grassland habitats of South America. Certain characteristic animals feed on these plants. Some animals live in only one or two habitats; the desman, for example, is a type of muskrat found only in fast-running mountain streams. Other animals, such as red foxes and brown rats, are able to survive in many different habitats. The coral reef shown here is one of the Earth's richest habitats in terms of species, but the water is poor in nutrients.

BIOME

A biome is a huge habitat, such as a tropical rain forest or a desert. The deserts of Africa, central Asia, and North America each have distinct kinds of plants and animals, but their ecology is similar. Each of these large habitats, or biomes, has a big cat as a top predator – the caracal (a kind of lynx) in Africa, the puma in North America, and Pallas's cat in central Asia. The major types of plants that grow in a biome are determined by its climate. Areas near the equator with very high rainfall become tropical rain forests, and in cold regions near the Arctic and Antarctic, only tundra plants can survive.

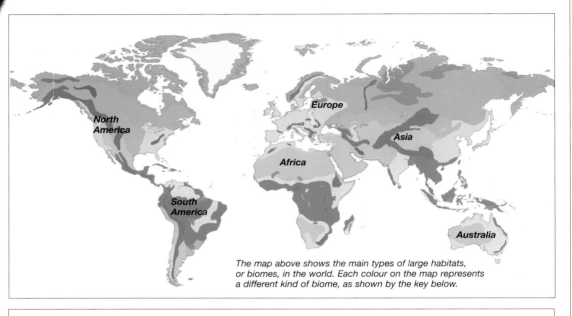

The map above shows the main types of large habitats, or biomes, in the world. Each colour on the map represents a different kind of biome, as shown by the key below.

Desert · Wetland · Savannah · Tropical rain forest · Temperate grassland · Temperate forest · Coniferous forest · Tundra · Mountains

PESTICIDES

Farmers and gardeners use pesticides to kill insects that are pests on vegetable and cereal crops. In 1972, the insecticide called DDT was banned in the United States because it caused great damage to wildlife. When DDT is sprayed on crops, some of it is eaten by herbivores such as mice and squirrels. The insecticide builds up inside the animal's body. A bird of prey such as a hawk eats the animal, and the DDT becomes concentrated (builds up) in the bird's body. The DDT causes the bird to make very thin or deformed eggshells, which break and kill the developing chicks inside. Since DDT was banned, the number of falcons has slowly risen.

Today, falcons and other birds of prey are rare. Many have died as a result of the pesticides used by farmers to kill insects on farm crops.

Find out more

ANIMALS
BIRDS
CONSERVATION
and endangered species
DESERT WILDLIFE
LAKE AND RIVER WILDLIFE
PLANTS
POLLUTION

ANCIENT EGYPT

THE RICH, FERTILE SOIL of the Nile Valley gave birth to Egypt, a civilization that began over 5,000 years ago and lasted more than 3,000 years. The River Nile made the black soil around it productive, and the civilization of Egypt grew wealthy. For much of its history Egypt was stable. Its pharaohs ruled with the help of officials called viziers who collected taxes and acted as judges. The Egyptians worshipped many gods and believed that when they died they went to the next world. Pharaohs built elaborate tombs for themselves; the best known are the magnificent pyramids. The Egyptians also made great advances in medicine. Gradually, however, the civilization broke down, leaving it open to foreign invasion. In 30 BCE the Romans finally conquered the empire.

PHARAOHS
The rulers of Ancient Egypt were called pharaohs, meaning "Great House". They were thought to be divine and had absolute power: all the land in Egypt belonged to them. People believed the pharaohs were the sons of Ra, the Sun god. Above is a famous pharaoh, Tutankhamun, who died when he was only 18.

The internal layout of the Great Pyramid

Grand Gallery

King's Chamber

Entrance

Escape shaft

Queen's Chamber

PYRAMIDS
The Egyptians believed in an eternal life after death in a "perfect" version of Egypt. After their bodies had been preserved by embalming, pharaohs were buried in pyramid tombs. The earliest pyramids had steps. People believed the dead king's spirit climbed the steps to join the Sun god at the top. Later, the pyramids were built with smooth slanted sides. However, people could rob the pyramid tombs easily, so later pharaohs were buried in unmarked tombs in the Valley of the Kings and guarded day and night.

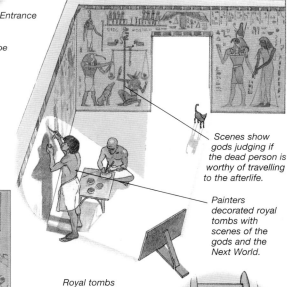

Scenes show gods judging if the dead person is worthy of travelling to the afterlife.

Painters decorated royal tombs with scenes of the gods and the Next World.

Painting of the time shows cattle being transported across the River Nile in special wide boats.

TRANSPORT AND TRADE
The quickest way to travel in Egypt was by water. Barges carried goods along the Nile, and Egyptian traders travelled to ports around the eastern Mediterranean and the Red Sea in wooden reed ships. Using a system called bartering, they exchanged gold, grain, and papyrus sheets for silver, iron, horses, cedar wood, and ivory.

Mediterranean Sea

Nile Delta

LOWER EGYPT

Red Sea

River Nile

UPPER EGYPT

Desert

Royal tombs were filled with food, jewellery, clothing, weapons, tools, and statues of servants.

Inside a tomb

RIVER NILE
Each year, the River Nile burst its banks and spread water and fertile silt over the land. This "inundation" of the Nile Valley made the land fertile for about 10 km (6 miles) on either side of the river. The Egyptians planned their agricultural system around this, farming the land by storing the floodwaters. The desert on either side provided a natural defensive barrier and a rich source of minerals and stone.

Water was drawn from ponds or lagoons with a shadoof.

People carried water to the land on their backs.

Seed was scattered by hand, then trodden in by animals and watered.

The Egyptians used wooden ploughs drawn by oxen.

The Egyptians fished from papyrus reed boats using baskets, nets, spears, and lines with hooks.

FARMING AND FISHING

Most Egyptians were farmers who worked for priests, wealthy landowners, or the pharaoh. They were paid in crops. They watered the lands with floodwaters trapped in lagoons or with water-lifting machines called shadoofs. Crops grown included emmer for bread, barley for beer, beans, onions, dates, melons, and cucumbers. People also fished from the Nile.

The royal name of Tutankhamun

HIEROGLYPHICS
The Egyptians developed picture writing, or hieroglyphics, around 3000 BCE. At first each object was shown exactly by its picture, or pictograph. Gradually the pictures came to stand for sounds. Groups of "sound hieroglyphs", or phonograms, were used to spell words.

NEFERTITI
Nefertiti was the wife of the pharaoh Ikhnaton, who ruled from 1367 to 1355 BCE. She had great influence over her husband's policies. Usually, however, the only women who held important titles were priestesses.

MEDICINE AND MAGIC
Egyptian doctors were the first to study the body scientifically. They also carried out some effective dentistry. However, many "cures" were based on magic.

Scarab beetles were sacred to the Egyptians, who used them as charms to ward off illness.

Headrest amulet

Relief of the time showing Ancient Egyptian medical tools.

ANCIENT EGYPT

c. 10,000-5000 BCE First villages on the banks of the Nile. Slow growth of the two kingdoms of Upper and Lower Egypt.

c. 2630 BCE First step pyramid built at Saqqara.

c. 2575 BCE During Old Kingdom period, bronze replaces copper. Pyramids built at Giza. Dead bodies are embalmed.

c. 2134 BCE Old Kingdom ends with power struggles.

c. 2040 BCE Middle Kingdom begins. Nobles from Thebes reunite the country. Nubia conquered.

c. 1640 BCE Middle Kingdom ends.

1550 BCE New Kingdom begins. Permanent army.

1400 BCE Egypt reaches height of its power.

1070 BCE Egyptian power begins to decline.

332 BCE Alexander the Great conquers Egypt.

51 BCE Cleopatra rules.

30 BCE Egypt becomes a Roman province.

MUMMIES
The Egyptians thought that if they preserved their bodies after death, they would "live" forever. So they made "mummies" – corpses that did not decay. Embalmers removed the liver, lungs, and brain from the dead body, leaving the heart inside. They then coated the body with saltlike natron crystals to preserve it, and finally wrapped the whole package in bandages.

An idealized portrait of the dead person was painted on the coffin.

The internal organs were wrapped in linen and placed in canopic jars.

Linen protected the body.

Coffin was richly decorated with hieroglyphs of spells to help the dead person in the afterlife.

Find out more
AFRICA, HISTORY OF
ALPHABETS
WONDERS
of the ancient world

ELECTRICITY

A FLASH OF LIGHTNING that leaps through the sky during a thunderstorm is one of the most visible signs of electricity. At almost all other times, electricity is invisible but hard at work for us. Electricity is a form of energy. It consists of electrons – tiny particles that come from atoms. Each electron carries a tiny electric charge which is an amount of electricity. When you switch on a light, about one billion billion electrons move through the bulb every second. Cables hidden in walls and ceilings carry electricity around houses and factories, providing energy at the flick of a switch. Electricity also provides portable power. Batteries produce electricity from chemicals, and solar cells provide electricity from the energy in sunlight. Lamps, motors, and dozens of other machines use electricity as their source of power. Electricity also provides signals which make telephones, radios, televisions, and computers work.

Electricity flows into homes through cables that run either underground or above street level on poles.

CURRENT ELECTRICITY

Electricity comes in two forms: electricity that flows, and static electricity, which does not move. Flowing electricity is called current electricity. Billions of electrons flow along a wire to give an electric current. The electricity moves from a source such as a battery or power station to a machine. It then returns to the source along another wire. The flow of electric current is measured in amperes (A).

Some power stations generate electricity by burning coal and oil. Other stations are powered by nuclear energy.

A transformer boosts the voltage (force) of the electricity to many thousands of volts.

Tall pylons support long cables that carry the electricity safely above the ground to all parts of an area.

Another transformer reduces the voltage of the electricity to levels suitable for domestic appliances.

CONDUCTORS AND INSULATORS

Electricity flows only through materials called conductors. These include copper and many other metals. Conductors can carry electricity because their own electrons are free to move. Other substances, called insulators, do not allow electricity to flow through them. This is because their electrons are held tightly inside their atoms.

Electrons flow through copper conductor.

Most plastics are insulators.

Batteries produce direct current, which flows one way around a circuit.

Battery pushes electric current around the circuit.

Power stations produce alternating current, which flows first in one direction and then the other.

Wires connect battery and bulb to form a circuit.

Bulb in bulb holder

ELECTRIC CIRCUITS

Electric current needs a continuous loop of wire to flow around. This is called a circuit. If the circuit is broken, the electricity can no longer flow.

SUPERCONDUCTORS

Ordinarily conductors, while letting most electricity flow through them, also resist it to some extent. So a measure of electricity is lost. However, some materials lose their resistance when very cold. They become superconductors.

A superconductor can produce a strong magnetic field which makes a small magnet hover above it.

STATIC ELECTRICITY

There are two types of electric charge, positive (+) and negative (–). Objects usually contain equal numbers of both charges so they cancel each other out. Rubbing a piece of amber (dried gum or resin from trees) against wool or fur makes it pick up extra electrons, which carry a negative charge. This charge is called static electricity. It produces an electric force which makes light objects, such as hair and feathers, cling to the amber.

GENERATOR

Generators produce electricity from the energy of movement. A coil of wire moves between the poles of a magnet. This produces an electric current in the coil. Small, simple generators that power bicycle lamps are called dynamos. Large generators in power stations produce huge amounts of electricity for homes and factories.

Basic generator

Coil of wire

Magnetic field produced by magnet.

A simple generator (above) contains a coil of wire that spins between the poles of a magnet. A current flows in the coil when it moves through the magnetic field.

Instead of a simple magnet, there is a set of electromagnets – coils that use electricity to produce a strong magnetic field.

Electromagnets spin inside another set of coils. This produces electricity in the outer set of coils.

A shaft connected to the turbine (a set of vanes) drives the generator.

In a hydroelectric power station, water falling from a dam spins a turbine.

Shaft of motor

Gears connect motor to wheels of car.

Coil of wire

Magnet produces magnetic field.

Electric current flows from battery into coil, producing a magnetic field.

The magnetic force pushes on the coil and makes it spin around.

ELECTRICITY FROM CHEMICALS

Chemical energy from food changes into movement in your muscles. Chemical energy can also change into electrical energy. This is how a battery works. Chemicals react together inside a battery and produce an electric current. When there are no fresh chemicals left, the current stops. Fuel cells also produce electricity from chemicals in the form of gases.

ELECTRIC EEL

The rivers of South America are the home of the electric eel. This eel has special organs in its long body that work like batteries to produce electricity. With a powerful electric shock, the electric eel can stun its prey.

Positive terminal

Powdered chemicals react together to release electrons.

Negative terminal

BATTERY

Connecting a battery in a circuit makes the chemicals inside react to produce an electric current. The battery provides a force that pushes electrons around the circuit. The energy provided by this force is measured in units called volts.

Inside the battery, the electrons flow from the positive terminal and back to the negative terminal.

ELECTRIC MOTOR

Many machines are powered by an electric motor, which contains a coil of wire placed between the poles of a magnet. The electric current fed to the motor flows through the coil, producing a magnetic field. The magnet pushes on the coil and makes it spin around and drive the shaft of the motor.

ELECTRIC SHOCKS

Living things make use of electricity. Weak electric signals pass along the nerves to and from the brain. These signals operate the muscles, maintain the heartbeat, and control the way in which the body works. A strong electric current can give an electric shock that damages the human body and may even cause death. *Never* play with the main electricity supply because of the danger of electric shock.

DISCOVERY

About 2,500 years ago, the Ancient Greeks found that rubbing amber (a yellow solid) produces a charge of static electricity. The Greek for amber is *elektron*, which is how electricity got its name. Around 1750, American scientist Benjamin Franklin (left) discovered that lightning is electricity and explained what electric charges are. At the end of the 18th century, Italian scientists Luigi Galvani and Alessandro Volta produced the first electric battery.

Benjamin Franklin (1706-90) studied the electrical nature of lightning by flying a kite during a thunderstorm.

A bird sitting on an electric cable does not get an electric shock. The electricity does not pass into its body because the bird is touching only one wire and does not complete an electric circuit.

Find out more

ATOMS AND MOLECULES
ELECTRONICS
ENERGY
FISH
MAGNETISM

ELECTRONICS

The semiconductor silicon comes from sand, which is a compound of silicon and oxygen.

A diode is made from the junction between pieces of n- and p-type semiconductors.

A diode allows current to flow through it in only one direction. The current is carried by the flow of holes and electrons.

If a battery is connected the other way around, holes and electrons cannot cross the junctions so current cannot flow.

ELECTRICITY is a source of power that drives machines and provides heat and light. Electricity is also used to produce signals that carry information and control devices. Using electricity in this way is called electronics. We are surrounded by thousands of electronic machines, including computers, MP3 players, telephones, and televisions. All these machines contain circuits through which electric currents flow. Tiny electronic components in the circuits control the flow of the current to produce signals. For instance, a varying current may represent sound in a telephone line, or a number in a computer. The most important electronic component is the transistor. A small radio receiver may contain a dozen transistors; a computer contains millions of transistors inside microchips.

SEMICONDUCTORS

Most electronic components are made of materials such as silicon, which are called semiconductors. Semiconductors control the flow of current because they contain a variable number of charge carriers (particles that carry electricity). In n-type semiconductors, the charge carriers are negatively charged electrons; in p-type semiconductors, the charge carriers are positively charged "holes" – regions where electrons are absent.

CIRCUIT BOARD

An electronic device such as a telephone contains an electronic circuit consisting of several components joined together on a circuit board. Every circuit is designed for a particular task. The circuit in a radio, for instance, picks up and amplifies (boosts) radio waves so they can be converted into sound.

Capacitor stores electric charge. In a radio circuit, capacitors help tune the circuit so that it picks up different radio frequencies.

Resistor reduces the amount of current flowing in the circuit.

Diode allows current to pass in only one direction.

Transistor boosts the strength of electrical signals.

Variable resistor allows the flow of current to be varied.

Wires are used to connect some components.

Microchip in plastic casing

Metal tracks on the underside of the board connect components.

CONTROLLING CURRENT

Electronic circuits do several basic jobs. They may amplify current; they may produce an oscillating current – one that rapidly changes direction, essential for generating radio waves; or they may switch current on and off.

Oscillation: Some circuits convert a steady one-way current (direct current, or DC) into a varying alternating current (AC).

Amplification: An amplifier circuit generates a strong AC current that is an accurate copy of a weaker AC current.

Switching: In computers, electronic circuits rapidly switch current on and off in a code that represents data.

MICROCHIPS
Microchips, or silicon chips, contain circuits consisting of millions of microscopic components. These circuits are squeezed onto the surface of a semiconductor less than 25 mm (1 in) square.

TRANSISTOR
Transistors lie at the heart of most electronic machines. They boost current and voltage in amplifier circuits, store information in computers, and perform many other tasks. Physicists William Shockley, John Bardeen, and Walter Brattain invented the transistor in 1947.

Find out more
COMPUTERS
ELECTRICITY
INFORMATION TECHNOLOGY
TECHNOLOGY
TELEVISION

ELIZABETH I

MORE THAN 400 YEARS AGO, one woman brought 45 years of peace and prosperity to England through her determination and wisdom. Queen Elizabeth I began her life as a neglected princess, whose mother had been executed by her father. She was ignored and imprisoned as a girl, but upon the death of her half sister, Queen Mary, Elizabeth became a strong and popular queen. She tried to end years of religious conflict between Catholics and Protestants by insisting that the Church of England should be only moderately Protestant, so that it included as many people as possible. Elizabeth avoided expensive foreign wars for many years. Her most dangerous conflict was with Philip II, king of Spain, who sent the Armada (fleet of ships) against England. The queen's court was a centre for poets, musicians, and writers. Her reign is often called England's Golden Age.

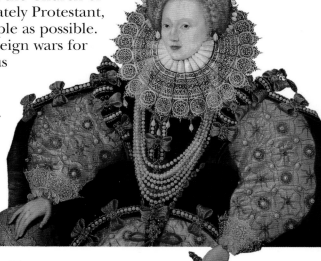

1533 Born, the daughter of Henry VIII and Anne Boleyn.

1536 Mother is executed for treason.

1554 Imprisoned in the Tower of London.

1558 Becomes queen.

1559 Establishes Protestant Church of England by the Act of Supremacy.

1587 Orders execution of Mary, Queen of Scots.

1588 Faces the Armada.

1603 Dies.

SIR WALTER RALEIGH

One of Elizabeth's favourite courtiers was Sir Walter Raleigh (1552-1618). In 1584 she knighted him, and later made Raleigh her Captain of the Guard. He made several voyages across the Atlantic, set up an English colony in Virginia, and brought tobacco and potatoes from the Americas to Europe.

ELIZABETHAN AGE

Elizabeth was the first monarch to give her name to an age. During her reign the arts of music, poetry, and drama flourished. Despite foreign threats and religious unrest at home, she won the loyalty and admiration of her subjects.

SPANISH ARMADA
In July 1588 Philip II, king of Spain, launched his Armada of nearly 150 ships to invade England and restore the Catholic religion. Sir Francis Drake (1540-96) sailed in command of a large group of warships to oppose the Armada. Aided by stormy weather, the English defeated the great fleet.

MARY, QUEEN OF SCOTS
Mary was Elizabeth's Catholic cousin and heir. Forced to abdicate her own throne in Scotland, she fled to England to seek Elizabeth's protection. Mary became involved in Catholic plots against Elizabeth, who reluctantly ordered her execution.

Find out more
HENRY VIII
STUARTS
TUDORS
UNITED KINGDOM, HISTORY OF

EMIGRATION AND IMMIGRATION

WHEN YOU EMIGRATE, YOU LEAVE the country of your birth and settle elsewhere to live and work. When you arrive in a new country, you become an immigrant. Since the 17th century, many British people have left to start new lives elsewhere, in North America, Australia, New Zealand, or African and Asian countries that were once part of the British Empire. In the same way, people from all over the world have arrived to settle in Britain. Some came from countries of the Empire, and later the Commonwealth, to work, because they held British passports. After Britain joined the European Union, large numbers of Europeans came to work in Britain. Other immigrants – refugees of war or religious or political persecution – come to Britain to seek asylum (safety).

EAST END OF LONDON
Many immigrants to Britain first landed at London's docks and so settled in the nearby East End. Huguenots (French Protestants) fleeing persecution in the 1680s and Jews escaping massacres in Russia and Eastern Europe in the 1880s both settled there. Synagogues show where the Jewish communities were. More recently, people from Bengal and Bangladesh have come to the area.

IMMIGRATION CONTROL
When immigrants arrive at a port or airport they must fill in forms to apply for permission to stay. Britain has always had some form of restriction on immigration, although people from the Empire were allowed in. In 1962, the law was changed so that black Commonwealth citizens could only enter if they had a job to come to. Since then, the law has been tightened many times, making it harder to enter the country.

EMPIRE WINDRUSH
During World War II (1939-45), many islanders from the British West Indies fought in the British armed services. Their islands were poor, and, after the war, some decided to move to Britain in search of jobs. In June 1948, the first group arrived on a boat, the *Empire Windrush*. More followed, and a West Indian community was established.

Some of the first 510 Jamaicans to sail to Britain in search of work arrive at Tilbury Docks.

EMIGRATION
For at least 400 years, more people left Britain than have arrived. In 1620, a group known as the Pilgrim Fathers left for North America because of religious persecution, while many more left because of poverty. Today, there are thousands of people in Canada, Australia, and elsewhere who can trace their families back to Britain.

EMIGRATION AND IMMIGRATION

1620 Pilgrims leave for New World.

1685 Huguenots flee France.

1880s Jews flee Eastern Europe.

1905 Aliens Act restricts entry of foreigners to Britain.

1948 *Empire Windrush* brings 510 Jamaicans to Britain.

1962 Commonwealth Immigration Act restricts immigration from Commonwealth.

1971 Immigration Act allows entry to those with British-born parents or grandparents.

2000s Increasing numbers of asylum seekers come to Britain.

Orphaned boys taken to Australia in the 1920s by Dr. Barnado's children's charity.

RACE RELATIONS
Racism is the belief that people of one culture or skin colour are superior to others. Many people who have settled in Britain have faced hostility and sometimes violence as a result of racism. In response, governments have made race discrimination illegal and have promoted equal opportunities for all Britons, black and white.

Find out more
BRITISH EMPIRE
GOVERNMENT AND POLITICS
UNITED KINGDOM, HISTORY OF

ENERGY

THE MOVEMENT OF A CAR, the sound of a trumpet, the light from a candle – all these things occur because of energy. Energy is the ability to make things happen. For example, when you throw a stone you give it energy of movement which shows itself when the stone smashes glass. All life on Earth depends on energy, almost all of which comes from the Sun. The Sun's energy makes plants grow, which provides the food that animals eat; the energy from food is stored in an animal's muscles, ready to be converted into movement. Although energy is not an object that you can see or touch, you can think of it as something that either flows from place to place, or is stored. For instance, energy is stored by water high at the top of a waterfall. As soon as the water starts to fall, the stored energy changes into moving energy which flows to the bottom of the waterfall.

WORK, ENERGY, AND POWER
When a force moves an object, energy is transferred, or passed, to the object or its surroundings. This transfer of energy is called work. The amount of work done depends on the size of the force and how far it moves. For instance, this weightlifter does a lot of work lifting a heavy weight through a large distance. Power is the rate of doing work. The weightlifter produces more power the faster he lifts the weight.

POTENTIAL ENERGY
Energy can be stored as potential energy until it turns into another form such as movement. Examples include water in a raised reservoir waiting to flow through turbines, chemical energy in a battery waiting to drive an electric current, and a coiled spring waiting to be released.

KINETIC ENERGY
An object such as an aeroplane needs energy to make it move. Moving energy is called kinetic energy. When the plane stops, it loses kinetic energy. This often appears as heat – for instance, in the plane's brakes.

TYPES OF ENERGY
Energy takes many forms, and it can change from one form into another. For example, power stations turn the chemical energy stored in coal or oil into heat energy which boils water. Turbines change the heat energy of the steam into electrical energy which flows to homes and factories.

ENERGY RESOURCES
The Earth's population uses a huge amount of energy. Most of this energy comes from coal, oil, gas, and the nuclear fuel uranium. However, these fuels are being used up and cannot be replaced. Today, scientists are experimenting with energy sources, called renewable resources, that will not run out. These include the Sun, wind, waves, and tides.

Heat energy, such as the warmth of the Sun, is carried by invisible waves called infrared or heat radiation.

Light is one form of energy that travels in waves. Others include X-rays and radio waves.

Sound waves are vibrations of the air, so they carry kinetic energy.

Some power stations produce electricity from nuclear energy, which comes from the nuclei (centres) of atoms.

Electrical devices turn the energy of electric currents into many other forms of energy, including heat, light, and movement.

A battery runs out when all its stored energy has been converted into heat in the wires, and heat and light in the bulb.

Oil and coal contain stored chemical energy which changes into heat and light when these fuels are burned.

ENERGY CYCLE
Energy cannot be created or destroyed; it can only change from one form into another. The only exception might seem to be when matter changes into energy in a nuclear reactor. However, the rule still applies because matter and energy are really the same and one can be converted into the other.

Rows of solar panels for producing electricity

Find out more
ELECTRICITY
FORCE AND MOTION
LIGHT
NUCLEAR ENERGY
SOUND
SUN
WATER
WIND

ENGINES

FOUR-STROKE ENGINE
Most car engines are four-stroke engines, which means that each piston makes a set of four movements.

Piston 4 rises and pushes waste gases out through exhaust valve.

Piston 2 rises and compresses (squeezes) fuel-air mixture.

Piston 3 is pushed down by expanding gases when the mixture explodes.

Spark plug produces electrical spark that ignites fuel-air mixture.

Valves open and close to admit and expel the fuel-air mixture.

Piston 1 moves down and sucks fuel-air mixture in through inlet valve.

The piston moves up and down inside the cylinder.

Most engines have between four and eight cylinders. These work in sequence to produce continuous movement.

Crankshaft changes the up-and-down movement of the pistons into circular movement, which drives the wheels.

WHEN PREHISTORIC PEOPLE discovered fire, they also found a way of obtaining energy; because burning releases heat and light. About one million years later, the steam engine was invented, and for the first time people could harness that energy and turn it into movement. Today, there are many different kinds of engines which drive the world's transport and industry. All engines serve one function – to use the energy stored in a fuel such as oil or coal, and change it into motion to drive machines. Before engines were invented, tasks such as building and lifting depended on the strength of people and their animals. Today, engines can produce enough power to lift the heaviest weights and drive the largest machines. The most powerful engine is the rocket engine; it can blast a spacecraft away from the pull of the Earth's gravity and out into space.

INTERNAL-COMBUSTION ENGINE
The engine that powers almost all the world's cars is the internal-combustion engine. It uses the power of gases created by exploding fuel to produce movement. A mixture of air and tiny droplets of petrol enters the engine's cylinders, each of which contains a piston. An electrical spark ignites (sets alight) the fuel mixture, producing gases which thrust each piston down.

ELECTRIC MOTORS
Petrol and diesel engines produce waste gases that pollute the air and contribute to the greenhouse effect (which causes the Earth's temperature to rise). Electric motors are clean, quiet, and produce no pollution. Several car manufacturers are developing cars powered by electric motors. Hybrid cars such as the Toyota Prius (below) use a combination of electric and petrol or gas power to provide good performance with low pollution.

DIESEL ENGINE
Many trains and lorries have powerful diesel engines, which are internal-combustion engines that burn diesel fuel instead of petrol. The engine works in the same way as a petrol-fuelled engine, but does not have spark plugs. Instead, each cylinder has an injector that squirts diesel fuel into the cylinder. The piston compresses the air, making it very hot. The hot air is all it needs to make the diesel fuel explode.

JET ENGINE

The jet, or gas turbine, engine now powers most high-speed aircraft. The engine blasts a jet of hot, fast-moving air backward out of its exhaust; this pushes the engine forward. Fans at the front of the engine spin and suck air into it and squeeze it at high pressure into several combustion chambers. There, flames of burning kerosene heat the air, which expands and rushes towards the exhaust. As the air streams out, it spins a turbine, which drives the fans at the front of the engine.

FRANK WHITTLE

In 1928, English pilot and engineer Frank Whittle (born1907) suggested the idea of the jet engine. Whittle's engine powered an experimental aircraft for the first time in 1941. However, the first jet-powered flight was made during the 1930s in Germany, where engineer Hans von Ohain had developed his own jet engine.

Burning kerosene fuel inside the combustion chambers heats the air and makes it expand violently.

Some of the air that enters the engine flows through the bypass duct.

Large fan spins, sucking air into the engine.

Hot air and exhaust gases rush out of the engine, spinning the turbine as they go.

Fast-spinning fans called compressors increase the pressure of the air and push it into the combustion chambers.

TURBOFAN ENGINE

A turbofan engine is a very efficient kind of gas turbine engine. Some of the air flows through a bypass duct around the main part of the engine. This increases the amount of air flowing through the engine, giving it more thrust. The duct also helps make the engine quieter.

STEAM ENGINE

The steam engine was developed during the 18th century and greatly changed people's lives. It led to the development of industry and transport. People left the land to work in the new factories which contained steam-powered machines, and steam railways allowed people to travel further and faster than ever before.

JAMES WATT

The first engine was a simple steam engine invented by the Greek scientist Hero in the 1st century CE, but it was little more than a toy. In 1712, the British engineer Thomas Newcomen built the first real engine. It was a huge steam engine used to pump water out of mines. In 1769, another British engineer, James Watt (left), greatly improved the steam engine. The unit of power, the watt, is named after him.

Boiler burns wood or coal, producing heat.

Hot air and smoke pass through pipes that run through the water tank. The heat turns the water into steam.

Steam and smoke escape through a valve and pour out of the smokestack.

Steam passes through a pipe to a cylinder. The steam pushes a piston back and forth inside the cylinder.

The movement of the piston drives the wheels of the train.

Find out more

AIRCRAFT
CARS
ELECTRICITY
SCIENCE, HISTORY OF
TECHNOLOGY
TRAINS

ENGLAND

ST. GEORGE'S FLAG
The red cross of St. George of England is the national flag.

MORE THAN EIGHTY PER CENT of the population of the United Kingdom, around 50 million people, live in England. The country has always been the largest, wealthiest, and most crowded region of Great Britain. The Industrial Revolution began in England in the late 1700s, causing a huge shift from agriculture to industry, and the emergence of industrial centres, such as Birmingham and Manchester. In the 19th and early 20th centuries, England was a major power as the centre of the British Empire. Today, England's manufacturing has declined but the country remains a centre for scientific research. Tourism based on England's heritage and traditions is also a major industry, employing thousands of people.

England stretches from Land's End in Cornwall, upwards to the border of Scotland. It covers 130,360 sq km (50,332 sq miles). It is divided into counties.

LONDON

London is England's capital, and a leading international centre for finance, business, theatre, art, and music. One of the biggest cities in Europe, London is a popular destination for millions of tourists every year. The city was founded by the Romans on the banks of the River Thames in 43 CE.

The famous statue of Eros stands in busy Piccadilly Circus in London.

RURAL ENGLAND
England is only a small country, but from the Yorkshire Moors in the north to the spectacular South Downs, it contains varied and beautiful countryside. Urbanization (the growth of towns) has destroyed much of England's rural areas. Preserving what remains has become an important issue.

THE ENGLISH LANGUAGE
Because the British Empire was so vast, English is spoken worldwide. More than 300 million people speak English as a first language, and it is the second or third language for another 600 million. It is the global language for air traffic control and science.

ARCHITECTURE
Most English people live in towns and cities, many of which are very crowded. Home ownership is valued, and town houses vary from from small terraced houses to apartment blocks. The most popular town houses include semi-detached houses, with their own gardens.

ENGLISH BREAKFAST
Traditional English cooking is variable, and not always liked by the people outside England. One popular speciality is the English breakfast with fried bread, eggs, bacon, sausages, tomatoes, and black pudding.

Find out more
INDUSTRIAL REVOLUTION
UNITED KINGDOM
UNITED KINGDOM, HISTORY OF

ENGLISH CIVIL WAR

IN 1649 CHARLES I, king of England, was put on trial for treason and executed. His death marked the climax of the English Civil War, also called the English Revolution, a fierce struggle between king and Parliament (the law-making assembly) over the issue of who should govern England. The struggle had begun many years before. Charles I believed that kings were appointed by God and should rule alone; Parliament believed that it should have greater power. When the king called upon Parliament for funds to fight the Scots, it refused to co-operate, and in 1642 civil war broke out. England was divided into two factions – the Royalists (also called Cavaliers), who supported Charles, and the Parliamentarians (also called Roundheads), who supported Parliament. Charles was a poor leader, and the Roundheads had the support of the navy and were led by two great generals – Lord Fairfax and Oliver Cromwell. By 1649 Cromwell had defeated Charles and declared England a republic. Despite various reforms, Cromwell's rule was unpopular. In 1660 the army asked Charles's son, Charles II, to take the throne and the monarchy was restored.

CHARLES I
King Charles I (reigned 1625-49) was the only English monarch to be executed. He ignored the Parliament, and ruled alone from 1629 to 1640. After a disagreement with the Parliament in 1642, Charles raised an army and began the civil war which ended his reign. The picture above depicts the scene of his execution.

Parliamentary (New Model) army

Royalist cavalry

Royalist officers wore wide-brimmed hats.

Pikeman

BATTLE OF NASEBY
At the Battle of Naseby in 1645 the heavily armed and well-organized pikemen and musketeers of Cromwell's "New Model Army" crushed the Royalists.

OLIVER CROMWELL
The English Republic (1649-60) was organized and ruled mainly by Lord Protector Oliver Cromwell (1599-1658). Cromwell was an honest, moderate man and a brilliant army leader. But his attempts to enforce religious purity upon England made him unpopular with many.

DIGGERS
During the turbulent years new political groups emerged. Some, such as the Diggers, were very radical. They believed that ordinary people should have a say in government and wanted to end private property.

RUMP PARLIAMENT
At the end of the English Civil War, all that was left of King Charles's parliament was a "rump" parliament, whose members refused to leave. In 1653 Cromwell, determined to get rid of any remnant of the king, dismissed Parliament. He pointed at the mace, the speaker's symbol of office, and laughingly called it a bauble (left).

Find out more
GOVERNMENT AND POLITICS
UNITED KINGDOM
UNITED KINGDOM, HISTORY OF

EUROPE

EURO
The European Union made a major move towards monetary union when the Euro was introduced as a single European currency. Eleven EU countries, including Germany and France, formally adopted the currency in 1999, and the Euro replaced the national currencies of 12 countries at the start of 2002 (Greece joining in with the original 11). Other EU countries, such as Britain and Denmark, kept their national currencies.

COMPARED TO ITS mighty eastern neighbour, Asia, Europe is a tiny continent. But the culture of Europe has extended far beyond its boundaries. Europe has a long history of wealth, industry, trading, and empire building. Much of its prosperity comes from its green and fertile land, which is watered by numerous rivers and plenty of rain. Yet the climate varies considerably across the continent. The countries of southern Europe border the Mediterranean Sea. Holiday-makers visit the coast of this enclosed sea to enjoy its long, hot summers. The far north, by contrast, reaches up into the icy Arctic Circle. There are also a number of high mountain ranges within Europe, including the Alps and the Pyrenees. The ethnic composition of Europe's 725 million people is as varied as the landscape. The continent is culturally diverse with a rich history. The Nordic people of the north have blond hair, fair skin, and blue eyes, while many Europeans in the south have darker skin and dark, curly hair.

Europe lies to the north of the Mediterranean Sea and overlooks the northern part of the Atlantic Ocean. It includes the surrounding islands, such as the British Isles and Iceland. The Ural Mountains in the Russian Federation mark the long eastern frontier with Asia.

To meet increasing competition from abroad, particularly from Japan, European companies have modernized their factories.

INDUSTRY
Large-scale industry began in Europe. Labor-saving inventions of the 18th and 19th centuries enabled workers in European factories to manufacture goods cheaply and in large numbers. The Industrial Revolution soon spread to other parts of the world, including the United States, India, and Japan. Manufacturing industries still play a vital role in most European countries.

Old European buildings may look picturesque, but the architecture is more than decorative. The mellow brick and stone provide essential protection against the cool, damp weather.

Austrian composer Johann Strauss Jr. (1825-99) named his famous waltz tune The Blue Danube after the river.

DANUBE RIVER
Europe's second-longest river is the Danube. The Danube flows from the Black Forest in Germany to the Black Sea and passes through nine European countries: Germany, Austria, Slovakia, Hungary, Croatia, Serbia, Romania, Bulgaria, and Ukraine.

CITIES
Most European cities pre-date those in Australia and America. Many are of ancient origin and have grown gradually over several centuries. As a result, they differ enormously in design and layout to their modern counterparts abroad. Originally designed to cope with small volumes of traffic, Europe's cities are composed of an irregular mixture of narrow winding streets, and wider boulevards. Modern cities, designed with current modes of transport in mind, are carefully planned and tend to follow a more uniform grid pattern.

TRADE

Europeans have always been great traders. Between the 15th and 18th centuries, the countries of Europe were the most powerful in the world. They took their trade to all corners of the globe, and their settlers ruled parts of the Americas, Africa, India, Southeast Asia, and Australia. Almost all of these regions are now independent, but many still retain traces of European culture.

European trade and money formed the basis of the world's banking system.

The people paint the houses white to reflect the heat of the sun.

SCANDINAVIA

A great hook-shaped peninsula encloses most of the Baltic Sea in northern Europe and extends into the Arctic Ocean. Sweden and Norway occupy this peninsula. Together with Denmark to the south, they make up Scandinavia. Finland, to the east of the Baltic, and the large island of Iceland in the North Atlantic, are often also included in the group.

In the warm climate of the Mediterranean region olives, oranges, lemons, sunflowers, melons, tomatoes, and aubergines grow well.

Goats and sheep are more common than cattle, which require richer pasture.

MEDITERRANEAN

Ten European countries border the Mediterranean Sea: Spain, France, Monaco, Italy, Slovenia, Croatia, Bosnia and Herzegovina, Montenegro, Albania, and Greece. A small part of Turkey is also in Europe. The Mediterranean people have traditionally lived by farming (above), but many of these countries now have thriving industries. Though the climate around the Mediterranean is much warmer than that of northern Europe, winters can still be quite chilly.

ART AND CULTURE

Europe has its own traditions of art and culture which are quite distinct from those of other parts of the world. Oil painting, classical music, and ballet had their origins in Europe. The traditions of European theatre, music, literature, painting, and sculpture all began in ancient times.

Tallinn (left), Estonia's capital city, is a major Baltic port.

BALTIC STATES

Lithuania, Latvia, and Estonia, low-lying agricultural countries on the eastern coast of the Baltic Sea, are together called the Baltic States. They were formed in 1918 and remained independent until 1940 when they were occupied by the Soviet Union. In 1991, Lithuania became one of the first of the former Soviet republics to achieve independence, followed a few months later by Estonia and Latvia.

Find out more

EUROPEAN UNION
EUROPE, HISTORY OF
MEDIEVAL EUROPE
NAPOLEON BONAPARTE
UNITED KINGDOM
WORLD WAR I
WORLD WAR II

STATISTICS
Area: 10,498,000 sq km
(4,053,309 sq miles)
Population: 727,247,000
Highest point: El' brus,
Caucasus Mountains
(European Russia)
5,642 m (18,511 ft)
Longest river: Volga
(European Russia)
3,688 m (2,290 miles)
Largest lake: Ladoga
(European Russia)
18,300 sq km
(7,100 sq miles)
Main occupations:
Agriculture,
manufacturing, industry
Main exports:
Machinery and transport
equipment
Main imports: Oil and
other raw materials

EUROPEAN UNION
In 1957, five European
countries agreed to
form the European
Economic Community (EEC).
In December 1991, the Maastricht
Treaty created the European Union
(EU). The EU flag (above) has
12 yellow stars on a blue background.
The Union now has 27 members.

ALBANIA
Area: 28,750 sq km
(11,100 sq miles)
Population: 3,639,000
Capital: Tirana

ANDORRA
Area: 468 sq km
(181 sq miles)
Population: 84,000
Capital: Andorra la Vella

AUSTRIA
Area: 83,850 sq km
(32,375 sq miles)
Population: 8,210,000
Capital: Vienna

BELGIUM
Area: 33,100 sq km
(12,780 sq miles)
Population: 10,414,000
Capital: Brussels

BELARUS
Area: 207,600 sq km
(80,154 sq miles)
Population: 9,649,000
Capital: Minsk

BOSNIA AND HERZEGOVINA
Area: 51,130 sq km (19,741 sq miles)
Population: 4,613,000
Capital: Sarajevo

BULGARIA
Area: 110,910 sq km
(42,822 sq miles)
Population: 7,205,000
Capital: Sofia

CROATIA
Area: 56,540 sq km
(21,830 sq miles)
Population: 4,489,000
Capital: Zagreb

CZECH REPUBLIC
Area: 78,370 sq km
(30,260 sq miles)
Population: 10,212,000
Capital: Prague

DENMARK
Area: 43,069 sq km
(16,629 sq miles)
Population: 5,501,000
Capital: Copenhagen

ESTONIA
Area: 45,125 sq km
(17,423 sq miles)
Population: 1,300,000
Capital: Tallinn

FINLAND
Area: 338,130 sq km
(130,552 sq miles)
Population: 5,250,000
Capital: Helsinki

FRANCE
Area: 551,500 sq km
(212,930 sq miles)
Population: 62,151,000
Capital: Paris

GERMANY
Area: 356,910 sq km
(137,800 sq miles)
Population: 82,330,000
Capital: Berlin

GREECE
Area: 131,990 sq km
(50,521 sq miles)
Population: 10,737,000
Capital: Athens

HUNGARY
Area: 93,030 sq km
(35,919 sq miles)
Population: 9,906,000
Capital: Budapest

ICELAND
Area: 103,000 sq km
(39,770 sq miles)
Population: 307,000
Capital: Reykjavik

IRELAND
Area: 70,280 sq km
(27,155 sq miles)
Population: 4,203,000
Capital: Dublin

ITALY
Area: 301,270 sq km
(116,320 sq miles)
Population: 58,126,000
Capital: Rome

KOSOVO
Area: 10,887 sq km
(4,203 sq miles)
Population: 2,217,000
Capital: Pristina

LATVIA
Area: 64,589 sq km
(24,938 sq miles)
Population: 2,232,000
Capital: Riga

LIECHTENSTEIN
Area: 160 sq km
(62 sq miles)
Population: 35,000
Capital: Vaduz

LITHUANIA
Area: 65,200 sq km
(25,174 sq miles)
Population: 3,555,000
Capital: Vilnius

LUXEMBOURG
Area: 2,586 sq km
(998 sq miles)
Population: 492,000
Capital: Luxembourg

MACEDONIA
Area: 25,715 sq km
(9,929 sq miles)
Population: 2,020,000
Capital: Skopje

MALTA
Area: 320 sq km
(124 sq miles)
Population: 405,000
Capital: Valletta

MOLDOVA
Area: 33,700 sq km
(13,000 sq miles)
Population: 4,321,000
Capital: Chisinau

MONACO
Area: 1.95 sq km
(0.75 sq miles)
Population: 33,000
Capital: Monaco

MONTENEGRO
Area: 14,026 sq km
(5,416 sq miles)
Population: 672,000
Capital: Podgorica

NETHERLANDS
Area: 37,330 sq km
(14,410 sq miles)
Population: 16,716,000
Capital: Amsterdam, The Hague

NORWAY
Area: 323,900 sq km
(125,060 sq miles)
Population: 4,661,000
Capital: Oslo

POLAND
Area: 312,680 sq km
(120,720 sq miles)
Population: 38,483,000
Capital: Warsaw

PORTUGAL
Area: 92,390 sq km
(35,670 sq miles)
Population: 10,708,000
Capital: Lisbon

ROMANIA
Area: 237,500 sq km
(88,934 sq miles)
Population: 22,215,000
Capital: Bucharest

RUSSIAN FED.
Area: 17,075,400 sq km
(5,592,800 sq miles)
Population: 140,041,000
Capital: Moscow

SAN MARINO
Area: 61 sq km
(24 sq miles)
Population: 30,300
Capital: San Marino

SERBIA
Area: 77,474 sq km
(29,913 sq miles)
Population: 7,379,000
Capital: Belgrade

SLOVAKIA
Area: 49,500 sq km
(19,100 sq miles)
Population: 5,463,000
Capital: Bratislava

SLOVENIA
Area: 20,250 sq km
(7,820 sq miles)
Population: 2,006,000
Capital: Ljubljana

SPAIN
Area: 504,780 sq km
(194,900 sq miles)
Population: 40,525,000
Capital: Madrid

SWEDEN
Area: 449,960 sq km
(173,730 sq miles)
Population: 9,060,000
Capital: Stockholm

SWITZERLAND
Area: 41,290 sq km
(15,940 sq miles)
Population: 7,604,000
Capital: Bern

UKRAINE
Area: 603,700 sq km
(223,090 sq miles)
Population: 45,700,000
Capital: Kiev

UNITED KINGDOM
Area: 244,880 sq km
(94,550 sq miles)
Population: 61,113,000
Capital: London

VATICAN CITY
Area: 0.44 sq km
(0.17 sq miles)
Population: 900
Capital: Vatican City

Volcano　Mountain　Ancient monument　Capital city　Large city/town　Small city/town

SCALE BAR
0　300　600　km
0　300　600　miles

POPULATION
More than 725 million people live in Europe and its population is highly urbanized. In Belgium and the Netherlands, more than 80 per cent of people live in cities. In the south and east, more people still live in rural areas.

N
W　E
S

Novaya Zemlya

Kara Sea

Ostrov Vaygach

Pechora Sea

Ostrov Kolguyev

North Cape

Barents Sea

Gora Narodnaya
1895m

Timan Ridge

RUSSIAN FEDERATION
(Asiatic Russia)

Pechora

Ural Mountains

ATLANTIC OCEAN

REVKJAVIK
ICELAND

Kölen

Lapland

Kebnekaise
2112m

Kola Peninsula

White Sea

Norwegian Sea

Northern Dvina

Lake Onega

RUSSIAN FEDERATION

Faeroe Islands
(to Denmark)

Scandinavia

NORWAY

SWEDEN

FINLAND

Lake Ladoga

Sukhona

Vyatka

Shetland Islands

Galdhøpiggen
2469m

OSLO

HELSINKI

Volga

Kuybyshev Reservoir

Outer Hebrides

Orkney Islands

STOCKHOLM

Gulf of Finland

TALLINN

MOSCOW
(MOSKVA)

Isle of Man
(to UK)

North Sea

Lake Vänern

Åland

ESTONIA

Volga Uplands

Gotland

Lake Peipus

Central Russian Upland

Newgrange
DUBLIN
IRELAND

UNITED KINGDOM

DENMARK

COPENHAGEN

Baltic Sea

LATVIA

RIGA

LITHUANIA

VILNIUS

North European Plain

Kirghiz Steppe

Avebury
Stonehenge
English Channel

THE HAGUE

LONDON

AMSTERDAM

NETHERLANDS

BERLIN

KALININGRAD
(part of Russ. Fed.)

MINSK

BELARUS

Don

Donets

Channel Islands
(to UK)

BELGIUM

BRUSSELS

WARSAW

POLAND

KIEV

Caspian Depression

Carnac

LUXEMBOURG

Rhine

Elbe

GERMANY

PRAGUE

CZECH REPUBLIC

Danube

Carpathian Mountains

Dniester

UKRAINE

Dnieper

Caspian Sea

PARIS

Seine

LIECHTENSTEIN

Gerlachovský Štít
2655m

FRANCE

Loire

SWITZERLAND

VADUZ

VIENNA

SLOVAKIA

BRATISLAVA

MOLDOVA

CHISINAU

Sea of Azov

El'brus
5642m

BERN

Matterhorn
4478m

AUSTRIA

BUDAPEST

HUNGARY

Massif Central

Alps

Mt Blanc
4807m

Po

SLOVENIA

LJUBLJANA

ZAGREB

Caucasus

SPAIN

Pyrenees

Rhône

CROATIA

BOSNIA AND HERZ.

SERBIA

ROMANIA

BELGRADE

BUCHAREST

Black Sea

LISBON

ANDORRA

LA VELLA

SAN MARINO

Adriatic Sea

SARAJEVO

KOSOVO
(disputed)

PORTUGAL

Tagus

MADRID

Ebro

MONACO

Corsica

ROME

MONTENEGRO

PODGORICA

PRISTINA

SOFIA

BULGARIA

Iberian Peninsula

Majorca

VATICAN CITY

Vesuvius
1277m

TIRANA

SKOPJE

Ibiza

Minorca

ITALY

MACEDONIA

Gibraltar
(to UK)

Balearic Islands

Sardinia

ALBANIA

GREECE

Ceuta
(to Spain)

Mediterranean Sea

Tyrrhenian Sea

Aegean Sea

T U R K E Y

A S I A

Melilla
(to Spain)

A F R I C A

Sicily

Ionian Sea

ATHENS

Crete

MALTA

VALLETTA

PYRENEES
The Pyrenees mountains lie on the border between France and Spain. The mountain range stretches from the Bay of Biscay to the Mediterranean Sea, a distance of 435 km (270 miles). The climate of the Pyrenees is mild and humid. The mountains offer fishing, sightseeing, and winter sports. There are also health spas with hot springs.

In 1992 UN peacekeeping forces entered war-torn Sarajevo, capital of Bosnia.

The majestic Pyrenees (left) form a spectacular natural border between Spain and France.

EASTERN EUROPE
This refers to countries such as Hungary and Poland that came under Soviet control in 1945. It also refers to what was the western Soviet Union. From 1989, the Communist regimes in Eastern Europe collapsed and were replaced by more democratic governments. Some countries kept their boundaries; others changed. There was also communist rule in Yugoslavia, a country that broke up in the early 1990s. After much bitter fighting, the nations of Bosnia and Herzegovina, Croatia, Kosovo, Macedonia, Montenegro, Serbia, and Slovenia, were formed.

EUROPEAN UNION

JEAN MONNET
French economist Jean Monnet (1888-1979) helped to set up the European Coal and Steel Community, and was its first president. He told the French government that this would prevent another war with Germany.

IN THE 75 YEARS BETWEEN 1870-1945, France and Germany fought each other three times. After the end of World War II in 1945, they decided to live together as friends, not enemies, by combining their industrial strength. Four other countries joined them, and by 1951 the European Steel and Coal Community was created. Seven years later, the six countries signed the Treaty of Rome to set up the European Economic Community. Since then, the Community has grown into a European Union (EU) of 27 countries, including Britain and Ireland. The EU has a huge impact on daily life in Europe, from the price of food to the colour of passports. Many Europeans, however, resist the idea of the EU becoming a "superstate" with its own army and constitution.

THE FLAG
The flag of the European Union was first used in 1955 and consists of 12 five-pointed stars on a blue background.

Countries of Europe which do not form part of the EU.

A meeting of the European Parliament in Strasbourg.

MEPs sit in a semi-circle.

EU MEMBERSHIP
The original members of the EU were France, Germany, Netherlands, Belgium, Luxembourg, and Italy. Britain, Ireland, and Denmark joined in 1973, Spain and Portugal in 1981, Greece in 1986, and Finland, Sweden, and Austria in 1995. Cyprus, Czech Republic, Estonia, Hungary, Latvia, Lithuania, Malta, Poland, Slovakia, and Slovenia joined in 2004. Bulgaria and Romania became members in 2007.

Original members

Current members

EUROPEAN PARLIAMENT

Every five years, the voters of Europe elect 751 Members of the European Parliament (MEPs) to represent them in Strasbourg, France. MEPs have the power to approve or throw out the Commission (the EU government), reject the annual budget, and question the Commission on its policies. The European Parliament is not as powerful as a national parliament, but it plays an important part in deciding how the European Union will develop.

Common passport allows holder to travel freely in the EU.

WHAT THE EU DOES
The EU looks after farming, fishing, economic, industrial, and cultural affairs. It helps the poorer parts of Europe by building roads, and paying for education and training projects. Everybody in the EU holds a common European passport.

The EU helps farmers to produce and sell food.

EUROPEAN UNION

1951 France, Germany, Italy, and the Benelux countries set up European Coal and Steel Community.

1957 ECSC members sign Treaty of Rome to set up European Economic Community (EEC) and Euratom, the atomic energy authority.

1967 ECSC, EEC, and Euratom merge to form the European Community.

1979 European Monetary System begins operation.

1993 Moves towards closer union result in the European Union (EU).

2004 Ten more countries join the EU.

2007 The EU expands to 27 countries when two more join.

Euro coins

EUROPEAN MONETARY UNION
EU countries first linked their currencies together in 1979. In 1999, 11 member countries joined the euro, or single currency. Euro bank notes and coins came into use in those countries in 2002, replacing national currencies such as the French franc and German mark. There are currently 16 members of the Eurozone, after Slovakia joined in 2009.

Find out more
EUROPE
EUROPE, HISTORY OF
TRADE AND INDUSTRY

HISTORY OF
EUROPE

EUROPE IS THE SECOND SMALLEST continent, but it has played an important part in world history. The Ancient Greek and Roman empires stretched into North Africa and the Middle East, and their art, thinking, and science are still influential today. More than a thousand years later, Portuguese and Spanish explorers sailed to new continents, and even around the world. This marked the start of a period of European dominance of world affairs that lasted 400 years. Throughout its long history, however, Europe's countries have rarely been at peace, and in the 20th century, quarrels between European nations led to two world wars. Since 1945, with the rise of the United States as a world superpower, Europe's global political influence is less, but it remains culturally important.

PREHISTORIC EUROPE
The first Europeans were primitive hunters who moved around in search of food and shelter. By about 5000 BCE, Europeans were growing crops, and domesticating animals. They settled in villages, and in northern Europe, they built large burial mounds for their dead.

GREECE AND ROME
In about 900 BCE, the Greeks set up powerful city states, such as Athens. Their merchants traded around the coast of the Mediterranean Sea, founding colonies from Spain to the Black Sea. Rome was founded in 753 BCE, and by 117 CE the Roman Empire controlled most of Europe, northern Africa, and the Middle East.

Roman aquaduct at Nîmes, southern France

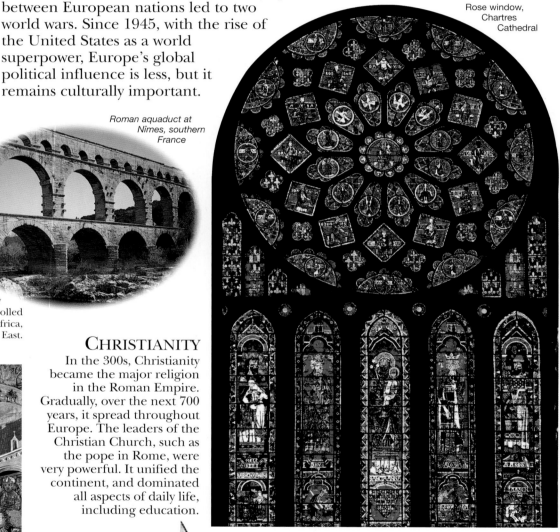

Rose window, Chartres Cathedral

CHRISTIANITY
In the 300s, Christianity became the major religion in the Roman Empire. Gradually, over the next 700 years, it spread throughout Europe. The leaders of the Christian Church, such as the pope in Rome, were very powerful. It unified the continent, and dominated all aspects of daily life, including education.

MEDIEVAL TRADE
Trade prospered in medieval Europe. In the 13th century, a group of towns around the Baltic and North Sea formed the Hanseatic League, trading from ports such as Lübeck and Bruges, and monopolising trade until the 1600s. Cloth, spices, and gold were sold at great trade fairs.

Portuguese caravel

EUROPEAN DOMINATION
In mid-1400s, the Portuguese set out to explore the coast of Africa in a new, fast ship – the caravel. They set up trading stations, and were followed by other European explorers and traders, who moved outward from Europe to all parts of the globe. Europeans soon came to dominate world trade, setting up colonies in the Americas, Asia, and Africa, and building vast empires.

THE ENLIGHTENMENT

In the 18th century, European thinkers began to reject old beliefs based on religion and superstition, and developed new ideas based on reason and science. An intellectual revolution, called the Enlightenment, broke out across Europe. New ideas about government led to the French and American revolutions. Religious toleration increased, and economics, philosophy, and science prospered.

WORLD WARS

In the 1900s, conflicts between European powers caused two devastating World Wars. World War I (1914-18) weakened Europe, but war broke out again in 1939. At its end in 1945, cities were in ruins, thousands were homeless, and two new "superpowers" – the USA and the Soviet Union – had emerged.

Russian tanks in the streets of Budapest, Hungary in 1956.

Intellectuals gather to discuss new ideas in science.

Kemal Ataturk (1881–1939), "Father of the Turks"

BREAK-UP OF EMPIRES

After World War I, the multinational empires of Germany, Austro-Hungary, Ottoman Turkey, and Russia broke up as the different nationalities within them created independent countries, such as Czechoslovakia and Poland. Kemal Ataturk abolished the old Islamic government of the Ottoman Empire, and created the non-religious country of Turkey.

COMMUNIST EUROPE

By 1945, Europe was effectively divided into Communist countries, dominated by the former Soviet Union, and non-communist nations influenced by the United States. Germany was split into two nations. Life was often harsh in Communist countries, and civil liberties were restricted. Revolts broke out in East Germany (1953), Hungary (1956), and Czechoslovakia (1968), but Russian troops put them down.

THE COLLAPSE OF COMMUNISM

By the late 1980s, Communism was losing its hold, and the Soviet Union (USSR) withdrew its support from Eastern Europe. In 1989, East Germans demonstrated for union with West Germany, and pulled down the wall that divided their capital city, Berlin. Germany was reunited the following year. Popular protests then overthrew Communist governments throughout Eastern Europe.

HISTORY OF EUROPE

5000 BCE Stone Age peoples begin to settle in villages.

900 Greek city states founded.

753 Rome founded.

117 CE Roman Empire at its height.

313 Christianity is tolerated throughout Roman Empire.

1000s Christianity spreads throughout Europe.

c. 1241 Hanseatic League established between Hamburg and Lübeck merchants.

1492 Columbus crosses Atlantic; leads to European dominance in the Americas.

1498 European explorers reach India.

1517 Reformation leads to emergence of Protestantism.

1700s Age of Enlightenment.

1800s European empires control most of Africa and Asia.

1914-18 World War I devastates Europe.

1939-45 World War II leads to division of Europe into Communist and non-communist sectors.

1957 Treaty of Rome sets up European Economic Community (EEC).

1989 Fall of Berlin Wall leads to end of Communism in Eastern Europe.

1991 USSR divided into 15 separate countries.

1991-99 Wars in the Balkans as Yugoslavia breaks up.

YUGOSLAVIA
In the 1990s, Yugoslavia fell apart as Serbia, the largest and most powerful province, tried to take control. Slovenia, Croatia, and Bosnia and Herzegovina all declared independence, leading to terrible atrocities on all sides. Serbia pursued "ethnic cleansing" – killing or expelling all non-Serbs, notably in Bosnia and Kosovo. War between Serbia and NATO – a military alliance of Western Europe and the USA – led to an uneasy peace in 1999.

Find out more
EUROPEAN UNION
MEDIEVAL EUROPE
WORLD WAR I
WORLD WAR II

EVOLUTION

AROUND 150 YEARS AGO, an English naturalist named Charles Darwin shocked the world when he wrote a book suggesting that humans were related to apes. Today Darwin's idea still forms the basis of what we call the theory of evolution. The word evolution means unfolding, and it is used to describe the way that all living things evolve, or change with time. There are three main parts to the theory. The first is called variation. All living things vary in size, shape, colour, and strength. No two animals or plants are exactly the same. The second part of the theory is that these variations affect whether or not a living thing can survive and breed. Certain features, such as colour, may mean that one animal or plant has a better chance of surviving than another. Some animals and plants have features that suit their surroundings. In other words, they are better adapted, and these useful features are called adaptations. The third part of the theory is inheritance. The adaptations that help a living thing to survive, such as its colour or shape, may be passed on to its offspring. If the offspring inherit the adaptations, they too will have a better chance of survival. Gradually, over many generations, the better-adapted plants and animals flourish, and those that are less well adapted die out. Many people believe that this process of evolution has led to the millions of different species that inhabit the Earth today.

NATURAL SELECTION
Charles Darwin wrote a book called *On the Origin of Species*, published in 1859, which explained his theory of evolution. Many people laughed at Darwin's idea that humans were related to animals. Above is a cartoon of the time, picturing Darwin as a monkey.

African elephant of today

Evolution of the elephant

Moenitherium *lived about 38 million years ago.*

Woolly mammoth *lived about two million years ago.*

Platybelodon *lived from 12 to 7 million years ago.*

Trilophodon *lived from 26 to three million years ago.*

EVIDENCE FROM THE PAST
Fossils, the remains of animals and plants preserved in rocks, provide evidence for evolution. They show how animals and plants have gradually changed through time. For example, each of the elephants shown above lived for a certain amount of time, as we know by the age of their fossilized bones. Scientists cannot be certain that the first type of elephant gradually evolved into the next, but it is unlikely that each elephant appeared, completely separate from the others. It is far more likely that these elephants were related. As we find more fossils, the relationships between various kinds of animals and plants become clearer.

EVIDENCE FROM THE PRESENT
Animals and plants alive today also provide evidence for evolution. In Hawaii, there are several kinds of honeycreepers that look similar. It is unlikely that this is by chance. More likely, these different honeycreeper birds all evolved from one kind of honeycreeper. This first honeycreeper flew to the islands five million years ago. Since that time, natural selection has produced several similar, but separate, species.

There are 28 species of honeycreepers on the Hawaiian Islands. Scientists believe they evolved from one species of bird.

Akiapolaau searches for insects with upper bill.

Kiwi beak and tubular tongue are suited to sipping nectar.

Maui parrotbill uses lower bill for chiselling into wood for insects.

Apapane has useful all-round beak.

Kona finch has strong bill for crushing seeds.

Original species of honeycreeper

Kauai akialoa has long beak for probing for insects.

HOW EVOLUTION OCCURS

Imagine some green frogs, living and breeding in green surroundings. Most of the young inherit the green colouring of their parents. They are well camouflaged and predators do not notice them in the grass. Their green colour is an adaptation which helps them to survive. A few of the young have different colours, because of variation. Predators can see them in the grass and these frogs are soon eaten – this is natural selection at work. Then the environment slowly changes to yellow as the grass dies. Now the green frogs show up on the sand, and predators eat them. Gradually, the following generations of frogs change from mainly green to mainly yellow. A new species has evolved.

Green, grassy environment

Green frogs survive because they are well camouflaged. Other frogs get eaten because they show up so much.

Predators easily spy frogs that are not camouflaged.

Yellow, sandy environment

New yellow species of frog has evolved.

CHANGING ENVIRONMENTS

As the environment changes, living things evolve. About 200 years ago in Britain, peppered moths had mostly light-coloured wings that matched the light-coloured tree trunks where they rested, so birds could not see them easily. During the Industrial Revolution, smoke from factory chimneys made the tree trunks darker in some areas. Light-coloured moths became easier to see. Gradually, more dark-coloured moths evolved, which were better camouflaged on the dark tree trunks.

The ichthyosaur is an extinct reptile. Its paddle-like front limb had many small bones.

The dolphin is a mammal. Its paddle has the typical bones of the mammal arm and hand.

The penguin is a bird that cannot fly. It has the typical bird's wing bones in its paddle.

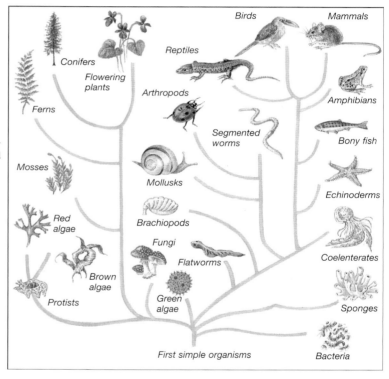

Ferns
Conifers
Flowering plants
Birds
Mammals
Reptiles
Arthropods
Amphibians
Mosses
Segmented worms
Bony fish
Red algae
Mollusks
Brachiopods
Echinoderms
Fungi
Flatworms
Coelenterates
Brown algae
Protists
Green algae
Sponges
First simple organisms
Bacteria

EVOLUTIONARY TREE

Scientists believe that all living things are related and that they have evolved from the same ancestors over millions of years. This chart is called an evolutionary tree. It has lines between the main groups of animals and plants alive today, showing which ones are most closely related.

CONVERGENT EVOLUTION

Evolution sometimes makes different animals and plants look similar. This is called convergent evolution. It means that different animals or plants that live in the same environment, such as the sea, gradually take on the same adaptations, such as body shape. All the animals shown above have evolved, or developed, the same streamlined body form, because this is the best shape for moving speedily through water.

Find out more

ANIMALS
DINOSAURS
FOSSILS
GENETICS
HUMAN BODY
PREHISTORIC LIFE
PREHISTORIC PEOPLES

EXPLORERS

TODAY, PEOPLE ARE AWARE of the remotest corners of the world. But hundreds of years ago, many did not know that countries apart from their own even existed. In the 6th century, the Irish Saint Brendan is said to have sailed across the Atlantic in search of a land promised to saints. But it was not until the early 15th century that strong seaworthy ships were developed and Europeans such as Christopher Columbus were able to explore in earnest. Turkish Muslims had been controlling the overland trade route between Europe and the Indies (the Far East – now East Asia) since the 11th century. They charged such high prices for Eastern goods that European merchants became eager to find a direct sea route to the Far East which would bypass the Turks. The sailors who searched for these routes found the Americas and other lands previously unknown to Europeans. Of course, people already lived in most of these "newly discovered" lands, and the results of these explorations were often disastrous. All too often, the new arrivals exploited and enslaved the native peoples, destroying their cultures.

VIKINGS
The Vikings came from Norway, Sweden, and Denmark. Looking for new lands in which to settle, they sailed to Iceland, Greenland, and North America in their long ships, navigating by the sun and the stars.

EARLY IDEAS
The first explorers had few maps. Early ideas about the shape of the world were hopelessly inaccurate. Many scholars thought the world was flat and that those who went too far might fall off the edge. Some believed that the world was supported by a tortoise (above).

PACIFIC ISLANDS
Europeans exploring the Pacific Ocean in the 1500s were amazed to find that prehistoric peoples had found the Pacific Islands before them. In about 3,000 BCE, the original Polynesians moved from southeast Asia to the islands in the western Pacific, sailing in fragile canoes. By 1000 CE, they had settled on hundreds of other islands.

Maori ancestors leaving for New Zealand

PERILS OF THE SEA
Early sailors faced many natural dangers such as storms, reefs, icebergs, and fog. The sea was an alien territory, and rumours and legends spoke of huge sea monsters which swam in unknown waters. These stories were probably based on sightings of whales and other marine creatures. They were exaggerated by returning sailors telling tall tales of their adventures. Writers and artists added more gruesome details to these descriptions and so the myths grew.

DISCOVERIES
Explorers took gold, treasure, and exciting new vegetables from the Americas to Europe; they also carried silks, jewels, and spices from the East. People in Europe were eager to obtain these and wanted more. This led to a great increase in trade with both East and West.

Silk from China

Potatoes from North America

Tomatoes and chillies from the Americas

Spices from South Asia

Chocolate was made from cacao beans from the Americas.

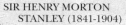

INQUISITIVE EUROPEANS

Once Europeans had an idea of the correct shape of the world, they set out to explore it more thoroughly. Some were driven by curiosity, some by greed, and some by a desire to convert the peoples who lived in faraway places to Christianity. All faced hardships and dangers.

SIR HENRY MORTON STANLEY (1841-1904)

Welshman Henry Stanley worked for a New York newspaper. He led an expedition into Africa to find the missing Scottish explorer David Livingstone. When he found him, he uttered the famous words "Dr. Livingstone, I presume?" Stanley later explored much of central Africa around Lake Victoria.

MARY KINGSLEY (1862-1900)

A fearless and determined Englishwoman, Mary Kingsley travelled in West Africa, trading and making scientific studies. On her travels, she was entertained by cannibals. She was one of the first to demand fair treatment for the people of Africa by their colonial rulers.

AMERIGO VESPUCCI (1454-1512)

The first European to explore the Brazilian coast, Italian-born Amerigo Vespucci gave his name to America. He was in charge of a school of navigation in Seville, Spain. Vespucci believed in a southwestern route to the Indies around South America.

FERDINAND MAGELLAN (1480-1521)

Leader of the first European expedition to sail around the world, Portuguese explorer Magellan proved that there was a southwestern route to the Indies through the Pacific.

VASCO DA GAMA (1469-1524)

Despite bad weather and hardships on the voyage, Portuguese-born Vasco da Gama reached the East African coast and proved that there was a southeastern route to India. He was the first European to sail around the southern tip of Africa.

Marco Polo's journey from Italy to China lasted more than 24 years.

Marco Polo leaving Venice

WONDERS OF CHINA

On his travels, Marco Polo became a favourite of Kublai Khan, the Mongol ruler. Marco later published a detailed account of his journey and the wonders he had seen. Few believed the account and it was years before Europeans realized that he had experienced a great civilization – the empire of China.

MARCO POLO

Marco Polo (1254-1324) was an Italian explorer. His father and uncle were merchants from Venice, Europe's greatest trading centre. They took the 17-year-old Marco with them on a journey from Italy to China.

Find out more

CARIBBEAN
CHINA
COLUMBUS, CHRISTOPHER
PIRATES

EYES

AS YOU READ THIS PAGE, you are using the two organs of sight – the eyes. Our eyes enable us to learn a great deal about the world around us. Each eyeball measures about 25 mm (1 in) across and sits in the front of the skull in the eye socket, or orbit. The eyes can swivel around in their sockets so that you can see things above, below, and to the side. Each eye has an adjustable lens and sees a slightly different view of the same scene. The eyes work together, controlled by the brain. This is called binocular vision. The lens of each eye allows rays of light to enter from the outside and project a picture onto the retina – the inner lining of the eye. The retina converts the light into nerve signals which travel along optic nerves to the brain, where images are formed.

EAGLE SIGHT
A golden eagle has extremely powerful eyesight. It can see rabbits and other prey from a distance of more than 1 km (half a mile).

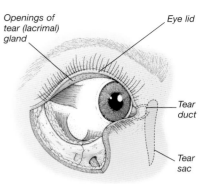

Openings of tear (lacrimal) gland

Eye lid

Tear duct

Tear sac

EYE SOCKETS
The eyelid and eyelashes protect the front of the eye. When you blink, the eyelids sweep moisture over the eyeball, keeping it clean. The moisture is produced in the tear glands above the eyes. These glands also produce tears when you cry. Tiny holes drain fluid through tear ducts into the tear sac, which empties inside the nose.

OUTER EYE
Light rays enter the curved front of the eye called the cornea, where they are partly focused. They pass through the pupil, which enlarges in dim conditions to let in more light and shrinks in bright conditions to protect the inside of the eye from too much light. The rays are then focused onto the retina by the lens.

Choroid, containing nourishing blood vessels

Muscles anchored at back of eye socket move the eye.

Cornea is like a transparent window in the front of the eyeball. The cornea partly focuses light rays.

Retina, bearing light-sensitive cells

Sclera – tough outer covering

Sclera

Pupil is a hole within the iris.

Iris makes pupil larger or smaller.

Fovea

EYEBALL
Three pairs of muscles turn the eyeball to look up, down, and from side to side and rotate it. Pads of fat cushion the eye and the optic nerve, which is stretched and pulled by eye movements.

Conjunctiva – thin covering layer

Lens fine-focuses light rays.

Aqueous fluid

Optic nerve to brain

Blind spot, containing no light-sensitive cells, where optic nerve leaves eye

INNER EYE
Inside the eye is the retina, which contains about 120 million rod cells, mainly around the sides, and seven million cone cells, mainly in the fovea. The image on the retina is upside down, but the brain turns it the right way up as it processes nerve signals from the eye.

Eye muscles

Vitreous fluid

RODS AND CONES
The retina contains millions of light-sensitive cells called rods and cones. The rods work best in dim light, while cones are sensitive to different colours. Rods and cones produce nerve signals when light falls on them.

CLEAR AND DEFECTIVE VISION
Clear vision depends on the lens bending light rays to the correct angle so that the rays form a sharp picture on the retina. In long-sighted people, the eyeball is too short and nearby objects appear blurry. In short-sighted people, the eyeball is too long, making distant objects out of focus. Glasses and artificial lenses, such as contact lenses, help the eye's own lens to focus the rays correctly, thus correcting defective vision.

LONGSIGHTEDNESS
Rays are focused behind the retina. A convex lens corrects the focus.

SHORTSIGHTEDNESS
Rays are focused in front of retina. A concave lens corrects the focus.

Find out more
CAMERAS
COLOUR
EARS
HUMAN BODY
LIGHT

124

FARMING

TO STOCK THE FOOD SHELVES of supermarkets in the world, farmers make nature and technology work in harmony. They use machinery to plough and reap great fields of wheat; they fertilize and irrigate greenhouses full of vegetables and orchards of fruit; and they rear animals indoors to fatten them quickly. Through this intensive agriculture, Western farmers feed up to ten people from land that once fed one. However, not all the world's farmers can be so productive. Those who have plots on hilly land cannot use machines. Instead they graze a few animals or cultivate the land with inefficient hand tools. Farmers in dry climates must be content with lower yields or choose less productive crops that will tolerate dry soil. And farmers who cannot afford machines and fertilizers are forced to use slower farming methods that have not changed for centuries.

SUBSISTENCE FARMING

In some developing countries, most farming families grow only sufficient food for themselves. This is called subsistence farming. In a good year it provides enough food for all. But a drought or an increase in the population may lead to famine and starvation.

Superwheat

CROPS

Almost all crops that are grown today are the descendants of wild plants. However, special breeding has created varieties that give high harvests. Grain crops such as wheat have especially benefitted. Modern varieties have much larger grains than traditional species. However, this new "superwheat" is not as resistant to disease as other varieties and must be grown carefully.

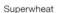
Ordinary wheat

Ploughing

Harvesting

Planting seeds

Spraying

FARM MACHINERY

Modern grain farming requires special machinery at different times of the year. In spring a plough breaks the soil into furrows for planting. A seed drill puts a measured amount of seed into the prepared soil and covers the seed so that birds do not eat it. A sprayer covers crops with pesticides to kill harmful diseases and pests. Finally a combine harvester cuts the crop and prepares it for storage.

A baler rolls up the straw – the cut stalks of wheat left after the grain has been harvested – and ties it into tight round bundles called bales.

ORGANIC FARMING

Some farmers in Western countries prefer to grow crops and raise animals in a natural or organic way. They do not use artificial pesticides or fertilizers. Organic food is more expensive. Some people believe it is safer and healthier to eat, but not all scientific evidence supports this view.

Organic farmers use natural fertilizers such as seaweed or animal dung to make the soil more productive.

In intensive chicken houses conveyor belts carry food to the hens in the crowded cages, and take away the eggs.

INTENSIVE FARMING

The purpose of intensive farming is to increase the production of crops and animals, and to cut food prices. Food animals such as chickens and pigs are kept indoors in tiny, overcrowded pens. Many people feel this is unnatural and cruel, and prefer to eat only "free-range" animals – animals that have been allowed to move freely in the farm.

Find out more

ANIMALS
PLANTS

FILMS

IN A PARIS café in December 1895, people sat down to watch the world's first motion picture. It was shown by two French brothers, Louis and Auguste Lumière, and though it consisted only of a few short, simple scenes, films have been popular ever since. The first films were silent, with titles on the screen to explain the story. A pianist accompanied the film with the right type of music – for example, fast and furious music during a chase scene. The United States took the lead in making films. Soon the public began to select its favourite actors and actresses, and the first film stars were created, such as Rudolph Valentino. In 1927, the first full-length "talkie" – film with sound – was shown, and from then on the public would settle for nothing less. Technical improvements continued. In the United States, Metro-Goldwyn-Mayer and a few other powerful studios made 95 per cent of the films. During the 1950s, television captured people's attention and the film industry went into decline. In recent years films have become popular again. Russia, Germany, France, and Japan have produced films that have influenced filmmaking throughout the world, and there are many national film industries.

CHARLIE CHAPLIN
The British actor Charles Chaplin (1889-1977) created a movie character that touched the hearts of millions: a silent little tramp with a funny walk.

HOLLYWOOD
Southern California, United States, had the ideal climate and scenery for making films. Between 1907 and 1913 a Los Angeles district called Hollywood became the centre of the American film industry. Not all stars were human: King Kong (above) was an animated model.

The senior electrician on the film set is called the gaffer.

Teams of expert makeup artists and dressers prepare an actress or actor for a day's shoot.

The art director designs the sets and chooses suitable locations for filming away from the studio.

A continuity worker makes sure that scenes shot out of order match each other. He or she notes the details of each shot, to ensure that there are no mistakes when the scenes are put in order.

Sound technicians follow the actors with microphones suspended from long poles (booms).

Lighting experts operate huge lamps, to ensure that the light looks as natural as possible in a film. Lighting is needed on location as well as in the studio.

The producer chooses the script, finds financial backing, picks the director and the technical teams, oversees the filming, and organizes publicity.

The director guides the actors' performances, the action, and the camera angles, and gives the film its style and character.

The cinematographer leads a team which also includes the camera operator and camera assistants, who help with focusing, load magazines, and operate the clapper board. Workers called grips move the camera down tracks or rails for the camera to run along smoothly.

FILM SET
Set builders make film sets – from city streets to tropical jungles – inside huge buildings like aircraft hangars, or outdoors on studio grounds. Hundreds of people are involved in getting things ready for the first filming of the day. When all is satisfactory, a red warning light goes on, the studio is told to stand by for a take (an attempt at a scene), sound and cameras roll, and the director shouts "Action!"

Acting on the big screen is very different from the theatre. In close-ups, every movement can be seen, and actors have to play their part with subtle facial expressions. They must also be able to act the story out of sequence.

Stuntmen and stuntwomen take the place of actors in dangerous action. They risk their lives performing stunts, such as falling from a great height, crashing a car, or leaping from a moving train.

SPECIAL EFFECTS

Special effects have created a vast new fantasy world in films. In a technique known as back projection, first used as early as 1913, the cinematographer projected a previously filmed background onto a screen from behind. Actors or models were then filmed in front of the screen, giving the impression that they were actually at that location. Glass screens painted with realistic backgrounds, studio sets wired up with controlled explosions, special smoke and wind machines, and stop-frame animation of models were all used to help bring make-believe scenes to life. As recently as the 1970s, life-like models were still being filmed in a studio to produce gruesome horror effects, such as the shark in *Jaws*, and convincing space battles, such as those in *Star Wars*. Today, almost all of these effects are created digitally using powerful computers.

The actors are filmed against a background of solid blue or green colour.

The actors are superimposed on a new background, and the wires supporting them are erased.

"BULLET-TIME" SLOW MOTION EFFECT

Each small hole in the scene above conceals a still camera taking a picture of the scene from a different angle. The series of shots is put together in sequence on computer, along with thousands of extra "in-between" frames created in software. The effect is of the camera moving around the action in extreme slow motion.

On computer, the coloured background is easily removed using a software filter – sometimes called "Chromakey".

SPIELBERG

Directors often become "stars" in their own right. Director Steven Spielberg was born in 1946. He shot his first film when he was 12 and won a contract with Universal Studios, Hollywood, after leaving college. He became the most successful American director of the 1970s, 1980s, and 1990s with blockbusters such as *Jaws* (1975) and *Jurassic Park* (1993), and Oscar winners such as *Schindler's List* (1993).

DIGITAL TRICKERY

Digital video editing software allows moviemakers to insert actors into almost any environment imaginable. Actors are filmed in front of a green or blue "matte" background, which is later replaced with a new scene – one either filmed elsewhere or created on computer. Real people can also be combined with computer-generated characters and models, as in *Harry Potter*, and whole armies can be created that have an "artificial life" entirely of their own, as in *Lord of the Rings*.

EDITING

The film editor sees that all the shots are in the right order, and that the film lasts the right amount of time. But editing is more complex than that. A good editor can improve the film by cutting out sequences that slow down the action or inserting close-up shots to make a scene more dramatic. Editing is a highly skilled process. In the past it involved physically cutting and taping together pieces of film, though now it is usually done digitally. Director and film editor work together for hours to get the right combination of shots in each scene.

DUBBING

The sound editor is responsible for assembling the soundtrack for the film. This consists of dozens of separate tracks, including all the dialogue, music, sound effects, and background sound. After editing, these sounds have to be balanced against each other and blended in a process called dubbing. Technicians known as mixers watch the film and operate controls on a sound console to get perfect timing and balance of sounds.

FILMS

1895 First public film show held in Paris.

1905 In the United States the first nickelodeon film theatre opens.

1907 Hollywood founded.

1927 *The Jazz Singer* (USA) is the first full-length film with sound.

1929 First Academy Awards.

1928 American cartoonist Walt Disney (1901-66) launches his most popular cartoon character, Mickey Mouse, in the film *Steamboat Willie*.

1935 First full-spectrum Technicolor feature, *Becky Sharp*, is released.

1953 First CinemaScope (wide screen) movie, *The Robe*, released.

1995 *Toy Story*, first completely computer-animated feature film, released.

2003 *Lord of the Rings* trilogy is the first film to win an award for Best Digital Acting Performance.

Find out more

CAMERAS
MUSIC
TECHNOLOGY
TELEVISION

FIRE OF LONDON

A plague doctor

IN 1666, THE WORST FIRE IN LONDON'S HISTORY raged for five days. It destroyed most of the business part of the city, wiped out 13,200 houses, 87 churches, including St Paul's Cathedral, and dozens of important halls and public buildings. Surprisingly, only nine people were killed. King Charles II and his brother the Duke of York took charge of fighting the fire. They stopped it from spreading further by blowing up houses in its path. Thousands of people were made homeless and had to camp in fields outside the city. However, the fire did destroy the rats that spread the terrible bubonic plague and the unhealthy buildings where the disease thrived. After the fire, the architect Sir Christopher Wren suggested a new layout for the city, but it was rejected by business men. Wren was also responsible for rebuilding St Paul's and more than 50 other churches. Diarist Samuel Pepys left a vivid account of the fire.

THE GREAT PLAGUE
In 1664-65, bubonic plague, the Black Death, swept through London, killing nearly 70,000 people. Doctors wore leather clothing, gloves, and bird-like masks to protect themselves. The beaks were stuffed with medicinal herbs to prevent the doctors catching the plague.

SAMUEL PEPYS
Pepys (1633-1703) was a civil servant at the Admiralty, and worked hard to make sure that England had a powerful navy. He is famous for his diary, which contains accounts of the Great Plague and the Great Fire. Pepys took the news of the fire to King Charles II, who acted quickly to fight it.

Old St Paul's Cathedral had been on the site since 1087.

Many people took to boats on the river to escape the flames.

Fire burned houses at the northern side of London Bridge.

HOW IT STARTED
The fire began very early on 2 September 1666, in Farriner's baker's shop in Pudding Lane. In those days most of the houses in London were built of wood, and were huddled close together in narrow streets. This allowed the fire to spread quickly. The warehouses on the banks of the River Thames were full of oil, tar, and corn. They too were wooden, and flames soon engulfed them. A Frenchman, Robert Hubert, later confessed to starting the fire. He was hanged.

A flaming urn, made of gilt bronze, tops the Monument.

THE MONUMENT
The government decided to build a memorial to remember the fire. Called the Monument, it was finished in 1677. It is nearly 62 m (203 ft) high, and stands the same distance west of the place where the fire started. It is the world's tallest free-standing stone column. People can climb the 311 steps to a viewing gallery.

The River Thames was a barrier that helped stop the spread of fire.

Houses and buildings on the south side of the river escaped fire.

The Monument

Old St. Paul's Cathedral

OLD ST PAUL'S
Old St Paul's was the fourth cathedral built on the site. Fire and Viking invaders destroyed the others. By 1664, the cathedral was in a very bad state, and repairs had begun in 1666, supervised by Sir Christopher Wren (1632-1723). When the fire destroyed the old building, Wren designed a new one.

Find out more
ARCHITECTURE
BLACK DEATH
STUARTS

FISH

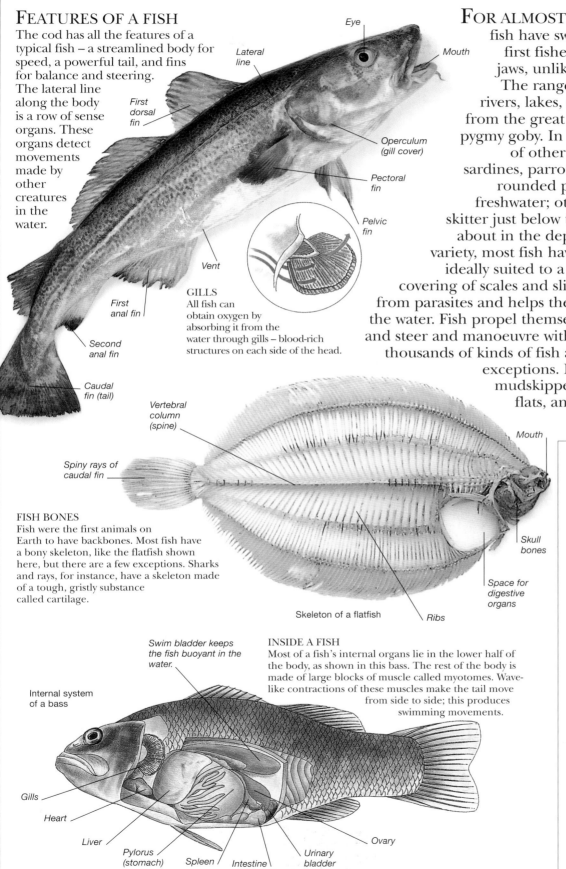

FEATURES OF A FISH

The cod has all the features of a typical fish – a streamlined body for speed, a powerful tail, and fins for balance and steering. The lateral line along the body is a row of sense organs. These organs detect movements made by other creatures in the water.

Eye

Lateral line

Mouth

First dorsal fin

Operculum (gill cover)

Pectoral fin

Pelvic fin

Vent

First anal fin

Second anal fin

Caudal fin (tail)

GILLS
All fish can obtain oxygen by absorbing it from the water through gills – blood-rich structures on each side of the head.

FOR ALMOST 530 MILLION YEARS, fish have swum in the oceans. The first fishes had no scales, fins, or jaws, unlike those we know today. The range of fish that live in our rivers, lakes, and seas is enormous – from the great whale shark to the tiny pygmy goby. In between are thousands of other fish, such as swordfish, sardines, parrotfish, and the comically rounded puffer fish. Some live in freshwater; others in saltwater. Some skitter just below the surface; others dart about in the depths. Despite their wide variety, most fish have a streamlined shape, ideally suited to a watery environment. A covering of scales and slimy mucus protects fish from parasites and helps them slip rapidly through the water. Fish propel themselves along by their tail, and steer and manoeuvre with their fins. Among the thousands of kinds of fish are some extraordinary exceptions. Lampreys have no jaws, mudskippers can skip across mud flats, and catfish can crawl and have no scales at all.

Vertebral column (spine)

Spiny rays of caudal fin

Mouth

Skull bones

Space for digestive organs

FISH BONES
Fish were the first animals on Earth to have backbones. Most fish have a bony skeleton, like the flatfish shown here, but there are a few exceptions. Sharks and rays, for instance, have a skeleton made of a tough, gristly substance called cartilage.

Skeleton of a flatfish

Ribs

Placoid (shark)

Cycloid (salmon)

Ganoid (gar)

Ctenoid (perch)

SCALES
Bony discs called scales are embedded in the skin. They protect the body and overlap to allow movement. Although there are four main kinds, most fish have the cycloid or ctenoid kind.

Swim bladder keeps the fish buoyant in the water.

Internal system of a bass

INSIDE A FISH
Most of a fish's internal organs lie in the lower half of the body, as shown in this bass. The rest of the body is made of large blocks of muscle called myotomes. Wave-like contractions of these muscles make the tail move from side to side; this produces swimming movements.

Gills

Heart

Liver

Pylorus (stomach)

Spleen

Intestine

Urinary bladder

Ovary

129

STRANGELY SHAPED FISH

Each kind of fish is suited to its own way of life. The long nose of the butterfly fish has a mouth at its tip and so can pick up food from rock crevices. Flying fish use their enlarged fins as "wings" for gliding as they leap out of the water. The bright colours on a lionfish warn other creatures of the deadly poison in its fin spines.

Lionfish

Flying fish

Long-nosed butterfly fish

SCHOOL OF FISH

Small fish often live in large groups called schools, or shoals, twisting and turning together as they search for food. A predator is sometimes so confused by their numbers and quick, darting movements that it cannot single out a fish to attack.

School of sea goldfish on a Red Sea coral reef

FEEDING

Fast predatory fish such as barracudas have long, slim, streamlined bodies and sharp teeth. Slower swimmers usually have more rounded bodies. Despite its shape, the parrotfish is an agile swimmer. It slips through cracks in the rock in search of food.

Parrotfish eating algae on a coral reef

Sea horses

SEA HORSE

Sea horse eggs are deposited by the female into the male's front pouch, where they develop for about four weeks. When the eggs hatch, the young sea horses emerge from the pouch.

Sea horses use their tails to cling to seaweed.

BREEDING

Most fish reproduce by depositing their eggs and sperm in the water, then leave the fertilized eggs to develop into fish. Some fish, such as sticklebacks and bowfins, look after the eggs and the young (called fry) once they have hatched. Other fish, such as some types of sharks, give birth to fully formed young fish after the eggs have developed in the mother's body.

MOUTHBREEDERS

Some cichlid fish, found in African lakes, keep their eggs safe inside their mouths. When the young hatch they swim out, then return to the parent's mouth for safety.

Cichlid fish and young

Royal gramma fish

EUROPEAN EELS

Adult eels lay eggs in the Sargasso Sea. The eggs hatch into larvae which swim north for the next three years. Upon reaching Europe they change into elvers and swim up streams. There, they grow into yellow eels, then adults.

Yellow eels change into adult eels, then return to the Sargasso Sea to breed.

Larvae swim north and change into elvers.

Eggs develop into larvae.

Young elvers travel inland along rivers, where they change into yellow eels.

TROPICAL OCEAN FISH

Fish, especially those from tropical waters, are among the brightest of all animals. Their dazzling colours and lively patterns have many different purposes. They help fish hide from predators among the coral, warn neighbouring fish to keep out of their territory, show other creatures that they are poisonous, or advertise for a mate.

Find out more

ANIMALS
DEEP-SEA WILDLIFE
LAKE AND RIVER WILDLIFE
OCEAN WILDLIFE
SEASHORE WILDLIFE

FLOWERS AND HERBS

Stamen (male parts)

Stigma receives pollen

Style

Anther with pollen

Ovary contains ovules (seeds).

Filament

Petals are brightly coloured to attract insects in search of nectar.

Sepals protect inner parts of flower.

The flower head contains the reproductive parts of the plant – as shown by this pink lily flower.

THE EXQUISITE BEAUTY, colour, and perfume of flowers have inspired artists and poets for centuries. Flowers are among the most brightly coloured of all living things. They include sun-loving desert marigolds, hardy poppies in the snowy Arctic, tropical orchids, and cultivated garden roses, as well as some tiny inconspicuous flowers. Without the thousands of different flowers and herbs that grow on the Earth, bees could not make honey, butterflies and hummingbirds would have no food, we would have no flowerbeds, and perfume would have no fragrance. For most of us, the word "flower" describes any flowering plant that is particularly colourful or pretty. To the botanist, who studies plants, however, a flower refers strictly to the reproductive part of a plant – its bloom or blossom. The word "herb" is an everyday name we give to smaller, less colourful flowering plants whose leaves and blossoms have a strong, pleasant scent and taste.

FLOWER STRUCTURE

Sepals are usually green and scaly, and protect the flower in its bud. They often drop off once the flower has blossomed. Petals may be large and colourful to attract bees and butterflies. The male cells lie in the pollen grains, contained in the anthers. The female cells are inside the ovary, below the stigma and style.

HERBS

Plants known as herbs usually have green, juicy stems, unlike trees and shrubs, which have hard, woody stems. Some herbs and other flowering plants are described as annuals because they grow, flower, produce seeds, and die all in one year. Others are known as biennials because their life cycle takes two years; perennials live for an indefinite number of years.

Thyme is a fragrant addition to meats, as a garnish, and for mouth, throat, and chest illnesses.

Basil is popular in Mediterranean cooking and is also used as an insect repellent.

HERB GARDEN

Tending the herb garden was once an important part of daily life because people relied on natural products which they grew themselves. Herbs are used to add flavour to food, scent the air, help us relax, and treat illnesses. Many of our modern medicines contain herbs; peppermint, for example, is used in many anti-indigestion pills. Herbal oils, known as essential oils, are extracted from herbs and used in the production of perfume and bath oils.

Parsley is a garnish, an ingredient in sauces, and a treatment for urinary illness.

Rosemary is a companion to lamb dishes, and brewed in tea for headaches and upset stomachs.

Sage flavours many dishes, from pork to poultry, and is used to treat sore throats and colds.

Bay adds flavour to casseroles and stocks.

Oregano (wild marjoram) is used for meat, stuffing, and pizza, and to aid digestion.

Tarragon is often used in French cooking.

Mint is used to make tea and mint jelly; it also clears a stuffy nose and eases indigestion.

131

Wild dog rose

POLLINATION

To produce a seed, the male cell in a pollen grain must fertilize a female cell in the ovule. For this to happen the pollen must travel from its anther to the female stigma. In some flowers, the pollen is small and light, with wings, and is blown from one flower to another by the wind.

Cultivated tea rose

HORTICULTURE

From the beginnings of civilization, people have cultivated flowers for their scent and colour. Today's garden roses have been bred from wild ancestors so that they have larger, more numerous, and more colourful petals, sweeter scents, and a longer flowering time. The art of gardening is called horticulture.

BEES AND FLOWERS
Bees help pollination. As a bee feeds on nectar and pollen, more pollen inside the flower sticks to the bee's legs and body and is carried by the bee to the next flower, where it pollinates the female parts.

NECTAR
Butterflies, moths, bats, and birds feed on the sweet, energy-rich nectar inside each flower. Bees convert nectar into honey in the beehive.

BIRD-OF-PARADISE FLOWER
The bird-of-paradise plant comes originally from riverbanks in southern Africa and is now grown in many parks and gardens. Each plant has brilliant orange flowers which form a shape that looks like the head and beak of a bird of paradise. The bird-of-paradise flowers rise one after the other from a long, stiff, green-pink casing.

Harebell

Common poppy

Oxeye daisy

Kangaroo paw

Passionflower

Cornflower

Snake's head fritillary

Common toadflax

Dogtooth violet

Water hyacinth

Lily of the valley flowers have a sweet scent. Their leaves are scented too.

PERFUME
A flower's smell attracts butterflies, bees, and people too. Lily of the valley and rose are used in the manufacture of perfumes and soaps.

WILD FLOWERS AND CONSERVATION

Many wild flowers are in danger of extinction. Marshes are drained, and forests are felled for farmland and buildings, so the flowers that grow there are destroyed. Rare and beautiful blooms are at risk because they are dug up illegally by plant collectors. To save rare flowers, the places where they grow must be protected. As forests are cut down, thousands of flowers are disappearing even before they are known to science.

Find out more
CONSERVATION
and endangered species
FOREST WILDLIFE
FRUITS AND SEEDS
PLANTS

FORCE AND MOTION

WHAT IS IT THAT MAKES objects move? Why does a boat float? How does a magnet work? Left to itself, any object would remain still, but when it is pushed or pulled, it begins to move. Something that pushes or pulls is called a force. Forces often produce motion, or movement. For example, an engine produces a force that pushes a car forward. There are several different kinds of forces. A magnet produces a magnetic force which pulls pieces of iron towards it, and a rubber band produces an elastic force when you stretch it. Liquids produce forces too. A boat floats because of the force of water pushing upwards on the hull. And a drop of water holds together because of a force called surface tension which makes all liquids seem as though they have an elastic skin around them. From the smallest particle inside an atom to the largest galaxy, the whole universe is held together by powerful forces. One of these forces is gravity, which holds us onto the surface of the Earth.

CHANGING DIRECTION
When you move in a circle, on a fairground ride for example, a constant force is needed to change the direction of your motion. This force acts towards the centre of the circle. On the ride shown above, the force comes from the tension in the ropes that support the seats.

ACCELERATION
The action of a force produces motion, making an object accelerate (speed up). For example, the force produced by the engine makes a ship accelerate. The stronger the force, the greater the acceleration.

INERTIA
It takes a strong force to start a heavier (more massive) object moving. In the same way, a strong force is needed to make it slow down and stop. This reluctance to start or stop moving is called inertia. The heavier the object, the greater its inertia.

Water and air resist motion, producing a force called drag. A small boat accelerates easily and soon reaches its cruising speed. But, drag increases as speed increases. When drag force balances the driving force of the engines, speed stays constant.

ACTION AND REACTION
A rowing boat moves by action and reaction. The force of the oars pushing on the water is the action. The moving water exerts an equal and opposite reaction on the oars. This reaction force pushes the boat forward.

NEWTON'S LAWS OF MOTION
In 1687, the English scientist Isaac Newton (1642-1727) published his three laws of motion. The first law explains that an object stays at rest or moves at a constant speed unless a force pushes or pulls it. The second law explains how force overcomes inertia and causes acceleration. The third law explains that when a force (or action) pushes one way, an equal force (or reaction) always pushes in the opposite direction.

FRICTION

When two surfaces rub against each other, they produce a force called friction, that opposes motion. For example, brakes use friction to slow a wheel down. Friction produces heat and wastes energy. Putting a layer of oil between the moving parts of a machine reduces friction and improves efficiency.

STATIC FORCES
When two teams in a tug-of-war pull equally hard on the rope, neither team moves. This is because the forces produced by the teams balance exactly. Forces that balance and produce no movement are called static forces. A bridge stays up because of the balance of static forces. Its weight pushing down is balanced by parts of the structure pushing up.

In an arch bridge, the piers (ends of the bridge) support the weight of the arch.

Find out more
ATOMS AND MOLECULES
ENERGY
ENGINES
GRAVITY
MAGNETISM

FOREST WILDLIFE

This map shows the main forest areas of the world.

North America
Europe
Asia
Africa
South America
Australia

☐ Temperate forest
☐ Coniferous forest
☐ Tropical forest

TREES ARE THE MOST IMPORTANT plants in a forest. They provide all kinds of animals, including monkeys, squirrels, and parrots, with food, homes, and escape routes from predators. The most common tree in any kind of forest often gives the forest its name, from the pine forests in the cold north, to the steamy teak forests in the tropical regions.

A temperate forest consists of different layers of vegetation. The forest floor is covered with leaf litter. Here, parts of trees and other plants rot into the soil, helped by the millipedes, worms, and other small creatures that feed on them. The next layer of the forest is called the herb layer. It consists of small flowers and ferns that grow wherever enough sunlight filters through the trees. Bushes, shrubs, and young trees make up the under-storey of the forest. Next is a layer of tall tree trunks, laced with trailing vines and creepers. The uppermost part of the forest is called the canopy. Leaves grow in the sunlight; insects, birds, and bats pollinate the flowers; and fruit ripens to feed a host of creatures.

LONG-EARED OWL
The long-eared owl swoops silently among the trees at twilight and during the night. These owls roost by day in a tree, and their mottled brown plumage provides good camouflage. The tufts on the feathers on this owl's head look like long ears – hence the name.

CONIFEROUS FORESTS
Pines and firs make up coniferous forests. These trees are evergreen – they keep their leaves all year, providing shelter for animals. The leaves are very tough, and only a few animals can eat and digest them. A few types of conifer, such as the larches, lose their leaves in autumn.

WOLVERINE
The wolverine of northern forests is an exceptionally strong animal for its size. It tackles animal prey much larger than itself and also eats carrion (dead animals), fruit, and berries. The wolverine is nicknamed the "glutton" because of its large appetite.

BROAD-LEAVED FORESTS
The trees in a broad-leaved forest are called deciduous trees because their leaves drop off in the autumn, to be replaced by new leaves the next year. These trees blossom in the spring, which is the main animal breeding time. The new shoots provide food for animals. In the autumn, animals feed on the fruit, nuts, and berries of these trees, so they can survive the winter.

Ferns, such as bracken, grow quickly and rapidly cover clearings. Bracken is common on every continent except Antarctica. It spreads by sending out branching underground stems.

Bluebells are one of the spring woodland flowers. Some bluebells have pink flowers; others have white ones.

Wood anemone

ROE DEER
The roe deer's reddish brown coat blends in well with the bracken where it lives. It lives alone for most of the year, feeding at twilight on the buds, shoots, and leaves of trees and shrubs.

Several heavy-bodied, strong-legged birds live in the forest, including pheasants such as the blue peacock shown here. These birds can fly but they often avoid danger by running into the dense forest undergrowth.

CONSERVATION

As the forests are cut down or burned, animals lose their homes. Tree-living creatures such as this American uakari monkey are most at risk. These monkeys depend on the flowers and fruit from the large old trees in rain forests. Worldwide conservation organizations are trying to stop the destruction of the rain forests in order to save monkeys and thousands of other creatures.

TANAGER

The paradise tanager is a noisy, active bird that lives high up in the rain forest canopy. Paradise tanagers keep their bright plumage all year and flutter from tree to tree in search of insects and ripe fruit.

TROPICAL FORESTS

In tropical forests, the climate is much the same all year round. High temperatures and heavy rainfall make tropical rain forests some of the richest places for wildlife. There are many more species of trees than in any other kind of forest, and thousands more kinds of animals.

SLOTH

Few animals move more slowly than the sloths of Central and South America. They hang from branches with their curved claws and eat leaves. Tiny green simple plants called algae grow on their coats, and this helps camouflage the sloths among the trees.

PARROT

The male and female eclectus parrots shown here are so differently coloured that for many years people believed they were two different species of birds. These parrots live in the forests of New Guinea and Australia. Like all parrots, they have huge bills for cracking seeds.

Several kinds of frogs, lizards, snakes, and squirrels have evolved, or developed, ways of gliding through the air from a high branch to escape from predators or to reach food. The gliding snake flattens its ribs as it leaps, to make a streamlined ribbon shape.

TOUCANET

With its large, light bill, the toucanet is an excellent berry picker. Its bright colours help it advertise for a mate in the breeding season. There are 42 kinds of toucanets, and they are all found in tropical South America. Toucanets nest in tree holes and eat birds' eggs and nestlings, fruit, insects, frogs, and lizards.

Atlas moth resting on a bromeliad flower

POISON ARROW FROG

It is so damp in rain forests that frogs spend their lives in the trees and do not need to find water elsewhere. Frogs lay their eggs, or spawn, in pools of rain which collect on leaves, fungi, and in flowers such as bromeliads, which grow on trees. Poison Arrow frogs live in the rain forests of South America. Their bright colours warn predators of the deadly poison in their skin.

ATLAS MOTH

The atlas moth is one of the largest moths in the world, with a wingspan of 30 cm (12 in). Today, atlas moths are rare. In the past, people killed thousands of them simply for their butterfly collections.

LEMUR

There are 19 different kinds of lemur. These mammals are related to monkeys, and they live in trees in Madagascar, an island off the east coast of Africa. Mouse lemurs weigh only 60 gm (2 oz).

Ground ginger is a spice made from the root of the ginger plant, which came originally from the forests of Asia.

Leaf roller ants curl up leaves on the forest floor and join the edges into a tube to make a nesting site.

Find out more

ANIMALS
BIRDS
CONSERVATION
and endangered species
ECOLOGY AND FOOD WEBS
FLOWERS AND HERBS

FOSSILS

THE FIRST PLANTS, the earliest animals, the beginnings of human life – we know about prehistoric times because of fossils. Preserved or mineralised for thousands or even millions of years, fossils may comprise, for example, parts of animals, moulds, footprints, and burrows. By studying fossils, we can learn what ancient creatures and plants looked like and how they lived. Most fossils are of plants and animals that lived in water. When the living plant or animal died, its soft parts rotted away, leaving the hard pieces such as bones or leaf veins. Gradually, layers of mud piled up and squeezed the remains of the plant or animal at great pressure. Slowly the mud, bones, and other remains fossilized, or turned to rock, in the place where they lay underground. Over many thousands of years, the movements of the Earth twisted and buckled the rocks, lifting the fossils closer to the surface of the soil. Sun, rain, and wind wore away the rocks and exposed the fossil.

Fossil collecting is a hobby that anyone can enjoy. You can find fossils in rocks, on beaches, and in quarries.

AMMONITE
Some of the most common fossils are the shells of sea creatures called ammonites. Ammonites were related to squid and octopuses. They were very widespread about 250 million years ago. The smallest ammonites measured less than 2 cm (1 in) across; the largest measured about 2.5 m (8 ft) across. Ammonites died out with the dinosaurs about 65 million years ago.

Fossil of a fish called Sparnodus – an ancestor of the sea bream

Fin on back for steering and stability

Backbone

Powerful two-lobed tail

Rear paddles

Long jaws and short, sharp teeth

Large eye socket

Ribs

Front paddle for steering

TYPES OF FOSSILS
When rock-forming minerals slowly replace the original parts of a dead creature or plant, they make a mineralized fossil. Sometimes the parts of a creature or plant rot away after being buried, leaving a hole in the rock; this is called a mould fossil. If the hole fills up with rock minerals, it becomes a cast fossil. The fossilized signs of animals, such as footprints, droppings, and tracks, are called trace fossils.

Mineralized fossil of a poplar leaf, 25 million years old

ICHTHYOSAUR
Sometimes the outline of an animal's skin is preserved as well as its bones. This happened to the ichthyosaur shown above – a sea reptile from about 150 million years ago. The ichthyosaur looked like a dolphin, so it probably led a life similar to that of dolphins. The outline of this fossil shows a fin on the back and a two-lobed tail. The dozens of sharp teeth in the long jaws tell us that this animal grabbed fish and other slippery prey.

Cast fossil of a creature called a trilobite, which lived in the sea

The word fossil literally means "dug up". People who study fossils are called palaeontologists.

Find out more
DINOSAURS
EVOLUTION
PREHISTORIC LIFE
ROCKS AND MINERALS

FRENCH REVOLUTION

THE EXECUTION OF LOUIS XVI
"Because the country must live, Louis must die."
With those words, the king of France was killed
on the guillotine on 21 January 1793.

"LIBERTY! EQUALITY! FRATERNITY!"
This slogan echoed through France in
1789 as the hungry French people united
to overthrow the rich noblemen who
ruled the country. The Revolution put
ordinary people in control of France and
gave hope to oppressed people all over
the world. The Revolution started when
the bankrupt king Louis XVI summoned
the French parliament for the first time
since 1614. Instead of helping him raise
taxes, they siezed power. In Paris, a crowd stormed the Bastille prison, the
symbol of royal authority. The king had to support the Revolution, but in
1792 France became a republic, and Louis was executed. Counterrevolution
broke out in parts of France in 1793, which led to a Reign of Terror that
undid many of the benefits of the revolution. In 1799 a military takeover put
Napoleon in power and ended the Revolution.

THE REVOLUTION

May 1789 Estates
General (parliament)
meets at Versailles.

July 1789 Paris crowd
storms Bastille prison.

Aug 1789 Declaration
of the Rights of Man.

June 1790 Nobility
is abolished.

June 1791 Louis XVI
tries to flee from Paris.

Aug 1792 King Louis
imprisoned.

Sept 1792 Monarchy
abolished and France
becomes a republic.

Mar 1793 Counter-
revolution in Vendée
region.

Sept 1793 Start of
Reign of Terror.

July 1794 Terror ends
when Robespierre
is overthrown.

Nov 1795 A new
republic, the Directory,
takes power.

Nov 1799 Napoleon
Bonaparte overthrows
Directory and assumes
power.

MAXIMILIEN ROBESPIERRE
When 35-year-old lawyer
Robespierre came to power in
1793, he took severe measures
to safeguard the Revolution.
He presided over the Reign
of Terror but was himself
executed in 1794.

Place de
Louis XV
National
Assembly
Royal
palace
Tuilleries
gardens
Place de
la Bastille
Place de
la Nation

PARIS
Although
the Revolution
engulfed the whole of
France, Paris was always
at the centre of events, with
guillotines set up in many
squares. Swords mark uprisings.

The red bonnet
worn by the
revolutionaries,
and the
republican
tricolor flag

MARIANNE
The new revolutionary
calendar started from
the day the king was
overthrown. Marianne –
a symbolic but
imaginary revolutionary
woman shown here on a
stamp – illustrated the
first month.

SANS-CULOTTES
The well-dressed aristocrats sneered
at the revolutionaries and called them
sans-culottes, or people without
trousers. The revolutionaries adopted
this name as their own. Their simple
clothes came to symbolize the new way
of life in revolutionary France.

REVOLUTIONARY WOMEN
Women were very active during
the Revolution and led many of
the marches. But women were
never allowed to vote or to
participate in the government,
and the Rights of Man (the
revolutionary charter of human
rights) did not apply to them.

Find out more
EUROPE
EUROPE, HISTORY OF
NAPOLEON BONAPARTE

FRUITS AND SEEDS

ALL FLOWERING PLANTS, from tiny duckweeds to mighty oaks, develop from seeds. Each seed contains an embryo (a young plant) plus a store of food for the embryo's growth. A fruit is the seed container; it protects the developing seeds until they are dispersed by animals, the wind, water, or the plant itself. Fruits include lemons, melons, cherries, and tomatoes. The hard little stones or pips inside are the seeds. Many fruits, such as oranges and blackcurrants, are an important source of food. They contain large amounts of vitamin C, necessary for good health. People have cultivated fruits for centuries; today, fruit growers produce millions of tonnes of fruit every year. Strangely enough, some foods that we call vegetables, such as cucumber, are in fact fruits, bursting with tiny seeds. So too are spices such as whole chillis and peppercorns. Yet rhubarb, which is often cooked as a fruit, is really the pink stem of a leaf.

Seeds (pips)

Core

There are more than 1,000 varieties of cultivated apples.

APPLE
The apple's flesh, which is what we eat, grows from the receptacle of the flower, so it is a false fruit. The apple core is formed from the ovary, and the pips inside are the seeds. Pears, quinces, and hawthorn berries are formed in the same way; they are also known as pomes.

TRUE AND FALSE FRUITS

Fruits have different names, depending on which part of the flower develops into the main part of the fruit. Fruits are usually described as either true or false fruits. A true fruit develops from the female parts of the flower. A false fruit is one that includes some other part of the flower, such as the receptacle, or flower base.

The bright red fruits of the mountain ash (rowan) develop from clusters of white flowers.

GRAPE
Berries are juicy, succulent true fruits with pips inside. They include grapevine berries, which we call grapes. About 5,000 kinds of grapes are used to make wine, or are dried into currants and raisins for cakes and biscuits. Other berries include gooseberries, tomatoes, and bananas. Citrus fruits, such as oranges, lemons, and grapefruits, are also berries.

PLUM DRUPE
Drupes are juicy, succulent true fruits like berries. Unlike berries, however, drupes do not have pips. Instead, they have a hard stone which contains the seed. Plums, cherries, and apricots are all drupes. A blackberry is a collection of drupes.

Cherry

Plum

Runner bean pod

PEA LEGUME
Legumes are dry, non-juicy fruits. Their seeds are contained in a long outer casing called a pod. Pods are found on pea and bean plants, as well as sweet peas and laburnums. We eat the fruits of pea and bean plants.

Pea

Pea pod

POPPY CAPSULE
Capsules are hard, dry fruits found on poppies, violets, snapdragons, and the horse chestnut tree. The poppy capsule is like a saltshaker. The tiny seeds fall through holes at the top when the wind blows.

NUT

A nut is a dry, hard-cased fruit such as an acorn or hazelnut, with only one seed inside. Most hard, woody fruits or seeds are called nuts, but the fruit of the walnut is actually a drupe, and the Brazil nut is really a seed.

Walnut fruit (drupe)

Walnut "nut" is the seed.

Outer shell of Brazil nut

Hard casing

Brazil "nuts" are the seeds of a South American tree. The seeds grow in melon-sized fruit pods.

Brazil nut (seed) that we eat

Seed cases

Seed head

Seeds

Sunflower seeds are used in margarine, animal food, and as a snack.

SUNFLOWER
The sunflower grows about 2.5 m (8 ft) high. After fertilization, the large flower ripens to form a plate-sized seed head. Sunflower seeds contain large amounts of vitamins and edible oil.

GERMINATION

Seeds need warmth, moisture, and air in order to germinate (grow). The seeds of certain tropical plants start to germinate within a few days; the seeds of most other plants remain dormant, or asleep, until conditions are right. Many tree and shrub seeds must pass through a cold winter before they can begin to grow.

Dormant seed

Radicle (young root)

First leaves

Young shoot

Root hairs begin to grow.

WHEAT
The seeds of cereals such as wheat and other grasses have only one seed leaf. These seeds are called monocotyledons.

RUNNER BEAN
A runner bean has a food store in the form of two seed leaves which are called cotyledons.

First true leaves open.

First true leaves

Shoot lengthens.

Plumule (young shoot)

Plumule grows upwards.

Testa (seed case) containing seed leaves

Radicle (young root) begins to grow.

Roots develop branches.

Roots lengthen.

HOW SEEDS ARE SPREAD

Plants have several ways of spreading their seeds. Some seeds have wings or parachutes that are blown by the wind. The coconut plant has seeds that float and are carried on water. The sweet pea has a pod that snaps open and flings the seeds out. Animals also disperse seeds. Birds eat berries and other fruits, then drop the seeds as they feed or pass them out after digestion.

Sycamore fruit has wings to carry it through the air.

Seed is contained inside fruit.

BIRDS
Birds and monkeys are the main seed spreaders for many fruits. Seeds stick to the bird's bill to be wiped off later on a branch or the ground.

ACORN
A large oak tree bears thousands of ripe fruits, called acorns. Animals cannot eat them all; a few survive to grow into new oak trees.

BURIERS
Squirrels bury nuts to eat during the winter. Sometimes squirrels forget where they have buried these nuts, and the forgotten seeds may sprout the following spring.

WIND
The light, winged, helicopter-shaped fruits of sycamore trees twirl in the wind, far away from the parent tree. Pines also have winged seeds. Many plants, such as cotton and dandelions, have seeds with fine silky plumes or parachutes that catch the breeze.

WATER
Aquatic plants such as water lilies and lotus flowers produce fruits that float away downriver on water currents. The fruits often grow into new plants far away from the parent plant.

Lotus flower lives in water. Its seeds float away downstream to grow elsewhere.

HOOKS AND BURRS
Numerous kinds of fruits and seeds have hooks and burrs on their outer casings. These hooks catch onto the fur or feathers of a passing mammal or bird and sometimes onto our shoes, socks, and clothing, to fall off later. Well-known hooked fruits are burdock, cleavers, agrimony, and South African grapple fruit.

EXPLOSIVE PODS
Fruits such as those of the lupin are still soft and fleshy when they shed their seeds. When they are fully ripe, the casing suddenly splits open, and the seeds pop out with explosive force.

DANDELION
Each time you blow on the head of a dandelion you spread the seeds on their feathery parachutes.

In autumn, the badger picks up many seeds on its fur as it pushes through undergrowth. The seeds eventually drop off and grow into new plants.

Find out more
BIRDS
FLOWERS AND HERBS
PLANTS
TREES

GENETICS

THE SCIENCE OF GENETICS has officially existed ever since the word "gene" was coined in 1909 by the Danish botanist Wilhelm Johannsen (1857-1927). He invented the term to describe the "particles" of inheritance that pass characteristics from one generation of plant or animal to the next. The field of genetics developed over the course of the 20th century, and produced important discoveries about how genes work. Scientists showed that genes are sections of the long molecules of deoxyribonucleic acid (DNA) that are connected together to form chromosomes. Genes contain the instructions by which plant and animal cells are built. Genes are passed from both parents to their children through sexual reproduction. By this process, called heredity, inheritable characteristics are passed from one generation to the next.

Each "rung" is a pair of chemicals called bases.

DNA

Deoxyribonucleic acid is the full name of DNA. It is the molecule that holds the coded instructions within genes. Its structure is a double helix, with chemical bonds that attach one side of the helix to the other, rather like the rungs on a ladder. Each "rung" is made up of a pair of chemicals selected from a choice of four chemicals, so the way in which genetic information is coded is actually very simple.

The sides of the "ladder" are made up of phosphate and sugar molecules.

The DNA molecule looks something like a twisted ladder in this model. In real life it is a chain of tens of thousands of atoms.

HEREDITY

When a plant or animal is created, it inherits a combination of genetic information from both of its parents. Heredity is the passing of characteristics from parents to children. It means that a baby inherits certain features from each of its parents, but it also ensures that each baby is usually different from its brothers and sisters.

Blue eye

Some of the features controlled by genes can be easily seen. The genes in this girl's cells make her eyes blue, her hair straight, and her skin fair.

Albino hamster has white fur and red eyes.

Hamster with normal colouring

MUTATION

When new DNA is being created, sometimes a mistake can occur during the copying process. These mistakes are called mutations, and they may appear as a defect or a new characteristic. If a mutation turns out to be useful, it may become common in future generations.

Children resemble their parents but are not identical to them.

Wavy hair

The genes in this boy's cells make his eyes brown, his hair wavy, and his skin dark.

GENES

Each chromosome consists of a long molecule of DNA. Normally the molecule is unravelled, but it coils up to give the chromosome its characteristic shape (right) when a cells divides. Each gene is a short section of the chromosome that contains the instructions needed to make a particular protein. This is just one of the large group of chemicals that control the features, such as eye colour. Humans have around 23,000 genes.

The sex chromosomes determine whether a cell is male or female. Males contain an XY pair, while females contain an XX pair.

CHROMOSOMES

The nucleus of a living cell contains a number of pairs of chromosomes. They are rather like filing cabinets that store all of the genetic information of the plant or animal. Chromosomes are arranged in pairs that carry identical or different forms of the same genes.

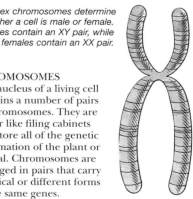

X chromosome

MENDEL

Gregor Mendel (1822-84), Austrian scientist, discovered the laws of heredity through experiments with pea plants. In 1866, he showed that features in a plant, such as the production of a smooth or a wrinkled pea, are determined by the genetic information given to the plant by its parents. He called this information "particles", some 43 years before the word "gene" was invented by the Danish scientist Wilhelm Johannsen (1857-1927).

Gregor Mendel was an ordained priest and combined this with his work as a scientist.

PATTERNS OF INHERITANCE

Different forms of the same gene are called alleles, and they can be dominant or recessive. Dominant alleles always show up, even if the information they carry comes from only one parent. Recessive means that a certain feature might not be seen in a plant or animal even though it is carrying the right alleles. Recessiveness is sometimes linked to gender.

Male cat carrying tortoiseshell allele

Female tortoiseshell cat

The cats produce male and female kittens. Only females can be tortoiseshell.

The second kitten, who carries two tortoiseshell alleles, does not have a tortoiseshell coat because he is male.

Only one kitten is tortoiseshell like her mother, because she carries two alleles and is female.

TWINS

If a fertilized human embryo splits in two it will develop into identical twins. Each twin shares the same genetic information. In fact, they are not entirely identical because each foetus develops in a slightly different way after the original split. Therefore identical twins can appear to be remarkably similar yet have quite different personalities. Non-identical twins develop from two separate embryos.

Identical twins are of the same sex because they come from a single embryo.

The world's media took a great interest in Dolly, the first large mammal to be cloned.

CLONING DOLLY

Clones are one or more identical organisms that share identical genes but unlike twins are not produced by natural reproduction. For many years, scientists have been interested in cloning identical copies of animals and plants. In 1996, scientists successfully cloned a sheep, known as Dolly. The experiment led to a worldwide debate about the ethics of cloning.

GM FOODS

The plants and animals that produce GM (genetically modified) foods have had their genes changed by scientists. In theory, genetic modification is just a way of speeding up the process of selection by breeding, which is already done in the natural way. There is much to be learnt before we can be sure that genetic modification is a safe thing to do.

GENETICS

1859 Darwin publishes his theory of evolution.

1866 Mendel establishes laws of inheritance.

1869 Friedrich Miescher isolates 'nuclein', later called DNA.

1905 X and Y sex chromosomes discovered.

1910 Thomas Morgan confirms chromosome theory of heredity.

1927 Genetic mutation in fruit flies created using X-rays.

1941 Proved that one gene produces one protein.

1944 Shown that DNA controls heredity.

1953 Watson and Crick discover the structure of DNA.

1966 Genetic code cracked.

1984 Discovery of DNA fingerprinting.

2003 Human genome project to identify genes, is completed.

Find out more
ATOMS AND MOLECULES
HUMAN BODY
REPRODUCTION

GOVERNMENT AND POLITICS

THE ADMINISTRATION OF A COUNTRY'S affairs is undertaken by a government whose policies direct decision making. Governments have many roles: they decide how money raised through taxes will be divided among the different public services, such as health, education, welfare, and defence. They also maintain the police for the safety of society and the armed forces for the defence of the nation. As a result of differing cultural and political traditions, government and policies vary from country to country. There are, however, three main types of government: republican, monarchical, and dictatorial. Most countries are republics, with people voting in an election to choose their government and head of state. In a monarchy, the head of the royal family is the head of state. Countries in which a single ruler has seized absolute power – often through a military takeover – are known as dictatorships.

PLATO
More than 2,000 years ago the Greek philosopher Plato wrote the first book about governments and how they rule people – what we today call politics. His book, *The Republic*, set out ideas for how a perfect state might be governed.

MONARCHY
In a monarchy a king or queen rules the country. Few modern monarchs have real political power, but four centuries ago, European monarchs made the laws and collected taxes.

PARLIAMENT

Many Western nations are democracies – they hold elections, in which the people vote for, or select, the next government from a range of political parties. Some countries, such as Britain and the Netherlands, have a parliamentary democracy. Elected politicians from different parties sit in parliament with the government and discuss the best way to run the country.

The government is usually from the political party with the greatest number of votes in the election, and the leader of this party becomes leader of the government and the country.

Parliament buildings in
The Hague, Netherlands

Thabo Mvuyelwa Mbeki is sworn in as president of the Republic of South Africa in 1999.

ANARCHISM
Not everyone believes in governments. Anarchists prefer a society without central control. The 19th-century picture below shows a bomb placed at a Paris opera house by French anti-government protestors.

PRESIDENCY

In a republic, such as South Africa, the people vote for their head of state. In this case, the president holds real political power, and is responsible for the administration of the country and for its foreign policy. In France, power is divided between the president and the prime minister. In some countries, such as India, the president is more of a symbolic figurehead, who takes on a ceremonial role, rather like that of some monarchs.

HOUSE OF LORDS
The House of Lords has some powers to amend or reject government legislation. It used to contain only hereditary peers, that is men who inherited titles such as earl from their fathers, as well as bishops and law lords. Many people thought this system undemocratic, so, in 1999, all but 92 hereditary peers were removed, leaving only peers chosen for life.

WESTMINSTER
The two Houses of Parliament – the House of Commons and the House of Lords – together with The Crown make up the Westminster government. Laws are proposed in either the Commons or the Lords, but all three must give assent to a bill (a proposed law) before it becomes an Act of Parliament, or law.

BRITISH MONARCHY
The monarchy once had great power but now plays a ceremonial role. The monarch has the right to be consulted about government policy, can chose a new prime minister, and can call a general election, although in practice she or he only acts on the advice of the prime minister.

Elizabeth II, current monarch of the UK

GOVERNMENT
The government runs the country. It proposes new laws to parliament, and takes decisions on every aspect of our daily lives. The British government consists of 20 or so ministers who sit in the Cabinet, plus another 90 or so junior ministers. The head is the prime minister, who always sits in the House of Commons and is usually the leader of the largest political party. Other ministers can sit in the Commons or the Lords.

CIVIL SERVICE
The civil service is the bureaucracy, or administrative machine, that carries out the instructions of the government once a law is passed. Civil servants collect taxes and duties, distribute benefits, and run the many government departments.

Government industrial chemists at work

THE SPEAKER
The Speaker of the House of Commons controls debates and keeps order in the Commons. She or he is a member of parliament (MP) and is elected at the start of each new session, once a year. Once elected, the speaker becomes neutral and may not cast a vote.

John Bercow MP, Speaker of the House of Commons from 2009

No. 10 Downing Street, the prime minister's official residence

POLITICAL PARTIES

Political parties are organizations formed to represent particular views in government or local councils. Britain has three main parties: the Labour, Conservative, and Liberal Democrat Parties. Since 1945, the government has always been either Labour or Conservative. Nationalist parties support independence for their own areas. Politicians who do not belong to a political party are called independents.

VOTING SYSTEMS

Most British elections are held under the first-past-the-post system, in which the person who gains the biggest number of votes wins. Other elections are based on proportional representation. In this system, seats are shared out according to the number of votes cast for each candidate or party.

Local governments are led by a mayor who wears a chain of office.

PRESSURE GROUPS

People form pressure groups to obtain action or change in a particular cause. Some groups, such as the environmental organization Greenpeace, campaign on a range of issues, often taking direct action such as confronting whaling ships. Others are concerned with local causes, such as stopping a hospital closure, or individual cases, such as freeing a wrongly convicted person in jail. Pressure groups can be very effective in achieving their demands or getting politicians to change their minds.

LOCAL GOVERNMENT

Every British city and town has its own city or district council. In rural areas, county and district councils share power. Local government looks after education, housing, social services, the environment, and public health, and carries out national government's orders.

DEVOLUTION

Until recently, parliament in London was the only law-making body in the country. In 1999, parliament agreed to devolve (hand down) power to parliaments in Scotland and Wales, giving them limited powers to make their own laws. Northern Ireland was also given a devolved assembly, in 1998, but it was not until 2007 that the local parties could agree to work together.

Inside of the new Scottish Parliament building

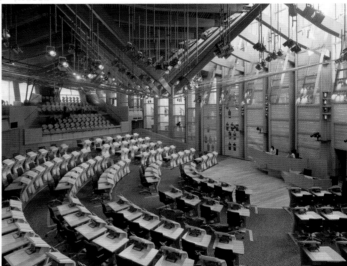

BRITISH GOVERNMENT

1265 Representatives from each county and town summoned to parliament, the first time "commoners" attend.

1300s Commons and Lords become separate Houses of Parliament.

1376 First speaker elected.

1642 English Civil War between King and parliament.

1688 Glorious Revolution: monarch cannot pass laws without parliament's consent.

1707 English and Scottish parliaments united.

1832 Property-owning men gain vote.

1835 Town councils set up.

1853 Modern civil service begins.

1867 Working-class men in towns gain the vote.

1872 Secret voting introduced to stop bribery of voters.

1911 Payment for MPs.

1911 Power of House of Lords reduced; House of Commons is supreme.

1918 Women aged 30 gain the vote.

1928 Every adult aged 21 has the vote.

1958 Life Peers first sit in the House of Lords.

1969 Voting age reduced to 18.

1999 Scottish parliament and Welsh Assembly meet for the first time.

1999 House of Lords reformed, only 92 hereditary peers remain.

CITIZENSHIP

Many people know little about the government and politics of Britain because they did not learn much about them at school. In 2002, a new subject, citizenship, became part of the national curriculum. Every child learns how the government works and how they can influence and take part in decisions through voting in elections.

Former prime minister Tony Blair and the children of the future.

Find out more
DEMOCRACY
ENGLISH CIVIL WAR
LAW

GRASSLAND WILDLIFE

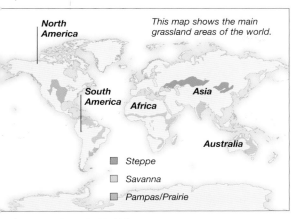

This map shows the main grassland areas of the world.

North America

South America

Africa

Asia

Australia

■ Steppe
□ Savanna
■ Pampas/Prairie

GRASSLAND AREAS
The main grassland areas in the world are the Asian steppes, African savannas and grasslands, North American prairies, and South American pampas, which blend into tropical Amazonian savanna. There are also tropical grasslands in parts of India and across Australia.

VAST AREAS OF AFRICA, the Americas, Asia, and Australia consist of grasslands – areas too dry for forests but not too dry for grasses. Grasses themselves are flowering plants that can grow again quickly after animals eat them. Grasses also recover quickly if fire sweeps across the plains in the hot, dry season. The fire burns only the upper parts of the grass, so the roots and stems are not damaged. Grasslands provide a home for many different animals; each survives by feeding on a different part of the grass plants. Zebras, for example, eat the coarse, older grass, while wildebeest (gnu) graze on new shoots. Thomson's gazelles nibble close to the ground. Grasshoppers, ants, and termites shelter among the grass stems and roots; these insects, in turn, are food for larger animals such as ant-eaters and armadillos. The lack of trees in grassland areas means that small animals and certain birds have to dig burrows for shelter and for breeding. Each type of grassland has bur-rowing rodents; prairie dogs and pocket gophers live in North America, susliks in Asia, ground squirrels in Africa, and vizcachas and tuco-tucos in South America.

Thistles grow in grassy areas throughout the world. Their prickles protect them against grazing animals. The flowers are often purple, and form fluffy white seed heads.

SOUTH AMERICAN PAMPAS
The largest mammals on the South American pampas are the pampas deer, guanaco, and rodents such as the viscacha, which burrows for shelter and safety. A fast-running bird called the rhea also lives on the South American pampas, feeding on grasses and other plants.

VISCACHA
The viscacha is related to the guinea pig. A male viscacha weighs about 8 kg (17 lb), almost twice the size of the female. Viscachas dig a system of burrows with their front feet and pile up sticks and stones near the various entrances. They eat mainly plant leaves and stems.

GIANT ANTEATER
With large claws on its second and third fingers, the giant anteater can easily rip a hole in an ants' nest or a termite mound as it searches for food. The giant anteater uses its long, sticky tongue to lick up the ants and termites. Its tongue measures about 60 cm (24 in) in length.

BURROWING OWL
The burrowing owl lives on the South American pampas. It often makes its nest in an empty burrow taken over from a viscacha. Burrowing owls eat grasshoppers, insects, small mammals, birds, lizards, and snakes.

PAMPAS GRASS
The white, fluffy seed heads of pampas grass are a familiar sight in parks and gardens. Wild pampas grass covers huge areas of Argentina, in South America. Pampas leaves have tiny teeth, like miniature saws, that easily cut human skin.

Tail protects anteater's body as it sleeps in a shallow hole, listening for predators such as pumas.

JACKAL
Golden jackals eat whatever they can find on the African savanna, including fruits, small mammals, eggs, birds, and the carcasses (dead bodies) of larger animals such as zebras.

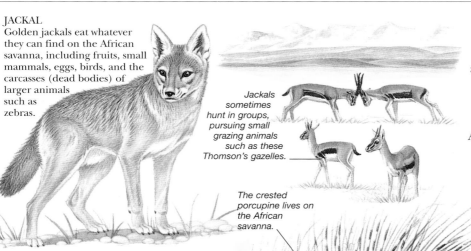

Jackals sometimes hunt in groups, pursuing small grazing animals such as these Thomson's gazelles.

The crested porcupine lives on the African savanna.

SAVANNA
The huge grassland areas of eastern and southern Africa are called savannas. These areas are home to the world's largest herds of grazing animals, including zebra, wildebeest, and hartebeest. Many large grazers wander from one area to the next, following the rains to find fresh pasture. Acacia and baobab trees dot the landscape, providing shade for resting lions, ambush cover for leopards, and sleeping places for baboons.

THOMSON'S GAZELLE
These swift-moving mammals live on the grassy plains of Africa in herds of up to 30 animals. They all have horns, but those of the male are larger than those of the female. Thomson's gazelles are often the prey of other grassland animals, such as the cheetah and the jackal.

CONSERVATION
Many grassland areas are now used as farmland, and the natural wildlife is being squeezed into smaller areas. As a result, these areas become overgrazed and barren. Grassland animals are also threatened by human hunters. In the past the Asian saiga antelope was killed for its horns. Today it is protected by law, but it is still seriously endangered with only 50,000 left in the wild.

A newborn saiga antelope is fluffy and has no horns.

CRESTED PORCUPINE
The crested porcupine has sharp spines on its back for protection. It warns enemies to stay away by rattling the hollow quills on its tail. If an intruder ignores these warnings, the porcupine runs backwards into the enemy, and the quills come away and stick into the intruder's flesh.

Wild peonies are found in many grassy habitats around the world. Many garden peony plants came originally from the hardy wild peonies that grow in grassland areas.

STEPPE
The vast plains of Asia are called steppes. In the western part of Asia the rainfall is more than 25 cm (10 in) each year, and grasses and other plants grow well. Towards the eastern part of Asia there is less than 6 cm (2.5 in) of rainfall yearly, and the grasses fade away into the harsh Gobi Desert. Saiga antelopes, red deer, and roe deer graze on the rolling plains.

GRASS SNAKE
The grass snake lives on riverbanks and in marshes, mainly in Europe and Asia. Grass snakes are good swimmers.

PALLAS'S CAT
This long-furred cat lives in mountains, high steppes, and open country across central Asia. At night it hunts for hares, birds, and mice.

Total body length of about 60 cm (24 in)

Strong, agile, stout body with short legs

Soft, thick fur to keep out the cold winds

BROOK'S GECKO
Sharp claws and sticky toe pads enable the gecko to climb well over smooth rocks, along crevices, and in cracks. The Brook's gecko is active at night, catching insects, and hides by day under rocks or in an empty termite or ant nest.

PALLAS'S SANDGROUSE
The mottled plumage (feathers) of Pallas's sandgrouse gives it excellent camouflage among the brownish grasses and stones of the Asian steppe. It needs little water and can survive on very dry, tough seeds and other plant parts.

Find out more
HORSES, ZEBRAS, AND ASSES
LIONS, TIGERS, and other big cats
LIZARDS
REPTILES

GRAVITY

FALLING

Earth's gravity makes falling objects accelerate (speed up). Their speed does not depend on how heavy they are: a light object falls as fast as a heavy object unless air slows it down. The Italian scientist Galileo Galilei (1564-1642) noticed this about 400 years ago.

A heavy rock weighs much more than an egg of the same size. However, both objects fall at the same rate and hit the ground at the same time.

THE EARTH MOVES around the sun, travelling about 50 times faster than a rifle bullet. A strong force holds the Earth in this orbit. This is the force of gravity; without it, the Earth would shoot off into space like a stone from a catapult. Everything possesses gravity; it is a force that attracts all objects to each other. However, the strength of the force depends on how much mass is in an object, so gravity is only strong in huge objects such as planets. Although you cannot feel it, the force of gravity is also pulling on you. The Earth's gravity holds you to the surface of the Earth, no matter where you are. This is because gravity always pulls towards the centre of the Earth. Sometimes you can see or feel the effects of gravity. For example, the effort you feel when you climb up a flight of stairs is because you are fighting against the force of gravity.

When you drop a ball, it falls because gravity is pulling it towards the centre of the Earth.

Gravity pulls all objects down towards the centre of the Earth.

MASS AND WEIGHT

An object's mass is the amount of material it contains. Mass stays the same wherever the object is in the universe. The weight of an object is the force of gravity pulling on it. Weight can change. Because the moon is smaller than the Earth, its gravity is weaker, about one sixth as strong as Earth's. Therefore, an astronaut on the moon weighs only one sixth of her weight on Earth, but her mass remains the same.

MOON AND EARTH

Gravity keeps the moon moving in its orbit around the Earth. The moon's gravity has effects on the Earth, too. When the moon is directly over the sea, its gravity pulls the sea water towards it, which produces a high tide; low tide follows when the Earth rotates away again.

Objects fall in the opposite direction on the other side of the Earth.

The force of gravity gets weaker as you go further from the centre of the Earth. On top of a high mountain, gravity is slightly weaker than at sea level; so objects weigh fractionally less.

EARTH'S GRAVITY

People on the opposite side of the Earth are upside down in relation to you. But they do not fall off into space. They are held on to the surface of the Earth just as you are. This is because the force of gravity pulls everything towards the centre of the Earth. Down is always the direction of the Earth's centre.

ISAAC NEWTON

British scientist Isaac Newton (1642-1727) was the first person to understand the force of gravity. In 1666, after watching an apple fall to the ground, he wondered whether the force of gravity that makes things fall also holds the moon in its orbit around the Earth. This was a daring idea, and it took Newton many years to prove it to be true. He declared his law of gravity to be a universal law – a law that is true throughout the universe.

CENTRE OF GRAVITY

It is best to carry a large, unwieldy object such as a ladder by holding it above its centre. The weight of the ladder balances at the centre, which is called its centre of gravity or centre of mass. An object with a large or heavy base has a low centre of gravity. This stops it from falling over easily.

Objects such as a loaded tray balance if supported directly beneath their centre of gravity.

Find out more

ASTRONAUTS
EARTH
PLANETS
SCIENCE, HISTORY OF
SUN
UNIVERSE

ANCIENT
GREECE

MANY WESTERN WORDS, monuments, ideas, and sources of entertainment have their roots in the world of Ancient Greece. About 2,500 years ago, the Greeks set up a society that became the most influential in the world. Greek architects designed a style of building that is copied to this day. Greek thinkers asked searching questions about life that are still discussed. Modern theatre is founded on the Ancient Greek plays that were performed under the skies thousands of years ago. And the Greeks set up the world's first democracy (government by the people) in Athens. However, only free men born in Athens were actually allowed to have a say in government. Ancient Greek society went through many phases, with a "golden age" between around 600 and 300 BCE. Arts and culture flourished at that time. The Macedonians, under Philip of Macedon, finally conquered the civilization, but it continued under Philip's son Alexander, who spread Greek culture and thinking throughout the Middle East and North Africa.

TEMPLE OF HERA
The Greeks built temples to worship their many gods. This temple at Paestum, Italy, was built to honour the goddess Hera, who was the protector of women and marriage.

PERICLES
As leader of Athens, Pericles (c.494–429 BCE) carried out a programme to beautify the city. This included the building of the Parthenon, a temple to the goddess Athena.

There were many busy markets in Athens, where people came to buy and sell their goods.

ATHENS
During the golden age, the Greek world consisted of independent, self-governing cities, known as city-states. With its own superb port at Piraeus, Athens was the most important city-state. It became the centre of Greek civilization and culture, attracting many famous playwrights and thinkers, such as Socrates. Athens practised the system of *demokratia* (democracy). People gathered together in the agora (marketplace) to shop and talk. The acropolis (high city) towered above Athens.

SPARTA
Spartan hoplites

The second major city-state of Greece, Sparta, revolved around warfare. Spartans led tough, disciplined lives. Each male Spartan began military training at the age of seven and remained a soldier until 60. Women kept very fit by running and wrestling. The fierce Spartan hoplites (foot soldiers) were feared throughout the Greek world.

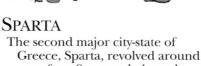

Athens (in Attica) and dependent states (shown in pink), c. 450 BCE

GREEK WORLD
The Greek world consisted of many city-states and their colonies, spread throughout the Mediterranean region.

NAVY
The Athenians possessed a powerful navy, consisting of a fleet of more than 200 triremes – warships powered by a square sail and rowed by 170 men seated in three ranks. The battle tactic involved rowing furiously and ramming the enemy's ship. In 480 BCE, during wars against the Persians, the Athenian navy crushed the Persian fleet at the sea battle of Salamis.

Modern reconstruction of a Greek trireme

ANCIENT GREECE

1500 BCE Minoan civilization (on island of Crete) at its height.

c. 1400 Mycenaean civilization, centred in great palaces on the Greek mainland, dominates Greece.

c. 1250 Probable date of the Trojan Wars between Mycenaeans and the city of Troy.

c. 1000 Establishment of the first city-states in mainland Greece.

776 First Olympic Games held at Olympia, Greece.

750s First Greek colonies founded.

c. 505 Democracy is established in Athens.

400s Golden age of Greek theatre.

490-479 Persian Wars; Greek states unite to defeat Persians.

490 Greeks defeat Persians at Marathon.

480 Greeks destroy the Persian fleet at the Battle of Salamis.

479 Final defeat of Persians at Plataea.

461-429 Pericles rules in Athens; Parthenon built.

431-404 Peloponnesian War between Athens and Sparta leads to Spartan domination of Greece.

359 Philip becomes king of Macedonia.

338 Philip of Macedonia conquers Greece.

336-323 Alexander the Great, son of Philip, sets up Greek empire in Middle East.

The main actors performed on the proskenion (stage).

All the actors were men, even those playing women's roles. They wore painted masks to hide their faces.

The audience bought stone tokens, which were like tickets, and sat in a semi-circle of tiered seats set into the hillside.

The chorus commented on the action of the play in song and dance.

The circular space in front of the stage was called the orchestra.

GREEK THEATRE
Drama was born in Athens. It began as singing and acting as part of a religious festival to honour the god Dionysus. The audience watched a series of plays; at the end of the festival, prizes were given for the best play and best actor. From these beginnings, playwrights such as Sophocles and Aristophanes started to write tragedies and comedies. Tragedies involved dreadful suffering; comedies featured slapstick humour and rude jokes.

THINKERS
Great thinkers from Athens dominated Greek learning and culture during the 5th and 4th centuries BCE. Socrates (469-399 BCE; above) was one of the most famous. He discussed the meaning and conduct of life. He also questioned people cleverly, often proving that their ideas were wrong. Socrates wrote no books himself, but one of his followers, Plato (427-347 BCE), made him the subject of many of his books.

VASE PAINTING
Painted scenes on Greek pottery give us clear clues about daily life in Ancient Greece. The paintings often show a touching scene, such as a warrior bidding his family farewell as he goes off to war. They also show the many gods that the Greeks worshipped.

Amphora (vase) from Attica shows Zeus, king of the gods, at the birth of Athena, his daughter.

Find out more
ARCHITECTURE
DEMOCRACY
GOVERNMENT AND POLITICS
WONDERS
of the ancient world
OLYMPIC GAMES

GUNPOWDER PLOT

IN THE LATE 1500s AND EARLY 1600s, Roman Catholics in England, urged on by the Catholic rulers of Spain, constantly schemed to replace England's Protestant rulers with Catholics. In 1605, a small group of Catholics hatched a plot to blow up James I and his government when the king opened a new session of parliament. The so-called Gunpowder Plot was due to take place on 5 November, but it failed because one of the conspirators warned his brother-in-law, Lord Mounteagle, not to attend parliament on that day. Mounteagle warned the government, and the cellars under parliament were searched. There, the king's soldiers found a young conspirator, Guy Fawkes, with 20 barrels of gunpowder. He was arrested, tortured, tried, and executed. The other plotters fled, but were later caught and were also executed.

RELIGIOUS INTOLERANCE
Anti-Catholic feeling was common in England and Scotland. Protestants distrusted Roman Catholics because they feared the political power of the pope. After the plot, fear of Catholics intensifed, and the conspirators were executed.

JAMES I
The first of the Stuart monarchs, James I was a staunch Protestant. He came to the throne in 1603, after the death of Elizabeth I. During Elizabeth's reign, Catholics had been persecuted. Mass was forbidden and Catholics could not hold high office. There were many Catholic plots. James I also distrusted Catholics. He angered them by refusing to reverse anti-Catholic laws.

Bates — Robert Winter — Christopher Wright — John Wright — Thomas Percy — Guy Fawkes — Robert Catesby — Thomas Winter

The House of Lords as the Queen formally opens parliament

STATE OPENING
Today, the British monarch still opens each session of parliament. There is a formal opening ceremony, at which the Queen reads out the government's programme for the year. It is the only day on which the Queen wears her crown, the symbol of her authority.

THE CONSPIRACY
The leader of the Gunpowder Plot was Robert Catesby (1573-1605), a wealthy Roman Catholic. He recruited 12 other conspirators, including Guy Fawkes, who was chosen to light the fuse and blow up the Houses of Parliament. The conspirators hoped that their actions would encourage a rebellion, which would lead to England becoming a Catholic nation. Thomas Tresham, one of the conspirators, gave the plot away.

Models of Guy Fawkes are still burned on Bonfire Night.

BONFIRE NIGHT
On 5 November 1605, supporters of the king celebrated the failure of the Gunpowder Plot by lighting bonfires. Ever since then, every year on 5 November, people in Britain remember the Gunpowder Plot. They build bonfires and let off fireworks. Children make dummy "guys" and ask people for a "penny for the guy". In some towns elaborate bonfire processions still take place.

Find out more
ELIZABETH I
GOVERNMENT AND POLITICS
HENRY VIII
STUARTS

HEART AND BLOOD

OUR BODIES CONTAIN about 4.5 litres (8 pints) of blood. Throughout life the heart, an organ inside the chest, pumps blood to every part of the body, keeping us alive. The heart is such a powerful pump that it takes only about a minute for each blood cell to travel all the way around the body and back to the heart. Travelling along tubes called blood vessels, blood carries oxygen and nourishment from digested food to every part of the body. Blood also carries away harmful waste products such as carbon dioxide. Blood consists of red and white blood cells, platelets, and a watery liquid called plasma. A drop of blood the size of a pinhead contains millions of red cells and thousands of white cells. About once every second the muscular walls of the heart contract, squeezing blood out of the heart and into blood vessels called arteries. The arteries divide many times until they form a network of tiny blood vessels called capillaries. The capillaries gradually join up again to form veins, which carry the blood back to the heart.

INSIDE THE HEART

The heart consists of two pumps, left and right, that work together. Each side has two chambers, an upper atrium and lower ventricle. Oxygen-poor blood from the body enters the right atrium through two big veins, the superior and posterior venae cavae. Blood passes into the right ventricle, which pumps it to the lungs to pick up along the pulmonary arteries – the only arteries to carry oxygen-rich blood. From there it passes to the left ventricle, which pumps it along the aorta and its branches to all parts of the body to deliver its oxygen before returning to the right atrium. Valves inside the heart ensure that blood flows in one direction only.

HUMAN HEART
The heart is protected by the rib cage. An adult's heart is the size of a clenched fist and weighs about 300 g (9 oz).

ARTERIES
These blood vessels carry blood away from the heart to the body. Arteries have thick walls that can resist high blood pressure produced when the heart beats. The coronary arteries deliver oxygen-rich blood to the walls of the heart itself.

CAPILLARIES
The tiny blood vessels that carry blood between the smallest arteries (arterioles) and the smallest veins (venules) are called capillaries. Capillaries allow oxygen and nutrients to pass through their walls to all the body cells.

VEINS
These blood vessels have thinner walls than arteries, as they are not subject to the high blood pressure created by each heartbeat. All veins, apart from the pulmonary veins, carry oxygen-poor blood from the body to the heart. Many have valves that prevent the backflow of blood from the heart. Skeletal muscles that surround veins help to squeeze blood towards the heart when they contract.

Labels on heart diagram: Superior vena cava, Aorta (main artery), Pulmonary artery, Left atrium, Pulmonary veins, Valve, Valves, Right atrium, Left ventricle, Valve, Right ventricle, Inferior vena cava, Descending aorta, Muscle

BLOOD CELLS

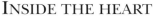

There are three types of blood cells. Red blood cells carry oxygen from the lungs to the rest of the body. White blood cells protect the body against illness and fight infection. Platelets, which are actually small cell fragments, help the blood to clot. All blood cells are produced in the bone marrow inside the bones.

Labels: White cell, Red cell, Platelets

HOW BLOOD CLOTS

When you cut yourself and blood flows out of the wound, platelets in the blood stick together and a fine meshwork of fibres forms. This meshwork traps more blood cells and forms a clot to seal the wound.

HEARTBEAT

On average, an adult's heart beats 60 to 70 times each minute. This rises to more than 150 beats after strenuous activity. Each heartbeat has three phases. During diastole (1) blood fills the two atria. They contract during atrial systole (2) to push blood into the ventricles that contract together during venticular systole (3) to pump blood into the arteries.

Blood leaks out where blood vessel is cut.

Platelets stick together, and clotting begins.

Tiny meshwork of platelets begins to form.

Blood clot forms, sealing the cut.

Blood enters atria (upper chambers).

Blood flows through to ventricles (lower chambers).

Ventricles contract to pump blood into arteries.

Atria refill with blood.

Find out more
BRAIN AND NERVES
HUMAN BODY
LUNGS AND BREATHING
MUSCLES AND MOVEMENT

HENRY VIII

THE SON OF HENRY VII, Henry VIII was the second of the Tudor monarchs, and probably the most famous king of England. Strong-willed, pleasure-loving, unpredictable, and obstinate, he inspired both admiration and fear. Henry wanted England to be a great power in Renaissance Europe, and used the money his father had amassed to establish Britain as a great naval force and to fight wars all over Europe. Resenting the power of the pope, who would not grant him a divorce from his first wife, Henry passed the Act of Supremacy in 1534. This set up the Church of England as a separate institution to the Catholic Church, and made the monarch its supreme head. Henry married six times, trying to produce a male heir.

1491 Born at Greenwich.

1509 Becomes king and marries Catherine of Aragon.

1533 Marries Anne Boleyn.

1536-39 Suppresses the monasteries.

1536 Anne Boleyn beheaded. Henry marries Jane Seymour.

1537 Son Edward born. Queen Jane dies.

1540 Henry marries Anne of Cleves; the marriage is annulled. Then marries Catherine Howard.

1542 Catherine is executed for treason.

1543 Henry marries Catherine Parr.

1547 Dies; buried at Whitehall.

Henry VIII enjoyed music, dance, games, sport, and hunting.

WAR AND PEACE
Henry sought glory through war with France. He strengthened the navy and had many powerful new ships built. At the Battle of the Spurs (1513), he led his army to victory, then in 1520 he organized a peace treaty between France and England at the ceremony of the Field of the Cloth of Gold. In 1544 he again made war with France. England captured Boulogne and France agreed to pay the king the sum of 2,000,000 crowns.

THOMAS CRANMER
Henry had many advisors. Those who disagreed with him were usually executed, but Thomas Cranmer (1489-1556), who supported Henry's marriage to Anne Boleyn, was made Archbishop of Canterbury in 1533.

Thomas Cranmer

THE SIX WIVES
Henry's first wife was Catherine of Aragon, mother of Mary I. Because no male heir was born, the king divorced Catherine and married Anne Boleyn, mother of Elizabeth I. For this, he was excommunicated by the pope. After Anne, Henry had four more wives: Jane Seymour, mother of King Edward VI; Anne of Cleves; Catherine Howard; and Catherine Parr, who outlived the king.

Anne Boleyn

THE ENGLISH REFORMATION
In 1534, Henry abolished the authority of the pope in England and founded the Church of England. This was the beginning of the English Reformation. Monasteries were closed and the king acquired their wealth and lands. The buildings fell into ruin or were destroyed.

Kirkstall Abbey, Yorkshire, destroyed in the Reformation.

Hampton Court Palace, which still exists today, was set in lavish gardens.

HAMPTON COURT
During Henry's reign, great houses were built by rich landowners and the king's courtiers, while many people lived in poverty. Henry himself oversaw the final building stages of Hampton Court, the largest house in England, begun by Cardinal Wolsey and built in brick, like many Tudor houses.

Find out more
REFORMATION
RELIGIONS
RENAISSANCE
TUDORS

HIBERNATION

MANY WARM-BLOODED ANIMALS need extra energy in order to stay warm in the cold winter months, but the source of that energy – food – is scarce in winter. Some animals survive winter by migrating to a warmer place; others, such as bats and hedgehogs, hibernate in a safe and unexposed place such as a nest, burrow, or cave. In true hibernation, the body processes slow down almost to a standstill – the heartbeat occurs only every now and then, and the animal takes only a few breaths per minute. The body temperature falls to only a few degrees above the outside temperature – as low as 0°C (32°F) in a hamster. If the outside temperature drops below zero, chemical reactions in the animal's body switch on to keep it from freezing to death. A hibernating animal feasts on extra food in the autumn so it can build up reserves of fat in its body and survive the winter months without food.

Senses such as hearing and sight are inactive during hibernation.

Dormouse curls up into a ball shape to reduce heat loss from its body.

Dormouse builds nest on or near ground, using stems, moss, and leaves.

Furry tail wraps around face for protection and insulation.

Up to half of body weight is lost during hibernation.

DORMOUSE

One of the best-known hibernators is the dormouse. In autumn it feeds eagerly to build up stores of body fat, then settles into a winter nest among tree roots or in dense undergrowth. Its heart slows to only one beat every few minutes, and its breathing slows down. Its body temperature also drops to a few degrees above the surroundings.

BLACK BEAR

The winter sleep of bears, skunks, and chipmunks is not as deep as the true hibernation of bats and mice. The American black bear's heartbeat slows but the body temperature drops by only a few degrees. This means that the bear can rouse itself from its sleep quite rapidly during a spell of slightly warmer weather. Although it wakes up, the bear does not eat and continues to live off its body fat until the spring. Some female bears give birth during the winter months.

TORPOR

To save energy, some small, warm-blooded animals such as bats and hummingbirds allow their bodies to cool and their heartbeat and breathing to slow down for part of the day or night. This is called torpor. Large animals such as bears do not become torpid because they would need too much energy to warm up again afterwards. Bats often huddle together as they hang upside down to prevent too much heat loss. When the cold season comes, bats fly to a special cave or tree called a hibernaculum, where they begin true hibernation.

AESTIVATION

Many desert animals sleep during the hot, dry season to survive the intense heat. This is called aestivation – the opposite of hibernation. Desert creatures which aestivate include lizards, frogs, insects, and snails. Before aestivation begins, snails seal their shell openings with a film of mucus that hardens in the heat.

Snails cluster on grass stems to aestivate, away from predators on the ground.

--- *Find out more* ---
ANIMALS
DESERT WILDLIFE
MAMMALS
POLAR WILDLIFE

HORSES
ZEBRAS, AND ASSES

FOR THREE THOUSAND YEARS before trains and cars were invented, horses were a fast, efficient method of transport. These swift, graceful creatures are easy for humans to train. Today there are more than 75 million domestic (tame) horses, and they are divided into more than 100 different breeds. Horses, asses, and zebras belong to the equid family, a group that includes donkeys and mules. Equids are long-legged mammals with hoofed feet, flowing tails, and a mane on the upper part of the neck. They can run or gallop with great speed. A keen sense of smell, good eyesight, and sharp hearing mean that they are always alert and ready to flee from danger. Horses, asses, and zebras are grazing animals that feed almost entirely on grasses, which they crop with their sharp front teeth.

TEETH
Experts can tell the age of a horse by the number, angle, and size of its teeth, and the way the teeth have worn down with use. Most adult horses have between 40 and 42 teeth.

UNICORN
The unicorn is an imaginary horselike creature. It often appears in legends and folktales as a symbol of purity.

Poll

Forelock

Eyes are on the side of the head for good all-round vision.

Large ears can swivel to detect which direction a sound comes from.

Mane covers upper neck.

Withers

Back

Flank

Croup

Dock

Muzzle

Long jaws and strong cheek muscles for chewing grass

Neck

Chest

Elbow

Horse uses long, coarse hairs of tail as a fly-whisk and as a social signal.

Knee

Heel

Frog

Sole

Horseshoe

Cannon

Bones

Fetlock

Pastern

Hoof

Today's domestic horse

Hyracotherium

THE FIRST HORSES
Hyracotherium, one of the first equids, lived in woodland areas more than 50 million years ago. It was only 60 cm (2 ft) high. Through evolution, horses gradually became larger and began to live in more open grassland areas.

HOOVES
Horses walk on the tips of their toes. On each foot is a strong, hard hoof: the core is made of bone and the outer coating is keratin. There is a pad on the sole of the hoof called the frog. The frog acts like a shock absorber when the horse runs. People also put metal horseshoes on a horse's hooves to protect them on hard roads and rough ground.

HORSES AND HUMANS
Domestic horses are trained to do many jobs, from pulling carts to carrying soldiers into battle. Many sports and leisure activities involve horses, such as show jumping, polo, rodeo, flat racing, and steeplechasing. Champion horses are worth millions of pounds, and the first prize at a famous horse race may be thousands of pounds.

ADULTS AND YOUNG
An adult male horse is called a stallion; an adult female is a mare. Young males are called colts; young females are fillies.

In some countries horses and mules are still used instead of cars. They are also used on farms to till fields, fertilize the crops, and pull produce to market.

Zebras live on the open grasslands of Africa.

ZEBRA

The zebra is the only member of the horse family with stripes. Although zebras look alike, each one has its own unique black and white markings. Like horses, zebras are social animals and live together in herds; young males, however, often live on their own until they are mature. As they become adults, male zebras battle with other males to collect a group, or harem, of females to breed with.

A zebra can run at about 65 km/h (40 mph) to escape from a predator such as a lion.

DONKEY
A donkey is a domesticated ass. Donkeys, together with horses and asses, have been hauling loads for people for thousands of years. They are often called beasts of burden. Another beast of burden, the mule, is the offspring of a female horse and a male donkey.

ASS

There are two kinds of wild ass – the African ass and the Asian ass. The African ass lives in dry, rocky areas of North Africa; the Asian ass is found in Asia. Asses need very little water and survive in the wild by eating tough, spiky grasses. Like other members of the horse family, the female ass has one young at a time, called a foal. The foal can walk a few minutes after birth.

A wild ass and a smaller domesticated ass

Przewalski's horse has a stiff upright mane.

PRZEWALSKI'S HORSE
Also called the Asian horse or "wild horse", Przewalski's horse is closely related to the domestic horse. Herds of these horses once lived on the high plains of Mongolia, in northern Asia. Today there are only a few hundred left in zoos and wildlife parks. Although introduced back into the wild, they must be kept away from domestic horses to avoid cross breeding.

GALLOPING
Horses move at a walk, trot, canter, or gallop, in increasing order of speed. When a horse gallops, all its hooves are off the ground for a split second during each stride. The fastest race horses can gallop at more than 65 km/h (40 mph) over a short distance.

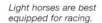

All four hooves lift off the ground in mid-gallop.

Light horses are best equipped for racing.

TYPES OF HORSES
There are three main kinds of horses – draught horses such as Shires; light horses such as Arabian horses; and ponies such as Shetland ponies. Draught horses pull ploughs, and light horses take part in races.

HOW WE MEASURE HORSES

Horses can be measured in hands from the ground to the withers (the highest point of the shoulder). One hand equals 10 cm (4 in). Shire horses are the largest and Shetland ponies are among the smallest horses.

Shire horse may be more than 180 cm (18 hands, 6 ft) at the shoulders and weigh more than 1,135 kg (2,500 lb).

Appaloosa is about 150 cm (15 hands, 5 ft) high.

Shetland pony is 120 cm (12 hands, 4 ft) high.

<hr>

Find out more

ANIMALS
GRASSLAND WILDLIFE
MAMMALS
MOUNTAIN WILDLIFE

HUMAN BODY

FROM THE MOMENT we are born to the moment we die, our bodies do not stop working for a second. The human body is a complex collection of more than 100,000 million living units called cells. There are more than 200 different types of cells, including nerve cells or neurons, muscle cells, fat cells, epidermal cells, blood cells, and gland cells that release secretions, such as hormones and enzymes. Each type of cell in the body does a particular job. Cells that do similar jobs are grouped together to form tissues, such as muscle tissue and nerve tissue. Tissues, in turn, are grouped together to form organs, which are separate structures within the body. The lungs, heart, liver, and kidneys are some of the main organs. Linked organs work together as systems, and each system carries out one or more major functions. For example, the heart, blood vessels, and blood form the circulatory system, which carries oxygen and nutrients around the body and carries away waste products. All the different systems work together, under the control of the brain, to produce a living, walking, talking human body.

THE BODY'S ABILITIES
The human body is capable of amazing feats of balance and co-ordination. Many animals can run faster or jump higher, but our bodies are very adaptable. An extremely complex brain controls the body and gives us the intelligence to use our physical abilities to the best advantage.

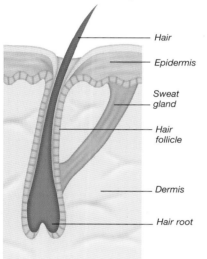

Hair
Epidermis
Sweat gland
Hair follicle
Dermis
Hair root

SKIN
The body is covered by skin. Skin is flexible and helps protect the body. It keeps water and harmful bacteria out, and keeps body fluids in. Skin is also wear-resistant because it continually renews itself. The base of the upper layer, or epidermis, divides constantly to make new cells. The new cells move upwards as if on a conveyor belt, to replace cells that are worn out.

CELL
Every second, millions of cells die and millions more replace them. An average cell measures about 0.025 mm (one thousandth of an inch) across, but there are many different kinds of cells in the body, each adapted for a certain job. Nerve cells are long and thin. Like wires, nerve cells conduct (carry) electrical nerve signals. Red blood cells are doughnut-shaped and contain chemicals that carry oxygen around the body. Epithelial cells on body surfaces, such as the lining of the mouth, are broad and flat and fit together like paving stones.

Skin cell
Red blood cell
Nerve cell
Bone cell
Muscle cell
Fat cell

NERVOUS SYSTEM
The brain and the nerves make up the nervous system. Nerves extend from the brain and spinal cord to all body parts, carrying signals in the form of tiny electrical impulses. The signals bring information from the sense organs to the brain and take instructions from the brain to the muscles. The brain controls many processes automatically, such as breathing, heartbeat, and digestion, without our having to think about them.

Brain stem
Cerebrum
Nerves
Spinal cord

Skull
Neck vertebrae
Rib cage
Humerus (upper-arm bone)
Elbow joint
Radius
Metacarpal (bone joining wrist with fingers)
Femur (thigh bone)
Patella (knee-cap)
Tibia (shinbone)
Tarsal (bone joining leg and foot)

SKELETAL SYSTEM
Two hundred and six bones form the body's strong internal framework. Some are connected at flexible joints; joints in the leg, for example, allow us to move. Others are fixed firmly together, as in the skull. The vertebral column, or backbone, supports the head at the top and the limbs on either side. The backbone also encases and protects the delicate spinal cord.

There are several stages of development in everyone's lifetime – from birth through childhood, adolescence, and adulthood, to old age.

GROWTH AND DEVELOPMENT

As the human body grows, it develops many skills. Babies learn to smile, sit up, crawl, walk, and talk. Learning continues at school. On average, the peak of physical abilities is reached at about 18 to 25 years of age. Later, more changes occur with age. The skin becomes wrinkled and less elastic, the joints are less flexible, bones become more brittle, muscles are less powerful, and there is some loss of height and greying of hair.

In many older people, decrease in physical strength is offset by the wisdom and knowledge gained from a lifetime of experience.

Neck muscles tilt and twist head.

Upper arm muscles bend and straighten elbow.

Chest muscles help in breathing.

Abdominal muscles shield digestive organs.

Buttock and thigh muscles are the most powerful muscles.

Muscles are joined to bones by tendons, such as the Achilles tendon in the heel.

Teeth

Mouth

Oesophagus (gullet)

Stomach

Large intestine

Small intestine

Rectum

Anus

Trachea (windpipe)

Lung

Heart

Kidney

Bladder

Veins return blood to the heart.

Arteries carry blood from the heart.

RESPIRATORY SYSTEM
The lungs, the airways, and the throat and nasal passages make up the respiratory system. The lungs absorb vital oxygen from the air. The blood transports this oxygen around the body, pumped through the blood vessels by the heart.

URINARY SYSTEM
The kidneys filter waste substances from the blood to form a fluid, urine, which is stored in the bladder.

MUSCULAR SYSTEM
There are about 650 muscles in the body. Some, such as the arm muscles, can be controlled at will, to pull on the bones of the skeleton and move the body. Others, such as the muscles of the heart and intestine, work automatically.

DIGESTIVE SYSTEM
The mouth, oesophagus, stomach, and intestines are part of the digestive system. These organs work together to break down food into particles that are small enough to pass through the lining of the intestine and into the blood. The mouth and teeth chop and chew food, and the stomach churns it with powerful digestive chemicals. The liver is the main organ for converting absorbed nutrients into forms more suitable for use by the various organs. The large intestine deals with wastes and leftover food.

Find out more
BRAIN AND NERVES
EARS
EYES
HEART AND BLOOD
LUNGS AND BREATHING
REPRODUCTION
SKELETONS
TEETH

HUMAN RIGHTS

MOST OF US BELIEVE that we have the right to be treated fairly and equally within society, regardless of our race, sex, religion, or social group. This equal treatment includes the right to vote, to work, and to be educated. When these rights are protected by law, they are called legal or human rights. In some countries, they are spelled out in the constitution. However, through history, many groups, including African-Americans, black South Africans, Native Americans, and women, have not been considered equal to others, and have had few, if any, civil or human rights. This kind of targetted mistreatment is called discrimination. In the 20th century, many different groups, including blacks, homosexuals, women, and people with disabilities, fought long and sometimes bitter campaigns to achieve their rights and obtain equal treatment within society.

MOHANDAS GANDHI
Human rights activists – those who fight for civil rights – use peaceful methods. They unite and mobilize people. In 1915, Mohandas Gandhi (1869-1948) began to lead the struggle against British rule in India. Using non-violent civil disobedience, Gandhi's fasts and marches helped lead to India's independence from British rule in 1947.

NELSON MANDELA
In 1948, the South African government introduced apartheid, under which the black majority had no civil rights. The African National Congress (ANC), headed by Nelson Mandela (b.1918), led a long fight against apartheid. It was finally repealed in 1991.

AFRICAN-AMERICAN RIGHTS
Until slavery was abolished in 1865, African-Americans were treated as property in the southern states. Following abolition, southern states introduced laws which segregated (separated) races, and made African-Americans second-class citizens. Under the leadership of Martin Luther King, Jr. (1929-68), a civil rights movement emerged. It used non-violent methods, such as sit-ins (see left), where African-Americans peacefully occupied segregated public places. Finally Congress passed the Civil Rights Act in 1964 and the Voting Rights Act in 1965. These laws outlawed discrimination on the grounds of race, colour, or religion in schooling, voting, and employment.

AMNESTY INTERNATIONAL
A worldwide human rights organization, Amnesty International was founded in 1961 following a legal appeal by a British lawyer, Peter Benenson, after he read about two Portuguese students who were imprisoned for raising their glasses in a toast to freedom. Amnesty works to obtain prompt and fair trials for all prisoners, to end torture and executions, and to secure the release of people imprisoned solely for their political or religious beliefs and who have not used or advocated violence. The organization has more than 2.2 million members and has its headquarters in London. In 1977, Amnesty International was awarded the Nobel Peace Prize for its work.

AMERICAN INDIAN MOVEMENT
Since the 1960s, Native Americans have become more forceful in demanding equal rights. In 1968, the American Indian Movement (AIM) formed to fight for civil rights and improved conditions on reservations. A militant organization, AIM conducted a number of high-profile protests. In 1973, they occupied Wounded Knee in South Dakota, the site of a massacre of Sioux people in 1890. Federal marshals surrounded the protestors, and a siege began in which two AIM members were killed. Since then, some Native Americans have won land rights, but discrimination still continues today.

Find out more
AFRICA, HISTORY OF
EMIGRATION
and immigration
EXPLORERS
LAW
SLAVERY
WOMAN'S RIGHTS

HUNDRED YEARS WAR

IN 1337, THE ENGLISH KING EDWARD III, whose mother was French, landed in Normandy, laid claim to the French crown, and began what historians call the Hundred Years War. To the people who fought it, it was more like a series of small wars separated by truces. It lasted through the reigns of five English and five French kings. Edward III failed to gain the French crown, and died in 1377. His heir, Richard II, took little interest in the war, but Henry V, who came to the throne in 1413, wanted to fight for the French crown and started the conflict again. Before 1420, the English won most of the battles, including Crécy (1346), Poitiers (1356), and Agincourt (1415), but by 1453, France had taken back all England's French lands, except Calais, which England lost in 1558.

ENGLAND AND FRANCE
Through royal marriages, the English already held large areas in the north and west of France. By the Treaty of Troyes in 1420, it was agreed that Henry V of England would become French king after the death of Charles VI of France.

English troops kept the sun behind them so that it shone directly into the eyes of the French soldiers.

French troops had to attack uphill.

Welsh and English archers fired faster than French cross-bow men.

French cavalry bogged down in the mud.

BATTLE OF CRÉCY
On 26 August 1346, Edward III's 8,000 troops were trapped at Crécy, but clever tactics and the skill of the English archers defeated a French army of 20,000. Edward's 16-year-old son, known as the Black Prince because of the black armour he wore, commanded his own troops in the battle.

HENRY V AND AGINCOURT
On 25 October 1415, Henry V (1387-1422) led his troops into battle at Agincourt. An English army of only 13,000 archers, pikemen, and cavalry defeated a French force of 50,000. Shakespeare described this English victory in *Henry V*.

ENGLISH LONGBOW
The longbow was normally made from yew, and the arrows were ash. In the 14th and 15th centuries, all English men were required by law to practise archery after church on Sundays, to be ready for war.

Archers practise with their longbows.

HUNDRED YEARS WAR
1338 Edward III of England claims French crown.

1346 Battle of Crécy.

1347 English capture Calais.

1356 Battle of Poitiers.

1415 Henry V declares war on Charles VI of France.

1415 Siege of Harfleur.

1415 Battle of Agincourt.

1419 English capture Normandy.

1420 Treaty of Troyes. Henry V marries King of France's daughter and claims French throne.

1428-29 Siege of Orléans.

1430 Joan of Arc taken.

1450 French reconquer Normandy.

1453 Battle of Castillon.

1453 Fall of Bordeaux ends war.

Find out more
CASTLES
EUROPE, HISTORY OF
NORMANS
SHAKESPEARE, WILLIAM
UNITED KINGDOM, HISTORY OF

INCAS

IN THE 12TH CENTURY, a tribe of Native Americans moved down from the Andes mountains in South America to settle in the fertile Cuzco valley. By the end of the 15th century they had conquered a huge territory of 1,140,000 sq km (440,000 sq miles) containing more than 10 million people. The Incas won this land with their powerful army and then controlled it with a remarkable system of communications. Inca engineers built a network of paved roads that crisscrossed the empire. Relays of imperial messengers ran along these roads (there were no horses or wheeled vehicles), travelling 250 km (150 miles) a day as they took messages to and from the capital city of Cuzco. At the head of the empire was the chief Inca, who was worshipped as a god and held absolute power over all his subjects. But in 1525 the chief Inca, Huayna Capac, died, and civil war broke out between two rivals for his throne. In 1532 a small force of Spanish soldiers arrived in the country and found it in disarray. They quickly overwhelmed the Incan army, and by 1533 the Inca empire was almost completely under Spanish rule.

South America

Inca empire

MACHU PICCHU
Covering an area of 13 sq km (5 sq miles), the fortress city of Machu Picchu was built on a series of terraces carved into the side of a mountain more than 2,280 m (7,500 ft) above sea level.

INCA EMPIRE
In 1525, at its height, the Inca empire stretched for more than 3,200 km (2,000 miles) along the Pacific coast of South America, ruling over much of present-day Ecuador, Peru, Bolivia, and Chile.

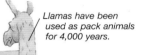

Llamas have been used as pack animals for 4,000 years.

An Inca woman weaving an elaborately designed piece of cloth.

QUIPU
The Incas did not read or write. Instead, they used quipus – lengths of knotted string – to record every aspect of their daily life. Historic events, laws, gold reserves, population statistics, and other items of information were all stored accurately in this way.

The colour of string, number of knots, and length of string on the quipu all meant different things.

The Incas were expert goldsmiths and often placed gold figurines (right) in their graves. Much of the Incan gold was melted down by Spanish invaders.

WEAVING
The Incas wove lengths of beautiful, colourful cloth with elaborate patterns. The wool they used came from the mountain animals – llamas, alpacas, and vicunas – that the Incas kept on their farms. Many of their designs depicted jaguars and pumas.

TERRACE FARMING
The Incas were expert at farming every available piece of fertile land in their mountainous empire. They built terraces along the steep hillsides and watered them with mountain streams so that crops could be grown and animals kept to feed all the people who lived in the cities.

___ *Find out more* ___
EUROPE, HISTORY OF
FARMING
SOUTH AMERICA
SOUTH AMERICA, HISTORY OF

INDIAN OCEAN

The Indian Ocean is bounded by Africa to the west, India and Australia to the east, and Asia to the north. In the south, it merges with the Antarctic Ocean. In the north, the Suez Canal gives access, via the Red Sea, to the Mediterranean.

MORE THAN 1,000 MILLION PEOPLE live in the countries that fringe the Indian Ocean, and on some of the 5,000 islands that are scattered across its surface. The world's third-largest ocean provides a major link between Europe and Asia. The monsoon winds, which bring heavy rainfall to many of the countries surrounding the ocean, also have an impact on the currents, which reverse direction completely between March and August. Early navigators used the winds and currents to carry them from Arabia to southern India and Indonesia, bringing Islamic religion and culture with them. Malays and Indonesians took the journey westwards, settling in Madagascar. Most of the islands of the Indian Ocean are small and uninhabited. However, many tourists are drawn to their beautiful palm-fringed beaches, and in some places tourism is beginning to supplement traditional ways of life based on fishing and farming.

MONSOON
The lands around the Indian Ocean are dependent on monsoon rainfall. Monsoons are seasonal winds, blowing from the southwest in summer and northeast in winter, that bring torrential downpours. Very heavy monsoon rains swell rivers, causing disastrous flooding often accompanied by diseases such as cholera. The Bay of Bengal is especially vulnerable to flooding.

SEYCHELLES
The island republic of the Seychelles consists of 40 scattered mountainous islands. These are surrounded by over 70 coral islands, which are low-lying and sparsely populated. The main islands are outstandingly beautiful; their hillsides blanketed with tropical vegetation, fringed by silvery-white beaches. Temperatures are constant throughout the year, reaching a daytime high of 30° C (86° F). The Seychelles attract year-round visitors from the northern hemisphere.

STILT FISHERMEN
There are less areas of shallow seas, where fish breed, in the Indian Ocean than in the Pacific or the Atlantic. Large-scale fishing, using trawlers and factory ships, has therefore not developed in the region. Most fishing takes place on a local basis, near island coastlines. Tuna is the most valuable catch. In Sri Lanka, fishermen – precariously perched on stilts – use poles and lines to catch their fish.

MADAGASCAN VILLAGE
Most Madagascans are descended from Malays and Indonesians, who crossed the Indian Ocean in the 7th century CE. These villagers come from the southeastern coast. The east coast is densely populated and poor. Most of Madagascar's ruling class come from the central plateau.

MADAGASCAR
The world's fourth-largest island lies off Africa's eastern coast. Most of the population is concentrated in the narrow strip of fertile land along the east coast, which has a humid, tropical climate. Farming dominates the economy. Rice and cassava are the main crops, while coffee and vanilla are grown for export. Poultry, sheep, pigs, and goats are all kept on a small scale. The government's attempts to modernize livestock farming have not been successful.

Find out more
AFRICA
ASIA
AUSTRALIA
OCEANS AND SEAS
OCEAN WILDLIFE

CHRISTMAS ISLAND
Area: 134.6 sq km
(52 sq miles)
Status: Australian external territory
Claimed: 1958
Population: 1,400
Capital: Flying Fish Cove

MADAGASCAR
Area: 587,040 sq km
(226,660 sq miles)
Population: 20,654,000
Capital: Antananarivo
Languages: Malagasy, French
Religions: Traditional beliefs, Christian, Muslim
Currency: Malagasy franc

MAURITIUS
Area: 2,040 sq km
(788 sq miles)
Population: 1,284,000
Capital: Port Louis
Languages: English, French, French Creole
Religions: Hindu, Roman Catholic
Currency: Mauritian rupee

SEYCHELLES
Area: 455 sq km
(176 sq miles)
Population: 87,476
Capital: Victoria
Languages: English, French, French Creole
Religions: Roman Catholic
Currency: Seychelles rupee

COMOROS
Area: 2,170 sq km
(838 sq miles)
Population: 752,000
Capital: Moroni
Languages: Arabic, Comoran, French
Religions: Muslim, Roman Catholic
Currency: Comoros franc

MALDIVES
Area: 300 sq km
(116 sq miles)
Population: 396,000
Capital: Male'
Languages: Dhivehi (Maldivian)
Religions: Sunni Muslim
Currency: Rufiyaa

REUNION
Area: 2,517 sq km
(972 sq miles)
Status: French overseas department
Claimed: 1649
Population: 802,000
Capital: Saint-Denis

ARAB DHOW
Dhows are Arab trading boats made of teak or coconut planks, sewn together with twine. They are lateen-rigged, which means that they have one, or sometimes two, triangular sails. Dhows are fast and manoeuvrable. They were a vital tool in the Arab exploration of the Indian Ocean from the 8th century CE. Using the monsoon winds, Arab merchants soon gained control of Indian Ocean trade and spread Islam as far as Indonesia.

THE MALDIVES
The Maldives consist of 1,800 low-lying coral islands, which form the crowns of ancient submerged volcanoes. None of the islands are higher than 1.8 m (6 ft), and all but 20 have fewer than 1,000 inhabitants. Rising sea levels, caused by global warming, threaten to submerge the islands.

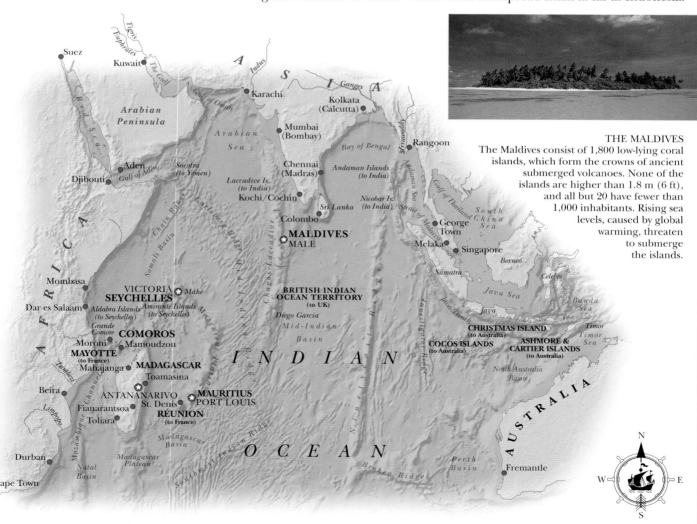

INDUSTRIAL REVOLUTION

THE WORLD WE LIVE IN TODAY, with its factories and huge cities, began less than 300 years ago in Britain, then spread to Europe and the United States. Beginning in about 1760, great changes took place that altered people's lives and methods of work forever, changes that are known today as the Industrial Revolution. Machines powered by water and, later, steam were invented to produce cloth and other goods more quickly. It took many workers to run these big machines, so poor people moved from the country into the new industrial towns to be near the factories. There were more jobs and higher wages in the cities, but life was often miserable. Although the Factory Act in 1833 banned young children in Britain from working in factories, there were no laws to control how long people worked each day, or to make sure the machines were safe.

FACTORY OWNERS
Robert Owen (1771-1858) was a generous British factory owner who tried to improve working conditions. Many other owners grew rich by demanding long hours of work for low wages.

NEW TOWNS
Factory towns were built as fast and as cheaply as possible. Large families were crowded into tiny houses, and the water supply was often polluted. Diseases spread rapidly, and many people died young.

Factory workers lived in overcrowded houses, which often became slums.

Barges on new canals carried factory goods from one town to another.

Chimneys from the new factories created a lot of smoke. This made the towns dirty and polluted.

NEW TECHNOLOGY
Stronger metals were needed to make machines, so cast iron and steel were developed. Steam to drive the new engines was made by burning coal to boil water. Coal mines were driven deep into the ground. Cotton cloth was the first product to be made completely by machine. The new goods were produced in large numbers so they were cheap to buy.

Cotton replaced wool as the main material for making clothes.

DAVY LAMP
In 1815 British inventor Sir Humphry Davy developed a miner's safety lamp.

Cast iron, which could be moulded into any shape, became common.

BEDSTEAD
Iron was even used for making beds.

1708 Englishman Abraham Darby invents coke-smelting of iron.

1733 John Kay, England, develops "flying shuttle", which mechanizes weaving.

1760 Start of Industrial Revolution, Britain.

1765 James Hargreaves, England, invents "spinning jenny". It increases output of spun cotton. Scotsman James Watt develops steam engine, which is used to drive machinery in cotton industry.

1769 Richard Arkwright's water frame used to spin strong thread. Speeds up production; early beginning of Factory Age, England.

1779 English weaver Samuel Crompton develops spinning "mule", which spins many threads at once.

1784 Henry Cort, England, develops puddling furnace and rolling mill. Produces high quality iron.

1789 First steam-powered spinning loom, England. Speeds up textile production.

1793 Eli Whitney's cotton gin mechanizes cotton production, United States.

1804 Englishman Richard Trevithick builds first railway locomotive.

1825 First public railway from Stockton to Darlington, England.

1828 Development of hot-blast smelting furnace, England.

1842 Mines Act, Britain, bans women and children from working underground.

1851 Great Exhibition, London, displays new industrial products and techniques.

1855 Bessemer converter developed in England. Changes pig iron into steel.

1870 Industrialization established in Britain, Germany, and United States.

MILLS
The first factories were water-driven cotton mills which produced cloth. They were noisy, dangerous places to work in. Mill owners employed many women and children because they could pay them lower wages than men.

STEAM HAMMER
Unlike humans, steam-powered machines could work tirelessly, turning out vast quantities of goods. This steam hammer, invented in 1839, could hammer iron forgings with tremendous power and great accuracy.

The Clifton suspension bridge, Avon

BRUNEL
Isambard Kingdom Brunel (1806-59) was probably the greatest engineer of the Industrial Revolution. His most famous bridge was the Clifton suspension bridge across the Avon Gorge. He also designed and built the Great Western Railway and the *Great Britain*, which was the first large steamship with an iron hull and a screw propeller.

CO-OPS AND UNIONS
Working people fought to improve their conditions. Some set up labour unions to fight for shorter hours and better pay. Others created co-op stores to provide wholesome food at reasonable prices. These stores later grew into a co-operative movement.

Find out more
FARMING
SCIENCE
SCIENCE, HISTORY OF
TRADE AND INDUSTRY
VICTORIANS

INFORMATION TECHNOLOGY

THE TERM "INFORMATION TECHNOLOGY", or IT for short, is used to describe technologies that handle, store, process, and transmit, or pass on, information. When people talk about IT, they usually mean the use of computers to store and pass on information, but radio, television, telephones, fax machines, and DVDs are also examples of information technology. Information technology in some form has existed since humans developed pictures and writing, while later inventions such as printing made information more widely available. But modern information technology is based on electronics; vast amounts of information, including pictures and sounds, can be stored as electric signals and transmitted anywhere in the world. Information technology is used in every part of our lives from schools and hospitals, to shopping. Its impact has been enormous, making the world truly a "global village".

An early dial telephone

Camera

EARLY IT
The telephone and the camera were the information technology tools of the 19th century. They had a great impact on society. With the telephone, people could talk to each other all around the world. Using the camera, they could make a record of their lives and families.

USING INFORMATION TECHNOLOGY
To use information technology, you need access to hardware and software. Hardware means the actual machinery, namely computers. Software refers to the programs or applications inside the computer, which actually run it. Programs range from word processing to multimedia and games. They are constantly being updated.

Touching this icon produces information as a piece of sound.

This icon takes the user to other similar pages of information.

MULTIMEDIA
Most computers take Digital Versatile Discs (DVDs), which can give information in multimedia form – words, pictures, and sounds. Multimedia programs are a good way to learn, because they give information in an interesting way and allow you to see how things work. Using the computer mouse, you can move from one bit of information to another.

DESKTOP PUBLISHING
Software programs known as desktop publishing (DTP) enable words and pictures to be moved around on screen. DTP is used in publishing, but it also means people can write and design fan magazines, posters, and newsletters in their own homes.

SPREADSHEETS
Some computers contain software programs called spreadsheets. A spreadsheet program stores figures or other information that needs to be shown in the form of tables or charts. The program can do calcuations, such as adding up, or working out percentages. Spreadsheets have many uses, including working out accounts or progress charts.

EARLY ELECTRONICS
The use of electronics in information technology has a long history. Materials and designs used for early technology may look dated, but the early inventions served the same purpose as today's modern examples.

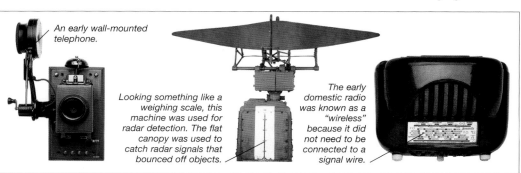

An early wall-mounted telephone.

Looking something like a weighing scale, this machine was used for radar detection. The flat canopy was used to catch radar signals that bounced off objects.

The early domestic radio was known as a "wireless" because it did not need to be connected to a signal wire.

OFFICE COMMUNICATION

In the early 20th century, a new kind of work place came into being – the office. Early offices contained manual typewriters and telephones. These were followed by machines powered by electricity, such as electric typewriters and photocopiers. Today, the modern office is totally computerized, and relies completely on information technology, from computers and e-mail to fax machines and picture scanners.

TRANSPORT
Information technology is important in transport, and is used to control airplanes, large ships, and even some cars. The cockpit of an aircraft in particular has become very sophisticated. The information supplied by the technology to the pilots is so accurate that pilots do not need to look out of the aircraft to fly safely, but can rely on the technology.

On-line shoppers can browse through pictures of items for sale displayed in virtual shops.

HOSPITALS
Information technology is very useful in hospitals, and medicine generally, and it is now possible to diagnose and treat many illnesses without physically looking inside the body. Scanning devices enable a doctor to monitor the development of an unborn baby on screen, checking on progress and identifying any problems at an early stage.

By using the image displayed on a monitor screen, the doctor can show a woman how her baby is developing inside her.

ON-LINE SHOPPING
E-commerce – buying and selling over the Internet – developed in the 1990s, and now many people shop on-line. To do so, you must pay with a debit or credit card. Fraud is a risk, but special programs keep credit card numbers safe.

The scanning device is held in the doctor's hand and moved over the woman's stomach, where it collects information that is shown on screen.

DISABILITY
Information technology has brought major advantages for people with disability. This is because the technology can be designed to make the most of each person's physical abilities. For example, word-activated processors are available for blind people, who can both receive and send sound messages. People with physical disabilities can communicate via e-mail, or access information through the Internet, without leaving home.

Find out more
COMPUTERS
ELECTRONICS
INTERNET
TECHNOLOGY

INSECTS

THE EARTH IS CRAWLING with insects; in fact, they make up the largest group of animals. There are at least one million different species, including beetles, butterflies, ants, and bees. Insects first appeared on Earth more than 500 million years ago and are found in almost every kind of habitat, from cold mountains to tropical rain forests. Although all insects have six legs and a body covered by a hard exoskeleton (outer skeleton), they vary enormously in size and shape. The goliath beetle weighs more than 100 g (3.5 oz); the tiny fairyfly is almost invisible to the human eye. Some insects cause problems for humans. Flies spread disease, and weevils and locusts eat farm crops. Parasites such as ticks and lice live and feed on farm animals and sometimes on humans, too. But insects are a vital part of nature. They pollinate flowers and other crops and are an important source of food for many birds, bats, and reptiles. Certain insects are also very useful to humans – without bees, for example, there would be no honey.

Tube-like casing of leg

Casing is thin and flexible at leg joint.

Leg joint

Seta (touch-sensitive hair)

Segment of abdomen

Thorax

Head

Wing

Eye

Back leg

Middle leg

Front leg

Antenna (feeler)

Claw

COCKROACH

A typical insect such as the common cockroach above has a body in three main parts. At the front is the head, which encloses the brain and bears the antennae, mouthparts, and eyes. In the middle is the thorax, where the six legs join. At the rear is the abdomen, which contains the digestive, reproductive, and sex organs. The hard, outer skeleton is made mainly of a substance called chitin.

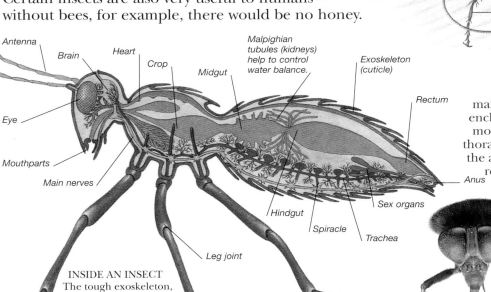

Antenna

Brain

Heart

Crop

Midgut

Malpighian tubules (kidneys) help to control water balance.

Exoskeleton (cuticle)

Rectum

Eye

Mouthparts

Main nerves

Hindgut

Spiracle

Trachea

Sex organs

Anus

Leg joint

INSIDE AN INSECT
The tough exoskeleton, or cuticle, surrounds and protects the soft internal organs. An insect breathes through tiny air tubes called tracheae, which form a network inside its body. The tubes open at holes called spiracles in the cuticle. Water-dwelling insects such as the grubs of pond beetles breathe through gills, which are formed from delicate folds of cuticle.

COMPOUND EYE
An insect's eye is made up of many rod-shaped units called ommatidia. The eye of a housefly has about 4,000 ommatidia. Each single ommatidium detects the amount and colour of light entering the eye, but it cannot form an image by itself. Together, all the thousands of ommatidia in the eye produce a mosaic-like view of the outside world made up of light and dark patches.

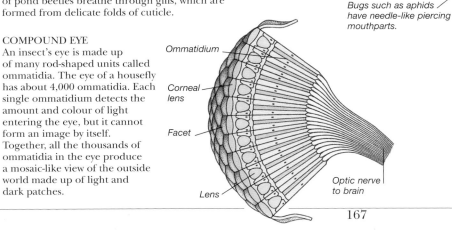

Ommatidium

Corneal lens

Facet

Optic nerve to brain

Lens

Bugs such as aphids have needle-like piercing mouthparts.

Housefly sucks up liquid food through its padded, sponge-like mouthparts.

Butterfly's tubular mouthparts work like a drinking straw.

FEEDING
Insects feed on almost anything – wood, blood, nectar, paper, shoe polish, seaweed, and other insects. The mouthparts of most insects, however, are specialized for eating a particular kind of food. Some mouthparts are adapted to bite, others to pierce, suck, sponge, scrape, and probe. The mouthparts have four main structures. The mandibles are hard jaws that bite and chew; the maxillae are secondary jaws; the labrum and labium are the upper and lower lips.

COURTSHIP

Some insects, such as the praying mantises shown here, have complicated courtship behaviour. After mating, the female mantis often grasps and eats the male mantis; the nutrients in the body of the male help the eggs to develop.

The praying mantis is the only insect that can turn its head to look directly behind.

ANTENNAE

Sense organs called antennae detect smells and vibrations in the air and in solid objects. Often, the male has larger, more branched antennae than the female. These help detect the scent that she releases into the air at mating time. Near the antennae there are often several tiny single-lens eyes called ocelli.

Indian beetle has antler-like antennae.

Weevil has elbow-jointed antennae.

METAMORPHOSIS

Most insects hatch from eggs. Some insects, such as the butterfly, hatch into a larva or caterpillar, which feeds voraciously and moults (sheds its skin) several times. It then forms a chrysalis and pupates, finally emerging as a mature adult butterfly. These great changes in form are known as complete metamorphosis. Other insects, such as grasshoppers, hatch into nymphs, which look like small versions of the parent but without proper wings. They moult in order to grow and finally become adult after the final moult when they have wings. This is called incomplete metamorphosis.

Female damselfly lays eggs on stem of reed.

Emerging nymph climbs up reed stem.

Adult emerges from nymph skin.

Young nymph (larva)

Older nymph (larva) develops wings.

LIFE CYCLE

A damselfly begins life as an egg in a pond or a stream. It passes through ten or more moults, taking up to two years altogether, before changing into an adult.

TYPES OF INSECTS

There are about 20 main groups of insects. Beetles and weevils form the largest single group of insects, which contains more than 350,000 species known to entomologists (scientists who study insects). Most insects have wings at some stage during their life cycle; bristletails, silverfish, and firebrats do not. Fleas are also wingless; their wings have disappeared during the course of evolution.

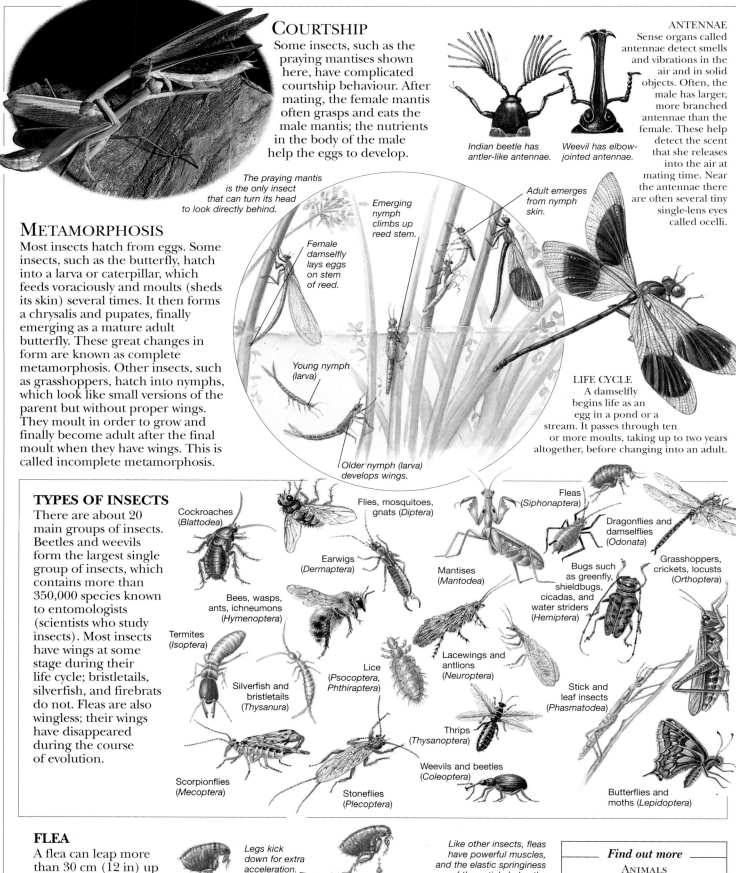

Cockroaches (*Blattodea*)

Flies, mosquitoes, gnats (*Diptera*)

Fleas (*Siphonaptera*)

Earwigs (*Dermaptera*)

Dragonflies and damselflies (*Odonata*)

Bees, wasps, ants, ichneumons (*Hymenoptera*)

Mantises (*Mantodea*)

Bugs such as greenfly, shieldbugs, cicadas, and water striders (*Hemiptera*)

Grasshoppers, crickets, locusts (*Orthoptera*)

Termites (*Isoptera*)

Silverfish and bristletails (*Thysanura*)

Lice (*Psocoptera, Phthiraptera*)

Lacewings and antlions (*Neuroptera*)

Stick and leaf insects (*Phasmatodea*)

Thrips (*Thysanoptera*)

Scorpionflies (*Mecoptera*)

Stoneflies (*Plecoptera*)

Weevils and beetles (*Coleoptera*)

Butterflies and moths (*Lepidoptera*)

FLEA

A flea can leap more than 30 cm (12 in) up into the air, which is similar to a person jumping 245 m (800 ft), or a 70-storey building, or St. Paul's Cathedral in London, England.

Legs kick down for extra acceleration.

Like other insects, fleas have powerful muscles, and the elastic springiness of the cuticle helps the legs to rebound quickly during movement.

St. Paul's Cathedral

Find out more

ANIMALS
ECOLOGY AND FOOD WEBS
EVOLUTION
FLOWERS AND HERBS
FOREST WILDLIFE
SPIDERS AND SCORPIONS

INTERNET

THE INTERNET IS A WAY for computers around the world to swap information. It started as a US military research project in 1969, but was opened to the public in 1988. At first, the Internet just carried email and simple data files. In the early 1990s the invention of the World Wide Web brought the Internet to the world's attention. It gave anyone an easy way to access information across the Internet. Today, words, pictures, music, videos, and any other type of data can be passed across the Internet almost instantly. This has changed the way we live and it is estimated that more than a quarter of the world's population now has Internet access.

A page from the Dorling Kindersley website.

This diagram is a representation of a tiny section of the Internet. Each small straight line is a connection between two computers.

HOW THE INTERNET WORKS

Computers can exchange information with nearby computers over connections called networks. The Internet (short for Inter-network) connects together separate networks, enabling computers all over the world to swap data. To send a data file, such as an MP3 music file, to a particular computer, the file is broken into chunks that are passed between these computers until they reach their destination. Computers usually swap data through wires as electrical signals, or fibre optic cables as pulses of light.

WORLD WIDE WEB
The World Wide Web (WWW, or "web") is a standard way of making information available over the Internet. When a user accesses information on the web, their computer requests data files, called web pages, from other computers on the Internet, called servers. On the user's computer, a program called a web browser displays the words and pictures from the web page on the screen. Web pages include links that, when clicked, access related pages. Search engines are programs that help users find useful pages. The user chooses words to search for – called search terms – and a special server creates a clickable list of relevant pages.

This transmitter/receiver is knowns as a "dongle" and connects a computer to the Internet using a mobile phone network.

Many mobile phones can now connect to the Internet. This Blackberry enables users to email while on the move.

CONNECTING TO THE INTERNET
A device called a modem, shown below, is required to translate messages into electronic data that can be sent from one computer to another and displayed on screen. To use the Internet from home, the user normally connects to a computer at an Internet Service Provider (ISP), a company that offers Internet connections for a small fee. A telephone network is used to connect to an ISP. For people on the move, mobile devices can connect to the Internet without using any wires by using a radio link, such as a mobile phone network.

A modem is used to connect a computer to the Internet via a telephone line.

USES FOR THE INTERNET
The ability to find information via the World Wide Web is just one of many uses for the Internet. Text messages can be swapped between messenger programs enabling real-time chat. Music and video can be compressed into manageable amounts of data so radio and television can be sent over the Internet. Video-phone calls, as shown, are also increasingly popular. Exchanging computer game data allows players across the the world to compete with one another.

Find out more
COMPUTERS
INFORMATION TECHNOLOGY
SATELLITES
TELEPHONES

IRELAND

OFF THE NORTHWEST COAST of Europe lies one of the most beautiful islands in the world. For centuries, writers and singers have praised the lush countryside and wild mountains of Ireland. Despite its beauty, Ireland is not a rich country and has few natural resources. It has no coal, no iron ore or vast reserves of oil. Nevertheless, Ireland's influence has been far-reaching, for the country is rich in its people and their distinctive Gaelic culture. Few corners of the world lack an Irish community whose members keep alive the memory and customs of their homeland. In 1973, Ireland (Eire) joined the European Economic Community (now the European Union). Until then, its powerful neighbour and former ruler, the United Kingdom, had always dominated the country's economy. As a member of the Union, Eire has become more prosperous and economically independent of the United Kingdom. New high-tech industries are replacing traditional agriculture and textiles as the main sources of employment.

Ireland is the smaller of the two main British Isles. The other – Britain – is to the east, and the Atlantic Ocean is to the west. Ireland is divided into Ireland (Eire), which is independent, and the province of Northern Ireland, which is part of the United Kingdom.

Blocks of peat – carbon-rich soil consisting of decomposed plant life – are dug up from the marshy countryside and left to dry before being used as fuel.

DUBLIN

The capital city of Ireland is Dublin. It lies on the Liffey river not far from the Irish Sea. The Vikings founded Dublin in the 9th century, and the city has many historic buildings and beautiful town squares.

COUNTRYSIDE

Wet west winds blow across Ireland from the Atlantic Ocean, soaking parts of the country with more than 200 cm (80 in) of rain each year. This makes the farmland very productive; about 16 per cent of the people work in farming and food processing industries.

GEOGRAPHY
Mountains to the south, west, and north surround Ireland's large, central plain. The plain is marshy in places, and there are many lakes, called loughs. Lough Neagh (right) in Northern Ireland, the biggest lake in the British Isles, is famous for its wildfowl and salmon.

The Ha'penny Bridge, which spans the Liffey river, is accepted as the symbol of Dublin. Opened in 1816, its name comes from the fee once charged to use it.

MUSIC

Ireland has a strong musical tradition. Irish rock and classical artists are well known internationally. The Corrs, U2, and Boyzone are all very successful Irish bands. Traditional Irish music and dancing is also very important to Ireland's cultural heritage.

INDUSTRY
Once renowned for its traditional industries of glass, lace, and linen, Ireland now also produces medicine, electronics, and other modern goods. Many people work in the tourism industry.

Pipes, fiddles, and banjos are all used in traditional Irish music.

Find out more
CELTS
EUROPE
TRADE AND INDUSTRY
UNITED KINGDOM
UNITED KINGDOM, HISTORY OF
VIKINGS

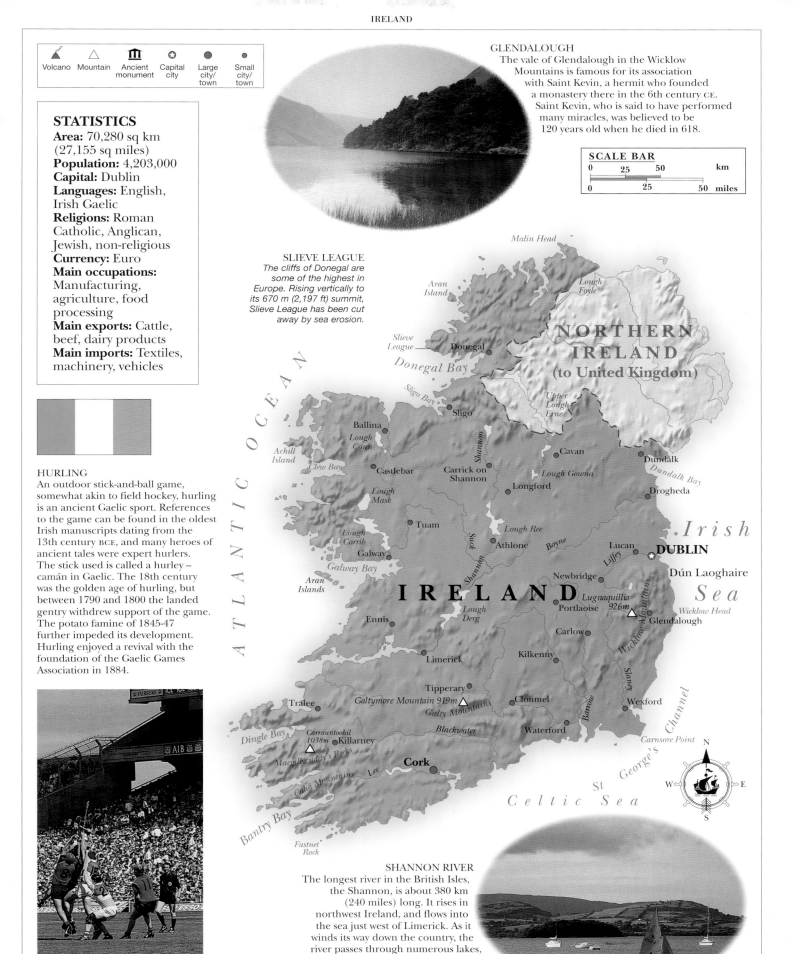

Volcano △ **Mountain** 🏛 **Ancient monument** ✪ **Capital city** ● **Large city/ town** ● **Small city/ town**

STATISTICS
Area: 70,280 sq km
(27,155 sq miles)
Population: 4,203,000
Capital: Dublin
Languages: English,
Irish Gaelic
Religions: Roman
Catholic, Anglican,
Jewish, non-religious
Currency: Euro
Main occupations:
Manufacturing,
agriculture, food
processing
Main exports: Cattle,
beef, dairy products
Main imports: Textiles,
machinery, vehicles

HURLING
An outdoor stick-and-ball game,
somewhat akin to field hockey, hurling
is an ancient Gaelic sport. References
to the game can be found in the oldest
Irish manuscripts dating from the
13th century BCE, and many heroes of
ancient tales were expert hurlers.
The stick used is called a hurley –
camán in Gaelic. The 18th century
was the golden age of hurling, but
between 1790 and 1800 the landed
gentry withdrew support of the game.
The potato famine of 1845-47
further impeded its development.
Hurling enjoyed a revival with the
foundation of the Gaelic Games
Association in 1884.

GLENDALOUGH
The vale of Glendalough in the Wicklow
Mountains is famous for its association
with Saint Kevin, a hermit who founded
a monastery there in the 6th century CE.
Saint Kevin, who is said to have performed
many miracles, was believed to be
120 years old when he died in 618.

SCALE BAR
0   25   50   km
0   25   50   miles

SLIEVE LEAGUE
*The cliffs of Donegal are
some of the highest in
Europe. Rising vertically to
its 670 m (2,197 ft) summit,
Slieve League has been cut
away by sea erosion.*

SHANNON RIVER
The longest river in the British Isles,
the Shannon, is about 380 km
(240 miles) long. It rises in
northwest Ireland, and flows into
the sea just west of Limerick. As it
winds its way down the country, the
river passes through numerous lakes,
the largest of which is Lough Derg.

IRON AGE

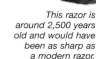

This razor is around 2,500 years old and would have been as sharp as a modern razor.

IRON AGE

4000 BCE First iron objects, made from meteoric iron, appear in the Middle East.

c. 1500 BCE People in the Middle East find out how to extract (smelt) iron from iron ore and how to work it by heating and hammering (wrought iron). The Hittites dominate the trade.

1000 BCE Iron Age begins in the Middle East and Greece. Iron-working also develops in India.

c. 800 BCE Use of iron spreads across Europe. Celts become expert workers in iron.

c. 400 BCE Chinese discover how to make cast-iron objects by melting iron ore and pouring it into moulds.

1760 CE Industrial revolution leads to a renewed use of iron. Also leads to great advances in ironworking techniques.

IN SEVERAL EARLY LANGUAGES the word for iron meant "metal from the sky". This was probably because the first iron used to make tools and weapons came from meteorites which fell to Earth from space. Ironworking probably began in the Middle East some 6,000 years ago. At first, people hammered iron while it was cold. Later they learned how to smelt iron – heat the iron ore so they could extract the iron and work with it properly. Unlike bronze, which early people also used, iron did not melt. Instead it was reduced to a spongy mass which people hammered and reheated until it was the right shape. Special furnaces were needed to reach the right temperature. The Hittites, who lived in what is now Turkey, were the first people we know of who traded in iron. But it was not until around 1000 BCE that knowledge of smelting spread and the Iron Age truly began. In western Europe, the Celts were one of the first peoples to make and use iron.

HILL FORT
The Celts fortified hill tops with ditches and ramparts. These forts were places of refuge in wartime; they were also administrative and trading centres, and enclosures for livestock.

IRONWORKING
Early furnaces were shallow stone hearths which people filled with iron ore and charcoal. Bellows helped raise the temperature to about 1,200°C (2,192°F), hot enough to make the iron workable. The Celts used deeper furnaces in which the iron collected at the bottom and impurities, called slag, gathered at the top.

Iron horseshoe

Heating iron ore in a furnace

Hammering the iron into shape

Iron pin

Spring

Brooch made of glass discs

CLOTHING
The Celts loved decoration. Celtic clothes were woollen, often with checked patterns. Richer men and women wore heavy twisted neckbands called torcs in gold or bronze, and cloaks fastened with ornate brooches.

TOOLS
People made useful tools from iron such as a saw with a serrated edge (far left) and tongs (left); the tongs were used to hold metal while beating it into shape.

WEAPONS
Iron weapons were greatly superior to bronze ones. They had much sharper edges and, thus, were more effective. This dagger has a handle shaped like a human figure.

Find out more
BRONZE AGE
CELTS
INDUSTRIAL REVOLUTION
METALS

LAKE AND RIVER WILDLIFE

THE WATER IN LAKES and rivers is teeming with all kinds of life. Grasses, reeds, and other plants grow along the water's edge, providing food and shelter for insects, nesting birds, and mammals such as water voles and muskrats. In rivers, the fast-flowing water sweeps away plants, but in lakes, tiny floating plants are food for small creatures such as water fleas and shrimps, which are in turn eaten by bigger fish. Larger floating waterweeds provide shade for basking fish. Fallen leaves, animal droppings, and rotting plant matter form a rich mud at the bottom of rivers and lakes, where worms, snails, and other small organisms live. Today, many lakes and rivers are suffering from serious pollution. Industrial chemicals, farm fertilizers, untreated sewage, and a host of other damaging substances discharged into lakes and rivers have upset or destroyed the natural wildlife balance.

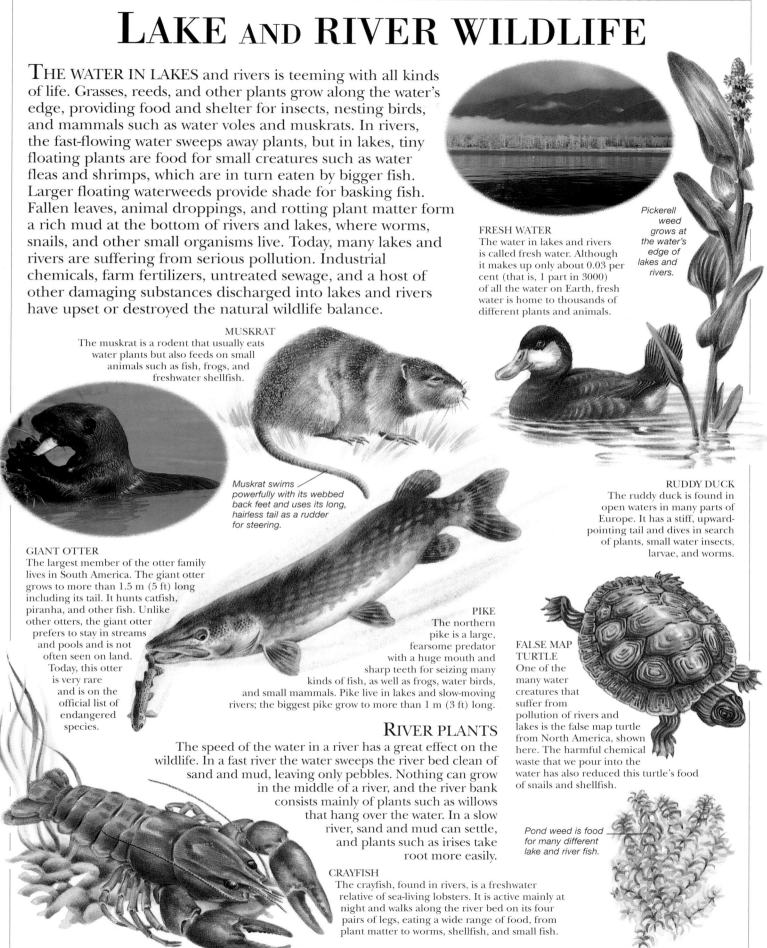

FRESH WATER
The water in lakes and rivers is called fresh water. Although it makes up only about 0.03 per cent (that is, 1 part in 3000) of all the water on Earth, fresh water is home to thousands of different plants and animals.

Pickerell weed grows at the water's edge of lakes and rivers.

MUSKRAT
The muskrat is a rodent that usually eats water plants but also feeds on small animals such as fish, frogs, and freshwater shellfish.

Muskrat swims powerfully with its webbed back feet and uses its long, hairless tail as a rudder for steering.

RUDDY DUCK
The ruddy duck is found in open waters in many parts of Europe. It has a stiff, upward-pointing tail and dives in search of plants, small water insects, larvae, and worms.

GIANT OTTER
The largest member of the otter family lives in South America. The giant otter grows to more than 1.5 m (5 ft) long including its tail. It hunts catfish, piranha, and other fish. Unlike other otters, the giant otter prefers to stay in streams and pools and is not often seen on land. Today, this otter is very rare and is on the official list of endangered species.

PIKE
The northern pike is a large, fearsome predator with a huge mouth and sharp teeth for seizing many kinds of fish, as well as frogs, water birds, and small mammals. Pike live in lakes and slow-moving rivers; the biggest pike grow to more than 1 m (3 ft) long.

FALSE MAP TURTLE
One of the many water creatures that suffer from pollution of rivers and lakes is the false map turtle from North America, shown here. The harmful chemical waste that we pour into the water has also reduced this turtle's food of snails and shellfish.

RIVER PLANTS
The speed of the water in a river has a great effect on the wildlife. In a fast river the water sweeps the river bed clean of sand and mud, leaving only pebbles. Nothing can grow in the middle of a river, and the river bank consists mainly of plants such as willows that hang over the water. In a slow river, sand and mud can settle, and plants such as irises take root more easily.

Pond weed is food for many different lake and river fish.

CRAYFISH
The crayfish, found in rivers, is a freshwater relative of sea-living lobsters. It is active mainly at night and walks along the river bed on its four pairs of legs, eating a wide range of food, from plant matter to worms, shellfish, and small fish.

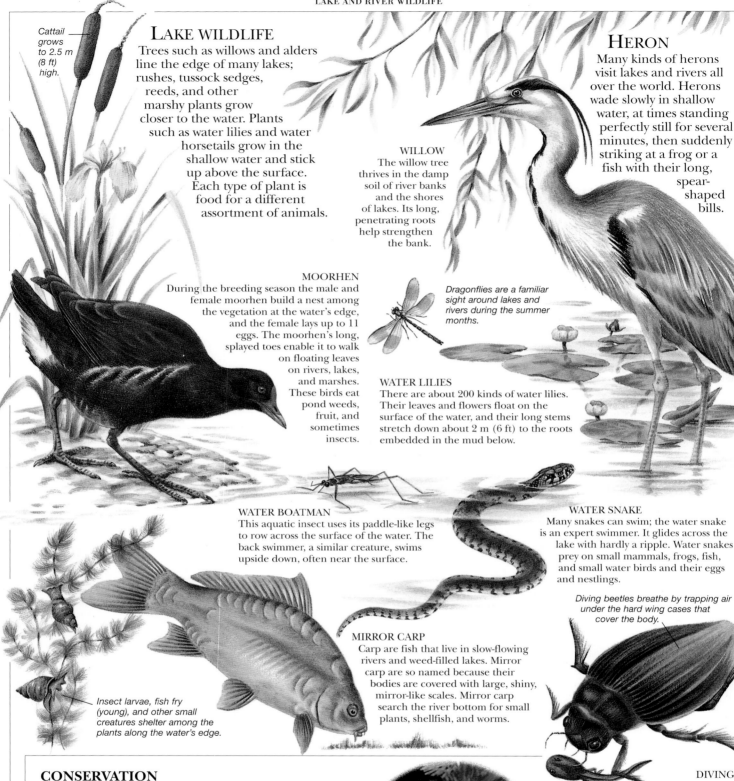

Cattail grows to 2.5 m (8 ft) high.

LAKE WILDLIFE
Trees such as willows and alders line the edge of many lakes; rushes, tussock sedges, reeds, and other marshy plants grow closer to the water. Plants such as water lilies and water horsetails grow in the shallow water and stick up above the surface. Each type of plant is food for a different assortment of animals.

WILLOW
The willow tree thrives in the damp soil of river banks and the shores of lakes. Its long, penetrating roots help strengthen the bank.

HERON
Many kinds of herons visit lakes and rivers all over the world. Herons wade slowly in shallow water, at times standing perfectly still for several minutes, then suddenly striking at a frog or a fish with their long, spear-shaped bills.

MOORHEN
During the breeding season the male and female moorhen build a nest among the vegetation at the water's edge, and the female lays up to 11 eggs. The moorhen's long, splayed toes enable it to walk on floating leaves on rivers, lakes, and marshes. These birds eat pond weeds, fruit, and sometimes insects.

Dragonflies are a familiar sight around lakes and rivers during the summer months.

WATER LILIES
There are about 200 kinds of water lilies. Their leaves and flowers float on the surface of the water, and their long stems stretch down about 2 m (6 ft) to the roots embedded in the mud below.

WATER BOATMAN
This aquatic insect uses its paddle-like legs to row across the surface of the water. The back swimmer, a similar creature, swims upside down, often near the surface.

WATER SNAKE
Many snakes can swim; the water snake is an expert swimmer. It glides across the lake with hardly a ripple. Water snakes prey on small mammals, frogs, fish, and small water birds and their eggs and nestlings.

Diving beetles breathe by trapping air under the hard wing cases that cover the body.

Insect larvae, fish fry (young), and other small creatures shelter among the plants along the water's edge.

MIRROR CARP
Carp are fish that live in slow-flowing rivers and weed-filled lakes. Mirror carp are so named because their bodies are covered with large, shiny, mirror-like scales. Mirror carp search the river bottom for small plants, shellfish, and worms.

DIVING BEETLE
The diving beetle is a fierce predator. It hunts tadpoles, small fish, aquatic worms, and insects.

CONSERVATION
The axolotl shown here is a kind of Mexican salamander. It cannot survive on land and is found only in lakes such as Lake Xochimilco, Mexico. Like many other lake and river creatures, the axolotl is threatened by pollution. Thousands of lakes in the world are now lifeless, because of the damaging substances that flow into them. Today, many lakes and rivers are being turned into nature reserves in order to protect the birds, fish, mammals, and other wildlife they contain.

Axolotl means "water beast".

Find out more

ANIMALS
BIRDS
FISH
MAMMALS
SNAKES

LANGUAGES

OUR ABILITY TO TALK is one of the skills that makes humans different from the rest of the animal world. Although some animals communicate with gestures, such as mating displays, human speech is much more highly developed. In English, for example, most people use a vocabulary (a list of words) of about 5,000 words in talking, and 10,000 in writing. A language is a way of organizing spoken sounds to express ideas. Human language developed over thousands of years, and people in different countries use different languages. Some languages share words with the languages of nearby countries. For instance, book is *libro* in both Italian and Spanish, and *livre* in French; in English we get the word library from the same source. There are now some 5,000 different languages and many dialects – local versions of major languages.

TOWER OF BABEL
At the beginning of this Bible story, everyone spoke the same language. But when people tried to build a tower to reach heaven, God became angry. He made many languages so people could not understand and help one another.

English is now spoken worldwide by more than a billion people, many as a second or third language.

More than a half of China's 1.3 billion population speak Mandarin Chinese.

France once ruled many countries in West Africa, and people there still speak French as well as their local languages.

There are at least 845 languages in India. Hindi and English are the official languages.

Some people have no difficulty in learning foreign languages and can speak several fluently; the record is about 28.

There are about 700 languages in Papua New Guinea.

LATIN
For many centuries, educated people of many nationalities spoke Latin as well as their native, or first, language. Throughout Europe, scholars, governments, and the Christian Church used Latin.

COMMON LANGUAGES

A map of national languages shows how European nations have spread around the world: for example, English settlers took their language to the United States, Canada, Australia, and New Zealand. Spain conquered much of South America, and Spanish is still spoken there. But many people using these languages also have their own local language, which is part of their native culture.

- Mandarin Chinese
- English
- Russian
- Spanish
- French
- Portuguese
- Arabic
- Other

SIGN LANGUAGE
Human speech and hearing make language possible. People who have difficulty speaking or hearing cannot use a spoken language. Instead, they communicate using hand signals. There are signs and gestures for all the common words, and signs for individual letters.

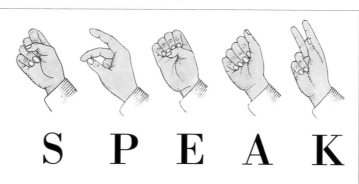

S P E A K

Find out more
ALPHABETS
FILM

LAW

EVERY SOCIETY HAS its own set of laws to safeguard the rights of its citizens and to balance individual freedom against the needs of the people in general. On the simplest level, there are laws to protect citizens from attack or robbery as they walk along the street. These and other similar rules are called criminal laws. However, the law does much more than provide simple protection. It also settles arguments between individuals. For example, if you believe that you have bought damaged goods, and the person who sold them disagrees, the law must decide who is right. The branch of law that deals with arguments such as these is called civil law. The law is very complex because it must meet the different needs and expectations of society's millions of members. It includes not only civil and criminal branches, but also other smaller divisions, such as family law, which settles arguments when people divorce. Understanding the law takes a long time; lawyers, who apply and interpret the law, study for many years. Most lawyers specialize in just one area of the law.

JUDGES
The judge helps the jury understand the laws relating to the trial, and passes sentence (decides the punishment) if there is a guilty verdict.

Witness answers questions

Jury of 12 people

Defence lawyer addresses the jury.

Defence tries to convince the jury that the prisoner is not guilty.

Prosecution tries to prove guilt.

FAIR AND JUST LAW
A statue representing justice wears a blindfold to show that the law does not favour any one person. However, not all law is good law, for governments can make laws that remove freedoms as well as ones that safeguard them. The scales show that justice weighs opposing evidence in the same way that a balance weighs goods. The sword represents punishment.

DEATH PENALTY
In past centuries a serious crime was punishable by death and, until the mid-19th century, hangings were public. Some countries still apply the death penalty, and in Europe people were executed for murder up to the mid-20th century.

JURY TRIAL
A person accused of a serious crime has the right to a trial by jury, a group of men and women (usually 12) chosen at random from the community. A prosecuting lawyer tries to convince the jury that the defendant – the accused person – is guilty. A defence lawyer sets out to prove the defendant's innocence. Witnesses tell the court what they know about the crime. The jury listens to the facts, or evidence, and decides whether the prosecution has proved guilt.

WORLD LAW
International problems call for worldwide co-operation. Air disasters, for example, may involve companies and individuals from many countries. Lawyers must agree on ways of establishing liability (blame) and compensating people for loss. Many countries share extradition treaties, so that criminals such as terrorists can be sent home for trial if they are caught elsewhere.

Passengers from many countries

Aeroplane made in the United States.

Accident happens over Spain.

ALTERNATIVES TO PRISON
Electronic tags locked to the ankles of criminals keep them at home and out of trouble. A box placed next to the offender's telephone monitors the range of the tag. If the wearer of the tag moves too far away, the box dials up a police central computer and sounds the alarm.

Offenders learn useful skills by following a schedule of duties such as working in the kitchen.

PRISON AND PUNISHMENT
People found guilty of serious crimes usually go to prison. This is to deter them from criminal activity in future and to protect others from danger for the term of their sentence. Prisons also aim to reform offenders – for example by teaching skills to improve their employment prospects on release.

TRIAL BY ORDEAL
In medieval England, justice was often barbaric. People accused of a crime had to prove they were innocent by undergoing an ordeal. They chose between a challenge, such as carrying a red-hot stone, or fighting their accuser. If they survived the ordeal, they were believed to be innocent.

COURTS
The Old Bailey, in London, houses the Central Criminal Court. There are many types of law court. In England and Wales these include crown and magistrate's courts, which handle criminal cases, and county courts for civil or non-criminal cases. The Scottish system differs, and includes district and sheriff courts.

Law Lords and clerks entering the High Court

BARRISTER AND SOLICITOR
There are two types of lawyer in Britain: barristers and solicitors. Barristers are trained to argue cases in court. Solicitors prepare cases that barristers present, and do legal work outside the courtroom.

The Law Courts, London

NON-CRIMINAL LAW
Most lawyers spend time dealing with non-criminal law, also known as civil law. This is concerned with rights and duties between citizens. It includes contract law, which is concerned with trade and other agreements between people, property law, and matters such as wills and divorce.

ADVERSARIAL SYSTEM
The British legal system is known as adversarial, because there are two sides, who argue to convince a jury that they are right. The side that brings a case to court is known as the prosecution, and the side that defends a charge in court is known as the defence. In civil cases, the prosecution is often known as "the plaintiff".

LAWS
In Britain, parliament makes laws. The courts then follow the law, but lawyers can appeal through the court system to try and change the law if it is unfair. The final decision is made by the Law Lords who sit in the House of Lords. British law is based on common law, which dates back to the Anglo-Saxons. Court decisions are based on precedent – previous decisions made on similar court cases.

Find out more
ANGLO-SAXONS
GOVERNMENT AND POLITICS
MEDIEVAL EUROPE

LEONARDO DA VINCI

A HIGHLY TALENTED ARTIST and scientist, Leonardo da Vinci was years ahead of his time. He was one of the greatest figures in the movement called the Renaissance, the revival of art and learning that began in Italy in the 15th century. Today, many people remember Leonardo for painting some of the most famous pictures of his time, but he achieved a great deal more than this. He designed castles and weaponry, invented machines, studied physics and mathematics, and made accurate scientific drawings of plants, animals, and the human body. He was probably one of the world's greatest all-round geniuses.

1452 Born near the village of Vinci, in Italy.

1466 Moves to Florence; works in studio of the artist Verrochio.

1482 Works as architect, engineer, and painter in Milan, in northern Italy.

1503 Begins *Mona Lisa.*

1503 Designs famous flying machine.

1513 Makes pioneering study of lenses and optics.

1515 Studies anatomy.

1516 Dies in France.

MONA LISA
Leonardo's best-known portrait is of Mona Lisa, the wife of a rich Florentine. The painting is famous for Mona Lisa's haunting smile, and for the softly blended colours, an effect known as *sfumato.* The painting is in the Louvre gallery in Paris.

MACHINERY

Leonardo's notebooks are crammed with designs for ingenious machines. Some of these devices, such as a pump, an armoured car, and a machine for grinding lenses, could actually have been built and used. Others, like his famous "ornithopter" flying machine with its flapping wings, would never have worked, but they were still ahead of their time.

RENAISSANCE MAN

In Leonardo's time, it was still possible for a person to become skilled in many different branches of learning – such a person was called a "Renaissance man". Leonardo produced new ideas in practically every area he studied. He wrote down many of these ideas in a series of beautifully illustrated notebooks.

ARCHITECTURE
Buildings and town planning fascinated Leonardo. He designed an "ideal city" which was never built. The streets of the city were arranged in a grid pattern, like a modern American town. He also designed bathhouses, together with drainage networks and systems for rubbish collecting, which were unknown at the time.

Flying machine

Tank design

ANATOMY
In the 16th century, people knew little about anatomy (the study of the human body and how it works). Leonardo was one of the first to dissect, or cut up, dead bodies and draw them, sketching every muscle and bone in detail. If his drawings had been published, they would have proved helpful to doctors and other scientists.

Find out more
PAINTERS
RENAISSANCE
SCIENCE, HISTORY OF

LIGHT

WITHOUT LIGHT, life on Earth would be impossible. Sunlight provides the energy to make plants grow and keep all living things alive. Light itself is a form of energy which travels as tiny packets of electromagnetic energy called photons. When photons enter our eyes they stimulate special light-sensitive cells so that we can see. Other forms of energy which travel as electromagnetic waves include radio waves, x-rays, and microwaves in microwave ovens. Just as there is a spectrum of colours in light, there is also an electromagnetic spectrum. In fact, light waves are also a type of electromagnetic wave, and the colours in light form a small part of the electromagnetic spectrum. Light waves and all other electromagnetic waves travel at 300,000 km (186,000 miles) per second, which is so fast that they could circle the world almost eight times in a second. Nothing in the universe can travel faster than light.

FLUORESCENT LIGHT
Most modern light bulbs are fluorescent tubes like this one. When an electric current is passed through the gas in the tube, gas atoms emit invisible, ultraviolet light. The ultraviolet light strikes phosphors – chemicals in the tube's lining – and makes them glow with a brilliant white light.

Electrical contact is made when the bulb terminal is screwed into the socket.

The electronics hidden inside the white plastic base control the light.

Inside a glass tube, an electric current flows through a gas (mercury vapour) making it emit invisible ultra-violet (UV) light.

A chemical coating inside the bulb converts the UV light into visible white light.

The explosion of gunpowder inside a firework produces a burst of coloured light.

Nuclear reactions inside the centre of the Sun produce intense heat and light. All stars produce light from nuclear reactions.

BRIGHTNESS OF LIGHT
The further you are from a light, the less bright it will seem. This is because light spreads out in all directions from its source. So when you are far away, the light is spread over a wide area. Many stars, for instance, are much brighter than our Sun, but their light is spread out over so vast an area that by the time it reaches us, the stars do not even seem as bright as a candle.

Some deep-sea fish have luminescent stripes and spots along their bodies that give out light.

Searchlights give out very intense light, often produced by an electric spark between two pieces of carbon.

SOURCES OF LIGHT
Many different objects give off light. The Sun, traditional electric light bulbs, and fireworks are incandescent, which means they glow because they are hot. But not all lights are hot. Chemicals, not heat, produce the glowing spots on the bodies of some deep-sea fish. All cool lights, including fluorescent lights, are called luminescent.

Shine a torch on a wall and watch the pool of light grow larger and dimmer as you move the torch further away.

A candle is a wide source of light, so it produces a fuzzy shadow.

Candles and lanterns give out light.

When things burn they give out light as well as heat.

LIGHT AND SHADOW
Light travels in straight lines, so, in most cases, it cannot go around obstacles in its path. When light rays hit a solid object, some bounce back and some are absorbed by the object, warming it up a little. The area behind receives no light rays and is left in shadow.

Current flowing through metal filament makes it glow white hot.

INCANDESCENT LIGHT BULB
In the middle of an incandescent electric light bulb is a tiny spiral of tungsten wire called the filament. When an electric current is sent through the filament, it warms up so much that it glows white hot. It is the brightly glowing filament that produces light.

Convex mirror produces images smaller than the object.

Concave mirror produces a magnified image.

CONVEX MIRROR

Mirrors that bulge outwards are called convex mirrors. Their curved shape reflects light from a wide angle, giving a much wider view than a regular mirror does. This has the effect of making all objects look small.

PLANE MIRROR

With a plane or flat mirror the reflection is exactly the same size as the object, but left and right are reversed. With both curved and plane mirrors, the reflection appears as though it were behind the mirror.

A flat mirror produces an image the same size as the object.

MIRRORS

Light passes easily through transparent substances such as glass and water, but not through opaque objects such as paper. Most opaque objects have a rough surface which scatters light in all directions. However, a mirror has a smooth surface, so it reflects light in a regular way. When you look at your face in a mirror, the light bounces straight back, producing a sharp image. Most mirrors are made of glass; your face is reflected from a shiny metal coating at the back of the mirror, not from the glass.

CONCAVE MIRROR

A concave mirror, which is curved inwards, forms two kinds of image. If the object is close to the mirror, the reflection is larger than the real thing. If the object is far away, the image formed is small and upside down.

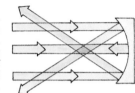

LENSES AND REFRACTION

Glasses, cameras, telescopes, and microscopes use lenses to create particular kinds of images. The lenses in a telescope, for example, produce a magnified view of a distant object. All lenses work on the principle that although light always travels in straight lines, it travels slower through glass than through air. If a light ray strikes glass at an angle, one side of the ray will hit the glass just before the other and will slow down earlier. The effect is to bend the light ray slightly, just as a car pulls to one side if it has a puncture. This bending of light is called refraction.

CONCAVE LENS

A concave lens is thicker at the edges than in the centre, so it spreads light rays out. If you look through a concave lens, everything appears smaller.

Focus

CONVEX LENS

Convex lenses bring light rays together. At the focus, where light rays from a distant object meet, they form an image of the object which can be seen on a screen.

Rays travel in straight lines in cool air

Upside-down image forms

Rays are bent as they pass into hot air

MIRAGE

In the hot desert, weary travellers are often fooled by the sight of an oasis. The oasis appears on the horizon, only to vanish as the travellers hurry towards it. What they have seen is an illusion called a mirage. In the example above, light rays travelling from the palm tree are bent upwards by the warm air. The observer's eyes interpret the light as having travelled in a straight line so he sees a watery reflection of the tree on the ground.

FIBRE OPTICS

Fibre optic cables are channels that carry light. They are flexible so they can carry light around corners. The fibres are long, thin filaments of glass; the light bounces back and forth along the inner surface of the glass. Fibre optics are valuable for seeing into awkward places. Doctors can use fibre optic endoscopes to see inside a patient's body without opening the body up.

Magnifying glasses are convex lenses.

Light refracts when it passes through water, because the water slows it down. This makes objects look as though they are bent.

Find out more

CAMERAS
COLOUR
EYES
PLANTS
SCIENCE, HISTORY OF
SUN
X-RAYS

LIONS
TIGERS, AND OTHER BIG CATS

FEW CREATURES ARE HELD in such awe as lions, tigers, cheetahs, and leopards, which we often call the big cats. These agile predators have strong, razor-sharp teeth and claws, muscular bodies, and excellent senses. Their beautiful striped and spotted fur breaks up their outline and camouflages them, allowing them to ambush unwary zebras, giraffes, and other prey. There are seven kinds of big cats. The tiger is the largest. A fully grown tiger may measure more than 3 m (10 ft) from nose to tail; a fully grown lion is almost as big.

The first large cats lived 45 million years ago. Many, including the lion, cheetah, and leopard, still inhabit parts of Africa. Snow leopards and lions dwell in the mountains and forests of Asia. Jaguars are the largest of the big cats in North and South America. They are equally at home swimming in lakes or climbing trees.

CUBS
Like all young big cats, tiger cubs have pale markings when they are born. After a few months, the pale stripes change to black and orange.

HUNTING PREY
Lions live mainly on savannas (grassy plains) and scrubland, and the females do most of the hunting. This picture shows two adult lionesses charging at a young gazelle, separating it from the rest of the herd.

LION PRIDE
Lions are the only big cats that live in groups, called prides, which may be up to 30 strong. The pride roams over an area of 100 sq km (40 sq miles) or more, depending on the abundance of prey in the area. The large male lions protect the pride's territory against other prides. The lions also defend the females against other males.

SKULL AND TEETH
Lions and other big cats have short, strong skulls with powerful jaws. Their spear-like canine teeth are used to grab hold of the victim's flesh. The large molar teeth cut flesh and gristle as the jaw opens and closes.

Lion has a thick, shaggy mane.

Large, strong canine teeth for tearing prey

The dominant male is the strongest member of the pride. It can measure 2.5 m (8 ft) in length, and 1 m (3 ft) high at the shoulder.

Large feet and sharp claws

CARNIVORES
Lions, tigers, and other big cats are true carnivores (flesh eaters). Lions usually eat large prey such as antelopes and zebras. One giraffe is often enough to feed a whole pride of lions.

CLAWS OUT

When a cat pounces on a victim or climbs up into a tree, it unsheathes its sharp claws. Muscles in the feet pull the claws out and draw back the sheaths.

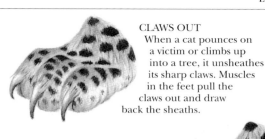

CLAWS IN

Most of the time, a cat's claws are protected in muscular sheaths. This keeps the claws sharp and less likely to break. The claws are extended when the cat cleans its feet.

LEOPARD

The leopard weighs about 60 kg (130 lb), and its body measures about 1.5 m (5 ft). Leopards are adaptable creatures. They can survive in hot tropical forests or on cold mountainsides. They may also live close to towns and villages.

CLIMBING

Leopards are excellent climbers. They sleep, rest, and watch for prey from the branches of trees. They also drag their uneaten food up into a tree to store it and to keep it away from scavengers.

PANTHER

The black panther (right) is a leopard or a jaguar with dark colouring. In daylight, its spots show black in its dark grey-brown fur.

JAGUAR

The jaguar (below) stalks its prey in the same way as the tiger. Jaguars eat a variety of other creatures, including tapirs, fish, frogs, rodents, sloths, and small caimans (South American crocodiles).

ROARING

Only the big cats can roar, and they do so loudly, although the jaguar and snow leopard roar only rarely. The roar is a way of expressing anger, and warns other creatures to keep away.

TIGER

Unlike most cats, the tiger does not mind water. A tiger sometimes pulls its dead prey near the water's edge, because it needs to take frequent drinks during a meal. Tigers stalk their prey through dense undergrowth, then bound over the last 15 m (50 ft) or so, taking their victim by surprise. On average, a tiger consumes about 18 kg (40 lb) of meat a day.

CHEETAH

No animal can outrun a cheetah over a short distance. Cheetahs can speed along at about 100 km/h (60 mph) – as fast as a car. Unlike other cats, the cheetah's claws are always extended, because it has no sheaths to withdraw them into. This gives the cheetah extra grip as it starts its run. If a stalking cheetah is detected before it gets within about 180 m (600 ft) of its prey, it does not make the final dash.

Lions

Tigers

Cheetahs

Leopards

CONSERVATION

Leopards and other big cats have been overhunted for their fur and because they attack livestock and, very rarely, people. The trade in big cats and fur products is now banned by an international agreement. The maps show the main areas of the world where these big cats still live.

Cheetah

Find out more

ANIMALS
CONSERVATION
and endangered species
ECOLOGY AND FOOD WEBS
FOREST WILDLIFE
MAMMALS
MOUNTAIN WILDLIFE
ZOOS

LITERATURE

LITERATURE INCLUDES PLAYS, poems, novels, and short stories. It is writing that carries strong and lasting value through offering the reader important insights into the nature of human emotions. For example, the English playwright William Shakespeare (1564-1616) often based his plays on old or well-known stories, and because Shakespeare was a very skilled writer and had a great understanding of human nature, his plays still excite audiences of all nationalities hundreds of years after they were written. Literature can be powerful, as it can express the writer's thoughts, ideals, and beliefs. Authors, or writers, have often used literature to protest injustice in the world, make a social criticism, and influence the opinions of peoples or governments. For instance, in *The Grapes of Wrath*, American novelist John Steinbeck (1902-68) drew public attention to the suffering of homeless farmers fleeing from Oklahoma to California during the Great Depression of the 1930s.

GULLIVER'S TRAVELS

English author Jonathan Swift (1667-1745) wrote *Gulliver's Travels* in 1726. Although he did not write the book for children, the first two parts have long been popular with young people.

When the people of Lilliput find Gulliver sleeping in their land, they tie him down on the ground so that he cannot move.

The arrogant and petty-minded Lilliputians represent the ruling class of 18th-century England.

PLOT

The collection of events that occur in a work of literature is called the plot. *Gulliver's Travels* tells the story of Lemuel Gulliver, a ship's surgeon. In the first part, Gulliver is shipwrecked in an imaginary land called Lilliput, where the people are only a few centimetres tall. In the second tale, he meets the giants of Brobdingnag. In the third story, Gulliver visits various strange lands. Finally he is marooned among the Houyhnhnms – a race of horses that are wiser and more intelligent than their repulsive human servants, the Yahoos. Rejected by the Houyhnhnms, Gulliver returns to England, where he is no longer able to tolerate the company of other humans.

Gulliver is visited by a Lilliputian noble.

THEME

Writers use their plots and characters to explore key themes such as love, death, morality, and social or political issues. *Gulliver's Travels* seems just an adventure story, but the underlying theme is 18th-century England, where the Lilliputians and other nationalities represent different types of people with their good and bad qualities.

CHARACTERS

An essential part of most literature is the writer's description of the characters – the people who take part in the plot. A writer portrays a character's personality by describing how they react to events in the story. For example, Swift shows that Gulliver is a kindhearted man by describing how he entertains the tiny Lilliputian people: "I would sometimes lie down, and let five or six of them dance on my Hand. And at last the Boys and Girls would venture to come and play at Hide and Seek in my Hair."

ORAL LITERATURE

Long before writing was invented, storytelling, or oral literature, was used to pass on myths and history. The heroine of a traditional Arabic story called *The Thousand and One Nights* is a storyteller named Scheherazade (right). Her cruel husband vows to kill her in the morning, but she charms him with a tale and so delays her death. Each night she tells another story and lives for one more day. After many stories her husband changes his mind and spares Scheherazade's life.

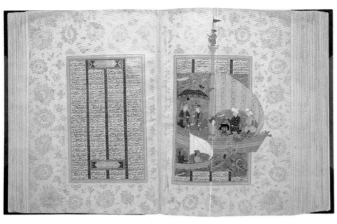

This copy of the Book of Kings *is written in Arabic script.*

EPICS AND SAGAS

Epics and sagas tell of legendary heroes and their deeds. An epic tells the story as a long poem, while a saga is written in prose. The national Persian epic, the *Book of Kings (Shah-nameh)* by Firdausi (c.935-1020), is 1,000 years old, and tells the story of Persian kings and their battles against monsters in mythical times. Other great epics include Homer's *Iliad* and *Odyssey*; Virgil's *Aeneid*; *Beowulf,* a 10th-century epic written in Old English; and John Milton's *Paradise Lost* and *Paradise Regained.*

BIOGRAPHY

A biography is a book that describes a person's life. In an autobiography the author writes of his or her own life. US writer Mark Twain (right) was portrayed in J. Kaplan's biography *Mr. Clemens and Mark Twain* (the title refers to Twain's real name, Samuel Langhorne Clemens).

POETRY

Poetry uses devices, such as rhythm and rhyme, to focus attention on the words. Rhythm is the use of sound patterns, such as repeated accents or beats, to make a line flow. One of the world's greatest poets was the American Walt Whitman (1810-92), whose poems express a great love of his country and its people. His collection of poems *Leaves of Grass* (1855) is considered one of his best works.

NOVELS

A novel is a long fictional (invented) story, written in prose. This form of writing only began in the early 17th century, and has had a dramatic rise in popularity because there are novels to suit all tastes. Some offer insights into everyday life, and some tell of fantastic adventures that keep you turning the pages. American author Louisa May Alcott wrote *Little Women* (1868-69), which tells the story of four sisters and their lives. This remains one of the best-loved children's books ever written. Many successful modern authors are now rewarded with high incomes from sales of their books, as well as from cinema films based on their novels.

Louisa May Alcott

DRAMA

Literature that is written to be performed by actors is called drama. Different countries have their own forms of drama. There is little scenery in Japanese Noh drama (below), which was first performed in the 14th century. The all-male actors use dance, mime, and masks for each performance, which can last for several hours. Noh drama is influenced by the religious beliefs of Buddhism and Shintoism.

Noh actors perform a programme of five plays, based on classical literature, romances, or poetry, accompanied by a chorus with an orchestra of drums and flute.

STORIES

Most stories describe a single incident or events that take place over a short period of time. There are children's stories about every subject ranging from adventures to ghosts. One of the best-known story writers was the Danish author Hans Christian Andersen (1805-75), who wrote tales such as *The Emperor's New Clothes* and *The Ugly Duckling.*

A Hans Christian Andersen story, The Princess and the Pea, *tells how a single pea beneath a heap of mattresses keeps a princess awake all night.*

Find out more

ALPHABETS
DICKENS, CHARLES
FILM
SHAKESPEARE, WILLIAM

LIZARDS

THE LARGEST GROUP of reptiles is the lizard family, with about 3,400 species. Lizards live in almost every habitat except the open sea and the far north. The huge Komodo dragon is the largest, and tiny geckos are the smallest – some are less than 2 cm (1 in) long. A typical lizard such as the iguana has a slim body, a long tail, legs that splay out sideways, and five-toed feet. There are many variations, however; skinks are often extremely long, with short legs. They seem to move effortlessly through loose soil with a wriggling motion. Snake-lizards are even more snake-like, with no front legs and small, paddle-shaped back legs. Several kinds of lizards, including the slow-worm, have lost their limbs during the course of evolution. Like other reptiles, most female lizards lay eggs, which they bury in the soil or hide under rocks until the young hatch.

Lizards can hear through their ear openings.

Green iguana

Long tail for balance

Typical scaly skin like other reptiles, such as snakes and crocodiles

Outstretched claws give extra balance.

CRESTED WATER DRAGON

This lizard is found in Asia and lives mainly in trees that grow close to water. Like most lizards, the water dragon is able to swim. Unlike most other lizards, however, which move on all four legs, the crested water dragon runs on two legs if it is threatened, which gives it more speed on land.

LIZARD TAILS
In the same way that a starfish regrows its arms, a lizard can regrow its tail. When a predator such as a bird or cat grabs a lizard by its tail, the lizard sheds the tail in order to escape. The vertebrae (backbones) along the tail have cracks in them, so the tail breaks off easily. The broken-off part of the tail often twitches for a few minutes, confusing the enemy while the lizard runs away. The tail grows back to its original length in about eight months.

Loose skin around neck looks like a huge collar.

The more the frilled lizard opens its mouth, the more the frill expands.

Tail waves around to frighten enemy.

Tree skink has lost the end of its tail.

Tail has regrown fully within a few months.

Tokay gecko

FRILLED LIZARD

The Australian frilled lizard has a flap of loose skin around its neck which folds flat along the body. The lizard raises the frill to make itself look bigger in order to scare away a predator. It also waves its tail and head around to alarm its enemy, then scuttles away.

TOKAY GECKO
The pads on the feet of the tokay gecko are covered with about one million microscopic hair-like structures which help the gecko grip on to surfaces. The rubber soles of plimsolls and walking boots look like the soles of the gecko's feet.

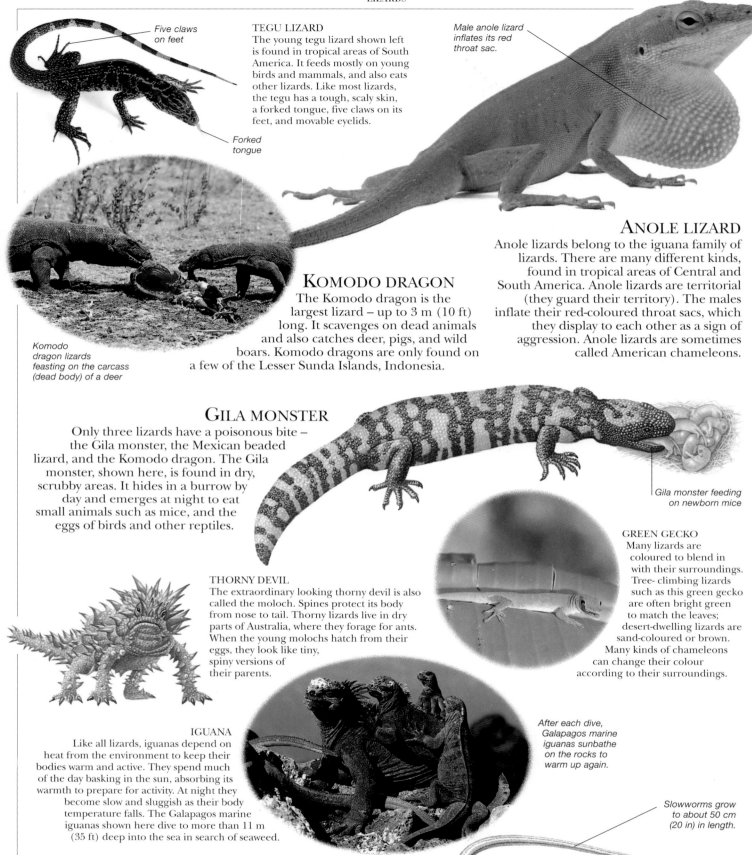

Five claws
on feet

Forked
tongue

TEGU LIZARD

The young tegu lizard shown left is found in tropical areas of South America. It feeds mostly on young birds and mammals, and also eats other lizards. Like most lizards, the tegu has a tough, scaly skin, a forked tongue, five claws on its feet, and movable eyelids.

Male anole lizard
inflates its red
throat sac.

ANOLE LIZARD

Anole lizards belong to the iguana family of lizards. There are many different kinds, found in tropical areas of Central and South America. Anole lizards are territorial (they guard their territory). The males inflate their red-coloured throat sacs, which they display to each other as a sign of aggression. Anole lizards are sometimes called American chameleons.

KOMODO DRAGON

The Komodo dragon is the largest lizard – up to 3 m (10 ft) long. It scavenges on dead animals and also catches deer, pigs, and wild boars. Komodo dragons are only found on a few of the Lesser Sunda Islands, Indonesia.

Komodo
dragon lizards
feasting on the carcass
(dead body) of a deer

GILA MONSTER

Only three lizards have a poisonous bite – the Gila monster, the Mexican beaded lizard, and the Komodo dragon. The Gila monster, shown here, is found in dry, scrubby areas. It hides in a burrow by day and emerges at night to eat small animals such as mice, and the eggs of birds and other reptiles.

Gila monster feeding
on newborn mice

GREEN GECKO

Many lizards are coloured to blend in with their surroundings. Tree- climbing lizards such as this green gecko are often bright green to match the leaves; desert-dwelling lizards are sand-coloured or brown. Many kinds of chameleons can change their colour according to their surroundings.

THORNY DEVIL

The extraordinary looking thorny devil is also called the moloch. Spines protect its body from nose to tail. Thorny lizards live in dry parts of Australia, where they forage for ants. When the young molochs hatch from their eggs, they look like tiny, spiny versions of their parents.

IGUANA

Like all lizards, iguanas depend on heat from the environment to keep their bodies warm and active. They spend much of the day basking in the sun, absorbing its warmth to prepare for activity. At night they become slow and sluggish as their body temperature falls. The Galapagos marine iguanas shown here dive to more than 11 m (35 ft) deep into the sea in search of seaweed.

After each dive,
Galapagos marine
iguanas sunbathe
on the rocks to
warm up again.

Slowworms grow
to about 50 cm
(20 in) in length.

SLOWWORM

The slowworm is not really a worm, but a lizard. It is not slow either; when disturbed, slowworms can wriggle away rapidly to safety. Slowworms are found in fields and scrubland in Europe, northern Africa, and southwest Asia. They feed on slugs, spiders, and insects. Unlike most lizards, slowworms give birth to fully formed young.

Find out more

DESERT WILDLIFE
EVOLUTION
REPTILES
SNAKES

LUNGS AND BREATHING

WE NEED OXYGEN TO LIVE, and we get oxygen by breathing air. When we breathe in, air is sucked through the nose or mouth, down the windpipe, and into the lungs, two powerful organs in the chest. The lungs absorb as much oxygen from the air as possible. The oxygen travels in the blood from the lungs to every part of the body. Our bodies use oxygen to release energy from sugars obtained from the food we eat. This also releases harmful carbon dioxide, which is breathed out of the body by the lungs. The whole process is called respiration. The lungs, together with the airways, throat, and nasal passages, form the respiratory system. Each lung is surrounded by two thin coverings or membranes called pleurae. The lungs themselves contain air tubes, blood vessels, and millions of tiny air sacs called alveoli. If you spread these air sacs out flat, they would cover the area of a tennis court.

HOW WE MAKE SOUNDS
We use the air flowing in and out of our lungs to make sounds. We speak, shout, laugh, and cry by making air flow over two small leathery flaps called the vocal cords. These are in the larynx (voice box), in the lower part of the throat. Muscles in the throat stretch the flaps tighter to change from low notes to high notes.

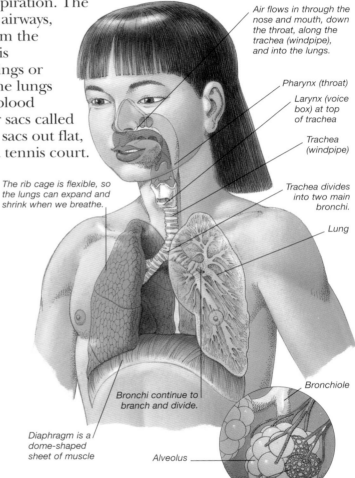

Air flows in through the nose and mouth, down the throat, along the trachea (windpipe), and into the lungs.

Pharynx (throat)

Larynx (voice box) at top of trachea

Trachea (windpipe)

Trachea divides into two main bronchi.

Lung

The rib cage is flexible, so the lungs can expand and shrink when we breathe.

Bronchiole

Bronchi continue to branch and divide.

Diaphragm is a dome-shaped sheet of muscle

Alveolus

Capillary blood vessels

The alveoli are grouped together like bunches of grapes. Tiny tubes called bronchioles bring fresh oxygen-containing air to the alveoli.

BREATHING

Lungs empty of air as you breathe out.

Diaphragm relaxes and rises.

Diaphragm contracts and flattens.

Lungs fill with air as you breathe in.

BREATHING OUT
When you breathe out, the diaphragm and chest muscles relax. The lungs are spongy and elastic, so they spring back to their smaller size after they have been stretched. This blows air back out of the lungs.

BREATHING IN
When you breathe in, the diaphragm contracts (becomes flatter) and pulls down the base of the lungs. Muscles between the ribs contract to swing the ribs up and out. These actions stretch and enlarge the lungs, so that air is sucked in.

LUNGFISH
Most animals that live on land have lungs. Many water animals, however, including most fish, breathe using feathery flaps called gills. Oxygen in the water passes through the thin gill coverings to the blood inside the fish's body. The lungfish shown here is an unusual animal because it has lungs and gills, so it can breathe in both ways and can survive out of water for a long time.

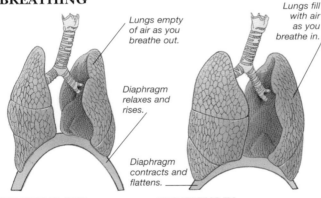

Air space inside alveolus

ALVEOLUS
Each alveolus is surrounded by a network of very fine blood vessels called capillaries. Oxygen passes from the air space inside the alveolus, through the lining, and into the blood. Carbon dioxide passes in the opposite way.

Find out more

BRAIN AND NERVES
HEART AND BLOOD
HUMAN BODY
MUSCLES AND MOVEMENT
OXYGEN
SKELETONS

MACHINES

INCLINED PLANE

Simple machines reduce the effort needed to move or lift an object, but the object has to travel a greater distance. The simplest machine is the ramp, or inclined plane. You need less force to push an object with a downwards load up an inclined plane than you need to lift it straight up. This is because the object moves a greater distance along the plane. The gentler the slope, the further you have to push, but the easier it is.

WHAT DO A SAW and a computer have in common? Both are machines. One is simple and the other is very complex, but both are tools that do work for us. Machines perform tasks that we would find difficult or even impossible to do. You cannot cut through wood with your bare hands, for example, but it is easy with a saw. Likewise, a computer can do calculations rapidly that would take you an enormous amount of time. All machines need a source of energy. Mechanical machines, such as a corkscrew, use the energy of movement. A motor or a person's muscles drive the machine with a certain amount of force called the effort. The machine then applies this movement but produces a larger force to move a load. For example, your fingers operate a can opener, but the blade of the can opener moves with much more force than that produced by your fingers. Many hand-powered machines help us perform tasks for which we do not have enough strength. They use devices known as simple machines. These include levers, gears, pulleys, and screws.

Effort

Steep slope – large effort

Force

Load

Gentle slope – small effort

Force

Load

SCREW

A screw moves forward a shorter distance than it turns. It therefore moves forward with a much greater force than the effort needed to turn it. The screw bites into the wood with great force and is held strongly.

Archimedes' screw (above) is an ancient device for raising water. As it turns, the screw shifts water along its thread instead of moving itself forward.

The screw makes use of the principle of the inclined plane.

The thread of the screw is like a slope wrapped around a cylinder.

PLOUGH

The plough has a cutting blade that bites into the soil and a V-shaped blade that turns the soil over.

PERPETUAL MOTION

Many inventors have tried to build a machine that, once started, would never stop. It would run on its own without any source of energy. However, such a perpetual motion machine is impossible. This is because all machines lose some energy as they work. Without a constant source of energy, a machine always slows down and stops.

In this machine, the motion of the balls was supposed to keep the wheel turning.

WEDGE

The wedge is a form of inclined plane. Instead of moving a load along a slope, the wedge is a slope that pushes a load aside or upward as it moves forward. The wedge pushes with greater force than the effort needed to move the wedge. Sharp blades are thin wedges that make cutting an easy task.

Effort

Axe is a kind of wedge

Force

Force

PULLEYS

Lifting a heavy load is easy with a pulley system. It contains a set of wheels fixed to a support. A rope goes around grooves in the wheels. Pulling the rope raises the lower wheel and the load. A pulley system allows you to lift a heavy load with little effort, but you must pull the rope a large distance to raise the load by a small amount.

Small effort, but the rope has to move a large distance.

Effort

Pulley

Object moves a small distance.

Force

Load

AUTOMATIC MACHINES

Many machines do not need to be operated by people. These are automatic machines. They contain mechanisms or computers to control themselves. These machines may simply perform a set task whenever it is required; automatic doors, for example, open as people arrive. Other machines are able to check their own work and change the way they operate to follow instructions. One example is an aircraft autopilot, which guides the plane through the skies.

Traffic lights are machines that control traffic automatically.

Fulcrum

A pair of scissors consists of two levers hinged together.

GEARS

Gears are intermeshing toothed wheels. They can increase force or speed depending on the relative size of the wheels and their number of teeth. A gearwheel driven by a smaller wheel turns less quickly than the smaller wheel but with greater force. A wheel driven by a larger wheel turns faster but with less force.

Mechanical clocks and watches contain gears that turn the hands at different speeds.

LEVER

A long stick propped up on a small object (a fulcrum) helps you move a heavy load. The stick is a simple machine called a lever. Pushing down on the end furthest from the fulcrum raises the other end with greater force, helping you move the load. Other kinds of levers can increase either the force applied to, or the distance moved by, a load.

Effort

Fulcrum

Force

Load

There are three types of lever. A crowbar is called a first-class lever. The fulcrum is between the load and the effort, which is the force that you apply.

Force

Fulcrum

A wheelbarrow is a second-class lever. The load lies between the fulcrum and the effort.

Load

Effort

Effort

WHEEL AND AXLE

Several machines use the principle of the wheel and axle. One example is the winch, in which a handle (the wheel) turns a shaft (the axle) that raises a load. The handle moves a greater distance than the load rises. The winch therefore lifts the load with a greater force than the effort needed to turn the handle.

Force

Fulcrum

Force

Effort

Load

A fishing rod is a third-class lever. The load moves a greater distance than the effort, but with less force. The effort pushes between the load and the fulcrum.

Load

STEERING WHEEL
The steering wheel on a car is an example of the wheel and axle. The shaft turns with greater force than the effort needed to turn the steering wheel.

Find out more
COMPUTERS
ENGINES
INDUSTRIAL REVOLUTION
ROBOTS
TECHNOLOGY

MAGNETISM

ORIGIN OF MAGNETISM
Iron contains millions of tiny magnets called magnetic domains. Normally, all the domains point in different directions so their magnetism cancels out. In a magnet, the domains point the same way so that their magnetism combines.

MAGNETIC FIELD
The area around a magnet in which its magnetic force works is called its magnetic field. For instance, a paper clip is pulled towards the magnet (right) when it is placed within the magnetic field of the magnet.

All magnets attract iron and steel objects but not plastic or wooden ones.

THE FORCE of magnetism is invisible, yet you can see its power when a magnet drags a piece of metal towards it. A material that attracts certain metals such as iron is called a magnet. Materials that are attracted by a magnet are called magnetic. Every magnet has two poles – places at which magnetic objects cluster. The Earth itself is a huge magnet; its magnetic poles are close to the geographical North and South Poles. One pole of a magnet is attracted to the Earth's northern magnetic pole and is called the magnet's north pole; the other is attracted to the south and is called the magnet's south pole. Materials that retain their magnetism all the time are called permanent magnets. An electric current flowing in a coil of wire produces a magnet called an electromagnet that can be switched on and off. Electromagnets are used in electric motors, loudspeakers, and many other devices.

LODESTONE
Magnetite is an iron ore that often possesses magnetism. It was once commonly called lodestone, which means "guiding stone", because early navigators used it as a compass.

MAGNETIC POLES

The north pole of one magnet and the south pole of another magnet attract each other.

A magnetic pole, such as a south pole, repels (pushes away) another pole of the same kind.

ELECTROMAGNETS
An electromagnet is a coil of wire. An electric current within the coil creates a magnetic field. The field can be made stronger by winding the wire around a piece of iron. Turning off the current switches off the magnetic field. Some cranes use an electromagnet instead of a hook.

The geographical North and South Poles lie on the Earth's axis, which is the line around which the Earth spins.

The pattern of lines shows the Earth's magnetic field. The field is strongest where the lines are closest together.

The magnetic north and south poles lie a small distance away from geographical North and South.

GEOMAGNETISM
The Earth produces a magnetic field which makes it seem as though it has a huge "bar" magnet inside it. Electric currents flowing within the Earth's liquid iron core cause the Earth's magnetism, which is called geomagnetism.

COMPASS
The needle inside a magnetic compass is a thin, light magnet, balanced so that it swings freely. The needle's north pole points towards the Earth's magnetic north pole, which is very close to the geographical North. People use magnetic compasses to navigate at sea and on land.

Find out more
EARTH
ELECTRICITY
METALS
SCIENCE

MAMMALS

THE ANIMAL GROUP CALLED MAMMALS includes the heaviest, tallest, and fastest animals on land – the elephant, the giraffe, and the cheetah. Mice, whales, rhinoceroses, bats, and humans are also mammals. Like birds, mammals are warm-blooded (endothermic), but three features set them apart from all other creatures. All mammals are covered in fur or hair, all feed their young on milk, and all have a unique type of jaw. The jawbone helps us to identify the fossilized bones of prehistoric mammals that lived on Earth millions of years ago. Mammals are also members of the group known as vertebrates because they all have vertebrae (backbones). Today there are more than 5,000 kinds of mammals, including carnivores (flesh eaters) such as tigers; herbivores (plant eaters) such as rabbits; and omnivores (flesh and plant eaters) such as bears. Cattle, sheep, goats, and most other farm animals are mammals, and many pets are mammals too, including cats, dogs, and guinea pigs. Mammals live nearly everywhere. They are found on land, in the sea, and in the sky, from the coldest Arctic to the most searing heat of the desert.

A mammal's body is covered in fur.

MARSUPIAL YOUNG
Marsupials are very tiny when they are born. At birth, a kangaroo is less than 2.5 cm (1 in) long. It crawls through its mother's fur into a pocket-like pouch on the abdomen, where it attaches itself to her teat and suckles milk.

A kangaroo's large tail is so strong that it can act as a prop for the kangaroo to lean on.

Young male joey

PLACENTAL MAMMALS
Most mammals, including monkeys, cats, and dogs, are called placental mammals because the young develop inside the mother's womb, or uterus, and are fed by means of the placenta. The placenta is a specialized organ embedded in the wall of the womb. It carries nutrients and other essential materials from the mother's blood to the baby's blood. These nutrients help the young to grow and develop. After the young are born, the placenta comes out of the uterus as afterbirth.

POUCHED MAMMALS
Kangaroos, opossums, wallabies, koalas, wombats, and bandicoots are all known as pouched mammals or marsupials. These animals carry their young in their pouches until the young are able to fend for themselves. Once it has left the pouch, the joey (young kangaroo) returns to the pouch to suck milk. Marsupials are found in Australia and New Guinea, South America, and North America. A few marsupials, such as the shrew opossum of South America, do not have pouches.

MONOTREME MAMMALS
Five kinds of mammals lay eggs. They are called monotreme mammals, and include the platypus and the four types of echidna (spiny ant-eater). All are found in Australasia. After about 10 days, the young hatch out of the eggs, then feed on their mother's milk.

PRIMATES
Monkeys, apes, and humans belong to a group called primates. Primates are able to grasp with their hands. Most primates have thumbs and big toes, with flat fingernails rather than claws. Members of the primate group range in size from the mouse lemur, which weighs only 60 g (2 oz), to the gorilla, which weighs up to 275 kg (610 lb).

SPINY ANTEATER
The short-beaked spiny ant-eater, or echidna, lays a single egg in a temporary pouch on its abdomen. The young echidna hatches, then sucks milk from mammary glands on its mother's abdomen.

MAMMAL GROUPS

There are about 27 main groups of mammals, some of which are shown below. Rodents make up half of all mammals; bats account for a quarter. There are only three kinds of elephant, and the aardvark is in a group of its own.

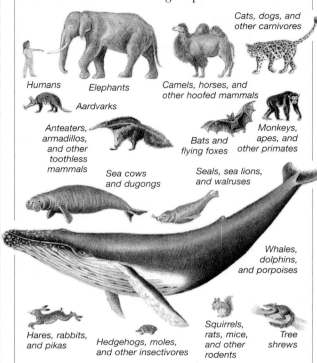

Humans

Elephants

Aardvarks

Camels, horses, and other hoofed mammals

Cats, dogs, and other carnivores

Anteaters, armadillos, and other toothless mammals

Bats and flying foxes

Monkeys, apes, and other primates

Sea cows and dugongs

Seals, sea lions, and walruses

Whales, dolphins, and porpoises

Hares, rabbits, and pikas

Hedgehogs, moles, and other insectivores

Squirrels, rats, mice, and other rodents

Tree shrews

Most puppies feed on their mother's milk for two or three months. A mother shrew suckles her young for four weeks; a mother whale feeds her youngster for six months or more.

MAMMAL MILK

Mammals are the only creatures that feed their young with milk. When the female is about to give birth, she starts to produce milk in mammary glands on the chest or abdomen. When the young are born, they suck the milk from the mother's teats. Mother's milk is an ideal food for the young – warm and nourishing, and full of special substances which protect the young from disease. As the babies grow larger and stronger, they take less milk and begin to eat solid foods. This process is called weaning.

GESTATION

The time between mating and birth, when the young develop in the mother's womb, is called the gestation or pregnancy period. In general, large mammals have longer pregnancies and fewer young than small mammals.

Rhinoceros

The gestation usually lasts for 15 months; one young is born.

Rabbit

Gestation usually lasts for 30 days; as many as eight young are born in a litter.

Dirty fur harbours pests and also lets heat escape, so many mammals spend time cleaning or grooming their fur.

HAIR AND FUR

Fur or hair protects the mammal's skin from injury and the sun's rays. It also keeps heat in and moisture out. The colours and patterns of the fur provide camouflage. Water-dwelling mammals such as beavers have special oily, waterproof fur. The porcupine's spines are modified hairs and the rhinoceros's horn is made from a hair-like fibrous substance.

ARMADILLO

Some mammals, such as armadillos and pangolins, have reptile-like scales instead of fur. The scales, or scutes, of an armadillo are made of a type of horn and bone that grows from the skin. Hairs grow between the scutes and also cover the animal's soft-skinned underbelly.

BODY TEMPERATURE

Mammals and birds are called warm-blooded animals because they can maintain a high body temperature even in cold conditions. Mammals do, however, need plenty of food to provide the energy for warmth. The heat to warm a mammal is produced by chemical reactions in the body, particularly in the muscles.

Huskies are able to stay warm in deep snow because of their thick fur.

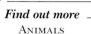

Find out more
ANIMALS
CONSERVATION
and endangered species
FOREST WILDLIFE
HIBERNATION
LAKE AND RIVER WILDLIFE
PREHISTORIC LIFE

MARSH AND SWAMP WILDLIFE

THE SALT AND FRESHWATER habitats of swamps and marshland are called wetlands. Marsh and swamp wildlife includes crocodiles, frogs, birds, fish, and countless plants. At different times of the year the water level of marshes and swamps rises and falls. In summer the land dries up, and in winter it floods. Wetlands are usually unsuitable for large mammals – except the African swamps where hippopotamuses live. Smaller mammals such as muskrats live in North American swamps, and the European marshes are home to many birds. The main plant life consists of reeds, rushes, saw grass, and cattail. Large trees are found only in the tropical mangroves, where the trees form dense thickets. Willows and other waterside trees grow in the higher, drier ground around the marsh.

PROBOSCIS MONKEY
This large-nosed monkey lives among the mangrove trees of river and coastal swamps. The proboscis monkey is a good swimmer. Proboscis monkeys eat leaves, flowers, and fruit.

CONSERVATION
Farming and industry threaten many swamplands, but some animals, such as the marsh harriers shown here, are protected. They live in the Coto Doñana National Park in Spain – one of Europe's most important wetlands.

PELICAN
Most of these fish-eating birds build their nests in remote marshland areas. Some species breed on the ground, some in trees. Others, such as spot-billed and Dalmatian pelicans, are very rare, because of destruction of their nesting sites.

Front fins help the mudskipper walk on mud and grip roots.

SWAMP RABBIT
This large rabbit from North America can swim well and dives to escape from predators. Swamp rabbits eat water plants, grasses, and other vegetation.

COTTONMOUTH
Most snakes are good swimmers and climbers, and they can travel through swamps with ease in search of prey. The cottonmouth, also called the water moccasin, is a North American swamp dweller with a very poisonous bite.

Swamp mud is usually so dense and waterlogged that, unlike normal soil, it contains almost no oxygen. The aerial roots of mangrove trees stick up above the mud, to absorb the oxygen they need to grow.

MUDSKIPPER
This unusual fish has a store of water in its large gill chambers which allows it to live out of water for long periods. From time to time it skitters over the mud to a pool to take in a new supply of water.

MARSHLAND
Marshes are nursery areas for many insects whose larvae live in water, such as dragonflies and mosquitoes. Insect larvae and worms form the main diet of many fish and water birds. Frogs, toads, and tadpoles are also eaten by larger creatures.

MANGROVE SWAMPS
Mangroves are trees that grow in muddy tropical swamps. Some kinds of mangrove trees grow in fresh water; others tolerate salty water and grow on the coast or in river estuaries. Their roots and trunks trap mud, and their seeds begin to grow while they are still attached to the parent tree. When the seeds drop into the mud, they quickly establish roots so they are not washed away.

Archer fish adjusts its aim if it misses, and fires again.

ARCHER FISH
The archer fish spits drops of water at insects on over-hanging twigs. The insects fall off the twigs, into the water, where the fish gulps them down.

The drops of water hit the insect like tiny bullets.

Find out more
BIRDS
FISH
LAKE AND RIVER WILDLIFE
MONKEYS AND APES
SEASHORE WILDLIFE
SNAKES

MAYA

DEEP IN THE TROPICAL FORESTS of Mexico, the Mayan people created one of the most amazing ancient civilizations, which reached its height between 250 and 900 CE. The Maya built cities with huge stone temples. Each city was the centre of a separate kingdom, with a king who was treated like a god. The Maya were great scholars who developed systems of mathematics and astronomy. They even created their own writing system and used it to carve inscriptions about their history on stone plaques that they set up in their cities. Despite their sophistication, the Maya had only the simplest technology. They used stone tools, and did not know about the wheel. By the 1500s the Spanish had conquered the region.

MAYAN CIVILIZATION
The Maya came from the Yucatan Peninsula and the highlands to the south, in what is now eastern Mexico. They also built cities in parts of modern Guatemala and Honduras.

Outer shell of stone concealed earth base and royal tomb.

Temple contains historic inscriptions.

Priests used the main staircase.

FLINT CARVING
Craftworkers made their tools out of stones such as flint or obsidian (a black, naturally occurring glass). They could work these materials to make a sharp edge. The Maya became highly skilled at this type of stoneworking, and made intricate carvings in strange shapes to show off their skill. Many were made to place in graves or as offerings to the gods.

PALENQUE
The Temple of the Inscriptions at Palenque was a famous Mayan pyramid. Deep inside the base was a secret chamber containing the tomb of a local king, Pacal, who died in about 684 CE. In the temple on top of the pyramid were stone tablets carved with glyphs that recorded the history of the local kings up to Pacal's reign. Its ruins still exist today.

People taking part in ceremonies could stand on the main stepped levels.

Stone ring acted as "goal".

Players used their elbows to hit the ball.

GLYPHS
Mayan writing was made up of a series of signs, which archaeologists call glyphs. Many of the glyphs were simplified pictures of the objects they stood for. Some represented sounds, which were used to build up words. Others were symbols that stood for different numbers. The Maya used glyphs to record their calendar, and to write inscriptions about their history.

Glyph describing a Mayan noble woman called Lady Xoc

Pot shaped like a jaguar

BLOOD SACRIFICE
Some Mayan communities believed that their gods would be pleased if people were killed in their honour. They also saw sacrificial blood as food for the gods. In some places a pot shaped like a jaguar, a beast sacred to the Maya, was used to collect the blood.

BALL GAME
Many cities had a ball court where people played a game with a rubber ball. Players wore padded clothing, and were only allowed to touch the ball with their hips, arms, or elbows. The aim was to get the ball through a small stone ring at the side of the court. Players who lost were sometimes put to death.

Find out more
BRONZE AGE
CENTRAL AMERICA
MEXICO

MEDICINE

TWO HUNDRED AND FIFTY YEARS AGO, people lived on average for just 35 years. Today, in the industrialized parts of the world, the average lifespan has increased to more than 70 years. Better food and hygiene have helped, but one of the main reasons for this change is the advances made in medicine. Medicine is the branch of science concerned with the prevention, diagnosis (identification), and treatment of disease and damage to the human body. Medical scientists are constantly searching for new ways of treating diseases. Treatments include drugs, radiation therapy, and surgery. Preventive measures, such as vaccinations against infections, are becoming an increasingly important part of modern medicine.

DIAGNOSIS
A doctor's first step with a sick patient is to diagnose the illness. This can be done in various ways – by asking the patient about his or her symptoms (physical feelings), by making a physical examination of the ill person, and by carrying out medical tests if necessary.

BRANCHES OF MEDICINE
Medicine is a huge subject and nobody can hope to know it all. Thus doctors, nurses, and other medical workers often become expert in a single area of medicine, a process which can take years and years of study.

Neurology is concerned with disorders of the brain and nerves.

Ophthalmology is the treatment of disorders of the eyes.

Orthopaedics is the care of the spine, bones, joints, and muscles.

Psychiatry is the study of mental health problems.

Cutting into the body to cure illness is called surgery.

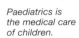
Dermatology is concerned with the skin and skin diseases.

Paediatrics is the medical care of children.

SURGERY
Medical treatments may include drugs or surgery. Surgery is the branch of medicine that involves operating, or cutting into the body, to treat the cause of an illness. Today surgery is so advanced that surgeons can sometimes repair or replace organs such as the kidneys and the heart.

RECOVERY
Recovery from an illness or an operation may take only a few hours or as long as several weeks. Much depends on the severity of the illness and the impact the treatment has on the body.

MEDICAL TECHNOLOGY
Modern medicine makes use of a wide range of technology. Latest developments include body scanners which use a strong magnetic field or ultrasound (very high-frequency sound waves) to produce an image of the interior of the human body. Such equipment has revolutionized medicine.

Doctors use MRI scanners to check patients for tumours or damage to the brain.

Rue is prescribed for some digestive disorders.

Catmint is a cold cure that was first used by prehistoric people.

Mint is used for settling a stomach upset.

HOLISTIC MEDICINE
The word *holistic* means "of the whole". The principle of holistic medicine is to treat the whole person – body and mind – rather than just the affected part. Holistic therapies (treatments) include acupuncture (stimulating the nerves by inserting needles into the skin) and aromatherapy (treatment using oils containing fragrant plant extracts).

Find out more
DISEASE
HUMAN BODY
MEDICINE, HISTORY OF
MUSCLES AND MOVEMENT
PLANTS
SCIENCE, HISTORY OF
TECHNOLOGY

HISTORY OF
MEDICINE

TREPANNING
Ten thousand years ago, the first doctors tried to cure an ill person by cutting a hole in his or her skull. Healers believed that the hole in the head released evil spirits that caused pain. This was known as trepanning.

SINCE THE EARLIEST TIMES, people have looked for ways of curing their illnesses. Early people believed that disease was a punishment from the gods. They also believed that priests and magicians could heal them. In Ancient Greece, people visited temples when they were ill and sacrificed animals to Asclepius, the Greek god of healing. They also drank and bathed in medicinal waters and followed strict diets in the hope of being cured. During the fifth century BCE the Greek doctor Hippocrates declared that it was nature, not magic, that caused and cured disease. Hippocrates was famed as "the father of medicine", and he and his followers wrote many medical books. The spirit of enquiry, which was part of the Renaissance (a cultural movement in 14th-century Europe), encouraged experiments that put European medicine on a firm scientific basis. Many people began to question the traditional ideas about medicine. Scientists such as Vesalius (1514-1564) began to study the bodies of dead people to learn more about disease and how to treat it. Since then, there have been many more discoveries in medicine, and the battle against disease continues.

HUMOURS
The Greek physician Galen (c. 130-200 CE) introduced the idea that the body contained four fluids called humours – blood, phlegm, yellow bile, and black bile. He believed that a person's mood depended on which of these four fluids ruled the body, and that if the fluids were not balanced, illness would result.

WILLIAM HARVEY
In 1628, an English doctor named William Harvey (1578-1657) discovered that blood constantly circulates around the body. He described how blood is pumped by the heart into the arteries and returns to the heart in the veins. He showed that valves in the veins stop the blood from flowing backwards. At first, Harvey was scorned for contradicting old ideas, but later he became physician to Charles I, king of England.

HERBALISM
For thousands of years, people have used herbs and plants in healing. Herbalists wrote lists of herbs and their uses. Monks were also famed for their knowledge of herbs. The first pharmacists, called apothecaries, used herbs to make potions, or medicines. But in Europe during the Renaissance many herbalists were accused of being witches. Many people are now turning to herbs as a natural way of treating illnesses.

Harvey drew detailed diagrams to explain his theory of circulation.

Carbolic acid sprayed continuously over operating area from a special pump.

ANTISEPTICS

Until the late 19th century, surgeons did not wash their hands or their medical instruments before operating on a patient. Many patients died from deadly infections following an operation. Joseph Lister (1827-1912), an English surgeon, guessed that infection with bacteria might be the cause of these deaths. In 1865, Lister developed an antiseptic spray called carbolic acid. This spray could destroy bacteria in the operating room, so there was a dramatic drop in the number of deaths following operations.

Leeches are parasites that attach themselves to a host. They secrete a substance that stops blood clotting while they feed on it.

BLOOD-LETTING

Doctors once believed that too much blood in the body was the cause of disease. They removed the excess blood by blood-letting. Doctors either cut open a vein to let the blood out, or they applied bloodsucking creatures called leeches to the body. The leech attached itself to the patient with its sucker, made a wound, then sucked out blood. The exact spot for blood-letting depended on what was wrong with the patient.

ALEXANDER FLEMING

Bacteria cause many of the illnesses that affect humans, so for years scientists tried to find a substance that would kill bacteria but would not harm human tissue. The Scottish bacteriologist Alexander Fleming (1881-1955) was the first person to identify an antibacterial substance. Fleming carried out his research in a laboratory at St. Mary's Hospital, London. In 1928, Fleming noticed that a mould that had accidentally developed on a dish of bacteria culture caused the bacteria to die. In 1941, the researchers Howard Florey and Ernst Chain purified the mould, *Penicillium*, to produce penicillin, the world's first antibiotic. Penicillin is widely used in the treatment of many diseases, including meningitis and pneumonia. Fleming shared the 1945 Nobel Prize for medicine with Florey and Chain.

HISTORY OF MEDICINE

c. 8000 BCE Early healers practise trepanning.

400s BCE Hippocrates, a Greek, begins scientific medicine.

1543 Vesalius publishes first scientific study of human body.

1615 Santorio, an Italian doctor, designs mouth thermometer.

1683 Anton van Leeuwenhoek, a Dutch scientist, discovers bacteria.

1796 Edward Jenner gives first smallpox vaccination.

1816 Rene Laennec, a French doctor, invents stethoscope.

1842 American surgeon, Horace Long, operates using general anaesthetic.

1895 Wilhelm Roentgen, a German physicist, discovers x-rays, which enable doctors to see inside the human body.

1898 Polish-born Marie Curie and her husband, Pierre Curie of France, discover the chemical element radium to treat cancer.

1928 Scottish bacteriologist, Alexander Fleming, discovers penicillin.

MEDICAL PIONEERS

Through the centuries many people have shaped modern medicine. The Flemish doctor Vesalius produced accurate drawings of the human body; Dutchman Anton van Leeuwenhoek (1632-1723) first discovered microbes, now called bacteria; and the English doctor Edward Jenner (1749-1823) discovered vaccinations – a way of preventing certain diseases by injection.

LOUIS PASTEUR
Frenchman Louis Pasteur (1822-1895) showed that bacteria caused disease. He invented pasteurization – the heating of milk and beer to destroy harmful bacteria.

SIGMUND FREUD
The Austrian doctor Sigmund Freud (1856-1939; below) was interested in finding out how the mind works. He treated patients with mental disorders by listening to them talk about their dreams and thoughts. This treatment was called psychoanalysis. In 1900, Freud published *The Interpretation of Dreams*, which explained his method.

Find out more

EGYPT, ANCIENT
GREECE, ANCIENT
LEONARDO DA VINCI
MEDICINE

MEDIEVAL EUROPE

FAIRS
Great fairs were held every year in towns, such as Winchester, England, which were on important trade routes. Merchants travelled from all over Europe to sell their goods at these fairs.

LORDS AND LADIES feasting in castle banquet halls, peasants working on the land, knights in armour – all these are associated with a time in European history known as the medieval period or the Middle Ages. This was a time of great change in western Europe between the 5th and 15th centuries. During the 5th century the Roman Empire fell, to be replaced by smaller kingdoms set up by invading Germanic tribes in Western Europe. Trade collapsed, and people had to make their living from the land. Gradually, powerful landowners or lords emerged and the feudal system developed. The early medieval period of Europe is sometimes called the Dark Age because the learning of Ancient Greece and Rome almost disappeared. But the Christian Church gave leadership to the people. Trade gradually improved. By about the 13th century the Middle Ages had reached their height. Feudalism governed society, and monasteries (where monks lived) were the centres of learning. The medieval times came to an end in the 15th century when the Renaissance swept through Europe.

Everyone gave part of their crops to the village church.

Windmill to grind grain

Farmers herding sheep through the village.

Most buildings in the village had thatched roofs.

Chopped wood served for repairs to the house and to make fire.

Travelling musicians entertained people at the fair. Sometimes there were dancing bears.

The village fair was held twice a year.

Ploughman working on the land around the village

The manor house was the largest house in the village. It was built of stone.

Stables

"Mystery" religious plays were popular throughout medieval Europe.

VILLAGE LIFE
Two or three huge open fields usually surrounded a medieval village. The lord of the manor owned the land, but the peasants farmed it, in scattered narrow strips, and kept most of what they grew. They worked hard all year round and paid taxes to the lord and the Church in the form of work and goods.

Shoemakers

TOWN SCENE

Trade increased in the later medieval period, making merchants wealthy and powerful. Towns became important trading centres with a new class of craftspeople. The craftspeople created organizations called guilds to control the prices and quality of their goods.

People bought fabric to make their own clothing.

The poultry trader sold geese.

FEUDALISM

Kings gave their vassals – powerful nobles – tracts of land called fiefs. In return for this land the vassals fought for the king when required. The vassals divided their land into manors (estates), which they gave to lesser nobles and knights. In return, the knights and lesser nobles worked for the lord of the manor, and had to fight for him when called on.

14th-century manuscript (right) shows feudal structure, with the king at the top.

A French medieval woman, Christine de Pisan (left), earned her living as a writer.

Hunting (above) was a popular sport for upper-class medieval women.

WOMEN

Peasant women worked very hard all their lives. They brought up their children, spun wool and wove clothing, and helped with all the farmwork. Upper-class women also led busy lives. They often ran the family estates while their husbands were away travelling around their lands, fighting against neighbouring lords, or on a Crusade to the Holy Land. Women also nursed the sick and provided education for children in their charge.

MEDIEVAL EUROPE

400 CE Roman empire begins to decline.

450 German tribes – Angles, Jutes, and Saxons – settle in Britain.

480s Franks set up kingdom in Gaul (now France).

800 Charlemagne, king of the Franks, unites western Europe.

900-1000s Europe is divided into feudal estates; there is widespread poverty and disease in the region.

1066 Normans conquer England.

1000s-1200s High Middle Ages: trade improves, population grows, towns develop, and learning flourishes.

c. 1100 First universities are founded.

1215 Magna Carta: English barons win power and rights from King John.

1300-1500 Late Middle Ages.

c. 1320 Renaissance, a rebirth of arts and learning, begins in Italy.

1337 Hundred Years' War begins between England and France.

1348 Black Death, a killing plague, reaches Europe. Eventually, it wipes out one third of the population of Europe.

1378-1417 Great Schism: Catholic Europe is divided in support of two different popes, Urban VI and Clement VII.

1454 Johannes Gutenberg, a German, develops movable type. Printing begins in Europe.

Find out more

BLACK DEATH
CASTLES
CRUSADES
EUROPE, HISTORY OF
RENAISSANCE
ROMAN EMPIRE

METALS

IMAGINE A WORLD WITHOUT METALS. There would be no cars or aeroplanes, and skyscrapers would fall down without the metal frames that support them. Metals have countless uses because they possess a unique combination of qualities. They are very strong and easy to shape, so they can be used to make all kinds of objects from ships to bottle tops. All metals conduct electricity. Some are ideal for wires and electrical equipment. Metals also carry heat, so they make good cooking pots. These qualities can be improved by mixing two or more metals to make alloys. Most metallic objects are made of alloys rather than pure metals. There are more than 80 kinds of pure metals, though some are very rare. Aluminium and iron are the most common metals. A few metals, such as gold, occur in the ground as pure metals; the rest are found as ores in rock. Metals can also be obtained by recycling old cars and tins. This reduces waste and costs less than processing metal ores.

Gold watch

Mercury thermometer

Copper wire

Silver-plated frame

PURE METALS

The rarity and lustre of gold and silver have been prized for centuries. Other pure metals have special uses. Electrical wires are made of copper, which conducts electricity well. Mercury, a liquid metal, is used in thermometers.

Aeroplane fuselage made of aluminium alloys

ALUMINIUM

The most common metal in the Earth's crust is aluminium. The metal comes from an ore called bauxite, which contains alumina, a compound of aluminium and oxygen. Aluminium is light, conducts electricity and heat, and resists corrosion. These qualities mean the metal and its alloys can be used in many things, including aircraft and bicycles, window frames, paints, saucepans, and electricity supply cables.

A lump of bauxite

Alumina poured in here *Carbon electrode* *Molten aluminium*

ELECTROLYSIS Passing an electric current through alumina separates it into aluminium and oxygen. This process is called electrolysis.

Thin, flexible aluminium foil is useful for cooking and storing food because it is nonreactive and can stand high temperatures.

ALLOYS

Most metal objects are made of steel or other alloys. This is because alloys are often stronger or easier to process than pure metals. Copper and tin are weak and pliable, but when mixed together they make a strong alloy called bronze. Brass is a tough alloy of copper and zinc that resists corrosion. Alloys of aluminium are light and strong and are used to make aircraft.

METAL FATIGUE
Metals sometimes fail even though they may be very tough and strong. Corrosion weakens some metals, as in the case of rusty steel. Repeated bending can cause metal parts to break, an effect called metal fatigue.

Keys may break after considerable use.

METALWORKING

There are many ways of shaping metal. Casting is one method of making objects such as metal statues. Hot, molten metal is poured into a mould where it sets and hardens into the required shape. Metal can also be pressed, hammered, or cut into shape.

WELDING
Metal parts can be joined by welding. Welders apply heat, from a gas flame or an electric spark, to the edges of two pieces of metal. The heat causes the edges to melt so that they can be joined together.

Find out more
BRONZE AGE
IRON AGE
MAGNETISM
ROCKS AND MINERALS
SCIENCE

MEXICO

THE WEALTH OF MEXICO has traditionally come from the land. Precious metals lie buried in the mountains and rich crops grow in the valleys. Oil flows from wells on the coast. The Mexican people began to exploit these advantages centuries ago. Farming supported most of the people, and from the country's mines came silver to make beautiful jewellery. The mineral wealth of the country attracted invading European soldiers in the 16th century, and Spain ruled Mexico for three centuries. A revolt against Spanish rule gave the Mexican people independence in 1821. The discovery of oil early in the 20th century brought new wealth to Mexico. The government invested this in new factories, and in social services to relieve hunger and improve health and education. In 1994, the North American Free Trade Agreement (NAFTA) reduced trade barriers between Mexico, Canada, and the United States, promising long-term economic benefits. However, the border between Mexico and the US has been strengthened as a result of US concern over the many illegal crossings made each year.

Mexico is part of the continent of North America and lies between the United States to its north and Central America to its south.

José Guadalupe Posada (1852–1913) drew humorous illustrations, many of which supported the Mexican revolution.

POLITICS AND REVOLUTION

Mexico was a Spanish colony from 1521 to 1821, when it became an independent republic. After a long period of political unrest, there was a revolution in 1910, in which half a million people died. From 1929, the Institutional Revolutionary party governed Mexico, but in 2000 it lost the presidential election for the first time. Mexico is now a fully functioning democracy.

MEXICO CITY

More than 19 million people live in and around Mexico City, the capital of Mexico, making it one of the most populated cities in the world. The city lies 1.6 km (1 mile) above sea level in a natural basin surrounded by mountains. These mountains trap the pollution from the city's industries. As a result, Mexico City is one of the world's most unhealthy cities, with an inadequate water supply, a lack of housing, and the constant threat of earthquakes adding to its many problems.

Cinnamon sticks

Sweet potatoes

Mangoes

Chillies

Beans

Corn

Bananas

Mexican artisans are skilled at making fine jewellery from the precious metals found in their country.

FARM PRODUCE

Only one-seventh of the population of Mexico works on the land, growing staple or food crops. Increasingly, however, farmers are growing coffee, cotton, sugar, and tomatoes for export. These cash crops take vital land away from the crops that the Mexican people themselves need for food. Most of the farmers are members of co-operatives, pooling their limited resources to help one another.

MINERAL WEALTH

Copper, silver, zinc, mercury, and other valuable metals are among the many minerals found in Mexico. Oil is the country's most important resource. In 1974, vast new reserves were discovered in the south of the country.

> *Find out more*
> MAYA
> NORTH AMERICA
> VOLCANOES

Volcano Mountain Ancient monument Capital city Large city/town Small city/town

STATISTICS
Area: 1,958,200 sq km (756,061 sq miles)
Population: 111,212,000
Capital: Mexico City
Languages: Spanish, Nahuatl, Maya, Zapotec, Mixtec, Otomi, Totonac, Tzotzil, Tzeltal
Religions: Roman Catholic, Protestant
Currency: Mexican peso
Main occupations: Subsistence farming, manufacturing, oil production
Main exports: Oil, cotton, machinery, coffee
Main imports: Machinery, vehicles, chemicals

SIERRA MADRE
The main mountain system of Mexico, the Sierra Madre, runs 2,400 km (1,500 miles) southeast from the border with the United States. There are three ranges, in the east, south, and west, and they enclose Mexico's central plateau. Mexico's third highest mountain, Volcán Iztaccihuatl (right), is in the Sierra Madre del Sur, the southern range. The mountain has three separate summits, and its name means "White Woman" in the Aztec language, because the peaks resemble a woman wearing a hood.

The tallest peak of Volcán Iztaccihuatl rises to 5,268 m (17,274 ft).

POPULATION
Most of northern Mexico is sparsely populated due to the hot, dry climate and lack of cultivable farmland. As people have migrated from the countryside in search of work, the cities have grown dramatically; almost 75 per cent of Mexicans now live in urban areas. Mexico city is home to almost a quarter of the population and is one of the world's largest cities. Rapid, unplanned growth has led to poor sanitation and water supplies.

GUANAJUATO
Spanish prospectors searching for gold founded Guanajuato (below) in 1554. The town is the capital of Guanajuato state in the mountains of central Mexico and rises more than 2,050 m (6,726 ft) above sea level. It is built in a ravine and has steep, winding streets.

RIO GRANDE
The Rio Grande flows from Colorado in the United States and forms much of Mexico's northern border. It crosses a vast arid region on its way to the Gulf of Mexico.

BAJA CALIFORNIA
Baja California is also called Lower California. The peninsula is in Mexico, and is not part of the US state with which it shares a name.

MEXICAN FABRICS
Mexican people have been expert weavers since ancient times. They produce brightly coloured fabrics with bold, geometric designs, such as the striped skirt worn by the girl on the left. Today most Mexican fabrics are mass-produced in large factories.

SCALE BAR
0   200   400   km
0   200   400   miles

MICROSCOPES

WITHIN ALL OBJECTS there is a hidden world, much too tiny for us to see. With the invention of the microscope in the 16th century, scientists were able to peer into this world and unravel some of the great mysteries of science. They discovered that animals and plants are made of millions of tiny cells, and later were able to identify the minute organisms called bacteria that cause disease. Early microscopes consisted of a single magnifying lens; today's microscopes have several lenses and can be used to see very tiny objects. Electron microscopes are even more powerful. Instead of light they use a beam of electrons – tiny particles which are normally part of atoms – to magnify objects many millions of times. Scientists use electron microscopes to study the smallest of living cells and to delve into the structure of materials such as plastics and metals.

Observer looks through eyepiece.

Objective lenses of different power can be swung into position when needed.

The objective lens produces an image which the eyepiece magnifies (makes larger).

The object being studied rests on a glass slide.

Condenser lenses concentrate a beam of light onto the object.

A strong beam of light strikes a mirror under the microscope. The beam shines onto the object from below.

Optical microscopes can reveal living cells such as these cells which come from a human cheek. They are magnified more than 200 times.

OPTICAL MICROSCOPE

The optical, or light, microscope has two main lenses: the objective and the eyepiece. High-quality microscopes contain several additional lenses which help to give a clear, bright image. Different objectives can be fitted which give a range of magnification from about 10 times to 1,500 times normal size.

INVENTING THE MICROSCOPE

EN L'AN 2000

Although the Romans used magnifying lenses about 2,000 years ago, the first true microscope appeared around 1590, built by Dutch spectacles makers Hans and Zacharias Janssen. In 1663, English scientist Robert Hooke studied insects and plants with a microscope. He found that cork was made up of tiny cells, a discovery of great scientific importance. Microscopes aroused great interest in microscopic life, as this old etching shows.

ELECTRON MICROSCOPES
Objects must be cut into thin slices in order to see them with a microscope. However, a scanning electron microscope can magnify a whole object such as this ant (right), which is about 15 times normal size.

With a scanning electron microscope the image appears on a monitor screen.

IMAGING ATOMS
Special electron microscopes can show individual atoms, which are so small that a line of 0.5 million atoms would only span the width of a human hair. This piece of silicon (above) is magnified 45 million times, revealing its atoms.

Find out more
ATOMS AND MOLECULES
MICROSCOPIC LIFE
TELESCOPES

MONEY

THE NEXT TIME YOU ARE about to buy something, look at your money. Coins and notes are just discs of metal and sheets of paper, yet the shop accepts them as payment for useful, valuable goods. Money is a token which people trade for goods of an agreed value, and strange objects have been used for money throughout the world. Tibetans once used blocks of dried tea! It does not really matter what you use as money, provided everyone can reach an agreement about what it is worth. Many early coins were made from precious metals, such as gold and silver, but in 11th-century China, paper bank notes, or bills, first appeared. Unlike gold, bank notes had no real value. However, the bank that issued them promised to exchange them for gold. English bank notes still have the same promise printed on them. The United States government stopped exchanging bills for gold in 1971.

MINT
A government-controlled factory called a mint produces coins. Each coin is stamped with a special design, including its value, and often the year of manufacture. This stamping process is known as "minting".

Some Native Americans used wampum belts made of clamshell beads for money.

The first Chinese coins were made of bronze in the shape of tools, such as the head of a hoe.

The weight of a coin made of precious metal indicates its value.

A strip of plastic or metal thread is embedded in the paper.

Specially made paper includes a watermark, which is visible only when the note is held up to the light.

The loops and whirls are machine-engraved and extremely difficult to copy.

The metal of a modern coin is almost worthless, so the value of the coin is stamped on it.

COINS
People from ancient Lydia (now Turkey) were the first to make coins, about 2,700 years ago. Their coins were made from electrum, a mixture of gold and silver. Today, coins are used only for small denominations (sums of money). Paper money is used for larger sums, because notes are more difficult to forge than coins.

BANK NOTES
Governments issue bank notes and guarantee their value. It is a crime for anyone else to copy and print bank notes. The crime is called forgery, or counterfeiting, and bank notes have complicated designs to make copying difficult. Thomas De La Rue & Company is one of the world's most successful bank note printers. Their specimen note includes various security features which make their notes very difficult to copy.

BANKS
Most people deposit, or store, their money in a bank. Banks keep this money safe in a vault or lend it to their other customers. The bank has an account, or record, of how much each of its customers has deposited. Banks pay out notes and coins when their customers need money to make purchases. People with bank accounts can also buy things by writing cheques – notes which the bank promises to exchange for cash.

The built-in computer chip contains your personal bank details.

The raised letters include your name, card number, and card expiry date.

CREDIT CARDS
A credit card is a piece of plastic that can be used in place of money. In many countries, credit cards have a built-in computer chip containing information that can be read by a machine when the card is used. The credit card company pays for the goods, and you pay the credit card company a month or so later.

Find out more
EUROPEAN UNION
ROCKS AND MINERALS
TECHNOLOGY
TRADE AND INDUSTRY

MONGOL EMPIRE

IN THE LATE 1100s a masterful chieftain united a group of wandering tribes into a powerful army. He was called Genghis Khan; the tribes were the Mongols. All were toughened by a harsh life spent herding on the treeless plains of northeastern Asia. Determined to train the best army of his time, Genghis built up a formidable cavalry force. Using their traditional composite bows and new weapons such as gunpowder, they were invincible. In 1211, the Mongols invaded China, then swept through Asia. They moved at incredible speed, concentrating their forces at critical moments. All their military operations were planned to the smallest detail. Looting and burning as they came, they struck terror into the hearts of their enemies. In 1227, Genghis Khan died, leaving a huge empire to his four sons, who extended it through Asia Minor into Europe. However, the empire broke apart as rival khans (Mongol kings) battled for control.

GENGHIS KHAN
Temüjin (1162-1227) was the son of a tribal chief. His father was murdered when Temüjin was still a child, and when he grew up he defeated his enemies, united all other tribes under his control, and took the title Genghis Khan, "prince of all that lies between the oceans". He aimed to conquer the world.

Armour-piercing arrow

Cavalry controlled horses with their feet to leave their hands free for fighting.

MONGOL KHANATES
After Genghis's death, the Mongol Empire divided into four khanates, or states, with different rulers. Kublai, grandson of Genghis, ruled the eastern khanate. The smaller western empires, although briefly united in the 1300s by Tamerlane the Great, gradually disintegrated.

COMPOSITE BOW
Mongols made their deadly bows out of wood, horn, and sinew, which gave the bows incredible power. The Mongols were superb archers, able to string, aim, and fire at full gallop. They developed armour-piercing arrows, whistling arrows for signalling, and even arrows tipped with grenades.

Strung bow

Unstrung bow

Horses in battle gear

MONGOL EMPIRE
1206 Temüjin unites all the tribes of Mongolia.
1219 Mongols invade Persia.
1223 Mongols invade Russia.
1237 Batu, grandson of Genghis Khan, invades north Russia.
1240 Batu invades Poland and Hungary.
1260 Mamelukes, Egyptian warriors, defeat Mongols.
1279 Kublai Khan defeats China.
1370 Tamerlane the Great conquers the western khanates.

YURTS
Tribes wandered the Mongolian steppes following their herds of sheep, goats, cattle, and horses. They lived in circular tents called yurts, which they took with them when they moved. The women drove wagons which held the yurts; the men hunted, looked after the herds, and traded for grain and metal. Mongols of today still live in yurts.

Find out more
ASIA, HISTORY OF
CHINA
EXPLORERS

MONKEYS AND APES

AMONG THE MOST INTELLIGENT creatures on Earth are the apes – chimpanzees, gorillas, gibbons, and orang-utans. They have large brains, long arms, fingers, and toes, and their bodies are covered in hair. In body shape and intelligence these creatures resemble humans. Apes and humans both belong to the larger group known as primates. Closely related to apes are monkeys, a larger group of animals that includes baboons, macaques, colubuses, and marmosets. Monkeys and apes have a similar body plan, although monkeys tend to be smaller. A pygmy marmoset weighs only 150 g (5 oz), whereas a huge male "silverback" gorilla weighs as much as 180 kg (400 lb). Both monkeys and apes have a rounded face, small ears, and large eyes which face forward. They use their front limbs like arms, and their hands can grasp strongly and manipulate delicately. Most monkeys have tails, which they use as a counterbalance as they swing through trees. In some monkeys the tail is strong and prehensile (grasping); apes, however, have no tails. Apes and monkeys feed on a variety of foods, including fruit, leaves, insects, and birds' eggs.

ORANG-UTAN

The richly coloured orang-utan is found in the forests of Borneo and Sumatra in southeast Asia. Orang-utans spend most of their time high up in the trees searching for fruit, shoots, leaves, and insects. They live alone, except where there is plenty of food.

Prehensile hand can grasp.

Arms are very long in relation to the body.

Shaggy coat of reddish-brown hair

Today, orang-utans are in danger of extinction because their forest homes are being cleared for timber and farmland.

GORILLA

Measuring up to 2 m (6 ft) in height, gorillas are the largest apes. Gorillas are slow, gentle creatures – unless disturbed – and they spend their time resting and eating leaves, stems, and shoots. Gorillas live in small family groups that travel slowly through the forest, eating some but not all of the food in one place before moving on to another area.

BREEDING
A gorilla group contains between five and 10 animals. There is one large male, several females, and their young of various ages. The young are born singly; a female gives birth about every four years.

PRIMATES
All monkeys and apes belong to the mammal group called primates. Other primates include bush babies, pottos, tarsiers, and humans. Today, many primates, including gibbons and the other apes, are on the official list of endangered species.

MACAQUE MONKEY
Monkeys and apes show behaviour that we describe as "intelligent". These creatures communicate well, have good memories, and are able to solve problems. A famous example is the Japanese macaque monkey, which discovered that by washing its food in water it could get rid of the dirt and sand on it. Other members of the troop saw what the monkey was doing and copied it.

GIBBON

A gibbon's muscular arms and hands are so long that the knuckles touch the ground even when the gibbon stands upright. Gibbons live in family groups of a male, a female, and two to four young. There are 14 kinds of gibbon; the largest is the siamang, which weighs about 10 kg (22 lb). The siamang is so heavy that it cannot swing out to the tips of thin branches as other gibbons can.

Gibbons feed mainly on fruit and young leaves.

The acrobatic gibbon swings through the trees of southeast Asia and rarely comes down to the ground.

Young chimpanzees spend much of their time playing with objects and chasing each other. This helps prepare the chimp to find food and fight off enemies in adult life.

Most monkeys and apes depend on trees for shelter and food, particularly in the rain forests.

COMMUNICATION

Many monkeys communicate by sounds. The howler monkey of South America produces extremely loud howling noises using its specialized larynx (voice box). These sounds warn other howler troops to stay out of the group's territory. The leading male howler is usually the main shouter and can be heard nearly 3 km (2 miles) away.

CONSERVATION

The forests where monkeys and apes live are being cut down at a great speed. Newly planted trees are soon removed for timber, so they do not provide homes for the local wildlife. Dozens of different kinds of monkeys are at risk. Among them is the woolly spider monkey of Brazil. Some non-profit organizations have taken up their cause. Their three-point programme works through rescue and rehabilitation, conservation education, and research.

BABOON

The African baboon can climb but usually walks or gallops on all fours. Baboons are easy to study because they live in open country, and scientists have learned much about their social life. Baboons live in troops. Each troop is based around senior females and their offspring. Growing males tend to live alone while they are maturing. When a male becomes an adult he joins a troop, but has to battle with other males to establish his rank. The troop protects itself against predators such as lions and against other baboon troops that stray into its territory.

CHIMPANZEE

Chimpanzees are the animals which remind us most of ourselves – because of their facial expressions and the way they play games, make tools, and solve puzzles. Chimpanzees live in groups which sometimes fight with neighbouring groups. Their main foods are fruit, leaves, seeds, flowers, insects, and sometimes larger creatures such as monkeys and deer. Chimpanzees live deep in the forests and open grassland of Africa. Pygmy chimps or bonobos are found only in the thick forests of the Democratic Republic of Congo (Zaire).

Find out more
ANIMALS
CONSERVATION
and endangered species
EVOLUTION
FOREST WILDLIFE
MAMMALS

MOON

Lava once flowed from the Moon's interior, following huge meteorite impacts more than 4,000 million years ago. The lava solidified into smooth-floored plains called seas, or maria.

OUR NEAREST NEIGHBOUR in space is the Moon. It orbits, or circles, the Earth keeping the same face pointed towards us. The Moon is a hostile place. It has no atmosphere to keep the temperature fairly even, as Earth does. Instead, temperatures range from a scorching 115°C (240°F) during the Moon's day to an icy -160°C (-260°F) at night. There is no water, so no plants or animals can live there. Great plains stretch over the Moon's surface, dotted with huge mountains and scarred by numerous craters. The Moon does not produce light of its own. We see the Moon because it acts like a huge mirror, reflecting light from the Sun. The Moon is a natural satellite – something that orbits around a planet or a star. There are many moons circling the other planets in the solar system.

Craters were formed by meteorite impacts. A few are a result of volcanic activity within the Moon.

BIRTH OF THE MOON
There have been many theories to explain the formation of the Moon. Scientists have suggested that the Moon may be a piece of the Earth that broke away millions of years ago. Today, however, most astronomers believe that the Moon was formed when an asteroid the size of Mars struck the Earth about 4.5 billion years ago.

The gravitational attraction of the Moon causes tides to rise and fall in the Earth's oceans.

1 New moon (moon invisible)
3 Half moon (first quarter)
5 Full moon
7 Half moon (last quarter)

2 Crescent moon
4 Gibbous moon (waxing)
6 Gibbous moon (waning)
8 Old moon

Moon seen from here

PHASES OF THE MOON
As the Moon orbits the Earth, different shapes, or phases, appear, depending on the amount of the sunlit side of the Moon that is visible from Earth.

LUNA 3
Until 1959, the far side of the Moon had never been seen. In October of that year, the Russian space probe *Luna 3* (right) sent back the first photographs of this part of the Moon.

OTHER MOONS
Our solar system contains more than 150 known moons. Nearly all circle the giant outer planets and are made of ice mixed with rock. The largest planet, Jupiter, has at least 63 moons, three of them larger than our own moon. One, Io (seen alongside Jupiter, left), is alive with active volcanoes. Another, Ganymede, is the largest satellite in the solar system. Some of Saturn's moons are very small and orbit in the outer sections of the planet's rings.

Armstrong's crew member, Edwin Aldrin, stands by the lunar module.

LUNAR LANDINGS
In 1966, the Russian *Luna 9* spacecraft made the first controlled landing on the Moon. It was only three years later, in July 1969, that American astronaut Neil Armstrong climbed down from the *Apollo 11* lunar module to become the first person on the Moon.

MOON FACTS

Distance from Earth	384,401 km (238,855 miles)
Diameter at equator	3,477.8 km (2,160.5 miles)
Time for each orbit	27 days, 7 hours, 43 minutes
Time between full moons	29 days, 12 hours, 43 minutes
Gravity at surface	1/6 of Earth's surface gravity
Brightness	1/425,000 brightness of Sun

Find out more
ASTRONOMY
EARTH
OCEANS AND SEAS
PLANETS
SPACE FLIGHT

MOUNTAINS

CONTINENTS COLLIDE and grind against one another, while hot, molten rock bubbles beneath the Earth's surface. These powerful forces thrust up mountains reaching as high as 8 km (5 miles). Many mountains are still growing, and those that formed long ago are slowly wearing away. Some mountains are volcanoes, made of layers of solidified lava which build up as the volcano erupts. There are mountains under the oceans and on other planets. The highest known mountain is on Mars; it is three times as high as Mount Everest.

The Earth has two vast mountain ranges. The Rocky Mountains and Andes run through North and South America; the mighty Himalayas, Alps, and Atlas Mountains stretch across Asia, Europe, and North Africa. These mountains are "young": they formed during the last 50 million years. Other ranges, such as the Urals in Russia, are much older and lower. The forces of erosion have worn them down since they were first formed more than 200 million years ago.

High on the mountaintop it is so cold that plants cannot grow. There is only snow and bare rock.

MOUNT EVEREST
The world's highest mountain is Mount Everest, on the border of China and Nepal. It rises to 8,850 m (29,035 ft). Above are Edmund Hillary of New Zealand (left) and Tenzing Norgay of Nepal who first climbed Everest in 1953.

MOUNTAIN CLIMBING
Mountain climbing requires special equipment, such as ropes to prevent falls, and crampons – steel spikes fixed to mountaineers' boots which grip ice.

Higher still, only plants that are adapted to the cold are able to grow.

Forests of pine trees grow higher up the mountain where it is colder.

AVALANCHE
Snow and ice can suddenly crash down a steep mountainside. This is called an avalanche, and it often occurs in spring as the snow melts.

MOUNTAIN ZONES
A high mountain has several zones, or regions, containing different kinds of plants. Forests cover the mountain's lower reaches. Further up is a zone of small, low-lying plants. Snow covers the summit, which is bare of plant life. Zones occur because the air becomes colder higher up the mountain.

Forests of broad-leaved trees and a wide range of other vegetation grow at the base of the mountain.

Formation of block mountains

Squeezing action pushes up blocks of rock.

Block wears away over many years to produce a mountain.

FAULTING AND FOLDING
As the continents move, they squeeze layers of rock. These movements produce huge cracks, or faults, and push up blocks of rock which form block mountains. The movements also make the Earth's surface buckle, forming fold mountains. Dome mountains appear when molten granite pushes the rock above it into a huge hump.

Formation of fold mountains

As layers of rock are squeezed, they form zigzag folds.

The rocks then crack and wear away at the top of the curve, forming jagged mountains.

EROSION
Ice, wind, and running water break up rock, slowly wearing it away over millions of years. This process of erosion carves out deep valleys and creates high peaks. Continuing erosion wears away the peaks, so that the mountains become lower and more rounded.

Find out more
CONTINENTS
EARTH
MOUNTAIN WILDLIFE
OCEANS AND SEAS
VOLCANOES

MOUNTAIN WILDLIFE

LAMMERGEIER
The lammergeier is one of the biggest vultures. It has a wingspan of about 3 m (10 ft) and soars over the high mountain peaks of Africa, Asia, and Europe. This bird of prey feeds mostly on carrion (bodies of dead animals).

THE MOUNTAIN RANGES of the world are home to all kinds of wildlife – from tiny beetles to huge bears. The lower slopes are often covered with lush vegetation and are rich in animal life. Higher up the mountain the temperature is lower, and there is less wildlife. Mammals living here have thick fur to survive the cold. In places too steep for most creatures to climb, sure-footed goats and chamois leap with ease over the rocks. Near the top of the mountain the wind is so strong that only powerful birds such as condors can fly. In some windy areas the insects have lost their wings during the course of evolution; wings would be useless to them. Spiders and wingless insects live higher up the mountain than any other creature. As you climb higher the temperature drops by 3.6°C (6.5°F) for every 300 m (1,000 ft) of height. Above about 2,400 m (8,000 ft) small shrubs grow, bent and twisted by the icy winds. Higher up still, only mosses and lichens grow, and at the very top there is permanent snow and ice.

CONSERVATION
Wildlife parks protect mountain animals such as the bobcat shown here. In the past people hunted the bobcat for its fur; today this cat is an endangered species.

This map shows the main mountain ranges of the world.

North America

Europe

Asia

Africa

South America

Australia

■ *Mountains*

The mountain goat is a North American relative of the European chamois. Its body is more thickset and sturdy, and it is three times the weight of a chamois. The mountain goat moves slowly and deliberately through deep snow.

CHAMOIS
A rubbery hoof pad allows the chamois to grip stony surfaces with ease as it leaps nimbly among rocks in search of grasses, herbs, and flowers. Chamois live in groups of up to 30 females and young. The males live alone except in the breeding season.

MOUNTAIN PLANTS
High up where trees do not grow, alpine flowers bloom in the short summer. The word *alpine* means above the tree line. The leaves of most alpine flowers grow low and flat so they are protected from the bitter winds. These flowers are pollinated mainly by flies, butterflies, and other insects that have survived the winter as eggs or as adults under the snow.

The trumpet gentian is named for its deep trumpet of petals. It grows in stony places and in damp, short turf at heights of 3,000 m (10,000 ft), in the Alps, Pyrenees, and Apennines of Europe.

Today the edelweiss is a protected plant in many areas.

The alpine longhorn beetle shown here suns itself on mountain flowers and feeds on their pollen.

SPECTACLED BEAR
The only bear in South America is the spectacled bear, so-named because of the markings around its eyes. It lives in the Andes Mountains and is found in warm, moist forests and mountains at heights of 3,500 m (11,500 ft). Spectacled bears eat a wide range of foods, including leaves, fruits, insects, eggs, small deer, and other mammals.

ROCK HYRAX
The small, furry, stoutly built hyrax of Africa is the closest living relative of the elephant – the largest animal on land. Rock hyraxes live at heights of up to 4,000 m (13,300 ft) in rocky places such as Mount Kenya.

Hyraxes eat mainly grasses.

Find out more
ANIMALS
BIRDS
CONSERVATION
and endangered species
FOREST WILDLIFE
LIONS, TIGERS,
and other big cats
MOUNTAINS

MUSCLES AND MOVEMENT

EVERY MOVEMENT YOU MAKE is powered by muscles. Muscles are controlled by nerve signals from the brain. There are three main types of muscle – skeletal, smooth, and cardiac. Skeletal muscle is also called striated muscle, and it covers the bones of the skeleton. It is attached to the bones by cords called tendons. When the muscle contracts, or shortens, it moves the bone. Skeletal muscles are also called voluntary muscles because they can be controlled at will. Smooth muscle is found in the digestive system, bladder, and blood vessels. It is called involuntary muscle because it works automatically, even when you are asleep. Cardiac muscle is found only in the heart. All muscles need energy in order to work properly. Blood carries oxygen and glucose (sugar) to muscles to provide them with fuel. As a muscle works harder, it needs more fuel, so the heart pumps faster to supply it with more blood.

KEEPING FIT
If skeletal muscles are not used regularly they gradually waste away. Regular exercise is an important part of staying healthy. Taking part in a sport, or exercising three or four times a week, helps keep a person fit.

Flexors move fingers.

Pectoralis moves shoulder and helps deep breathing.

Deltoid raises arm.

Trapezius pulls shoulder back and up.

Rectus abdominis strengthens front of abdomen.

Skeletal muscle looks striped under the microscope.

Gluteus maximus, used in walking and climbing.

Gastrocnemius bends foot downwards.

Biceps femoris (hamstring) moves knees and hips.

Sartorius bends and rotates thigh.

Smooth muscle has no stripes under the microscope.

HUMAN MUSCLES
A simple movement such as lifting your arm involves dozens of muscles, acting together in sequence with split-second timing. About 650 muscles move the various parts of the skeleton. Muscles work in teams. The largest muscle is called the gluteus maximus, in the buttock. The smallest muscles are the tiny muscles of the small bones inside the ear. Altogether, muscles make up to half an adult's body weight.

Biceps contracts and shortens.

Elbow bends.

Triceps relaxes.

Biceps relaxes and lengthens.

Triceps contracts and shortens.

Elbow straightens.

BICEPS AND TRICEPS MUSCLES
Muscles can pull, but they cannot push. Many, such as the biceps and triceps muscles in the upper arm, are arranged in opposing pairs. The biceps muscle in the arm contracts to pull on the forearm bones and bend the elbow. The triceps muscle in the arm contracts to straighten the elbow.

Epimysium (muscle sheath)

Fascicle (bundle of fibres)

Muscle fibre

Blood vessel

Myofibril

Healthy muscle has a good flow of oxygen.

Unhealthy muscle has fatty deposits.

INSIDE A MUSCLE
Each muscle consists of a bundle of thin fibres. Each of these fibres is made up of even smaller myofibrils. Myofibrils contain long, interlocking groups of molecules called actin and myosin. Actin and myosin molecules slide past each other in ratchet fashion in order to make the muscle contract.

Find out more
BRAIN AND NERVES
HEART AND BLOOD
HUMAN BODY
LUNGS AND BREATHING
SKELETONS

MUSHROOMS
TOADSTOOLS, AND OTHER FUNGI

Champignon mushrooms grow in a ring in meadows and in gardens. Many people used to believe these were magic fairy rings.

BRIGHTLY COLOURED TOADSTOOLS, delicate mushrooms, and the furry green mould on a rotting piece of bread all belong to a unique group of organisms called fungi. Fungi are neither plants nor animals. They are the great decomposers of the natural world. Fungi feed by releasing chemicals called enzymes which rot away whatever they are feeding on. The dissolved nutrients and minerals are absorbed and recycled by the fungi. Many kinds of fungi grow in damp woodlands and lush, grassy meadows, especially during autumn. There is no scientific difference between mushrooms and toadstools, but toadstools are often more colourful, and some are extremely poisonous. The part of a mushroom that we eat is called the cap. It contains spores – minute cells which grow into new mushrooms when they are released from the cap. Some harmful fungi cause diseases on plants and ringworm in humans. Yeast is a fungus used to make bread dough rise. Another fungus is used to make the antibiotic drug penicillin.

MOULD
The decaying parts of plants and animals are rotted away by pinmould, which grows on damp bread, and is the blue mould growing on this peach.

BEEFSTEAK FUNGUS
This fungus grows on trees. It is called the beefsteak bracket because it looks like a piece of undercooked steak.

Ring where rim of cap was attached to stalk — Cap — Gills inside cap — Stalk — Young cap

Spores are released from between the gills of mature caps.

EDIBLE FUNGI
Many mushrooms and other fungi are edible; some are not only delicious but also are a good source of minerals and fibre. Cultivated mushrooms are farmed in dark, damp sheds on beds of peat. Collecting wild fungi to eat can be very dangerous. Some deadly poisonous fungi look just like edible mushrooms.

OYSTER MUSHROOM
The oyster mushroom is common on beech trees; its cap looks like the shell of an oyster. Oyster mushrooms are tasty and keep well when they are dried.

FIELD MUSHROOM
During the autumn, field mushrooms spring up overnight in damp pastures and meadows.

MOREL
Prized for its flavour, the morel's cap is crisscrossed with patterned ridgework.

CHANTERELLE
The funnel-shaped cap of the chanterelle mushroom is yellow and smells like an apricot. It is found in oak, beech, and birch woods. It grows slowly, preserves well, and is much prized by chefs.

GIANT PUFFBALL
When the giant puffball ripens, its top breaks open, and clouds of tiny spores puff out with the slightest breeze or the smallest splattering of rain.

DUTCH ELM DISEASE
Dead and dying elm trees are a familiar sight in Europe and North America. A deadly fungus carried on the bodies of elm bark beetles, which live on elm trees, has killed millions of trees. The fungus grows through the bark, blocking the water-carrying tubes inside the trunk.

POISONOUS FUNGI
People die every year from eating poisonous fungi. Some of these are brightly coloured toadstools which are easily recognized. Others, such as the destroying angel, look harmless, but cause death rapidly if they are eaten.

Death cup

The bright red fly agaric toadstool is poisonous. Small amounts can cause unconsciousness.

The harmless-looking death cup is one of the most poisonous fungi. Less than 28 g (1 oz) can kill a person in only a few hours.

Fly agaric

Find out more
FOREST WILDLIFE
FRUITS AND SEEDS
PLANTS
TREES

MUSIC

MUSICIANS MAKE MUSIC by carefully organizing sounds into a regular, pleasing pattern to entertain listeners. Notes are the starting point for all music. A note is a regular vibration of the air which musicians create with musical instruments or with their voices. The more rapid the vibration, the higher the pitch of the note – the higher it sounds to a listener. Certain notes sound better together than others. Most music uses these notes, organized into a scale. A scale is a series of notes that increase gradually and regularly in pitch. Musicians usually play or sing notes at fixed time intervals. We call this regular pattern of notes the rhythm or meter of the music. A melody or tune is a combination of the rhythm, the notes the musician plays, and their order. The melody is the overall pattern that we hear and remember – and whistle or hum days or perhaps weeks later.

Ancient musicians of Ur in Sumer (now southern Iraq) played lyres, flutes, pipes, and percussion instruments.

THE FIRST MUSIC
The chanting of prehistoric people was probably the earliest music. The oldest surviving musical instruments are mammoth bones from northern Eurasia; musicians may have banged them together or blown them to make notes about 35,000 years ago.

The clef shows the pitch at which to play the music. This is the treble clef.

The key signature shows which key the music is in. A key is a series of related notes.

A curved tie line joining two identical notes means they must be played as one unbroken note.

The shape of each note tells the musician how long to play it. This is a quarter note.

Allegro — *The speed of the music is often written in Italian. Allegro means "quickly".*

The time signature shows the musician the meter in which to play the piece. This is four-four or common time.

Rests show where the musician should pause.

mf — *Dynamic markings indicate how loudly to play the music – mf stands for mezzo forte, or moderately loud.*

When eighth notes are next to each other their hooks are usually joined together.

All music is divided into equal measures, each of which has the same number of beats, as indicated by the time signature. The bar marks the end of the measure.

A crescendo shows that the music gets gradually louder.

The position of the notes on or between the five horizontal staff lines indicates their pitch. Musicians use letters of the alphabet as names for each of the eight notes in an octave.

c d e f g a b c

NOTATION
Composers need a way of writing down the music they create. Musical notation is a code of symbols and signs that records every aspect of the music. In the 9th century, monks began to use musical notation to help them remember the tunes of holy songs. The system in use today had developed fully by about 1200 CE.

JAZZ
The essential ingredient of jazz is improvisation – the musicians make up some or all of the music as they play it. Black musicians created the very first jazz music at the beginning of the 20th century in New Orleans, U.S.A. Jazz is a mixture of blues, religious gospel, and European music.

Charlie "Bird" Parker (1920-55) popularized a new form of jazz, called "bebop", in the 1940s.

CHAMBER MUSIC
Classical – rather than pop – music for small groups of instruments is called chamber music. Chamber music was so called because it began as music for enjoyment in chambers, or rooms, in the home. Composers wrote different types of music for theatres or churches. Today, performances of chamber music often take place in concert halls.

TRADITIONAL MUSIC

In much traditional music the composer is unknown, and the music itself may not be written down. Performers are often non-professional musicians who learn the tunes "by ear" – by listening to each other play – so they do not need a written score. Musicians sometimes make small changes as they play, so there are often many slightly different versions of the same traditional melody.

Buddhist monks blow large horns as part of their religious ceremonies.

Cheerleaders keep time with marching music and encourage spectators to join in songs and chants.

MILITARY AND MARCHING MUSIC

Music with a strong, steady beat helps soldiers march in step. Today, military bands are not the only ones to play marching music. American high schools and football teams often have their own marching bands, which entertain the crowds at halftime and on special occasions.

RELIGIOUS MUSIC

Music has always played an important part in religion. In religious ceremonies, music inspires people to think about their God or gods. It accompanies religious songs and sacred dances. Composers also choose religious themes for music that is not part of worship: *Messiah* by the German composer George Frideric Handel (1685-1759) sets part of the Bible to music.

ROCK MUSIC

During the 1950s a new form of popular music was heard for the first time. Rock and roll songs had a powerful beat and words that young people could relate to. This form of music began in the United States, where it grew from traditional rhythm and blues played by black musicians. Over the years it has influenced many other musical forms.

American-born singer Elvis Presley (1935-77) sold millions of rock and roll records and starred in 33 movies.

CLASSICAL MUSIC

Classical music has become increasingly popular in recent years, partly thanks to the efforts of young musicians such as violinist Vanessa Mae. Mae started writing her own music at age nine, and by age 18 had made several records and performed in classical concerts all over the world. She has also mixed classical with modern by combining the sounds of acoustic and electric violins.

Find out more

FILMS
MUSICAL INSTRUMENTS
SOUND
UNITED STATES OF AMERICA

MUSICAL INSTRUMENTS

THE POUNDING BEAT of an electric guitar might seem far removed from the delicate trill of a classical violin, yet these two instruments make their different sounds in a similar way. Both use a stretched string to create the vibrations we hear as music. The guitar and the violin evolved in a similar manner, but they actually belong to different families of musical instruments. String instruments such as the violin make their notes when the musician plucks the strings or draws a stretched bow – a bundle of horsehair – across them. Electric instruments, such as the electric guitar, produce weak vibrations that must be amplified for the audience to hear the music. There are five other groups: woodwind, percussion, brass, keyboard, and electronic. This short list includes a huge variety: some instruments, such as the hollow wooden flute, are very simple; others, such as the synthesizer, are highly complex.

CONCH HORNS
Conch sea shells made fine trumpets in ancient times – as they still do in modern Peru.

STRING INSTRUMENTS
Vibrating strings stretched across these instruments make the musical note: the finer the string and the shorter its length, the higher the note. The size of the instrument also affects its sound. The small violin, for example, produces higher sounds than the large double bass. Musicians pluck the strings of guitars, harps, and lutes, and usually use a bow to play the violin, viola, cello, and double bass.

Playing the violin

CELLO
The four cello strings make a rich, mellow sound.

VIOLIN
To play the violin the musician holds it under the chin.

WOODWIND INSTRUMENTS
Blowing into a woodwind instrument makes the air inside vibrate; this produces the musical notes. Covering the holes in the tube with fingers or keys changes the length of the vibrating air, producing different notes. The instruments with the shortest tubes, such as the piccolo, make the highest notes. Other woodwind instruments are the bassoon, English horn, saxophone, clarinet, oboe, and flute.

FLUTE
To play a side-blown flute such as this one, you blow across the tube.

Upper joint

Keys

Body joint

Keys

Head joint

Lip plate

Blowhole

Bell joint

Reed

OBOE
The mouthpiece of an oboe is a double reed (a piece of thin wood). The instrument makes a clear, sad sound.

Reed

Tip

OBOE REED
Most professional oboe players make their own reeds by binding two pieces of split cane to a tube called a staple.

Staple

A flautist playing a side-blown concert flute

Playing the oboe

A wood frame pulls horsehair tight across the bow. Sliding the bow across the strings makes them vibrate.

215

BRASS

Some of the most exciting sounds in music come from brass instruments. This group includes the French horn, trumpet, bugle, cornet, trombone, and tuba. The instruments are long tubes of brass or other metal curved around for easier handling. Sounds produced by the musician's lips on the mouthpiece vibrate down the tube. Pressing the valves opens more of the tube, making the pitch of the note lower. The trumpet has a long history. When the Egyptians buried King Tutankhamun more than 3,000 years ago, they placed a trumpet in his tomb.

Playing the horn

THE CORNET
Musicians in military and brass bands often play the cornet, which is descended from the horns that were blown to announce the arrival of a mailcoach. The cornet is one of the smallest brass instruments, with a tube about 1.5 m (4.5 ft) long.

Cornet player

FRENCH HORN

Uncurled, this horn is 5 m (16 ft) long. It developed from an 18th-century hunting horn and makes a rich, warm sound. The Austrian composer Wolfgang Amadeus Mozart created four pieces of music for the French horn.

PERCUSSION

Bells, gongs, and drums are percussion instruments and there are many more, because all over the world people find different objects, such as beads and seeds, that make a noise when beaten or shaken. Some percussion instruments, such as the xylophone and timpani, are tuned to play definite notes.

SNARE DRUM
The wire spring on the bottom skin of the snare drum vibrates when the player strikes the top skin.

Bass strings

Treble strings

Tuning pins

Sounding board

KEYBOARDS
Hammers strike strings in the piano when the pianist presses a key. Pedals keep the note sounding when the key is released.

Iron frame

Pedals

Keyboard

Dampers

Hammers

TRADITIONAL INSTRUMENTS

Musicians in symphony orchestras play only a few of the world's vast range of musical instruments. Many more are used in the traditional or folk music of individual countries. Some of these instruments developed unique shapes in different parts of the world, as musicians explored the music-making potential of local materials. However, some are remarkably similar: the bagpipes are played in Europe, Asia, and Africa.

A flute player from Thailand

ELECTRONIC INSTRUMENTS

These instruments can produce an exciting array of sounds, by either simulating existing instruments or synthesizing completely new sounds. The musician can feed sounds into the memory of the instrument and then play them back together to simulate a whole orchestra.

Find out more
ELECTRONICS
FILM
MUSIC
SOUND

NAPOLEON BONAPARTE

15 August 1769 Born on the island of Corsica.

1779-85 Military school

1799 Becomes ruler of France.

1804 Crowned Emperor.

1812 Defeated in Russia.

1814 Exiled to island of Elba in the Mediterranean.

1815 Returns to France; defeated at Waterloo.

5 May 1821 Dies in exile on the island of St. Helena.

IN A LAVISH CEREMONY IN 1804, Napoleon Bonaparte crowned himself Emperor of the French. He was an unlikely figure to lead his country, and spoke French with a thick Corsican accent. Yet he was one of the most brilliant military leaders in history. Napoleon first caught the public eye in 1793, when he commanded an attack against the British fleet occupying the French port of Toulon. In 1795 he crushed a revolt in Paris and soon led the French armies to victory in Italy. By 1799, Napoleon was strong enough to take power with the help of the army. He made himself First Consul and restored the power of the French government after the chaos left by the French Revolution. He introduced many social reforms, laying the foundations of the French legal, educational, and financial systems. Napoleon was a military genius who went on to control Europe from the English Channel to the Russian border. But he suffered a humiliating defeat in Russia, and when the British and Prussians beat him at the Battle of Waterloo in 1815, Napoleon was sent out of France into exile on a British island in the South Atlantic. He died six years later.

NAPOLEONIC EMPIRE

At the height of his power in 1812, Napoleon ruled Europe from the Baltic to the south of Rome, and his relations ruled Spain, Italy, and parts of Germany. The rest of Germany, Switzerland, and Poland were also under French control, and Denmark, Austria, and Prussia were allies. Only Portugal, Britain, Sweden, and Russia were independent.

EMPEROR
On 2 December 1804, Napoleon crowned himself Emperor of the French in a ceremony at Notre Dame Cathedral in Paris. He had already changed his Italian-sounding name, Buonaparte, to the French name of Bonaparte. Now he was to be known as Napoleon I.

1812 AND THE RETREAT FROM MOSCOW

Napoleon invaded Russia in June 1812 with a force of more than 500,000 men. The Russians retreated, drawing the French army deeper into the country. Napoleon captured the capital, Moscow, but was forced to retreat because he could not supply his army. The harsh Russian winter killed many troops as they returned to France.

INVASION OF ENGLAND
In 1805 Napoleon assembled an army of 140,000 soldiers by the English Channel and drew up plans to invade England which he called "a nation of shopkeepers". These plans included crossing the Channel by ship and balloon, and digging a tunnel under the sea. The invasion was cancelled when the British admiral Nelson defeated the French fleet at the Battle of Trafalgar.

Find out more
EUROPE
EUROPE, HISTORY OF
FRENCH REVOLUTION

NEW ZEALAND

THE ISLAND NATION of New Zealand is a fascinating mixture of cultures and peoples. Maori people were the original inhabitants of the country, which they call Aotearoa, and they still live there, together with the descendants of the early British settlers and immigrants from other European and Asian countries. Only 4.2 million people live in New Zealand, and there are few large towns. The people are young – more than half of them are less than 35 years old – and the number of births per 1,000 of population is among the highest of all developed nations. A former British colony, New Zealand became fully independent in 1947. It is a leading Pacific nation and has strong links with many of the small islands in the region, such as Niue. The landscape of New Zealand is varied. There are towering mountains, glaciers, volcanoes, lakes, hot springs, sandy beaches, rolling hills, and plains.

New Zealand lies in the Pacific Ocean, east of Australia. There are two large islands – the North Island and the South Island – and many smaller ones, making a total area of 268,670 sq km (103,733 sq miles).

KIWI
New Zealand lies far from other land masses, and as a result its wildlife has developed in an unusual way. The kiwi, which cannot fly, is the most famous of all New Zealand creatures. There are several other species of flightless birds.

WELLINGTON

The capital of New Zealand is Wellington, which stands at the southern tip of the North Island. The city lies around a large natural harbour and is a busy port. Older wooden buildings stand close to recent structures built in a more modern style.

Sheep shearers work very quickly: some can clip a lamb in under a minute.

MAORI CULTURE
The Maoris, a Polynesian people, arrived in New Zealand around 950 CE. from islands in the Pacific. Today their descendants keep alive the rich culture of wood carving, weaving, and music and dance, which they brought with them.

FARMING

New Zealand has a warm, moist climate which is ideal for many types of farming. Sheep and cattle ranching are the biggest businesses. There are two cattle and 13 sheep for every human in New Zealand. The country exports more dairy produce and lamb than any other nation and is the second largest exporter of wool. Over the past 15 years production of other crops, such as kiwi fruit, oranges, and lemons, has increased. Newly built fishing boats have helped New Zealand's fleet increase its catch, and today the country is a major seafood exporter.

SOUTH ISLAND

Although the South Island is the largest New Zealand island, it has fewer inhabitants than the North Island. The western side of the island is covered by the Southern Alps, a region of mountains and glaciers, parts of which have not been explored. The rest of the island consists of farmland, grazing land for sheep and cattle, and a few ports and coastal cities.

Find out more

BRITISH EMPIRE
EMIGRATION AND IMMIGRATION
FARMING
MOUNTAINS
PACIFIC OCEAN

Volcano   **Mountain**   **Ancient monument**   **Capital city**   **Large city/town**   **Small city/town**

SCALE BAR

0   50   100   km

0   50   100   miles

STATISTICS

Area: 268,680 sq km (103,730 sq miles)
Population: 4,213,000
Capital: Wellington
Languages: English, Maori
Religions: Anglican, Presbyterian, Roman Catholic, Methodist, non-religious
Currency: New Zealand dollar
Main occupations: Agriculture
Main exports: Butter, wool, lamb, fruit, vegetables, fish, cork, wood, textiles
Main imports: Manufactured goods, iron, steel

SOUTHERN ALPS
On the west coast of the South Island the Southern Alps nearly reach the shore of the Tasman Sea. The terrain is mountainous and steep, with only a few passes between the east and west coasts.

Sutherland Falls, 580 m (1,904 ft)

Aged 19, Jonah Lomu (right) became the youngest ever All Black team member. He was voted player of the tournament at the 1995 World Cup.

AUCKLAND
The city of Auckland stands at a point where the North Island narrows to a strip less than 1.5 km (1 mile) wide. The Pacific lies to the east, and the Tasman Sea to the west, so Auckland has two harbour areas and is New Zealand's chief port. Auckland is important as a distribution centre, particularly for New Zealand's vital dairy industry, and high-rise buildings tower over the city's business centre. Auckland has a mixed population: a third of the people who live in the city are Polynesian.

RUGBY
Rugby is New Zealand's favourite sport. The national team, the All Blacks, are world famous. They are named after their black shirt and shorts. The All Blacks perform the *haka*, a Maori dance, before each international game. Rugby was introduced to New Zealand by Charles John Monro, a New Zealander educated in England. The first game was played by Nelson College and Nelson Football Club in 1870.

MOUNT TARANAKI
The peak of Mount Taranaki in the southwest of the North Island is 2,517 m (8,260 ft) high, so the volcano is visible from many kilometres away. Taranaki is now extinct, but Ruapehu and Ngauruhoe, in the centre of the island, are occasionally active.

Three Kings Islands
North Cape
Cape Reinga
Great Exhibition Bay
Paihia
North Island
Ruawai
Great Barrier Island
Auckland
Whitianga
Tasman Sea
Bay of Plenty
Hamilton
Rotorua
East Cape
Raukumara Range
North Taranaki Bight
Lake Taupo
Taupo
Gisborne
New Plymouth
Cape Egmont
Mount Taranaki 2518m
Mount Ruapehu 2797m
Hawke Bay
Hastings
South Taranaki Bight
Wanganui
Palmerston North
Masterton
Cape Farewell
D'Urville Island
Tasman Bay
Nelson
Picton
WELLINGTON
Cape Palliser
Karamea Bight
Cape Foulwind
Westport
Cook Strait
Cape Campbell
Clarence
Greymouth
Kaikoura
Southern Alps
South Island
Fox Glacier
Pegasus Bay
Christchurch
Mt Cook 3744m
Canterbury Plains
Ashburton
Milford Sound
Lake Wakatipu
Waitaki
Timaru
Canterbury Bight
Queenstown
Clutha
Lake Te Anau
Te Anau
Otago Peninsula
Fiordland
Waiau
Dunedin
Invercargill
Foveaux Strait
Stewart Island
South West Cape

NEW ZEALAND

PACIFIC OCEAN

N W E S

219

NORMANS

BAYEUX TAPESTRY
Dating to the 11th century, the Bayeux tapestry was produced to record the Norman Conquest of England. It shows scenes of battle, and can be seen today at Bayeux, in France.

TODAY, SOLID STONE CASTLES in England, Sicily, and France stand as reminders of the Normans, warriors from northern France, who transformed Europe during the 11th and 12th centuries. The Normans were descendants of the Norsemen, or Vikings, and were formidable fighters. They settled in northern France during the early 900s in an area now known as Normandy. The Normans were not only warriors but also skilled administrators. Their dukes created a complex and efficient society, dividing their kingdom into areas called fiefs. A knight controlled each fief. The Normans reached their height of power under William, Duke of Normandy, who led the conquest of England in 1066. They quickly transformed England into a Norman kingdom, building castles to defend their conquests, as well as churches, monasteries, and cathedrals. By the mid-12th century, the Saxons and Normans had begun to merge into one nation, ruled by the Plantagenet dynasty. In 1204 the king of France conquered Normandy and took it over.

WILLIAM THE CONQUEROR
William, Duke of Normandy (c. 1028-87), was a brilliant, but ruthless general and administrator. He led the Norman invasion of England and, after defeating the Saxon king, Harold II, was crowned king of England.

Sovereign states

SCOTLAND

Unconquered territory

Conquered territory

IRELAND

WALES ENGLAND

Paris

BRITTANY

AQUITAINE

DOMESDAY BOOK
In 1085, King William I ordered a complete survey of England. Known as the Domesday Book, it contained thorough details of people, goods, animals, and lands for almost the whole country.

ARCHITECTURE
The Normans were skilled architects. They built strong castles to guard their conquests, such as the Tower of London, which stands to this day. They also built churches, cathedrals, and monasteries. Norman churches have intricately carved arches over the doors and windows, and massive walls and pillars.

EMPIRE
At the height of Norman power, Henry II (reigned 1154-89) ruled England and much of France, and a separate group of Normans had conquered southern Italy and Sicily.

Find out more

ARCHITECTURE
BRITAIN, ANCIENT
CASTLES
UNITED KINGDOM, HISTORY OF
VIKINGS

NORTH AMERICA

The North American continent stretches from the Arctic Circle to the Tropics and is flanked by the Atlantic, Pacific, and Arctic Oceans. The five Great Lakes of North America form the largest area of fresh water in the world.

THE NORTH AMERICAN continent is a region of great contrasts. Impressive mountain chains – the Appalachians and Rockies – run down its east and west coasts, enclosing a vast, and mostly flat, landscape, criss-crossed by mighty rivers such as the Mississippi and Missouri. The north is blanketed with coniferous forests. The central Great Plains are grasslands, once grazed by huge herds of buffalo. In the north the Arctic region is permanently frozen, while in the south arid deserts and rocky canyons bake in year-round sunshine. Tropical forests cover southern Mexico, and in the southeastern USA, semi-tropical wetlands harbour many endangered species. Native Americans are descendants of the peoples who first settled the continent over 25,000 years ago. They were displaced by European colonists who explored and settled on the continent from the 16th century. Successive waves of immigrants, first from Europe, and then from the rest of the world, continued to settle in North America, drawn by its wealth of natural resources, its fertile prairies, and its vibrant cities – home to most of its population.

THE BIG FREEZE
Severe winter weather is common in the centre of the continent, especially around the Great Lakes, which often freeze over in winter. Chicago, on Lake Michigan, is prone to severe snowstorms, which can cut off the city. In 1998, a freak icestorm in the Canadian Great Lakes region froze power lines, blacking out the area for several days.

ROCKIES
The Rocky Mountains form the backbone of the American continent, separating the great plains of the east from the high plateaux and basins of the west. Stretching from the Canadian Arctic to New Mexico, they are highest in Colorado, where some 254 mountains are over 4,000 m (13,000 ft). The highest point, Mt Elbert, is 4,312 m (14,149 ft).

AUTUMN IN NEW ENGLAND
The climate of North America ranges from the hot rainforests of Yucatán to the frozen Arctic. The eastern coast of the USA has four distinct seasons. The colours of autumnal leaves, especially the bright red of the maple, is a famous sight which attracts many tourists.

TUNDRA IN ALASKA

Tundra is a Finnish word meaning "treeless heights". It describes the landscape of Alaska (above), where the only vegetation is lichens, mosses, turf and low-lying shrubs. The average temperature is below freezing and in winter it can plummet to -32°C (-89.6°F). These low temperatures leave a layer of permanently frozen soil which can reach depths of 1,525 m (5,000 ft).

Moose live in the subarctic forests. They have huge antlers, long legs and fleshy muzzles.

GRAND CANYON

Canyons are dramatic, deep rock formations created by the eroding flow of a river. The most famous is the Grand Canyon in Arizona, formed by the Colorado River. It is 350 km (220 miles) long, and plunges to depths of 1,820 m (5,970 ft). The processes of erosion started about 5-6 million years ago. Some of the rocks at the base are 2 billion years old – the oldest rocks known in the USA.

Limestone, sandstone, shale and granite are eroded at different speeds, giving the Grand Canyon its distinctive layered colours.

Manatees grow to an average length of 3 m (10 ft). These huge, gentle creatures are found in Florida's shallow coastal waters.

FLORIDA EVERGLADE

The Everglades (left) is a vast area of semi-tropical marshland which stretches across the southwestern part of Florida. A series of low islands, called "hammocks", are home to a great variety of trees, ranging from tropical hardwoods, such as mahogany, to bay trees, eucalyptus and mangroves. Over 400 species of bird are found in the Everglades, and other animals such as alligators, tree frogs, and otters thrive in the swampy conditions. The Everglades' unique ecosystem is supported by a cycle of dry winters and wet summers.

MISSISSIPPI

At 6,020 km (3,740 miles) long, the Mississippi is the main river artery of the USA and one of the busiest commercial waterways in the world. It rises in northern Minnesota, flowing south and receives the waters of the Missouri and Ohio rivers in its middle reaches. It drains into the Gulf of Mexico, where it forms a delta which is moving the shoreline out to sea at a rate of nearly 10 km (6 miles) every 100 years.

This bison's thick hair and beard accentuate its size.

This satellite image (above) shows the Mississippi and Missouri rivers converging at St Louis during flooding in 1993.

A barn and yellow canola crop on the Great Plains just east of Washington

GREAT PLAINS

The Great Plains, which stretch across the centre of North America, were once areas of grassland (prairie) grazed by huge herds of buffalo (bison). Over-hunting wiped out the buffaloes and, as the frontier of pioneer settlement moved further west throughout the 19th century, the Plains were settled by farmers. Today, this is one of the most intensively farmed regions in the world, a vast producer of both maize and wheat.

BISON

The so-called American buffalo that used to roam the Great Plains of North America is actually a bison. A fully grown bison stands 2 m (6.6 ft) high and weighs more than 900 kgs (1,985 lbs). Traditionally the bison provided food and clothing for the Native Americans living on the Plains. Up until the 18th century, the bison population flourished as the Native American method of hunting had little effect on numbers. It was not until the "white man" arrived with rifles that the herds were dramatically reduced. During construction of the railways in the 19th century, whole herds were shot to feed the rail workers. Today, only 40,000-50,000 bison remain. Most live in reserves, protected by American law.

URBAN LIFE

Much of the North American continent, such as the drier south and west, is sparsley populated, but there are great concentrations of population and industry in urban areas – especially in the temperate regions along the coasts and the shores of the Great Lakes. New York City (right) lies at the centre of a vast conurbation of cities, which stretches from Boston to Washington D.C. Accessible to both the Atlantic Ocean and the Hudson River, New York City developed as a major port. Today, it is the USA's main financial, commercial, and cultural centre. Toronto is the largest urban area in Canada. It is an important commercial, financial, and industrial centre. The city and its surrounding area produce more than half of Canada's manufactured goods.

BALD EAGLE

The bald eagle, the only eagle native to North America, has been the US national bird since 1782. It has a wingspan of 2 m (7 ft), and is found mainly along the coasts. It is a protected species in the USA.

OIL RIG

The USA has an abundance of natural resources, including oil, coal, and minerals. Oil was found along the coast of East Texas in 1901. After Alaska, Texas is the USA's main oil-producing state. Oil is transported to refineries on the Gulf Coast by pipeline, tanker, and train. Houston is the capital of the oil business, although it is also the centre of high-tech industries and home to the space shuttle programme.

NATIVE AMERICANS

The first people to settle North America crossed into the continent from Asia more than 25,000 years ago. As they settled, they adapted to many different climatic conditions, resources, and terrain. Today, after centuries of conflict with European settlers, many Native Americans now live on Government reservations. The Navajo are the largest tribe in the USA. Most of them live in a large reservation in the Southwest. The tribe is famous for weaving and silverwork and many of their hand-made artefacts are sold to tourists.

NATURAL HAZARDS

A chain of volcanoes stretches from the US-Mexican border to the southern end of South America. Popocatapetl, one of Mexico's many dormant volcanoes, is 5,452 m (17,888 ft) high, with a crater 152 m (500 ft) deep. Central Mexico is also vulnerable to earthquakes, which often hit the country's most heavily populated regions. In 1985, an earthquake in Mexico City killed some 9,500 people.

El Castillo, the temple-pyramid at Chichén-Itzá is 22m (73ft) high. It stands in the main plaza of the city.

DESERT

The barren deserts of the Southwest are harsh and arid places, swept by fierce wind eddies and baked by searing heat. Only the hardiest animals, such as snakes, lizards, and reptiles, can survive these conditions. Spiny-leaved Joshua trees thrive in the desert, and can live for up to 1,000 years.

Joshua trees grow in the higher and cooler parts of California's desert.

Rugged formations of pink and grey rocks and boulders form a stark desert vista.

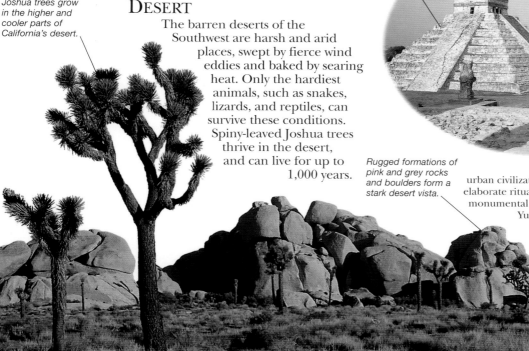

CHICHEN-ITZA

The history of Mexico's urban civilizations dates back to c. 1150 BCE, and the elaborate ritual centres of the Olmec. The Maya built monumental cities and temples in the jungles of the Yucatán from c. 200 CE. They are thought to be the first American civilization to develop a writing system. The Mayan pyramid-temple at Chichén Itzá dates to the 12th century CE.

Find out more

CANADA
MEXICO
PILGRIMS
UNITED STATES OF AMERICA

Volcano △ Mountain 🏛 Ancient monument ✦ Capital city ● Large city/town ● Small city/town

ALASKAN GLACIERS
Glaciers are large masses of ice that form when winter snowfall exceeds summer melting. They may be several hundred metres thick. As they move down the valley, they grind and scour the valley floor, leaving rock fragments in their wake. Many of Alaska's glaciers spread over lowlands at the foot of mountain ranges. The Hubbard Glacier forms the longest glacial valley in North America. It is 150 km (93 miles) long, and moves very slowly, at an average rate of about 5 cm (2 in) a day.

MOUNT ST HELENS
The volcano of Mount St Helens in Washington state, USA, has erupted 20 times over the past 4,500 years, most devastatingly in 1980. After several days of volcanic activity, the mountain's height was reduced by 1,100 m (3,600 ft). A resulting avalanche reached speeds of 250 km/h (155 mph), and destroyed 10 million trees. A layer of ash 8 cm (3 in) deep, blanketed surrounding towns.

BERING STRAIT
The Bering Strait separates Asia and North America. It is 85 km (53 miles) wide at its narrowest point. Sea levels were much lower in the last Ice Age, exposing a land bridge. Humans, plants, and animals crossed to America by this route 35-20,000 years ago.

MONARCH BUTTERFLY
Every winter thousands of monarch butterflies migrate from northern USA and Canada to southern California and Mexico. They travel up to 130 km (80 miles) a day.

TOTEM POLE
The Native American tribes of western Canada lived as hunters and fishers. They built towering wooden totem poles, carved with animal and human figures, as a sign of a family's status, as a mark of respect, or as a memorial. Ancient wood carving is now being revived in the region.

CALIFORNIAN REDWOODS
When dinosaurs roamed the Earth, some 60 million years ago, gigantic redwood trees covered much of North America. Today, they are restricted to the northwest coast of the USA. They are the world's tallest trees, reaching heights of 112 m (368 ft).

SCALE BAR
0 500 1000 km
0 500 1000 miles

NORTHERN IRELAND

LYING JUST ACROSS THE IRISH SEA from Scotland, Northern Ireland is part of the United Kingdom. It covers an area of 14,121 sq km (5,452 sq miles), and has a population of just over 1.7 million people, split between a Protestant majority and a slightly smaller number of Roman Catholics. Also known as Ulster, Northern Ireland consists of the six counties of Antrim, Londonderry, Tyrone, Fermanagh, Armagh and Down. Remaining part of the United Kingdom when southern Ireland split away in 1920, Northern Ireland has had a troubled history, dominated by religious and political conflict. Since the late 1990s, peace initiatives have been taking place. In 1998, Catholics and Protestants agreed to share power in a self-governing assembly, but it has proved difficult to make this arrangement work.

Northern Ireland occupies the northeastern part of Ireland. It is bordered by the Republic of Ireland to the south and west, with the Irish Sea to the east.

BELFAST

Belfast is the biggest city in Northern Ireland, and capital of the province. Sitting on the northeast coast, Belfast is a major UK port and manufacturing centre, which was once world famous for its engineering works and shipyards. The *Titanic*, for instance, was built in Belfast. Political troubles have divided the city in recent years.

GIANT'S CAUSEWAY
A major landmark, the Giant's Causeway lies off the coast of County Antrim on the north coast. The thousands of rocks that make up the Causeway are shaped like hexagons, or eight-sided columns. They were created when lava from underground volcanoes cooled in the sea some 60 million years ago. Its name comes from a legend that giants built a causeway to Scotland so they could cross the Irish Sea.

LINEN
The textile industry is one of Northern Ireland's chief industries. Linen-making is traditional. Woven from flax, linen from Northern Ireland is among the finest in the world. Farming and engineering are also important to the economy.

MUSIC
There is a long tradition of music-making in Northern Ireland, and many famous musicians have been born there. Music varies from the pipe and drum bands of the Orange Order, through to traditional Gaelic music and more modern pop music.

The famous singer Van Morrison grew up in Northern Ireland.

PEOPLE
Many of Belfast's children have grown up surrounded by violence, caused by the long-running conflict between Protestants and Roman Catholics. Most Protestants wish to remain part of the United Kingdom, although some favour self-government. Many Roman Catholics would like to unite with the Republic of Ireland in the south.

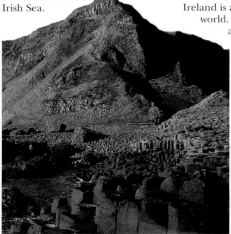

ORANGE ORDER
The Orange Order (supporter, left), a society to support Protestantism, was founded in 1795. It was named after William of Orange, who became the first Protestant king of Britain.

Find out more
IRELAND
UNITED KINGDOM
UNITED KINGDOM, HISTORY OF

NUCLEAR ENERGY

THE ATOMS THAT MAKE UP everything in the universe are the source of a huge amount of energy called nuclear energy. Nuclear energy produces the searing heat and light of the Sun, the deadly explosions of nuclear weapons, and vast amounts of electricity in nuclear power stations. Nuclear energy is based on the fact that matter and energy are different forms of the same thing, and one can be converted into the other. In a nuclear reaction, a tiny amount of matter changes into an enormous amount of energy. The nuclear reaction occurs in the nuclei (centres) of atoms. This can happen in two ways: when the nucleus of a heavy atom splits, in a process called fission, and when two lightweight nuclei join together, in a process called fusion. In nuclear weapons, fission or fusion occurs in a split second. By contrast, nuclear power stations produce electricity from fission reactions that work at a controlled rate.

Experimental nuclear fusion reactor near Oxford, England

Hydrogen nucleus with extra neutron

Neutron

Hydrogen nucleus with two extra neutrons

Helium nucleus

NUCLEAR FUSION
Scientists are trying to build reactors that use nuclear fusion, a process which produces less dangerous waste than nuclear fission (below). Nuclear fusion occurs when hydrogen atoms smash together and join to form heavier atoms of helium. However, nuclear fusion is extremely difficult to achieve. Hydrogen atoms must be held by a magnetic field and heated to a temperature higher than that in the Sun's centre for fusion to occur.

Neutron hits nucleus of uranium atom.

Fission occurs, releasing energy and neutrons.

Reactor core contains pellets of uranium dioxide fuel held in fuel rods. Two thimble-sized pellets would produce enough electricity for a person for one year.

If neutrons travel too rapidly, they bounce off uranium atoms without producing fission. The fuel is surrounded by water, which slows the neutrons down so they produce fission. A material that slows neutrons in a reactor is called a moderator.

Control rods absorb neutrons and slow down the nuclear reaction. In an emergency, the control rods drop into the reactor core and shut off the nuclear reaction.

Pump for high-pressure water system

NUCLEAR FISSION
Nuclear power stations produce energy from the fission of atoms of uranium within uranium oxide pellets. The impact of a particle called a neutron makes an atom of uranium split, releasing heat energy and two or three neutrons. The neutrons strike other uranium atoms and make them divide. Soon, many atoms split, producing a huge amount of energy.

Protective clothing worn when handling nuclear waste

The high-pressure water flows through pipes in a steam generator which transfers its heat to a separate water system. The water in this second system boils to form steam.

Water is pumped around the reactor core at high pressure in a sealed circuit. The nuclear reactions heat the water to more than 300°C (570°F), but the high pressure keeps it from turning into steam.

Steam spins turbines that drive generators, producing electricity.

A third water circuit acts as a coolant, changing the steam back into water which returns to the steam generator once again.

Pressurized water reactor (PWR)

NUCLEAR RADIATION
Some waste from nuclear power stations is radioactive – it produces deadly nuclear radiation consisting of tiny particles or invisible waves that can damage living cells. Some radioactive waste may last for thousands of years, so it is buried underground in sealed containers. Many people are concerned about the dangers of nuclear waste and are demanding an end to nuclear energy production.

NUCLEAR POWER STATION
A fission reaction becomes continuous only if there is a certain amount of fuel present, called the critical mass. In a nuclear reactor, rods contain uranium fuel. The fuel rods are placed close together to provide the critical mass that starts the reaction.

Find out more
ATOMS AND MOLECULES
COLD WAR
ELECTRICITY
ENERGY
LIGHT
SCIENCE, HISTORY OF
SOVIET UNION, HISTORY OF

NUMBERS

3

WHEN WE WANT TO KNOW how many things we have, or measure how large something is, we use numbers. Numbers are symbols that describe an amount. There are only ten number symbols: 0, 1, 2, 3, 4, 5, 6, 7, 8, and 9, but they can be put together in many different ways to make other numbers of any size. As well as counting and measuring, numbers can also be used to work out time and distances, or to put things in order. The skill of working with numbers is called arithmetic. Early humans probably used their fingers and thumbs to count. Because we have ten digits – eight fingers and two thumbs – we developed a system of counting that was based on tens. This is called the decimal system, after the Latin word for ten. Numbers are just as important as words for passing on information. They can be written down, so that other people can read and use them.

FRACTIONS
Sometimes the number 1 has to be divided into portions. Parts of a whole number are called fractions.

COUNTING
When people needed to count higher than ten, they used objects such as pebbles to represent multiples of ten. So, five pebbles and three fingers stood for the number 53. Making calculations with pebbles led to the invention of the abacus, and later the slide rule, and calculator.

Calculator

Using fingers

Ruler

Pebbles

Cardinal numbers

A fraction, two-thirds

A decimal fraction, ten and sixty-five hundredths

NUMBERS IN HISTORY
People have invented many different ways of representing numbers with symbols. The modern decimal system has now been taken up all over the world, but older systems are still used in a few places. Even the Ancient Roman system is used sometimes, especially on clock faces.

The Babylonians invented a number system based on ten about 3,500 years ago, but the symbols took a long time to write down.

I   II   III   IV   V   VI   VII   VIII   IX   X

The Ancient Roman number system goes back to about 500 BCE. It is an awkward system, but it is still sometimes used today.

In about 200 BCE the Hindus used a number system based on ten. About 1,400 years ago they modified it to include zero.

By the 15th century, Hindu-Arabic numbers had replaced Roman numerals as the most popular number system.

0 1 2 3 4 5 6 7 8 9 10

Today, most countries use a modern version of the Hindu-Arabic number system, because it makes calculations easy.

Cricket scoreboard

USING NUMBERS
If you look around, you will see how numbers are used in everyday life. For example, scoreboards, speed limits, distances, prices, TV channels, and the time of day are all shown using numbers. Page numbers in the index of this book show where to find the topics that interest you. Money is also divided into units to make it simple to understand.

TYPES OF NUMBER
Whole numbers that stand for quantities, such as 1, 2, or 3, are called cardinal numbers. Numbers that put things in order, such as 1st, 2nd, or 3rd, are known as ordinal numbers. In a fraction, the number below the line shows how many parts the whole is divided into; the number above shows how many of those parts are being described.

Find out more
ALPHABETS
COMPUTERS
SCIENCE
SCIENCE, HISTORY OF

OCEANS AND SEAS

YOUR FEET MAY BE RESTING firmly on the ground, but more than two thirds of our planet is covered with water. Oceans and seas make up 71 per cent of the Earth's surface. They influence the climate, supply us with food, power, and valuable minerals, and provide a home for a fascinating range of plant and animal life.

The oceans and seas began millions of years ago when the Earth cooled from its original molten state. Water vapour escaped from inside the Earth in volcanic eruptions, cooled, and fell as rain. It filled vast hollows and basins surrounding rocky land masses. These gradually moved around to form the continents and oceans as they exist today. As rivers formed on the land and flowed into the seas, they dissolved minerals from the rocks, making the oceans and seas salty.

OCEAN HUNTERS
Fishing boats sail the oceans and seas to bring us the fish and other sea creatures that we eat. The best fishing grounds are in shallow seas, where the water teems with fish. But catches must be controlled; otherwise the numbers of fish will fall as the fish fail to breed.

Sun

Rise in water level

Moon

Earth

SPRING TIDES
High, spring tides occur when the Earth, Sun, and Moon are in line.

TIDES
Twice a day the level of the seas rises and falls. These changes in level are called tides. They are caused mainly by the pull of the Moon's gravity on the Earth. When the Moon lies directly over the ocean, its gravity pulls the water towards it. Water also rises on the opposite side of the Earth, because the Earth itself is pulled towards the Moon.

THE WORLD'S OCEANS AND SEAS
Oceans are vast bodies of water, usually separating the continents. The Pacific Ocean, which is the largest and deepest, lies between America and Asia and covers more than a third of the globe. The others, in order of size, are the Atlantic, Indian, Southern, and Arctic oceans. The Arctic Ocean lies between the land masses around the North Pole and is largely covered by ice. Seas, bays, and gulfs are smaller bodies of water that lie between arms of land, or between islands and land masses. Some, such as the Caspian and Dead seas, are entirely surrounded by land and are really not seas but large lakes.

Pacific Ocean

Indian Ocean

North Pacific Ocean

Southern Ocean

The Southern Ocean surrounds Antarctica. It includes all the waters between 60 degrees South latitude and the continent of Antarctica.

Atlantic Ocean

Indian Ocean

The Arctic Ocean is an ice-covered ocean at the North Pole.

OCEAN CURRENTS
The water in the oceans is constantly moving in great circular streams, or currents, which can flow about as fast as you walk. Winds blow the surface layer of the oceans to form these currents, which carry warm or cold water along the shores of continents, greatly affecting the weather there. Sometimes, currents flow deep below the surface, moving in the opposite direction to surface currents. For example, surface currents carry warm water away from the equator, while currents deep beneath the sea bring cold water back to the equator. Most seas have strong currents. But the waters of the Sargasso Sea, which lies in the North Atlantic Ocean, are almost still, causing the sea to become choked with seaweed.

NORTH AMERICA

North Atlantic Drift

Gulf Stream

Gulf of Mexico

EUROPE

The Gulf Stream broadens out, slows down, and becomes the North Atlantic Drift. A slow current is called a drift.

THE KON TIKI EXPEDITION
Early peoples may have used the currents to travel across oceans. In 1947 the *Kon Tiki* expedition, led by Norwegian explorer Thor Heyerdahl, tested this theory by sailing a light wooden raft from Peru to the Polynesian Islands.

GULF STREAM
Water heated by the Sun flows out from the Gulf of Mexico. This warm current crosses the Atlantic Ocean and flows around the shores of western Europe. There the winter weather is mild, while places on the other side of the ocean away from the current are freezing cold.

Long, wide ocean
ridges run through
most oceans.

Undersea
mountains rise
from the seabed.

Long, deep trenches
lie near the edges
of some oceans.

UNDER THE OCEANS

A strange landscape lies hidden beneath the oceans. There are huge cliffs, great ranges of mountains, and deep chasms, all far larger than any on land. Much of the ocean floor is a vast flat plain which lies up to 6 km (4 miles) below the surface. Trenches descend as deep as 11 km (7 miles), more than the height of the highest mountain on land. Undersea mountains and volcanoes rise from the plain, many poking their summits above the waves to form islands. The seas around the shores of most continents are not very deep. Most offshore islands are high land rising from the shallow seabed. Coral reefs and atolls grow up from the seabed in warm seas.

Some volcanoes rise
from the deep ocean
floor to form islands.

Many
continents
extend out into
the ocean and
have a wide under-
sea continental shelf
which is about 130 m
(400 ft) deep.

Large offshore islands
rise from the ocean floor
or continental shelf.

The continental shelf
ends in a cliff called
the continental slope.

OCEANOGRAPHY

Our knowledge of the oceans comes from oceanographers, who study the oceans. They sail in special ships with instruments that take samples of the water and mud on the seabed, chart ocean currents, and map the ridges and trenches in the ocean floor. The scientists also dive in submersibles and use underwater robots to see the strange creatures that live in the depths. Satellites look down from space and send back information about the oceans.

WAVES

The surface of the sea is restless, even on the calmest day. Waves ceaselessly rise and fall, eventually reaching the land to lap or crash on the shore. Waves are caused by winds blowing over the ocean. The energy from waves can be used to power generators and produce electricity. However, tsunamis, huge waves that can reach heights of 30 m (100 ft), are very powerful and destructive. Sometimes wrongly referred to as tidal waves, tsunamis are in fact caused by earthquakes and volcanic eruptions.

SHORES AND COASTS

High land at the shore ends in cliffs, and low land slopes gently to form beaches. The waves hurl stones at the base of cliffs, causing rocks to fall and form coasts with bays and headlands. Strange rock formations and caves may result. The waves batter the rocks and break them up into pebbles and then into sand. Beaches form at the base of cliffs, and the sea also sweeps pebbles and sand along the shore to form beaches elsewhere.

Water reaches base of
circle in trough of wave.

Water reaches top of
circle in crest of wave.

Crest topples over
to break on shore.

HOW WAVES MOVE

The water in a wave does not move forwards. It moves in a circle, so the water only goes up and down as a wave passes. The approaching shore holds back the base of the wave, making the top of the wave move faster to break on the shore.

Find out more
CONTINENTS
DEEP-SEA WILDLIFE
EARTHQUAKES
INDIAN OCEAN
OCEAN WILDLIFE
PACIFIC OCEAN
SEASHORE WILDLIFE

OCEAN WILDLIFE

LIFE BEGAN IN THE OCEANS millions of years ago. Today, oceans cover 71 per cent of the planet's surface and provide homes for countless fish, octopuses, seals, sharks, and jellyfish. Ocean wildlife is at its richest in the warm shallow waters of coral reefs, where dazzlingly colourful angelfish and butterfly fish live. In deeper waters, whales, dolphins, and porpoises are found. Most plants and animals live close to the water's surface. Sunlight filters through the surface, allowing microscopic organisms such as diatoms to flourish. An intricate web of small animals feeds on these tiny organisms; larger sea creatures eat the smaller ones, and so on, up the food chain to the large predators such as sharks. Today, many marine plants and animals are threatened; we dump chemical wastes in the oceans, fertilizers flow into the oceans from rivers, and we catch so many fish that fish-eating sea mammals such as seals and dolphins have to compete with us for their food.

Seabirds

COELACANTH
The coelacanth is a survivor from prehistoric times, although scientists first discovered it in 1938. The coelacanth lives around the Comoro Islands, off southeast Africa, and in the eastern Indian Ocean, in water 70–400 m (230–1,300 ft) deep. Adult coelacanths measure about 1.7 m (5.5 ft) in length. Today this fish is threatened because of fish collectors and souvenir hunters.

Common squid

Finback whale

PLANKTON
Billions of tiny organisms float in sea water. Together they are called plankton, from the Greek word *planktos*, meaning "wanderer". Plankton are food for many fish and other sea creatures.

FINBACK WHALE
The finback whale is the second largest living animal (the blue whale is the largest) and is found from the Poles to the tropics. Finbacks grow to about 25 m (85 ft) in length and weigh 73 tonnes (71 tons). They feed by straining shrimplike creatures called krill from the water, using fringes of baleen hanging from the upper jaws.

OPEN OCEAN
Many animals in the open sea are streamlined (sleek in shape) so that they can swim away quickly from predators and chase after prey. There are fish of all shapes and sizes in the open ocean, as well as enormous schools of jellyfish, and mammals such as seals. Sea birds such as albatrosses, petrels, and shearwaters feed at the surface.

SAND TIGER
Sharks are the most aggressive hunters in the ocean. The ferocious sand tiger shark hunts even before it is born, when it is still in its mother's womb. There are 10–15 embryo sharks in the womb, and as they develop, they eat each other until there are only one or two left. The survivors are born fully formed, then swim away to begin their fish-eating lives, growing to 3.5 m (12 ft) in length.

SARDINE
Pacific sardines are related to herrings. Other members of the herring family are the sprat and the shad. All of them are hunted by bigger ocean dwellers such as seals.

HERRING
There were once vast shoals of herring in the oceans; they were an easy catch for fishing boats, and people valued them for their tasty flesh. Today, herring is much less common because people have overfished the oceans. Herring feed on plankton.

SWORDFISH
This spear-nosed hunter is one of the fastest fish in the sea; it can swim in bursts at speeds of 95 km/h (60 mph). The swordfish resembles the marlin and sailfish, and weighs up to 675 kg (1,500 lb). Swordfish injure their prey with sideways slashes of the sword, and then devour them.

Swordfish

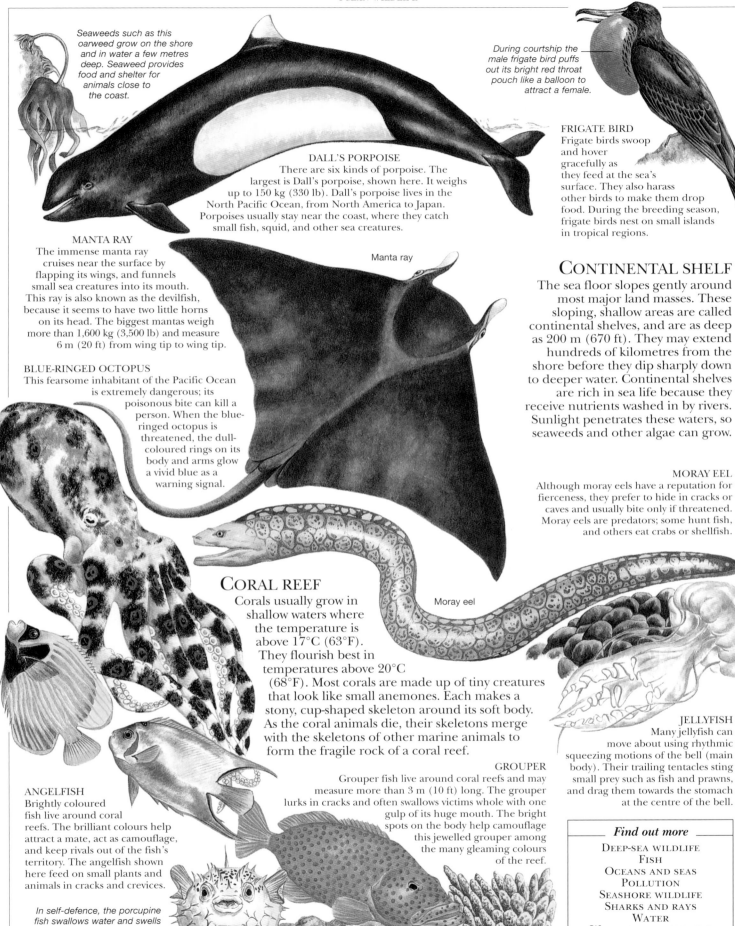

Seaweeds such as this oarweed grow on the shore and in water a few metres deep. Seaweed provides food and shelter for animals close to the coast.

During courtship the male frigate bird puffs out its bright red throat pouch like a balloon to attract a female.

DALL'S PORPOISE
There are six kinds of porpoise. The largest is Dall's porpoise, shown here. It weighs up to 150 kg (330 lb). Dall's porpoise lives in the North Pacific Ocean, from North America to Japan. Porpoises usually stay near the coast, where they catch small fish, squid, and other sea creatures.

FRIGATE BIRD
Frigate birds swoop and hover gracefully as they feed at the sea's surface. They also harass other birds to make them drop food. During the breeding season, frigate birds nest on small islands in tropical regions.

MANTA RAY
The immense manta ray cruises near the surface by flapping its wings, and funnels small sea creatures into its mouth. This ray is also known as the devilfish, because it seems to have two little horns on its head. The biggest mantas weigh more than 1,600 kg (3,500 lb) and measure 6 m (20 ft) from wing tip to wing tip.

Manta ray

CONTINENTAL SHELF
The sea floor slopes gently around most major land masses. These sloping, shallow areas are called continental shelves, and are as deep as 200 m (670 ft). They may extend hundreds of kilometres from the shore before they dip sharply down to deeper water. Continental shelves are rich in sea life because they receive nutrients washed in by rivers. Sunlight penetrates these waters, so seaweeds and other algae can grow.

BLUE-RINGED OCTOPUS
This fearsome inhabitant of the Pacific Ocean is extremely dangerous; its poisonous bite can kill a person. When the blue-ringed octopus is threatened, the dull-coloured rings on its body and arms glow a vivid blue as a warning signal.

MORAY EEL
Although moray eels have a reputation for fierceness, they prefer to hide in cracks or caves and usually bite only if threatened. Moray eels are predators; some hunt fish, and others eat crabs or shellfish.

Moray eel

CORAL REEF
Corals usually grow in shallow waters where the temperature is above 17°C (63°F). They flourish best in temperatures above 20°C (68°F). Most corals are made up of tiny creatures that look like small anemones. Each makes a stony, cup-shaped skeleton around its soft body. As the coral animals die, their skeletons merge with the skeletons of other marine animals to form the fragile rock of a coral reef.

JELLYFISH
Many jellyfish can move about using rhythmic squeezing motions of the bell (main body). Their trailing tentacles sting small prey such as fish and prawns, and drag them towards the stomach at the centre of the bell.

GROUPER
Grouper fish live around coral reefs and may measure more than 3 m (10 ft) long. The grouper lurks in cracks and often swallows victims whole with one gulp of its huge mouth. The bright spots on the body help camouflage this jewelled grouper among the many gleaming colours of the reef.

ANGELFISH
Brightly coloured fish live around coral reefs. The brilliant colours help attract a mate, act as camouflage, and keep rivals out of the fish's territory. The angelfish shown here feed on small plants and animals in cracks and crevices.

In self-defence, the porcupine fish swallows water and swells into a ball shape with its spines poking outwards.

Find out more
DEEP-SEA WILDLIFE
FISH
OCEANS AND SEAS
POLLUTION
SEASHORE WILDLIFE
SHARKS AND RAYS
WATER
WHALES AND DOLPHINS

Volcano Mountain Ancient monument Capital city Large city/town Small city/town

STATISTICS
Area: 790,225 sq km (305,106 sq miles)
Population: 8,490,000
Number of independent countries: 12
Languages: English, local languages and dialects
Religions: Protestant, Roman Catholic, Hindu
Highest point: Mount Wilhelm (Papua New Guinea) 4,509 m (14,793 ft)
Main occupations: Agriculture, fishing

FIJI

Area: 18,270 sq km (7,054 sq miles)
Population: 945,000
Capital: Suva
Currency: Fiji dollar

KIRIBATI

Area: 710 sq km (274 sq miles)
Population: 113,000
Capital: Bairiki
Currency: Australian dollar

MARSHALL ISLANDS

Area: 181 sq km (70 sq miles)
Population: 65,000
Capital: Delap District
Currency: U.S. dollar

MICRONESIA

Area: 2,900 sq km (1,120 sq miles)
Population: 107,000
Capital: Palikir
Currency: U.S. dollar

NAURU

Area: 21.2 sq km (8.2 sq miles)
Population: 14,000
Government Centre: Yaren
Currency: Australian dollar

PAPUA NEW GUINEA

Area: 462,840 sq km (178,700 sq miles)
Population: 6,057,000
Capital: Port Moresby
Currency: Kina

PALAU

Area: 497 sq km (192 sq miles)
Population: 21,000
Capital: Koror
Currency: U.S. dollar

SAMOA

Area: 2,840 sq km (1,027 sq miles)
Population: 220,000
Capital: Apia
Currency: Tala

SOLOMON ISLANDS

Area: 289,000 sq km (111,583 sq miles)
Population: 596,000
Capital: Honiara
Currency: Solomon Islands dollar

TONGA

Area: 750 sq km (290 sq miles)
Population: 121,000
Capital: Nuku'alofa
Currency: Tongan pa'anga

TUVALU

Area: 26 sq km (10 sq miles)
Population: 12,000
Capital: Fongafale
Currency: Australian dollar

VANUATU

Area: 12,190 sq km (4,706 sq miles)
Population: 219,000
Capital: Port-Villa
Currency: Vatu

NEW CALEDONIA
The Isle of Pines (above) is one of the smallest inhabited islands in the New Caledonia group. Like many of the Pacific Islands, New Caledonia is governed by a larger, more powerful country. France rules New Caledonia, and French aid provides one-third of the country's income. Most of the rest comes from the export of nickel – the islands have 40 per cent of the world's reserves of the metal.

DEPENDENCIES
Besides the twelve independent nations listed at the top of the page, there are many other island groups in the Pacific. Most of these islands depend on aid from a larger country, and some have very low populations. Pitcairn for example, is a British colony and is home to less than 100 people.

PAINTERS

ARTISTS USE PAINT in the same way that writers use words to convey ideas on paper. Painters capture the likeness of a face or a flower, but they can do much more than just paint a realistic image. Painters work skilfully with colour, texture, and shape to create all kinds of eye-catching images of the world as they see it. Many cultures throughout history has produced its own great painters, from Giotto in the 14th century to Picasso in the 20th century. There have been many different groups, or movements, in painting, such as classicism, cubism, and pop art. Painters change the way we see the world. Rembrandt's portrait paintings, for example, are powerful studies from real life, whereas Salvador Dali's strange surrealist (dreamlike) landscapes are drawn from his imagination. Painters use all kinds of paint to create a picture – thick blobs of oil colour daubed onto a canvas with a palette knife; delicate brushstrokes of water-colour on a sheet of paper. Some painters dab paint on with sponges, rags, even their fingers; others flick paint onto a surface. Whatever the medium (materials) used, each great painter has his or her own distinctive style.

EARLY PAINTERS
The artists of ancient Egypt decorated the walls of tombs with scenes of gods and goddesses and of hunting and feasting. The Minoan people of early Greece painted their houses and palaces with pictures of dancers, birds, and flowers. Roman artists painted gods and goddesses and scenes from classical mythology.

MEDIEVAL PAINTERS
Up until the 14th century, Western artists painted mostly Christian subjects – the life of Christ and the saints. Painters used rich colours and thin layers of gold to make these religious paintings. These early artists used different methods of painting people from later Western painters, but although the paintings may look flat to us, they are no less powerful. Artists worked on wood panels for altarpieces and painted directly on church walls.

People in medieval paintings sometimes look stiff and expressionless, like the figures in this 11th-century picture (left) of an emperor, a saint, and an angel.

The Sistine Chapel ceiling, painted by Michelangelo.

RENAISSANCE
One of the greatest periods in European painting was the Renaissance, which reached its height in Italy in the late 15th and early 16th centuries. During the Renaissance, painters developed more realistic styles of painting. They studied perspective and the human body, painted more realistic landscapes, and developed portrait painting.

MICHELANGELO
Michelangelo Buonarroti (1475-1564) is one of the best-known Italian Renaissance painters. Much of his work was for Pope Julius II, who commissioned him to paint the ceiling of the Sistine Chapel in the Vatican, in Rome, between 1508 and 1512.

Michelangelo had difficulty in reaching certain parts of the ceiling in the Sistine Chapel, so he built a scaffold and sometimes lay on his back to paint.

GIOTTO
The Italian artist Giotto (c.1266-1337) painted at the beginning of the Renaissance. He brought a new sense of naturalness to paintings. The painting shown above is called *The Flight into Egypt*. It shows Mary and Jesus on a donkey being led by Joseph.

REMBRANDT
Most people know the Dutch artist Rembrandt Harmenszoon van Rijn (1606-69) only by his first name. He is well known for his portraits which are full of expression. The painting shown here is one of many self-portraits.

ROMANTIC MOVEMENT
During the late 18th and early 19th centuries, painters such as the French artist Eugène Delacroix (1798-1863) began a new style of painting, which became known as the Romantic Movement. The romantics used bright colour and a free handling of paint to create their dramatic pictures. The English painter J.M.W. Turner (1775-1851) painted landscapes and seascapes flooded with light and colour.

EASTERN PAINTERS
While European art was developing, Eastern artists were evolving their own styles of painting. The Chinese observed nature accurately and painted exquisite pictures with simple brushstrokes in ink on silk and paper. Some Japanese artists, such as Hokusai (1760-1849), made beautiful prints.

This painting is by the modern Japanese painter Kaii Higashiyama (born 1918); it is called Flowery Glow.

PICASSO
Many people believe that the Spanish painter Pablo Picasso (1881-1973) was the most creative and influential artist of the 20th century. From a very young age, Picasso was extremely skilful at drawing and painting. His restless personality led him to paint in many different styles. One style was his "blue period" of painting, when he concentrated on blue as the main colour for his pictures. In 1907, Picasso painted a picture called *Les Demoiselles D'Avignon*, which shocked many people – it was a painting of human figures represented by angular and distorted shapes. This led to a style of painting called cubism.

This is a detail from the painting by the French artist Fragonard (1732-1806) called The Swing.

The Poppy Field, by Claude Monet

This photograph shows Picasso with a painting of his children, Claude and Paloma. He is on his way to show this painting at an exhibition of his work.

MONET
Claude Monet (1840-1926) was the leader of the impressionists. He painted many pictures of the flowers in his garden at Giverny and in the French countryside, including the picture above right, called *The Poppy Field*. Seen close up, the picture consists of many brushstrokes of different colours, but from a distance the dabs of colour come together to form a field of red flowers.

IMPRESSIONISM
At an exhibition in Paris in 1874 a painting by the French artist Claude Monet caused an uproar. Art critics and the public were used to seeing realistic objects in pictures, but Monet and his fellow artists, known as impressionists, painted in dabs of colour to create the effect of light and shade. Other great artists of the impressionist movement were Camille Pissarro, Pierre Auguste Renoir, Edgar Degas, Mary Cassatt, and Alfred Sisley.

HOCKNEY
David Hockney (born 1937) is a well-known British painter. He is famous for his pictures of California, especially paintings of swimming pools such as this one, called *A Bigger Splash*. Hockney works with many different materials, including photographs and colour photocopies.

MODERN PAINTERS
Since the beginning of the 20th century, painters have experimented with different ways of creating pictures. Picasso and Georges Braque stuck fabric, sand, and newsprint on to canvases to make collages. Piet Mondrian painted in straight lines and right angles. Action painting was developed by the American artist Jackson Pollock, who splashed paint onto huge canvases on his studio floor.

Find out more

ARCHITECTURE
COLOUR
LEONARDO DA VINCI
LIGHT
RENAISSANCE

PEASANTS REVOLT

IN JUNE 1381, A MAJOR UPRISING occurred in England when angry peasants marched on London in protest against an unfair poll tax and harsh working conditions. Known as the Peasants' Revolt, it was the most important uprising by ordinary people in English history. The leaders were Wat Tyler, Jack Straw, and John Ball, a former priest. They led 100,000 men from Kent and Essex to London burning buildings and looting along the way. They also murdered the Archbishop of Canterbury, and some government ministers. Richard II, the 14-year-old king, met the peasants at Smithfield and agreed to abolish serfdom and the poll tax. Most peasants dispersed, but Tyler was killed. After the revolt, Richard failed to keep his promises, but such a heavy poll tax was not imposed again, and serfdom gradually disappeared.

WAT TYLER AND JACK STRAW
Wat Tyler led the Kentish rebels. Jack Straw, a thresher, led a group who set fire to buildings, including the palace of John of Gaunt, the king's uncle.

MORE REVOLTS
Rebellions broke out in St Albans, Hertfordshire, Bury St. Edmonds, Suffolk, Cambridgeshire, Huntingdonshire, Norfolk, and Sussex. Most of the outbreaks were fairly short-lived. The violence frightened the government and after the revolt Jack Straw and John Ball were executed.

Gold noble

Groat

POLL TAX
Poll means "head", and the poll tax was levied on every person over the age of 14. In 1377, parliament imposed a poll tax of one groat to meet the costs of the Hundred Years War. In 1380, it was raised to one shilling (5p) per head, a huge amount then. This sparked off the revolts.

Peasants and Richard II at Smithfield, London

Wat Tyler falls from his horse and is killed.

RICHARD II
Grandson of Edward III, Richard II (1367–1400) became king in 1377, aged 10. He used courage and daring to suppress the Peasants' Revolt. He was deposed by Henry IV in 1400 and was either murdered or died of starvation.

Agricultural tools of the 1300s

Scythe

Sickle

WEAPONS
The peasants had few real weapons they could use in a revolt. Instead they took with them the tools of their trade – pitchforks, scythes, billhooks, and sickles – all of which could cause ugly wounds. As the revolt progressed, many peasants looted swords and daggers.

Pitchfork

SERFDOM
Farming was hard in the 1300s. Many peasants were serfs, or villeins, who effectively belonged to the lords of the manor, and were forced to pay heavy dues. However, after the Black Death (1347-50), which killed thousands, surviving peasants were able to demand higher wages and better working conditions.

___ *Find out more* ___
BLACK DEATH
FARMING
HUNDRED YEARS WAR
MEDIEVAL EUROPE
UNITED KINGDOM, HISTORY OF

ANCIENT PERSIANS

CYRUS THE GREAT
Cyrus (ruled 550-529 BCE) founded the Persian Empire. During his reign many different peoples, including Babylonians, Egyptians, Greeks, and Syrians, lived in the Persian Empire.

MORE THAN 3,000 YEARS AGO, the present-day country of Iran was home to various tribes, including the Medes and the Persians. For many years, the Medes ruled the area, but in 550 BCE Cyrus, the Persian king of a small state called Ashan, conquered the Medes and set out to create a vast kingdom. Within 30 years Persia had become the most powerful nation in the world, and the Persian Empire covered all of Mesopotamia, Anatolia (Turkey), the eastern Mediterranean, and what are now Pakistan and Afghanistan. For more than 200 years the Persian Empire was the greatest the world had ever seen. The Persians were skilled warriors, horse riders, and craft workers. They were also highly organized. Under Darius I, also called Darius the Great, the empire was divided into provinces called satrapies. A network of roads linked the provinces and enabled people to trade easily. Darius introduced a postal system and a single currency to unify the empire. The empire flourished until the Greek leader Alexander the Great conquered Persia in 331 BCE.

People bringing gifts to the royal palace

Reliefs show people arriving for a festival on New Year's Day

PERSEPOLIS
In about 520 BCE Darius I began to build the city of Persepolis. Building continued in the reign of Xerxes I (486-465 BCE). Persepolis was the site of many beautiful buildings, including the royal palace. The city was used only once a year at New Year, when the peoples of the empire brought tributes (gifts) to the king.

Remains of Persepolis include statues such as the carved head of this horse in the Central Palace.

PERSIAN EMPIRE
Sardis
Nineveh
Babylon
Susa
Jerusalem
Parsagadae
Persepolis
Thebes

At its height, the Persian Empire stretched from the borders of India to the River Nile in Egypt. Susa was the administrative capital of the empire, Persepolis was the royal capital, and the two cities were linked by a 2,700-km- (1678-mile-) long Royal Road.

ZOROASTRIANISM
The Persian people followed the teachings of a prophet named Zoroaster, who lived from about 628 to 551 BCE. Zoroastrianism was the main religion in Persia until the country became Muslim in the 7th century CE.

Zoroastrian priests carried a mace with a bull's head as a symbol of the priests' religious battle against evil.

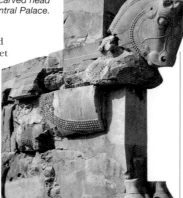

PERSEPOLIS TODAY
When Alexander the Great invaded the Persian Empire, he burned Persepolis to the ground. But the ruins of the city, including the royal palace, can still be seen today in southern Iran.

ANCIENT PERSIANS

550 BCE Cyrus the Great defeats the Medes peoples and forms the Persian Empire.

538 BCE Cyrus conquers the Babylonian Empire.

529 BCE Cyrus dies.

525 BCE Persians conquer Egypt.

521-486 BCE Reign of Darius the Great.

510 BCE Persians invade southeast Europe and central Asia.

499-449 BCE Persian Wars between Persian Empire and Greek states, because Persian kings felt threatened by the democracy of Greece.

490 BCE Greeks defeat Persians at the Battle of Marathon.

480 BCE Greek navy defeats Persians at the Battle of Salamis.

334 BCE Alexander the Great invades Persia.

331 BCE Alexander defeats Persians at the Battle of Gaugamela. Persian Empire collapses.

Find out more
ASSYRIANS
BABYLONIANS
EGYPT, ANCIENT
EUROPE, HISTORY OF
GREECE, ANCIENT

PHOENICIANS

Phoenicians made purple dye from the liquid produced by crushing murex seashells.

A TINY GROUP OF CITIES perched along the coast of the Mediterranean produced the most famous sailors and traders of the ancient world. These seafaring people were called the Phoenicians. The cities of Phoenicia were linked by the sea, and they traded in many goods, including purple dyes, glass, and ivory. From 1200 to 350 BCE the Phoenicians controlled trade throughout the Mediterranean. They spread their trading links to many points around the coast. Their most famous trading post was Carthage on the north coast of Africa. During its history, Phoenicia was conquered by several foreign empires, including the Assyrians, Babylonians, and Persians. These foreign rulers usually allowed the Phoenicians to continue trading. But in 332 BCE Alexander the Great conquered Phoenicia, and Greek people came to live there. The Greeks brought their own culture with them, and the Phoenician culture faded away.

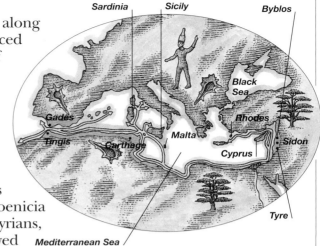

Mediterranean Sea

PHOENICIA
Phoenicia lay on the coast of the eastern Mediterranean roughly where Lebanon is today. The Phoenicians spread throughout the Mediterranean, to Carthage, Rhodes, Cyprus, Sicily, Malta, Sardinia, Gades (Cadiz), and Tingis (Tangier).

When arriving at a new place to trade, the Phoenicians would lay their goods out on the beach and let the local people come and look at what they had brought.

Sculptures show that Phoenician men wore distinctive conical hats.

Phoenician glassware, such as this glass jar, was a luxury in the ancient world.

Phoenicians traded in a vast array of goods from the Mediterranean, including metals, farm animals, wheat, cloth, jewellery, and gemstones.

PHOENICIAN SHIPS
The Phoenicians' ships were famous all over the Mediterranean, and were the main reason for the Phoenicians' success as traders. The ships had oarsmen, sails, and heavy keels, which enabled them to sail in any direction.

DYEING
The Phoenicians were the only people who knew how to produce a vivid purple dye from murex shells. The dye was considered to be exceptionally beautiful but it was also very expensive. Only high government officials, for example, could wear purple dyed cloth in the Roman Empire.

PHOENICIAN GLASSWARE
Ancient Egyptians made glass many years before the Phoenicians did, but Egyptian glass was cloudy, whereas Phoenician glass was clear. The Phoenicians were able to make clear glass because their sand contained large amounts of quartz.

BYBLOS

The Phoenician port of Byblos was famous for its trade in papyrus – a kind of paper made in Egypt by pressing together strands of papyrus reeds. The Greeks called papyrus *biblos* after the port of Byblos. A number of our words concerned with books, such as Bible, and bibliography (a list of books), come from *biblos*.

The papyrus reed grows in the warm, damp conditions of the River Nile in Egypt.

Find out more
AFRICA
ALPHABETS
ASSYRIANS
BABYLONIANS
GREECE, ANCIENT
PERSIANS, ANCIENT
SHIPS AND BOATS
SUMERIANS

PILGRIMS

ON A BLUSTERY SEPTEMBER DAY in 1620, a small ship set sail from the port of Plymouth, England, bound for North America. The 102 settlers on board hoped that in the New World they could worship freely in their own way, which they had not been able to do in England. Because of their Puritan faith, and because they started one of the colonies that would later grow into the United States, the group became known as the Pilgrims. The Pilgrims landed in what is now Massachusetts and established a settlement called Plymouth. The first winter was hard. The settlers had little food, and it was difficult to farm and fish. But with help from the local Native Americans, the settlement eventually prospered. The Pilgrims replaced their wooden homes with more secure dwellings and started trading furs with the Native Americans. More groups of Puritans came to join the original settlers; together they created one of the first successful European settlements in North America.

16 September 1620 Mayflower sets sail from Plymouth.

19 November Cape Cod is sighted.

Cape Cod Bay

21 November Mayflower anchors in Provincetown harbour.

26 December Plymouth colony founded, Massachusetts.

MAYFLOWER
The Pilgrims sailed to North America in a two-masted ship, the *Mayflower*. The ship was about 30 m (90 ft) long and was built to carry wine and other cargo.

EARLY SETTLEMENT
The first settlements in Plymouth were built of wood from the local forests. The chimneys were made of sticks held together with clay, and the roofs were waterproofed with bark.

Splitting logs to make planks

Food had to be cooked in the open.

Every member of the family had to work hard to build a house and plant crops for food.

GOVERNMENT
The early Plymouth settlers elected their own government which met annually to make laws and levy taxes.

PURITANISM
The Puritan religion stressed hard work and obedience and disapproved of frivolity and idleness.

The Pilgrims held prayer meetings outside until they built churches.

PURITANS
The people known as the Puritans wished to purify the Church of England of its pomp and ritual. They dressed in simple clothes and tried to live in accordance with the Bible.

THANKSGIVING
In the autumn of 1621, the Pilgrims celebrated their first successful harvest. They invited the local Native Americans to join them in a feast of thanksgiving. Thanksgiving, which became a national holiday in 1863, is celebrated in the United States on the fourth Thursday in November.

Find out more
EXPLORERS
NORTH AMERICA
RELIGIONS
UNITED STATES, HISTORY OF

PIRATES

IN TALES ABOUT PIRATES, shady figures row through the moonlight to bury treasure on tropical islands. The reality of a pirate's life, though, was very different from the storybook version. Most pirates were simply criminals who robbed ships at sea and often murdered the crews. Pirates first appeared when trading ships began to cross the Mediterranean about 4,000 years ago. They have flourished ever since in every ocean of the world, but were particularly active from 1500 to 1800. Some pirates, such as Blackbeard, cruised the Caribbean Sea, which was also called the Spanish Main. Others, such as Captain Kidd, attacked ships in the Indian Ocean. Sometimes countries at war encouraged piracy, but only against enemy shipping. They called the pirate ships privateers and gave them letters of marque – official licences to plunder enemy ships. Pirates still exist in the waters off Somalia. They hijack ships, take them into their own ports, and demand ransoms for the ships' owners.

TREASURE MAPS
Buried pirate treasure, marked with an X on a map, is largely the invention of adventure writers. Most of the time pirates attacked lightly armed merchant ships, stealing food and weapons.

PIRATE SHIPS
Traditional pirate vessels were generally small, fast, and manoeuvrable. They floated high in the water so they could escape into shallow creeks and inlets if pursued. They were armed with as many cannons as possible. Some cannons were heavy guns which fired large metal balls; others were lighter swivel guns which fired lead shot.

ANNE BONNY
Anne Bonny was born in Ireland. She fell in love with the pirate "Calico Jack" Rackham and sailed with him. On a captured ship she met another woman pirate, Mary Read. The women pirates were arrested in 1720 but escaped the gallows, as they were both expecting babies.

BLACKBEARD
One of the most terrible pirates was Edward Teach. His nickname was Blackbeard, and his favourite drink was rum and gunpowder. In battle he carried six pistols and wore burning matches twisted into his hair. He died on a British warship in 1718.

SPANISH DOLLAR
The pirate's currency was a Spanish gold dollar worth eight reales (called *real de a ocho*). The pirate term "pieces of eight" comes from the habit of cutting these into eight pieces, each worth one real.

> *Find out more*
> SHIPS AND BOATS

PLANETS

EARTH IS ONE of eight major planets moving around the Sun. Planets are large balls of rock, metal, gases, and liquids orbiting a star. In our solar system, all the planets travel in the same direction around the Sun, each revolving in an elliptical (oval) orbit. Through a telescope, the planets appear as discs of light moving slowly across the night sky. They do not, however, produce light themselves, but reflect light from the Sun. All the planets except Mercury are surrounded by a layer of gas called an atmosphere. The four smaller planets, such as Earth, have a rocky surface, but the four giant planets are mostly gas and liquid. The giant planets are each surrounded by rings. There is a huge difference in temperature between the planets nearest to the Sun and those farthest away. Mercury is hotter than an oven by day, while Neptune is about 200°C (392°F) below freezing. As far as we know, Earth is the only planet that supports life. However, the Sun is one of millions of stars, and planets have already been discovered orbiting hundreds of them. Another planet somewhere might support life.

THE SUN
The Sun is a star – a vast ball of hot gas, far larger than any of the planets.

MARS
Mars is a small, dry planet with a red, rocky surface. It is cold – about -23°C (-9°F) – and has two polar caps of ice and frozen gas. Mars has two tiny moons named Phobos and Deimos.

JUPITER
Jupiter is the largest planet in the solar system. It has no solid surface as it is made up of a mixture of liquids and gases, with belts of swirling gas forming an atmosphere around it. It is a cold planet, surrounded by a ring of dust, and orbited by more than 60 moons.

Mars
Earth
Venus
The Moon

MERCURY
Mercury is so close to the Sun that it has no atmosphere or oceans. It has a rocky surface that rises to a temperature of about 350°C (662°F).

VENUS
Thick clouds cover the whole surface of Venus. They trap the Sun's heat, making Venus the hottest planet in the solar system. The surface temperature of Venus is about 480°C (896°F).

EARTH
The Earth has an atmosphere of air and oceans filled with water. The Earth's average temperature is 22°C (72°F). A source of energy and liquid water are essential for life on the planet. If the Earth were hotter, the water would evaporate; if it were colder, the water would freeze.

ASTEROIDS
Thousands of tiny bodies called asteroids orbit the Sun, mainly travelling in a belt between Mars and Jupiter. Dating from the earliest days of the solar system, most asteroids are lumps of rock and metal just a few kilometres in diameter. Jupiter's gravitational pull can send asteroids into erratic orbits, causing them to collide with planets and other asteroids. Many objects made of ice and rock are also known to exist in the Kuiper Belt, an area in the solar system beyond the orbit of Neptune.

PLANET PICTURES
Space technology has shown us what the other planets in the solar system look like and what they are made of; it has also established that these other planets are unlikely to support life. The images shown right and at the foot of the next page were taken from a variety of spacecraft.

The heavily cratered surface of Mercury is revealed in this photograph taken by the Messenger spacecraft.

Photograph taken by the Pioneer-Venus probe shows thick yellowish clouds covering the surface of Venus.

Picture of the Earth taken by the Meteosat weather satellite. Colours have been enhanced using a computer.

This snapshot of Mars was created from a series of images taken by NASA's Hubble Space Telescope.

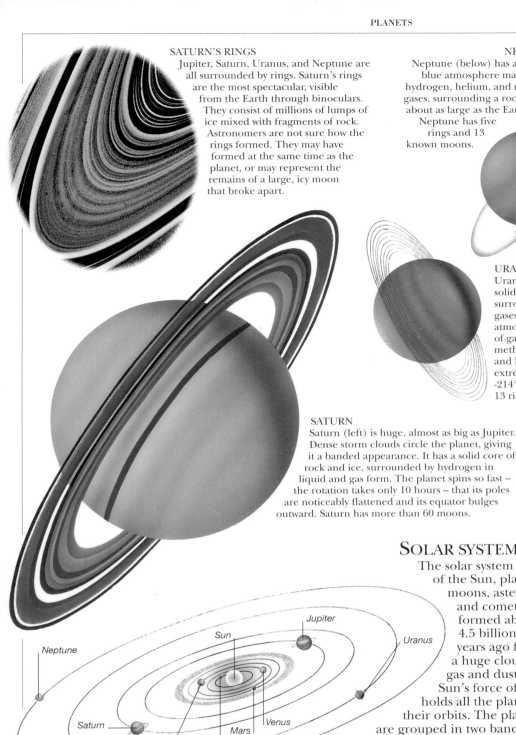

SATURN'S RINGS

Jupiter, Saturn, Uranus, and Neptune are all surrounded by rings. Saturn's rings are the most spectacular, visible from the Earth through binoculars. They consist of millions of lumps of ice mixed with fragments of rock. Astronomers are not sure how the rings formed. They may have formed at the same time as the planet, or may represent the remains of a large, icy moon that broke apart.

NEPTUNE

Neptune (below) has a striking blue atmosphere made up of hydrogen, helium, and methane gases, surrounding a rocky core about as large as the Earth. Neptune has five rings and 13 known moons.

DWARF PLANETS

Some of the largest asteroids that are big enough to be spherical are classed as dwarf planets. Ceres in the asteroid belt is one. The others are all in the Kuiper Belt beyond Neptune. One of these is Pluto. Pluto used to be classed as a major planet until 2006 but its path is more elliptical and tilted compared with the orbits of the major planets, and it is smaller than the Moon. The dwarf planet Eris is a little larger than Pluto.

URANUS

Uranus (left) has a solid core of metal surrounded by ice and gases. Its blue-green atmosphere is made of gases, including methane, hydrogen, and helium. Uranus is extremely cold – about -214°C (-353°F). It has 13 rings and 27 moons.

SATURN

Saturn (left) is huge, almost as big as Jupiter. Dense storm clouds circle the planet, giving it a banded appearance. It has a solid core of rock and ice, surrounded by hydrogen in liquid and gas form. The planet spins so fast – the rotation takes only 10 hours – that its poles are noticeably flattened and its equator bulges outward. Saturn has more than 60 moons.

SOLAR SYSTEM

The solar system consists of the Sun, planets, moons, asteroids, and comets. It formed about 4.5 billion years ago from a huge cloud of gas and dust. The Sun's force of gravity holds all the planets in their orbits. The planets are grouped in two bands. The inner band consists of Mercury, Venus, Earth, and Mars; in the outer band are Jupiter, Saturn, Uranus, and Neptune.

Neptune

Sun

Jupiter

Uranus

Saturn

Earth

Mercury

Mars

Venus

VOYAGER SPACECRAFT

We have incredible pictures of the planets and their moons because space probes have flown to all of the planets except Pluto. *Voyager 2* was one of the most successful interplanetary spacecraft. It travelled for over a decade photographing the planets, and in 1990, made its way out of the solar system. *Voyager 2* made use of the gravity of the planets to give it an extra push on its long journey – a similar effect to stepping off a merry-go-round while it is moving.

Voyager 1 *picture of Jupiter showing the Great Red Spot which is thought to be a huge storm.*

Image taken by Voyager 1 *showing Saturn and its rings, which are thought to consist of a mixture of ice and rock.*

Voyager 2 *image of Uranus. Its atmosphere looks blue because the methane gas it contains cuts out red light.*

Voyager 2 *photograph of Neptune. The two dark blurs are enormous storms in Neptune's atmosphere.*

Find out more

ASTRONOMY
GRAVITY
MOON
SUN
UNIVERSE

PLANTS

LIFE ON EARTH could not exist without plants. Humans and animals need plants for food and oxygen. The cereal you eat for breakfast, the orange juice you drink, even the jeans you wear, are all derived from plants. Trees provide us with wood for fuel, furniture, and tools. In almost every country, flowers and vegetables are grown by the millions for food and pleasure. Scientists use plants to make drugs such as digitalis (from foxglove) and morphine (from poppies). Plants range from tiny mosses to gigantic coniferous trees so tall you cannot see their tops. What they all have in common is their unique ability to capture and use the Sun's light as an energy source. This process is called photosynthesis, and it powers all plant life and growth. About 400,000 plants are already known to us, from rare exotic flowers to common garden vegetables. Even more plants await discovery, especially in tropical regions. Today, however, more than 25,000 different trees, flowers, and other plants are in danger of extinction due to the destruction of their natural habitats.

FLOWERS
The flowers of a plant contain both male and female reproductive parts, the pollen and ovule cells. If pollinated the ovule develops into a seed.

LEAVES
Green leaves capture light energy from the Sun by the process known as photosynthesis.

STEM
Sturdy stem supports leaves and flowers and carries water and food to leaves and fruit.

Inside a leaf

Upper epidermis

Air spaces

Leaf vein

Palisade cell containing chloroplasts

Mesophyll cell

Guard cells

Stoma

Seed is inside fruit (bean pod).

FRUIT
The fruit contain seeds which eventually grow into new plants. The large fruit on this plant are called beans.

STRUCTURE OF A PLANT
During its lifetime, a typical flowering plant such as this runner bean grows a stem, roots, shoots, leaves, flowers, and fruit. Trees, which are huge plants, have a trunk – a stiff, woody stem full of fibres.

Carbon dioxide is taken in from air through tiny holes called stoma.

Light energy from Sun

Oxygen is given off into the air through stoma.

Water is taken in from soil through roots.

PHOTOSYNTHESIS
In order to grow, plants use energy from sunlight. This process is called photo-synthesis. A green substance called chlorophyll is contained in the cells of a plant's leaves. Chlorophyll captures energy in the light waves from the Sun, then carries out chemical reactions in which carbon dioxide gas from the air is combined with water from the soil. This process creates sugars and other substances which the plant uses for energy and growth.

Xylem (water-carrying tube)

Cortex

Phloem (sap-carrying tube)

Root hair

Root cap

Inside a root

ROOTS
From the soil, the roots take in water and minerals which pass to the leaves and fruit through tiny tubes in the stem. Roots also anchor the plant firmly in the ground.

REPRODUCTION
Most plants reproduce sexually. Pollen fertilizes the ovules in the ovaries, which ripen into fruit that contains seeds. Other plants, such as the potato, reproduce asexually. They grow by tubers which develop into new plants that look like the parent plant.

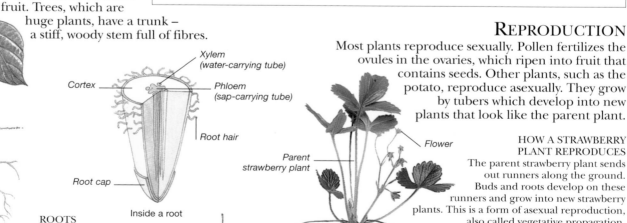

Flower

Parent strawberry plant

HOW A STRAWBERRY PLANT REPRODUCES
The parent strawberry plant sends out runners along the ground. Buds and roots develop on these runners and grow into new strawberry plants. This is a form of asexual reproduction, also called vegetative propagation.

Runner | New strawberry plant

MAIN GROUPS OF PLANTS

The plant kingdom is made up of many different groups. These groups are divided into flowering and non-flowering plants, as shown here.

Seaweed is an alga that grows in sea water and attaches itself to rocks.

Moss grows on logs and walls and in moist, shady woodland areas.

Lichen is now classified as a fungi. It has no true leaves, stems, or roots.

Liverworts are small non-flowering plants related to mosses.

Horsetails were among the earliest plants on Earth.

Microscopic plants are so small that we can see them only through a microscope.

Club mosses are among the first plants to develop with true stems.

Coniferous trees include fir trees and pine trees. They are also called evergreen trees.

WEEDS

A weed is simply a plant growing where it is troublesome to humans. Most weeds grow fast, come into flower quickly, then spread their seeds. Some weeds, such as the convolvulus shown above, have pale, delicate flowers; others are colourful, such as the dandelions and buttercups that grow on lawns.

Ferns grow in all parts of the world. Some are as large as trees; others are tiny and look like moss.

Weeds are unwanted flowering plants that include dandelions, nettles, and buttercups.

Fruit trees provide many kinds of fruit, including apples, lemons, and bananas. All are rich in vitamins.

Bushes are woody plants that are smaller than trees. They usually have one main stem.

Vegetables are edible flowering plants that are rich in vitamins and minerals. They include carrots, potatoes, spinach, tomatoes, and beans.

True flowering plants include roses, tulips, and other garden plants.

Deciduous trees are also called broadleaved trees. They lose their leaves each autumn.

Shrubs are woody plants with more than one main branch growing from the ground.

Herbs have scented leaves. They include basil and oregano.

Grasses include lawn grass and cereals such as wheat, rice, barley, and corn.

FOOD FROM PLANTS

We grow plants for food on farms and in gardens, too. Food plants include cereals such as rice, fruit such as oranges, and vegetables such as carrots. Spices such as cinnamon are parts of plants and are used for flavouring. Some plant parts cannot be eaten because they are bitter, sour, or poisonous. Potatoes are an important food crop, but we eat only the tuber that grows underground. The fruit and leaves of the potato plant, which grow above ground, are poisonous.

CHOCOLATE

Inside every large fruit, or pod, of the tropical cacao tree are about 40 cacao beans. These beans are roasted, shelled, then ground into a paste. The cacao paste is mixed with sugar at a high temperature to make chocolate.

THE BIGGEST FLOWER

The giant rafflesia is a parasitic plant. It has no leaves and draws its food from the liana creepers it lives on. It has the world's largest flower, at 1 m (3 ft) across. Because of its smell, it is also called the stinking giant.

MISTLETOE

This plant "steals" its food and energy by growing and feeding on trees. It grows high up in the branches, and its roots grow into the bark and absorb the tree's nutrients.

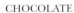

CARNIVOROUS PLANTS

Some plants obtain extra food from animals. One plant, commonly called the Venus's-flytrap, usually grows in swamps, where the soil is poor. Flesh-eating or carnivorous plants trap and digest insects and other small creatures.

When a small creature touches sensitive hairs on the leaves of the Venus's-flytrap, the leaves snap shut with one of the fastest movements in the plant world.

Venus's-flytrap flower

The flytrap shuts in one fiftieth of a second, when trigger hairs at the base of each leaf are moved.

Find out more

FARMING
FLOWERS AND HERBS
FOREST WILDLIFE
FRUITS AND SEEDS
MEDICINE
POLLUTION
TREES

POLAR WILDLIFE

THE NORTH AND SOUTH POLES are the coldest places on Earth. But despite freezing temperatures, icy water, and biting winds, many different plants and animals live near the Poles and are found nowhere else in the world. All survive because they have adapted to the harsh conditions. Plants in these regions are low-growing, to protect them from the cold wind, and they complete their life cycle during the few short weeks of summer. Polar animals, too, have adapted to the cold conditions; some have thick fur or feathers; others have a layer of fatty blubber to conserve body warmth. The biggest animals, the great whales, roam the waters of Antarctica, near the South Pole, and the largest bear, the polar bear, lives in the Arctic, near the North Pole. Many other warm-blooded animals, including wolves, foxes, reindeer, hares, and lemmings, also live here. Polar animals are often white in colour for camouflage on the ice. The cold seas are also teeming with life, particularly in summer. Around Antarctica, ocean currents bring up nutrients from the deep sea to feed the plankton, which in turn feeds animals such as krill.

NORTH POLE
In the central Arctic Ocean at the top of the globe, there are vast areas of drifting ice several metres thick.

SOUTH POLE
At the bottom of the globe, the continent of Antarctica is almost completely covered by a massive sheet of ice.

ARCTIC SKUA
The skua snatches food from other birds such as gulls and puffins. It pesters them in midair until they drop their catch of fish.

NARWHAL
The narwhal belongs to the whale family. It hunts in small groups among pack ice searching for cod, flatfish, shrimps, and squid. Narwhals have only two teeth. In the male, the left tooth usually develops into a tusk, which can measure up to 2.5 m (8 ft) long.

POLAR BEAR CUBS
Young polar bears are born in winter in a den made by their mother under the snow. The cubs stay in the den for four months, feeding on their mother's milk, then begin to learn how to hunt. The cubs leave their mother at about two years old.

BEARDED SEAL
Bearded seals live all around the Arctic region, mainly in shallow water. They eat shellfish on the seabed, as well as crabs and sea cucumbers. In the breeding season, male bearded seals make eerie noises under water. The female seals give birth to pups on ice floes in the spring.

HOODED SEAL
In summer, hooded seals migrate north to the waters around Greenland. They hunt deep-water fishes such as halibut and redfish, as well as squid. They spend the winter further south, off northeastern North America, resting on ice floes and rarely coming onto land.

The male hooded seal inflates the hood – a sac of loose skin on its nose – to scare off other males.

POLAR BEAR
The huge polar bear is covered in thick, water-repelling fur, except for its footpads and the tip of its nose. Polar bears have an excellent sense of smell for locating prey, and they can bound across the ice at great speed. An adult polar bear weighs about half a tonne. It is so strong that a single blow of its paw can kill a person.

Claws are very sharp for gripping prey.

Polar bears eat seals, fish, birds, and small mammals. They also scavenge on the carcasses (dead bodies) of whales.

CONSERVATION

Today, polar bears and whales are protected from hunting by law. But many polar animals are still threatened by oil spills, overfishing, and global warming melting the ice. Fishing boats catch huge quantities of fish, which affects the numbers of animals that depend on fish for food.

KRILL

The shrimp-like creatures shown left are called krill. They are the main food for baleen (whalebone) whales, such as the blue whale, which scoop up thousands of krill from the ocean every day.

PENGUINS

There are 17 different kinds of penguins; all live in the southern hemisphere. Penguins cannot fly, but they are expert swimmers and divers. They can speed along in the water after fish and squid using their flipper-shaped wings.

EMPEROR PENGUIN

The emperor penguin has a bright orange bib around its neck. To escape the leopard seal, it dives out of the water with great speed. It breeds in the coldest place on Earth – on Antarctic ice where the average temperature is -20°C (-4°F). After the female penguin has laid an egg, the male penguin keeps it warm between his feet and belly for about 60 days. The newborn chicks stay warm by standing on their parents' feet.

ICE FISH

The blood of most fish freezes solid at about –35°C (-32°F), and the waters in the polar regions sometimes drop even lower. The ice fish, also called the crocodile fish, has special chemicals in its blood to stop it from freezing.

LEOPARD SEAL

The four main kinds of seals around Antarctica are the leopard, crabeater, Ross, and Weddell seals. The leopard seal measures up to 3 m (10 ft) in length. It patrols the pack ice and island coasts hunting for penguins and other seals, especially crabeater seals.

There is little life on the continent of Antarctica itself, apart from a few mosses, lichens, and tiny creatures such as mites.

TUNDRA

The lands on the edge of the Arctic Ocean are bleak and treeless. This region is called the tundra. The brief summer in the Arctic allows small plants such as sedges, cushion-shaped saxifrages, heathers, mosses, and lichens to grow. These plants provide food for many insects and the grazing caribou. Birds such as snow geese breed along the shores and migrate south in autumn.

MUSK OX

The musk ox is a type of goat. It is the only large mammal that can survive winter on the tundra. The musk ox's thickset body has dense underfur and a thick, shaggy outer coat of tough hairs. Musk oxen stand together in a herd for warmth and as protection against predators such as wolves.

SNOW GOOSE

About 100 kinds of birds migrate to the tundra to breed in spring. Snow geese arrive two weeks before there are any plants to eat, but they have a store of body fat which allows them to make a nest and lay eggs before they eat. Later they feed the chicks on the newly growing grasses.

Dwarf willows are among the world's smallest shrubs. They grow low and spread sideways to stay out of the icy winds.

ARCTIC SAXIFRAGE

The cushion shapes of tundra flowers such as saxifrage and crowberry help prevent the plants from freezing. These plants also provide shelter for the tiny creatures living inside them.

Find out more

ANIMALS
ANTARCTICA
ARCTIC
FISH
OCEANS AND SEAS
SEASHORE WILDLIFE
WHALES AND DOLPHINS

POLLUTION

OIL ON BEACHES, vehicle exhaust fumes, litter, and other waste products are called pollutants, because they pollute (dirty) our environment. Pollutants can affect our health and harm animals and plants. We pollute our surroundings with all kinds of chemical waste from factories and power stations. These substances are the unwanted results of modern living. Pollution itself is not new – a hundred years ago factories sent out great clouds of poisonous smoke. Today, there are many more factories and many more pollutants. Pollution has spread to the land, air, and water of every corner on Earth, even to Antarctica and Mount Everest. Scientists are worried that the gases released by factories and vehicles are even changing the atmosphere and causing the surface temperature of the planet to heat up. We can reduce pollution by recycling waste and using biodegradable materials that eventually break down in the soil.

ACCIDENTAL POLLUTION
As well as everyday pollution, there is also accidental pollution – for example, when a ship leaks oil and creates a huge oil slick in the ocean. This kind of pollution causes damage to the environment and kills millions of fish and sea birds, like the oil-covered birds shown above.

ACID RAIN
Vehicle exhausts produce fumes that contain nitrogen oxides. The coal we burn in power stations produces sulphur dioxide. When these two substances mix with water in the air, they turn into acids, then fall as acid rain. Acid rain damages trees, eats into buildings, and kills wildlife in rivers. Today, it is possible to reduce the amount of sulphur dioxide given off by power stations, but the process is expensive.

ATMOSPHERIC POLLUTION
Ozone is a kind of oxygen present in the atmosphere. It forms a protective layer that blocks out the Sun's ultraviolet radiation, which can cause skin cancer in humans. Chemicals called CFCs (chlorofluorocarbons) destroy the ozone.

GLOBAL WARMING
Burning fossil fuels releases carbon gases into the atmosphere. They act like the panes of glass in a greenhouse, trapping the heat. Many scientists now believe that the Earth is becoming too warm. If the Earth becomes just a few degrees warmer, sea levels will rise, drowning low-lying coastal cities.

Many factories release pollutants as a by-product.

Farmers spray crops with fertilizers to help them grow, and pesticides to control pests and weeds, but these chemicals harm the other kinds of wildlife that live and feed on the crops.

RECYCLING
If we save the glass, metal, plastics, and paper that we use every day, they can be recycled and used again. This helps preserve the Earth's natural resources. Recycling cuts down litter, reduces air and water pollution, and can save energy. Many towns have "bottle banks" to collect glass for recycling.

TRAFFIC POLLUTION
Lorry, car, and bus exhausts belch out lead (which can damage the nervous system), carbon monoxide, carbon dioxide, and nitrogen oxides, which cause acid rain and the smog called photochemical smog. Some of these harmful substances are reduced by special catalytic converters attached to vehicle exhausts.

Ships leak oil into the sea, which is harmful to sea creatures.

Every day we drop litter on the ground – sweet wrappers, paper bags, empty tin cans, bottles, and cigarette packets. Litter is ugly, unhygienic, and a fire risk, and it can kill animals that eat it.

WASTE DUMPING
In many parts of the world people bury toxic (poisonous) chemicals and other dangerous waste products. These substances leak into the soil and water, killing wildlife. We treat the seas as waste dumps, and the North Sea is now seriously polluted. For the wildlife in the seas to survive, we must produce less harmful waste products.

HOLES IN THE OZONE LAYER

In the late 1970s, scientists detected "holes" in the ozone layer above the South and North Poles. Probably caused by air pollutants, such as CFCs and methane, the "holes" seemed to be growing larger. In 1987, more than 30 countries signed an agreement called the Montreal Protocol, which has sharply reduced the production of CFCs worldwide.

The dark patch is the "hole" in the ozone layer above the Antarctic.

An aerosol is a mixture of product and propellant.

The can is pressurized by the propellant gas.

HOUSEHOLD POLLUTION

Some of the polluting gases that were destroying the ozone layer came from household devices. The most damaging were chlorofluorocarbons (CFCs), used as propellants in aerosol cans and inside the cooling systems of refrigerators. Today, in the move to reduce pollution, less harmful gases have replaced CFCs.

CLEANING UP

Neutralizing chemicals can be used to clean up pollution. Spilt oil, for example, can be countered with detergents. But unfortunately these chemicals can do just as much damage as the original spill. Sometimes the only way to clean up is to physically remove the pollutant. Sadly the damage is often already done, although it may not be very obvious.

Where possible, mechanical scoops remove spilt oil sludge.

Special V-shaped paddles are used to push the oil sludge into heaps.

OIL BARRIER

Crude oil is a particularly harmful chemical pollutant. However, because oil floats on water, an oil slick created by a spillage from a wrecked tanker can be contained by barriers. The oil must then be dispersed or collected quickly because, if it is left, it will eventually thicken and sink. Also, oil barriers cannot withstand storms.

ENERGY SAVING

Much of the pollution that we produce is the result of burning fossil fuels in power plants and motor vehicles. Generators and engines can be made more efficient so that they use less fuel. Individuals too can save energy and reduce pollution by making use of energy-efficient light bulbs and other appliances in the home, and by using cars less.

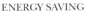

Energy-saving lamps reduce pollution, but just switching off lights helps even more.

RAIN FORESTS

Since 1945, more than half of the world's rain forests have been destroyed. They are cut down for timber or burnt to clear space for farmland. Burning produces carbon dioxide, contributing to global warming. Scientists are increasingly concerned about the impact of this on the environment.

Find out more
ATMOSPHERE
CLIMATES
CONSERVATION
and endangered species
ENERGY

PREHISTORIC LIFE

2,000 MILLION YEARS AGO
The earliest forms of life were bacteria and blue-green algae. The algae grew in rings or short columns called stromatolites, which are fossilized in rocks. Today, stromatolites still form in shallow tropical seas.

WHEN PLANET EARTH FORMED more than 4,600 million years ago, there was no life. Torrential storms raged, lightning bolts flashed, volcanoes poured out poisonous gases, and there was no atmosphere to protect the Earth from the sun's radiation. Slowly, warm shallow seas formed. In these seas the first forms of life appeared, protected by the water. We call these early beginnings "prehistory" because they happened before written history. Fossils – the preserved remains of plants and animals – provide the only records of prehistoric life. We know from fossils more than 2,000 million years old that some of the earliest forms of life were bacteria. Gradually, plants called blue-green algae evolved, or developed. These produced oxygen – the gas that plants and animals need for life. Oxygen was released into the air from the sea and formed a protective blanket of ozone in the atmosphere. The ozone screened out the sun's radiation, and living things began to invade the land and take to the air. Millions of kinds of animals and plants have existed since the first signs of life – some, such as insects, have thrived; others, such as the dinosaurs, have died out as the Earth's environment has changed.

Some of the earliest remains of the life on Earth are fossils called stromatolites.

600 MILLION YEARS AGO
Rare fossils of soft-bodied creatures show us that many different animals had evolved by this time. They included the first kinds of jellyfish, corals, sea pens, and worms.

Sea pens existed 600 million years ago.

One of the first fishes, about 390 million years old

390 MILLION YEARS AGO
Fish were the first creatures with backbones. They evolved quickly into many different kinds. Gradually, they developed jaws and fins. The first small land plants, such as mosses, appeared on the swampy shores.

Trilobites were common 450 million years ago. They are ancient relatives of crabs.

450 MILLION YEARS AGO
Fossils from this time are much more common, because animals had developed hard shells that preserved well. They include trilobites, nautiloids, sea urchins, and giant eurypterids, or sea scorpions, more than 2.5 m (8 ft) long.

Cooksonia was one of the first land plants to appear on Earth.

HOW WE KNOW THE AGE OF FOSSILS

Stages	Million years ago (mya)
Neogene period	23–today
Paleogene period	65.5–23
Jurassic and Cretaceous periods	199.6–65.5
Triassic period	251–199.6
Carboniferous and Permian periods	359.2–251
Devonian period	416–359.2
Ordovician and Silurian periods	488.3–416
Cambrian period	542–488.3
Pre-cambrian period	4,500–542

Scientists called palaeontologists find out how old a fossil is from the age of the rocks around it. This is called relative dating. They also measure the amounts of radioactive chemicals in the rocks and fossils to find out when they formed. This is called absolute dating.

Prehistoric time is divided into different stages, called eras, which are further divided into periods. Each of these stages lasted for many millions of years. If you dig deep down into the Earth's surface, you can find fossils of animals and plants that lived during the different periods.

350 MILLION YEARS AGO
As plants became established on land, they were soon followed by the first land animals, such as millipedes and insects. Woody trees that looked like conifers stood more than 30 m (100 ft) high. Sharks and many other fish swam in the seas.

Insects such as the dragonfly evolved about 350 million years ago.

300 MILLION YEARS AGO
The first amphibians had crawled out from the water about 50 million years earlier. Gradually, they developed stronger limbs and thicker skins, so they could live on land. They still had to return to the water to lay their eggs. Giant ferns and horsetails grew in the warm swamps.

150 MILLION YEARS AGO
Dinosaurs ruled the land. Reptiles such as plesiosaurs ruled the seas, and other reptiles, the pterosaurs, flew in the air. There were also birds and mammals at this time. Ammonites were common in the seas.

Mosasaur was one of the first sea reptiles. Its sharp teeth show that it was a meat eater, and it probably hunted fish.

The first bats existed about 50 million years ago.

65 MILLION YEARS AGO
Trees with blossoms, such as the magnolia, began to appear on Earth more than 100 million years ago. Later, about 65 million years ago, dinosaurs and many other living things became extinct (died out). During the next few million years different kinds of mammals and birds became more common.

Sabre-toothed cats existed 19 to 2 million years ago. Their huge teeth enabled them to attack and kill large prey.

EXTINCTION

There is concern over the fact that many animals and plants are in danger of dying out, or becoming extinct. But ever since life began, animals and plants have died out, to be replaced by others. This process is part of nature. As the conditions on Earth change, some living things cannot adapt; they eventually become extinct. Scientists believe that 99 per cent of all the different plants and animals that ever lived have died out naturally. In prehistoric times there were mass extinctions when hundreds of different things died out together. These extinctions were often due to dramatic changes in climate. About 225 million years ago, 90 per cent of all the living things in the sea died out. Today, animals and plants are dying out more quickly because humans damage and destroy the areas where they live.

STEGOSAURUS
This dinosaur lived about 150 million years ago in North America. It became extinct about 140 million years ago.

NEANDERTHAL PEOPLE
These people lived from about 120,000–35,000 years ago. They were smaller than humans, and are now thought not to be ancestral to them. It is debated, however, whether they interbred with humans.

GREAT ICE AGE

About 2 million years ago, several ice ages gripped the Earth, with warmer stretches between. Humans evolved – probably in Africa – and spread around the world. In the north, they hunted woolly mammoths, woolly rhinos, and sabre-toothed cats. About 18,000 years ago, ice sheets covered much of northern Europe, northern Britain, and North America.

Find out more
DINOSAURS
EVOLUTION
FOSSILS
PREHISTORIC PEOPLES
REPTILES

PREHISTORIC PEOPLES

PREHISTORIC PEOPLES

COMPARED WITH the rest of life on Earth, human beings arrived quite recently, after the dinosaur age and the age of mammals. The whole story of human evolution is incomplete, because many parts of the fossil record have never been found. Human-like mammals first emerged from the ape family about five million years ago in central Africa. They came down from the trees and began to walk on two legs. Hominins, or early humans, were more apelike than human and lived in the open. Over millions of years they learned to walk upright and developed bigger brains. These large brains helped them to develop language and the ability to work together. Hominins lived in groups and shared work and food, wandering through the countryside gathering fruits, roots, nuts, berries, and seeds, and hunting animals. Standing upright left their hands free to make tools and weapons, shelters and fire. They lived in caves and in shelters made from branches and stones. These early humans spread slowly over the rest of the world and soon rose to dominate life on Earth.

PREHISTORIC PEOPLES

c. 7,000,000 BCE Apes and hominins begin to evolve in different ways.

c. 2,500,000 BCE First stone tools made. Palaeolithic (Old Stone) Age begins.

c. 2,000,000 BCE *Homo erectus* appears.

c. 350,000 BCE First Neanderthals (an early form of *Homo sapiens* – "wise man") develop.

c. 50,000 BCE First modern people, *Homo sapiens*, develop.

c. 8,000 BCE Neolithic (New Stone) Age begins.

c. 7,000 BCE Farming villages and pottery.

c. 3,500 BCE Sumerians in Mesopotamia develop writing. Sumerians begin to live in cities.

c. 3,000 BCE Metal tools and weapons begin to replace stone.

HUMAN OR APE?
Humans have smaller jaws and larger brains than apes. The human hand has a longer thumb; apes have longer fingers. The human pelvis and thigh allow upright motion, giving the spine an S-shaped curve. Human legs are longer than arms; apes have the reverse. Unlike apes, humans cannot use their big toes as extra thumbs; the foot has adapted to walking and can no longer grasp.

WISDOM TOOTH
Early people needed wisdom teeth in order to eat roots and berries. Today, we no longer need wisdom teeth, and many people do not even develop them.

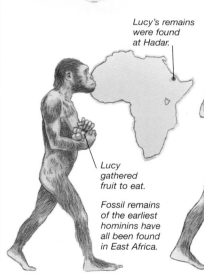

LUCY
In 1974, archaeologists discovered a complete fossil hominin skeleton in Ethiopia, northeastern Africa. She was nicknamed Lucy, after the Beatles' song *Lucy in the Sky with Diamonds*. Lucy was 3 million years old. Although nearly human, she was probably not one of our direct ancestors.

When alive, Lucy was about the same height as a 10-year-old girl, and weighed 27 kg (60 lb).

Lucy's remains were found at Hadar.

Lucy gathered fruit to eat.

Fossil remains of the earliest hominins have all been found in East Africa.

Homo habilis

Simple stone tool

Simple clothing

Homo erectus made more advanced tools, such as this spear.

Homo erectus

Sophisticated carving

Sewn leather clothing

Neanderthal man

Rough woven cloth

Modern people wear shoes.

MODERN PEOPLE
When humans learned to domesticate animals and grow crops, they stopped wandering and settled down on farms. Thus towns began to develop.

FROM HOMININS TO HUMANS

About 2.3 million years ago hominins called *Homo habilis* (meaning "handy man") shaped crude stone tools and built rough shelters. Other, more advanced hominins, called *Homo erectus*, moved out of Africa into Europe and Asia. They lived in camps, made use of fire, and probably had a language. After the Ice Age, Neanderthals lived in Europe. Neanderthals looked much like people today, wore clothes, made flint tools and fire, and buried their dead. They vanished about 30,000 years ago and were replaced by "modern people", who invented farming about 9,000 years ago and began to settle down in communities. Shortly after, the first civilizations began.

Find out more
BRONZE AGE
EVOLUTION
FOSSILS
PREHISTORIC LIFE
STONE AGE

RAIN AND SNOW

THE WATER THAT FALLS from the sky as rain or snow is taking part in a continuous cycle. It begins when the water on the Earth's surface evaporates, or dries out, and enters the air as invisible water vapour. Rising air carries the vapour into the sky. The air cools as it rises, and the water vapour turns into tiny water droplets. These droplets are so small that they float in the air, and a cloud forms. A rain cloud contains millions of water droplets which merge together to form larger drops. When these drops become too large and heavy to float, they fall to the ground as rain and the cycle starts all over again. If the air is very cold, the water in the cloud freezes and forms snowflakes or hailstones. However, rainfall and snowfall are not equal all over the world. Deserts have hardly any rain at all; tropical regions can have so much rain that there are severe floods, while in the polar regions snow falls instead of rain.

LIFE-GIVING RAIN
Rain is vital to life on Earth. Plants need water to grow, providing food for us and other animals. Rain also fills the rivers and lakes which provide our water supply.

WATER CYCLE
Water enters the air from lakes, rivers, seas, and oceans through the process of evaporation. In addition, plants, animals, and people give out water vapour into the atmosphere. The vapour stays in the air for an average time of 10 days and then falls as rain or snow. It joins the sea, rivers, and underground watercourses, and the cycle begins once more.

Trees and other plants release water vapour into the air from their leaves.

Cloud begins to form from water vapour in the atmosphere.

Water joins rivers and streams and flows down to the sea.

Water droplets fall from a cloud especially over high ground where the air is cooler. The general name for rain, snow, sleet, hail, mist, and dew is precipitation.

Water seeps underground through a layer of porous, or permeable, rock and flows down to the sea.

Wind and the sun's heat cause water to evaporate from the oceans and other large areas of water.

RAINBOW
If the sun shines on a shower of rain, you may see a rainbow if you are looking towards the rain and the sun is behind you. The raindrops in the shower reflect the sun's light back to you. As the sunlight passes through the raindrops, it splits up into a circular band of colours. You see the top part of this circle as a rainbow.

SNOW AND HAIL
In cold weather, the water in a cloud freezes and forms ice crystals. These crystals stick together and fall as snowflakes. The snow may melt slightly as it falls, producing sleet. In some clouds, strong air currents can toss frozen raindrops up and down. Each time they rise and fall, the frozen drops collect more ice crystals and water, and frozen layers build up like the skin around an onion. Eventually they become so heavy that they fall to the ground as hailstones.

ICE CRYSTAL
A microscope reveals that snowflakes are made of tiny six-sided ice crystals. No two crystals are exactly the same.

Find out more
COLOUR
RIVERS
STORMS
WATER
WEATHER
WIND

REFORMATION

ON 31 OCTOBER 1517, German monk Martin Luther pinned a list of 95 theses, or complaints, on a church door in Wittenberg, Saxony. This sparked off a movement known as the Reformation because its followers demanded the reform of the Catholic Church, then the most powerful force in Europe. Many, like Luther, believed it was corrupt, and attacked its wealth and the sale of indulgences (pardons for sins). In 1521, Luther was expelled from the Church. He set up his own church which became known as Protestant because its followers "protested" against what they felt were the errors of the Catholic Church. Protestantism spread through Europe. Then, in a movement called the Counter-Reformation, the Catholic Church began to reform itself. The Counter-Reformation led to religious persecution and bitter civil wars.

MARTIN LUTHER
Martin Luther (1483-1546) inspired the Reformation. He attacked the sale of indulgences and said that no amount of money paid to the clergy could pardon an individual for his sins. Only through faith could people be saved.

War started after two Protestants were thrown out of a window in Prague.

Battle scene during Thirty Years' War

Catholic and Protestant | Protestant | Catholic

PROTESTANTISM
By 1560, Europe had two main religions – Roman Catholic and Protestant. Protestantism began in Germany. Many German rulers adopted the new religion so that they could break away from the control of the Pope and the Holy Roman Emperor (the "political" Catholic ruler).

THIRTY YEARS' WAR
The Thirty Years' War lasted from 1618 to 1648. It began as a religious struggle between Catholics and Protestants in Germany. Then it grew into a war between the Habsburg rulers of the Holy Roman Empire and the kings of France for possession of land. In 1648, the Catholic side acknowledged it could not extinguish Protestantism.

COUNCIL OF TRENT
The Counter-Reformation began when Catholic leaders met at the Council of Trent in 1545. The council established the main principles of Catholicism and set up places for training priests and missionaries. During this time the Jesuits, an important teaching order founded in 1534, became popular.

INQUISITION
In 1231, the Pope set up the Inquisition – a special organization that searched out and punished heretics (those who did not conform to the Catholic faith). Inquisitors arrested, tortured, and executed alleged heretics and witches (above). During the Reformation, 300 years later, the Inquisition tried to crush the new Protestant churches, but failed.

___ *Find out more* ___
EUROPE
EUROPE, HISTORY OF
HENRY VIII
RELIGIONS
UNITED KINGDOM, HISTORY OF

RELIGIONS

PEOPLE HAVE ALWAYS SEARCHED for answers to life's mysteries and unexpected events. This questioning may have led to the growth of religions, to give meaning to life and death. Most religious people believe in a god or several gods. Gods are thought of as supreme beings who created the world or who control what happens in it. Religions may be highly organized, and teach people how to live, with a set of beliefs and rituals to follow. There may be special places in which to worship, and a spiritual leader for guidance. Some religions believe there is a spirit or a god in every object, from animals to rocks. Many believe in a life after death. Other religions have less formal rules, and people follow beliefs in their own way. The world's six major organized religions are Christianity, Judaism, Islam, Hinduism, Buddhism, and Sikhism.

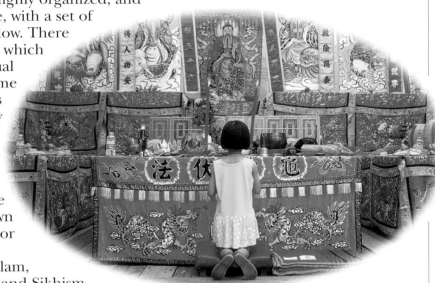

MOTHER GODDESSES
Pregnant female figures mostly found in domestic locations may have been worshipped as a symbol of the making of new life.

RELIGION AND ART
Many people use art, architecture, and sculpture to convey their religious ideas, and to show the important icons of their religion. This Christian sculpture of the Virgin Mary holding Jesus shows her crowned as the Queen of Heaven.

GODS
Many religions worship either a single God, or several gods. There may be myths or stories associated with the god, which demonstrate an important lesson. Ganesha (right) is the Hindu god of wisdom. According to legend, his father accidentally cut off his head and in desperation replaced it with that of an elephant.

WORSHIP AND PRAYER
Each religion has its own system of worship and prayer. Worship shows reverence towards a god or deity, in a public ceremony or service. It often takes place in a special building, such as a mosque or church. Prayers can be spoken or thought during worship or in private, and are a thanksgiving or request to a god or holy object. The girl above prays during the Buddhist Festival of Hungry Ghosts in Singapore.

JERUSALEM
Jerusalem is sacred to three religions. Jews pray at the Wailing Wall, the ruins of a temple destroyed in 70 CE. The Dome of the Rock mosque is holy to Muslims as the place where Prophet Muhammad rose to heaven. The Church of the Holy Sepulchre is built on the site of the crucifixion and burial of Jesus Christ.

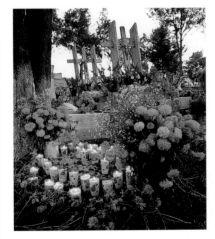

DEATH AND HEAVEN
Many faiths believe that the human body is a temporary container for the soul. After death the soul may be reborn in another body or go to heaven as a reward for good deeds on earth. Most religions have special rituals or funerals to honour and remember the dead, such as the Day of the Dead in Mexico (above). Candles are lit to help dead relatives find their way to the land of the living.

SACRED TEXTS
Many religions have texts which teach and guide. Muslims read the Qur'an, Christianity is based on the Bible, Buddhists follow the Dharma, and the Talmud (above) is central to Judaism.

257

JUDAISM

The religion of the Jewish people, Judaism, began over 4,000 years ago. Jews worship one God. They believe that God has made the Jews his chosen people. The Jewish festival of Passover, held in the spring, commemorates the time when the Jews left their exile in Egypt to return to Israel.

Plate with Passover meal

HINDUISM

The Hindu religion developed in India thousands of years ago. Hindus have many gods, but they are all part of one great power, called Brahman. Hindus believe that when we die, we are reborn as a person, animal, or plant. The better our deeds in one life, the better our rebirth. The Hindu festival of Diwali celebrates the victory of good over evil.

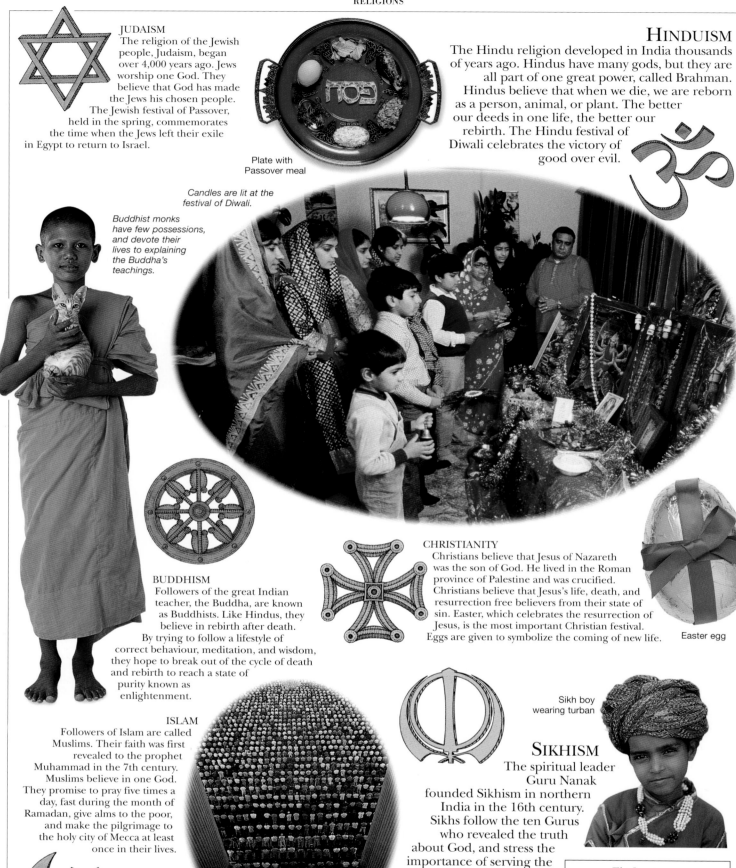

Candles are lit at the festival of Diwali.

Buddhist monks have few possessions, and devote their lives to explaining the Buddha's teachings.

BUDDHISM

Followers of the great Indian teacher, the Buddha, are known as Buddhists. Like Hindus, they believe in rebirth after death. By trying to follow a lifestyle of correct behaviour, meditation, and wisdom, they hope to break out of the cycle of death and rebirth to reach a state of purity known as enlightenment.

CHRISTIANITY

Christians believe that Jesus of Nazareth was the son of God. He lived in the Roman province of Palestine and was crucified. Christians believe that Jesus's life, death, and resurrection free believers from their state of sin. Easter, which celebrates the resurrection of Jesus, is the most important Christian festival. Eggs are given to symbolize the coming of new life.

Easter egg

ISLAM

Followers of Islam are called Muslims. Their faith was first revealed to the prophet Muhammad in the 7th century. Muslims believe in one God. They promise to pray five times a day, fast during the month of Ramadan, give alms to the poor, and make the pilgrimage to the holy city of Mecca at least once in their lives.

When they pray, Muslims face the direction of Mecca.

Sikh boy wearing turban

SIKHISM

The spiritual leader Guru Nanak founded Sikhism in northern India in the 16th century. Sikhs follow the ten Gurus who revealed the truth about God, and stress the importance of serving the community, as well as worship. Male (and some female) Sikhs wear the turban to show their faith and their membership of the Sikh community.

Find out more
ASIA
CRUSADES
EUROPE, HISTORY OF
HENRY VIII
REFORMATION

RENAISSANCE

ITALY IN THE 15TH CENTURY was an exciting place. It was here that educated people began to develop new ideas about the world around them and rediscovered the arts and learning of Ancient Greece and Rome. For a period of about 200 years that became known as the Renaissance (rebirth) people made great advances in education, technology, and the arts. Helped by the invention of printing, the Renaissance gradually spread from Italy to the rest of Europe. Although the Renaissance mainly affected the wealthy, it had a huge impact on the way that everybody lived and perceived the world around them. The Renaissance produced great artists such as Michelangelo and Raphael. It also produced a new way of thinking called humanism, as scholars and thinkers such as Erasmus began to challenge the authority of the Roman Catholic Church. Humanism gave human beings more importance. It meant that artists such as Leonardo da Vinci began to produce realistic images instead of symbolic scenes. Scientists challenged old ideas about the nature of the universe, and conducted pioneering experiments.

COPERNICUS
By observing the movement of planets and stars, astronomers such as Nicolaus Copernicus (1473-1543) began to challenge ideas about the solar system which had been accepted since the time of the Ancient Greeks. Copernicus was first to suggest that the Earth revolves every 24 hours and that it travels around the Sun once a year. Many people did not accept his findings until many years later.

TECHNOLOGY
Renaissance scientists invented or developed new scientific instruments to help them in their work. The armillary sphere, a skeleton sphere with the Earth in the centre, was used to measure the position of the stars. Galileo invented the useful proportional compass, which could be set at any angle.

Armillary sphere

Proportional compass

Galileo at work

GALILEO
Galileo Galilei (1564-1642) was an Italian astronomer and physicist. He disproved many of the Ancient Greek thinker Aristotle's theories, including the theory that heavy objects fall faster than light ones. He perfected a refracting telescope and observed that the Earth and all the planets of the solar system revolve around the Sun.

RENAISSANCE MUSIC
When the first music was printed in Italy in the late 15th century, new musical styles began to spread throughout Europe. Non-religious music became more common, showing the influence of the humanist approach to life which characterized the Renaissance period. Music became more harmonious and melodic than before. William Byrd (1543-1623), left, was the first Englishman to have his music printed in England. He was a well known organist, first at Lincoln Cathedral, and then later at the Queen Elizabeth I Chapel Royal in London. He was also a composer with more than 470 works to his name, making him one of the masters of European Renaissance music.

ERASMUS
Desiderius Erasmus (1466-1536), a Dutch priest, wanted to reform the Roman Catholic Church. He criticized the superstitions of the clergy, and published studies of the Old and New Testaments, giving a better understanding of the Bible. A leading humanist, he questioned the authority of the Church – a shocking idea at the time.

BOTTICELLI

The paintings of Sandro Botticelli (1444-1510) show many of the features typical of Renaissance art: clear lines, even composition, and an emphasis on human activity. Renaissance artists painted realistic, mythological, and Biblical subjects. Most tried to make their paintings as realistic as possible by using perspective to give scenes an appearance of depth. Above is the Botticelli painting *Venus and Mars*.

MEDICIS

The Medicis were a great banking family who ruled Florence for more than 300 years. They became very powerful. Many of them, particularly Lorenzo "the Magnificent" (1449-92), encouraged artists such as Michelangelo, and helped them financially.

MICHELANGELO

Michelangelo (1475-1564) was a very skilled Italian artist and sculptor. His marble statue of David (left) is one of the finest examples of Renaissance sculpture. People admired the statue's youthful strength and beauty, which demonstrated the new realistic style of art.

Dome rises more than 120 m (400 ft) from the floor of the church.

Begun in 1505, the building took 150 years to complete.

ST. PETER'S

Situated in Vatican City, Rome, Italy, St. Peter's Church has a rich history. Ten different architects worked on its construction. Michelangelo designed the dome. The Italian architect Bernini (1598-1680) designed the inside of the church and the majestic piazza outside the church. St. Peter's houses many fabulous works of art, and marble and detailed mosaics decorate the walls.

SCULPTURE

Renaissance sculptors made great use of marble, copying the style of Ancient Roman statues. A new understanding of anatomy inspired sculptors to carve nude figures, with accurate depictions of muscles and joints. Some sculptors even dissected corpses to discover how the human body works.

ARCHITECTURE

Renaissance architecture was modelled on classical Roman building styles. Architects featured high domed roofs, vaulted ceilings, decorative columns, and rounded arches in their buildings. One of the most influential architects was Andrea Palladio (1508-80). The classical designs used by Palladio for his many villas and palaces were widely copied by later architects.

RENAISSANCE

1420-36 Architect Filippo Brunelleschi develops the system of perspective.

1430-35 Donatello's sculpture of David is the first large nude statue since the Roman Empire.

1480-85 Sandro Botticelli paints *The Birth of Venus*.

1497 Leonardo da Vinci paints *The Last Supper*.

1501 Petrucci publishes first printed music in Venice.

1501-04 Michelangelo sculpts *David*.

1502 Leonardo paints the *Mona Lisa*.

1505 Architect Donato Bramante begins the new St. Peter's in Rome. Completed in 1655.

1508 Artist Raphael begins to decorate the Pope's apartments in the Vatican.

1508-12 Michelangelo decorates the Sistine chapel.

1509 Erasmus writes *In Praise of Folly*, criticizing the Church.

c.1510 Renaissance art in Venice reaches its peak with artists such as Titian, Veronese, and Tintoretto.

1513 Death of Pope Julius II.

1532 Niccolo Machiavelli's book *The Prince* is published, suggesting how a ruler should govern a state.

1543 Astronomer Copernicus claims that the Earth and the other planets move around the sun.

1564 Death of Michelangelo.

1565 Architect Palladio begins to build the Villa Rotunda in Venice.

1593 Galileo develops the thermometer.

1608 Galileo develops the telescope.

Find out more

ARCHITECTURE
ASTRONOMY
LEONARDO DA VINCI
MEDIEVAL EUROPE
PAINTERS

REPRODUCTION

FOR LIFE TO CONTINUE on Earth, humans and other animals must produce young. The process of creating new life is called reproduction. Human beings reproduce in much the same way as other mammals. From birth, a woman has many tiny pinhead-sized ova (egg cells) in two organs inside the abdomen called ovaries. From puberty onwards, one of these egg cells is released each month as part of the menstrual cycle. Throughout life, a man produces small tadpole-shaped cells called sperm in sex organs called the testes. During sexual intercourse, sperm cells leave the man's body and enter the woman's body, swimming towards her ovaries. If a sperm meets a ripe egg cell, the two join together. This is called fertilization. The egg cell can only be fertilized for about 24 hours after ovulation. Once fertilized, the egg travels to the uterus to continue its development. During the following nine months the tiny egg develops into a fully formed baby, ready to be born.

FOETUS
A developing baby, or foetus, lives inside the uterus, cushioned from bumps, bright lights, and noise by a surrounding fluid called the amniotic fluid. However, the baby can hear the regular thump of the mother's heartbeat and the gurgling of food in her intestines.

SEX ORGANS
The main female sex organs, the ovaries, are inside the abdomen. The main male organs, the testes and penis, hang outside the abdomen. Other differences between males and females, such as the woman's breasts, are called secondary sexual characteristics.

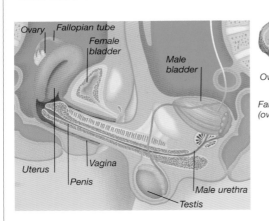

Ovary
Fallopian tube
Female bladder
Male bladder
Uterus
Penis
Vagina
Male urethra
Testis

FEMALE SEX ORGANS
About 300,000 eggs are stored in each ovary. During one menstrual cycle, an egg ripens and leaves the ovary, moving into the Fallopian tube, or oviduct. If it is not fertilized by a sperm, it reaches the uterus, dies and breaks down, then leaves the body during the process called menstruation.

Ovary
Fallopian tube (oviduct)
Uterus (womb)
Vagina

MALE SEX ORGANS
Each testis makes more than 250 million sperm cells every day. The cells are stored in the testis itself and in a long, winding tube called the epididymis. If they are not released, they break down and are reabsorbed into the bloodstream.

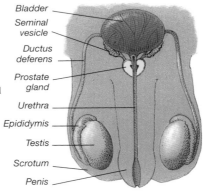

Bladder
Seminal vesicle
Ductus deferens
Prostate gland
Urethra
Epididymis
Testis
Scrotum
Penis

SEXUAL INTERCOURSE

During sexual intercourse, the man's penis becomes stiff enough to insert into the woman's vagina, which also enlarges. After a while muscular contractions squeeze sperm cells from the man's testes out of the penis and into the vagina, in a fluid called semen. This process is called ejaculation. The sperm cells swim through the uterus, propelled by their tails, and travel along the Fallopian tube. Sometimes, one of these sperm cells reaches the egg cell and fertilizes it, resulting in pregnancy.

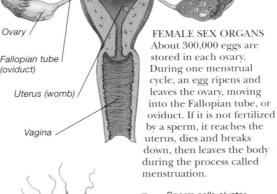

Sperm cells cluster around egg cell in Fallopian tube.

Only one sperm penetrates egg to fertilize it.

Barrier around dividing cells keeps out other sperm cells.

Fertilized egg divides into two cells within 36 hours, four within 48 hours, then eight, and so on.

Embryo enters uterus about four days after fertilization as a solid ball of 32 cells.

FERTILIZATION
An egg cell begins to divide and develop into a baby only when it is joined by a sperm cell. After intercourse, hundreds of sperm cells may reach the egg, but only one breaks through the outer layer. Once this occurs, genetic material in the sperm – the instructions needed to make a new human – joins the genetic material inside the egg. The coming together of sperm and egg and their genes is called fertilization.

PREGNANCY

About one week after fertilization, the now hollow ball of cells embeds itself in the blood-rich lining of the uterus where it absorbs nutrients. The cells continue to divide and change, forming the first body tissues such as blood vessels and nerves. Gradually the ball of cells folds and twists into the basic body shape of the baby. Meanwhile, other cells form the placenta, a saucer-shaped organ, in the lining of the uterus. The placenta is fed with blood from the mother, and oxygen and nutrients pass to the baby through the umbilical cord. This lifeline consists of three blood vessels; the largest vein carries nutrients and oxygen-rich blood to the baby, and the smaller ones carry waste and blood low in oxygen back to the placenta.

5 WEEKS
The developing baby is now about 10 mm (½ in) long. It has a recognizable head, back, and heart, and the beginnings of a mouth and eyes. The limbs are forming as small buds. At this stage, the developing baby is called an embryo.

8 WEEKS
The baby is about 25 mm (1 in) long, and all the major parts of the body have formed – even the fingers and toes. The developing baby is now called a foetus.

12 WEEKS
Its cells actively multiplying, the foetus continues to grow and develop rapidly. Features such as fingernails, toenails, and eyelids are now visible. The baby is about 13 cm (5 in) long. There are still 28 weeks to go before it is born.

PUBERTY

Babies and children have sex organs, but they are not able to release egg or sperm cells. At puberty, which generally starts when people are between 10 and 15 years old, chemicals called sex hormones are released into the bloodstream from hormonal glands. These sex hormones cause the sex organs to mature (become fully developed). Other changes occur at this time too, particularly a spurt in growth.

In a boy, the testes produce a sex hormone called testosterone. This makes hair grow on the face and body. It also makes the voice deeper, encourages muscle development, and sets off production of sperm.

In a girl, the ovaries produce progesterone and oestrogen, which cause the breasts to develop and fatty tissue to form, giving the body a more rounded shape. From puberty onwards, a woman's body also undergoes a monthly process called the menstrual cycle, as shown below. Changing levels of hormones thicken the uterus lining and enrich it with blood, which will nourish a fertilized egg if it implants.

1st week	2nd week	3rd week	4th week
Lining of uterus breaks down and passes out of the vagina during menstruation or a period.	Lining starts to thicken again in preparation for next egg. Next egg begins to ripen in ovary.	Ripe egg is released from ovary. Egg can be fertilized for up to 24 hours in Fallopian tube.	Egg reaches uterus and implants if fertilized, or breaks down if not fertilized.

BIRTH

Birth is the process that ends pregnancy and pushes a baby out of the uterus, usually after 38-40 weeks of pregnancy. When the baby has reached full term (left), it is about 50 cm (20 in) long. Labour is triggered by the hormone oxytocin and by changes in the level of other hormones in the mother's blood. During labour the cervix widens to allow birth to take place, and powerful contractions in the uterus push the baby out through the vagina, usually head first. If a baby is born feet first it is called a breech birth. The baby then takes its first breaths and the umbilical cord is cut. The placenta is expelled from the uterus a few minutes later as afterbirth.

PREMATURE BABIES
If a baby is born before the 37th week of pregnancy it is called premature and may have difficulty breathing. The baby is placed in an incubator and monitored very carefully until it is strong enough to breathe for itself.

A doctor checks the heartbeat of a premature baby in its incubator.

Find out more
ANIMALS
HUMAN BODY

REPTILES

SCALY-SKINNED ANIMALS such as alligators, turtles, and snakes are called reptiles. Some reptiles live in water and some on land; most are found in the warmer parts of the world. There are six main groups; lizards, snakes, worm lizards, turtles and tortoises, crocodiles and alligators, and the tuatara. Tortoises and turtles are the only reptiles with shells. Lizards make up the largest group, with about 4,300 different kinds, yet there is only one kind of tuatara. Reptiles are among the most ancient of all animals. The ancestors of today's reptiles were the dinosaurs. Dinosaurs roamed the Earth for about 150 million years, then suddenly died out 65 million years ago. Today, there are more than 8,000 kinds of reptiles, from the long reticulated python, measuring 10 m (33 ft), to the tiny dwarf gecko, only 33 mm (1.3 in) in length. Unlike warm-blooded (endothermic) mammals, reptiles are cold-blooded (ectothermic) – they need the warmth of the Sun to give them the energy to move.

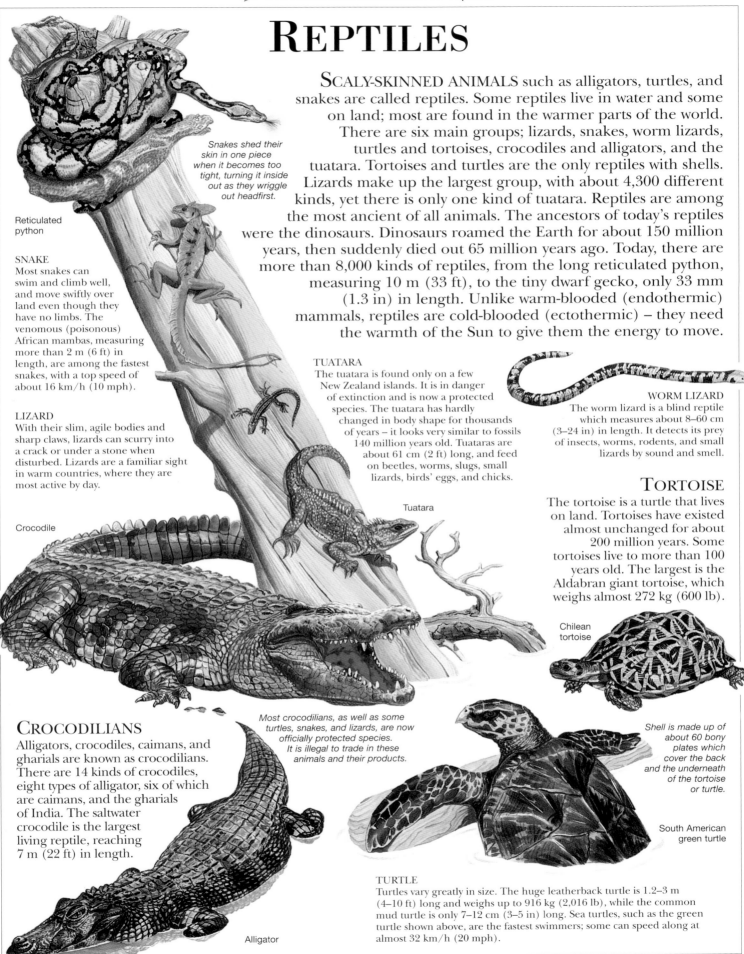

Snakes shed their skin in one piece when it becomes too tight, turning it inside out as they wriggle out headfirst.

Reticulated python

SNAKE
Most snakes can swim and climb well, and move swiftly over land even though they have no limbs. The venomous (poisonous) African mambas, measuring more than 2 m (6 ft) in length, are among the fastest snakes, with a top speed of about 16 km/h (10 mph).

LIZARD
With their slim, agile bodies and sharp claws, lizards can scurry into a crack or under a stone when disturbed. Lizards are a familiar sight in warm countries, where they are most active by day.

Crocodile

TUATARA
The tuatara is found only on a few New Zealand islands. It is in danger of extinction and is now a protected species. The tuatara has hardly changed in body shape for thousands of years – it looks very similar to fossils 140 million years old. Tuataras are about 61 cm (2 ft) long, and feed on beetles, worms, slugs, small lizards, birds' eggs, and chicks.

Tuatara

WORM LIZARD
The worm lizard is a blind reptile which measures about 8–60 cm (3–24 in) in length. It detects its prey of insects, worms, rodents, and small lizards by sound and smell.

TORTOISE
The tortoise is a turtle that lives on land. Tortoises have existed almost unchanged for about 200 million years. Some tortoises live to more than 100 years old. The largest is the Aldabran giant tortoise, which weighs almost 272 kg (600 lb).

Chilean tortoise

CROCODILIANS
Alligators, crocodiles, caimans, and gharials are known as crocodilians. There are 14 kinds of crocodiles, eight types of alligator, six of which are caimans, and the gharials of India. The saltwater crocodile is the largest living reptile, reaching 7 m (22 ft) in length.

Most crocodilians, as well as some turtles, snakes, and lizards, are now officially protected species. It is illegal to trade in these animals and their products.

Shell is made up of about 60 bony plates which cover the back and the underneath of the tortoise or turtle.

South American green turtle

TURTLE
Turtles vary greatly in size. The huge leatherback turtle is 1.2–3 m (4–10 ft) long and weighs up to 916 kg (2,016 lb), while the common mud turtle is only 7–12 cm (3–5 in) long. Sea turtles, such as the green turtle shown above, are the fastest swimmers; some can speed along at almost 32 km/h (20 mph).

Alligator

BREEDING

Most reptiles lay eggs, from which the young hatch. Snake and lizard eggs usually have a leathery, flexible shell. The eggs of crocodiles and tortoises are hard and rigid, and the temperature at which the eggs are incubated determines the sex of the hatchling. The loggerhead turtle, shown here, digs a deep hole in the beach sand and lays its eggs under the cover of darkness. The eggs take several weeks to hatch and are at risk from foxes and monitor lizards, which dig them up and eat them. After hatching, the young turtles have to avoid sea birds and crabs as they scuttle down to the sea.

The female loggerhead turtle swims ashore and crawls up the beach at night to lay eggs.

The female turtle lays about 100 eggs in the sand.

BLUE-TONGUED SKINK

The reptiles tongue has several uses. Lizards and snakes use it to detect their surroundings. The tongue flicks out to pick up chemicals in the air and carries them back to Jacobson's organs, special sensory organs in the roof of the mouth. When in danger, the Australian blue-tongued skink opens its mouth wide, thrusts out its bright blue tongue, hisses, and puffs up its body to frighten away a predator.

SCALES

A reptile's scaly skin provides good protection against predators and stops the animal from drying out. The arrangement of the scales helps scientists identify species. Some reptiles, such as chameleons, have special cells in the skin. These cells make the coloured pigments inside the skin expand or contract. This is how the chameleon changes its colour, for camouflage.

WALL GECKO

Wall geckos have tiny, sticky pads on their toes, which enable them to run up smooth glass windows and upside-down across the ceiling.

Some geckos are smaller than the human palm.

TEMPERATURE REGULATION

We often describe reptiles as cold-blooded, but this is not strictly true. Reptiles cannot generate body heat internally, in the way that mammals do, but they can control their body temperature by their behaviour. Reptiles bask in the Sun to absorb warmth, then hide in the shade when they become too hot.

During the hot midday Sun the lizard stays in the shade to avoid overheating.

At dawn the lizard sunbathes with the length of its body facing the Sun to absorb maximum heat.

At dusk the lizard basks with its head facing the Sun to keep up its body temperature.

LARGEST AND SMALLEST REPTILES

The saltwater crocodile is the largest reptile, although some snakes, such as the reticulated python, are longer, growing to 10 m (33 ft) in length. The largest lizard is the Komodo dragon, a type of monitor lizard. The smallest of all reptiles are some kinds of geckos, only about a centimetre long when fully grown.

COELOPHYSIS

The first reptiles appeared on Earth more than 300 million years ago and gradually took over from amphibians as the largest animals on land. Dinosaurs, such as the *Coelophysis* shown here, were early reptiles that evolved about 200–220 million years ago. *Coelophysis* was about the size of an adult human.

Coelophysis probably hunted lizard-like reptiles and other small animals of the time.

Find out more

ANIMALS
DINOSAURS
LIZARDS
MARSH AND SWAMP WILDLIFE
SNAKES

RIVERS

WATER RUNS DOWN from high ground, cutting out a channel in the rock as it moves. This flowing water forms a river, which can be fed by a melting glacier, an overflowing lake, or a mountain spring. Rivers shape the landscape as they flow: the water sweeps away soil and eventually creates deep valleys in the land. One of the world's deepest valleys, cut by the River Kali Gandak through the Himalayas, is 5.5 km (3.4 miles) deep. Rivers also flow deep underground, slowly wearing away limestone rocks to form caves.

Rivers are important for transport and as a source of water, which is why most big cities lie on rivers. The longest rivers are the River Nile in Africa, which is 6,670 km (4,145 miles) long, and the River Amazon in South America, which is 6,448 km (4,007 miles) long.

Rain feeds the river system.

RIVER SYSTEM

Small rivers and streams feed a large river with water. A river system consists of the whole group of rivers and streams. A watershed, or high ridge, separates one river system from another. Streams flow in opposite directions on either side of a watershed.

TRIBUTARIES
The streams and rivers that flow into a big river are called its tributaries.

WATERFALL
The river plunges over a shelf of hard rock to form a waterfall.

GORGE
The waterfall slowly wears away the rock, cutting a deep gorge.

RAPIDS
Fast, swirling currents form where water flows down a steep slope. These parts of the river are called rapids.

Weathering on the valley sides breaks up soft rock and soil. This material falls into the river and is carried away by the current.

RIVER VALLEY
The river carries along stones and mud, which grind against the river-bed and sides, deepening and widening the V-shaped valley.

NIAGARA FALLS
The Niagara River plunges almost 55 m (180 ft) at Niagara Falls, which is situated on the border of the United States and Canada.

OXBOW LAKE
The river cuts through the neck of a loop by wearing away the bank. Material is deposited at the ends of the loop, eventually forming a lake.

FLOODS
Rivers can overflow with heavy rain, or when water surges up from the sea. Flooding is severe in low-lying places, such as parts of Brazil in South America, which are often hit by tropical storms. Destruction of surrounding forests may be increasing the flow of water, making floods worse.

FLOOD PLAIN
Further down the river, the valley flattens out. This area, called the flood plain, is sometimes submerged during floods. The river runs through the plain in loops called meanders.

USES OF RIVERS

Great rivers that flow across whole countries carry boats that take goods from place to place. Some rivers have dams which build up huge stores of water in reservoirs. This water is used to supply towns and cities, irrigate crops, and generate electricity in hydroelectric power stations. Rivers are also a source of fish, but many rivers are now polluted by farms and factories.

DELTA
The river sometimes fans out into separate streams as it reaches the sea. The streams dump mud which forms an area of flat land called a delta.

Some rivers do not form deltas, but flow into the sea through a single wide channel called an estuary.

RIVER RHINE
The River Rhine is an important trade route. Barges carry goods between towns in northern Europe.

Find out more
FISH
LAKE AND RIVER WILDLIFE
MARSH AND SWAMP WILDLIFE
RAIN AND SNOW
SHIPS AND BOATS
WATER

ROBOTS

WHEN PEOPLE THINK OF ROBOTS, they often imagine the metal monsters of science fiction movies. However, most robots at work today look nothing like this. A robot is a computer-controlled machine that carries out mechanical tasks. The Czech playwright Karel Capek invented the word *robot*, which comes from a Czech word meaning "forced labour". Indeed, robots do jobs that would be dangerous or boring for people to do. Many factories have robots that consist of a single arm that is fixed in one spot. The robot simply repeats a task that it has been instructed to perform, such as spray-painting car parts. Today, engineers are developing much more sophisticated robots. These robots can move around, and their electronic detectors enable them to sense their surroundings. They also have "intelligence", which means that they can respond to what they see and hear and make decisions for themselves. Intelligent robots are designed to act as guards and firemen, and may travel into space to study distant worlds.

SCIENCE FICTION ROBOTS
The robots of science fiction, such as C3-P0 from the film *Star Wars*, are often anthropoid (human-like). In reality, anthropoid robots are rare. However, Japanese engineers have built experimental robots with two legs.

Held too tightly – loosen grip.

Brain sends nerve signals to muscles in the hand, adjusting the strength of the grip so the egg is neither dropped nor squashed.

Held too loosely – tighten grip.

Touch sensors in your hand detect how hard you are pressing on the egg.

FEEDBACK
When you pick up an egg, your senses begin sending signals to your brain. From this information, your brain automatically adjusts the movement of your hand and the pressure of your fingers. This adjustment is called feedback. Advanced robots control their actions by feedback from electronic detectors such as lasers, television cameras, and touch sensors.

ROBOT ARM
Sophisticated robots work in factories, assembling, spraying, and welding components (parts). A skilled welder or painter will have programmed the robot by leading it (or a similar robot) through the task. Some robots can understand simple spoken instructions too. Robots often have sensors such as laser vision systems which help the robots to find and work on complex parts.

SPACE ROBOT
In January 2004, two unmanned exploration rovers, *Spirit* (right) and *Opportunity*, touched down on Mars. They photographed the planet and analysed samples of rock. Robot space probes such as these are designed to obey instructions from controllers on Earth, but decide for themselves how to carry out the orders.

Space probes need to be able to work independently because radio instructions could take minutes or even hours to travel from Earth.

REMOTE CONTROL
Mobile robots do dangerous jobs such as repairing and dismantling nuclear reactors and detonating concealed bombs. These robots are remotely controlled – a human operator controls the general actions of the robot from a safe distance, and onboard computers control detailed movements.

This bomb disposal robot runs on tracks so that it can climb into awkward places. It carries cameras to send back pictures to the operator, and a gun for detonating the bomb.

Find out more

COMPUTERS
SCIENCE
TECHNOLOGY

ROCKS AND MINERALS

GIANT'S CAUSEWAY
The steps of this unusual rock formation in Northern Ireland are made of columns of basalt, rock which developed when lava from a volcano cooled and set. The rock cracked into columns as it cooled.

WE LIVE ON THE SURFACE of a huge ball of rock, the Earth. The landscape everywhere is made up of rocks. Most are covered by soil, trees, or grass. Others, such as Uluru (Ayers Rock) in Australia, a massive lump of sandstone 348 m (1,142 ft) high, rise from the ground and are visible. The oldest rocks on Earth are about 4,000 million years old. Other rocks are much more recent, and new rocks are forming all the time. All rocks contain substances called minerals. Marble consists mainly of calcite, for example, and granite contains the minerals mica, quartz, and feldspar.

Rocks form in different ways: from molten rock within the Earth, from the fossils of animals and plants, and by the action of heat and pressure on ancient rocks inside the Earth. But no rocks, however hard, last forever on the Earth's surface. They are slowly eroded, or worn away, by the action of wind, rain, and other weather conditions.

HOW ROCKS FORM
All rocks started out as clouds of dust in space. The dust particles came together and formed the rocks that make up the planets, moons, and meteorites. There are now three main kinds of rocks on the Earth's surface: igneous, sedimentary, and metamorphic rocks. Each kind of rock forms in a different way.

Bubbles of gas trapped in the lava created holes in this piece of rock.

When lava from a volcano cools on the Earth's surface, it forms basalt.

IGNEOUS ROCKS
Deep underground the heat is so intense that some rock is molten (melted). When it cools, this molten rock, or magma, sets hard to produce an igneous rock. This may happen underground, or the magma may rise to the surface as lava and solidify.

Mud and pebbles are buried and squashed together, producing a hard sedimentary rock called conglomerate.

SEDIMENTARY ROCKS
Ice, wind, and running water wear away rocks into pebbles and small particles called sediment. Layers of sediment containing sand, clay, and animal skeletons are buried and squeezed so that they slowly change into hard rocks called sedimentary rocks.

Limestone contains the remains of shellfish. Chalk, another kind of limestone, is made of the skeletons of sea animals.

Sedimentary rocks, such as conglomerate, form on the beach at the mouth of a river.

River carries sediment from the land to the sea.

Lava flows from a volcano and solidifies, forming basalt, an igneous rock.

Red-hot magma heats surrounding limestone, turning it into marble.

Hot magma solidifies, forming granite, an igneous rock.

Shale forms from clay at the river bed.

Clay forms shale, a sedimentary rock that crumbles easily. This rock is slate, the metamorphic rock which forms from shale.

METAMORPHIC ROCKS
Heat and pressure deep underground bake and squeeze sedimentary and igneous rocks. The minerals within the rocks change, often becoming harder. In this way they form new rocks called metamorphic rocks. After millions of years, the top rocks are worn away and metamorphic rocks appear on the surface.

Heating and compressing limestone turns it into marble, a hard metamorphic rock.

When magma slowly cools deep underground, it often forms granite, a hard rock which is used as a building material.

MINERALS

An impressive rock collection will feature rocks that contain beautiful mineral crystals. Minerals are the different substances of which rocks are made. For example, limestone and marble contain the white mineral calcite. Minerals include precious stones such as diamonds, and ores – minerals that contain metals such as iron and aluminium. Almost all metals are produced by mining and quarrying ores, and then treating the ores to extract their metals.

DESERT ROSE
The mineral gypsum forms petal-shaped crystals in deserts and dry regions. This happens as water dries up, leaving mineral deposits behind. The crystals often look like flowers, so they are called desert roses or gypsum flowers.

TURQUOISE
Jewellers cut beautiful gemstones and ornaments from turquoise, a blue-green mineral that often runs in a thin vein through other rocks.

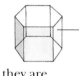

HALITE
Table salt comes from the mineral halite. Halite forms where sea water dries at the shore. Underground deposits of halite are the remains of ancient salt lakes. Pure salt has no colour, but impurities in halite give it a pink colour.

SULPHUR
Yellow crystals form when molten sulphur cools. Large underground deposits in places such as the United States provide sulphur for making rubber and chemicals.

CRYSTALS

Minerals often form crystals – solids which grow in regular shapes with flat sides. Light sparkles from crystals because they are often transparent and have smooth, shiny surfaces. Each mineral forms crystals with particular shapes, such as columns and cubes. Crystals grow from molten minerals or minerals that are dissolved in liquids, such as water.

Hexagonal crystals form in six-sided columns.

Cubic crystals form in four-sided columns.

GALENA
Glistening grey crystals of galena stick out from a piece of white limestone. Galena forms cubic crystals. It is the main ore in which lead is found, and it often appears as a vein in limestone. Lead is combined with sulphur in galena. Smelting the ore by heating it in a furnace removes the sulphur and leaves lead metal.

Some minerals, such as solecite, form needle-shaped crystals.

Crystals form in columns, such as in this piece of the mineral beryl.

QUARTZ
Quartz is one of the most common minerals. Electronic clocks and watches contain small cut pieces of quartz that control time-keeping with great accuracy.

USES OF ROCK

Rocks in one form or another surround us in towns, cities, and the countryside. Hard rocks such as granite, sandstone, and limestone provide good building materials for houses and walls, and roads contain fragments of crushed rock. Soft rocks have uses too. Heating clay or shale with crushed limestone produces cement for making concrete and laying bricks. Bricks themselves are made by baking clay in moulds.

The first tools were made of stone. Early people broke pieces of rocks and stone to make sharp cutting implements such as axes.

Sculptors work rocks, stones, and pure minerals to make statues and ornaments.

Find out more
ATOMS AND MOLECULES
EARTH
FOSSILS
IRON AGE
METALS
SCIENCE
VOLCANOES

ROMAN EMPIRE

TWO THOUSAND YEARS AGO a single government and way of life united most of western Europe, the Middle East, and the north coast of Africa. The Roman Empire was based on good organization and centralized control. Towns in different countries were planned in exactly the same way. A network of stone-paved roads (parts of which remain today) connected every area to Rome. The reign of the first emperor, Augustus, began a long period of stability known as the Pax Romana, or Roman Peace, which lasted for about 200 years. Strong border defences manned by the Roman army protected the empire, while a skilled civil service governed it. Trade flourished and the people were united. The empire reached the height of its power in about 200 CE and then began to decline slowly. It was divided into two parts in 395. In 476, barbarian tribes conquered Rome, putting an end to the Western Empire. The Eastern Empire (based in Constantinople, now called Istanbul, Turkey) continued until 1453.

GRAFFITI
The Romans were fond of making fun of each other. This caricature was found on a wall in Pompeii. It is a mockery of a leading local citizen – probably a noble, judging from his laurel wreath.

Temple where people worshipped their gods.

Traders sold their wares at market stalls.

Public baths

CITY LIFE

Roman cities were carefully planned with straight streets, running water, and sewers. The forum, or central market-place, was surrounded by shops, law courts, and the town hall. The rich, always Roman citizens, lived in fine villas; the poor lived in apartment-style buildings. There were many temples. Most of the hard work was done by slaves, who had none of the rights granted to citizens, such as access to the baths.

COLOSSEUM
Emperors paid for expensive public games, such as chariot racing, in order to be popular with the crowds. In Rome a massive theatre called the Colosseum held 45,000 people, who watched gladiators and wild animals fight to the death.

ROMAN BATHS

The Romans loved bathing. They scraped off the dirt, rubbed oil into their skin, relaxed in steam rooms, swam in warm pools, and plunged into icy water.

The hypocaust system circulated hot air under the floors and through the walls to heat houses and baths.

People rubbed oil, which they carried in oil flasks, on their bodies.

Bathers scraped the sweat and dirt off their bodies with strigils.

Commanding officers often wore crests on their helmets so that their men could recognize them in battle.

ROMAN ARMY

The power of the empire depended on the might of its professional armies, or legions. Soldiers belonging to a legion (about 5,000 men) were called legionaries. They were highly trained and well equipped with spears, shields, and short swords. They built roads and forts to defend their conquests. Upon retirement, veteran soldiers were often given land in colonies throughout the empire.

ROMAN EMPIRE

c.753 BCE First settlement built.

509 BCE Last king of Rome driven out of city. Republic established.

275 BCE Italy conquered. Expansion overseas begins.

364-146 BCE Punic Wars against Carthage end with Roman control of Spain and North Africa, and the destruction of Carthage.

71 BCE Slaves revolt, led by Spartacus.

52 BCE Gaul (France) conquered by Julius Caesar.

44 BCE Caesar assassinated.

27 BCE Augustus becomes first emperor.

43 CE Claudius conquers Britain.

117 CE Empire reaches its greatest size.

284 CE Empire splits into two halves.

410 CE Visigoths sack Rome.

476 CE Western part of the Empire falls.

THE ROMAN EMPIRE
At its height the Roman Empire stretched from the Middle East to Britain. The inhabitants were of many different races and spoke many different languages.

HADRIAN'S WALL
The emperor Hadrian ordered a wall to be built across northern Britain to defend Roman lands from the fierce, unconquered tribes who lived in the mountains of Scotland. The wall, parts of which can still be seen today, was 120 km (75 miles) long, and studded with forts. The army built defensive ditches, fortress bases, and signal towers along it.

TECHNOLOGY AND CRAFTS

The Romans were highly skilled engineers and craftworkers. Their towns had water supplies and drains, and rich people lived in centrally heated houses. The houses often had detailed mosaics on the floors. Artisans worked with glass, metals, bone, and clay to make beautiful objects that have lasted to this day.

Keys were made of metal.

Decorated clay oil lamp

Glass jar for holding liquids

Find out more

AFRICA, HISTORY OF
ARCHITECTURE
BYZANTINE EMPIRE
EUROPE, HISTORY OF
SLAVERY

SATELLITES

Polar orbit, used by Earth observation satellites

Geostationary orbit, used by communications satellites

Elliptical orbit, used by spy satellites

SATELLITE ORBITS

A communications satellite takes exactly 24 hours to orbit the Earth, so it appears to remain fixed over one spot. This kind of orbit is called geostationary. A polar orbit allows a satellite to see the whole Earth in a series of strips. In an elliptical orbit, a satellite can pass low over a selected part of the Earth.

Solar panels generate electricity from sunlight to power the satellite.

Radar altimeter provides data on wind speed, ocean currents, and tides.

WHEN AIRCRAFT and balloons first took to the skies, the people in them were amazed at their new view of the world. From hundreds of metres up they could see the layout of a large city, the shape of a coastline, or the patchwork of fields on a farm. Today, we have an even wider view. Satellites circle the Earth, not hundreds of metres, but hundreds of kilometres above the ground. From this great height, satellites provide a unique image of our planet. Some have cameras that take photographs of land and sea, giving information about the changing environment on Earth. Others plot weather patterns or peer out into space and send back data (information) about planets and stars. All of these are artificial satellites that have been launched into space from Earth. However, the word satellite actually means any object that moves around a planet while being held in orbit by the planet's gravity. There are countless natural satellites in the universe: the Earth has one, which is the Moon.

Infra-red scanner measures water vapour in the atmosphere and the temperatures of seas and cloud tops.

Earth observation satellite ERS-2

Antenna for transmitting data back to Earth

ARTIFICIAL SATELLITES

There are many types of artificial satellite. Weather satellites observe rain, storms, and clouds, and measure land and sea temperatures. Communications satellites send radio and television signals from one part of the Earth to another. Spy satellites observe military targets from low altitudes and send back detailed pictures to ground stations. Earth observation satellites monitor vegetation, air and water pollution, population changes, and geological factors such as mineral deposits.

MAPPING THE EARTH

Resources satellites take pictures of the Earth's surface. The cameras have various filters so they can pick up infra-red (heat) radiation and different colours of light. Vegetation, for instance, reflects infra-red light strongly, showing up forests and woodlands. Computer-generated colours are used to pick out areas with different kinds of vegetation and minerals.

Satellite map image of San Francisco Bay, California. Clearly visible are two bridges: the Golden Gate Bridge on the left and the Bay Bridge on the right.

SPUTNIK 1

On 4 October 1957, the Soviet Union launched *Sputnik 1*, the world's first artificial satellite. *Sputnik 1* carried a radio transmitter that sent signals back to Earth until it burned up in the atmosphere 92 days later.

NATURAL SATELLITES

There are around 200 known natural satellites, or moons, in the solar system. Most of these orbit (move around) the four giant outer planets: Jupiter, Saturn, Uranus, and Neptune. The largest moons are bigger than Mercury, the smallest planet; the smallest moons are only a few kilometres across and have irregular, potato-like shapes.

The planet Jupiter with two of its moons, Io (left) and Europa (right)

Find out more

ASTRONOMY
SCIENCE, HISTORY OF
SPACE FLIGHT
TECHNOLOGY
TELEPHONES
TELEVISION

SCIENCE

THERE ARE MANY FORMS OF SCIENCE, and together they study the nature and behaviour of the universe and everything in it. Science comes from the Latin word for "to know". Scientists find out what they want to know by practical methods. They observe, take measurements, make experiments, and write down the results. There are four main categories (types) of science: natural sciences, physical sciences, technological sciences, and social sciences. Natural sciences include the life sciences, such as biology and botany, and earth sciences, such as geology. Physical sciences include physics and chemistry. Technological science includes engineering, and uses information discovered by scientists to make or build things in the real world. Social sciences study people, and include anthropology and psychology. All the sciences depend on mathematics.

A glass rod in a beaker of water looks bent because light waves travel slower through water than through air.

PHYSICS

Physics is the study of matter and energy, and how they work together. Because there are many different kinds of matter and forms of energy, there are many different branches of physics. Optics, for example, looks at the different way light waves can behave. For instance, they travel at different speeds through space, air, glass, or water.

SCIENTIFIC METHOD

Scientific method involves using observation and hypotheses (theories) to explain things, and then testing these hypotheses with experiments. To be sure that their results are accurate, scientists always follow strict rules when making an experiment. In an experiment only the conditions under test must change, everything else must be kept the same. In this way, differences in results should only be caused by the experimenter's deliberate changes.

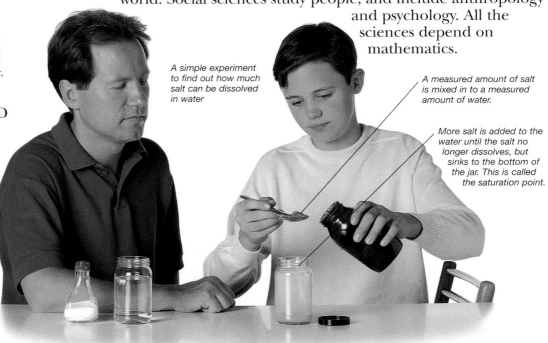

A simple experiment to find out how much salt can be dissolved in water

A measured amount of salt is mixed in to a measured amount of water.

More salt is added to the water until the salt no longer dissolves, but sinks to the bottom of the jar. This is called the saturation point.

EARTH SCIENCES

Geography and geology are earth sciences. Earth scientists study the structure of our planet and the way it changes. The study of rocks and fossils can tell us a lot about the way the planet and its life have evolved. Since Earth is a living planet, the earth sciences are linked to the life sciences.

Shoot grows up towards the sun.

Bean shoot

LIFE SCIENCES

Any of the sciences that study living things is called a life science. Biology is the study of life of all kinds, botany is the study of plants, and zoology is the study of animals. Because animal and plant life depend on each other, scientists also study them together. Ecology is the study of the relationships between living things of all kinds and how they fit in with and affect their environments.

Geologists study rocks and crystals.

Chrysocolla

Cyanotrichite

SOCIAL SCIENCES

The sciences that study people are called social sciences. There are various kinds. Anthropology is the study of life and culture of the whole of humanity. Sociology studies the way humans behave together in groups; it looks at how families work, how society is made up, what makes it change, and how the changes affect people. Psychology is also a social science, but it looks at how people behave as individuals.

Roots absorb water and nutrients.

Find out more
EARTH
MEDICINE
ROCKS AND MINERALS
SCIENCE, HISTORY OF
TECHNOLOGY

HISTORY OF
SCIENCE

SPACE TRAVEL, computers, and reliable medical care are just a few of the things that owe their existence to scientists and inventors. Scientists study the natural world, from distant galaxies to tiny atoms, and try to explain what they see. The work of a scientist is based on a cycle of experiment, observation, and theorization (making theories). For instance, in the 17th century, English scientist Isaac Newton experimented with sunlight passing through a prism. From the spectrum (bands of colours) that he observed, he suggested the theory that white light is a mixture of colours. Inventors are people who think of a new idea that can be put into practice. An invention may be the result of a scientific discovery, such as the laser, which Theodore Maiman (born 1927) built because of his knowledge of light and atoms. However, this is not always the case. Early people invented the lever before they knew how it worked. Whatever their chosen fields, scientists and inventors have one thing in common: they are people of rare insight who make discoveries new to the world.

ANCIENT TIMES
Early people first invented tools about 2 million years ago. About 10,000 years ago, people began to settle in communities and started farming and building. The first civilizations grew up in the Middle East, Africa, India, and China. There, people studied the Sun and stars, built simple clocks, developed mathematics, and discovered how to make metals and pottery.

This stone blade was used about 200,000 years ago in Egypt.

The plough was invented in about 4000 BCE.

The wheel was invented in about 3500 BCE.

The pump was invented in the 2nd century BCE.

GREEKS AND ROMANS
From about 600 BCE, the Greeks began to study their world. Great philosophers (thinkers) such as Pythagoras developed the "scientific method" – the principle of observation and experiment that is still the basis of science today. The Greeks studied mathematics and astronomy and invented simple machines. At around the same time, the Romans used Greek scientific ideas to help them build great structures.

Hero of Greece built the first simple steam engine in the 1st century CE.

ARCHIMEDES
Greek scientist Archimedes (287-212 BCE) explained how levers and pulleys work and discovered how things float. This idea is said to have come to him while he was in his bath.

A balloon first carried people in 1783.

Archimedes's screw was a device for raising water.

In 1608, Dutch optician Hans Lippershey invented the telescope.

ISAAC NEWTON
In 1687, Isaac Newton (1642-1727) published the daring idea that gravity is a universal force, keeping planets and moons in their orbits as well as causing things to fall to the ground. Newton also put forward the famous laws of motion, and found that white light is composed of the colours in the rainbow.

LEONARDO DA VINCI
The great Italian artist and inventor Leonardo da Vinci (1452-1519) designed many machines, including a parachute and a helicopter. However, these machines were never built.

1000-1600 CE
During this period, Arabic civilizations made several discoveries, particularly about the nature of light. After about 1000 CE, people in Europe began to use the scientific method of the Ancient Greeks. Polish astronomer Nicolaus Copernicus (1473-1543) suggested that the Earth orbits the Sun, and Andreas Vesalius (1514-64), a Flemish doctor, made discoveries about human anatomy.

In 1438, Johannes Gutenberg of Germany (c.1398-1468) invented the modern printing process.

1600-1800
Italian scientist Galileo Galilei (1564-1642) made discoveries about force, gravity, and motion. Modern astronomy began in 1609 when German astronomer Johannes Kepler (1571-1630) discovered the laws of planetary motion and Galileo built a telescope to observe the heavens. During the 1700s, the first engines were built by inventors such as James Watt (1736-1819) of Scotland. Chemistry advanced as scientists discovered how everything is composed of chemical elements such as oxygen and hydrogen.

1800-1900

The invention of the battery by Italian Alessandro Volta (1745-1827) led to discoveries about electricity and magnetism by scientists such as Englishman Michael Faraday (1791-1867) and many electrical inventions such as electric light. Englishman John Dalton (1766-1844) and other scientists found out that everything is made of tiny atoms. Frenchman Louis Pasteur (1822-1895) showed that bacteria cause disease, which led to better health care. Transport advanced with the invention of locomotives, powered ships, and cars.

In 1804 Englishman Richard Trevithick invented the steam locomotive.

The telephone was invented by a Scottish-American, Alexander Graham Bell, in 1876.

In 1895 Italian scientist Guglielmo Marconi invented radio transmission.

THOMAS EDISON
Thomas Edison (1847-1931) was one of the world's most successful inventors. He made more than 1,000 inventions, including the record player (patented 1878) and a system for making motion pictures. Edison was also one of the inventors of the electric light bulb.

1900 TO THE PRESENT

Scientists delved into the atom, finding electrons and the nucleus, and then studied the nucleus itself. This led to the invention of nuclear power and to the science of electronics, which brought us television and the computer. Scientists also explored living cells and found new ways of fighting disease. Astronomers studied stars, planets, and distant galaxies. The invention of aircraft and space flight allowed people to travel into the air and out into space.

WRIGHT BROTHERS
In 1903, the world watched in wonder as Orville Wright (1871-1948) and his brother Wilbur (1867-1912) made the first powered aeroplane flight.

Several scientists developed television during the 1920s. The first public television service started in the 1930s.

Theodore Maiman and Charles Townes invented the first working laser in 1960.

Artificial satellites were first launched in 1957.

WILLIAM SHOCKLEY
Computers, televisions, and other electronic devices depend on the transistor, invented in 1948 by a team of scientists headed by William Shockley (born 1910). Now millions of transistors can be packed into a tiny microchip.

In 1946 a team of American scientists built the first fully electronic computer.

ALBERT EINSTEIN
In 1905 and 1915, the German scientist Albert Einstein (1879-1955) proposed his theories of relativity. They showed that light is the fastest thing in the universe, and that time would slow down, length would shorten, and mass would increase if you could travel at almost the speed of light. The Sun's source of energy and nuclear power, and how black holes can exist in space are explained by his discoveries.

MAX PLANCK
In about 1900, German scientist Max Planck (1858-1947) published his quantum theory, which explained the nature of energy and led to many new ideas. For example, although we usually think of light as waves, quantum theory explains how light sometimes seems to behave as tiny particles called photons.

HISTORY OF SCIENCE

5000 BCE Metal objects first made in Middle East.

400 BCE Greek scientist Democritus suggests that all things are made of atoms.

105 CE Chinese inventor Ts'ai Lun makes paper.

650 CE Persians invent the windmill.

1000 CE Chinese use gunpowder in warfare.

1657 Dutchman Christiaan Huygens constructs pendulum clock.

1712 English engineer Thomas Newcomen builds first practical steam engine.

1775 Englishman Joseph Priestley discovers oxygen.

1789 French scientist Antoine Lavoisier explains chemical reactions.

1803 English scientist John Dalton explains existence of atoms.

1826 Frenchman Joseph Niépce takes first photograph.

1879 Thomas Edison (US) and Englishman Joseph Swan invent electric light bulb.

1885 German engineer Karl Benz builds first car.

1888 German scientist Heinrich Hertz discovers radio waves.

1898 French-Polish scientist Marie Curie discovers radium.

1911 English scientist Ernest Rutherford discovers nucleus of the atom.

1924 US astronomer Edwin Hubble discovers galaxies and, in 1929, the expansion of the universe.

1942 Italian scientist Enrico Fermi builds first nuclear reactor.

1959 Soviet Union launches first space probe.

1969 ARPANET (first version of the Internet) goes live.

1993 The World Wide Web developed.

Find out more
ATOMS AND MOLECULES
GRAVITY
LEONARDO DA VINCI
MEDICINE, HISTORY OF
RENAISSANCE
SCIENCE
TECHNOLOGY

SCOTLAND

ST. ANDREW'S CROSS
The cross of St. Andrew, patron saint of Scotland, is called the saltire.

FROM EDINBURGH TO THE HIGHLANDS, the Scottish people are proud of their unique culture. Scotland is part of the United Kingdom, but has kept some of its independence. Scottish banks print their own pound notes, the legal system is different to that of England and Wales, Scottish university courses last four years, not three as in England, and Scottish students sit Higher Still examinations, not A-levels. Since 1999, Scotland has also regained its parliament. Because it is so far north, Scotland has short days in winter, but long hours of daylight in summer. The old industries have declined, but new jobs have been created in service industries and through North Sea oil.

Scotland and its islands are the most northerly parts of the United Kingdom.

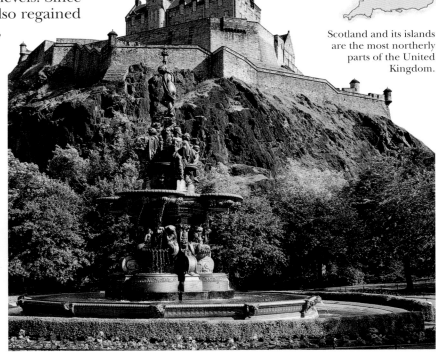

HIGHLANDS
The north of Scotland contains the Highlands, a rugged but beautiful mountainous region that includes Ben Nevis, the highest mountain in Britain, and spectacular lochs (lakes). Scotland covers an area of 78,742 sq km (30,394) sq miles). Of its population of about 5.1 million people, most live further south in the so-called Lowlands, near the cities of Glasgow and Edinburgh.

KILTS AND SPORRANS
Tartan and kilts are unique to Scottish culture. A kilt is like a skirt and is made from tartan, a checked woollen material. Traditionally, the kilt is worn with the sporran, special shoes, and sometimes a dagger tucked into a sock. There are many different tartans. Each belongs to a special clan, or tribe.

Sporran

EDINBURGH
The capital of Scotland is the city of Edinburgh. The kings of Scotland used to rule the country from Edinburgh, and the newly created Scottish parliament has its home there. The volcanic crag at the centre is topped by Edinburgh Castle, and dominates the city's skyline. Every year, Edinburgh hosts an internationally renowned arts festival.

WHISKY
Scotland is famous for its whisky. Many different distilleries across the country produce hundreds of malt whiskies varying in taste and colour. Traditional Scottish dishes include porridge, and haggis, made from spiced sheep's innards mixed with oats.

HIGHLAND GAMES
The champions of Scotland's traditional sports compete at the annual Highland Games. The Games have a long history, and include events such as putting the shot and throwing the hammer. It also includes a unique event – tossing the caber. For this, athletes compete with each other to pick up and toss (throw) the caber – a large tree trunk – as far as possible.

Find out more
STUARTS
UNITED KINGDOM
UNITED KINGDOM, HISTORY OF

SEASHORE WILDLIFE

SEASIDE DANGERS
Most of these baby turtles, hatching from eggs buried by their mother in the sand, will die. They are food for gulls, crabs, lizards and other hunters. Humans also steal the eggs. Conservation efforts are now being made to protect turtles.

A SEASHORE is formed wherever the land meets the sea, and can be a polar ice cliff or a tropical beach. The endless motion of the waves, and the tide going in and out, means the shore changes constantly with time. Each seashore has its own selection of plant and animal life that is specially adapted to an environment governed by the rhythm of the tides. Inhabitants of the seashore must survive pounding waves, salty sea water, fresh rainwater, drying winds, and hot sunshine. Plants thrive along rocky coasts and in some muddy areas, providing food and shelter for creatures, but they cannot grow on shifting sand or pebbles. Here the inhabitants depend on the tide to bring new supplies of food, in the form of particles floating in the water. Successful seashore animal groups include molluscs and crustaceans, both of which are protected by hard casings.

Gulls hover over the sea looking for fish, while waders hunt around the shore.

Seagull

Many sea birds patrol the coast, searching for food or scavenging on the dead bodies of cast-up sea creatures.

Lace coral can survive harsh rubbing by the wave-washed sand grains. It provides a refuge for animals in its lacy folds.

Common starfish

SANDY BEACHES
Waves roll and tumble the tiny grains of sand on the beach. Plants cannot get a firm hold on this type of shore, so they usually grow higher up. Although the sandy beach often looks deserted, dozens of creatures are just below the surface. Sand makes an ideal hiding place for burrowing creatures. Many filter food from the sea water when the tide is in or digest tiny edible particles in the sand.

WADING BIRDS
Waders probe into sand or mud with their long, narrow bills to find shellfish and worms. Large species with the longest bills, such as the curlew (above), reach down several centimetres for deeply buried items. Smaller waders, such as the black-bellied dunlin, take food from just below the surface.

GHOST CRAB
There are hundreds of kinds of shore crabs along the world's coastlines. They are the seashore's "cleaners"; they can consume almost anything edible – living or dead. The ghost crab (above right) takes its name from its ghostly pale colour.

EGG CASES
Sharks and rays lay their eggs near the shore, anchored to seaweeds or rocks by clinging tendrils. When the young fishes hatch, the egg cases, known as "mermaid's purses", come free and are often washed up on the shore.

RAZOR CLAM
So called because it looks like an old-fashioned cut-throat razor, the razor clam has a hinged shell. The mollusc inside digs quickly by pushing its strong, fleshy foot into the sand and then pulling the shell down.

The burrowing sea anemone's arms spread out to sting and catch small prey. Its stalk, up to 30 cm (12 in) long, is used to hold on to the sand.

SAND HOPPER
Sand hoppers are crustaceans which feed on rotting vegetation. They swarm over seaweed which has washed up on shore and, when in danger, leap away on their strong back legs, hence their name.

WEEVER FISH
The weever lies half buried in the sand, waiting to gobble up small fishes, crabs, and shrimps. It has poisonous spines on its fins, which give a nasty sting if the fish is stepped on.

SAND EEL
Many animals, from puffins to herrings, feed on the sand eel shown here. In turn, the sand eel eats even smaller fishes, as well as worms and plankton. It is not a true eel, but an eel-shaped member of the perch group. It lives in shallow water.

SALT MARSHES

Salt marshes form at the back of the shore, where the tide floods flat areas of land near a river's mouth. Plants such as cordgrass, glasswort, eelgrass, sea club rush, and sea starwort are able to survive in the salt that builds up in the soil. Birds such as geese, gulls, and terns can feed on salt marshes all year round, especially in winter, when inland areas are frozen hard. Some birds use salt marshes as summer breeding grounds, some as stop-overs while migrating.

Some large seaweeds are called kelps, such as sugar kelp and oarweed.

CLIFFS

Only a few very agile land animals, such as snakes, can reach precarious cliff ledges. So the ledges are safe nesting sites for a variety of birds, from gannets to gulls, razorbills, and cormorants. A few plants, like thrift ("sea pink"), also gain a foothold, provided they can withstand strong winds and salty spray.

Periwinkles seal themselves to the rock with mucus as the tide retreats, to keep them from losing water and drying out.

SEAWEED

There are three main kinds of rocky-shore seaweeds, also known as algae: brown, red, and green. They do not have roots, stems, or leaves. Instead, most anchor themselves to the rocks by structures called holdfasts. The larger brown and red weeds have stem-like stipes, ending in leaflike blades known as laminae or fronds.

ROCKY SHORES

Rocks provide a firm surface for seaweeds, and many creatures shelter among the fronds. But the weeds still face problems. Waves smash them against the hard stony surface, and they are regularly submerged by salt water, then left high and dry at low tide. Shellfish cling to the rocks, and a variety of fishes and crabs adapt themselves to the ever-changing conditions, hiding from predators in holes and crevices.

WHELKS

These rocky-shore scavengers hunt for dead or dying animals. They are relatives of land snails and find prey by "smelling" the water, which they draw in through a periscope-like siphon.

ANEMONES

These jellyfish relatives use their tentacles to sting small fishes, shrimps, and other creatures, and draw them into the body cavity through the mouth. When the tide goes out, the tentacles fold inwards for protection.

Barnacle

CHITON

Chitons are also called "coat of mail shells" because they look like chainmail armour. Each chiton has an eight-part shell set into its broad, fleshy body. It can grip a rock very firmly. These molluscs feed on small algae from the rock surface.

MANTIS SHRIMP

The mantis shrimp, a crustacean, hides in a hole waiting for prey. When a fish or other victim approaches, the shrimp stuns it by a lightning blow from its club-shaped second "leg".

Branching holdfast provides shelter for small animals

Red seaweed

SEA STAR

The biscuit sea star feeds on shellfish, sea squirts, corals, sponges, and other animals. It glides along on dozens of tiny, sucker-tipped hydraulic tube feet located on its underside.

Find out more

CONSERVATION
and endangered species
FISH
LAKE AND RIVER WILDLIFE
MARSH AND SWAMP WILDLIFE
OCEANS AND SEAS
OCEAN WILDLIFE
POLLUTION

WILLIAM SHAKESPEARE

THE GREATEST PLAYWRIGHT of all time was probably the Englishman William Shakespeare. He was born in Stratford-upon-Avon, where he went to school, and later married. When he was in his 20s, he went to London to work as an actor, and a playwright. His plays were very successful, and 37 of them survive. Some, such as *Hamlet*, are tragedies, that end with the death of the hero or heroine. Others, such as *Twelfth Night*, are comedies, full of amusing characters who get into terrible difficulties that are eventually sorted out. Shakespeare also wrote histories that are based on real-life situations, such as *Henry IV*. Most of Shakespeare's plays are written in an unrhymed verse form called blank verse. They are famous worldwide for their use of language, fascinating characters, and wide appeal.

1564 Born, Stratford-upon-Avon, England.

1582 Marries Anne Hathaway.

1592 Writes his first plays in London.

1594-99 Produces early comedies, and many history plays.

1599 Globe Theatre constructed.

1600-08 Writes many of his greatest tragedies.

1616 Dies in Stratford-upon-Avon.

THE GRAMMAR SCHOOL
With its rows of wooden desks, the old grammar school still stands in Stratford. Shakespeare was probably educated here.

KING'S MEN
In the 1590s, Shakespeare joined a troupe of actors called the Lord Chamberlain's Men, and became their resident writer. When James I came to the throne in 1603, they gained his support and became known as the King's Men. They had their own theatre, the Globe, near the River Thames in London.

Male actors played female roles.

The audience stood around the stage.

Henry Wriothesley

POETRY
Shakespeare was a fine poet, and wrote a series of 14-line love poems called sonnets. They are addressed to two different people, "a dark lady" and Mr. W.H. Some scholars believe that Mr. W.H. may have been Henry Wriothesley, the Third Earl of Southampton, who was Shakespeare's patron.

WAS IT BACON?
In the 19th century, some people thought that the learned writer Francis Bacon(1561-1626) had written Shakespeare's plays, because Shakespeare had not gone to university. But there is no real evidence that proves this.

English actress, Maggie Smith, in a performance of A Midsummer Night's Dream.

A MIDSUMMER NIGHT'S DREAM
One of Shakespeare's most popular plays, *A Midsummer Night's Dream*, is a comedy. The play has a huge cast of characters, including two young couples who fall in and out of love, a group of workmen, and the king and queen of the fairies, who create hilarious confusion with their magic.

Find out more
ELIZABETH I
HENRY VIII
LITERATURE
TUDORS

SHARKS AND RAYS

A PERFECT SHAPE FOR SPEED, an incredible sense of smell, and a mouth brimming with razor-sharp teeth make sharks the most fearsome fish in the sea. Sharks have existed for 350 million years, and their basic shape has hardly changed at all during this time. As adults, they have no predators and fear nothing in the ocean. The great white shark is the largest predatory fish, at more than 9 m (27 ft) in length and 2.7 tonnes (2.7 tons) in weight. Dozens of huge teeth line its jaws. The great white shark prowls the ocean, eating any kind of meat, alive or dead, and often swallows its prey in one gulp. Sharks have to keep moving in order to take in enough oxygen, and the great white travels more than 500 km (300 miles) in a day. Most fish have bony skeletons, but sharks and their relatives, the rays, have skeletons made of a substance called cartilage. Rays are flat-bodied, with a wide mouth on the underside and blunt teeth for crushing clams and other shellfish. Rays live close to the seabed and move gracefully by flapping their huge wings.

Good sense of smell for hunting

Long tail used for rounding up fish in the water

The thresher shark lashes the water with its tail to sweep fish into a group. Then, with its mouth open, the shark charges through, gobbling them up.

Excellent eyesight for spying prey

THRESHER SHARK

This shark measures 6 m (20 ft) in length. It lives mainly in the warm coastal waters of the Atlantic and Pacific oceans but sometimes strays north in summer.

FIN
A shark's dorsal (back) fin cuts the sea's surface as the shark circles before attacking. The dolphin's fin is more crescent-shaped.

Stingrays have a poison spine on the tail.

STINGRAY

There are about 100 kinds of stingrays – the biggest measures 4 m (12 ft) across.

Huge wings

Shark tooth

Sharks' teeth have a serrated edge so they can saw through flesh.

TEETH
Sharks have many rows of teeth. As they grow, the teeth move from inside the mouth to the outside edge, where they are used for tearing flesh. Eventually the teeth wear away or break off, only to be replaced by the teeth behind.

SKIN
Shark skin is covered with toothlike scales, and has a texture like sandpaper.

Dorsal fin

Dorsal fin

WHALE SHARK

The harmless whale shark cruises slowly through the tropical oceans, feeding by filtering tiny floating animals (plankton) from the water. It is a peaceful creature and is the biggest fish of any kind, at 15 m (50 ft) long.

Upper lobe of caudal fin (tail)

Pectoral fin

Nostrils are excellent at detecting the smell of blood in the water.

SWIMMING MACHINE
The shark's swimming power comes from its tail. The larger upper lobe drives it down with each stroke and helps keep the body level; otherwise the creature's weight would tilt its head down. A shark cannot swivel its fins to stop quickly. It must veer to one side instead.

HAMMERHEAD
The eyes and nostrils of the hammerhead shark are on the two "lobes" of its head. Hammerheads prey on stingrays, unharmed by the poison in their spines.

A human can swim safely with the gentle whale shark, the biggest fish in the sea.

Find out more
ANIMALS
FISH
OCEANS AND SEAS
OCEAN WILDLIFE

SHIPS AND BOATS

Traditional craft such as this Chinese junk are still used in some parts of the world.

EVER SINCE OUR EARLIEST ancestors discovered that wood floats on water, ships and boats have played a major part in human history. The first boats helped people cross streams and rivers and carried hunters into shallow waters so they could go fishing. Better ways of building ships and boats began to develop when people left their homes to explore new territories. Since more than two thirds of the Earth is covered by water, these early explorers had to go out to sea to discover new lands, and they needed vessels that could make long voyages. Ships and boats changed and improved over thousands of years as distant nations began to trade and opposing navies fought battles at sea. Today, there are thousands of different types of ships and boats. Ships are seagoing vessels; boats are generally smaller and travel on coastal or inland waters.

SHIPBUILDING
Modern ships are built of steel plates welded together. Ship builders make all the parts separately and finally assemble the ship in the shipyard. After months of sea trials to check its safety, the ship is ready for service.

The captain commands the ship from the bridge, which houses the steering wheel and navigation instruments such as compasses, radar equipment, and charts.

A crane (called a derrick), driven by steam or electricity, is used to load and unload cargo.

Weight of ship pushing downwards

Upthrust from water pushing upwards

HOW SHIPS FLOAT
Although metal is very heavy, a ship contains large spaces filled with air. The hull (main body) of a ship pushes water out of the way, and the water pushes back on the ship with a force called upthrust. The upthrust balances the weight of the ship and keeps it afloat.

Propeller

Rudder

RUDDER AND PROPELLER
A rotating propeller forces the ship through the water, and the rudder steers the ship. When the rudder twists, the weight of water thrusting against it turns the ship.

A powerful diesel engine drives one or more propellers at the stern (back) of the ship.

Cabins for crew to sleep in when not on duty

Main body of the ship is called the hull.

Cargo is stored in a large compartment below the deck, called a hold. Large modern cargo vessels may have 12 or more holds. Ships that carry fresh food have refrigerated holds.

The front end of a ship is called the bow.

CARGO SHIP
Every year, cargo ships carry millions of tonnes of goods across the world's oceans. Some cargo ships, called container ships, carry huge loads piled up in large, steel boxes that stack together like building blocks. The largest ships of this kind carry more than 10,000 such containers.

KINDS OF SHIPS
There are many kinds of ships. They range from passenger vessels to cargo ships that carry goods of all types to and from the world's ports.

FERRY
Ferries take people and goods across a stretch of water. Large ferries carry cars, trucks, and trains as well as people.

OIL TANKER
Oil is transported at sea in huge tankers. The engines and bridge are at the stern to give more storage space.

CRUISE LINER
Liners are large ships that carry passengers on scheduled routes. Most liners are like floating hotels and take tourists on lengthy cruises.

TRAWLER
Trawlers are engine-powered fishing boats that drag a net (the trawl) along the sea bed in order to catch fish that swim near the bottom of the sea.

HISTORY OF SHIPS AND BOATS

The development of ships began more than 6,000 years ago with rafts and reed boats, and continues today with the introduction of nuclear-powered ships and boats made of light, strong plastics.

HIDE BOAT
About 6,000 years ago the Ancient Egyptians used boats made of a wicker framework covered with animal skins. In about 3200 BCE the Egyptians invented sails.

TRIREME
The Greeks invented the trireme (above) in about 650 BCE. It had sails and lines of rowers to carry it along at speed. The Romans built similar ships for trade and war.

Groups of rowers were positioned on two levels.

CLIPPER
Fast sailing ships called clippers (above) appeared during the 19th century, the height of the age of sailing. They carried many sails and had sleek lines to increase speed. Clippers were used mainly for trade.

STEAMSHIPS
Oceangoing steamships (below) took to the seas early in the 19th century. The earliest vessels had paddles connected to the engine and sails to gain extra speed in high winds. Ships with propellers entered service during the 1840s.

KINDS OF BOATS

Different boats have different uses. Many boats, such as yachts, are pleasure craft; tugs and fishing boats, however, are the workhorses of coastal waters.

POWERBOAT
Powerboats are small, fast boats driven by powerful petrol or diesel engines. They are used either for pleasure or for racing.

TUGBOAT
Tugs tow larger vessels, guiding them through difficult or shallow waters at sea or on inland waterways such as canals.

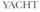

YACHT
Yachts are pleasure boats. They have engines or sails. Racing yachts are built purely for speed and are made of strong, light materials.

HYDROFOIL

A boat's engine has to work hard to overcome the resistance of the water. Light, fast boats called hydrofoils avoid this problem because they rise up on skis at high speeds. With the hydrofoil travelling so rapidly, water behaves as if it were a solid, so the hydrofoil skims over the water surface just like an aeroplane wing in air.

Any force can be divided into two parts at right angles to each other. The part along the length of the boat drives the boat forwards.

Air rushing past the sail produces a force that tends to move the boat at right angles to the wind.

Wind rushing past sail

Wind pushing on sail

HOW A BOAT SAILS
Modern sailing boats do not need the wind behind them to move – they can travel in almost any direction. In the same way that air rushing over the wings of an aeroplane produces an upward force called lift, wind moving past a sail produces a force at right angles to the sail. Adjusting the sail makes the boat move in different directions.

Centreboard prevents boat from drifting with the wind and stops the boat from capsizing.

With the wind behind the boat, the sail is stretched out across the boat.

Direction of wind

Direction of movement

A sailing boat cannot travel directly into the wind. Instead, it must follow a zigzag path. This is called tacking.

The boat heads into the wind with the sail drawn in as tightly as possible.

With the wind to the side of the boat, the sail is drawn in more tightly. The boat travels fastest with the wind in this position.

Direction of movement

Find out more
COLOMBUS, CHRISTOPHER
OCEANS AND SEAS
RIVERS
TECHNOLOGY
TRADE AND INDUSTRY
WIND

SKELETONS

INSIDE THE HUMAN BODY, hundreds of bones link together like scaffolding to form the skeleton. Without a skeleton, the body would collapse. The skeleton holds the body rigid and gives shape to all the softer parts. It also protects the organs – the skull surrounds the brain, and the ribs act as a protective cage around the lungs and heart. The skeleton is also an anchor for the muscles, which move the different parts of the body. Bone is made of living cells surrounded by a framework of minerals, particularly calcium and phosphate, and tough fibres of a substance called collagen. In a newborn baby, many of the bones are made of a soft, rubbery substance called cartilage. As a baby grows, the cartilage is gradually replaced by hard bone. Our wrists and ankles are among the last to become bone. In later life, bones gradually become more fragile and brittle, and break more easily.

INTERNAL SKELETONS

Humans and other mammals, fish, birds, and reptiles all have an inner skeleton, or endoskeleton, made up of many separate bones. The central part of the skeleton is the spine (vertebral column or backbone). The spinal joints can move only a little, but the spine as a whole is very flexible. Some creatures, such as worms, have no bones. Instead the pressure of fluid inside their bodies helps them keep their shape. They are said to have a hydrostatic skeleton.

Lizard has an internal skeleton, like other vertebrates.

JOINTS

Bones are linked together at joints. There are several types of joints, including fixed, hinge, and ball-and-socket joints. Fixed joints, such as those between the separate bones in the skull, cannot move. Hinge joints, such as those in the elbow, allow movement in one direction only. Ball-and-socket joints, such as the hip, allow the bones to swing in two directions and also to twist.

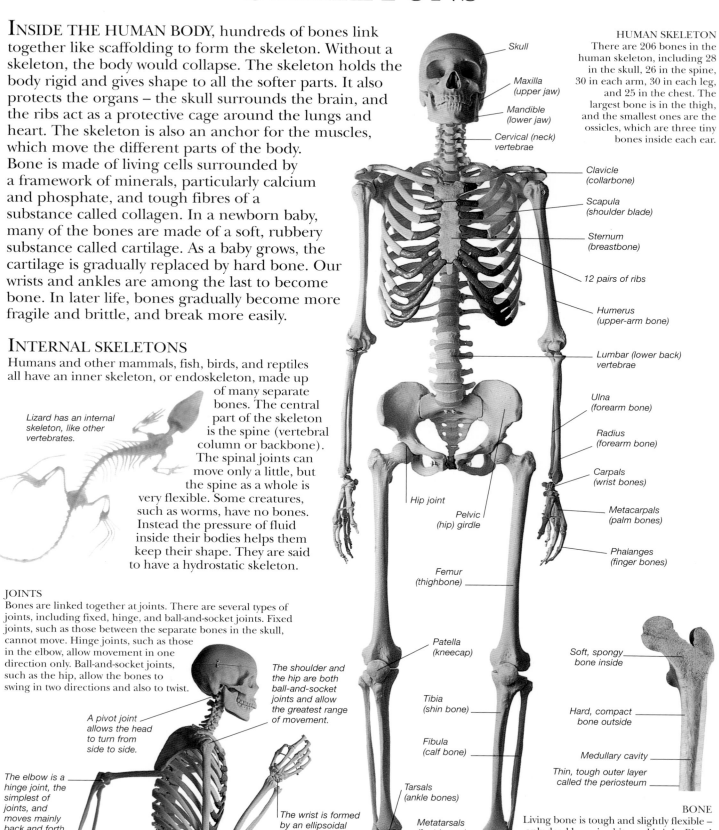

Skull

Maxilla (upper jaw)

Mandible (lower jaw)

Cervical (neck) vertebrae

HUMAN SKELETON
There are 206 bones in the human skeleton, including 28 in the skull, 26 in the spine, 30 in each arm, 30 in each leg, and 25 in the chest. The largest bone is in the thigh, and the smallest ones are the ossicles, which are three tiny bones inside each ear.

Clavicle (collarbone)

Scapula (shoulder blade)

Sternum (breastbone)

12 pairs of ribs

Humerus (upper-arm bone)

Lumbar (lower back) vertebrae

Ulna (forearm bone)

Radius (forearm bone)

Carpals (wrist bones)

Metacarpals (palm bones)

Phalanges (finger bones)

Hip joint

Pelvic (hip) girdle

Femur (thighbone)

Patella (kneecap)

Tibia (shin bone)

Fibula (calf bone)

Tarsals (ankle bones)

Metatarsals (foot bones)

Phalanges (toe bones)

The shoulder and the hip are both ball-and-socket joints and allow the greatest range of movement.

A pivot joint allows the head to turn from side to side.

The elbow is a hinge joint, the simplest of joints, and moves mainly back and forth.

The wrist is formed by an ellipsoidal joint which can be flexed or extended and moved from side to side.

Soft, spongy bone inside

Hard, compact bone outside

Medullary cavity

Thin, tough outer layer called the periosteum

BONE
Living bone is tough and slightly flexible – only dead bone is white and brittle. Blood vessels pass through small holes in the bone's surface, and carry a steady supply of blood to the bone. Some bones contain a jelly-like substance called red bone marrow, which makes blood cells.

SPINE

The spine, or backbone, runs down the back of the body. It supports the skull and upper body, and allows them to twist and bend. Animals, known as vertebrates, which include humans, get their name from the flexible row of spine bones, called vertebrae, which protect the spinal cord. The spine can flex and bend because each vertebra can move slightly against the next one.

Human spine

The many girders that make up the Eiffel Tower act in the same way as the bones of a skeleton, keeping the structure upright.

The spine is made up of 26 linked vertebrae. Fibrous discs between vertebrae act as shock absorbers during walking, and allow the spine to bend.

The coccyx, or "tail".

Earthworm

The body of an earthworm is filled with pressurized fluid.

The circular wall of a wading pool is held up by the water contained within it.

HYDROSTATIC SKELETON

Some skeletons are made from materials that are not rigid at all. Instead, they are divided into compartments that can be filled with fluid, and this hydrostatic pressure makes them rigid. Many of the microscopic cells which form plants and animals keep their shape in this way, and so do some artificial objects.

Beetle

CHITIN

Insects, spiders, and scorpions have skeletons on the outside rather than the inside of their bodies. They are made of a tough plastic-like substance called chitin. This is built up from layers of fibre arranged in different directions, rather like plywood.

Chitin

Volkswagen "Beetle"

Nicknamed "beetle" because of its shape, this car's bodywork is an exoskeleton.

EXTERNAL SKELETON

Skeletons that cover the outside of the body of animals such as insects are called exoskeletons. Many objects made by people also have exoskeletons, rather than internal ones. Modern cars, for instance, are made like this. Flat sheet metal is moulded into curved shapes to make a strong outer shell to protect the inside.

PNEUMOSTATIC SKELETON

Just as hydrostatic skeletons are inflated with liquid to make them more rigid and provide support, some animals are supported by structures filled with gas. Gases are much lighter than liquids so they enable animals, such as the Portuguese man-of-war, to float on and be blown across, the surface of the water.

The Portuguese man-of-war floats on the surface of the ocean supported by a gas-filled bladder.

Compressed air pushes the structure of this inflatable life raft into shape, and holds it rigid.

Tentacles hang from the gas-filled bladder.

Find out more
ANIMALS
HUMAN BODY
MUSCLES AND MOVEMENT

SLAVERY

FIVE THOUSAND YEARS AGO the Sumerians put their prisoners to work on farms as slaves. The workers had no rights and no pay, and their masters regarded them as property. In ancient Greece and Rome, slaves produced most of the goods and also worked as household servants. During the 16th century, European nations began to colonize the Americas, and imported thousands of Africans to work as slaves on their plantations and silver mines. Between 1500 and 1800, European ships took about 12 million slaves from their homes to the new colonies. By the 19th century, those against slavery set up movements in the United States, and Britain, to end it. Slavery was formally abolished in the British Empire and the United States in the mid-1800s. Sadly, it continues today in many parts of the world, most often affecting children and immigrants.

ROMAN SLAVES
Most wealthy Roman citizens owned slaves. Some slaves lived as part of the family; others were treated very badly. Some earned manumission (a formal release from slavery) through loyalty to a master.

TRIANGLE OF TRADE

The British trade in slaves was known as the triangular trade. Ships sailed from British ports laden with goods such as guns and cloth. Traders exchanged these goods with African chiefs for slaves on the west coast of Africa. The slave ships then carried their cargo across the Atlantic to the Americas and the Caribbean. Here, slaves were in demand for plantation work, so the traders exchanged them for sugar, tobacco, rum, and molasses. The ships then returned to Britain carrying this cargo, which was sold at huge profits.

NORTH AMERICA

Ships sailed back to Europe with goods.

Britain

Tobacco

Ships departed from Britain carrying guns and cloth.

AFRICA

Slave coast

SOUTH AMERICA

Ships carried slaves across the Atlantic.

Rum, sugar, and molasses

Slave ship

SLAVE SHIPS
Slavers (slave traders) packed their ships with Africans to sail on what was known as the middle passage across the Atlantic. The slaves were chained and kept below deck for most of the voyage. Unclothed and underfed, thousands of Africans died on the Atlantic crossing.

SLAVE REBELLIONS
Many Africans fought against slavery. In 1791, one of the most famous rebellions began in the French colony of Haiti. A slave named Toussaint L'Ouverture led an army of slaves against the French soldiers in a rebellion that lasted 13 years. L'Ouverture was captured and died in prison in 1803. In 1804, Haiti gained independence and became the world's first black republic.

SLAVE MARKET

Once the slaves reached the West Indies or the southern states of America, they were auctioned at a slave market. Here, they were treated like animals. Families were sometimes separated, and people were sold singly to plantation owners. Slaves were put to work on cotton, sugar, and tobacco plantations. Many received cruel treatment, and severe whipping was a common punishment for slaves who tried to escape.

SLAVERY AND WEALTH

England dominated the slave trade, and some British cities became very rich as a result. Bristol and Liverpool, for instance, imported goods such as sugar and tobacco produced by slaves in the West Indies. Ships from both cities carried slaves from Africa to American plantations.

Ships in Bristol harbour

COTTON

African slave labourers were made to grow sugar in Brazil and the Caribbean. Later, tobacco was also grown. By the late 1700s there were huge cotton plantations in North America, and the British textile industry began to flourish, stimulating the Industrial Revolution. Cotton was made into cloth in Glasgow and Manchester.

AM I NOT A MAN & A BROTHER

GRANVILLE SHARP

In 1772, British clerk Granville Sharp defended a black immigrant named James Somerset in a legal case known as the Somerset Case. This established that slavery was not recognized in Britain, and a slave who stepped on British soil was automatically free. The ruling was seen as officially abolishing slavery in England.

ABOLITIONISTS

On both sides of the Atlantic, Quakers, evangelical Christians, and liberal thinkers fought to abolish slavery. In Britain, Granville Sharp, and William Wilberforce (1759-1833), formed the Anti-Slavery Society in 1787-88. Members campaigned for the abolition of slavery and the freeing of all slaves. As part of the campaign, pottery owner Josiah Wedgwood produced a special medal. In 1833, the Slavery Abolition Act freed slaves in the British Empire.

ANTI-SLAVERY MOVEMENT

In 1840, a World Anti-Slavery Convention took place in London, with delegates from the United States. Women took an active part in the abolition movement, often linking their situation with that of slaves. American feminists Lucretia Mott (1793-1880) and Susan B. Anthony (1820-1906) were leading campaigners.

OLAUDAH EQUIANO

Africans themselves played a part in the anti-slavery movement. One of the best-known African anti-slavery campaigners was Olaudah Equiano (1745-97). Born in Nigeria, he was captured with his sister when he was eleven, and taken to Britain as a servant. His autobiography was influential and is one of the earliest important works by an African written in English.

Find out more

AFRICA, HISTORY OF
HUMAN RIGHTS
INDUSTRIAL REVOLUTION
SUMERIANS
UNITED STATES, HISTORY OF

SNAKES

LONG, LEGLESS, SCALY, and slithering, snakes are a very successful group of reptiles. They are found everywhere except the coldest regions, highest mountain peaks, and a few islands. Most snakes can swim and climb well. All snakes are hunters. Some, such as pythons and boa constrictors, squeeze and suffocate their prey to death; others, such as cobras, paralyse their victims with a poisonous bite. Fast-moving snakes such as sand snakes hunt down insects, small birds, and mammals. Blind snakes are burrowers that eat ants and termites. More than 400 kinds of snakes are venomous (poisonous), but only some can give a fatal bite to humans. Deadly poisonous snakes include cobras, boomslangs, and mambas.

FANGS
The pair of hollow teeth at the front of the upper jaw are called fangs. The fangs lie flat along the jaw and swing forward when the snake strikes. Muscles pump venom from glands down the fangs into the victim.

RATTLE
Rattlesnakes are so named because they shake the tip of the tail (the rattle) to scare off predators. The rattle consists of a row of hollow tail segments which make a noise when the snake shakes them.

Rattle at tip of tail

SNAKE CHARMING
This is an ancient entertainment in Africa and Asia. Snake charmers fascinate snakes with movements that make the snakes sway to the music.

Snake's long belly has large scales called ventral scutes which overlap like tiles on a roof.

Emerald tree boa constricts or squeezes its prey.

RATTLESNAKE
At more than 2 m (7 ft) long, the eastern diamondback is the largest rattlesnake, and the most poisonous snake in North America. The rattlesnake feeds mainly on rats, rabbits, and birds. Unlike many other snakes, which lay eggs, the rattlesnake gives birth to about 10 live young in late summer.

MILK SNAKE
The non-venomous milk snake shown left is found all over North America, down to the north of South America. It looks similar to the poisonous coral snake, but the milk snake has yellow bands bordered by black, whereas the poisonous coral snake has black bands bordered by yellow. The milk snake hunts small mammals, birds, and other reptiles, including rattlesnakes. It coils around its prey and chokes it to death.

YOUNG SNAKES
Some snakes are described as viviparous, because they give birth to fully formed young. Others lay eggs in a burrow or under a log, leaving the young to hatch and fend for themselves. Certain kinds of pythons coil around the eggs and protect them until they hatch.

CONSTRICTOR
Boas and pythons are called constrictors because they constrict or coil around their prey and suffocate it. There are 72 kinds of boas and pythons; they include some of the largest snakes on Earth. Anacondas are boas of the Amazon region in South America. These massive snakes reach more than 8 m (25 ft) in length and weigh 225 kg (500 lbs).

The sea snake's body follows S-shaped curves, pushing sideways and backwards.

Young grass snake hatches from its egg head first and flicks its tongue to sense its surroundings.

SEA SNAKE
There are more than 60 kinds of sea snakes – the yellow-bellied sea snake shown left is the most common. It measures up to 80 cm (32 in) in length, preys on fish, and gives birth to about five young at sea. Sea snakes spend their lives swimming in the warm waters of the Indian Ocean, around Southeast Asia and Australia, and in the western Pacific.

Find out more
ANIMALS
DESERT WILDLIFE
FOREST WILDLIFE
REPTILES
SPIDERS AND SCORPIONS

SOUND

WE LIVE IN A NOISY WORLD. The roar of city traffic, the music from a piano, the bark of a dog, all come to our ears as sound waves travelling through the air. Sound is generated when a disturbance sets air moving; for example, when someone plucks a guitar string. We hear sounds when sound waves – tiny vibrations in the air – strike our eardrums. Sound waves need a substance to travel through. This substance may be a liquid, such as water; a solid, such as brick and stone; or a gas, such as air.

Sounds such as musical notes have a certain pitch. A high-pitched sound makes the air vibrate backward and forward more times each second than a low-pitched sound. The number of vibrations per second is called the frequency of the sound and is measured in hertz (cycles per second). Humans cannot hear sounds with frequencies above about 20,000 hertz, or below about 30 hertz.

LOUDNESS AND DECIBELS
The sound of a train is louder than the sound of a whisper because the train produces larger vibrations in the air. The loudness of sound also depends on how close you are to its source. Loudness is measured in decibels (dB). A jet airliner taking off is rated at about 120 dB; the rustling of leaves is about 33 dB.

ECHOES
If you shout in a large hall or near mountains, you can hear your voice echo back to you. An echo occurs when a sound bounces off a surface such as a cliff face and reaches you shortly after the direct sound. The clarity of speech and music in a room or concert hall depends on the way sounds echo inside it.

SPEED OF SOUND
Sound travels in air at a speed of about 1,224 km/h (about 760 mph). It travels more slowly when the temperature and pressure of the air are lower. In the thin, cold air 11 km (7 miles) up, the speed of sound is about 1,000 km/h (620 mph). In water, sound travels at 5,400 km/h (about 3,350 mph), much faster than in air.

The distance from one region of highest pressure to the next is called the wavelength of the sound. The higher the pitch, or frequency, of the sound, the shorter the wavelength.

Region of high-pressure air

Region of low-pressure air

The noise of the boat's engine sends sound waves through the water.

SOUND WAVES
A sound wave consists of air molecules vibrating backward and forward. At each moment the molecules are crowded together in some places, producing regions of high pressure, and spaced out in others, producing regions of low pressure. Waves of alternately high pressure and low pressure move through the air, spreading out from the source of the sound. These sound waves carry the sound to your ears.

HARMONICS
In a musical note, secondary frequencies, called harmonics, are mixed with the main frequency. Harmonics are characteristic of different instruments, which is why a note played on a piano sounds different from the same note played on a violin. Harmonics bring life to the sound of musical instruments: an electronically produced sound of a single pure frequency sounds artificial and dull.

RESONANCE
An object such as a glass gives out a musical note when struck because it has its own natural frequency of vibration. If you sing a musical note of this frequency, the object vibrates at its natural frequency, pushed by the sound waves that hit it. This is called resonance. A very loud sound can make a glass resonate so strongly that it shatters.

Find out more
EARS
MUSIC
MUSICAL INSTRUMENTS
TELEPHONES

SOUTH AMERICA

THREE VERY DIFFERENT TYPES of landscape dominate the triangular continent of South America. Along the western coast the towering Andes Mountains reach to more than 6,900 m (22,600 ft) in height. Dense rain forest covers the hot and humid northeastern area. Further south are great open plains of grass and scrub. There are huge mineral deposits and rich farming lands. Despite this, some of the 12 nations which make up the continent are under-developed.

Until about 170 years ago, Spain and Portugal ruled almost all of South America. Most people still speak Spanish or Portuguese. The population is made up of three groups: those descended from European settlers; Native Americans; and people of mixed ancestry. Many people are desperately poor and can barely afford to buy food. Large sections of the population are uneducated and cannot read or write. Many South American governments are insecure or unstable. Most have borrowed large sums of money from wealthier nations. The cost of repaying these debts makes it hard for some countries to develop. But Brazil and Argentina are emerging as major economic powers.

South America lies south of the isthmus of Panama, between the Atlantic and Pacific oceans. It covers 17.8 million sq km (6.9 million sq miles).

Care of the Argentine cattle is the job of cowboys called *gauchos*.

USING THE LAND

Large herds of beef cattle roam the grasslands of the Pampas, supporting the meat-packing trade in Argentina, Uruguay, and Paraguay. Corn (maize) is grown as a staple crop right across the continent. Coffee is grown as a cash crop in Brazil and Colombia, while coca plants grown in Bolivia, Peru, and Colombia, provide most of the world's cocaine, an illegal drug.

ANDES MOUNTAINS
Stretching the entire length of the continent, the Andes mountain chain is 47,250 km (4,500 miles) long. As well as mineral deposits, the Andes have rich farming land in mountain valleys and on the Altiplano, a large plateau in Peru and Bolivia.

Roads crossing the Andes follow routes through the few low passes.

PERU
With a population of more than 29 million, Peru is one of the larger South American countries. It includes a long stretch of the Andes and part of the rain forest. Many people live on mountain farms and are very poor. Others work on plantations growing coffee, sugar, and cotton for export. Oil has recently been discovered and is bringing some wealth to Peru.

Coffee is still picked by hand in parts of South America.

LAKE TITICACA
In the Andes mountains on the border between Peru and Bolivia, Lake Titicaca is the highest large lake in the world. The lake's surface is 3,812 m (12,507 ft) above sea level. Some parts are 180 m (600 ft) deep. Although large ships operate on the lake, the local people still use reed to build their traditional fishing boats.

BOLIVIA

The mountain nation of Bolivia has no coastline. Its only links with the rest of the world are railways and roads running through Peru and Chile. Although there are large deposits of oil, tin, and silver in the high Andes, the nation remains very poor. About 70 per cent of the population are Aymara or Quechua Native Americans who grow just enough food in the mountains to feed themselves. Some farmers make extra money by growing the coca plant, which is processed to make the illegal drug cocaine.

A woman from Bolivia in traditional dress

SOCCER

Supported passionately, soccer is a favourite sport in most South American countries. Argentina, Brazil, and Uruguay have been very successful in international competitions. In 1930, Uruguay became the first country to host the World Cup. Uruguay also managed to win the tournament in the same year. World Cup victories in 1958, 1962, 1970, 1994, and 2002 mean that Brazil has won this fiercely contested event more times than any other country in the world.

Argentinian football fans parade the streets, demonstrating support for their national soccer team. Argentina won the Fédération Internationale de Football Association (FIFA) World Cup in 1978 and 1986.

The Native Americans of South American forests live in large huts shared by many families. They sleep in hammocks hung between the posts of the huts.

NATIVE AMERICANS

The first peoples of South America were Native Americans. In the lowlands, Native Americans lived in small villages and gathered food from the forest, but in the Andes they built great civilizations. The arrival of European explorers destroyed these great cultures, and today only a few remote tribes still live in the forest as their ancestors did. However, the destruction of the rain forest for farming and mining threatens to eliminate these last traces of Native American society.

FALKLAND ISLANDS

Located in the Atlantic Ocean, the Falkland Islands were discovered by the English navigator John Davis, in his ship *Desire* in 1592. In 1690, the islands were named after Viscount Falkland, treasurer of the British navy. Islas Malvinas, the Argentinian name, comes from "Les Malouines", the name given to the islands by French sailors in the 1700s. The islands were occupied at various times by England, Spain, France, and Argentina.

Rockhopper, Magellanic, and Gento penguins are common on the Falkland Islands.

AMAZON

The longest river in South America is the Amazon, which rises in the Andes and flows 6,516 km (4,050 miles) to the Atlantic. For most of its length the river flows through a rain forest which covers 6.5 million sq km (2.5 million sq miles). In recent years much of the rain forest has been cut down to provide farmland. Although the destruction continues, it is now beginning to slow down.

Find out more
AZTECS
INCAS
MEXICO
MOUNTAINS
SOUTH AMERICA, HISTORY OF

MINERALS IN CHILE

Copper is Chile's largest export. Chuquicamata (above) is the country's most productive copper mine. Metallic minerals are plentiful along the length of the Andes mountains. They are formed over thousands of years by pressure and heat during mountain-building processes. The Atacama Desert in the northern third of the country stores copper, silver, gold, and abundant deposits of sodium nitrate.

* Countries covered on other pages.

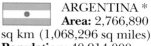 ARGENTINA *
Area: 2,766,890 sq km (1,068,296 sq miles)
Population: 40,914,000
Capital: Buenos Aires

BOLIVIA
Area: 1,098,580 sq km (424,162 sq miles)
Population: 9,775,000
Capital: Sucre, La Paz
Languages: Spanish, Quechua, Aymará
Religions: Roman Catholic
Currency: Boliviano
Main occupations: Subsistence farming, mining, trading
Main exports: Gold, silver, zinc, lead, tin, oil, natural gas

 BRAZIL *
Area: 8,511,970 sq km (3,286,472 sq miles)
Population: 198,739,000
Capital: Brasília

CHILE
Area: 756,950 sq km (292,258 sq miles)
Population: 16,601,000
Capital: Santiago
Languages: Spanish, Amerindian languages
Religions: Roman Catholic, non-religious
Currency: Chilean peso
Main occupations: Mining, agriculture
Main exports: Copper, fresh fruit, fishmeal, salmon, wine, lithium, molybdenum, gold

COLOMBIA *
Area: 1,138,910 sq km (439,733 sq miles)
Population: 45,644,000
Capital: Bogotá

 ECUADOR
Area: 283,560 sq km (109,483 sq miles)
Population: 14,573,000
Capital: Quito
Languages: Spanish, Quechua, other Amerindian languages
Religions: Roman Catholic, Protestant, Jewish
Currency: U.S. dollar
Main occupations: Oil production, agriculture, fishing
Main exports: Oil, bananas, fish

FRENCH GUIANA
Area: 83,533 sq km (32,252 sq miles)
Population: 221,500
Capital: Cayenne
Status: French department

GUYANA
Area: 214,970 sq km (83,000 sq miles)
Population: 772,000
Capital: Georgetown
Languages: English Creole, Hindi, Tamil, Amerindian languages, English
Religions: Christian, Hindu, Muslim
Currency: Guyana dollar
Main occupations: Subsistence farming, mining, forestry
Main exports: Gold, sugar, bauxite, diamond, timber, rice

PARAGUAY
Area: 406,750 sq km (157,046 sq miles)
Population: 6,996,000
Capital: Asunción
Languages: Guaraní, Spanish
Religions: Roman Catholic
Currency: Guaraní
Main occupations: Agriculture
Main exports: Energy, cotton, oilseeds, soya

PERU
Area: 1,285,220 sq km (496,223 sq miles)
Population: 29,547,000
Capital: Lima
Languages: Spanish, Quechua, Aymará
Religions: Roman Catholic
Currency: Nuevo sol
Main occupations: Subsistence farming, fishing, manufacturing
Main exports: Oil, fish, cotton, coffee, textiles, copper, lead, coca leaves, sugar

 SURINAM
Area: 163,270 sq km (63,039 sq miles)
Population: 481,000
Capital: Paramaribo
Languages: Pidgin English (Taki-Taki), Dutch, Hindi, Javanese, Saramacca, Carib
Religions: Christian, Hindu, Muslim
Currency: Surinam dollar
Main occupations: Agriculture, forestry, mining, fishing
Main exports: Bauxite, gold, oil, rice, bananas, citrus fruits, shrimp, aluminium

URUGUAY
Area: 174,810 sq km (67,494 sq miles)
Population: 3,494,000
Capital: Montevideo
Languages: Spanish
Religions: Roman Catholic, Protestant, Jewish, non-religious
Currency: Uruguayan peso
Main occupations: Agriculture, tourism, manufacturing
Main exports: Wool, meat, rice

INCA TERRACES
These terraces near Cuzco, Peru, were built by the Incas to enable cultivation of the hillside. They are still farmed by descendants of the Inca people today.

VENEZUELA
Area: 912,050 sq km (352,143 sq miles)
Population: 26,815,000
Capital: Caracas
Languages: Spanish, Amerindian languages
Religions: Roman Catholic, Protestant
Currency: Bolivar
Main occupations: Mining, agriculture, oil production
Main exports: Coal, bauxite, iron, gold, bitumen fuel, steel, aluminium, oil, coffee

At a height of 979 m (3,212 ft), the majestic Angel Falls in Venezuela (above), is the highest uninterrupted waterfall in the world. It was named after bush pilot Jimmy Angel.

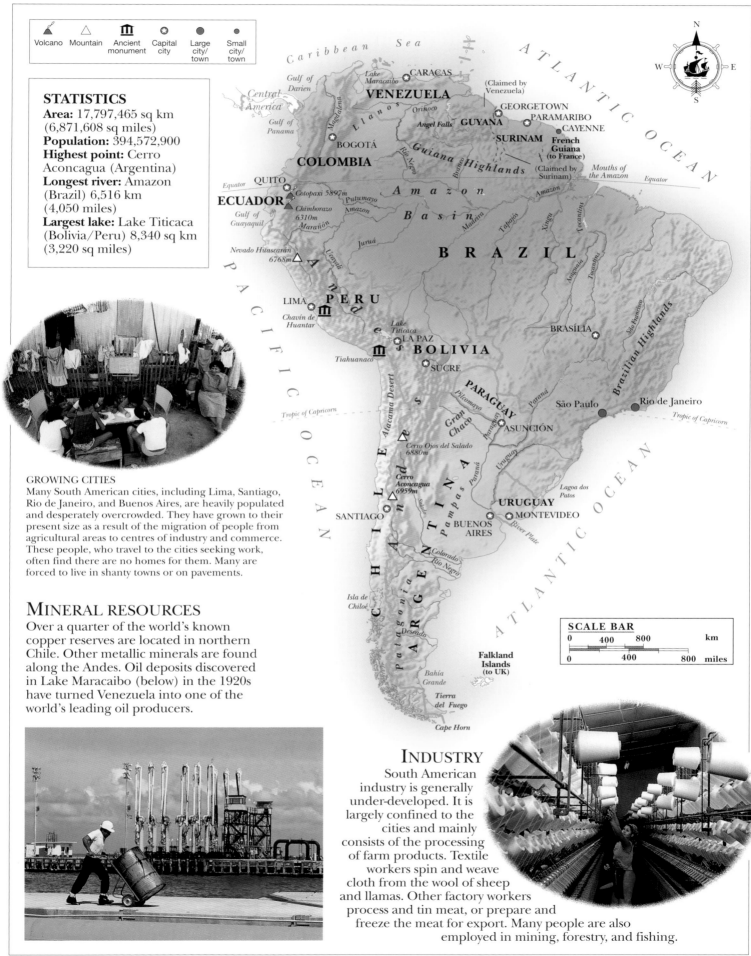

Volcano | Mountain | Ancient monument | Capital city | Large city/town | Small city/town

STATISTICS
Area: 17,797,465 sq km
(6,871,608 sq miles)
Population: 394,572,900
Highest point: Cerro
Aconcagua (Argentina)
Longest river: Amazon
(Brazil) 6,516 km
(4,050 miles)
Largest lake: Lake Titicaca
(Bolivia/Peru) 8,340 sq km
(3,220 sq miles)

GROWING CITIES
Many South American cities, including Lima, Santiago,
Rio de Janeiro, and Buenos Aires, are heavily populated
and desperately overcrowded. They have grown to their
present size as a result of the migration of people from
agricultural areas to centres of industry and commerce.
These people, who travel to the cities seeking work,
often find there are no homes for them. Many are
forced to live in shanty towns or on pavements.

MINERAL RESOURCES
Over a quarter of the world's known
copper reserves are located in northern
Chile. Other metallic minerals are found
along the Andes. Oil deposits discovered
in Lake Maracaibo (below) in the 1920s
have turned Venezuela into one of the
world's leading oil producers.

INDUSTRY
South American
industry is generally
under-developed. It is
largely confined to the
cities and mainly
consists of the processing
of farm products. Textile
workers spin and weave
cloth from the wool of sheep
and llamas. Other factory workers
process and tin meat, or prepare and
freeze the meat for export. Many people are also
employed in mining, forestry, and fishing.

SCALE BAR
0 400 800 km
0 400 800 miles

HISTORY OF
SOUTH AMERICA

Attendants, uniformly dressed, carry the dead king on a bier.

Gold mask

Dead Chimu king is prepared for burial in a sitting position.

Chimu burial ceremony

CHIMU EMPIRE

The Chimu empire centred on the vast capital city of Chan Chan, in what is now northern Peru. The empire covered much of the Pacific coast of South America and reached the height of its power in the 15th century. Around 1470, the Incas conquered the Chimu empire, and Chan Chan fell into ruin. The Chimu are remembered as a highly civilized society. The royal dead were buried with a wealth of funeral offerings.

FOR THOUSANDS OF YEARS, the continent of South America developed independently from the rest of the world. Great cultures rose and fell, among them the Nazcas, Chimus, and Incas, all of which developed highly advanced civilizations of great wealth and achievement. In 1532 the Spaniards invaded the Inca empire and within a few years ruled over most of the continent. The Portuguese established control over Brazil. Soon Spanish and Portuguese became the main languages of South America, and for the next 300 years the affairs of South America were decided in Europe. The native peoples were almost wiped out by disease and ill treatment. When Spain and Portugal became involved in the Napoleonic wars in Europe, the South Americans seized the chance to win their independence. Afterwards, the new countries were ruled by European families who had settled in South America. Many more Europeans arrived during the 19th and early 20th centuries. The nations of South America have only recently begun to control their destinies.

Line of demarcation 1494

Portuguese territories

Spanish territories

SOUTH AMERICA

200 BCE-600 CE Nazca empire in Peru.

600 City-states of Tiahuanaco and Huari in Peru.

1000-1470 Chimu empire in Peru.

1200 Inca empire in Bolivia, Chile, Ecuador, and Peru.

1494 Treaty of Tordesillas divides New World between Spain and Portugal.

1499-1510 Amerigo Vespucci explores coast of South America; the continent is named after him.

1530 Portuguese colonize Brazil.

1532-33 Spanish led by Francisco Pizarro conquer Inca empire.

1545 Silver discovered in Peru.

1808-25 Liberation wars: Spanish and Portuguese colonies

1822-89 Empire of Brazil

1879-84 Border wars between Peru, Chile, and Bolivia.

1932-35 War between Paraguay and Bolivia over disputed territory.

1946 Juan Perón becomes president of Argentina.

1967 Che Guevara killed in Bolivia.

TREATY OF TORDESILLAS
In the 1494 Treaty of Tordesillas, Spain and Portugal divided the non-European world between them. They drew a rough line down the South American continent, giving Spain the lands to the west and Portugal the lands to the east of the line.

SPANISH DOMINATION
From 1532 to 1810, Spain controlled the whole of South America apart from Portuguese-owned Brazil. The vast Spanish Empire there was divided into three viceroyalties – New Granada in the north, Peru in the centre, and Rio de la Plata in the south. On the right is Santiago, the patron saint of Spanish soldiers.

NATIVE AMERICANS
The Native Americans were put to work as slaves in the silver mines. They were also forced to labour in the big plantations of sugar and other crops that were exported to Europe. Most Native Americans died of poor conditions, overwork, and European diseases they had no immunity against.

SIMÓN BOLÍVAR

In 1808, Spain was involved in a war with French emperor Napoleon Bonaparte; the South American colonies took this opportunity to declare their independence. Led by Simón Bolívar (1783-1830) and José de San Martín (1778-1850), the colonies fought against Spanish control; all gained their freedom by 1825. Bolívar hoped to unite all of South America, but many disliked his dictatorial approach. In 1822, Brazil declared its independence from Portugal, leaving only Guiana in the north under European control.

ROMAN CATHOLIC CHURCH

When the Spanish arrived in South America, they brought the Roman Catholic religion with them. Catholic priests tried to stamp out local religions and convert the Native Americans to their faith. In the end the priests were forced to include parts of the old Native American religions in their services. In some places, the priests tried to protect the Native Americans against Spanish rulers who were cruel to them, but most priests upheld the Spanish colonial government. During the 20th century the Catholic Church began to take a more active role in supporting the poor against powerful landlords and corrupt governments.

Bolívar leads soldiers into battle

Pedro arrives in Recife (formerly Pernambuco), a prosperous town in the empire.

Stamp bearing a portrait of Pedro II

BRAZILIAN EMPIRE

From 1822 to 1889 Brazil was an empire. Under Emperor Pedro II (1825-1891) roads and railways were built, and the coffee and rubber industries began to prosper. Thousands of immigrants poured into the country from Italy, Portugal, and Spain. In 1888, the African slaves who had been brought over to work the plantations were freed. This angered many landowners, as they had been using the slaves as cheap labour. The landowners withdrew their support from Pedro, and in 1889 the army took over the empire and a republic was declared.

ERNESTO "CHE" GUEVARA

One of the most popular heroes of the 20th century, Che Guevara (1928-1967) was born into a rich Argentinian family. Guevara was a doctor before choosing to spend his life supporting revolutions against oppressive South American governments. In 1959, he helped Fidel Castro overthrow the Cuban government. Guevara served under Castro until 1965. In late 1966 he moved to Bolivia, where he based himself in the countryside among peasants. In 1967, he was killed by the Bolivian army. His death made him a hero for revolutionaries everywhere. In 1997, he was reburied in Cuba.

JUAN PERÓN

From 1946 to 1955, Argentina was ruled by President Juan Perón (1895-1974). Poor people living in the cities supported Perón and his wife, Eva. He introduced many reforms but did not allow anyone to oppose him. After the economy weakened in the early 1950s, and after Eva died (1952), Perón was much less popular. In 1955, the army overthrew him. In 1973, he again held power but died the following year. His third wife, Isabel Martínez de Perón, succeeded him as president.

Find out more

CENTRAL AMERICA
INCAS
MEXICO
SOUTH AMERICA

HISTORY OF THE
SOVIET UNION

IN 1922, A NEW NATION came into being. The Union of Soviet Socialist Republics, or the Soviet Union, was the new name for Communist Russia, led by Vladimir Lenin (1870-1924). The years following the 1917 Revolution were difficult. Civil war between Communists and anti-Communists had torn Russia apart. More than 20 million people had died. When Lenin died, Joseph Stalin took over as dictator. In a reign of terror, he eliminated all opposition to his rule. He started to transform the Soviet Union into a modern industrial state. The huge industrial effort made the Soviet Union strong. It survived German invasion in 1941, although World War II (1939-1945) cost the nation many lives. After 1945 the Soviet Union became a superpower, but it still had difficulty providing enough goods for its people. In 1985, Mikhail Gorbachev came to power. He introduced reforms and began a policy of openness with the West. In 1991, the Communist Party was declared illegal, and the Soviet Union broke up.

INDUSTRIALIZATION
Stalin introduced a series of Five-Year Plans to increase production of coal, steel, and power. The plans were successful for the country, but workers had little reward for their efforts and many were used as slave labour.

Posters showing muscular workers encouraged people to work hard.

This shows how collective farms were organized under Stalin. The collective included a school where children were educated, a factory, and a hospital. The collective had to send fixed deliveries of crops to the State.

School, hospital, and factory

Workers' homes

Private plots for fruit, vegetables, and poultry

Grazing land for pigs, sheep, and cattle

Land for growing crops

COLLECTIVE FARM
Stalin wanted to get rid of all the old-fashioned peasant farms and increase productivity. He reorganized the land into *kolkhozy* (giant collective farms), controlled by the government. The government took the land and livestock of millions of *kulaks* (richer peasants); those who protested were sent to work in prison labour camps. Most of the collectives' products were exported, or sent to the government to feed the city workers.

JOSEPH STALIN
Born in poverty in Georgia, in the south-west of the Russian Empire, Joseph Stalin (1879-1953) was a follower of Lenin. After Lenin's death, Stalin seized power and destroyed his opponents. He formed a secret police force to arrest, torture, and execute millions of suspected enemies. These ruthless "purges" enabled Stalin to remain unchallenged as Soviet leader until his death.

ALEXANDRA KOLLONTAI
Communism was supposed to introduce equality into Soviet society. However, while women worked alongside men in heavy industry, they were not allowed to hold real power. But a woman named Alexandra Kollontai (1872-1952) did become a member of Stalin's government. She made many important speeches and wrote several articles about peace and women's rights.

WORLD WAR II

In 1941, German armies invaded the Soviet Union and reached the gates of Moscow, the capital. The Soviets resisted heroically. Stalingrad and Leningrad survived long and bitter sieges. New factories in the east began to produce advanced weapons, such as the T-34 tank, in large numbers. In 1943, Soviet armoured forces, led by Marshal Zhukov, fought and won the largest tank battle ever. But the Soviets paid a high price for victory. They suffered more military casualties than any other country in the war. More than 20 million people died.

SOVIET UNION

1917 Russian Revolution

1922 Soviet Union formed.

1924 Lenin dies and is replaced by Stalin.

1941-45 More than 20 million Soviets die in World War II.

1955 Warsaw Pact, an alliance of Communist states, created.

1962 Soviet Union builds missile bases on Cuba. US Navy blockades island. Soviet Union removes missiles.

1980 Soviet invasion of Afghanistan.

1988 Soviet troops withdraw from Afghanistan.

1991 Soviet Union breaks up as Lithuania, Latvia, and other republics declare their independence.

CHERNOBYL

In 1986 there was a major disaster at Chernobyl, near Kiev. A nuclear power plant exploded, killing at least 30 people and injuring hundreds more. Radioactive dust and smoke blew all over Europe and exposed thousands of people to contamination. Instead of keeping this disaster secret, the Soviets followed their new policy of *glasnost*, or openness, and warned the rest of the world of the danger.

SPACE RACE

On 4 October 1957, the whole world listened in amazement to a strange beeping sound that came from space. The Soviet Union had launched the first satellite, called *Sputnik 1*, into orbit around Earth. It was followed four years later by Yuri Gagarin (left), the first human in space.

COLLAPSE OF COMMUNISM

After his appointment in 1985, Soviet premier Mikhail Gorbachev introduced policies of *glasnost* (openness) and *perestroika* (economic reform) to improve the poor state of the Soviet economy. People under Soviet control began to demand more freedom. The Communist Party ceased to be the only political party. In Romania, the Communist dictator, Nicolae Ceausescu, was overthrown and executed in 1989. In the Soviet Union, anti-Communist demonstrations took place. People destroyed statues of Lenin and other Communist leaders. In Moscow, the statue of Felix Dzerzhinsky, head of the hated KGB, or security police, was toppled.

GORBACHEV AND YELTSIN

Throughout the late 1980s, Soviet people suffered from terrible economic hardship. Many thought that the changes brought about by Gorbachev's policy of *perestroika* were too slow. Mikhail Gorbachev (right) resigned in 1991. Boris Yeltsin (left) became the leader of the new Russian Federation. The Soviet Union broke up as the republics formed their own governments. Yeltsin resigned in 1999, and was replaced by Vladimir Putin who served as president until 2008.

Find out more

COLD WAR
COMMUNISM
SATELLITES
SPACE FLIGHT
WOMEN'S RIGHTS
WORLD WAR II

SPACE FLIGHT

SPACE SHUTTLE

Between 1981 and 2010, America's space shuttles made more than 130 flights to Earth orbit, carrying a crew of several astronauts. They took off like rockets, but landed like aircraft. Their cargo bay was large enough for a satellite. Two shuttles were destroyed in accidents – *Challenger* in 1986, and *Columbia* in 2003.

A large fuel tank fed the main engines. It broke away at a height of 110 km (70 miles), just eight minutes after launch.

Smaller engines guided the shuttle into orbit.

The booster rockets broke away at a height of about 47 km (29 miles). They were recovered from the ocean and used again.

A spacecraft must reach a speed of about 28,000 km/h (17,500 mph) in order to get into orbit. If it attains a speed of 40,000 km/h (about 25,000 mph), it can break free from the Earth's gravity and travel out into space. This speed is called the Earth's escape velocity.

UNTIL THE MIDDLE OF last century stories about space flight were found only in science fiction books. Today, rockets blast off regularly. They place satellites in Earth orbit, send astronauts and cargo to the International Space Station, and launch spacecraft to explore the solar system. Space flight became a reality after the development of powerful rocket engines, capable of giving a spacecraft or satellite the speed it needs to reach Earth orbit. For its journey from Earth into space, a spacecraft is attached to the top of a launch vehicle (rocket), which is powered by rocket engines and carries huge amounts of fuel. The exploration of the solar system is one of the most exciting aspects of space flight. Humans have only travelled as far as the Moon, a journey of just three days. However, robotic spacecraft have travelled for years to explore the distant planets, returning amazing images and information collected by their cameras and instruments.

SPACE ROCKET
Spacecraft are carried into space by launch vehicles, or rockets. The launch rocket consists of several parts called stages, each with its own rocket engine. Each stage breaks away as it uses up its fuel, eventually leaving only the spacecraft to fly in space. Spacecraft that return to Earth use a small engine to slow them down until they fall out of orbit.

At the launch pad, a tall gantry enabled astronauts to enter the shuttle. The shuttle's rocket engines fired, and the spacecraft lifted off to begin its journey into space.

SOYUZ SPACECRAFT
The Russian Soyuz spacecraft can carry three cosmonauts. It is launched on a rocket and is used to ferry people to and from the International Space Station. The habitable parts are the Orbital Module and the Descent Module. The cosmonauts travel back to Earth in the Descent Module. The Orbital and Service modules separate from the Descent Module and burn up in the atmosphere.

The contents of the Orbital Module includes a toilet and communications equipment. A small window allows the crew to see ahead.

The heat-resistant Descent Module is used for the launch and the journey back to Earth.

As the spacecraft rotates, the solar panels point toward the Sun.

The Service Module houses the temperature control systems, an electric power supply, and long-range radio telecommunications.

ORION SPACECRAFT
The Orion spacecraft is expected to take its first astronauts into space in about 2014. It is NASA's replacement for the Space Shuttle and will be launched by an Ares rocket. At first, it will be used to go to and from the International Space Station. It is pictured here about to dock on the right. Later it may take astronauts as far as the Moon.

Once in orbit, the shuttle might launch a satellite, go to repair the Hubble Space Telescope, or dock at the International Space Station.

At the end of its mission, the shuttle turned around and fired its engines to slow it down.

INTERPLANETARY FLIGHT

Some aircraft are designed to explore objects in the solar system. They are equipped with cameras and all kinds of sensors that take images and collect information, which is beamed back to Earth by radio.

Radio antenna to communicate with Earth

Once the shuttle was travelling slowly enough, it left its orbit and began to descend towards Earth.

Instruments for studying Jupiter's surface

FIRSTS IN SPACE

1957 The first artificial satellite, *Sputnik 1* (Soviet Union), goes into orbit around the Earth.

1959 *Luna 3* (Soviet Union), the first successful space probe, flies past the Moon and sends back the first picture of the Moon's far side.

1961 Russian Yuri Gagarin becomes the first person to fly in space, making one orbit of the Earth.

1962 *Mariner 2* (US), the first successful planetary space probe, flies past Venus.

1969 Neil Armstrong becomes the first person to walk on the Moon.

1971 The first space station, *Salyut 1* (Soviet Union), goes into orbit.

1981 US space shuttle *Columbia* makes its first test flight into space.

1986 European space probe *Giotto* sends back close-up pictures of the nucleus (centre) of Halley's Comet.

1995 *Discovery* (US) is the first shuttle mission to be flown by a female pilot, Eileen Collins.

2001 Businessman Dennis Tito becomes the first space tourist, aboard the Russian craft *Soyuz*.

When the shuttle entered Earth's atmosphere, friction of the air made the heat-proof underside of the shuttle glow red-hot.

GALILEO
In 1995, the *Galileo* spacecraft entered orbit around Jupiter. After eight years studying the planet and its moons, it was crashed into Jupiter so there was no risk of Earth bacteria contaminating any of Jupiter's moons.

Atmospheric entry probe

A parachute lowered the entry probe into Jupiter's atmosphere.

The spacecraft released a probe containing instruments that measured conditions in Jupiter's atmosphere. They worked for only 75 minutes because they heated up as the probe plunged deeper until it was totally crushed by the pressure.

Heat shield

The shuttle came to a halt with the help of a parachute at the back.

The shuttle glided down towards a runway, just like an ordinary aircraft.

INSIDE THE ISS

While on board the International Space Station (ISS), astronauts conduct experiments and repair equipment under weightless conditions. The space station is currently under construction, due to be completed in 2010.

Solar panels rotate to point at the Sun.

Thermal control panels regulate temperature.

SPACE STATION

People can make the longest space flights on board space stations – large spacecraft that spend several years in orbit around the Earth. Smaller spacecraft carry teams of astronauts to the space station, where they will live and work for weeks or months at a time. Supplies and relief crews come aboard in spacecraft that dock, or link up, with the space station.

Pressurized modules provide living quarters and laboratories.

Spacecraft dock at ports in positions like this one.

International Space Station

Radiators turn edge-on to the Sun to lose excess heat.

Remote sensing instruments look down on Earth.

Find out more
ASTRONAUTS
and space travel
ATMOSPHERE
GRAVITY
MOON
PLANETS
SATELLITES

SPIDERS AND SCORPIONS

FEW ANIMALS ARE MORE FEARED but less understood than spiders and scorpions. We often call these scurrying little creatures insects, but they really belong to the group of animals called arachnids, along with ticks and mites. Insects have six legs; spiders and other arachnids have eight legs. There are about 40,000 kinds of spiders and 1,400 kinds of scorpions. All are carnivorous (meat eaters). Scorpions hunt down their prey and kill it with their pincers. If the prey is big, or struggles, the scorpion uses the sting in its tail. Many spiders capture insects by spinning a silken web. The silk of some webs is stronger than steel wire of the same thickness. Not all spiders spin webs, however; some catch their prey by dropping a net of silk onto it. A few spiders, such as the trap-door spider, rush out at their victim from a burrow. Some scorpions and several spiders are dangerous to humans, including the Australian funnel web spider and the Durango scorpion of Mexico.

WEB
Spiders make webs with a special silken thread from glands at the rear end of the body. Tubes called spinnerets squeeze out the thread like toothpaste. The silk hardens as the spider's legs pull it out.

GARDEN SPIDER

Thousands of spiders live in our houses and gardens, feeding on flies, gnats, and moths. The common garden spider spins a beautiful, complicated web called an orb web, often between the stems of plants. Some spiders lie in wait for their prey in the centre of the web; others hide nearby. Many orb-web spiders spin a new web almost every day.

The female black widow has a deadly bite.

SPIDERLINGS
Young spiders are called spiderlings. They hatch from eggs inside a silken cocoon and feed on stores of yolk in their bodies. After a few days, weeks, or months, depending on the weather, they cut their way out of the cocoon and begin to hunt for food.

BLACK WIDOW
The female black widow spider is so named because it sometimes kills its mate. This spider is also one of the few spiders that can kill humans. The female black widow shown here is standing near its eggs, which are wrapped in a silken egg sac or cocoon.

TARANTULA
True tarantulas are shy spiders which live mainly in burrows. False tarantulas, such as the big spider shown here, include various large, hairy hunting spiders from North and South America. They are also called bird or monkey spiders. Their bite is painful to humans, but it is less poisonous than the bite of smaller spiders such as the black widow.

FOOD
Spiders eat animal prey. Their most common victims are insects, worms, sow bugs, and other spiders. The spider's venom subdues or paralyses the prey while the spider wraps it up in a silk bag to eat later.

YOUNG SCORPIONS
Scorpions are born fully formed. At first the female scorpion carries the young on its back, where they are well protected from predators. After the young have moulted (shed their skin) for the first time, they leave their mother to fend for themselves.

Mother carries the young on her back.

Imperial scorpion

The sting is connected to twin poison glands at the end of the tail.

SCORPION

Scorpions live mainly in warm regions, lurking beneath rocks or in cracks or burrows. Most feed at night, ambushing or hunting down their prey. They feed mainly on insects and spiders. The scorpion uses the sting at the end of the tail in self-defence, as well as to subdue its prey.

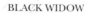

Scorpion's large pincers are called pedipalps. They seize, crush, and tear the prey, then pass it to the jaws.

Find out more
ANIMALS
DESERT WILDLIFE
SNAKES

STARS

IF YOU LOOK AT THE SKY ON A CLEAR dark night, it is possible to see up to about 3,000 of the billions of stars in our galaxy. Although they appear as tiny dots, they are, like our closest star the Sun, huge, hot balls of gas, deep in space. Some stars are gigantic – if placed in the centre of our solar system, they would stretch beyond the Earth's orbit. Others are far smaller, about the size of our planet, and give off only faint light. Stars are unimaginably distant. Light from even our nearest star (apart from the Sun) takes more than four years to reach us.

Ancient skywatchers noticed that stars seem to form patterns in the sky. They imagined that the shapes represented pictures called constellations. These constellations, such as the Great Bear, are still useful for learning the positions of the stars. Astronomers identify the brightest stars with individual names, or by their constellation combined with a Greek letter, such as alpha, beta, or gamma. For instance, the second brightest star in the constellation of Cygnus (the Swan) is Beta Cygni, or Albireo.

BLACK HOLE
The remains of a very massive star may collapse into a tiny volume, forming a black hole. The gravitational pull of a black hole is so strong that matter and radiation, such as light, cannot escape from it.

NEUTRON STAR
A supernova may leave a neutron star – a spinning ball with a mass greater than the Sun's, yet only about 16 km (10 miles) across. As a neutron star spins, it sends out a powerful beam of radiation.

SUPERNOVA
When a massive star dies, it collapses in less than one second. This is followed by a colossal explosion called a supernova. The explosion produces other substances which scatter through space in an expanding gas cloud.

RED SUPERGIANT
Some dying stars grow into huge, cool stars called red supergiants, which can be up to 1,000 times the diameter of the Sun. A red supergiant contains many substances formed by nuclear reactions.

A group of growing stars in a cluster.

The gas and dust in a mini-globule pack closer together, and it spins faster and gets hotter. The mini-globule has become a protostar (a young star).

Death of a massive star

Temperature at centre of red supergiant is about 10 billion°C (18 billion°F).

STAR STARTS TO SHINE
When the centre of the protostar reaches about 10 million°C (18 million°F), nuclear reactions begin which slowly change hydrogen into helium. The protostar begins to shine, and has become a true star.

The planetary nebula survives only for a few thousand years.

White dwarf

NEBULA
Stars are born from great clouds of dust particles and hydrogen gas, called nebulae. The word nebula (plural nebulae) comes from the Latin for "mist".

BIRTH OF A STAR
Gravity pulls parts of a nebula into blobs called globules. These get smaller and spin faster, finally breaking up into a few hundred "mini-globules". Each of these will eventually become a star.

Death of a star about the size of the Sun

RED GIANT
As a sunlike star runs low in hydrogen, it swells into a cooler, larger star called a red giant. This will happen to our own Sun in about 5,000 million years.

LIFE AND DEATH OF A STAR
Throughout the universe, new stars form and old stars die. The birthplaces of stars are clouds of gas and dust scattered through space. Stars the size of the Sun shine for about 10 billion years. The most massive stars (which contain 100 times as much matter as the Sun) shine very brightly, but live for a shorter time – only about 10 million years.

PLANETARY NEBULA
At the end of its life, a red giant blows off its outer layers of gas. These make a glowing shell called a planetary nebula, which eventually disperses. At the centre is a white dwarf, a tiny hot star that is the burned out core of the red giant. It will outlast the nebula by billions of years.

CONSTELLATIONS
Modern astronomers group stars into 88 constellations. Each has a Latin name, such as Ursa Major (the Great Bear) or Corona Australis (the Southern Crown). The "sun signs" of astrology have the same names as the 12 constellations of the zodiac – the band of sky along which the Sun and planets appear to pass during the course of a year.

When the constellation of Orion (above) is in the night sky, it can be seen from anywhere on Earth.

TWINKLING STARLIGHT
Nuclear reactions inside a star heat the star up from the centre, causing it to emit light and heat from its surface. A star appears to flicker or twinkle because its light passes through the Earth's atmosphere, which is a constantly shifting blanket of gases. Seen from a travelling spacecraft, stars shine steadily because there is no surrounding atmosphere to disturb the path of the light.

STAR BRIGHTNESS
A star's brightness is called its magnitude. The brightest magnitudes are the smallest numbers, so magnitude 1 stars are brighter than magnitude 2 stars. How bright a star looks depends on its distance and how much light it emits.

VARIABLE STARS
Many stars, called variable stars, appear to vary in brightness. Some stars constantly swell and shrink, becoming alternately fainter and brighter. Other variables are really two stars that circle each other and block off each other's light from time to time.

Double stars circle around each other. When one star is in front of the other, the brightness dims. When both stars can be seen, the brightness increases.

Some variable stars are produced by exploding stars. The explosion makes the star appear much brighter than usual for a period that can last from a few days to a few years.

PARALLAX
Astronomers use a technique called parallax to measure the distance of a star from the Earth. As the Earth moves around the Sun, the closest stars seem to move very slightly compared with stars further away. Astronomers measure the position of a star once, and then again six months later. From their measurements they can then calculate the distance of a star.

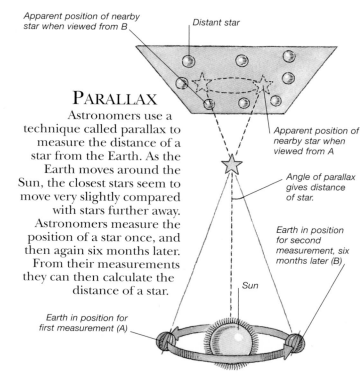

Apparent position of nearby star when viewed from B

Distant star

Apparent position of nearby star when viewed from A

Angle of parallax gives distance of star.

Earth in position for second measurement, six months later (B)

Sun

Earth in position for first measurement (A)

STAR QUALITIES
The colour of a star's light corresponds to the surface temperature of the star: red stars are the coolest, blue stars are the hottest. A star's brightness (the amount of energy it gives out) is linked to its mass (the amount of material it contains): heavier stars are brighter than lighter stars. Astronomers can use the colour and brightness of the light emitted from a star to help calculate its size and distance from the Earth.

Neutron stars (pulsars) are the smallest stars. They have about the same mass as the Sun, but are only about 16 km (10 miles) in diameter.

White dwarfs are small stars at the end of their life; some are smaller than the Earth.

Yellow dwarfs, or medium-sized stars, are about the same size as the Sun.

Giants have diameters between 100 and 1,000 times larger than that of the Sun.

Supergiants are the largest stars, with diameters up to 1,000 times that of the Sun.

Find out more
ASTRONOMY
ATMOSPHERE
BIG BANG
GRAVITY
PLANETS
SUN
TELESCOPES
UNIVERSE

STONE AGE

MORE THAN TWO MILLION YEARS AGO, stone was the most valuable raw material known to people. They made stone tools and weapons, usually from flint. These early people were called hominins, and were more apelike than us. They gradually learned to make specialized implements, such as knife blades. Stone Age people moved constantly, looking for hunting areas and setting up camps in small groups. A few groups lived in caves during the coldest seasons. They gathered fruits, berries, and roots, and hunted wild animals. By the start of the Mesolithic Age (Middle Stone Age; 15,000 years ago) many types of larger animals had died out. Mesolithic people, who were "modern people" (*Homo sapiens*) like us, used new stone-edged tools to fish and hunt deer and wild pigs. About 10,000 years ago some Neolithic (New Stone) Age people learned how to domesticate animals and grow crops. They settled on farms.

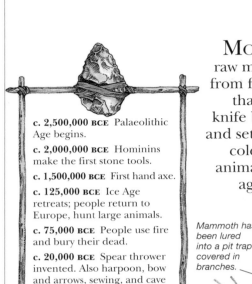

c. 2,500,000 BCE Palaeolithic Age begins.

c. 2,000,000 BCE Hominins make the first stone tools.

c. 1,500,000 BCE First hand axe.

c. 125,000 BCE Ice Age retreats; people return to Europe, hunt large animals.

c. 75,000 BCE People use fire and bury their dead.

c. 20,000 BCE Spear thrower invented. Also harpoon, bow and arrows, sewing, and cave painting.

c. 12,500 BCE Mesolithic Age.

c. 9500 BCE Neolithic Age.

c. 3000 BCE Metal tools and weapons replace stone.

MAMMOTH HUNT

From about 50,000 years ago, "modern people" hunted wild animals. By co-operating in groups and using their superior brainpower, they could kill creatures much larger than themselves. They sometimes slaughtered large numbers of deer and similar creatures by driving whole herds over cliffs. Elephant-like woolly mammoths were popular game; they are now extinct.

Mammoth has been lured into a pit trap covered in branches.

Hunters killed prey with sharp stone weapons.

Woman cooks a hare on a spit over the fire.

Dwelling places made from animal hides and mammoth bones kept out the cold wind.

Stretching hide to make clothing.

Man is using a bone hammer to chip away at a flint core.

MAKING FLINT TOOLS AND WEAPONS

1 The first flint implements were crude. People used the sharp edge of a broken rock as a cutting tool.

2 Later tools were much better. The toolmaker prepared a flint core by skillful chipping.

3 Hitting the core with a bone hammer made flakes, each one a special tool.

HAND AXE
The hand axe was the first deliberately shaped tool made by humans. It was gripped at the rounded end and used to cut meat or dig roots. Popular for over a million years, it was used longer than any other tool.

This flint hand axe was found in a desert area near Thebes, Egypt.

Find out more
BRITAIN, ANCIENT
EVOLUTION
PREHISTORIC PEOPLES
ROCKS AND MINERALS

STORMS

TORNADOES

The most violent storms are tornadoes, or whirlwinds. A twisting column of rising air forms beneath a thunder cloud, sometimes producing winds of 400 km/h (250 mph). The air pressure at the centre is very low, which can cause buildings to explode. A waterspout is a tornado over water, formed when water is sucked up into the funnel of air. Dust devils are tornadoes which have sucked up sand over the desert.

Severe storms build up as moist air, heated by warm land or sea, rises. Storm clouds develop as the rising air cools and rain forms. Air rushes in to replace the rising air, and strong winds begin to blow.

ABOUT 2,000 thunderstorms are raging throughout the world at this very moment, and lightning has struck about 500 times since you started reading this page. Storms have enormous power: the energy in a hurricane could illuminate more light bulbs than there are in the United States. A storm is basically a very strong wind. Severe storms such as thunderstorms, hurricanes, and tornadoes all contain their own strong wind system and blow along as a whole. Certain areas, such as the region around the Gulf of Mexico, are hit regularly by severe storms because of the local conditions. Storms can cause great damage because of the force of the wind and the devastating power of the rain, snow, sand, or dust which they carry along. One of the most destructive forces of a hurricane is a storm surge. The level of the sea rises because of a rapid drop in air pressure at the centre of the storm. This rise combines with the effect of the wind on the sea to create a huge wall of water which causes terrible damage if it hits the coast.

The base of the tornado is fairly narrow – about 1.5 km (1 mile) across.

The rising air spirals up the column, sucking up dirt and objects as heavy as trucks from the ground.

DESTRUCTION AND DEVASTATION
Winds of 320 km/h (200 mph) leave a trail of destruction (below) when the hurricane strikes the shore. The strongest winds are in a belt around the calm eye.

THUNDER AND LIGHTNING

Thunder clouds often form on hot, humid days. Strong air currents in the cloud cause raindrops and hailstones to collide, producing electric charges. Lightning flashes in giant sparks between the charges, and often leaps to the ground. A burst of heat from the flash makes the air nearby expand violently and produces a clap of thunder.

HURRICANES

When warm, moist air spirals upward above tropical oceans, it forms a hurricane – a violent storm which is also called a typhoon or a cyclone. The spin of the Earth causes the storm winds to circle around a calm centre called the eye. The eye usually moves along at about 25 km/h (15 mph). It can measure as much as 800 km (500 miles) across.

Negative charges in the bottom of the cloud attract positive charges in the ground. Eventually, a huge spark of lightning leaps from the cloud to the highest point on the ground.

Buildings are protected by lightning rods – strips of metal on the roof which attract the lightning and lead the electricity safely to the ground.

Find out more
CLIMATES
RAIN AND SNOW
WEATHER
WIND

STUARTS

COAT OF ARMS
The Stuart coat of arms included the English and Scottish lions, the Irish harp, and the French fleur-de-lys.

IN 1603, THE LAST TUDOR MONARCH – Elizabeth I – died without leaving an heir. Her cousin, James Stuart, already James VI of Scotland, took over the English throne as well, becoming James I of England. The Stuarts united England and Scotland peacefully, but there were deep differences between King and Parliament over the power of the monarch. In 1642, these differences led to civil war. James I's son, Charles I, was executed in 1649, and England became a republic under Cromwell. In 1660, the Stuarts were restored (brought back to power) under Charles II. However, when his Catholic brother James II came to the throne in 1685, people resented his religion and his harsh laws. He was banished to Scotland and his son-in law, the Protestant William of Orange, became king. The last Stuart was Queen Anne, James II's second daughter.

JAMES I
A vain man, James I believed God had made him ruler, and he ignored Parliament for much of his reign. Instead, he relied on the advice of favourites, and this weakened his government. However, James did achieve peace with Spain, England's old enemy. He also ordered an important new English translation of the Bible.

Headdress with stiffened frill

Dark coat over brocade vest

Fitted bodice trimmed with bows

Upper-class man from about 1670

Noblewoman of the Stuart period

Felt hat

Leather shoes with buckles

RESTORATION

After Oliver Cromwell's death, parliamentary leader George Monck (1608-70) negotiated with the exiled Charles II, and Britain became a monarchy again. During what historians call the Restoration, Charles II led a pleasure-seeking life, quite different to the Puritanism of Cromwell and his followers.

STUARTS

1603-25 Reign of James I.

1605 Gunpowder Plotters try to blow up parliament.

1625-49 Reign of Charles I.

1642-49 English Civil War.

1649-60 England becomes a republic.

1660 Monarchy restored.

1660-85 Reign of Charles II.

1666 Great Fire of London.

1685-88 Reign of James II.

1688 "Glorious Revolution" brings William of Orange to Britain.

1689-1702 Reign of William and Mary.

1702-14 Queen Anne rules, the last of the Stuart dynasty.

QUEEN ANNE
The last Stuart ruler was Queen Anne (1665-1714),She had a troubled life, and her reign was also difficult, as England waged a long war against France. However, British forces under John Churchill, Duke of Marlborough, gained victories which made England more powerful overseas. The decorative arts, such as furniture-making, flourished during Anne's reign.

Queen Anne table with cabriole legs

GLORIOUS REVOLUTION

In 1688, British leaders opposed to James II's Catholicism, invited Protestant Dutch King William of Orange to rule Britain. William, who reigned jointly with his wife, Mary, agreed a Bill of Rights forbidding the introduction of laws or taxes without Parliament's approval. Known as the "Glorious Revolution", this marked the start of modern constitutional monarchy, by which Parliament has greater powers than the king or queen.

Find out more
ENGLISH CIVIL WAR
FIRE OF LONDON
TUDORS
UNITED KINGDOM, HISTORY OF

SUMERIANS

THE WORLD'S FIRST CITIES were built on the banks of the Tigris and Euphrates rivers in what is now Iraq. About 5,000 years ago, the people of Sumer, the area of southern Iraq where the two rivers flow together, began to build what would become great, bustling cities. They made bricks from the riverside mud to build houses and massive temples. The Sumerians also developed one of the world's earliest writing systems, by making marks in soft tablets of clay, which they left in the sun to harden. Their earliest cities, such as Ur and Uruk, became famous all over the Middle East as Sumerian merchants travelled abroad trading food grown in the fertile local fields. The Sumerians flourished until about 2000 BCE, when desert tribes invaded.

MESOPOTAMIA
The land between the Tigris and Euphrates rivers is known as Mesopotamia. The home of the Sumerians was in southern Mesopotamia and Ur was one of their greatest cities.

GILGAMESH
The Sumerians created the earliest written story that has survived to modern times. Written on clay tablets, the story tells of Gilgamesh, King of Uruk and the son of a goddess and a man. Gilgamesh begins as a cruel king, but be becomes a hero when he kills two fearsome monsters. Later, Gilgamesh visits the underworld to try to search for immortal life.

Cuneiform script consisted of wedge-shaped marks made with a reed writing-stylus.

ZIGGURAT
At the centre of each Sumerian city was a stepped tower called a ziggurat, topped by a temple. By building their ziggurats high, the Sumerians believed that they were reaching up to the heavens, so that each temple could become a home for one of Sumer's many gods and goddesses. Only priests were allowed to worship in the temples.

SUMER
The land between the two rivers was fertile but dry. Farmers dug canals to bring water to their fields, and found that this meant they could produce huge harvests – there was usually enough to sell. The Sumerians found other useful resources near the rivers. They used reeds for boat-building and simple houses, and clay for making bricks and pottery.

Mud-brick ziggurat towered over the city.

Palm trees provided dates and wood.

Sumerians travelled along the rivers in boats made from local reeds. Fishermen used similar boats.

Reed beds grew on the banks of the river

Farmers scattered seeds by hand.

Oxen pulled wooden ploughs.

Brickmakers poured soft mud into a mould.

Reed huts were common in southern Mesopotamia.

Neatly trimmed beard typical of Mesopotamian fashion.

SARGON
Originally the servant of a king of Kish, in Akkad, north of Sumer, Sargon rose to become Akkad's ruler. In around 2325 BCE, he conquered Sumer, Mesopotamia and the eastern territory of Elam. He made Mesopotamia into a united country for the first time. Sargon was a powerful king who protected merchants, and built up flourishing trade.

Bricks were left to bake dry in the hot sun.

Workers dug up clay to make bricks.

> ### Find out more
> ALPHABET
> BRONZE AGE
> SLAVERY

SUN

THE NIGHT SKY is full of stars, so distant that they are mere points of light. The Sun is also a star, but we are closer to it than to any other star. Along with the other planets of the solar system, the Earth moves around the Sun, trapped in orbit by the force of gravity. The Sun sustains nearly all life on Earth with its light and heat. The Sun is a ball of glowing gases, roughly three-quarters hydrogen and one-quarter helium, along with traces of other elements. Within its hot, dense core, hydrogen particles crash together. This produces nuclear reactions that release enormous amounts of energy, keeping the core of the Sun very hot. The energy travels outwards and leaves the Sun's surface mainly as light, and infrared and ultraviolet radiation. Energy sources that humans use to provide power originate from the Sun. For example, coal is the remains of ancient plants, which trapped the Sun's energy.

STORY OF THE SUN
The Sun formed just under 5,000 million years ago from a cloud of hydrogen, helium, and dust, which contracted under its own gravity. The contraction heated the cloud until nuclear reactions began, converting hydrogen into helium. At this point the Sun began to shine steadily. It is believed that the Sun will continue to shine for another 5,000 million years before it runs out of hydrogen fuel and begins to die.

SOLAR FLARES
Huge explosions on the Sun's surface, called solar flares, fire streams of electrically charged particles into space.

CORONA AND SOLAR WIND
The corona is a thin atmosphere of gases that extends for millions of kilometres around the Sun. A blast of electrically charged particles, called the solar wind, blows out from the corona at a rate of millions of tonnes each second. The Earth is protected from these particles by its magnetic field, but they can damage spacecraft and satellites. Coronal Mass Ejections are sudden blasts of great clouds from the corona. These are thought to cause auroras – coloured lights in the sky above the Earth's poles – and magnetic storms.

Energy travels outwards in the form of heat and electromagnetic waves such as infrared, light, and radio waves.

Relatively cool and dark areas, called sunspots, form on the surface of the Sun. Sunspots develop in places where the Sun's magnetic field becomes particularly strong.

Great streamers of glowing hydrogen gas, called prominences, frequently soar up from the Sun. Prominences are often about 60,000 km (more than 37,000 miles) long.

Light from the Sun takes about eight minutes to reach the Earth.

Core extends to about 175,000 km (about 110,800 miles) from the Sun's centre.

The hot, glowing surface of the Sun is called the photosphere (sphere of light). It is about 400 km (250 miles) deep.

A glowing red layer of hydrogen gas called the chromosphere (sphere of colour) lies above the photosphere. The chromosphere is a few thousand kilometres deep.

Warning: Never look at the Sun, either directly or through dark glasses. The intense light could seriously damage your eyesight.

The Sun's diameter is 109 times that of the Earth. More than 1,300,000 globes the size of the Earth could fit into the Sun.

SOLAR ENERGY
Electronic devices called solar cells convert sunlight into electricity. Solar cells power satellites and produce electricity in experimental houses and cars. In 2003, the solar-powered *Nuna II* car (below) drove across Australia at an average speed of 96.8 km/h (60 mph).

Umbra is the centre of the moon's shadow, where the Sun is completely hidden.

Penumbra is the outer part of the moon's shadow, where part of the Sun can be seen.

SUN FACTS
Earth–Sun distance	149.6 million km (92.9 million miles)
Diameter at equator	1,392,000 km (864,950 miles)
Time to rotate once	25.4 days
Temperature at surface	5,500°C (10,000°F)
Temperature at centre	15,000,000°C (27,000,000°F)

SOLAR ECLIPSES
When the Moon passes between the Earth and the Sun, the Sun is hidden. This is called a solar eclipse. A total solar eclipse occurs at places on the Earth where the Sun appears to be completely hidden (although prominences, chromosphere, and corona can be seen). Elsewhere the eclipse is partial, and parts of the Sun can be seen.

Find out more
ASTRONOMY
ENERGY
STARS

TECHNOLOGY

Bone and pebble hammers

Flint flake

THE INVENTION OF STONE TOOLS more than two million years ago marked the beginning of technology. For the first time in history, people found that cutting or chopping was easier to do with tools than with bare hands. Technology is the way in which people use the ideas of science to build machinery and make tasks easier. Although technology began in prehistoric times, it advanced rapidly during and after the Industrial Revolution, beginning in the 18th century. Since that time technology has dramatically changed our world. It has given us fast, safe transport, materials such as plastics, increased worldwide communications, and many useful daily appliances. Perhaps the greatest benefits of technology are in modern medicine, which has improved our health and lengthened our lives. Advances in technology have been mainly beneficial to humans and our lifestyle. However, increased technology has a negative side, too – it has produced weapons with the power to cause death and destruction. Technology and development have caused many environmental problems such as ozone depletion, and is often dependent on non-renewable resources, such as oil, which has a limited life. Governments and other organizations are now trying to use new technology to find solutions to these problems.

EARLY TECHNOLOGY
Humans living during the Stone Age developed a variety of tools for everyday purposes. They used rounded pebbles and bones as hammers to form cutting tools from a strong stone called flint. Flint was chipped and flaked to produce a sharp cutting edge like a blade.

COMPUTERS
The development of computers has been one of the most important recent advances in technology. The invention of the microchip (right) changed the emphasis of producing goods from mechanical to electronic. This meant that many tasks which had previously been done manually were now automated. Computers perform many different tasks and are used in banking, architecture, manufacturing, and a range of other businesses. Computers also aid new technology, because they can help develop new machines.

Threshing machines help farmers separate the heads from the stalks of rice plants. Previously, this job had to be done by hand.

Microchips lie at the heart of a computer. These tiny devices store and process huge amounts of information at high speed.

SMALL-SCALE TECHNOLOGY
People in poorer countries cannot afford to buy the technological goods that are common in richer parts of the world such as North America and Europe. Their primary concern is feeding and housing their families, and they tend to use smaller, simpler machines, such as windmills that drive pumps for irrigation.

Synthetic clothing materials are lightweight, machine-washable, and allow ease of movement.

The cyclist's helmet is made from plastic and polystyrene. It has an aerodynamic shape to increase the speed of the cyclist.

Disabled members of the community can participate in more activities because of advanced technology, such as this specially designed tricycle.

Wheel technology, developed in 3500 BCE, revolutionized machines and modes of transportation.

LIFESTYLE
In the western world, technology has generally made daily life easier. Washing machines, cars, and cash machines all make daily tasks more convenient, providing more time for leisure, hobbies, and sports. People also now have the time and means to travel to other countries to experience different cultures and environments.

MEDICAL TECHNOLOGY
Inventions such as x-ray machines and brain scanners help doctors to detect and treat illness. Doctors can transplant organs, implant tiny electronic pacemakers to keep a heart beating, and repair damaged tissue with plastic surgery. Medical technology, such as glasses, contact lenses, or hearing aids, also helps to improve the daily lives of many people affected by impaired vision or hearing. Prosthetic (artificial) limbs are also being improved and now allow their users more movement and flexibility.

Laser surgery can correct many eye defects without needing to cut the eye.

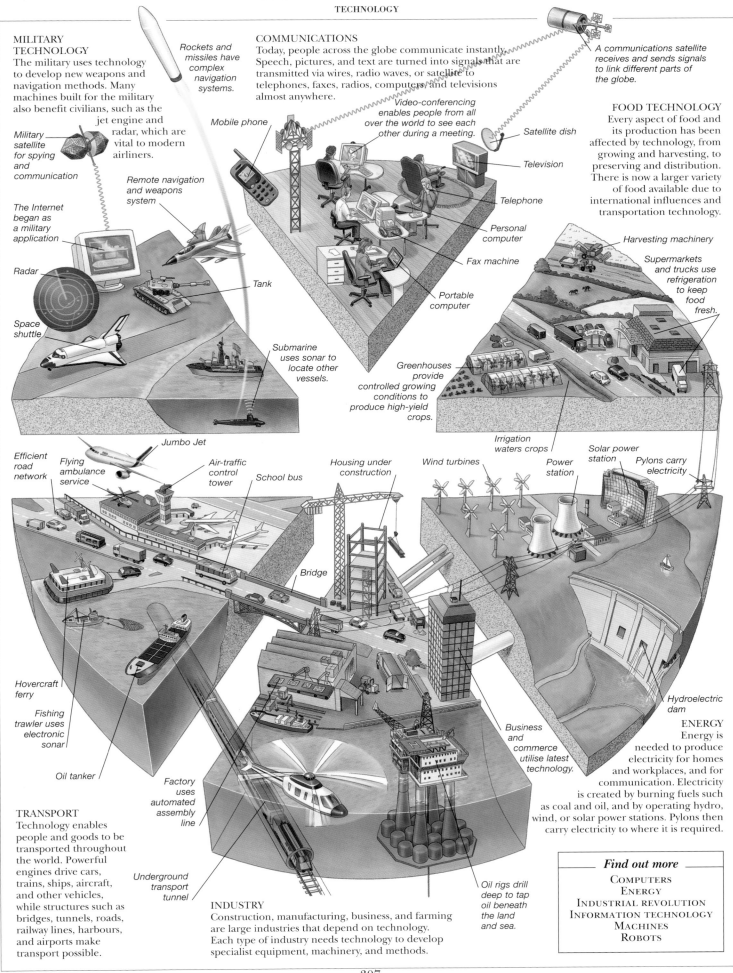

MILITARY TECHNOLOGY
The military uses technology to develop new weapons and navigation methods. Many machines built for the military also benefit civilians, such as the jet engine and radar, which are vital to modern airliners.

Rockets and missiles have complex navigation systems.

Military satellite for spying and communication

The Internet began as a military application

Radar

Space shuttle

Remote navigation and weapons system

Tank

Submarine uses sonar to locate other vessels.

COMMUNICATIONS
Today, people across the globe communicate instantly. Speech, pictures, and text are turned into signals that are transmitted via wires, radio waves, or satellite to telephones, faxes, radios, computers, and televisions almost anywhere.

A communications satellite receives and sends signals to link different parts of the globe.

Mobile phone

Video-conferencing enables people from all over the world to see each other during a meeting.

Satellite dish

Television

Telephone

Personal computer

Fax machine

Portable computer

FOOD TECHNOLOGY
Every aspect of food and its production has been affected by technology, from growing and harvesting, to preserving and distribution. There is now a larger variety of food available due to international influences and transportation technology.

Harvesting machinery

Supermarkets and trucks use refrigeration to keep food fresh.

Greenhouses provide controlled growing conditions to produce high-yield crops.

Irrigation waters crops

Wind turbines

Power station

Solar power station

Pylons carry electricity

Jumbo Jet

Efficient road network

Flying ambulance service

Air-traffic control tower

School bus

Housing under construction

Bridge

Business and commerce utilise latest technology.

Hydroelectric dam

Hovercraft ferry

Fishing trawler uses electronic sonar

Oil tanker

Factory uses automated assembly line

Underground transport tunnel

ENERGY
Energy is needed to produce electricity for homes and workplaces, and for communication. Electricity is created by burning fuels such as coal and oil, and by operating hydro, wind, or solar power stations. Pylons then carry electricity to where it is required.

TRANSPORT
Technology enables people and goods to be transported throughout the world. Powerful engines drive cars, trains, ships, aircraft, and other vehicles, while structures such as bridges, tunnels, roads, railway lines, harbours, and airports make transport possible.

Oil rigs drill deep to tap oil beneath the land and sea.

INDUSTRY
Construction, manufacturing, business, and farming are large industries that depend on technology. Each type of industry needs technology to develop specialist equipment, machinery, and methods.

Find out more
COMPUTERS
ENERGY
INDUSTRIAL REVOLUTION
INFORMATION TECHNOLOGY
MACHINES
ROBOTS

TEETH

EVERY TIME WE EAT we use our teeth to bite, chew, crunch, and grind food. Teeth enable us to break up food into small pieces so that our bodies can digest it and use it. A tooth has three main parts – the crown of the tooth, which shows above the gum; the neck, which shows at gum level; and the root, which is hidden in the jawbone. The root of the tooth is fixed securely in the jaw by a substance called cementum. A tooth has three layers – creamy white enamel on the outside (the hardest substance in the body); a layer of dentine beneath; and the pulp cavity in the centre. The pulp contains many nerves, which connect to the jawbone. There are four main kinds of teeth; each kind is shaped for a different job. Chisel-like incisors at the front of the mouth cut and slice food; longer, pointed canines tear and rip food; and flat, broad premolars and molars crush and grind it. During our lives, we have two sets of teeth – milk teeth as children, and a second set of teeth as adults.

HEALTHY TEETH
It is important to take care of your teeth to keep them healthy. Teeth should be cleaned with a toothbrush and toothpaste at least twice a day. Dental floss should be used regularly. Sugary foods are damaging to teeth and cause tooth decay.

Enamel
Pulp cavity
Dentine
Gum
Blood vessels
Root
Jawbone
Cementum
Nerve
Cross-section of a molar

JAWS
The upper jaw is fixed to the skull and does not move. Powerful muscles in the cheeks and the side of the head pull the lower jaw up towards the upper jaw, so that the teeth come together with great pressure for biting. Other muscles pull the lower jaw sideways, so that we can chew with both up-and-down and side-to-side movements. Teeth are an important first step in the process of digesting food.

Temporalis muscle pulls jaw up.

Lateral pterygoid muscles move jaw from side to side.

DENTISTS
Dentists use X-rays (right) to see the roots of teeth and to identify any cavities. In the past, dentists extracted decaying teeth, but now only the affected parts are removed and the hole is filled with hard artificial materials. The white areas on this X-ray are fillings and two crowns on posts.

STRUCTURE OF A TOOTH
Teeth have one, two (like this molar), three, or occasionally four roots, which anchor them securely in the jawbone and withstand the pressure of biting and chewing. Blood vessels which carry nutrients and oxygen, and nerves which transmit sensation, pass out through tiny holes in the base of each root.

Part of tooth shows below the gum line.

MILK TEETH AND ADULT TEETH
Children have 20 milk teeth which gradually fall out and are replaced by a second set of permanent adult teeth. Adults have 32 teeth in total. Each jaw has 4 incisors, 2 canines, 4 premolars, and 6 molars (2 of which are wisdom teeth). Wisdom teeth grow when a person is about 20, although some may never push through the gum.

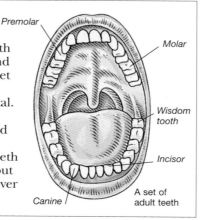

Premolar
Molar
Wisdom tooth
Incisor
Canine
A set of adult teeth

TUSKS
Animals use their teeth for more than just eating food. Large teeth help to defend against enemies, or when battling with rivals during the mating season. The warthog's tusks shown here are huge canine teeth – like the tusks of a walrus. Tusks are used to frighten off predators and, sometimes, to dig up food.

Find out more
DIGESTION
HUMAN BODY
SKELETONS

TELEPHONES

Earpiece

A loudspeaker, called the receiver, contains a thin metal disc that vibrates, converting electric signals into sound waves.

Silicon chip

Electronic circuits generate signals corresponding to each button as it is pressed. They also amplify (boost) incoming electric signals and send them to the receiver.

TELEPHONE HANDSET
A small direct (one-way) electric current flows in the wires connected to a telephone handset. Signals representing sounds such as callers' voices, computer data, and fax messages consist of rapid variations in the strength of this current.

Microphone

Soundwaves of the user's voice strike a microphone called the transmitter, creating an electrical signal that is sent down the telephone cable.

The electric cable connects to the telephone network, allowing access all over the world.

WITH THE PUSH of a few buttons on the telephone, it is possible to talk to someone nearly anywhere else in the world. By making instant communication possible, the telephone has done more to "shrink" the world than almost any other invention. A telephone signal can take several forms on its journey. Beneath the city streets it travels in the form of electric currents in cables, or as light waves in thin glass fibres. Telephone signals also travel as radio waves when they beam down to other countries via satellites, or when they carry messages to and from mobile phones. Many electronic devices "talk" to each other by sending signals via telephone links. Computers exchange information and programs with one another, and fax machines use telephone lines to send copies of pictures and text to other fax machines across the world within seconds.

TELEPHONE NETWORK
Computer-controlled telephone exchanges make the connections needed to link two telephones. When a person dials a telephone number, automatic switches at the local exchange link the telephone lines directly. International calls travel along undersea cables or, in the form of radio waves, by way of satellites.

Communication satellites orbit the Earth at such a height and speed that they remain stationary over the same part of the globe all the time. They receive telephone signals from one country on Earth, boost the signals, then beam them back down to another country.

Words and pictures printed by a fax machine have jagged edges because they are made up of thousands of dots.

Fibre-optic cables use light waves to carry thousands of phone calls at one time.

FAX
A facsimile, or fax, machine scans a page by measuring its brightness at thousands of individual points. It then sends signals along the telephone wire, each representing the brightness at one point. A printer inside the receiving fax machine prints a dot wherever the original picture is dark, making a copy. Today, email is increasingly replacing the fax.

ALEXANDER GRAHAM BELL
The inventor of the telephone was a Scottish-American teacher named Alexander Graham Bell (1847-1922). In 1875, Bell was experimenting with early telegraph systems. For this he used vibrating steel strips called reeds. He found that when a reed at one end of the line vibrated, a reed at the other end gave out a sound. In 1876, Bell patented the world's first practical telephone.

PORTABLE PHONES
A cordless telephone has a built-in radio transmitter and receiver. It communicates with a unit connected to a telephone line in a home. Mobile phones (left) work with the aid of powerful relay stations such as cellular exchanges. Mobile phones are becoming increasingly versatile. Many now also function as cameras and can connect to the Internet.

Find out more
INTERNET
SATELLITES
SOUND
TECHNOLOGY

TELESCOPES

FROM FAR AWAY, a person looks like a tiny dot. But with a telescope, you can see a clear, bright image that reveals all the details of that person's face. Large modern telescopes make it possible for astronomers to make images of extremely faint objects in the universe, such as galaxies billions of light years away, or small icy worlds at the edge of the solar system. Less powerful telescopes are important too: they are valuable tools for mapmakers, sailors, and bird watchers. Telescopes have helped scientists make some of the greatest discoveries about the universe. In 1609, the Italian scientist Galileo first turned a telescope to the skies. His observations led him to suggest that the Earth moved around the Sun and was not the centre of the universe, as people believed at that time. Since then, astronomers have continued to build ever bigger and better telescopes and to make new and unexpected discoveries with them.

OPERA GLASSES
Opera glasses are the simplest kind of binoculars. They consist of two small telescopes placed side by side.

Eyepiece lenses are adjustable to match the strength of each eye.

Prisms "fold up" the light inside the binoculars, which magnifies objects as much as a long telescope.

A prism is a triangular-shaped piece of glass.

BINOCULARS
Binoculars are more complex than opera glasses. They contain a system of lenses and prisms that makes them powerful yet small in size.

Light enters the front of the binoculars.

The Keck telescope, right, does not use lenses, like binoculars, but a large primary mirror made up of smaller segments. Each segment is adjusted by a computer to an accuracy 25,000 times smaller than a human hair.

REFLECTING TELESCOPE
Most astronomers use reflecting telescopes, the best telescopes for picking up the faint light from distant stars. A large curved mirror catches the light and concentrates it to form an image. For observing directly by eye, a smaller mirror then carries the image to a lens called the eyepiece. In large telescopes used by professional astronomers, the light goes into an electronic instrument or camera and the observations are stored in a computer.

The secondary mirror bounces light back down to tertiary mirror.

The structure keeps all parts in same relative positons as telescope turns and tilts.

The tertiary mirror reflects light to cameras and scientific instruments.

Cameras and scientific instruments.

The primary mirror is made from 36 small hexagons that work like a single mirror. Together, these segments collect light and reflect it to focus on the secondary mirror.

RADIO TELESCOPES
Stars and other objects in space give out invisible radio waves as well as light. Astronomers study the universe with radio telescopes, which are large dish-shaped antennas that pick up radio waves from space. Radio astronomy has led to the discovery of dying stars and distant galaxies that would not have been seen from their light alone.

The eyepiece lens focuses the image into the observer's eye.

The objective lens is a convex lens which concentrates the light to form an image.

The middle lens turns the image the right way up.

REFRACTING TELESCOPE
A large lens at the front of a refracting telescope refracts, or bends, the light to form an image of a distant object. The eyepiece lens is at the back. Some refractors have a third lens in the middle. Without this lens, the telescope would produce an upside-down image.

Find out more
ASTRONOMY
LIGHT
MICROSCOPES
SCIENCE, HISTORY OF

TELEVISION

SINCE ITS INVENTION early in the 20th century, television has become one of the world's most important sources of opinion, information, and entertainment. Television gives us the best seats in the theatre, at a rock concert, or at the Olympic Games. It also beams us pictures of war and disaster, the conquering of space, and other world events as they happen. Television programmes are actually electronic signals sent out as radio waves by way of satellites and underground cables. A television set converts the signals into sound and pictures. People can watch pre-recorded films and record broadcast programmes to play at a later time using digital versatile discs (DVDs) or a personal video recorder (PVR). Lightweight video cameras can also be used to make home movies. Closed-circuit (nonbroadcast) television cameras are used to guard shops and offices, monitor traffic conditions, and survey crowds at sports events.

Operator controls camera on movable stand.

Autocue

Presenter reads the news from the autocue into the camera.

TELEVISION STUDIO
Within the space of a few hours, a studio might be used for a game show, a play, a variety show, and a panel discussion, so studio sets have to be changed very rapidly. Presenters and people working behind the cameras receive instructions from the control room via headphones. Most programmes are recorded, sometimes months before they are broadcast.

CONTROL ROOM
The director and vision mixer sit in the control room (shown above) in front of a bank of screens showing pictures from several sources, such as from cameras at various angles in the studio and at outside broadcast locations, from digital recording machines, and from satellites. Other screens show still photographs, captions, and titles. The vision mixer is instructed by the director which image to broadcast on screen and for how long. Sound is also mixed in at the same time. The producer has overall control of the final programme.

AUTOCUE
The presenter reads the script from an autocue. The words are displayed on a monitor screen and reflected in a two-way mirror in front of the camera lens. An operator on the studio floor controls the speed at which the words move.

OUTSIDE BROADCAST
Outside broadcast teams use portable cameras when mobility is important, as in a news report, and large, fixed cameras for events such as football games. The pictures are recorded on videotape or beamed back to the studio via a mobile dish antenna.

Sound is recorded through a sound boom.

Sections of digital recording are cut, edited, and reordered.

The editor watches the original recordings and puts together the final programme.

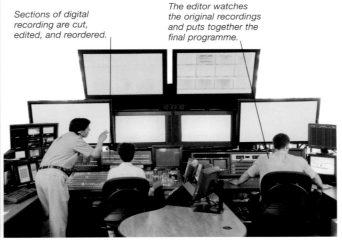

EDITING SUITE
When a programme is not broadcast live, an editor gathers all the material recorded from each camera and selects the best sections and edits them together in the right order. This is done in an editing suite (left) with specialist equipment. Editing allows filming to be done out of sequence, and from many different angles. Smooth editing can be crucial to the flow and final cut of a programme.

TELEVISION RECEIVER

A television receiver picks up signals broadcast by television stations and converts them to moving pictures on a screen. Images appear to move because 25-60 pictures appear each second. The most common type of screen is the LCD (Liquid Crystal Display). LCDs are made up of millions of tiny dots of light called pixels. Each pixel contains a red, a green, and a blue subpixel – different combinations of these three colours can produces all the colours that make up a picture. The subpixels are controlled by groups of liquid crystals. Electronic circuits in the TV work out which pixels need to be switched on to make a picture. They pass electric signals through the liquid crystals, which act like tiny light switches to turn each subpixel on or off.

2. A special filter lets through only vertical beams of light.

4. Coloured filters change the white light beams into red, green, or blue light.

No light reaches the glass so this subpixel is dark.

7. Human eye sees different combinations of light beams as different colours.

1. Light source at back of screen (backlight) gives out white light

3. Electricity makes liquid crystals twist or untwist. Twisted crystals twist the light beams, too.

5. Filter lets through only the beams of light that have been twisted horizontal by the liquid crystals.

6. The light from the switched-on subpixels reaches the glass screen and combines to form a pixel.

How liquid crystals control pixel colours in an LCD screen

NEW TECHNOLOGIES

Today's widescreen TV sets have flat plasma screens or liquid crystal displays, but these will be replaced by ultra-thin organic LED displays (OLED). High Definition (HD) broadcasts and screens use more pixels to give better picture quality. At home, personal video recorders (PVRs) store video on computer hard disc drives. Movies and TV shows can now be downloaded from the Internet, too. Digital broadcasting uses binary code to carry TV signals with better quality sound and pictures. And with interactive television, viewers can select what to watch and when from a wide range of options.

Pocket digital video player

High-definition flatscreen television

Personal video recorder

TELEVISION TRANSMISSION

Television signals can reach a viewer by several routes. Usually, transmitters broadcast television signals directly to homes as ultrahigh frequency (UHF) radio waves. Alternatively, the signals are sent up to a satellite, which transmits them over a larger region. Individual homes receive the satellite broadcast via dish antennas (right). In other cases, a ground station picks up the signals and sends them out along cables.

Satellite television sends signals from the TV station to homes via a satellite.

Television station

House aerial picks up UHF signals.

Cable television

Cable feeds the signal into the house to the receiver.

The horn collects concentrated incoming waves

Camcorder

INVENTION

In 1926, Scottish engineer John Logie Baird (1888-1946) gave the first public demonstration of television. At about the same time, the Russian American engineer Vladimir Zworykin (1889-1982) invented the electronic camera tube, which was more sophisticated than Baird's system and is the basis of today's television sets. In 1956 the U.S. company Ampex first produced videotape; videocassette recorders appeared in 1969, produced by Sony of Japan.

VIDEO CAMERAS

Today's video cameras or "camcorders" are tiny in comparison with the giant studio cameras used in the early days of TV. They fit easily in the palm of one hand. Most are now digital and record high-quality video sequences – including stereo sound as well – in the form of binary code stored on magnetic tape, optical DVD discs, memory cards, or a hard disc drive built into the camera.

Find out more
CAMERAS
ELECTRONICS
INFORMATION TECHNOLOGY
SOUND
TECHNOLOGY

TIME

HOUR FOLLOWS HOUR as time passes. Time always flows steadily in the same direction. Behind us in time lies the past, which we know. Ahead lies the future, which we cannot know. We cannot change time, but we can measure it. People first measured time in days and nights, which they could easily see and count. They also measured time in months, by watching the phases of the Moon, and in years, by watching the cycle of the seasons. Today, we have clocks and watches that can measure time in fractions of a second.

In 1905, German physicist Albert Einstein proposed the scientific theory of relativity. This says that time is not constant, but that it would pass more slowly if you could travel very fast (near the speed of light), or in strong fields of gravity. Scientists believe that time may even come to a stop in black holes deep in space.

HOURGLASS
Sand draining through an hourglass shows the passing of time. It takes one hour for the sand to run from the top to the bottom bulb.

In reality, the Earth is 400 times further away from the Sun than it is from the Moon.

Earth | Moon | Sun

YEARS AND MONTHS
A year is based on the time the Earth takes to go once around the Sun, which is 365.26 days. Months vary from 28 to 31 days. They were originally based on the time between full moons, which is about 29.5 days.

The International Date Line is at 180 degrees longitude.

3 p.m. in Moscow, Russian Federation

INTERNATIONAL DATE LINE
The western side of the International Date Line is one day ahead of the eastern side. When you cross the line, the date changes.

12 noon in London, Britain

TIME ZONES
The world is divided into 24 regions, called time zones, each with a different time of day. This was done to avoid having several time differences within one area, and to ensure that all countries have noon during the middle of the day.

2 p.m. in Cairo, Egypt

UNIVERSAL TIME
The time at the prime meridian is used as a standard time known as Universal Time (UT) or Greenwich Mean Time (GMT).

The prime meridian is at 0 degrees longitude.

7 a.m. in New York City, USA

The Earth spins counterclockwise when looking down at the North Pole. It goes clockwise viewed from above the South Pole.

UNITS OF TIME
One full day and night is the time in which the Earth spins once. This is divided into 24 hours: each hour contains 60 minutes, and each minute contains 60 seconds. The Babylonians fixed these units about 5,000 years ago, using 24 and 60 because they divide easily by 2, 3, and 4.

9 a.m. in Rio de Janeiro, Brazil

DAYS AND NIGHTS
The Sun lights up one half of the Earth, where it is day. The other half, away from the Sun, is dark, and there it is night. Days and nights come and go because the Earth spins once every 24 hours. But the day and night may last different lengths of time because the Earth is tilted at an angle to the Sun.

The Hindu calendar is based on lunar months. Diwali, the Festival of Lights, marks the start of the new year, which falls in October or November.

CALENDARS
The date is fixed by the calendar, which contains 12 months with a total of 365 days. Every fourth year is a leap year which has one extra day, February 29. Leap years are years that divide by four, such as 2008 and 2012. The calendar contains leap years because the Earth takes slightly longer than 365 days to go once around the Sun. Prehistoric peoples may have used monuments such as Stonehenge, in southern England (below), to measure the Sun's position and find the exact length of the year.

Twice a year the Sun is overhead the Equator at 12 noon.

Find out more
BABYLONIANS
EARTH
MOON
SCIENCE
STARS
SUN
UNIVERSE

TRADE AND INDUSTRY

WITHOUT TRADE AND INDUSTRY, people would have to create everything they needed to live. If you wanted a loaf of bread you would have to grow wheat, grind the wheat to make flour, mix the dough, and bake it in an oven. You would also need to build the mill and make the oven! Industry organizes the production of bread, so that just a few farmers, millers, and bakers can make bread for everyone. Similarly, industry supplies us with most other essential and luxury goods, from fresh water to cars. Trade is the process of buying and selling. Trade gets the products from the people who make them to the people who need them. And through trade, manufacturers can buy the raw materials they need to supply their factories and keep production going. Together, the trade and industry of a nation are sometimes called the economy.

SILK ROAD
Trade between different regions and peoples goes back to ancient times. The Silk Road was one of the earliest and most famous trade routes. Traders led horses and camels along this route between 300 BCE and 1600 CE, carrying silk from China to Europe.

INTERNATIONAL TRADE
Goods move around the world by sea, land, and air. This international trade takes materials such as oil from the countries that have a surplus to those that have no or insufficient oil deposits. International trade is also necessary because goods do not always fetch a high price in the country where they are made. For example, many clothes are made by hand in countries where wages are low. But the clothes are sold in another country where people are richer and can pay a high price. Money earned this way helps less rich countries pay for their imports.

India exports cotton textiles to Europe.

India exports tea to the Russian Federation.

India imports cars from Japan.

India imports oil from the Middle East.

India exports rice to Australia.

Imports

Exports

IMPORTS AND EXPORTS
Goods that are traded internationally are called imports and exports. Goods that one country sells to another are called exports; imports are goods that a country buys from another. In most nations, private businesses control imports and exports. But in others, the government imposes strict controls on what can be bought and sold.

TRADE AGREEMENTS
Some countries sign trade agreements in order to control trade between them. The agreement may simply fix the price at which the two countries buy and sell certain goods, such as tea and wheat. The European Union (EU) has a complicated network of trade agreements which allow free exchange of goods between member countries. The EU also restricts trade with countries that are not members of the Union. This helps encourage industry within the Union.

Imports

Exports

To pay for imports (goods bought from foreign countries) ...

...every country must export goods, and sell them abroad.

BALANCE OF PAYMENTS
Each country pays for imports with the money it earns by selling goods in other countries. This balance between imports and exports is called the balance of trade, or the balance of payments. Countries that do not export enough must borrow money from abroad to pay for imports.

FACTORIES

Some industry takes place in people's homes, but workers in factories make most of the products that we buy. In a factory each person has a small task in the manufacturing process. He or she may operate a large machine or assemble something by hand. No one person makes an entire product. This process of mass production makes manufacturing cheaper and quicker. Most factories are owned by large companies; a few factories are owned by governments or by the people who work in them.

The restaurant industry provides the service of cooking and serving food.

SUPPLY AND DEMAND

Companies set up factories to produce goods that they think people will want to buy. They sell the goods at a price that allows the company to make a profit. As long as there is a demand for the goods, the factory will continue to supply them. When fewer people buy the goods that the factory makes, prices drop to try to attract buyers, and workers in the factory may lose their jobs.

A factory starts by making a small number of umbrellas.

Shops put a few umbrellas on sale at a high price.

Many people need umbrellas and buy them, increasing demand.

The factory employs more people to make more umbrellas.

When everyone has an umbrella, demand for umbrellas falls.

Prices drop, and the factory needs fewer umbrella workers.

SERVICE INDUSTRIES

Not all industries make objects for sale. Some industries provide a service in return for money. A garage, for instance, might charge a fee to adjust a car so that it runs more efficiently. People pay for this service rather than do the work themselves.

The engine comes from a factory in Spain.

A French factory makes the body from British steel.

A modern car is so complex that one factory cannot make every part. So, many factories build car components, and an assembly plant builds the vehicle.

The transmission is made in Germany.

Final assembly of the car may take place in Spain.

MANUFACTURING

The basic form of industry is manufacturing. This means working on materials to manufacture, or make, a finished product. Almost everything we use is the product of manufacturing, and most manufacturing takes place in large factories. However, craftsworkers manufacture goods alone or in small groups. Some goods go through many stages of manufacturing. For example, workers making cars assemble manufactured components or parts which, in turn, have been made in many other factories, often in other countries.

TRADE UNIONS

During the 19th century, workers began to form trade unions in order to obtain better pay and conditions for their members. If a union cannot achieve its aims, its members may go on strike – stop work – until their demands are met.

The successful strike of women workers in a London match factory in 1888 encouraged other workers to join unions.

Find out more

CHINA
EUROPEAN UNION
INDUSTRIAL REVOLUTION
MACHINES
MONEY
PIRATES

TRAINS

WHEN THE FIRST RAILWAYS were built more than 150 years ago, many people said they were the most wonderful of all inventions. Others said the snorting, smoking steam engines were like ugly, metal monsters. Trains and railways certainly changed our world. Not only did embankments and cuttings alter the landscape, but also, for the first time, people and goods could be carried long distances in vast quantities – and at speeds undreamed of. Railways also allowed cities to grow more than ever before. Today, large networks of railways stretch through many countries. If the tracks of the world's main rail routes were laid end to end, they would circle the Earth more than 34 times. Trains are an efficient method of transport. They use less fuel and produce less pollution than cars and trucks because they carry large cargoes in a single journey. Because of the damage road vehicles do to our environment, many people believe trains are the best form of transport for the future.

All carriages are air-conditioned to maintain a comfortable, fresh atmosphere.

Electric trains pick up a high-voltage current from overhead cables through an arm called a pantograph.

Windows are designed to reduce outside noise.

Air-powered suspension systems with large shock absorbers help give a smooth ride.

TRUCKS
All trains run on "trucks" of four or more wheels. The trucks swivel to allow the train to go around curves.

The driver's cab is equipped with a computer screen to check for faults in the train, and a radio to keep in contact with the signalling centre and other trains on the line.

Streamlined shape reduces air resistance, allowing the TGV to speed to its destination with a minimum of power.

LOCOMOTIVE
The part that pulls or pushes a high-speed train like the TGV is called the power car. It contains powerful motors to drive the train. Most high-speed trains have a power car at each end.

Wheel

POINTS
Track-laying vehicles usually weld the rails into one continuous track as they are laid, which allows the train to run very smoothly. Intersections in the rails, called points, move trains onto a new stretch of track.

Rod moves points.

A short pair of rails in the points turns so that the train moves onto the new track.

Normally the train goes straight on.

The track rests on beams of wood or concrete called sleepers.

HIGH-SPEED TRAIN
The Train à Grande Vitesse (TGV), a high-speed electric train in France, is one of the world's fastest trains, able to reach 300 km/h (186 mph). But the TGVs have to run on specially built tracks with gentle grades and curves.

RICHARD TREVITHICK
In 1804, a steam locomotive (right) built by Englishman Richard Trevithick ran on rails for the first time. Trevithick thought that steam power had a future, and bet that his steam engine could haul 9 tonnes (9 tons) of iron 15 km (9.5 miles) along a mine railway in Wales. Trevithick won his bet; the engine carried not only the iron but also 70 cheering coal miners who climbed aboard.

The Rocket, *built by English engineer George Stephenson in 1829, was a new design that heralded the age of the passenger train.*

A front truck was introduced on early American locomotives to give a smoother ride around curves.

During the mid-1800s, England's railway system developed into a large network.

Engines could reach 200 km/h (126 mph) by the 1930s – the peak of the steam age.

Steam locomotives of the 1930s were very sophisticated compared to the first engines.

UNDERGROUND TRAINS
In crowded cities, underground trains are the quickest way to travel. The first underground system was opened in London in 1863. Now many cities have their own network. The Metro in Paris is one of the most efficient underground systems in the world.

STEAM RAILWAYS
Railways date back 4,000 years to the Babylonians, who pushed carts along grooves. But the age of railways really began in the early 1800s when steam engines first ran on rails. In 1825, the first passenger line opened in England; 30 years later, vast railway systems stretched across Europe and North America. By the 1890s, steam engines could reach speeds of more than 160 km/h (100 mph).

SIGNALS AND SAFETY
Trackside signals tell the driver how fast to go and when to stop. In the past, signals were mechanical arms worked by levers in the signal box. Nowadays they are usually sets of coloured lights controlled by computers that monitor the position of every train.

MAGLEVS AND MONORAILS
One day we may be whisked along silently at speeds of 480 km/h (300 mph) on trains that glide a small distance above special tracks, held up by magnetic force – which is why they are called maglevs (for magnetic levitation). Some countries, such as China, already have maglev lines. Other new designs include monorail trains, which are electric trains that run on, or are suspended from, a single rail.

The Shanghai maglev

ORIENT EXPRESS
Some trains have become famous for their speed, some for their luxury, and others for the length of their route. From 1883, the *Orient Express*, for example, provided a first-class service from Paris to Constantinople (Istanbul), Turkey. It still travels part of this route today. The world's longest train route is the *Trans-Siberian Express*, which runs 9,438 km (5,864 miles) across Siberia.

Find out more
ENGINES
INDUSTRIAL REVOLUTION
SCIENCE, HISTORY OF
TECHNOLOGY

TREES

WITHOUT PLANTS such as trees there could be no life on Earth. Trees take in carbon dioxide from the air and give off oxygen by the process of photosynthesis, so maintaining the balance of the atmosphere. Tree roots stabilize the soil so it is not washed away by the rain, and their leaves give off vast amounts of water vapour, which affects the balance of the world's weather. Forests cover about 39 million sq km (15 million sq miles) of the planet's surface. Trees vary greatly in size, from towering redwoods to dwarf snow willows, that are only a few centimetres high. They supply food for millions of creatures, and produce wood to make buildings, furniture – even the pages of this book.

Giant sequoia trees are the largest living things – more than 84 m (270 ft) high, and 2,000 tonnes (1,970 tons) in weight; an elephant weighs about 5 tonnes (5 tons).

Leaves

English oak tree in spring and autumn

Buds

Oak bark

Acorns are the fruits of the oak tree; they develop from the pollinated female flowers during autumn.

The roots of a deciduous tree may reach out sideways to the same distance as the tree's height.

CONIFEROUS TREES

Pines, firs, cedars, and redwoods are called coniferous trees, or conifers, because they grow their seeds in hard, woody cones. The long, narrow leaves, called needles, stay on the tree all winter. These trees are also called evergreens, because they stay green all year.

CONES
Each tree has its own type of cone, which develops from the fertilized female flowers.

Larch cone

Scots pine needles grow in pairs.

Pine cone

Arolla pine needles

Conifer roots usually spread out sideways.

BROAD-LEAVED TREES

Oaks, beeches, willows, and many other trees are called broad-leaved because their leaves are broad and flat, unlike the sharp needles on coniferous trees. Some broad-leaved trees are also called deciduous, because their leaves die and drop off in autumn.

Sitka spruce cone turns brown as it ripens.

NEEDLES
Every conifer has distinctively shaped needles that grow in a certain pattern. Sitka spruce needles are long and sharp.

Needle

Sitka spruce is an evergreen coniferous tree often seen in forest plantations.

LEAVES
Broad-leaved trees can be recognized by the shape of their leaves and the pattern in which the leaves grow on the twigs. In winter, you can identify a bare tree by its bark, buds, and overall shape.

Leaves of the holly tree are spiky.

Japanese maple leaves have deep notches.

The gingko tree has fan-shaped leaves.

Rowan or mountain ash trees have compound leaves.

Sweet chestnut leaves have a jagged edge.

318

GROWTH

All trees grow from small seeds inside their fruit. Each seed contains a food store and a tiny embryo tree. The seed begins to grow when the temperature and moisture of the soil are suitable. A young tree is called a sapling.

Shoot grows from between seed leaves.

First true leaves develop and seed case falls away.

Seed case splits.

Beech seed (or beechnut) is contained in hard seed case.

Root begins to emerge.

Root and stem of seedling grow longer.

SEASONAL GROWTH

In temperate regions, where there are definite seasons each year, trees grow during spring and summer. Growth occurs mainly at the ends of the tree, the tips of the branches, and the roots. The twigs lengthen, and flowers and leaves appear from the buds. Root tips grow longer and push their way through the soil. The roots and branches thicken, as does the tree trunk, so that the tree's girth, or waistband, also increases in size.

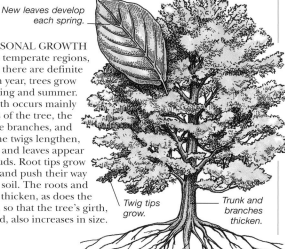

New leaves develop each spring.

Twig tips grow.

Trunk and branches thicken.

Roots become fatter.

Root tips lengthen.

TREE TRUNK

During spring and early summer, when growth is rapid, tree trunks thicken. Large thin-walled cells form light-coloured wood. Slower growth during the rest of the year produces thick-walled cells that make darker-coloured wood. One light-coloured ring plus one dark ring indicates one year's growth. Some tropical trees grow all year round; they have faint rings or none at all.

Bark cambium (growing area) of young tree

INSIDE A TREE

Counting the rings on a section of trunk can tell us the age of a tree. This is a section of a very old giant sequoia tree.

1800 CE Washington, D.C., becomes U.S. capital.

1400 CE Joan of Arc burned at the stake.

800 CE Charlemagne crowned emperor.

Native Americans used the smooth bark of birch trees to make canoes.

Young bark is smooth.

Bark grows from the inside and pushes the older bark outwards.

Old bark cracks and flakes.

BARK

The tree's bark is its skin. It shields the living wood within, stops it from drying out, and protects it from extreme cold and heat. Bark prevents damage from moulds, but some animals, such as deer and beavers, eat the bark, and a few wood-boring beetles can tunnel through. A tree with no leaves can be identified by the colour and texture of its bark.

The rough bark of the cork tree is stripped off every eight to 10 years; it is used to make bottle stoppers and floor tiles.

Coconut palm tree

PALM TREES

The 2,700 kinds of palm tree are found in warm Mediterranean and tropical regions. These tall, straight trees provide many products, including palm oils, dates, and coconuts from the coconut palm.

The outer husk of the coconut is used to make coconut matting (above). Coconuts are a valuable source of milk, edible fats, and animal food.

Native Americans carved whole tree trunks to create totem poles.

WOOD

Each year we use thousands of tonnes of wood for building, as fuel for cooking and heating, and to make tools, furniture, and paper. As the world's population grows, vast areas of forest are cut down, particularly in South America, where much of the tropical rain forest has been destroyed.

In the past, loggers had to float logs to the sawmill.

Whole tree trunks are used to make telephone poles.

Find out more

FOREST WILDLIFE
FRUITS AND SEEDS
PLANTS
POLLUTION

TUDORS

THE TUDORS CAME TO the throne in 1485. Before that, there had been years of civil war between two rival ruling family groups, the House of York and the House of Lancaster. But during the Tudor period, which ended in 1603, England enjoyed a time of lasting peace. Rulers such as Henry VII, who united the warring houses, and Elizabeth I, improved the economy, making the country a richer place. It was also a golden age for the arts, with major poets, great playwrights, and fine composers creating important works. However, there were damaging disputes over religion, with the official faith of England changing repeatedly until Elizabeth I became queen. Under her, the Protestant Church of England became established as the national religion.

HENRY VII
The first Tudor king was Henry VII (r. 1485-1509). His name was Henry Tudor, and the dynasty (ruling house) took its name from him. A member of the House of Lancaster, he married Elizabeth of York to unite their two houses. He kept other noble families under control, banning their armies, and defeating two rivals to the throne.

THE TUDORS
1485 Battle of Bosworth: Henry Tudor defeats Richard III. He rules as Henry VII.

1497 Henry supports voyages to America by John and Sebastian Cabot.

1509-47 Henry VIII reigns.

1534 Henry VIII rebels against the pope and becomes head of the Church of England.

1547-53 Edward VI reigns.

1553-58 Reign of Mary I.

1554 Mary marries Philip of Spain, creating an alliance between the two countries.

1558-1603 Reign of Elizabeth I, last of the Tudors.

DAILY LIFE
In Tudor times, most people lived in the countryside, and there was much poverty. Many country people had a difficult life, working hard and earning little. A few made money farming sheep and exporting the wool to Europe. In the towns, merchants and craftworkers could make a good living. Some of their houses still survive.

Framework made of strong oak timbers

Gaps between timbers filled in with wattle (thin strips of wood) and daub (mud or clay).

Roof covered with baked clay tiles

Overhang, or "jetty", gave more room on the upper floor.

This house, belonging to a wealthy Tudor merchant, had two storeys. Its central hall reached up through both levels.

Fireplace had a brick chimney, to keep heat away from the timbers.

MARY TUDOR
England was a Protestant country when Mary Tudor (r. 1553-58) became queen. Mary married Philip II of Spain, and made England Catholic again. She ordered that Protestants who refused to change their faith were to be burned at the stake, for which she earned the nickname "Bloody Mary".

Protestants being burned at the stake.

Large central hall provided living space for the family.

Lute

MUSIC AND ENTERTAINMENT
The Tudors enjoyed good food and drink, dancing, and music. Some of England's greatest composers lived during the Tudor period. They included Thomas Morley and John Dowland, who wrote songs and music for the lute, and Thomas Tallis and William Byrd, who composed choral music.

Find out more
ELIZABETH I
HENRY VIII
STUARTS

UNITED KINGDOM

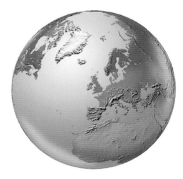

The United Kingdom is just off the northwest coast of Europe. To its east lies the North Sea. The Atlantic Ocean washes its northern and western coasts. The English Channel separates the country from mainland Europe.

THE UNITED KINGDOM of Great Britain and Northern Ireland was formed under the Act of Union of 1801. It is made up of England, Wales, and Scotland, which together form the island of Great Britain, and the province of Northern Ireland. In the late 1990s, the British government devolved power to regional governments by creating new parliaments in Northern Ireland, Scotland and Wales. The English countryside is famed for its gently sloping hills and rich farmland. Wales and Scotland are mostly wild and mountainous. Much of Northern Ireland is low-lying and marshy. In Wales and parts of Scotland, many of the people speak a language of their own. Britain is a multicultural country, for the English, Scots, Welsh, and Irish are all separate peoples. In the last 100 years refugees and immigrants from Europe, Africa, Asia, and the Caribbean have settled in Britain, bringing with them their own languages and religions. Britain once controlled a vast empire that stretched around the world. In recent years its economy has declined, but the discovery of oil in the North Sea has helped to make the country self-sufficient in energy.

Distinctive red double-decker buses and black taxis ferry Londoners around their city.

LONDON

When the Roman armies invaded Britain almost 2,000 years ago, they built a fortified town called Londinium to safeguard the crossing over the River Thames. By 1100, the city of London had grown in size to become the capital of the entire country. Today, London is a huge city of more than 7 million people and is the political, financial, and cultural centre of Britain. Tourists come from all over the world to admire the historic buildings, particularly the Tower of London (left), an 11th-century fortress.

Cricket began in Britain, and is the country's national sport. Many villages have their own teams.

CITY OF LONDON

The ancient heart of London is called the City. London is one of the world's leading financial centres, and most of the nation's banks and businesses have their headquarters here. The modern building shown on the left is the Lloyd's Building, where the world's shipping is registered and insured.

ENGLAND

The biggest and most populated part of the United Kingdom is England. Many people live in large towns and cities, such as London, Birmingham, and Manchester. Parts of the southeast and the north are very crowded. The English countryside is varied, with rolling farmland in the south and east and hilly moors in the north and west. England is dotted with picturesque villages where old houses and shops are often grouped around a village green.

The rose is the national flower of England.

JERSEY AND GUERNSEY

The Channel Islands of Jersey and Guernsey are closer to France than they are to Britain. The French coast is just 24 km (15 miles) away from Jersey, the largest island. Close to Jersey and Guernsey are some smaller islands that are also part of the Channel Islands group. All of the islands have a mild climate, so one of the principal occupations is the growing of vegetables. The warm weather and ample sunshine also attract holidaymakers, who in the summer months swell the islands' usual population of 150,000.

Thousands of colourful flowers are used to decorate floats for Jersey's "Battle of the Flowers" festival.

"Mad Sunday" motor cyclist on the Isle of Man

NORTHERN ENGLAND

The north of England has traditionally been the most heavily industrialized part of the United Kingdom. During the Industrial Revolution of the 19th century, factories and mills made goods for export to a British empire that covered half the world. Today the industrial cities of the north remain, but many of the factories stand empty because manufacturing is more profitable in other parts of the world. Northern England is also famous for its natural beauty; in the northwest is a rugged, mountainous region called the Lake District. Here deep lakes separate steep hills which rise to a height of more than 975 m (3,200 ft). The Lake District is beautiful and attracts many visitors and tourists.

FISHING INDUSTRY

The waters of the northeast Atlantic are among the world's richest fishing grounds. But EU regulations, designed to reduce catches and conserve fish stocks, are causing widespread discontent amongst fishermen.

ISLE OF MAN

The Isle of Man is part of the United Kingdom but enjoys a certain amount of independence. The Manx people, as islanders are called, have their own government, called the Tynwald, which makes many decisions about how the island is run. There is also a Manx language, though it is now used only for formal ceremonies. Manx independence has a long history, and between 1405 and 1765 the island was a kingdom separate from England.

PEOPLE

The United Kingdom is densely populated, with most of the people living in urban areas, particularly in the southeast of England. Almost 10 per cent of the total population of the country lives in London. The southeast is also the most prosperous area. Other parts of the country are less crowded. For example, the Highlands in Scotland have less inhabitants today than 200 years ago.

The United Kingdom has many fishing ports, like this one in Scotland.

SHETLAND AND ORKNEY

To the northeast of Scotland, two groups of islands form Britain's most northerly outposts. Orkney and Shetland comprise about 170 islands in all, but only the larger islands are inhabited. The landscape is bleak and there are few trees. The land is too poor to make farming profitable, and the traditional local industry is fishing. The islands are also famous for their hand-knitted wool clothes: Fair Isle has given its name to a distinctive knitting pattern.

A Welsh village has the longest placename in the United Kingdom.

LLANFAIRPWLLGWYNGYLLGOGERYCHWYRN-DROBWLLLLANTYSILIOGOGOGOCH

WALES

Farming, forestry, and tourism are the most important occupations in the rural regions of Wales. Farms tend to be small and average 40 hectares (16 acres) in size. Farmers in the upland regions keep cattle and sheep. Wales was once one of the main coal-producing areas in the world. There were 630 collieries in the region in 1913. However, the coal industry declined in the years after the first World War.

PUBLIC HOUSES

Public houses, more usually called pubs, developed from inns which offered travellers food, drink, and shelter. The pub played a part in British culture, too. In the *Canterbury Tales* by Geoffrey Chaucer (1340-1400), pilgrims on their way to Canterbury in southeast England rest at pubs and tell each other tales. Many of the plays of William Shakespeare (1564-1616) were performed in the yards of London pubs. Today the pub is a social centre where adults meet to discuss the events of the day. Pubs often entertain their customers with music or poetry, and many British rock bands began their careers playing in a pub.

The leek is the Welsh National emblem.

By custom, the first son of the British king or queen becomes Prince of Wales, and wears a gold crown.

EISTEDDFOD

Every year a festival of poetry, music, and drama celebrates and promotes the Welsh language. This National Eisteddfod began in the 7th century. Today colourful choirs and orchestras compete for awards at the event.

SCOTTISH TOURISM

Tourism is an important source of income for Scotland. People are lured to the region by its beautifully wild Highland scenery. Scotland is steeped in history and visitors often take the opportunity to visit its many ancient castles. For centuries, Scotland was dominated by struggles between rival families, known as clans. Today one of the most popular tourist souvenirs is tartan – textiles woven in the colours of the clans.

Most of Scotland consists of high mountains and remote glens or valleys.

The Scottish emblem is the thistle.

The Irish shamrock emblem

NORTHERN IRELAND

Prior to the the 1960s, the economy of Northern Ireland was based on manufacturing, engineering, shipbuilding, and textiles. Heavy industry was concentrated in Belfast where shipbuilding (above) was the largest employer. However, civil disorder after 1968 had a detrimental effect on the economy and, as across the whole of the UK, the manufacturing industry has been in decline since then.

Find out more

ENGLAND
NORTHERN IRELAND
SCOTLAND
WALES

| Volcano | Mountain | Ancient monument | Capital city | Large city/ town | Small city/ town |

SHETLAND ISLANDS

STATISTICS

Area: 244,880 sq km (94,550 sq miles)
Population: 61,634,000
Capital: London
Languages: English, Welsh, Scottish Gaelic, Irish Gaelic
Religions: Anglican, Roman Catholic, Presbyterian, Muslim, Methodist
Currency: Pound sterling
Main occupations: Finance, engineering, oil and gas production, manufacturing, agriculture
Main exports: Oil, natural gas, chemicals, electronics, cars, aircraft
Main imports: Machinery, fruit and vegetables, metals, raw materials

ENGLAND
Area: 130,423 sq km (50,356 sq miles)
Population: 51,456,000
Capital: London

SCOTLAND
Area: 78,133 sq km (30,167 sq miles)
Population: 5,169,000
Capital: Edinburgh

WALES
Area: 20,766 sq km (8,017 sq miles)
Population: 2,980,000
Capital: Cardiff

NORTHERN IRELAND (no official flag)
Area: 14,695 sq km (5,674 sq miles)
Population: 1,759,000
Capital: Belfast

SCALE BAR

0   50   100   km

0   50   100 miles

ENGLISH CHANNEL
British people call the narrow stretch of sea that separates their country from France the English Channel; but the French call it La Manche, which means "The Sleeve".

NORTH SEA OIL

The discovery of oil under the North Sea greatly benefitted the British economy from the 1980s. Construction and operation of the oil drilling platforms provided many jobs, and money from oil sales allowed the British government to cut taxes.

CHANNEL ISLANDS

HISTORY OF THE
UNITED KINGDOM

IN 1801, THE UNITED KINGDOM came into being with the Act of Union. Before that there had been four separate nations: England, Wales, Scotland, and Ireland. However, England had begun taking over the government of Wales in the 1000s, Ireland in the 1100s, and had shared a joint monarchy with Scotland since 1603. The United Kingdom is a small country, but by 1850 it had become the richest and most powerful nation in the world, controlling the largest empire in history. Even today, the Commonwealth includes more than 40 independent countries that were once British colonies. The United Kingdom has often been forced to fight long and bitter wars, but has survived and prospered because of its island position and its strong navy. The British system of laws and government by Parliament has become a model which many other nations have copied.

PALAEOLITHIC SETTLERS
A quarter of a million years ago, during mild conditions between two Ice Ages, people began to settle in Britain. They walked across the bridge of land which joined Britain to Europe at the time.

BATTLE OF HASTINGS

In 1066, a battle changed the course of English history. A Norman army led by William the Conqueror defeated an English king, Harold of Wessex, at Hastings, in southern England. William's descendants have ruled the country ever since. As king, he built castles in his new kingdom and gave land to powerful barons. They in turn give land to local lords for agreeing to fight for them. Peasants farmed the land of the local lord, and paid rent in produce and money. This system was called feudalism.

HENRY VIII
A truly multitalented king, Henry VIII was an expert at many things, from jousting and archery to lute-playing and languages. His impact on England was tremendous. In 1541, he forced the Irish Parliament to recognize him as king of Ireland. He also broke from the Roman Catholic Church, in order to divorce his wife, and became head of a new Church of England. Henry was an absolute ruler who executed anyone who displeased him, including two of his six wives.

MAGNA CARTA
The Magna Carta (Great Charter) of 1215 was an agreement between the king and the nobles of England. The charter promised that the king would not abuse his royal power to tax the nobles. This important moment in English history was the start of the belief that even kings must obey certain laws of the land.

UNITED KINGDOM

43 CE Ancient Romans, under Claudius, invade Britain and make it part of their empire.

411 Romans leave Britain.

c. 500 Christian missionaries arrive in Britain and preach Christianity to the people.

UNION FLAG
The flag of the United Kingdom is made up from the red crosses of St. George of England and St. Patrick of Ireland, plus the white St. Andrew's cross of Scotland, on a blue background. Wales has its own flag.

c. 870 Viking conquest of Britain begins.

1066 Normans invade Britain.

1215 Magna Carta agreement between the king and the nobles of England.

1282 Edward I, king of England, conquers Wales.

1485 Battle of Bosworth. Henry VII becomes the first Tudor king.

1534 Parliament declares Henry VIII head of the Church of England.

1588 English navy defeats the Spanish Armada (fleet) sent by Philip II, king of Spain.

CHARLES II
The Parliamentary army defeated and executed King Charles I during the English Civil War (1642-51). For nine years Oliver Cromwell (1599-1658), a member of Parliament, and his army ruled the country as a republic. In 1660, Charles' son returned from travels abroad (above) and claimed the throne as King Charles II. The nation, weary of the republic, welcomed him.

ADMIRAL NELSON
The most famous and daring commander of the British Royal Navy was Admiral Horatio Nelson (1758-1805), who defeated the Spanish and French at the Battle of Trafalgar (1805). Before the battle he said "England expects every man to do his duty". Nelson was fatally wounded in the battle.

CHARTISTS
During the 19th century, British people fought for the right to vote. Groups such as the Chartists (1837-48) organized demonstrations demanding a fairer system with representation for all, a secret voting system, and regular elections. Above is a Chartist riot being crushed by the police.

IMMIGRATION
The United Kingdom has become a multiracial and multicultural society, with immigration mainly from Commonwealth countries in the Caribbean, and from many of the Asian nations. This picture, taken in the 1960s, shows new arrivals from Jamaica receiving meals at a hostel set up to provide support for immigrants.

WELFARE STATE
In 1945, following the end of World War II, a Labour government came into power and introduced a welfare state and universal free education. This placed most hospitals under public control. It also provided welfare for people "from the cradle to the grave", including free medical treatment under the National Health Service.

European Parliament building in Strasbourg, France

CONSTITUTIONAL CHANGES
In 1973 Britain joined the European Community (now the European Union). Gradually, more power over matters such as trade has moved from the British parliament in London to European institutions in Brussels. In 1907 Scotland and Wales voted for "devolution", decentralizing power away from London to local institutions, including a Scottish parliament in Edinburgh.

UNITED KINGDOM

1642-51 Civil War between the King and Parliament.

1660 Charles II becomes King of England.

1707 Act of Union unites England, Wales, and Scotland.

1801 Ireland united with Great Britain.

1900 Britain is the strongest, richest country in the world.

1914-18 Britain fights in World War I.

1931 Commonwealth of Nations is established.

1939-45 Britain fights in World War II.

1945 Welfare state introduced.

1973 Britain becomes a member of the European Community (now the EU).

1997 Scotland votes in favour of its own parliament.

Find out more
ELIZABETH I
ENGLISH CIVIL WAR
EUROPEAN UNION
INDUSTRIAL REVOLUTION
NORMANS
UNITED KINGDOM
VICTORIANS

REGIONAL HISTORY OF
UNITED KINGDOM

ALFRED THE GREAT
Known as the "Great", Alfred was the grandson of Ecgberht of Wessex (r. 829-39), the first person to unite England.

FOR MUCH OF ITS HISTORY, the United Kingdom has been anything but united. England, Wales, Scotland, and Ireland were all once separate countries and have often split into rival kingdoms themselves. Since the 1100s, England has tried to unite the countries of the British Isles under its rule. In 1171 England invaded Ireland, although it failed to win control; a century later, England conquered Wales. Until the 1600s, Scotland and England were deadly enemies. They were only united when a Scottish king inherited the English throne. The United Kingdom as we know it came into being in 1801, when the final Act of Union was passed between Ireland and the rest of the country, athough most of Ireland left the union in 1922. Today, the separate parts of the country are regaining control of their affairs from London.

Conwy Castle was built during the 1200s. Conwy is on the north coast of Wales.

Melrose Abbey

SCOTLAND

The first true king of Scotland was Kenneth MacAlpin, who united the country north of the River Forth in 843. By 1018 the country was united within roughly its present borders. For the next 200 years Scottish kings fought a long series of border wars with England. They built many stone castles, as well as several abbeys, such as Melrose.

INVASION OF WALES

In 1277, the English King Edward I demanded that the Welsh Prince Llywelyn Yr Ail accept him as the ultimate ruler of Wales. Llywelyn refused and so Edward invaded. After the death of Llywelyn in 1282, Wales became part of England. In order to keep control, Edward built 10 great stone castles throughout the principality.

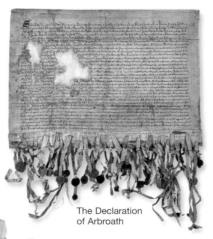

Robert the Bruce

Hero of Scottish independence, Robert the Bruce led 30,000 men to victory against an English army of 100,000 under King Edward II at the Battle of Bannockburn.

BANNOCKBURN

In 1290 Margaret, the young queen of Scotland, died without an heir. The Scottish lords asked Edward I of England to choose a successor, but in 1296 he took direct control of Scotland. William Wallace (c. 1274-1305) – Braveheart – rose in revolt against English rule but was executed in 1305. Robert the Bruce (1274-1319) continued the fight, finally defeating the English army at Bannockburn in 1314.

The Declaration of Arbroath

DECLARATION OF ARBROATH

After their victory at Bannockburn, the Scots expected the English to leave them alone. This did not happen, so in 1320 the Scottish lords and bishops met at Arbroath to draw up a petition to Pope John XXII, asking him to recognize Scottish independence. In 1328, the English finally recognized Scotland as an independent nation.

INVASION OF IRELAND

In 1155, Pope Adrian IV authorized King Henry II to bring the Irish Church into line with the Catholic Church in Rome. Henry invaded in 1171, forcing the Irish bishops to submit to Rome at the Rock of Cashel. The invasion marked the start of English involvement in Ireland.

Rock of Cashel

UNION OF ENGLAND AND SCOTLAND

In 1603, Elizabeth I of England died. Her heir was her distant cousin, James VI of Scotland. He also took over the English throne as James I, so uniting the two countries. Scotland kept its own parliament, Church, and judicial system until 1707, when the Act of Union united the two parliaments in London. In 1999, Scotland once again had its own parliament.

James I of England and VI of Scotland

BATTLE OF THE BOYNE

In 1688, Catholic King James II was forced off the English throne. Irish Catholics objected and started a rebellion. They asked James to lead them, and he brought troops from France. However, in 1690, the Protestant English King William III defeated the Catholics at the Battle of the Boyne.

CULLODEN

After Queen Anne died in 1714, the British throne went to the German King George I. Many Scots believed that Catholic James Edward Stuart (1688-1766), son of James II, should be king. In 1715, they rose in revolt. The rebellion failed, but in 1745, the Scots tried again under Charles Edward Stuart (1720-88), known as Bonnie Prince Charlie. They were defeated at Culloden Moor in 1746.

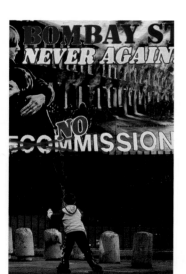

NORTHERN IRELAND

During the 19th century, Irish Catholics campaigned for Home Rule for Ireland. Northern Irish Protestants objected to this. In 1920-22 the British government divided Ireland, setting up separate states in northern and southern Ireland, each with its own parliament. Many Northern Irish Catholics, continue to campaign for a united Ireland free of British rule.

GOOD FRIDAY

In 1972 the Northern Ireland parliament was closed because it could not keep the peace between Protestants and Catholics. Eventually, US senator George Mitchell and the British minister Mo Mowlam worked out an agreement to share power between all political parties. It was signed on Good Friday, 10 April, 1998. However, there have been problems making power-sharing work.

DEVOLUTION

For some years, many people in Scotland and Wales have wanted devolution, the passing of power from England to their own parliaments. In 1998, the British government held a vote on devolution in both countries. A Scottish parliament and a Welsh Assembly were then set up. They both met for the first time in 1999.

Many football fans, such as this young Scot, paint their country's flag on their faces in support of their national team.

THE REGIONS OF THE UNITED KINGDOM

871-899 Alfred rules England.

1018 Malcolm II unites Scotland.

1171 Henry II invades Ireland.

1200s Wales united.

1277-84 England conquers Wales.

1296 Edward I of England rules Scotland.

1314 English defeated at Bannockburn and driven out of Scotland.

1320 Scottish lords draw up Declaration of Arbroath.

1536 Act of Union between England and Wales.

1603 Scottish and English crowns unite.

1690s Protestants take complete control of Ireland.

1707 Act of Union between Scotland and England.

1746 Scots defeated at Culloden.

1801 Act of Union between Britain and Ireland.

1920-22 Ireland divided into north and south.

1999 Scotland and Wales get devolved government.

Find out more
ENGLAND
NORTHERN IRELAND
SCOTLAND
WALES

UNITED NATIONS

IN 1945, AT THE END of World War II, the nations that opposed Germany, Italy, and Japan decided that such a war must never be repeated. They set up the United Nations, with the aim of preventing future conflicts, and drew up the United Nations Charter. The United Nations (UN) met for the first time in San Francisco in 1945. Today, 192 nations belong to the UN. The UN consists of six main organs: the General Assembly, the Security Council, the Secretariat, the Economic and Social Council, the Trusteeship Council, and the International Court of Justice. Each is concerned with world peace and social justice. The UN also has agencies which deal with global issues such as health. Each member nation of the UN has a seat in the General Assembly; 15 nations sit on the Security Council. The UN is not without problems. Its members often disagree, and it suffers financial difficulties.

LEAGUE OF NATIONS
In 1919, the victors of World War I including Great Britain, founded the League of Nations to keep peace. But in 1935 the League failed to prevent Italy from invading Ethiopia. In 1946, the League's functions were transferred to the UN. Haile Selassie, emperor of Ethiopia, is seen addressing the League, above.

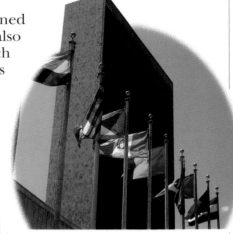

UNITED NATIONS
The headquarters of the UN in New York City, United States, is where the General Assembly and Security Council meet, as well as many of the specialist agencies of the organization. Politicians from every member nation come to New York to address the UN, and many international disputes and conflicts are settled here.

SECURITY COUNCIL

The aim of the Security Council is to maintain peace in the world. It investigates any event which might lead to fighting. The council has five permanent members – Britain, the United States, the Russian Federation, France, and China – and 10 members elected for two years each.

UN SYMBOL
The symbol of the United Nations (above) consists of a map of the world surrounded by a wreath of olive branches, symbolizing peace.

UNICEF
The United Nations Children's Fund (UNICEF) is one of the most successful agencies of the UN. UNICEF was originally founded to help child victims of World War II. The fund now provides education, health care, and medical help for children across the world, particularly in areas devastated by war or famine. Much of its work takes place in the poorer countries of Africa and Asia.

Children in underdeveloped countries are immunized against disease, thanks to UNICEF.

PEACEKEEPING
The UN is sometimes called on to send a peacekeeping force to a country in order to prevent war. In 1989, a UN force was sent to Namibia, southern Africa, to supervise the elections that led to Namibia's independence. More recently, a UN peacekeeping mission was established to help uphold a peace agreement in Darfur, southern Sudan.

Find out more
EUROPE, HISTORY OF
GOVERNMENT AND POLITICS
WORLD WAR I
WORLD WAR II

UNITED STATES OF AMERICA

ON THE FLAG OF the United States, 50 identical stars represent the country's 50 states. But the states themselves could not be more different. If the stars showed their areas, the largest, for Alaska, would be nearly 500 times bigger than the star for the smallest state, Rhode Island. If the stars showed population, Alaska's star would be the smallest, and the star for California, which has the most people, would be more than 50 times larger. The states vary in other ways, too. The Rocky Mountains in the western states reach more than 4,400 m (14,400 ft) in height, but flat plains extend for hundreds of kilometres across the country's centre. At Barrow, Alaska, the most northerly town, the average temperature is just -13°C (9°F), yet in Arizona temperatures have reached 57°C (134°F). Since 1945, the USA has played a leading role in world affairs. The nation is the most powerful in the Western world. American finance, culture, and politics have spread outward from the United States. Products made in the United States are available in every country. Decisions made by American politicians affect the lives of many people throughout the world.

The United States covers much of the continent of North America. It reaches from the Atlantic to the Pacific oceans and from the Mexican border to Canada. The nation covers a total of 9.37 million sq km (3.68 million sq miles).

NASA

The United States is a world leader in technology, particularly in space research. The National Aeronautics and Space Administration (NASA) spends millions of dollars every year on satellites and spacecraft. In 1969, Neil Armstrong, commander of NASA's *Apollo 11*, became the first man to walk on the moon. One of NASA's recent successes is the space shuttle, a reusable spacecraft.

Operatives monitor data in a NASA space shuttle control centre.

STATE AND FEDERAL GOVERNMENT
The United States is a democracy and has a written constitution which sets out how government works. State governments, which meet in the state capital, have the authority to make laws affecting their own residents. The states were once nearly self-governing, but today the federal, or national, government has more power. It makes decisions on foreign policy and can pass laws which affect the entire country.

NEW YORK CITY

At the mouth of the Hudson River on the east coast of the United States is New York City, the country's biggest city. It is also one of the oldest. New York was founded in the 1620s and is now an urban area with 8 million people. The city is the financial heart of the nation and houses the offices of many large companies and dozens of theatres, museums, and parks. Skyscrapers more than 300 m (1,000 ft) tall dominate the city centre, Manhattan.

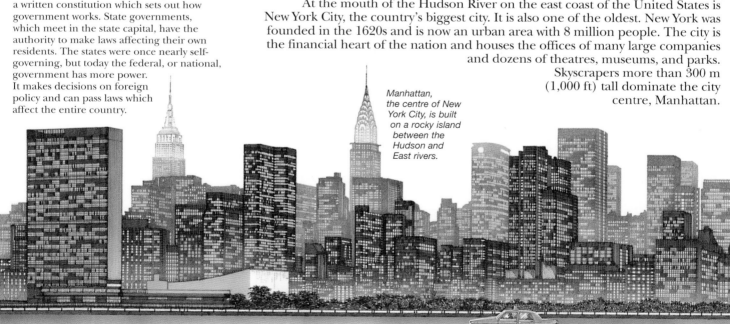

Manhattan, the centre of New York City, is built on a rocky island between the Hudson and East rivers.

HAWAII AND ALASKA

Hawaii, a group of tropical islands in the Pacific Ocean, became the fiftieth US state in 1959. The islands produce pineapples, sugar, and coffee. Polynesians first settled Hawaii in the 700s, and many native Polynesians still live here. Alaska lies outside the main part of the United States, too, separated from the other states by Canada.

The Sugar Train *on the Hawaiian island of Maui*

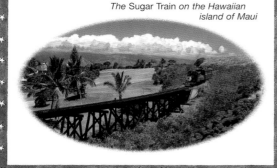

CALIFORNIA

In 1848 gold was discovered in California, and many people rushed to the region to prospect for it. California is still the state with the most inhabitants. About 36 million people live there. Most of the state has a mild, sunny climate and produces vast amounts of fruit. Many towns in California have become resorts. Modern industries have started up in California; the so-called Silicon Valley, for example, is a centre for the computer business.

Cable cars still carry passengers up some of the 43 hills on which the city of San Francisco, California, is built.

AMERICAN PEOPLE

Native Americans, the original Americans, now make up only a small part of the total population of more than 307 million. Most people are the descendants of settlers from overseas and speak English. They live in the same neighbourhoods and mingle in everyday life. Their cultures have also mingled, producing a new form of English different from that spoken in England. Some groups, such as the Chinese and the Italians, also keep their own traditions and language alive in small, urban communities.

The Grand Canyon is a favourite tourist attraction, and many people ride to the bottom on mules.

BASEBALL
Baseball is the USA's top sport, and was first played between two organized teams in 1846.

HOLLYWOOD
Hollywood, in Los Angeles, was founded in 1887 as a community for Christians. Today, it is the centre of America's film industry. Many movie studios are based here, and actors, actresses and other celebrities live and work nearby. The area is a big tourist attraction. Visitors come to spot the stars and to take photos of the Hollywood sign (right) in the Hollywood Hills.

BLUES
During the 17th, 18th, and 19th centuries thousands of Africans were brought to America as slaves. Slavery was outlawed in 1865, and since then black writers, artists, and musicians have made their mark on American culture. The popular music known as blues originated among slaves in the southern states of America.

Famous blues singer B.B. King (born 1925) has played his guitar, named Lucille, in concerts all over the world.

GRAND CANYON
There are many natural wonders in the United States; one of the most impressive is the Grand Canyon in Arizona. The Colorado River took thousands of years to cut the canyon by natural erosion through solid rock. It is 29 km (18 miles) wide in places and more than 1,800 m (6,000 ft) deep.

> **Find out more**
>
> ASTRONAUTS
> and space travel
> COLOMBUS, CHRISTOPHER
> GOVERNMENT AND POLITICS

Legend
Volcano	Mountain	Ancient monument	Capital city	Large city/town	Small city/town

STATISTICS
Area: 9,372,610 sq km (3,681,760 sq miles)
Population: 307,212,000
Capital: Washington, DC
Languages: English, Spanish, Italian, German, French, Polish, Chinese, Tagalog, Greek
Religions: Protestant, Roman Catholic, Jewish, non-religious
Currency: US dollar
Main occupations: Research, manufacturing, agriculture
Main exports: Energy, raw materials, food, electronics, cars, coal
Main imports: Oil

MIDWEST
The United States is the world's largest exporter of wheat and produces nearly half of the corn on Earth. This enormous quantity of food is grown on the open plains that cover the Midwest between the Mississippi River and the Rockies. Grain farming is highly mechanized, with giant machines operating in fields hundreds of hectares in size. The United States also produces one quarter of the world's oranges, one seventh of the world's nuts, and half of the world's soya beans.

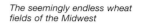

The seemingly endless wheat fields of the Midwest

INDUSTRY
Most of the industries in the United States are the largest and most profitable of their type in the world. America has abundant mineral deposits, raw materials, and energy sources. The most economically important industries in the US include car manufacturing, food processing, textile and clothing manufacture, and the computer industry. "Silicon Valley" in California is a world centre for micro-electronics. New York City is the nation's financial capital while Washington has an important aerospace industry.

BORDER
The border between Canada and the USA is the world's longest land border between any two countries.

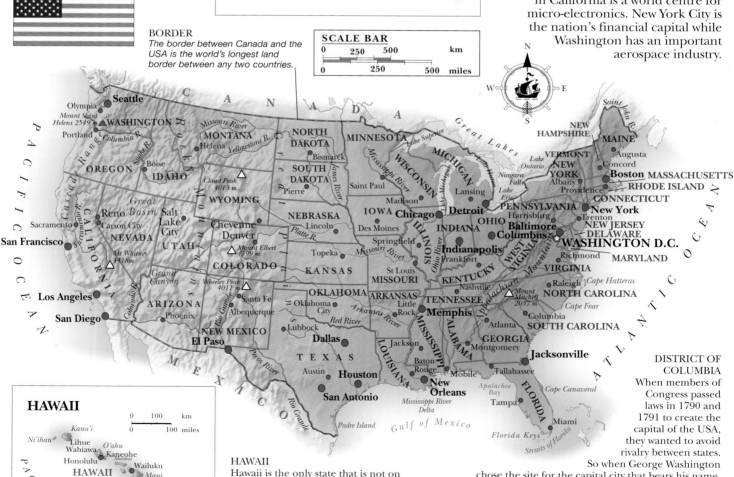

ALASKA

HAWAII

HAWAII
Hawaii is the only state that is not on the North American mainland. The eight main islands of the group are some 3,380 km (2,100 miles) southwest of San Francisco. Although most of the population lives on the island of Oahu, Hawai'i itself is the biggest island.

DISTRICT OF COLUMBIA
When members of Congress passed laws in 1790 and 1791 to create the capital of the USA, they wanted to avoid rivalry between states. So when George Washington chose the site for the capital city that bears his name, the region was created as a special district, called the District of Columbia (D.C.). However, D.C. is not a state, and although the people who live there take part in Congressional elections, their delegate in the House of Representatives cannot vote.

HISTORY OF THE
UNITED STATES

TODAY, THE UNITED STATES OF AMERICA is the most powerful nation on Earth. Yet, just 230 years ago the United States was a new and vulnerable nation. It occupied a narrow strip of land on the Atlantic coast of North America and had a population of only about four million people. Beyond its borders lay vast areas of unclaimed land. Throughout the 19th century, American settlers pushed the frontier westwards across that land, fighting the Native Americans for control. At the same time, millions of immigrants from Europe were arriving on the East Coast. By 1900, the nation's farms and factories were producing more than any other country. That wealth and power led to its involvement in international affairs and drew it into two world wars. But the country continued to prosper. Since 1945 the system of individual enterprise that inspired the founders of the United States has made its people among the world's richest. American business, influence, and culture have spread to every other nation in the world.

FOUNDING FATHERS

The United States originally consisted of 13 states, each with its own customs and history. In 1787 George Washington and other leaders, sometimes called the Founding Fathers, drew up the United States Constitution, a document that established a strong central government. The Constitution, which also safeguards the rights of the states and those of their people, has been in force since 1789.

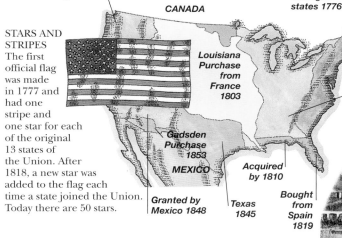

Oregon 1846

CANADA

13 original states 1776

STARS AND STRIPES
The first official flag was made in 1777 and had one stripe and one star for each of the original 13 states of the Union. After 1818, a new star was added to the flag each time a state joined the Union. Today there are 50 stars.

Louisiana Purchase from France 1803

Acquired by 1783

Gadsden Purchase 1853

MEXICO

Acquired by 1810

Granted by Mexico 1848

Texas 1845

Bought from Spain 1819

GROWTH OF THE UNITED STATES
The 13 original colonies on the East Coast gained their independence from Britain in 1783, and acquired all the land as far west as the Mississippi River. In 1803 the vast area of Louisiana was bought from France, and by 1848 the United States had reached the Pacific Ocean.

FALL OF THE SOUTH
The Civil War ended in 1865, leaving the South in ruinous poverty. The hatred and bitterness caused by the war lasted for many years as the central government took temporary control of the defeated southern states.

SPREAD OF THE RAILWAY
In 1860 there were more than 48,000 km (30,000 miles) of railways in the eastern United States, but almost none had been built west of the Mississippi River. On 10 May 1869, the first continental railway was completed, and the two coasts of America were joined for the first time. A ceremony was held at Promontory Point in Utah to mark the occasion. The growth of the national railway network helped unify the country.

IMMIGRATION

During the 19th century many Europeans crossed the Atlantic in search of new freedoms and opportunities. The United States welcomed Irish people escaping famine, eastern European Jews fleeing persecution, and countless others. By 1890, half a million immigrants were arriving each year in the United States. As a result, the country became a mixture of many different cultures and religions.

INDUSTRY

The United States offered an endless supply of raw materials to 19th-century industrialists, who soon took advantage of these resources. Manufacturers such as Ransom Olds pioneered mass production of cars and many other goods. In the Olds Motor Works, cars moved along a production line, with workers at intervals each performing a single task. This technique made assembly faster, and Henry Ford and other manufacturers quickly adopted it.

Immigrants arriving in the United States were examined at a reception centre on Ellis Island, New York.

THE UNITED STATES AT WAR

Until the United States entered World War I in 1917, its armed forces had rarely fought overseas. After the war ended the United States tried once again to stay out of conflicts abroad. But in 1941 the Japanese attacked Pearl Harbor naval base in Hawaii, bringing the U.S. into World War II. Since 1945, the U.S. has fought in several overseas wars, notably in Korea (1950-53) and Vietnam (1961-73).

The Iwo Jima monument in Arlington National Cemetery is a memorial to Americans who died in World War II. It shows Marines raising the flag on Iwo Jima Island in the Pacific. Many US soldiers died in the battle for the island.

JOHN F. KENNEDY

In 1960, John F. Kennedy (1917-63) became the youngest man ever elected president. In 1961, Kennedy approved the invasion of Communist Cuba by US-backed Cuban exiles. The invasion, at the Bay of Pigs, was a disaster, and Kennedy was severely criticized. In 1962 the Soviets stationed nuclear missiles on the island. For one week, nuclear war seemed unavoidable, but Kennedy persuaded the Soviet Union to remove the missiles and averted the war. Kennedy's presidency ended tragically on 22 November 1963, when he was assassinated during a visit to Dallas, Texas, United States, after serving for exactly 1,000 days in office.

CHICAGO DAILY NEWS

PRESIDENT IS KILLED
Texas Sniper Escapes; Johnson Sworn In

Story Begins on Next Page

EQUAL OPPORTUNITIES

Since 1789, the US Constitution has guaranteed every citizen equal rights. In reality, many minority groups are only now starting to achieve equality. The photograph shows Barack Obama, the United States' first African American president.

UNITED STATES

1783 The 13 colonies win their freedom from Britain.

1787 Constitution is drafted.

1789 George Washington becomes the first president.

1790-1800 A new capital, Washington, D.C., is built on the Potomac River.

1803 Louisiana Purchase doubles size of the country.

1845 Texas joins the Union.

1848 US defeats Mexico and acquires California and other territories.

1861-65 Civil War ends slavery

1869 First transcontinental railroad is completed.

1917-1918 US fights in World War I.

1929 Economic depression.

1941 United States enters World War II.

1963 President Kennedy assassinated.

1969 Neil Armstrong walks on the moon.

1991 US leads United Nations forces against Iraq in the Gulf War.

2001 Islamic terrorists destroy the World Trade Center.

2003 US invades Iraq.

Find out more
CARS
COLD WAR
EMIGRATION AND IMMIGRATION
PILGRIMS
TRADE AND INDUSTRY
UNITED STATES OF AMERICA
VIETNAM WAR
WORLD WAR II

UNIVERSE

THE VAST EXPANSE OF SPACE that we call the universe contains everything there is. It includes the Sun, the planets, the Milky Way galaxy, and all other galaxies too. The universe is continually growing, and each part is gradually moving further away from every other part. We know about the universe by using powerful telescopes to study light, radio waves, x-rays, and other radiations that reach Earth from space. Light travels nearly 9.5 billion km (6 billion miles) in a year. We call this distance a light-year. The light from a distant star that you can see through a telescope may have travelled thousands of years to reach us. Most scientists believe that the universe was created by a massive explosive event that happened billions of years ago. This idea is called the Big Bang theory. Many scientists now believe that visible matter makes up only 7 per cent of the universe and that the rest is dark matter and dark energy.

Milky Way has a halo of stars and gas.

MILKY WAY
The Sun is just one of 100 billion stars in the large spiral galaxy we call the Milky Way. Like most other spiral galaxies, the Milky Way has curved arms of stars radiating from a globe-shaped centre. The Milky Way is 100,000 light-years across, and the Sun is 30,000 light-years from its centre.

GALAXIES

Galaxies, which contain gas, dust, and billions of stars, belong to one of three main groups – elliptical, irregular, or spiral. Most galaxies are elliptical, ranging from sphere shapes to egg shapes. A few galaxies are irregular. Others, such as the Milky Way, are spirals. The universe consists of billions of galaxies of all types.

Pieces of paper represent clusters of galaxies.

GALAXY CLUSTERS
Most galaxies belong to groups called clusters, which may contain thousands of galaxies of all types. These clusters form "walls" with great voids in between, so that the universe is like a foam.

In this image the galaxies are yellow and red, and the blue haloes around them represent dark matter.

Balloon expands in the same way that the universe is expanding.

THE EXPANDING UNIVERSE
You can get an idea of how the universe is expanding by imagining several small pieces of paper glued onto a balloon. Each piece represents a cluster of galaxies. As you blow up the balloon, all the paper pieces move further away from one another. In the same way, galaxy clusters are moving further away from one another. The further a cluster is, the faster it travels away from us.

THE INVISIBLE UNIVERSE
When scientists estimate the mass of a galaxy cluster, the figure usually turns out to be much more than the mass of the visible galaxies alone. The extra, invisible matter is called dark matter, and no-one knows what it is. Dark matter and ordinary matter together account for only 30% of the universe. Scientists call the remaining 70% dark energy. Dark energy is like a force that acts against gravity and pushes the galaxies apart. It is causing the expansion of the universe to speed up.

LOOKING BACK IN TIME
If you look through a telescope you can see galaxies millions of light-years away. You are not seeing them as they are now but as they were long ago, when their light first set out on its journey – so in a sense, you are looking into the past.

Dinosaurs lived on Earth 65–215 million years ago.

Galaxy is 100 million light-years away. Light left this galaxy when the dinosaurs lived on Earth.

Find out more
ASTRONOMY
BIG BANG
EARTH
LIGHT
MOON
PLANETS
SPACE FLIGHT
STARS
SUN
TELESCOPES

335

VICTORIANS

UNDER THE RULE OF QUEEN VICTORIA, the British people enjoyed a long period of prosperity. Profits gained from the Empire overseas, as well as from industrial improvements at home, allowed a large, educated middle-class to develop. Great advances were made in the arts and sciences. In the cities, department stores were opened for the convenience of those with cash to spend. Domestic servants were employed in many homes, although vast numbers of people remained poor and lived in slums. Public transport, police forces, clean water supplies, and sewage treatment were introduced to ease conditions in the new towns. Like Victoria, middle-class people set high moral standards, and devised programmes to "improve" the lives of the poor. The Victorians thought themselves the most advanced society in the world.

QUEEN VICTORIA
Victoria (1819-1901) is best remembered dressed all in black and in mourning for her husband Albert, who died in 1861. Queen Victoria had great dignity and was highly respected by her subjects.

CRYSTAL PALACE
In 1851, a new building was erected in Hyde Park, London, to house the Great Exhibition. It was made entirely of glass and cast iron. Joseph Paxton designed it so it could be moved later and rebuilt in south London.

VICTORIAN STYLE
Victorians loved elaborate decoration. Almost all Victorian objects, from lamp posts to teaspoons were covered in carvings, patterns, and other ornamentation. Large houses and public buildings, such as St. Pancras station, London (right), were built in the style of ancient castles, cathedrals, and palaces.

St. Pancras station

THE GREAT EXHIBITION
In 1851, Prince Albert organized the first international exhibition in Britain. More than 6 million people visited the Crystal Palace (above) to celebrate the industrial age. The 14,000 exhibits included a 24-ton lump of coal, a railway engine, the Koh-i-noor diamond from India, and a stuffed elephant.

Egg whisk

Laundry starch

Servant's bell

Black grate polish

DOMESTIC LIFE
Servants were a feature of every upper- and middle-class household. Maids worked long hours for little or no pay, sometimes only for board and lodging. In 1871, more than ⅓ of British women aged 12-20 were "in service".

VICTORIANS

1837 Victoria becomes queen.

1842 Mines Act prevents women and children from working underground in mines.

1851 Great Exhibition held in London.

1863 First underground railway (the Metropolitan Line) opens, London.

1864 Factory Act bans children under eight years old from factory work.

1881 First electric street lighting is installed.

1882 Married Women's Property Act gives married women legal ownership of their property.

1891 Primary education in state schools made free.

1901 Queen Victoria dies.

MUSIC HALLS

Working people went to music halls for cheap and popular entertainment. Audiences could eat and drink while enjoying melodramas, acrobats, comedians, and singers. Sentimental songs were especially popular.

Acrobats performed exciting feats on stage in music halls.

The Martini-Henry rifle appeared around 1871. It had a range of 275 m (300 yards).

EMPIRE BUILDING

During Victoria's reign, there were dozens of small-scale wars as the various European nations carved out empires in Africa and Asia. The people who already lived in these places stood little chance against trained troops equipped with rifles and automatic guns.

The Gatling gun fired bullets at a rate of 1,000 rounds per minute.

HMS Warrior

IRONCLAD BATTLESHIPS
Britain kept a huge navy to protect and control an empire which spanned the world. Fast gunboats and powerful battleships – with armour-plated wooden hulls for protection – sailed to areas where there was trouble, defending British political and commercial interests wherever these were threatened.

SOCIAL REFORM
In Victorian times, a new industrial era resulted in a wealthy middle class. However, it also created a vast working class who often suffered terrible living and working conditions. Some boys worked as chimney sweeps in wealthy homes (above). Their plight was publicized by Charles Kingsley's novel *Water Babies*, and reformers such as Lord Shaftesbury campaigned for new labour laws.

Find out more

BRITISH EMPIRE
INDUSTRIAL REVOLUTION
SHIPS AND BOATS
UNITED KINGDOM, HISTORY OF

VIETNAM WAR

VIETNAM WAR

1859 France begins to colonize Vietnam.

1954 Vietnamese defeat French.

1956 Viet Cong lead rebellion against South Vietnamese government.

1961 United States sends advisers to train South Vietnamese army.

1964 Gulf of Tongkin clash between North Vietnamese and US naval craft leads to war.

1965 United States begins bombing of North; first US combat troops arrive in South.

1968 Tet (Vietnamese New Year) offensive by Viet Cong

1968 American troops massacre My Lai villagers.

1968 Antiwar protests in the US

1973 Cease-fire signed in Paris; American troops leave Vietnam.

1975 Vietnam reunited under Communist control.

BETWEEN 1956 AND 1975 Vietnam was the scene of one of the most destructive wars in modern history. In 1954, Vietnam defeated French colonial forces and was divided into two countries – a Communist North and a non-Communist South Vietnam. The Viet Cong (Vietnamese Communists) rebelled against the South Vietnamese government and, helped by North Vietnam under Ho Chi Minh, fought to reunite the country. This brought in the United States, which believed that if Vietnam fell to the Communists, nearby countries would fall too. During the 1960s the United States poured troops and money into Vietnam, but found itself in an undeclared war it could not win. Despite intensive bombing and the latest military technology, the Viet Cong were better equipped and trained for jungle warfare. Casualties in Vietnam were appalling, and strong opposition to the war developed in the United States. A cease-fire was negotiated, and in 1973 all American troops were withdrawn. Two years later North Vietnam captured Saigon, capital of South Vietnam, and Vietnam was united as a Communist country.

VIETNAM
Vietnam is in Southeast Asia. The war was fought in the jungles of South Vietnam and in the skies above North Vietnam. Viet Cong fighters received supplies from the North along the Ho Chi Minh trail. At the end of the war, the country was reunited with its capital at Hanoi. Saigon, the southern capital, was renamed Ho Chi Minh City.

TROOPS
The first American military personnel arrived in Vietnam during 1961 to advise the South Vietnamese government. By 1969 there were about 550,000 American troops in Vietnam.

DESTRUCTION
The lengthy fighting had a terrible effect on the people of Vietnam. Their fields were destroyed, their forests stripped of leaves, and their houses blown up, leaving them refugees. Thousands were killed, injured, or maimed.

COSTS
It is unlikely that the exact cost of the Vietnam war will ever be known, but in terms of lives lost, money spent, and bombs dropped, it was enormous. Both sides suffered huge casualties and emerged with seriously damaged economies.

The United States spent $150 billion on the war; there are no figures for what North Vietnam spent.

Four times as many bombs were dropped by the American Air Force on Vietnam than were dropped by British and American bombers on Germany during the whole of World War II.

More than one million South Vietnamese and between 500,000 and one million North Vietnamese died in the war; over 58,000 American soldiers and nurses lost their lives.

The US Air Force bombed the jungle with chemicals to strip the leaves off the trees. Much of Vietnam is still deforested today.

Find out more
ASIA, HISTORY OF
COMMUNISM
UNITED STATES, HISTORY OF

VIKINGS

BETWEEN THE 8TH AND 12TH CENTURIES CE, fierce warriors called Vikings terrorized the people of Europe. They came from Norway, Sweden, and Denmark, where the weather was cold and the soil was poor, to look for loot. At first they made lightning raids on coastal villages and isolated farms. They stole horses and food, captured prisoners for slaves, and robbed churches of their gold and silver. Later they conquered and settled in parts of England, France, Germany, Ireland, Italy, Russia, and Scotland. The Vikings were the finest shipbuilders of the time, and their swift, light boats could travel far from their homelands. They settled in Iceland and Greenland and were the first Europeans to reach North America. Although they are chiefly remembered for their conquests, most Nordic people lived peacefully in small settlements and worked as farmers, merchants, and craftsworkers.

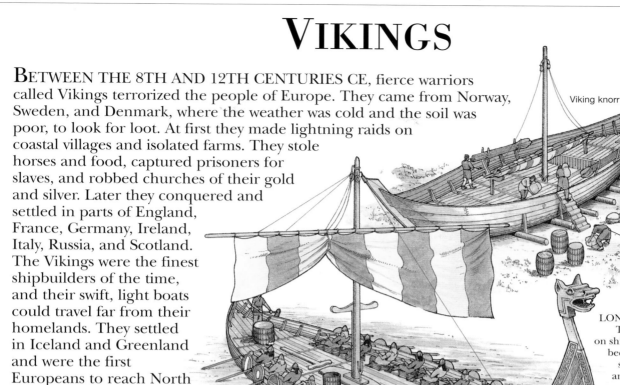

Viking knorr

Villagers loaded up the knorrs with farm produce, for trading purposes.

Viking longship

LONGSHIP AND KNORR

The Vikings depended on ships for transportation, because their lands were surrounded by the sea and covered with dense forests, which made travel difficult. They built magnificent longships out of wood cut from the vast Scandinavian forests. A longship carried about 80 warriors, who rowed and sailed the ship and also fought battles when they reached land. The Vikings also built smaller ships called knorrs, which they used for trading and transporting goods.

WARRIORS

Viking warriors usually fought with swords and battle axes, although some used spears, and bows and arrows. They carried wooden shields, and some wore armour made of layers of thick animal hides. Viking chieftains often wore metal helmets and chainmail armour.

Swedish helmet (7th century)

A warrior used both hands to swing the long-handled battle axe at an enemy.

The sword was among the fearsome weapons carried by the Vikings.

BURIALS
Important Vikings were buried with their ships. Relatives placed the body in a wooden cabin on the deck. Sometimes, dogs, horses, cattle, and slaves were buried with their owners. The body of a great warrior might be burned on a pile of wood or placed on the deck of a longship which was then set alight.

Relatives have surrounded the body with the dead person's most treasured possessions, including his horse.

VIKING FAMILIES

Some Vikings lived in bustling trading towns, such as York, England. But most lived in isolated farming settlements. Everything the family needed had to be made or grown on the farm. Viking women had more rights than many other European women of the time. For instance, they were allowed to get divorced if they wished.

Find out more

EUROPE, HISTORY OF
NORMANS

VOLCANOES

LIVING IN THE SHADOW of a volcano can be a source of constant fear. An active volcano can erupt with little warning: smoke and hot ash billow from the crater at the volcano's summit, and red-hot lava flows down the slopes, setting fire to everything in its path. Volcanoes are caused by the movement of vast slabs of rock, called plates, in the Earth's surface. When the plates collide or spread apart, molten rock from deep underground is forced to the surface, at or near the place where the plates meet. There are about 850 active volcanoes in the world. Most lie in a belt called the Ring of Fire, which surrounds the Pacific Ocean. Volcanoes also occur in the ocean, where they form underwater mountains or islands, such as Hawaii.

Cloud of ash and gas pours out from crater.

Magma rises up the main pipe and branch pipes. If thick, slow-flowing lava blocks the main pipe, the volcano may explode.

Magma chamber forms deep underground.

Volcano builds up with layers of ash and solidified lava.

VOLCANIC ERUPTIONS

A volcano lies over a deep chamber of red-hot, molten rock, called magma. Pressure from hot gases forces the magma up to the surface. The molten rock, now called lava, melts a hole through the rock above and flows out. Layers of lava and volcanic ash cool and solidify, building up a cone-shaped mountain with a central pipe through which lava flows. Most volcanoes do not erupt continuously. Between eruptions, active volcanoes are called dormant. Extinct volcanoes are those that are no longer active.

Red-hot lava flows down side of volcano.

Earth's crust is formed of layers of different kinds of rock. Close to the centre of the Earth, the intense heat melts the rock.

MAGMA
A volcano's shape depends on the magma it produces. Thick magma produces a steep cone; runny magma results in a flattened, shieldlike volcano. Some volcano cones are made only of ash.

LAVA
Molten rock which has escaped to the Earth's surface is called lava. A bubbling lake of molten rock fills the crater of the volcano, and fountains of fiery lava leap high into the air. Glowing streams of lava pour out of the crater and flow down the sides of the volcano like rivers of fire. The lava has a temperature of about 1,100°C (2,000°F), which is hot enough to melt steel.

PUMICE
Lava containing bubbles of gas hardens to form a rock called pumice, which is peppered with tiny holes. The holes make pumice very light; it is the only rock that can float in water.

POMPEII
In 79 CE, Mount Vesuvius in Italy erupted. Clouds of ash shot into the air, while pyroclastic flows (clouds of hot ash and air) swept down the mountain, burning all in their paths. Archaeologists have uncovered much of Pompeii, where the bodies of the victims left hollows in the ash. The plaster cast below is made from such a hollow and shows the last moments of a person killed by a pyroclastic flow. Vesuvius last erupted in 1944. It could erupt again at any time. Another volcanic disaster occurred on the island of Krakatoa, Indonesia, in 1883.

GEYSERS
A jet of boiling water which suddenly shoots up from the ground is called a geyser. Hot rock deep below the surface heats water in an underground chamber so that it boils. Steam forces the water out in a jet. When the chamber refills and heats up, the geyser blows again.

Find out more
CONTINENTS
EARTH
EARTHQUAKES
MOUNTAINS
ROCKS AND MINERALS

WALES

FROM THE WILDS OF ITS NORTHERN mountains to the industrial valleys of the south, Wales covers an area of 20,761 sq km (8,014 sq miles). It has a population of almost 3 million and is the smallest country in the United Kingdom. Wales has been under English control since the late 13th century, although in 1999 a Welsh Assembly was introduced, giving Wales limited self-government. Until recently, coal mining was a major industry, particularly in the south, but by the 1990s most mines had closed, causing widespread unemployment. Sheep and cattle farming have remained economically important. Wales has a strong national identity, with its own language and a long tradition of music and song. Welsh choirs are famous worldwide.

WELSH DRAGON
The Welsh flag carries a red dragon, the national symbol of Wales.

Wales lies on a peninsula (land jutting into the sea) in western Great Britain. It is bordered by England on its eastern border and the Irish Sea to the west.

CARDIFF
Located on the south coast of Wales, Cardiff is the country's capital and the largest city. It is also the headquarters of the new Welsh Assembly. For many years Cardiff was a major port, exporting coal from the valleys in the south. The port has declined, but the city is still an administrative and business centre.

WELSH COUNTRYSIDE
Much of Wales is extremely beautiful, particularly around St. David's Bay on the Pembrokeshire coast in the west. Welsh landscape is varied. Snowdonia, in the north of the country, has spectacular mountain scenery, and is a national park. Green hills cover mid-Wales. The southeast is industrial.

PRINCE OF WALES
Edward I of England conquered Wales in 1284, but told the Welsh he would find them a prince who had never spoken English. He then held up his baby son as Prince of Wales at Caernarfon (Caernarvon) Castle. The title passes to the heir to the British throne. Today, Prince Charles is the Prince of Wales.

RUGBY
The national sport of Wales is Rugby Union. The game plays an important part in daily life and Welsh teams play at national and international level. The Millennium Stadium in Cardiff is the world's finest.

Neil Jenkins, Welsh rugby star

KEEP WALES TIDY
PLEASE TAKE YOUR LITTER HOME

EWCH A'CH SBWRIEL GYDA CHI
CADWCH GYMRU'N DACLUS

MAX PENALTY
£1000
COSB UCHAF

WELSH LANGUAGE
Wales is bilingual, that is two languages – Welsh and English – are officially recognized. Road signs are in Welsh and English, and many people in the north speak Welsh as a first language. Teaching Welsh in schools has revived interest in traditional Welsh culture. Poets, speakers, and choirs compete at traditional festivals called *eisteddfods*.

Find out more
ENGLAND
UNITED KINGDOM
UNITED KINGDOM, HISTORY OF

WATER

WE ARE SURROUNDED by water. More than 70 per cent of the Earth's surface is covered by vast oceans and seas. In addition, 10 per cent of the land – an area the size of South America – is covered by water in the form of ice. However, little new water is ever made on Earth. The rain that falls from the sky has fallen billions of times before, and will fall billions of times again. It runs down the land to the sea, evaporates (changes into vapour) into the clouds, and falls again as rain in an endless cycle. Water has a huge effect on our planet and its inhabitants. All plants and animals need water to survive; life itself began in the Earth's prehistoric seas. Seas and rivers shape the land over thousands of years, cutting cliffs and canyons; icy glaciers dig out huge valleys. Water is also essential to people in homes and factories and on farms.

The force of surface tension holds water molecules together so that they form small, roughly spherical drops.

SURFACE TENSION

The surface of water seems to be like an elastic skin. You can see this if you watch tiny insects such as water striders walking on water – their feet make hollows in the surface of the water, but the insects do not sink. This "skin" effect is called surface tension. It is caused by the attraction of water molecules to each other. Surface tension has another important effect: it causes water to form drops.

Molecules at the surface have other molecules pulling on them only from below. This means there is a force pulling on this top layer of molecules, keeping them under tension like a stretched elastic band.

In the body of the liquid, each water molecule is surrounded by others, so the forces on them balance out.

WATER FOR LIFE

All plants and animals, including humans, are made largely of water and depend on water for life. For instance, more than two thirds of the human body is water. To replace water lost by urinating, sweating, and breathing, we must drink water every day to stay healthy. No one can survive more than four days without water.

ICE

Water freezes when the temperature drops below 0°C (32°F). Water expands, or takes up more space, as it freezes. Water pipes sometimes burst in very cold winters as the water inside freezes and expands.

STATES OF WATER

Pure water is a compound of two common elements, hydrogen and oxygen. In each water molecule there are two hydrogen atoms and one oxygen atom; scientists represent this by writing H_2O. Water is usually in a liquid state, but it can also be a solid or a gas. If left standing, water slowly evaporates and turns into water vapour, an invisible gas. When water is cooled down enough, it freezes solid and turns to ice.

WATER

Salty water boils at a higher temperature and freezes at a lower temperature than fresh water, which is why salt is put on roads in winter to keep ice from forming.

WATER VAPOUR

Water boils at 100°C (212°F). At this temperature it evaporates so rapidly that water vapour forms bubbles in the liquid. Water vapour is invisible; visible clouds of steam are not water vapour but are tiny droplets of water formed when the hot vapour hits cold air.

Water falls as rain and is collected in lakes and artificial reservoirs.

Water is cleaned in a treatment plant.

Water tank stores clean water.

Once the water is treated, it is pumped up into a high tank, ready to be used.

With the water high above the ground, the tap can be opened and the water runs out.

WATER TREATMENT

Water in a reservoir is usually not fit to drink. It must pass through a treatment centre which removes germs and other harmful substances. Chlorine gas is often dissolved into the water to kill bacteria and viruses. In addition, the water is stored in huge basins so that pieces of dirt sink to the bottom; filters made of stones and sand remove any remaining particles.

Water can provide an unlimited supply of power, unlike the underground resources such as coal and gas.

SOLUTIONS

Pure water is rarely found in nature because water dissolves other substances to form mixtures called solutions. For example, sea water is salty because there are many minerals dissolved in it. Water solutions are vital to life; blood plasma, for instance, is a water solution.

Sugar dissolves in water, making a sweet-tasting sugar solution.

The sugar disappears when it is completely dissolved.

HYDROELECTRIC POWER

People have used water as a source of power for more than 2,000 years. Today, water is used to produce electricity in hydroelectric (water-driven) power stations. Hydroelectric power stations are often built inside dams. Water from a huge lake behind the dam flows down pipes. The moving water spins turbines which drive generators and produce electricity. Hydroelectric power produces electricity without causing pollution or using scarce resources.

If three identical holes are drilled in the side of a water-filled container, water spurts out much further from the lowest hole because of the weight of the water above.

WATER PRESSURE

Water rushes out of a tap because it is under pressure; that is, it is pushed from behind. Pressure is produced by pumps that force water along using pistons or blades like those on a ship's propeller. Water pressure is also created by the sheer weight of water above. The deeper the water, the greater the pressure. If you dive into a pool, you can feel the water pressure pushing on your eardrums.

POLLUTION AND DROUGHT

In many places, such as East Africa, there is insufficient rain and constant drought. Plants cannot grow, and people and animals must fight a constant battle for survival. Fresh, clean water can also be difficult to obtain even in places with lots of rain. This is because waste from cities and factories pollutes the water, making it unsafe to drink.

Fire fighters connect their hoses to fire engines which contain powerful pumps. The pumps increase the pressure so that the water can reach flames high up in buildings.

Deep underground water stores exist below the surface of the Earth. After a drought, these stores dry out; it may take years for them to be refilled.

Find out more
EARTH
ELECTRICITY
OCEANS AND SEAS
POLLUTION
RAIN AND SNOW
RIVERS

WEATHER

WEATHER DESCRIBES CONDITIONS, such as rain, wind, and sunshine, that occur during a short period of time in a particular place; climate is the overall pattern of weather in a region. From one moment to the next the weather can change. A warm, sunny day can be overtaken by a violent storm. Dark clouds form, high winds blow, and rain lashes the ground, yet it may be only a few minutes before the sunny weather returns. However, in some parts of the world, such as in parts of the tropics, the weather barely changes for months at a time. There it is always hot, and heavy rains fall. Meteorologists are scientists who measure and forecast the weather. They do this by studying clouds, winds, and the temperature and pressure of the Earth's atmosphere. But despite the use of satellites, computers, and other technology in weather forecasting, weather remains a force of nature that is hard to predict.

The air over the Sahara Desert is so stable and dry that rain seldom falls.

Clouds hang over the hot and rainy tropics of Central Africa.

Swirls of cloud mark patterns of winds.

Snow and ice cover the cold Antarctic continent.

WORLD WEATHER
The Sun is the driving force for the world's weather. The heat of the Sun's rays produces wind and evaporates water from the seas, which later forms clouds and rain. The direct heat above the equator makes the weather hot, while the poles, which get less of the Sun's heat, are cold and cloudy.

MEASURING THE WEATHER
Several thousand weather stations on land, ships, and aircraft measure weather conditions around the world. The stations contain instruments that record temperature, rainfall, the speed and direction of wind, air pressure, and humidity (the amount of water vapour in the air). Balloons called radiosondes carry instruments to take measurements high in the air. Weather satellites in space send back pictures of the clouds.

A scale of hours on the recorder shows at what times the Sun was shining.

SUNSHINE RECORDER
The more direct sunshine a region receives, the warmer it becomes. An instrument called a sunshine recorder measures daily hours of sunshine. The glass ball works like a powerful lens, focusing the Sun's rays, which leave a line of burn marks on a piece of cardboard.

The wind spins the cups, and the wind speed is shown on a dial.

Rain pours through a funnel into a container. After every 24 hours the collected water is poured into a measuring cylinder that gives a reading of the day's total rainfall.

Barograph gives a permanent record of air pressure on a chart.

ANEMOMETER
The Sun's heat produces winds – moving currents of air that flow over the Earth's surface. Meteorologists use anemometers to measure wind speed, which shows the rate of approaching weather.

RAIN GAUGE
Droplets of water and tiny ice crystals group together to form clouds, and water falls from the skies as rain and snow. Meteorologists measure rainfall, which is the depth of water that would occur if the rain did not drain away.

BAROGRAPH
A barograph measures air pressure. This is important in weather forecasting because high pressure often brings settled weather; low pressure brings wind and rain.

CLOUDS

Low-lying clouds at the top of a hill cause the air to become cold, foggy, and damp. This is because the clouds contain many tiny droplets of water. Clouds form in air that is rising. The air contains invisible water vapour. As the air ascends, it becomes cooler. Colder air cannot hold so much vapour, and some vapour turns to tiny droplets or freezes to ice crystals, forming a cloud. Slow-rising air produces sheets of cloud. Air that is ascending quickly forms clumps of cloud.

CLOUD FORMATION

There are three main kinds of clouds, that form at different heights in the air. Feathery cirrus clouds float highest of all. Midway to low are fluffy cumulus clouds. Sheets of stratus clouds often lie low in the sky; grey stratus bears rain. Cumulonimbus cloud, a type of cumulus cloud, towers in the sky and often brings thunderstorms.

Cirrus clouds
Anvil of cumulonimbus clouds
Cirrocumulus
Cumulonimbus
Altostratus
Altocumulus
Cumulus
Stratocumulus
Stratus
Ground level

16 km (10 miles)
13 km (8 miles)
9.7 km (6 miles)
6.4 km (4 miles)
3.2 km (2 miles)

CIRRUS CLOUDS
Cirrus clouds form high in the sky so they contain only ice crystals. Cirrocumulus (above) and cirro-stratus also form at high altitudes.

CUMULUS CLOUDS
Separate masses of cloud are called cumulus clouds. Altocumulus is medium-high patchy cloud, and low stratocumulus contains low, dense clumps of cloud.

AIR MASSES AND FRONTS

Huge bodies of air, called air masses, form over land and sea. Air masses containing warm, cold, moist, or dry air bring different kinds of weather as they are carried by the wind. A front is where two air masses meet. The weather changes when a front arrives.

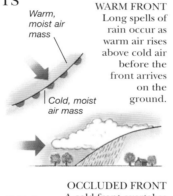

Warm, moist air mass
Cold, moist air mass

WARM FRONT
Long spells of rain occur as warm air rises above cold air before the front arrives on the ground.

COLD FRONT
Cold air moves in under warm air, bringing heavy rain followed by showers.

Cold air mass
Warm air mass

OCCLUDED FRONT
A cold front overtakes a warm front, lifting warm air above it. Rain also falls along an occluded front.

Cold air mass
Warm air mass
Cold air mass

WEATHER FORECASTING

The weather centres in different countries receive measurements of weather conditions from satellites and observers around the world. They use this data to forecast the weather that lies ahead. Supercomputers do the many difficult calculations involved and draw charts of the weather to come. Forecasters use the charts to predict the weather for the next few days, producing weather reports for television, newspapers, shipping, and aircraft.

Lines called isobars give the air pressure, which is measured in millibars.
LOW indicates regions of lowest air pressure.
HIGH indicates regions of highest air pressure.
Red semicircles indicate the advancing edge of a warm front.
Blue triangles indicate the advancing edge of a cold front.

WEATHER CHART
A weather forecaster predicts the day's weather using a chart showing air pressure and fronts over a large region. Lines called isobars connect regions with the same atmospheric pressure. Tight loops of isobars of decreasing pressure show a low, where it is windy and possibly rainy. Isobars of rising pressure indicate a high, which gives settled weather.

HIGHS AND LOWS
The pressure of the air varies from time to time and from place to place. Regions of low pressure are called cyclones or lows. The air rises and cools, bringing clouds and rain. An anticyclone, or high, is a region of high pressure. The air descends and warms, bringing clear, dry weather. Winds circle around highs and lows, as can be seen in this satellite picture of a cyclonic storm.

Find out more
ATMOSPHERE
CLIMATES
EARTH
RAIN AND SNOW
STORMS
WIND

WHALES AND DOLPHINS

TEN MILLION YEARS before humans first lived on Earth, whales were swimming in the oceans. Whales are among the most intelligent of all creatures. They are also the largest living animals, and among the gentlest and most graceful. Whales, dolphins, and porpoises make up a fascinating group of mammals. They are warm-blooded, but unlike seals, they have no fur; a thick layer of fatty blubber under the skin keeps them warm. The whale group is divided into those with teeth (toothed whales) and those without teeth (baleen whales). There are dozens of different toothed whales, including the friendly bottle-nosed dolphin and the ferocious killer whale, which eats almost anything in the sea. Toothless or baleen whales include the humpback and blue whales, which feed by sieving small sea creatures, such as krill, into their mouths. Since all whales and dolphins breathe air, they must swim to the surface of the water regularly. Whales and dolphins swim by moving their tails up and down; fish move their tails from side to side. Whales have suffered greatly from hunting by humans, and 21 kinds are on the official lists of endangered species. Today, whaling is not allowed, in the hope that the population of whales will increase.

THE SOCIABLE DOLPHIN
One of the most playful creatures in the world is the dolphin. This sociable animal lives in "schools" of up to 1,000. They race through the waves, and sometimes can be seen scooting along in front of boats.

BLUE WHALE
The blue whale is the largest animal that is alive today, and it roams all oceans. Blue whales can live to 80 years of age. The skin on the blue whale's throat has many grooves, and expands hugely as the whale feeds.

Baleen plates for feeding

Blowhole (nostrils)

Throat pleats

PORPOISE
There are six different kinds of porpoise. Common, or harbour, porpoises such as the one shown here are often seen in shallow water close to harbours and beaches.

Dorsal (back) fin

BOTTLE-NOSED DOLPHIN
Of all the animals on Earth, the delightful, highly intelligent bottle-nosed dolphin is one of the friendliest and most gentle toward humans.

BLUE WHALE CALF
A baby blue whale weighs about 2.7 tonnes (2.7 tons) when it is born, and measures 8 m (25 ft) in length. The baby whale, or calf, suckles milk from its mother for about seven months before it can start to use the baleen in its own mouth.

TEETH AND BALEEN
Toothed whales, such as the bottle-nosed dolphin shown above, have dozens of sharp teeth for gripping fish and other slippery prey. Baleen whales, such as the right whale shown left, have comb-like baleen plates, also known as whalebone, for sieving krill from the sea.

BREEDING
Like other mammals, a male and a female whale come together to mate. The female usually gives birth in warm seas, because the newborn calf has very little blubber to keep it warm. Most large whales produce just one calf every other year.

Tail fluke

Calf returns to surface, breathes out and rests.

Calf holds its breath and dives under mother.

Calf sucks and swallows milk from its mother's nipple on her underside.

Calf lies by mother's side on surface of water and breathes in air.

MOTHER'S MILK
A newborn whale must learn to breathe air at the surface within a few minutes of birth, or it will drown. It must also dive down to suck milk from its mother's nipples. During the first few days the calf learns how to suckle, then surface for air.

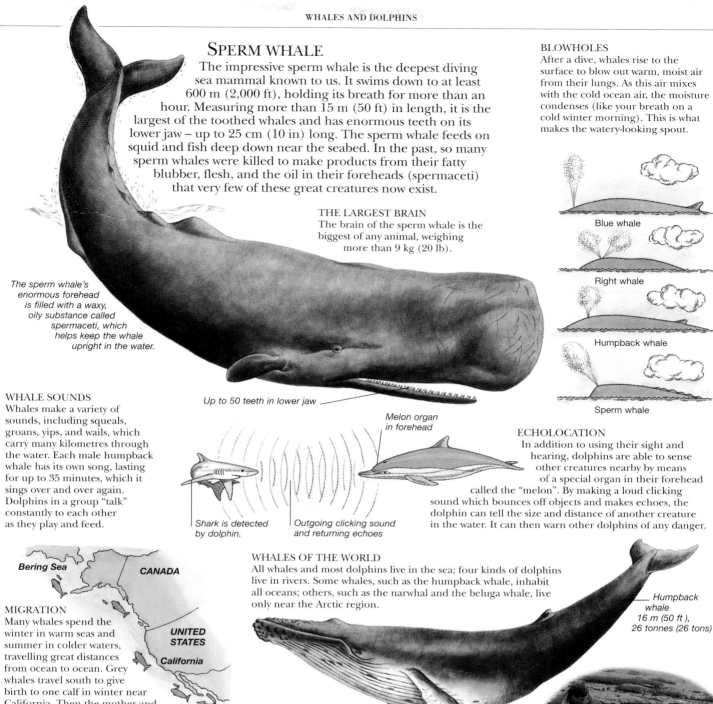

SPERM WHALE

The impressive sperm whale is the deepest diving sea mammal known to us. It swims down to at least 600 m (2,000 ft), holding its breath for more than an hour. Measuring more than 15 m (50 ft) in length, it is the largest of the toothed whales and has enormous teeth on its lower jaw – up to 25 cm (10 in) long. The sperm whale feeds on squid and fish deep down near the seabed. In the past, so many sperm whales were killed to make products from their fatty blubber, flesh, and the oil in their foreheads (spermaceti) that very few of these great creatures now exist.

THE LARGEST BRAIN
The brain of the sperm whale is the biggest of any animal, weighing more than 9 kg (20 lb).

The sperm whale's enormous forehead is filled with a waxy, oily substance called spermaceti, which helps keep the whale upright in the water.

Up to 50 teeth in lower jaw

BLOWHOLES
After a dive, whales rise to the surface to blow out warm, moist air from their lungs. As this air mixes with the cold ocean air, the moisture condenses (like your breath on a cold winter morning). This is what makes the watery-looking spout.

Blue whale

Right whale

Humpback whale

Sperm whale

WHALE SOUNDS
Whales make a variety of sounds, including squeals, groans, yips, and wails, which carry many kilometres through the water. Each male humpback whale has its own song, lasting for up to 35 minutes, which it sings over and over again. Dolphins in a group "talk" constantly to each other as they play and feed.

Melon organ in forehead

Shark is detected by dolphin.

Outgoing clicking sound and returning echoes

ECHOLOCATION
In addition to using their sight and hearing, dolphins are able to sense other creatures nearby by means of a special organ in their forehead called the "melon". By making a loud clicking sound which bounces off objects and makes echoes, the dolphin can tell the size and distance of another creature in the water. It can then warn other dolphins of any danger.

Bering Sea

CANADA

UNITED STATES

California

MIGRATION
Many whales spend the winter in warm seas and summer in colder waters, travelling great distances from ocean to ocean. Grey whales travel south to give birth to one calf in winter near California. Then the mother and baby begin a long journey up the coast toward the Bering Sea and the Arctic Ocean.

WHALES OF THE WORLD
All whales and most dolphins live in the sea; four kinds of dolphins live in rivers. Some whales, such as the humpback whale, inhabit all oceans; others, such as the narwhal and the beluga whale, live only near the Arctic region.

Humpback whale 16 m (50 ft), 26 tonnes (26 tons)

BIGGEST ANIMAL EVER

Blue whales are larger than the dinosaurs were – up to 30 m (100 ft) in length. They are the heaviest animals ever, weighing 136 tonnes (134 tons) – about as heavy as 2,000 people.

Killer whale (orca) 8 m (25 ft), 3.5 tonnes (3.5 tons)

Beluga, 1.5 tonnes (1.5 tons)

Pacific white-sided dolphin, 90 kg (200 lb)

STRANDINGS
Whales sometimes swim too close to the land and are stranded. Without water to support their bodies, they cannot breathe, and soon die.

Human diver, 2 m (6 ft) in length. Blue whale 30 m (100 ft) in length.

Ganges river dolphin, 90 kg (200 lb)

Narwhal, 1.5 tonnes (1.5 tons)

> ### *Find out more*
> ANIMALS
> FISH
> MAMMALS
> OCEANS AND SEAS
> OCEAN WILDLIFE

WIND

AS A GENTLE BREEZE or a powerful hurricane, wind blows constantly around the world. Winds are belts of moving air that flow from one area to another, driven by the Sun's heat. Warm air is lighter than cold air, so warm air rises as it is heated by the Sun, and cold air flows in to take its place. This sets up a circular current of air which produces winds. Light, warm air exerts less pressure on the Earth than cold air, creating an area of low pressure toward which cold air flows. Similarly, cold air sinks and produces an area of high pressure from which air flows outward. The greater the difference in pressure between two areas, the stronger the winds. Weather forecasters use the Beaufort scale to measure the speed of wind. It runs from 0 to 12: for example, force 2 is a light breeze; force 12 is a hurricane. The size and shape of areas of land and water affect local winds, which are often given special names, such as the chinook in North America and the sirocco in Italy.

WIND DIRECTION
A wind is often named according to the direction from which it is coming. For example, a wind which comes from the west is called a westerly. Windsocks (above) and vanes are used to show wind direction.

At the equator, the Sun's heat warms the air. In this area, the air rises, causing a belt of calm air called the doldrums.

Horse latitudes
Path of air
Doldrums

When the air has risen very high, it cools and sinks back to the Earth in the horse latitudes.

Doldrums
Path of air
Horse latitudes

Polar easterlies

Westerlies

The westerlies are warm winds which blow away from the horse latitudes in the direction of the poles.

Horse latitudes

NE trade winds

The trade winds flow from the horse latitudes toward the equator.

Equator

In between the westerlies and the trade winds is an area of calm called the horse latitudes. The name may refer to the many horses that died on ships that were becalmed in this region.

SE trade winds

Horse latitudes

Westerlies

The polar easterlies are cold winds which blow away from the poles.

WORLD WINDS

Besides local and seasonal winds, there are certain winds that always blow. These are called prevailing winds. There are three main belts of prevailing winds on each side of the equator. They are called the trade winds, the westerlies, and the polar easterlies. The direction they blow in is affected by the spin of the Earth. They are angled toward the left in the southern hemisphere and toward the right in the northern hemisphere.

WIND TURBINES
The earliest ships used wind power to carry them across the sea. Wind also powers machines. Windmills were used in Iran as long ago as the 7th century for raising water from rivers, and later for grinding corn. Today huge windmills, or wind turbines, can produce electricity; a large wind turbine can supply enough electricity for a small town. Wind turbines cause no pollution but they are large and noisy and take up huge areas of land.

A wind farm in the United States uses 300 wind turbines to produce electricity.

MONSOONS
Seasonal winds that blow in a particular direction are called monsoons. For example, during the summer in southern Asia, the wind blows from the Indian Ocean toward the land, bringing heavy rains. In winter, the wind blows in the opposite direction, from the Himalayas towards the ocean.

Find out more
CLIMATES
ENERGY
STORMS
WEATHER

WOMEN'S RIGHTS

UP UNTIL TWO HUNDRED YEARS AGO women had few rights. They were not allowed to vote, and were considered the property of their fathers or husbands. By the middle of the 19th century, women were demanding equality with men. They wanted suffrage – the right to vote in elections – and an equal chance to work and be educated. They demanded the right to have their own possessions, to divorce their husbands, and to keep their children after divorce. The fight for women's rights was also called feminism. The first organized demand for the vote occurred in the United States in 1848. By the 1920s, women had won some battles, particularly for the vote and greater education. In the 1960s, women renewed their call for equal rights. This new wave of protest was named the women's liberation movement, and led to laws in many countries to stop discrimination against women.

Yet today, in a few countries, women are still denied full voting rights.

WORKING WOMEN
In the United States about 43 per cent of workers are women. But few hold important positions, and most earn less than men doing the same jobs.

WOMEN'S RIGHTS

1792 Mary Wollstonecraft publishes *A Vindication of the Rights of Woman.*

1848 First Women's Rights Conference, USA calls for voting rights for women.

1893 New Zealand is first country to grant voting rights to women.

1903 Emmeline Pankhurst launches Women's Social Political Union in Britain.

1918 British women over 30 earn voting rights.

1920 The United States grants vote to women over 30.

1960 World's first woman prime minister in Sri Lanka.

1963 US Federal Equal Pay Act outlaws paying women less than men for the same job.

1970 First Women's Liberation Conference, UK.

1970 Equal Pay Act, Britain.

1979 United Nations approves Convention on the Elimination of All Forms of Discrimination Against Women.

EMILY DAVISON
In 1913 British suffragette Emily Davison leaped under the king's horse at a race and died. Her protest drew attention to the Votes for Women campaign.

SUSAN B. ANTHONY
One of the leaders of the suffrage movement in the United States, Susan B. Anthony (1820-1906) helped launch *Revolution*, the first feminist newspaper.

SUFFRAGETTES

In 1905, a British newspaper used the word suffragette to insult women who were fighting for the vote. However, the suffragettes themselves were delighted. People have used the name ever since. Many suffragettes broke the law and went to prison for their beliefs. Women who used peaceful means to obtain the vote were called suffragists.

Suffragettes publicized their campaign by chaining themselves to the railings of famous buildings.

FORCE FEEDING
In 1909, suffragettes in prison refused to eat. Warders fed them by pouring food down tubes that they forced through the women's noses and into their stomachs. It was painful and seriously injured some women. Force-feeding ended in 1913.

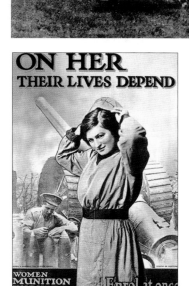

ON HER THEIR LIVES DEPEND

WOMEN MUNITION WORKERS   Enrol at once

WOMEN AT WAR
During World War I (1914-18), women in Britain worked to keep factories going while the men fought. They proved that women were just as capable as men. In 1918, British women over 30 got voting rights. Two years later, all American women also gained the vote.

WOMEN'S LIBERATION MOVEMENT
During the late 1960s and 1970s, the women's liberation movement fought for further improvements in women's rights. Women everywhere demonstrated for equal pay, better health care, and an end to pornography and violence against women.

Find out more
DEMOCRACY
HUMAN RIGHTS
LAW
WORLD WAR I

WONDERS
OF THE ANCIENT WORLD

TWO THOUSAND YEARS AGO Ancient Greek and Roman tourists visited the world's great landmarks just as we do today. Ancient "travel agents" compiled lists of amazing things that travellers should see. These "wonders" were outstanding examples of human artistic or engineering achievement. The seven most commonly listed monuments to human endeavour are called the Seven Wonders of the Ancient World. They all had qualities that made them stand out from the rest. Some were the most beautiful statues, others the largest structures of the day. Of the seven wonders, only one, the Great Pyramids, can still be seen today. The Hanging Gardens, the Temple of Artemis, the Statue of Zeus, the Mausoleum, the Colossus, and the Lighthouse at Pharos have all vanished or are in ruins.

PYRAMIDS
Three pyramids were built at Giza, Egypt, in about 2600 BCE as tombs for three Egyptian kings. The largest, made from more than two million huge blocks of limestone, stands 147 m (482 ft) high.

HANGING GARDENS
In 605 BCE Nebuchadnezzar II, king of Babylon, built the Hanging Gardens in his kingdom. He planted many exotic plants on a brick terrace 23 m (75 ft) above the ground. Machines worked by slaves watered the plants.

MAUSOLEUM
The Mausoleum at Halicarnassus (in modern Turkey) was a huge marble tomb built for Mausolus, a rich governor. It stood 41 m (135 ft) high, with a base supporting 36 columns, under a stepped pyramid. An earthquake destroyed most of the mausoleum.

LIGHTHOUSE
The Greek architect Sostratos designed the world's first lighthouse. It was built around 304 BCE on the island of Pharos, Alexandria, Egypt. It stood about 134 m (440 ft) high. A fire burned at the top to mark the harbour entrance.

TEMPLE OF ARTEMIS
This, the largest temple of its day, was dedicated to Artemis, goddess of the moon and hunting. Built almost entirely of marble by the Greeks at Ephesus (in modern Turkey), it burned down in 356 BCE, leaving only a few broken statues.

COLOSSUS
The bronze statue of the sun god Helios towered 37 m (120 ft) over the harbour entrance on the island of Rhodes in the Aegean Sea. Built in 292 BCE, it was about the same size as the Statue of Liberty in New York.

ZEUS
The great Statue of Zeus, king of the Greek gods, stood 12 m (40 ft) high at Olympia, Greece. Phidias, a famous Greek sculptor, created the statue in about 435 BCE. The god's robes and ornaments were made of gold, and the skin was of ivory.

LOCATION OF THE WONDERS
The map shows the location of the Seven Wonders of the Ancient World. Travellers visited many of them by ship. Most of the wonders were destroyed by earthquakes or fire, but some remains can still be seen in the British Museum in London, England.

Find out more
ARCHITECTURE
BABYLONIANS
EGYPT, ANCIENT

WORLD WAR I

BETWEEN 1914 AND 1918, a terrible war engulfed Europe. The war was called the First World War, or the Great War, because it affected almost every country in the world. It began because of the rivalry between several powerful European countries. Fighting started when the empire of Austria and Hungary declared war on Serbia. Soon, other countries joined the war. They formed two main groups: the Allies, composed of Britain, France, Italy, Russia, and the United States, versus the Central Powers – Germany, Austria-Hungary, and Turkey. In the beginning everyone thought the war would be short and glorious. Young men rushed to join the armies and navies. But it soon became clear that none of the opposing armies was strong enough to win a clear victory. Thousands of troops died, fighting to gain just a few hundred feet of the battlefield. In the end, the war, which some called the "war to end all wars", had achieved nothing. Within a few years a worse war broke out in Europe.

ARCHDUKE FERDINAND
On 28 June 1914, a Serbian terrorist shot Franz Ferdinand, heir to the throne of Austria and Hungary. Germany encouraged Austria to retaliate, or fight back, by declaring war on Serbia. A month after the assassination, World War I had begun.

COUNTRIES AT WAR
The war involved nearly 30 countries – more countries than any previous war. There was fighting in the Middle East, Africa, and the Pacific. However, most of the war was fought in Europe. The western front in northern France was a line of trenches that stretched from Switzerland to the English Channel. Soldiers on the eastern front fought in what is now Poland. Fighting took place on land, at sea, and in the air.

Allied countries are green, Central Powers are pink, and neutral countries are shown in beige.

Norway
Denmark
Sweden
Russia
Great Britain
Netherlands
English Channel
Poland
Germany
Belgium
Austria-Hungary
France
Italy
Spain
Romania
Serbia
Bulgaria
Montenegro

RED BARON
World War I was the first war in which airplanes were used for fighting. Germany's Manfred von Richthofen (the Red Baron) became one of the first air aces.

YPRES
The Belgian city of Ypres was a battleground several times during World War I. It was here that the Germans first used poison gas on the western front. By 1918 the town was devastated (left).

TRENCH WARFARE
The armies advanced as far they could, then dug trenches for shelter. Life in the trenches was miserable. Soldiers were often up to their knees in mud. Lice and rats added to their discomfort. When soldiers left the trenches to advance further, the enemy killed them by the millions with machine guns. Each side also had artillery – guns that fired huge shells – which killed many more and churned up the battlefield into a sea of mud.

U-BOATS
German submarines called underwater boats, or U-boats, sank many cargo ships in the Atlantic, causing food shortages in Britain.

LUSITANIA
On 7 May 1915, a German U-boat torpedoed the British passenger liner *Lusitania*. More than 100 American passengers drowned, some of whom were very rich and famous. This angered many Americans and turned them against Germany. The sinking helped to bring the United States into the war on the Allied side.

WORLD WAR I
June 1914 Assassination of Archduke Franz Ferdinand

July 1914 Austria-Hungary declares war on Serbia.

August 1914 Germany declares war on Russia and France and invades Belgium. Britain declares war on Germany and Austria-Hungary.

May 1915 Italy joins Allies.

July 1916 Allies use tanks for the first time in France.

April 1917 United States enters the war.

March 1918 Russia signs treaty with Germany. Germany's final huge attack at Marne fails.

September 1918 Allies begin their final attack.

November 1918 Germany signs armistice, ending the war.

PROPAGANDA
Wartime posters and newspapers aimed to persuade people that the enemy was evil and that war must go on. The message of this propaganda, or government-controlled news, was that everyone should help by fighting, working, raising money, and making sacrifices. The poster (left) shows a frightening image of Germany with its hands on Europe.

WOMEN WORKERS
As thousands of men went off to war, women took over their jobs in the factories. Most women worked long hours, and many had dangerous jobs, such as making ammunition. Their efforts disproved the old idea that women were inferior to men, and eventually led to women gaining the right to vote. But when the troops returned after the war, there was massive unemployment, and women lost their jobs.

COMMUNICATION
People at home had little idea of the real conditions of the war. Officers read mail from soldiers and censored, or cut out, information that told the true story. Troops returning home were often too sickened by life in the trenches to explain what it was really like or to tell how many soldiers had been killed or wounded.

GERMANS
Until 1918, it looked as if Germany and her allies might win. But they were outnumbered, and when the British navy blocked the ports and cut off supplies of food and vital war materials, the German people rioted. They demanded food and peace, and the Kaiser – the German emperor – gave up his throne. Germany then made a peace treaty called the Treaty of Versailles with the Allied forces. The Germans lost much land and took the blame for starting the war.

DEATH TOLL
Germany and Russia each lost nearly two million soldiers in the war. Britain lost nearly one million. In all, 10 million died.

Find out more
EUROPE, HISTORY OF
WOMEN'S RIGHTS
WORLD WAR II

WORLD WAR II

IN 1939, GERMAN TANKS and bombers attacked Poland, and the bloodiest war in history began. Like World War I, World War II was a global war and was fought on the ground, in the air, and at sea. The war was a result of the rise to power of the German National Socialist or Nazi party, led by Adolf Hitler. The Nazis wanted to wipe out the memory of defeat in World War I. Within a year, German armies, with help from Italy, had occupied much of Europe. Only Britain opposed them. In 1941, Hitler invaded the Soviet Union. But the Soviet people fought hard and millions died. In the Pacific, the Japanese formed an alliance, called the Axis, with Germany and Italy. Japanese warplanes bombed the American naval base at Pearl Harbor, in Hawaii. This brought the United States into the war, and they joined the Soviet Union and Britain to form the Allies. By May 1945, Allied forces had defeated the Nazis in Europe; Japan surrendered in August. When the war ended, 45 million people had died and much of Europe was in ruins. Two new "superpowers" – the Soviet Union and the United States – began to dominate world politics.

HITLER
In 1933, Adolf Hitler came to power in Germany as leader of the Nazi party. The Nazis were fascists: they were against Communism and believed in strong national government. The Nazis ruthlessly crushed anyone who opposed them. They enslaved and murdered Jews, gypsies, and other minorities, whom they blamed for all of Germany's problems, from defeat in World War I to unemployment and inflation.

British Spitfire

German Messerschmitt

The growth of Nazi Germany

Norway

Sweden

Dunkirk

Britain

Soviet Union

France

Poland

Nazi Germany

Czechoslovakia

Austria

Hungary

INVASION
In 1938, Hitler took control of Austria and parts of Czechoslovakia. Britain and France did not oppose him, and he went on to invade Poland. Britain and France then declared war on Germany. German troops smashed into France in 1940, sweeping aside the armies of Britain and France. Fleets of fishing boats and pleasure steamers from the southern coast of England helped the Royal Navy to rescue the retreating Allied soldiers from the beaches at Dunkirk, on the coast of France.

BLITZ
Between August and October 1940, the British Royal Air Force fought the Luftwaffe – the German air force – in the Battle of Britain, and finally won. Without control of the skies, Hitler could not invade Britain. His bombers began to bomb British cities during the night. This "blitzkrieg" or blitz, killed 40,000 people, mostly civilians.

EVACUATIONS
During the bombing of major cities, such as London, thousands of British children were evacuated to country towns and villages where they were much safer.

MIDWAY

Japan conquered many Pacific islands and invaded mainland Asia. However, the United States fleet defeated the Japanese at the Battle of Midway, which took place between 4-7 June 1942. The battle turned the Pacific war in favour of the Allies.

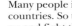

The Soviet advance

The defeat of Hitler's Germany, 1944-45

Britain

Held by Germany at end of war

Liberated by Allied forces — **France**

Neutral

Spain

Advance of Allies

RESISTANCE

Many people in Europe hated the Nazi occupation of their countries. So they formed secret resistance movements to spy on and fight the enemy. They used hidden radios (above) to work behind the battle lines. Resistance workers risked torture and death if they were discovered.

PEACE IN EUROPE

By the spring of 1945, the Allies had recaptured most of occupied Europe and began to cross the Rhine River into Germany. In the east, the Soviet army swept toward Berlin, Germany's capital. Crushed between these two powerful forces, the German armies surrendered. Hitler committed suicide, and the biggest and most expensive war in human history ended.

D-DAY

In June 1944, Allied troops invaded occupied Europe in the greatest seaborne landing ever mounted. Invasion day was code-named D-day. The D stood for deliverance. After a bitter struggle, and aided by resistance fighters, the Allied forces broke through, and the German soldiers retreated or were taken as prisoners.

CONCENTRATION CAMP

After Germany surrendered, Allied troops discovered horrifying concentration (prison) camps throughout Europe, where the Nazis had imprisoned up to 26 million people they considered "undesirable", including millions of Jews. The prisoners were starved and tortured, and many were eventually gassed to death.

VE DAY

On May 8, 1945, the Allies celebrated VE (Victory in Europe) Day. However, there were still another three months of bitter fighting in the Pacific. In August 1945, US planes dropped two atom bombs on Japan, destroying the cities of Hiroshima and Nagasaki. This was done to force Japan to surrender quickly and so save Allied lives that would be lost if the Allies invaded Japan. Within a few weeks the Japanese surrendered and the war ended.

WORLD WAR II

1 September 1939 Germany invades Poland. Britain and France declare war on Germany two days later.

April 1940 Germany invades Denmark and Norway.

May 1940 Germany invades Belgium, the Netherlands, and France.

June 1940 Germans enter Paris, and France signs an armistice (peace agreement) with Germany.

April 1941 Germany invades Greece and Yugoslavia.

June 1941 Germany invades the Soviet Union.

September 1941 Siege of Leningrad (Soviet Union) begins; lasts over two and a half years.

December 7, 1941 Japanese planes attack Pearl Harbor. The United States, Britain, and Canada declare war on Japan.

February 1942 Japanese capture many Pacific islands.

August 1942 German attack on Stalingrad (Soviet Union) begins.

November 1942 Under General Montgomery the British defeat Germany, led by Rommel, at El Alamein, Egypt. Allied troops land in French North Africa to fight Germany and Italy.

January 1943 German armies besieged in Stalingrad surrender.

May 1943 German armies in North Africa surrender to the Allies.

July 1943 Allies invade Sicily.

September 1943 Allied forces land in Italy. Italy surrenders.

June 1944 Allied forces land in Normandy, north-west France, in the D-day invasion.

May 1945 German forces surrender; war in Europe ends.

August 1945 Allies drop atomic bombs on Japan.

September 2, 1945 Japan signs an unconditional surrender, ending World War II.

Find out more

EUROPE, HISTORY OF
NUCLEAR ENERGY
UNITED NATIONS
UNITED STATES, HISTORY OF
WORLD WAR I

X-RAYS

To THE EARLY pioneers of medicine, the thought of looking through the body of a living person would probably have seemed like magic. But today it is routine for doctors and dentists to take pictures of their patients' bones and teeth with an x-ray camera. X-rays are invisible waves, like light or radio waves. They can travel through soft materials just as light passes through glass. For example, x-rays can travel through flesh and skin. But hard materials such as bone and metal stop x-rays, so bone and metal show up as a shadow on an x-ray picture. X-rays have many uses: scientists use them to probe into the molecular structure of materials such as plastics, and engineers make x-ray scans of aircraft to find cracks that could cause mechanical failure. In addition, the Sun, stars, and other objects in space produce x-rays naturally.

WILHELM ROENTGEN
The German scientist Wilhelm Roentgen (1845-1923) discovered x-rays in 1895. Roentgen did not understand what these rays were, so he named them x-rays.

Array of photodiodes – electronic detectors that produce electrical signals when x-rays hit them

Scanner is lined with lead to prevent x-rays from escaping.

A metal object such as a pistol does not allow x-rays to pass through it, so the pistol shows up on screen.

Conveyor belt carries suitcases into the scanner.

Computer receives electrical signals from the photodiodes and converts them into an image of the case.

X-ray tube produces x-rays.

X-RAY TUBE
Like a light bulb, an x-ray tube is filled with an inert (non-reacting) gas, but produces x-rays instead of light.

A strong electric current heats a wire. The energy from the electric current knocks some electrons out of the atoms in the wire.

Monitor screen displays contents of case to security guards.

As the electrons crash into the target, atoms of the metal produce the x-ray beam.

A powerful electric field pulls electrons at high speed toward the metal target.

BAGGAGE SCANNER
Airports have x-ray scanners (left) to check baggage for weapons and other dangerous objects. An x-ray tube produces a beam of x-rays, and a conveyor belt carries each suitcase into the path of the beam. Electronic detectors pick up the x-rays once they have passed through the case. A computer uses signals from the detectors to build up a picture of the contents of the case.

MEDICAL X-RAYS
Doctors and dentists use x-ray machines to look inside their patients' bodies without using surgery. The machine makes an x-ray picture using a digital sensor, or on a piece of photograpic film. The photograph is a negative, and bones show up in white. Large doses of x-rays are harmful, so x-ray examinations must be carefully controlled as a precaution.

X-RAYS IN SPACE
Satellites containing x-ray telescopes orbit the Earth. The telescopes detect x-rays coming from the Sun and stars, and from objects such as black holes. The satellites send x-ray pictures back to Earth. Astronomers use these pictures to discover and understand more of the universe.

Find out more
ATOMS AND MOLECULES
MACHINES
MEDICINE, HISTORY OF
SCIENCE
STARS

ZOOS

PEOPLE BEGAN TO KEEP animals in zoological gardens, or zoos, more than 3,000 years ago, when rulers in China established a huge zoo, called the Gardens of Intelligence. Today, most cities have a zoo, wildlife park, or aquarium, which provide a chance to observe and study hundreds of different animals. However, many people do not agree on the value of zoos. Zoo supporters say that zoos give people the opportunity to be close to animals, which they would never otherwise experience; zoos help us appreciate the wonder of the natural world; and zoo staff carry out scientific research and important conservation work, such as breeding rare species. Zoo critics believe that it is wrong to keep animals in captivity; the creatures behave unnaturally, and in poorly run zoos they suffer because of stress, unsuitable food, dirty conditions, and disease.

EARLY ZOOS
In early zoos, animals such as elephants were taught to perform for the visitors, as shown in this picture. Animals are no longer trained to perform for the public. The purpose of a zoo is to enable people to see how wild animals behave in their natural surroundings. The ideal solution is to save wild areas, with their animals and plants, and allow people to visit these, but this is not always possible.

This huge birdcage is called an aviary.

Tons of animal food are delivered to the zoo each week from all over the world, including eucalyptus leaves from Australia for the koalas.

Storehouse, where food is stored. Zoo trucks take food from here to the animals.

Display boards and guide books full of information provide education.

Gardeners take care of the zoo grounds and look after all of the plants.

Signposts around the zoo direct visitors to different areas.

Thousands of school-children visit zoos each year with their teachers.

Zoo vans collect dirty straw from each of the animal houses.

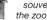
Zookeeper delivering straw to animals

Zoos have restaurants and cafés, where visitors can eat, drink, and relax.

Visitors can buy souvenirs in the zoo shop.

Zookeepers hose down the animal houses every day with water.

HOW ZOOS ARE RUN
A zoo employs zookeepers to look after the animals, zoologists (scientists who study animals), veterinarians, accountants, architects, cooks, gardeners, builders, and many other people. The zoo manager must keep all of these people organized because there are many jobs to do, such as ordering the correct food for each animal and running the souvenir shop and the restaurants. Visitors have to pay an entrance fee toward the upkeep of the zoo, but most zoos also need government funds.

MODERN ZOOS
In some zoos, such as the San Diego Zoo, United States, (left), animals range free in large enclosures with trees and other natural features. People view the animals through glass panels rather than iron bars. You can even see the animals from an open-topped bus. In most countries, inspectors can arrive unannounced to check the welfare of the creatures. A few zoos still treat their captives badly, and organizations such as Zoo Check work toward ensuring better conditions in zoos.

Find out more
ANIMALS
CONSERVATION
and endangered species

Page numbers in **bold** type have most information in them.

A

aardvarks 192
aboriginal Australians 40, 41, 44, 45
absolute dating 252
acceleration 133
acid rain 250
acorns 139, 318
Acre city of 84
acropolis, Athens 148
Act of Union (1707) 328
Act of Union (1801) 321, 325, 327
Act of Supremacy 152
action and reaction 133
actors 126, 127, 149, 278
acupuncture 72, 195
addax 89
Adelaide, Australia 42
adversarial system 177
Aegean civilizations 56
aerosols 251
aestivation 153
Africa 7-12, 123, 146
  East 343
  history 11-12, 55
  North 8
  slave trade 284-285
  West 8
African-American rights 158
African National Congress 12, 158
African Union 12
ageing 157
AIDS 94
ailerons 14
AIM see American Indian Movement
air 38, 187, 234
aircraft 13-14, 38, 108, 110, 166, 200
  autopilot 189
  fighting 351, 353
  and international law 176
  loudness 287
air masses 298
air pressure 344, 345
air-traffic control 79
Akkad 304
Alaska 24, 221, 224, 330, 331, 332
Albania 75
Albert, Prince 336
albino animals 140
Alcock, John 14
Alcott, Louisa May 184
Alexander the Great 47, 158, 240, 241
Alfred the Great 16, 17, 327
algae 252, 277
alimentary canal 91
All Blacks 219
alleles 141
alligators 263
alloys 200
alphabets 15
Alps 209, 210
aluminium 200
alveoli 187
Amazon, River 265, 289
amber 104
American Civil War 333
American Indian Movement 158
ammonites 136, 253
Amnesty International 158
amniotic fluid 261
amphibians 18, 19, 81, 253
amplification 105
anacondas 286
anarchism 142
anatomy 178
  see also human body
ANC see African National Congress
Andersen, Hans Christian 184
Andes 160, 209, 210, 288, 289, 290

anemometer 344
anemones 276, 277
Angel Falls 290
angelfish 231
anglerfish 85
Anglo-Saxon Chronicle 17
Anglo-Saxons 16-17, 177
animals 18-19, 99
  camouflage 264
  and colour 76
  endangered species 81-82, 89, 146, 210
  hibernation 153
  migration 347
  seed dispersal 139
  senses 95
  in warfare 205
  working 155, 160, 304
  zoos 356
  see also amphibians; mammals; reptiles; wildlife
Anne, queen of England 303, 328
anole lizards 186
Antarctica 20-21, 74, 248, 249
anteaters 145, 191
antennae 168
anthers 131
Anthony, Susan B. 285, 349
anthropology 272
anticyclones 345
Antilles 62
antiseptics 197
anti-slavery movement 285
antlions 168
ants 135, 145
aorta 151
apartheid 12, 158
apes 206-207, 254
Apollo moon landing 208, 330
Appalachians 199
Appaloosa horse 155
apples 138
Arabs 26, 30, 34, 57, 162, 273
arachnids 19, 298
Arbroath, Declaration of 327
archaeology 17, 340
arch bridges 133
archers 65, 159, 205
arches 22, 23
Archimedes 273
Archimedes' screw 188, 273
architecture 22-23, 42
  ancient wonders 350
  Caribbean 61
  English 111, 320, 336
  European 113
  Norman 220
  Renaissance 260
  skyscrapers 59, 330
Arctic 24-25, 36, 74, 113, 221, 248-249
Arctic Ocean 25, 26, 228
Arctic tern 347
Argentina 145, 288, 283
  soccer team 289
Aristarchus 35, 97
Aristophanes 149
Aristotle 259
arithmetic 227
Armada, Spanish 106
armadillos 89, 145, 192
armies 142
  Australian 44, 55
  of British Empire 55
  English 112
  Ottoman 233
  Roman 270
Armstrong, Neil 33, 208, 330
aromatherapy 195
art 237, 238
  aboriginal 41
  Ancient Greek 149
  Aztec 46
  Chinese 72
  European 114
  religious 257

Renaissance 178, 260
  see also rock paintings
arteries 151, 157
arthritis 94
Asclepius 196
asexual reproduction 246
Ashanti peoples 7
Asia 26-31, 83, 205
  art 238
  history 30-31
  steppes 30, 145, 146
  Southeast 26, 27, 30, 31
asses 154-155
assassinations 334, 351
asteroids 244, 245
astrology 300
astronauts 33, 234, 296, 297
astronomy 34-35, 194, 273, 274, 300, 310
Atacama Desert 290
Ataturk, Kemal 119
Athens, Greece 148, 149
Atlantic Ocean 36-37, 83, 122
atlas moth 135
Atlas mountains 209
atmosphere 38, 96, 244
atolls 229
atom bombs 354
  see also nuclear weapons
atoms 53, 335
Atrebates 67
Auckland, New Zealand 219
Augustus, Roman emperor 269
aurora borealis 25
auroras 305
Australia 40-45
  history 44-45, 54, 55, 107
  Uluru 40, 41, 267
Austria 351, 353
autobiography 184
avalanches 209
aviaries 356
axles 189
axons 52
Ayers Rock see Uluru
Aymara people 289
Azores 36
Aztecs 46

B

Babbage, Charles 80
Babel, Tower of 175
babies 157, 166, 261-262, 282
baboons 207
Babylon, city of 47, 350
Babylonians 47, 227, 313, 317
backbone see spine
Bacon, Francis 278
bacteria 86, 94, 197, 252
badgers 139
Baffin Bay 60
Baird, John Logie 312
Baja California, Mexico 202
balance 95, 156
balance of payments 314
bald eagle 223
ball game, Mayan 194
Ball, John 239
balloons, hot-air 273
Baltic States 114
Bangladesh 107
banking 114, 204
bank notes 204
Bantu people 11
baobab trees 88, 146
barographs 344
Baroque era 23
barristers 177
bartering 101
Baryonyx 92, 93
basalt 267
baseball 331
bass (fish) 129
Bastille Day 61
Bastille prison 137

Batman, John 42
bats 81, 95, 153, 192, 253
batteries 103, 104, 105, 274
bauxite 200
Bay of Pigs, Cuba 334
beaches 54, 386, 276
beaks 50, 120
bears 24, 153, 210, 248
Beaufort scale 348
beavers 192
Bede, The Venerable 17
bees 66, 132, 167, 168
beetles 102, 167, 168, 174, 210, 212, 319
Beijing, China 70
Belfast, Northern Ireland 323
Belgium 116, 324
Belize 68
Bell, Alexander Graham 274, 309
Bengal 107
Bengal, Bay of 161
Benin, Kingdom of 11
Ben Nevis 275
Benz, Karl 64
Beowulf 17, 184
Bering Strait 26, 224
Berlin, Germany 75, 119
Bermuda Triangle 37
Bernini, Gian Lorenzo 260
berries 192
Bible 47, 175, 241, 242, 257, 259, 303
biceps 211
Big Bang 48, 335
bills see beaks
binary code 80, 312
binoculars 310
binocular vision 124
biography 184
biology 272
  see also animals; plants; wildlife
bioluminescence 85
biome 100
bird-of-paradise flower 132
birds 19, 49-50, 104
  endangered species 82
  evolution 120, 121
  seed dispersal by 82
birth 262
bison 222
Blackbeard 243
black bears 153
Black Death 51, 239
black holes 35, 299
Black Prince 159
black widow spider 298
bladder 157
Blitz 353
blood 151, 157, 211
  circulation 156, 196
blood-letting 197
blood plasma 343
lues 193
Bluetooth 80
blue whales 346, 347
boas 286
boats 133, 162, 235, 280-281, 304
  see also barges; ships
bobcats 210
body see human body
body temperature 192
Boleyn, Anne 152
Bolivar, Simon 293
Bolivia 289, 293
bone 282
  see also skeletons
Bonfire Night 150
Bonny, Anne 243
books 47, 241
  see also literature
Bosnia and Herzegovina 116, 119
botany 131, 272
  see also plants
Botany Bay 44
Botticelli, Sandro 260
bottle-nosed dolphins 346

Boudicca (Boadicea) 67
bows and arrows 205
  longbows 159
brain 52, 156
Braque, Georges 238
brass 200
brass instruments 216
Brazil 123, 265, 288, 292, 293
breathing 157, 187, 234
breeding, captive 82
Brendan, Saint 122
bridges 133, 164, 170
Brisbane, Australia 42
Bristol, England 285
Britain, ancient 53, 67
  Romans and 270
British Empire 54-55, 107, 111, 321, 336, 337
  colonies 12, 40, 44, 54, 236
Britain, Great see United Kingdom
broad-leaved trees 134, 318
bronchi and bronchiole 187
bronze 172, 200
Bronze Age 53, 56
Brown, Arthur Whitten 14
Bruce, Robert the 327
Brunei 27
Brunel, Isambard Kingdom 164
bryozoans 19
Budapest, Hungary 119
Buddhism 22, 30, 184, 257, 258
  Tibetan 71, 72
buffalo see bison
bugs 168
buildings see architecture
burial mounds 17, 118
burials, Viking 339
Burke, Robert O'Hara 45
Burma (Myanmar) 26
burrowing creatures 145, 276, 286
Burundi 8
bushes 247
Bushmen 9
butterflies 82, 131, 132, 168, 224
Byblos 241
Byrd, William 259, 320
Byzantine Empire 57
Byzantium see Istanbul

C

cacti 81, 89
Cairo, Egypt 7
calcite 268
calendars 313
California, USA 330, 331, 332
  see also San Francisco
camera obscura 58
cameras 58, 165
  digital 58
  movie 126
  video (camcorders) 311, 312
camouflage 264
Canada 24, 59, 60, 222, 224
  history 54, 55
Canadian Mounted Police 59
Canadian Shield 60
canals 69, 163, 304
Canary Islands 36
Canberra, Australia 40, 42
cancer 94
canine teeth 308
cannibals 123
canoes 319
Canterbury Tales 323
Canute, king of England 16
canyons 60
Cape Verde Islands 10
capillaries 151, 187
capital cities
  Africa 9
  Asia 28, 73, 162

Atlantic territories 37
Australia 42
Caribbean 62
Central America 69
Europe 115
North America 60
Pacific Islands 236
South America 290
UK 324
USA 332
Capitalism 75, 78
capital letters 15
carbolic acid 197
carbon dioxide 38, 151, 187, 234, 246, 318
cardinal numbers 227
cargo ships 280
Caribbean region 61-62, 77, 243, 284, 326
carnivores 99, 181, 191
carnivorous plants 247
carp 174
cars 63-64, 104, 109, 283, 315
  exhausts 250, 251
  production line 334
  solar-powered 305
  steering wheels 189
Carthage 241
cartilage 279, 282
Cashel, Rock of 327
Caspian Sea 29
Castro, Fidel 78, 293
castles 65-66, 220, 275, 327
Catesby, Robert 150
cathedrals 118, 128, 220
Catherine of Aragon 152
cats 141, 146, 210
  big 100, 181-182
  sabre-toothed 253
cattle farming 41, 218, 288
Cavaliers 112
Cayley, Sir George 14
Ceausescu, Nicolae 295
cellos 215
cells 156
  blood cells 151, 156
  nerve cells 52, 156
Celts 53, 67, 172
centipedes 19
Central America 68-69
cerebral hemispheres 52
Ceres 245
CFCs 250, 251
Chad 8
chalk 267
chameleons 186, 264
Channel Islands 322, 324
Chaplin, Charlie 126
Charles I, king of England 112, 196, 303, 326
Charles II, king of England 112, 128, 303, 326
Charlie, Bonnie Prince 328
Chartists 326
Chartres Cathedral 118
Chaucer, Geoffrey 323
cheetahs 182
chemicals
  energy from 104
  polluting 250
chemistry 163
Chernobyl disaster 295
Chicago, USA 221
Chichen-Itza 223
chickenpox 94
chickens 125
child labour 337
Chile 290
chillies 122, 138
Chimu empire 292
China 26, 30, 31, 70-73, 205, 317, 356
  art 238
  Communism 70, 78
  knowledge 58
  languages 72, 175
  money 204

River Yangtze 27, 29, 73
Shang dynasty 56
writing 15, 72
chlorophyll 246
chocolate 122, 247
cholera 94
chordates 18
Christianity 16, 118, 198, **258**
and art 237
Crusades **84**
and Jerusalem 257
missionaries 55
and Ottoman Empire 233
Roman Empire and 57, 118
see also Protestantism
chromosomes 140
chrysalis 168
Chrysler Building 23
churches 17, 220, 237
Churchill, John *see* Marlborough, duke of
Churchill, Winston 75
Church of England 106, 152, 325
Church of the Holy Sepulchre 257
circuits, electric 103
circulatory system 156, 196
CITES (Convention on International Trade in Endangered Species) 82
cities 113
ancient 46, 269
see also capital cities; towns
citizenship 144
civil law 177
civil rights 158
civil service 143
civil wars
Africa 8, 10
American 333
Central America 68
English **112**, 326
Russia 294
clans 323
classical music 213, 214
cliffs 277
Clifton suspension bridge 164
climate **74**
Antarctica 20
Asia 27, 146, 161
Atlantic Ocean 36
Central America 68
Europe 113, 114, 116
North America 221, 330
see also weather
climbing 209, 234
clocks 189
cloning 141
closed-circuit television 311
clothes 113
historic and traditional 172, 303, 322
clotting, blood 151
clouds 38, 96, 255, 302, **345**
cnidarians 19
Cnut *see* Canute
coal 24, 163, 305
and pollution 250
Welsh 323, **341**
coast *see* beaches; seashore
coats of arms 303
cobras 88
coca 288
cochlea 95
cockroaches 167, 168
coconuts 139, 319
cocoons 298
cod 129
coelacanths 230
Coelophysis 264
coffee 26, 288, 293
coins 204
Cold War 36, **75**
colonies *see* British Empire; *and particular countries*
Colorado River 221, 331
Colosseum, Rome 269
Colossus of Rhodes 350
colour **76**, 312
Columbus, Christopher 77
comedies (drama) 149, 278
Commonwealth, British 55, 107, 325, 326
communications **307**, 309, 352
Communism 31, **78**, 87, 116, 119

China 70, 78
North Korea 75
Soviet Union 75, 78, 119, **294-295**
Vietnam 338
compasses
magnetic 36, 60, **190**
proportional 259
composers 79-80, 165-166, 188, 274, **306**, 309
on aircraft 13, 14, 166
in cars 64
production of 71
in trains 316
and weather forecasting 345
concave shape 180
concentration camps **354**
Concorde 13
concrete 268
conductors 103
congenital diseases 94
conglomerate 267
coniferous trees 134, 318
conquistadors 46
conservation **81-82**, 86, 89, 182
forests 135
grasslands 146
lakes and rivers 174
polar regions 249
wetlands 193
wild flowers 132
Constantine the Great 57
Constantinople *see* Istanbul
constellations 299, **300**
Constitution, US 333, 334
constrictors 286
continental drift 83, 97
continental shelf 229, 231
continents **83**, 97
convergent evolution 121
convex shape 180
convicts 44, 54
Cook, James 44
Copernicus, Nicolaus 97, **259**, 163
copper 200, 290
Copper Age 56
coral islands 161, 162
coral reefs 43, 100, 130, 229, 230, **231**, 235
corals 231, 276
core, Earth's 96
cork 319
corn (maize) 288
cornea 124
Coronal Mass Ejections 305
corona, Sun's 305
corrosion 200
cosmonauts 33, 296
Costa Rica 69
cotton 163, **285**
cottonmouth snake 193
cotyledons 139
Coubertin, Baron Pierre de 232
Counter-Reformation 256
courts 177
crabs 276
crafts
African 8, 11
Native American 223
Roman 270
cranes 190, 280
Cranmer, Thomas 152
crayfish 173
credit cards 166, **204**
crested water dragon 185
cricket (sport) 61, 321
crickets 81, 168
critical mass 226
crocodiles 81, 263, 264
Cromwell, Oliver 112, 303, 326
crops **125**
cruise liners 20, **280**, 352
Crusades **84**
crustaceans 19, 276
crust, Earth's **96**, 97, 98
Crystal Palace 336
crystals 268
Cuba 61, 78, 293, 334
cubism 238
Cugnot, Nicolas 64
cuckoos 50
cuneiform 15, 47, 56
currency 40, 113, 117
pirates' 243
currents, electric 103, 104, 105

currents, ocean 161, **228**, 248
currents, river 265
Cuzco, Peru 160
Cycladic culture 56
cycling 232
disabled 306
cyclones 302, 345
Cyrillic alphabet 15
Cyrus the Great 47, 240
Czechoslovakia 87, 119, 266, 353

D · E

Daimler, Gottlieb 64
Dalai Lama 71
Dali, Salvador 237
Dalton, John 39, 274
dams 265
damselflies 168
dance, traditional 10, 235
dandelions 139
Danes 16
Danube, River **113**
Darius I, king of Persia 240
Dark Age 198
dark energy 335
dark matter 335
Darwin, Charles **120**
date palms 89
Davis, John 289
Davison, Emily 349
Davy Lamp 163
Day of the Dead 257
days 313
D-day landings **354**
DDT 100
death 257, 258
death penalty 176
decibels 287
deciduous trees 134, 247, 318
decimal system 227
decolonization 55
deep-sea wildlife 85-86
deer 134, 146
Delacroix, Eugène 238
deltas 265
democracy **87**, 142, 148, 330
Democritus 39
dendrites 52
Denmark 25
see also Danes
dentists 102, 308
dermatology 195
deserts 26, 43, 70, 74, 100, 223, 290
aestivation 153
cold 88
dust devils 302
hot 89
mirages 180
wildlife 88-89, 153, 223
see also Sahara Desert
desktop publishing 165
detritivores 99
devolution 144, 328
diagnosis 195
diaphragm 187
Dickens, Charles **90**
dictatorships 142
diesel fuel 109
digestion **91**, 157
digital technology 58, 127, 311, 312
Diggers 112
dinosaurs 92-93, **253**, 263, 264, 335
Dionysus 149
Diplodocus 93
disabilities 158, 166, 306
discrimination 158
diseases **94**, 212
diving 234
diving beetles 174
Diwali 258, 313
DNA (deoxyribonucleic acid) 39, **140**
dodo 82
dogs 95
huskies 24, 192
doldrums 348
Dolly the sheep 141
dolphins 121, **346-347**
Dome of the Rock 257
domes 22

Domesday Book 220
donkeys **155**
Doppler Effect 48
dormice 153
dovecotes 66
Dowland, John 320
Downing Street 143
drag 133
dragonflies 174
Drake, Sir Francis 106
drama *see* theatre and drama
drought **343**
drugs 246
Druids 67
drums 8, **216**
DTP *see* desktop publishing
dubbing 127
Dublin, Ireland 170
ducks 173
dungeons 65, 66
Dunkirk rescue 353
dust devils 302
Dutch Elm Disease **212**
DVDs 165, 311
dwarf planets 245
dwarf stars 300
dyeing 241
dynamos 104
eagles 88, 124, 223
Earhart, Amelia 14
ears 88, **95**, 211
Earth 96-97, 99, 244
atmosphere **38**, 96
continents 83
cooling 228
energy resources 108
gravity 97
life 48, 96, 97, 108, 252, 255
Renaissance ideas of 259
satellites' view of 271
and time 313
earthquakes 83, **98**, 201, 234
earth sciences 272
earthworms 283
East Africa 343
East India Company 54
East Timor 29
Easter 258
Easter Island 235
Eastern Europe 75, 87, **116**
echidna 191
echinoderms 19
echoes 287
echolocation **347**
ecology 99-100, 272
see also environment; pollution
ecosystem 99
Edinburgh, Scotland 275
Edison, Thomas 274
editing
film 127
television 311
education, 7, 68, 144
Edward I, king of England 327, 341
Edward III, king of England 159
Edward the Confessor 16
eels 85, 104, **130**, 231, 276
eggs 50, 264, 276
human 261
Egypt, Ancient **101-102**
beliefs 101
boats 281
decorative arts 237
hieroglyphics 15, 102
papyrus 241
pyramids 101, 350
science 101, 102
Tutankhamun 101, 216
Egypt, modern 7, 84
eidelweiss 210
Eiffel Tower 283
Einstein, Albert 274, 313
Eire *see* Ireland
Eisteddfods 323, 341
ejaculation 261
elections 87, 142, 144
electric eels 104
electric motors 104, 109
electric shocks 104
electrolysis 200

electromagnetism 179, 190, 305
electronic tags 176
electronics 58, 79, 80, **105**, 165-166, 274, 312
musical instruments 216
electrons 39, 103
elephants 82, 120, 192
Elizabeth I, queen of England **106**, 150, 303
Elizabeth II, queen of Great Britain 55, 143, 150
El Salvador 68
email 169
embryos 261, 262
emigration **107**
emperor penguins 249
enamel (teeth) 308
endoscopes 180
endoskeletons 282
energy **108**, 109, 307
atomic 226
dark 335
geothermal 97
heat 108
kinetic energy 108
light 179
potential 108
and respiration 234
saving 251
solar 108, 305
engines **109-110**, 133
car 64
jet 13, 14, 110
rocket 109, 234
England 113, 321
history **16-17**, 51, 106, 217, 220, 239, 320, **325-326**
see also British Empire; United Kingdom
English Channel 324
English Civil War 112, 326
English language 111, 175
Enlightenment 119
entomologists 168
environment 20, 81, 94, 121, 306
see also ecology; pollution
enzymes 91, 156, 212
Ephesus, Turkey 350
epics 184
epidemics 94
epidermis 156
epiglottis 91
epithelial cells 156
Equator 74, 97, 344, 348
Equiano, Olaudah 285
equids 154-155
Erasmus, Desiderius 259
Eris 245
erosion 209
Eskimos *see* Inuits
Estonia 114
estuaries 265
Ethiopia 329
ethnic cleansing 119
Euphrates, River 26, 47, 304
Euro 113, 117
Europe **113-119**
Celts 67
colonies 12, 30, 31
history **118-119 198-199**
languages 175
see also Eastern Europe; Scandinavia; Southeast Europe
European Parliament 117, 326
European Union 107, 115, **117**, 170, 314, 326
evacuations 353
evaporation 255
Everest, Mount 29, 38, 73, **209**
Everglades, USA **222**
evergreen trees 134, 247, 318
evolution **120-121**, 253, **254**
executions 176
exercise 211
exoskeleton 19, 167, 283
exosphere 38
experiments, scientific 272
exploration 118, **122-123**, 280
of Africa 11
of the Americas 77
of Asia 31
of Australia 44, 45
by the British 55, 106

exports 314
extinctions 18, 81-82, 93, **253**
eyes **124**, 140, 179
insects' 167
laser surgery 306
Eyre, Edward 45

F · G

Factories 90, 110, 113, 315
Industrial Revolution 163-164
and pollution 250
robots 266
faeces 91
Fairfax, Thomas 112
Fair Isle 322
fairs 198
falcons 100
Falkland Islands 37, 54, **289**
Fallopian tubes 261
false fruits 138
family law 176
famine 8, 171, 233
fangs, snakes' 286
Faraday, Michael 274
Far East 26, 27
farming **125**
Africa 8
Ancient Egypt 101, 102
Asia 27, 29, 70, 161
Australasia 41, 44, 218
Canary Islands 36
Caribbean 61
Central America 68, 69
collectives 294
Europe 114, 170
history 56, 198, 339
Inca terraces 160, 290
intensive 125
North America 60, 201, 332
and pollution 250
Russia/Soviet Union 294
South America 288
UK 323, 341
farm machinery **125**, 188, 306
faults, geological 83, 98, 209
Fawkes, Guy 150
fax machines 309
feathers 49, 50
feminism 349
ferns 134, 247
ferries 280
fertilization 261
fertilizers 250
festivals, religious 257, 258
feudalism 198, **199**, 325
fibre optics **180**, 309
Field of the Cloth of Gold 152
Fiji 235
films 40, **126-127**, 193
cameras 58
finback whale 230
fins 129, 279
Firdausi 184
fire 109, 145, 234
Fire of London **128**
fish 19, 43, **129-130**, **230-231**
bioluminescence 85, 179
breathing 187, 234
deep-sea 85-86
fossilized 136, 252
fresh water 173, 174
polar regions 25, 249
seashore 276
sense organs 95
swamps 193
fishing **228**
ancient world 102, 304
Atlantic Ocean 36, 322
Canada 59
New Zealand 218
overfishing 86, 230, 249
stilt fishermen 161
fission
nuclear 226
fitness 211
flags
Africa 9
Asia 28, 73, 162
Atlantic territories 37
Australasia 43, 219
Canada 60
Caribbean 62
Central America 69
Europe 115, 117
Pacific Islands 236
South America 290

UK 324, 325, 328
USA 332, 333
fleas 51, 168
Fleming, Alexander 197
flies 167, 168
flight, history of **14**, 178
flint working 119, 301, 306
flood plains 265
floods 265
Florence, Italy 260
Florey, Howard 197
Florida, USA 222
flowers **131-132**, 134, 138,
   139, 146, 246, 247
   alpine 210
   festival 322
   roses 132, 321
flu (influenza) 94
fluorescent light 179
flutes **215**, 216
flying fish 130
foetus 261, 262
fold mountains 209
food 18
   chains and webs
      99-100, 230
   digestion **91**, 157
   and disease 94
   fruits 138
   GM 141
   national specialities 72,
      111, 275
   plants 247
   technology 307
football, soccer 289, 328
force 133
force feeding 349
Ford cars **64**, 334
forests 74, 100, 132, 209,
   221, 318
   wildlife 134-135
forgery 204
forum, Roman 269
fossil fuels 250, 251
fossils 92, 120, 136, 191, **252**
Founding Fathers 333
four-stroke engine 109
foxes 99, 100
fractions 227
Fragonard, Jean 238
France 117, **137**, 142, 353
   architecture 23, 118
   colonies 54, 59, 61, 236
   history 67, 152, 159,
      217, 220
   TGV 316
Franklin, Benjamin 104
Franz Ferdinand,
   Archduke 324
free-range animals 125
French horns 216
French language 15, 175
French Revolution **137**, 217
frequencies 287
Freud, Sigmund 197
friction 133
frilled lizard 185
frogs 18, 99, 121, 135
fronts, weather 345
fruits 68, **138-139**, 247
fuel cells 104
fulcrum 189
fungi **212**
fur, mammals' 192
furnaces 172
fur trade 54
Gagarin, Yuri 33, 295
Gaia theory 97
Galapagos Islands 81, 186
galaxies 35, 48, 310, **335**
galaxy clusters 335
Galen 196
Galileo Galilei 35, 147, **259**,
   273, 310
Galileo spacecraft 297
Galvani, Luigi 104
Gama, Vasco da 31, **123**
game reserves 10
gamma rays 35
Gandhi, Mohandas 158
Ganesha 257
gardens 131, 132
Garnier, Jean Louis
   Charles 23
gases 283
Gates, Bill 80
gauchos 288
gazelles 89, 145, 146
gears 189
geckos 146, 185, 186, 264
geese 249, 277
gemstones 268

generators 104
genes **140-141**
genetically modified
   foods 141
genetics 140-141
Genghis Khan 205
geology 272
   see also fossils; rocks
geomagnetism 190
George I, king of Great
   Britain 328
George V, king of Great
   Britain 55
geothermal energy 97
Germany 117, 119, 256
   and World War I 352
germination 139
gestation 192
geysers 340
Giant's Causeway 267
giant stars 299, 300
gibbons 207
Gila monster 186
Gilgamesh 304
gills 129, 167, 187, 234
ginger 135
Giotto 237
giraffes 18
glaciers 21, 224
glass 180, 241
   stained 118
glasses 124
Glendalough, Ireland 171
global warming 24, 250
Globe Theatre 278
Glorious Revolution 303
glucose 211
glypha 119
GM *see* genetically
   modified foods
GMT *see* Greenwich
   Mean Time
goats 210
Gobi Desert 88, 146
gods and goddesses 257
gold 10, 53, 160, 200, 204
   rushes 45, 54, 331
Golden Gate bridge 271
Gondwanaland 83
Good Friday Agreement 328
Gorbachev, Mikhail 75,
   294, **295**
gorges 265
Gorgosaurus 92
gorillas 191, **206**
Gothic architecture 22,
   23, 42
government 142-144
graffiti 80
Grand Canyon **221**, 331
granite 267
Grapes of Wrath, The 183
grasses 145, 154, 247
grasshoppers 145, 168
grassland wildlife 145-146
grass snakes 146, 286
gravity 33, 38, 133, **147**, 228,
   273, 305
Great Barrier Reef 40, 43
Great Bear Lake 60
Great Britain (steamship) 164
Great Dividing Range 41
Great Exhibition 336
Great Lakes 221, 222
Great Plains, USA 221, **222**
Greece, Ancient 118,
   148-149
   architecture 22
   democracy 87
   Homer 184
   knowledge 34, 35, 39 97,
      104, 110, 196, 259, 273
   Olympic Games 232
   slaves 284
   temples 22, 148, 350
   theatre 149
   triremes 149, 281
   wonders 350
   see also Alexander
      the Great
Greek alphabet 15
greenhouse effect 74,
   109, 250
Greenland 24, **25**, 339
Greenpeace 81, 144
Greenwich Mean Time 313
growth, human 157
Guadeloupe 61
Guanajuato, Mexico 202
Guatemala 68, 194
Guernsey 322
Guevara, Che 293

guitars 215
Gulf of Mexico 36, 222,
   228, 302
Gulf Stream 36, **228**
Gulliver's Travels 183
gulls 50, 276, 277
gunpowder 65, 179
Gunpowder Plot 150
Gutenberg, Johannes 273
gypsum 268

H·I·J

habitat 100
   loss of 81 82
Habsburgs 256
Hadrian's Wall 270
hail **255**, 302
Haiti 284
halite 268
hammerhead sharks 279
Hammurabi, king of
   Babylon 47
Hampton Court Palace 152
hamsters 140, 153
Han Chinese 71
hand (measurement) 155
Handel, George Frideric 214
Hanging Gardens of
   Babylon 350
Hanseatic League 118
hardware 80, 165
harems 233
harmonics 287
Harold II, king of England
   16, 325
harvesting 125
Harvey, William 196
hatchetfish 86
Hawaii 120, 235, **331**,
   332, 334, 340
HD (High Definition) 312
health *see* medicine
   and healing
heart **151**
heart disease 94
heat 200
heat energy 108
hedgehogs 88, 153
helium 48, 226, 305
helmets 270, 306, 339
Henry II, king of England
   220, 327
Henry V, king of
   England 159
Henry VII, king of
   England 320
Henry VIII, king of
   England **152**, 325
herbalism 131, **196**
herbivores 99, 191
herbs **131-132**, 247
hereditary diseases 94
heredity 140, 141
herons 174
herring 230
hertz 287
Heyerdahl, Thor 228
hibernation **153**
hieroglyphics 15, 102
Higashiyama, Kaii 238
Highlands, Scottish 275,
   322, 323
Hillary, Edmund 209
hill forts 172
Himalayas 29, 30, 209, 265
Hindi language 15
Hindu-Arabic numbers 227
Hinduism 30, 257, 258, 313
Hippocrates 196
hippopotamuses 193
Hiroshima, Japan 354
Hitler, Adolf **353-354**
HIV 94
Ho Chi Minh 338
Hockney, David 238
Hokusai 238
holistic medicine 195
Holland *see* Netherlands
Hollywood 126, **331**
Holocaust 354
Homer 184
hominins 254, 301
Homo erectus 254
homosexuals 158
Honduras 68, 194
Hong Kong 72
hooves 154
hormones 156, 262
Horn of Africa 10

horse latitudes 348
horses **154-155**
   in warfare 205
horsetails 247
horticulture 132
hospitals 166, 326
hourglass 313
House of Commons 143
House of Lords 143,
   150, 177
Howard, Katherine 152
howler monkeys 207
Hoyle, Fred 48
Hubble, Edwin 35, 48
Hubble Space Telescope 34
Hudson's Bay Company 54
Huguenots 107
human beings 19, 206
   evolution 253, **254**
human body **156-157**
   brain 52
   digestion 91
   heart and blood 151
   muscles and
      movement 211
   reproduction 261-262
   skeleton 18, 156, **282-283**
   teeth 308
   water 342
humanism 259
human rights 70, **158**
   see also slavery; women
hummingbirds 49, 50, 153
humours (medicine) 196
Hundred Years War **159**, 239
Hungary 116, 119, 324
hunting 199, 222, 301
hurricanes 302
huskies 24, 192
hydroelectric power
   265, **343**
hydrofoils 281
hydrogen 48, 226, 305
hypocaust 269
hypothalamus 52
Hyracotherium 154
hyraxes 210
ice **255**, 342
ice ages 74, 224, 253
ice-breakers 24
ice fish 294
ice hockey 59
Iceland 36, 339
Iceni 270
ice shelves 21
ichthyosaurs 92, 121, 136
igloos 24
igneous rocks 267
iguanas 185, 186
Iguanodon 93
immigration 107
   to America 221, 242,
      333, 334
   to Australia 45
   to Brazil 293
   to UK 107, 321, 326
immune system 94
imports 314
Incas 160, 290, 292
incisors 308
inclined plane 188
independence movements
   55, 68, 201, 284, 292, 293
India 22, 26, 30, 54, 87, 142
   ancient observatory 35
   independence 31, 55, 158
   languages 15, 27, 175
   see also Hinduism
Indian Mutiny 54
Indian Ocean 98, 161-162,
   230, 243
Indians *see* Native
   Americans
Indian subcontinent 26, 27
Indonesia 27, 29, 31,
   162, 235
Indus Valley Civilization
   26, 30
Industrial Revolution 111,
   113, 121, 163-164, 285,
   306, 322
industry 307, 314-315
   Asia 71, 72
   Central America 68
   Europe 113, 170
   Soviet Union 294
   UK 322, 323
   USA 332, 334
inertia 133

information technology
   165-166
infrared rays 35, 108
Inquisition 256
insecticides 100
insects 19, **167-168**
   larvae 174, 193
   mountain 210
   prehistoric 253
   skeletons 283
   water 342
insulators 103
interactive television 312
internal-combustion
   engine 109
international date line 313
International Space Station
   33, 296, 297
International Union for the
   Conservation of Nature
   and Natural Resources 81
Internet 80, 166, **169**, 312
Internet Service Provider 169
intestines 91, 157
Inuits 24, 54, 59
inventors 273-274
invertebrates 19
ionosphere 38
Iran 240, 348
Iraq 26, 47, 304
Ireland 170-171, 325,
   327, 328
   see also Northern Ireland
iris (eye) 124
iron 39, 41, 164, 172, 200
   cast 163
   and magnetism 190
Iron Age 53, 56, **172**
Iron Curtain 75
irrigation 8, 89, 102,
   304, 306
Ishtar Gate 47
Islam (Muslims) 257, **258**
   in Africa 8
   in Asia 30, 57, 161, 162
   Crusades 84
   Ottoman Empire
   and 233
islands, formation of 229
Isle of Man 322
isobars 345
ISP *see* Internet
   Service Provider
IT *see* information
   technology
Italy 178, 329
   Renaissance 259-260
Iwo Jima 294, 334
jackals 146
jaguars **181**, **182**, 194
James I, king of England
   (James VII of Scotland)
   150, 278, 303, 328
James II, king of England
   303, 328
Jamestown, Virginia 54
Janissaries 233
Japan 15, 27, 29, 31
   art 238
   Noh drama 184
   pagodas 22
   robots 266
   and World War II 31,
      353, 354
Java, Indonesia 29
jaws 191, **308**
Jaws (film) 127
jazz 213
jellyfish 231, 283
Jenner, Edward 197
jerboas 88
Jersey 322
Jerusalem 47, 84, 257
Jesuits 256
Jesus Christ 237, 257, 258
Jews 107, 233, 257, 258
   Holocaust 354
Johannsen, Wilhelm 140
Johnson, Amy 14
joints 156, 282
Joshua trees 223
jousting 65
Judaism 258
judges 176
Jupiter 208, **244**, 245,
   271, 297
juries 176
Justinian I, Byzantine
   emperor 57

K·L·M

kangaroos 191
Karakoram Mountains 26
Keck telescope 310
Kennedy, John F. 334
Kenneth MacAlpin, king of
   Scotland 327
Kepler, Johannes 273
keratin 50
keyboards (music) 216
Kidd, Captain 243
kidneys 157
Kikuyu people 7
Kilimanjaru 7, 10
killer whales 346, 347
kilts 275
kinetic energy 108
kingfishers 99
King Kong 126
King, Martin Luther 158
Kingsley, Charles 337
Kingsley, Mary 123
King's Men 278
kittens 141
kiwis 218
knights 65, 199
Komodo Dragon *186*, 264
Kon Tiki 228
Koran 257
Korea 27
   see also North Korea;
      South Korea
Korean War 75, 334
Kosovo 119
Krakatoa 340
krill 230, 248, **249**
Kublai Khan 123, 205
Kuiper Belt 244, 245
Kurile Islands 29
lacewings 168
Lake District, England 322
lakes **173-174**
   Africa 10,
   Asia 29
   dry 43, 45
   Europe 170, 171
   North America 60
   oxbow 265
   South America 288
   wildlife 173-174
lammergeier 210
lampreys 129
languages **175**
   alphabets 15
   in China 72
   English 111, 175
   in India 27
   old UK languages 322, 341
lantern fish 85
lasers 273, 274
laser surgery 306
Latin 175
Latvia 114
Laurasia 83
lava 96, 267, **340**
law **176-177**
LCD (liquid crystal display)
   58, 312
lead 268
leaf litter 134
leaf roller ants 135
League of Nations 329
leap years 313
leaves 139, 246, **318**
Lebanon 241
leeches 197
Leeuwenhoek, Anton
   van 197
Leeward Islands 62
legends *see* myths and
   legends
legions 270
Lemaître, George 48
lemurs **135**, 191
Lenin, Vladimir 78, 294
Leningrad *see* St Petersburg
lenses **180**, 310
Leonardo da Vinci **178**,
   259, 273
leopards 181, 182
letters of marque 243
Levassor, Emile 64
levers **189**, 273
lice 167, 168
lichens 246, 249
life 244, 252, 255
light 35, 38, 48, 76, 108,
   124, **179**, 273, 335
   starlight 299, 300
light bulbs 179, 251, 274

lighthouses 350
lighting
  film 126
lightning 103, 104, **302**
light-years 335
Lilienthal, Otto 14
limestone **267**, 268
Lindbergh, Charles 14
lions 18, **181**
liquids 133
Lister, Joseph 197
literature 90, **183-184**
  see also stories; theatre
  and drama
Lithuania 114
Little Women 184
liver 91, 157
Liverpool, England 285
liverworts 246
Livingstone, David 55, 123
lizards 88, 92, 135, **185-186**,
  263, 264, 282
llamas 160
Llasa, Tibet 71
Lloyds building 23, 321
Llywelyn Yr Ail 327
locusts 167, 168
logging *see* timber
London 107, 111, 143, 239,
  321, 322
  buildings 23, 177, 321, 336
  Fire of 128
  Globe Theatre 278
  pubs 323
  Tower of 220, **321**
  underground 317
  Westminster Abbey 16
longbows 159
longships 339
longsightedness 124
lotus flowers 139
Louis XVI, king of
  France 137
Louisiana Purchase 333
L'Ouverture, Toussaint 284
Louvre gallery 178
Lucy (hominin) 254
Lumière, Louis and
  Auguste 126
lungfish 187
lungs 157, **187**
lupins 139
Lusitania 352
lute 320
Luther, Martin 256
Macao (Macau) 31, 72
macaque monkeys 206
macaws 50
Macedonia
  ancient 148
machines 163, 164, **188-189**,
  306-307
  Leonardo's designs
  178, 273
Machu Picchu 160
Madagascar 135, **161**
Magellan, Ferdinand 123
maglevs 317
magma 267, **340**
Magna Carta 325
magnetism 133, **190**
magnetic poles 60, 190
magnetic storms 305
magnifying glasses 180
magnitude (brightness) 300
Maiden Castle, England 53
Maiman, Theodore 273, 274
malaria 94
Malawi 12
Malaysia 26, 27
Maldives 162
mambas 263
mammals 18, 19, 88, 121,
  191-192, 210
mammoths, woolly 120,
  253, 301
manatees 222
Mandela, Nelson 12, 158
mangrove swamps 193
manors 198
manta rays 231
mantis shrimp 277
mantle 96
manufacturing 315
manuscripts 17
Maoris 218
Mao Zedong 31, 78
marble 267, 268
Marconi, Guglielmo 274
Marlborough, duke of 303
Marne-la-Vallée, France 23
Mars 209, **244**, 245, 266

marshes **193**, 222
  salt marshes 277
marsupials 191
Martinique 61
Marx, Karl 78
Mary, mother of Jesus 257
Mary Tudor (Mary I) 320
Mary II, queen of
  England 303
Mary, queen of Scots 106
Mary Celeste 37
Masai people 7
mass 147
Mass, Christian 150
mathematics 194, 227
Mausoleum of
  Halicarnassus 350
Maya 68, **194**, 223
Mayflower 242
Mbeki, Thabo Mvuyelwa 142
measles 94
Mecca, Saudi Arabia 258
Medici family 260
medicine and healing
  195-197
  African 8
  Chinese 72
  herbs 131
  history of 51, 102, **196-197**
  information technology
  166
  technology and 306, 355
medieval era *see* Middle Ages
Mediterranean region 113,
  114, 118, 241
Melanesia 235
Melbourne, Australia 40, 42
Mendel, Gregor 141
menstrual cycle 261, 262
mental health 197
mercury (chemical) 200
Mercury (planet) **244**, 245
Mesolithic Age 301
Mesopotamia 47, 56, 304
  cuneiform 15, 47, 56
mesosphere 38
metal fatigue 200
metals **200**, 268
metalworking 53, 56, 67, **200**
metamorphic rocks 267
metamorphosis 168
meteorites 93, 97, 172, 208
meteorologists 344
meteors 38
methane 251
Mexico **201-202**, 221, 223
  Day of the Dead 257
  early peoples **46**, 68,
  194, 223
Mexico City 61, **201**, 202, 223
Michelangelo Buonarroti
  237, 260
microchips 80, 105, 306
Micronesia 235
micro-organisms 94
microscopic life 230
  plants 247
Microsoft 80
mid-Atlantic ridge 36
Middle Ages **198-199**, 237
Middle East 26, 27, 172, 233
*Midsummer Night's
  Dream, A* 278
Midway 235, 354
Midwest, USA 332
migration, animal 347
military technology 307
milk, mothers' 192
milk teeth 308
Milky Way 335
millipedes 19
mills 164
Milton, John 184
minerals **267-268**
  Asia 26
  Chile 290
  Mexico 201
  North America 59
  polar regions 20, 24
mining 10, 11, 24, 41, 45,
  163, 341
Minoan culture 56, 237
mint (herb) 131, 195
mint (money factory) 204
mirages 180
mirrors 180
  in telescopes 310
missionaries 55
Mississippi, River 222
Mitchell, George 328
moats 65
mobile phones 169, **309**

Moctezuma II, Aztec
  emperor 46
molars 308
molecules **39**, 287
  water 342
molluscs 88
moloch *see* thorny devil
Mona Lisa 178
monarch butterflies 224
monarchies 142, 143
monasteries and abbeys 17,
  152, 198, 307
Monck, George 303
Monet, Claude 238
money 204
Mongol Empire 30, 71,
  123, **205**
Mongolia 155
mongoose 88
monkeys 82, 135, 193,
  206-207
monks
  Buddhist 30, 71, 72
  Christian 17, 196, 213
Monnet, Jean 117
monocotyledons 139
monorails 317
monsoons 161, 348
months 313
Montreal Protocol 251
Monument, the 128
Moon (Earth's) 97, 147,
  208, 228, 271, 313
  missions to 33, 208, 296
moons (planets) 208,
  244, 271
moorhens 174
moose 221
moray eels 231
Morley, Thomas 320
Mosasaur 253
Moscow, Russia 295
mosques 57, 257
mosquitoes 168
mosses 247, 249
moths 89, 121, 135, 168
motion 133
motors, electric 104, 109
motte and bailey 66
Mott, Lucretia 285
mould 212
mountain ash 138, 318
mountains 38, 74, 83, 100,
  209-210
  Antarctica 21
  Asia 26, 29, 30,
  Australasia 41, 218, 219
  Europe 113, 116, 170
  North America 59, 202,
  221
  South America 288
  UK 275, 323, 341
  underwater 36, 229
  wildlife 210
  see also volcanoes
movement, bodily 211
movie cameras 58
Mowlam, Mo 328
Mozart, Wolfgang Amadeus
  216
mudskippers 129, **193**
Muhammad 257, 258
mules 155
multimedia 165
mummies 102
muscles 52, 157, **211**, 234
  of fish 129
mushrooms 212
music **213-216**, 287
  blues 331
  early 16, 259, 320
  instruments 215-216
  traditional 8, 72, 170,
  214, 216
music halls 337
musk ox 249
muskrats 173, 193
Muslims *see* Islam
mutation 140
Myanmar *see* Burma
Mycenaean culture 56
myofibrils 211
myths and legends 183

N·O·P

NAFTA *see* North American
  Free Trade Agreement
Nagasaki, Japan 354
naked mole rats 89
Namibia 329

Nanak, Guru 258
Napoleon Bonaparte 137,
  217, 293
narwhals 248
NASA (National
  Aeronautics and Space
  Administration) 34, 296,
  330
National Health Service 326
Native Americans 59, 221,
  223, 242, 331
  canoes 193
  Caribbean 77
  Central America 68
  rights of 158
  South America 160,
  289, **292**, 293
  totem poles 224, 319
  wampum 204
NATO (North Atlantic
  Treaty Organization)
  75, 119
natural gas 36, 59
natural sciences 272
Navajo people 223
navies
  in Cold War 36
  English 128, 152
  Greek 148
navigation 30, 161, 190
Nazis **353-354**
Neagh, Lough 170
Neanderthal people
  253, 254
nebulae 35, 39, 299
nectar 132
Nefertiti, queen of Egypt 102
Nelson, Horatio 326
Neolithic Age 53, 301
Neptune 38, 244, **245**
nerve cells *see* neurons
nerves 52
nervous system 52, 156
nests 50
Netherlands (Holland)
  116, 142
neurology 195
neurons (nerve cells) 52
neutrinos 35
neutrons 39, 226
neutron stars 299, 300
New Caledonia 235, 236
Newcomen, Thomas 110
New England, USA 221
New Orleans, USA 213
New Testament 259
Newton, Isaac 133, 147, **273**
New Year, Chinese 70
New York City 23, 222, 329,
  330, 332
New Zealand **218-219**, 263
  history 55
Niagara Falls 265
Nicaragua 68
nickel 236
Nigeria 7, 8
nights 313
Nile, River 10, **101**, 265
nitrogen 38
Nobel prizes 197
  for peace 158
Noh drama 184
nomads 30, 74
Normandy, France 159, 220
Normans 66, 320, 325
North Africa 8
North America 221-224
  see also Canada; Mexico;
  United States of America
North American Free Trade
  Agreement 201
North Atlantic Drift 228
Northern Ireland 144, 170,
  321, **323**, 328
  Giant's Causeway 267
northern lights 305
North Korea 27, 75
North Pole 24, 25, 97
  magnetic 60, 190
  wildlife 248-249
North Sea 250
North Sea Oil 275, 321, **324**
Norway 24, 25
notation, musical 213
notornis 82
novels 183, 184
nuclear energy 226
nuclear fission 226
nuclear fusion **226**
nuclear missiles 334

nuclear power 39, 45,
  226, 274
  Chernobyl disaster 295
nuclear radiation 226
nuclear reactors 226
nuclear weapons 39, 75,
  226, 354
nucleus (atoms) 39
Nullarbor Plain 43
numbers 227
nutritional diseases 94
nymphs 168
oak trees 139, **318**
OAU *see* Organization of
  African Unity
Obama, Barack 334
oboes 215
observatories 34, 35
obsidian 194
oceanography 229
oceans and seas 74, 96, 97,
  228, 252, 342
  currents 161, **228**, 248
  tides 208, 228
  volcanoes 340
  wildlife 85-86, 230
  see also Atlantic Ocean;
  Indian Ocean; Pacific
  Ocean
octopuses 231
oesophagus 91
oestrogen 262
office communication 166
oil **390**, 306
  Atlantic Ocean 36
  Brunei 27
oil barriers 251
oil spills 250, 251
oil tankers **280**
Old Bailey 177
Olds Motor Works 334
Old Testament 259
Oliver Twist 90
Olmecs 61, 223
Olympia, Greece 232, 350
Olympic Games **232**
ommatidia 167
omnivores 99, 191
ophthalmology 195
optics 272
oral literature 183
orang-utans 206
orbits 271
orchids 81
ordinal numbers 227
ores 200, 268
organic farming 125
Organization of African
  Unity 12
organs 18, 19, 156, 157
  fish 129
Orient Express 317
Orion spacecraft 296
Orkney Islands 53, 322
Ornithischians 92, 93
orthopaedics 195
oscillation 105
ossicles 95
ostriches 49
otters 173
Ottoman Empire 57,
  119, **233**
outback 41
ovaries
  human 261, 262
  plant 131, 246
Owen, Robert 163
owls 134, 145
oxbow lakes 265
oxen 249, 304
oxygen 38, 39, 97, 151,
  157, 187, 211, **234**, 246,
  252, 318
oxygen cycle 234
oxytocin 262
ozone layer 20, 38, **250**,
  251, 252, 306
Pacific Islands 122, **235-236**,
  331, 354
Pacific Ocean 83, 228,
  235-236
  Ring of Fire 340
paediatrics 195
pagodas 22
painters **237-238**
Pakistan 26, 27
palaeontologists 136, 252
Palenque, Mexico 68, **194**

Palestine 84
Palladio, Andrea 260
Pallas's cat 146
Pallas's sandgrouse 146
palm trees 89, 319
pampas 100, 145, **288**
Panama 68
Panama Canal 69
pandas 71
Pangaea 83
Panhard, René 64
panthers 182
Papua New Guinea 175, **235**
papyrus 241
parallax 300
parasites **167**
Paris, France 137, 217
  Eiffel Tower 283
  Metro 317
Parisii 67
Parker, Charlie 213
parliaments 87, 142
  English 112, 143, 144,
  150, 177, 303, 325
  European 117, 326
  UK regions 275, 321,
  326, 328
Parr, Catherine 152
parrotfish 130
parrots 50, 135
Parthenon 22, 148
Parthians 47
particles 35, 39, 48
Passover 258
passports 117
pasteurization 197
Pasteur, Louis 197, 274
Paxton, Joseph 336
peacocks 50, 134
Pearl Harbor 334, 353
Peasants' Revolt 239
pediments 23
Pedro II, emperor of
  Brazil 293
pelicans 193
penguins 20, 82, 121,
  249, 289
penicillin 197, 212
penis 261
peonies 146
Pepys, Samuel 128
percussion 216
perestroika 295
Pericles 148
peristalsis 91
periwinkles 277
permafrost 26
Perón, Juan and Eva 293
perpetual motion 188
Persepolis, Iran 240
Persians 31, 47, 184, **240**
Persian wars 149
personal computers 79
personal video recorder
  311, 312
Perth, Australia 42
Peru **288**, 292
  Incas **160**, 290, 292
pesticides 100, 125, 250
pests 167
petals 131
petrol 109
pharaohs 101
Pharos lighthouse 350
Philip II, king of Spain
  106, 320
Philip II of Macedon 148
Philippines 27
philosophers, Greek 149
Phoenicians 15, 241
photography **58**
  space 244-245
photons 179
photophores 85
photosynthesis 234, 246, 318
physical sciences 272
physics 272
pianos 216
Picasso, Pablo **238**
Piccadilly Circus 111
Picnic at Hanging Rock 40
pigeons 49
pike 173
pilgrims 107, **242**
pine cones 318
pirates 243
Pitcairn 236
pixels 312
placenta 191, **262**
plague 128,
  see also Black Death

Planck, Max 274
planetary nebula 299
planets 96, 97, **244-245**
　atmospheres 38
　moons 208
plankton 230, 248, 279
Plantagenets 220
plantations 61, 68, 284, 292
plants 99, **131-132**, **246-247**
　aquatic 139, 173, 174
　desert 88, 89
　endangered species 81
　fruits and seeds 138-139
　grassland 145, 146
　mountain 210
　polar regions 248, 249
　oxygen cycle 234
　prehistoric 252, 253
　seashore 276, 277
plastics 39
plastic surgery 306
platelets 151
plate tectonics **83**, 98, 340
Plato 78, 142, 149
plesiosaurs 92
ploughs 125, 188, 273, 304
plums 138
Pluto 245
Plymouth, USA 242
pneumostatic skeletons 283
poaching 82
pods 138, 139
poets **184**, 278
poison arrow frogs 135
poisonous fungi 212
poisonous snakes 286
Poland 353
polar bears 35, 248
Polaroid cameras 58
polar regions 20, 24, 74, 348
　wildlife 248-249
poles see North Pole;
　South Pole
police 59, 142
politics **142-144**, 232
pollination **132**, 167, 246
Pollock, Jackson 238
poll tax 259
pollution 38, 74, 81, 86, 94,
　96, 109, **250-251**
　car filters for 63
　and drought 343
　Industrial Revolution 163
　lakes and rivers 173, 174
　Mexico City 201
　oceans 230
　rivers 265
Polo, Marco **123**
Polynesia 235
Polynesians 40, 122, 218, 331
Pompeii 269, **340**
Popocatepetl 223
Pope(s) 118, 152, 233, 237,
　256, 327
poppies 132, 138
porcupines 146, 192
porpoises 231, **346**
Portugal,
　exploration and colonies
　31, 72, 118, 123, 288, 292
Portuguese man-of-war 283
potatoes 106, 122, 246, 247
potential energy 108
Potsdam Conference 75
pottery see ceramics
poultry 125
poverty 288
　Victorian Britain 90,
　336, 337
power stations 103, 104,
　108, 343
　and pollution 250
Prague 256
prairies 60, 145
prawns 19
prayer 257
praying mantises 168
precious stones 268
pregnancy 192, **261-262**
prehistoric life 252-253
　see also dinosaurs; fossils
prehistoric peoples 118,
　254, 273
　Britain 81, 325
　calendars 313
　and fire 109
　music 213
　Neaderthals 253
　Pacific 122
　tools 172, 268, 273,
　301, 306
　see also Bronze Age; cave

paintings; Iron Age;
　Stone Age
premature babies 262
presidency 142
Presley, Elvis 214
pressure groups 144
prime ministers 142, 143
primates 191, **206-207**
printers (machines) 58, 80
printing 19, 76, 165, 259, 273
prism 76
prisons 176
proboscis monkey 193
production line 334
progesterone 262
prominences (Sun) 305
propaganda 352
propellers 280, 281
prosthetic limbs 306
Protestantism 106, 150,
　256, 320
　in Ireland 328
Protoceratops 93
protons 39
protostars 299
protozoa 18
Prudhoe Bay 25
Przewalski's horse 155
psychiatry 195
psychoanalysis 197
psychology 272
pterosaurs 92, 253
Ptolemy 77
puberty 262
Puerto Rico Trench 36
pulleys **189**, 273
pulp (teeth) 308
pulsars 35, 300
pumice 340
punctuation 15
punishments 176
pupae 168
puppies 192
Puritans 242, 303
Putin, Vladimir 295
pygmies 7
pygmy hogs 81
pygmy shrews 18
pyramids
　American 46, 68,
　194, 223
　Egyptian 101, 350
Pyrenees 116
Pythagoras 273
pythons 263, 286

Q · R

quantum theory 274
quarks 39
quartz **268**
quasars 35
Quebec, Canada 54, 59
Quechua people 289
quipus 160
rabbits 192, 193
race relations 107, 158
　see also apartheid
racing cars 64
radar 13, 35
radar detection 165
radiation, nuclear 226
radio 165, 165, 169, 274
radioactive decay 96
radioactive waste 226
radioactivity 295
radio telescopes 310
radio waves 35, 309,
　311, 312
rafflesia, giant 247
rain **255**, 342, 344
rainbows 76, **255**
rain forests 74, 82, 100, 251
　Amazon 288, 289, 319
　Asia 26
　wildlife 135
rain gauges 344
Raj 54
Raleigh, Sir Walter 106
Ramadan 258
rapids 265
rats 100, 128
rattlesnakes 286
rays (fish) 231, 276, **279**
rays (science) 35
Reagan, Ronald 75
receiver, television 312
Recife, Brazil 293
rectum 91
recycling 200, **250**
red blood cells **151**, 156

red giants and
　supergiants 299
red shift 48
redwood trees 224
reflecting telescopes 310
reflexes 52
Reformation 152, **256**
refracting telescopes 310
refraction 180
refrigerators 251
refugees 107, 321
reincarnation (rebirth) 258
relative dating 252
relativity, theory of, 274, 313
religions 30, 214, **257-258**
religious tolerance 119, 233
Rembrandt 237, 238
Renaissance 178, 196, 198,
　237, **259-260**
renewable resources 108
reproduction
　human 261-262
　plant 246
reptiles 19, 92, 121, 253,
　263-264
　see also particular
　animals
republics 142
reservations 223
reservoirs 265, 343
resistance movements 354
resonance 287
respiration 157, 187, 234
Restoration 303
Resurrection 258
retina 124
revolts 51, 67, 119, 239
　by slaves 284
revolutions 137, 201,
　217, 293
Rhine, River 265
rhinoceroses 82, 192
　woolly 253
Rhode Island, USA 330
Rhodes, Cecil 55
rhubarb 138
rhythm 213
rib cage 187
rice 27, 29, 70, 72, 306
Richard I "the Lionheart",
　king of England 84
Richard II, king of
　England 239
Richter scale 98
Richthofen, Manfred
　von 324
Rio Grande 202
rituals 257
rivers 228, 265, 267
　Arctic 35
　Asia 26, 27, 304
　Europe 113, 115, 171
　North America 202,
　221, 222
　South America 289
　wildlife 173-174
roadrunners 89
Robespierre, Maximilien
　137
robots 266
rock and roll 214
Rocket (locomotive) 317
rockets 296
　engines 109, 234
rock music 214
rock paintings 41
　see also cave paintings
rocks **267-268**
　liquid 96
　pumice 340
　seashores 277
Rocky Mountains 59, 209,
　221, 330
rodents 145, 173, 192
rods and cones 124
Roentgen, Wilhelm 355
Roman alphabet 15
Roman Catholicism
　in the Americas 68, 293
　in England 106, 150,
　303, 325
　humanism and 259
　in Ireland 327, 328
　Reformation and 256
Roman Empire 22, 57, 67,
　101, 118, **269-270**
　aqueducts 118
　art 237
　and Christianity 57, 118
　fall of 198
　learning 259, 273

and London 111, 321
　Pompeii 269, **340**
　slaves 284
Romania 295
Roman numerals 227
Romantic movement 238
Rome, city of (ancient) 269
　see also Vatican City
roots 139, **246**, 318
roses 132, 321
Rosetta Stone 15
Ross Ice Shelf 21
Roundheads 112
rowan see mountain ash
Royalists 112
rubber 293
rudders 280
rugby 219, 341
Rump Parliament 112
runner beans 139
Russia (pre-Soviet) 217
Russian Federation 26, 29
　see also Soviet Union
Russian Revolution 294
Rutherford, Ernest 39
Rwanda 8

S · T

sacrifice 46, 194
Sahara Desert 7, 8, 11, 74,
　89, 344
Saigon, Vietnam 338
St David's Bay, Wales 341
St Helens, Mount 224
St Paul's Cathedral 128
St Peter's Basilica 260
St Petersburg (*formerly*
　Leningrad), Russia 295
saints 122, 171
Saladin 84
salamanders 81, 174
salivary glands 91
salt 268, 272, 342
salt marshes 277
Samarkand 30
San Andreas fault 83, 98
sand eels 276
sand hoppers 276
San Diego Zoo 356
sand tiger shark 230
San Francisco, USA 98,
　271, 331
San Martín, José de 293
sans-culottes 137
Santa Maria 77
São Tomé and Principe 10
saplings 319
Sarajevo, Bosnia 116
sardines 230
Sargasso Sea 130, 228
Sargon, king of Akkad 304
satellites 34, 35, **271**, 274,
　295, 305
　communications 309
　weather 344
　x-ray telescopes 355
saturation point 272
Saturn 208, **245**
Saurischians 92
savanna 7, 145, **146**
saxifrages 249
scales, animal 129, 192, 264
scales, musical 213
Scandinavia 16, 114
　see also Vikings
scanners, baggage 355
　medical 166, 195, 306
scarab beetles 102
Scheherazade 183
Schindler's List 127
science 272-274
　history of 259, **273-274**
science fiction 266
scientific method 272
scientific research 20, 21,
　33, 111
Scilly Islands 36
scissors 189
scorpionflies 168
scorpions 298
Scotland 106, 144, 270, **275**,
　321, 325, 327, 328
　Highlands 275, 322, 323
　Shetland and Orkney 322
　tourism 323
screws 188
sculpture 260, 268
scutes 264
sea see oceans and seas
sea cucumber 86

sea horses 130
seals (animals) 81, 82,
　248, 249
seaplanes 13
searchlights 179
seashore 229, **276-277**
sea snakes 286
seasons 97
sea stars 277
seaweed 231, 247, **277**
sedimentary rocks 267
seed drill 125
seeds **138-139**, 319
seismology 98
Selassie, Haile 329
semen 261
semiconductors 105
senses 52
Seoul, South Korea 29
sepals 131
sequoia trees 318, 319
Serbia 119, 324
serfdom 239
servants 336
service industries 315
sex hormones 262
sex organs 261
sexual intercourse 261
Seychelles 161
Seymour, Jane 152
shadows 179
Shakespeare, William 159,
　183, **278**, 323
Shang dynasty, China 56
Shanghai, China **71**, 317
Shannon, River 171
sharks 18, 130, 230, **279**
　egg cases 276
Sharp, Granville 285
sheep 41, 218
　cloned 141
shellfish 277
Shetland Islands 322, 324
Shetland ponies 155
Shintoism 184
shipbuilding 280, 323
ships 133, **280-281**
　Ancient Egyptian 101
　battleships 337
　cruise liners 20, **280**, 352
　ice-breakers 24
　junks 71, 280
　Phoenician 241
　pirate 243
　sailing 40, 77, 118,
　242, **281**
　slave ships 284, 285
　steamships 164, 281
　triremes 149, 281
　Viking 280
Shire horses 155
Shockley, William 105, **274**
shopping 166
shortsightedness 124
shrubs 247, **249**
Siberia 26, **446**
Sicily 51, 220
sickle cell anaemia 94
sieges 57, 65, 84, 295
Sierra Madre, Mexico 202
signals, railway 317
sign language
　for the deaf 175
Sikhism **258**
silent movies 126
silicon 105
Silicon Valley, USA 332
silk 122
Silk Road 26, 30, 314
silver 200, 201, 292
silverfish 168
Singapore 27, 31, 257
Sistine Chapel **237**
Skara Brae, Orkney 53
skeletal muscle 211
skeletons 18, 156, **282-283**
　of birds 49
　external 19, 167, 283
　of fish 129
skin 140, 156
skinks 185, 264
sky 38
skyscrapers 59, 330
slate 267
slavery 11, 61, 158,
　284-285, 292
　abolition **285**
　in ancient world 269, **284**
　rebellions 284
　slaves, freed 293
sleep 52

Slieve League 171
sloths 135
slow-motion effect 127
slow-worms 186
smell 49, 132
smelting 172
Smith, Maggie 278
snails 153
snake lizards 185
snakes 88, 89, 135, 146, 174,
　193, **263**, **286**
snake's head fritillary 132
snakeskins 82
snow 255
Snowdonia 341
snow geese 249
snow leopards 82
snowmobiles 24
soccer 289, 328
social reform 337
social sciences 272
Socrates 149
software 80, 165
soil 318
solar cells 103, 305
solar eclipses 305
solar energy 108, 305
solar flares 305
solar system 48, 96, 244,
　245, 259
solar wind **305**
solicitors 177
Somalia 243
Somerset, James 285
sonnets 278
Sophocles 149
sound 95, 187, **287**
　waves 48, 108, **287**
sound barrier 13, 14
South Africa (country) 12,
　142, 158
South America **288-293**
　history 292-293
　pampas 100, 145, **288**
Southeast Asia 26, 27, 30, 31
Southern Ocean 20, 228
South Korea 27, 29, 31, 75
South Pole 20
　magnetic 190
　wildlife 248-249
Soviet Union 116, 119,
　294-295
　Cold War 36, 75
　Communism 75, 78, 119,
　294-295
　and Cuba 334
　space programme 33,
　208, 295, 296, 297
　and World War II 353, 354
Soyuz spacecraft 296
space 96
spacecraft 234, 245, **296-297**
space flight **33**, 295, **296-297**, 330
　moon landings 33,
　208, 296
space probes, robot 266
space shuttle 296-297
spacesuits 33
space telescopes 34
spadefoot toads 81
Spain 66, 106, 193
　colonies and empire 68,
　160, 201, 288, 292, 293
　conquistadors 46, 160
Spanish language 175
Sparnodus 136
Sparta 148
special effects 127
spectacled bear 210
spectrum **76**, 273
speech 15
sperm 261
sperm whales 347
spices 122, 135, 138, 247
spiders 81, 210, 283, **298**
Spielberg, Steven 127
spina bifida 94
spinal cord 52, 156, 283
spine 156, 282, **283**
spiral staircases 66
Spitsbergen, Arctic 24
sponges 18, 19
spores 212
sports 154, 171, 275, 331
　Olympic Games **232**
　winter 59, 232
spreadsheets 165
spruce, sitka 318
Sputnik **271**, 295
spy satellites 271

squid 19, 86, 95
squirrels 139
Sri Lanka 27, 30, 161
stained glass 118
Stalin, Joseph 75, **294**
stamens 131
Stanley, Henry Morton 123
starfish 276
starlings 49
stars 35, 39, 48, 179, **299-300**, 305, 310
stars and stripes 333
static electricity 103, 104
static forces 133
steam hammer 164
steam power 110, 163, 273
trains 274, 317
steamships 164, 281
steel 163
Stegosaurus 253
Steinbeck, John 183
stems, plant 246
Stephenson, George 317
steppes 30, 145, **146**
stick insects 168
stigma 131, 132
stingrays 279
stirrup bone 95
stoma 246
stomach 91
Stone Age 53, 56, **301**, 306
stoneflies 168
Stonehenge 53, 313
stories 183, 184, 304
storms 302
Strasbourg, France 117, 326
Stratford-upon-Avon, England 278
stratosphere 38
Strauss, Johann, Jr. 113
strawberry plants 246
string instruments **215**, 320
stromatolites 252
Stuart, John McDouall 45
Stuarts **303**, 328
see also Charles I; Charles II; James I; James II
stunts 126
stupa 22
Sturt, Charles 45
submarines 36
U-boats 352
subsistence farming 125
Sudan 329
suffrage 87, **349**
suffragettes 349
sugar plantations 61, 68, 284, 292
Suleiman the Magnificent 233
sulphur 268
sulphur vents 86
sultans 233
Sumerians 56, 284, **304**
Sun 96, 97, 108, 179, 226, 252, 299, **305**
and climate 74, 344
and plants 99, 246
and rainbow 76
reptiles and 264
and time 313
see also solar system
sunflowers 138
sunset and sunrise 38
sunspots 305
superconductors 103
supergiants 299
supernova 35, 299
supply and demand 315
surface tension 133, **342**
surfing 40
surgery **195**, 197
suspension bridges 164
Sutton Hoo, England 17
swamps **193**, 222
Swift, Jonathan 183
switching 105
swordfish 230
sycamores 139
Sydney, Australia 40, 44
synagogues 107
Syria 11
tadpoles 99
tai chi 78
Taiwan 71, 73
Tallinn, Estonia 114
Tallis, Thomas 320
Talmud 257
tamarins 82
Tamerlane the Great 30, 205
tanks 178, 295
Tanzania 7

Taranaki, Mount 219
tarantulas 81, **298**
tartans 275, 323
Tasmania 41
taste 91
taxes 142, 239
tea 73
tears 124
technological sciences 272
technology 163, 195, **306-307**
Renaissance 259
Roman 270
teeth 254, **308**
animals' 154, 181, 279, 286
tegu lizard 186
telegraph systems 309
telephone poles 319
telephones 165, 274, **309**
telescopes 34, 35, 180, 259, **310**, 335, 355
television 126, 169, 274, 311-312
temperate regions 74, 100, 134, 319
temperature, body 192
Temple of Artemis 350
temples
Buddhist, in Central America 46, 68, 194
Greek 22, 148, 350
Roman 269
Sumerian 304
tendons 211
Tenochtitlán **46**
Tenzing Norgay 209
termites 145, 168
terns 25, 277
terrorism 232
testes 261
testosterone 262
Texas, USA 223
textiles 160, 202, 285
TGV 316
Thames, River 128, 321
Thanksgiving 242
theatre and drama 184
Greek 148, **149**
religious plays 198
see also Shakespeare, William
thermometers 200
thermosphere 38
Thirty Years' War 256
thistles 145
Thomson's gazelles 145, 146
thorny devil 186
Thousand and One Nights, The 183
Three Gorges Dam 27
thresher shark 279
threshing 306
throat 187
thunderstorms 302
Tiananmen Square 70
Tibet 70, 71, 72, 73, 204
ticks 167
tides 208, 228
tigers **181-182**
Tigris, River 26, 47, 304
Tikal, Guatemala 68
timber 26, 59, 60, 319
time **313**, 335
tissues 156
Titicaca, Lake 288
toads 81
toadstools 212
tobacco 106, 285
Toltecs 46
Tonga 235
tongues 91
toothed whales 346
tornadoes 302
Toronto, Canada 59, 222
torpor 153
tortoises 81, **263**
torture 158, 256
totem poles 224, 319
toucanets 139
Tower of London 220, **321**
towns 111, 163, 199
see also cities
trachea 187
trade 122, **314-315**
ancient world 101, 241, 269
animal products 82
Europe 114, 118
imperial 54
medieval 199
North America 59, 201
see also slavery

trade agreements 314
trade routes 26, 30, 36, 122
trade unions 164, 315
trade winds 348
traffic pollution 250
tragedies (drama) 149, 278
trains 60, 109, 110, 164, 222, **316-317**
steam 274, 317
US railways 333
transistors **105**, 274
transmitters 309, 312
transport 154, 166, 274, 307, 321
see also aircraft; cars; ships; trains
Trans-Siberian Railway 317
trawlers 280
treasure maps 243
treaties
Antarctic 21
INF 75
Nanking 71
Rome 117
Tordesillas 292
Troyes 159
Versailles 352
trees 134, 139, 174, 224, 246, 247, **318-319**
prehistoric 252, 253
sacred 67
see also forests; timber
trenches, ocean 229
trench warfare 324
Trent, Council of 256
trepanning 196
Tresham, Thomas 150
Trevithick, Richard 274, 317
trials 176, 177
triceps 211
trilobites 136, 252
triremes 149, 281
tropics 52, 130, 135, 344
troposphere 38
Truman, Harry 75
trumpet gentian 210
trumpets 216
tsunamis 98, **229**
Tuareg peoples 7, 8, 74
tuatara 263
tubers 246, 247
Tudors 320
see also Elizabeth I; Henry VIII
tugboats 281
tundra 26, 74, 100, 221, **249**
Tuojiangosaurus 93
turbans 258
turbines 108, 110
turbofan engines 110
Turkestan 71
Turkey 122, 172, 204, 350
and Ottoman Empire 119, **233**
Turner, J.M.W. 238
turquoise 268
turtles 173, **263**, 264, 276
tusks 308
Tutankhamun 101, 216
Twain, Mark 184
twins 141
Tyler, Wat 239
typhoid 94
typhoons 302
Tyrannosaurus rex 92

U · V · W

ultraviolet rays 35, 96
Uluru (Ayers Rock) 40, 41, 267
umbilical cord 262
underground trains 317
UNICEF 329
unicorn 154
union flag 325
United Kingdom (Britain) **321-326**
emigration and immigration 107
government 143-144
history 325-326
Industrial Revolution 163-164
regional history 327-328
see also Britain, ancient; British Empire; Commonwealth, British; England; Northern Ireland; Scotland; Wales

United Nations **329**
United Nations Environment Programme 81
United States of America 221-224, **330-334**
African-American rights 158
borders 201
Civil War 333
Cold War 36, 75
Depression (1930s) history 333-334
independence
national symbol 223
natural resources 223
and Pacific islands 235
pilgrims 242
slavery 284-285
space programme 296, 297
Vietnam War 334
women's rights 349
and world wars 352, 353, 354
see also Native Americans
universal time 313
universe 39, 48, **335**
upthrust 280
Ur 56, 304
Urals 54, 29, 209
uranium 41, 45, 226
Uranus 245
urbanization 111, 222
urinary system 157
Uruguay 289
UT *see* universal time
uterus 261, 262
vaccinations 197
vagina 261
Valentino, Rudolph 126
Valley of the Kings 101
valleys 265
variable stars 300
vassals 199
vault (architecture) 22
VCR *see* videocassette recorder
VE day 354
vegetables 246, 247
veins 151, 157
Venezuela 290
Venice, Italy 123
ventricles 151
Venus 35, **244**, 245
Venus's flytrap 247
vertebrae 283
vertebrates **18-19**, 191, 283
Vesalius 196, 197, 273
Vespucci, Amerigo 123
Vesuvius, Mount 340
Victoria, Italy 151
Victoria, queen of England 198-199
Victorians 54, 198-199
video cameras 311, 312
videocassette recorders 311, 312
video-phone calls 169
Viet Cong 338
Vietnam War 334, **338**
Vikings 16, 122, 170, 220, **339**
villages 198, 321
villi 91
violets 81, 132
violins 215
viperfish 85
Virgil 184
Virginia, USA 106
viruses 94
viscachas 145
vitamin C 138
viziers 101
Volcán Iztaccihuatl 202
volcanoes 74, 83, 96, 97, 209, **340**
Atlantic Ocean 36
Central America 68
New Zealand 219
North America 223, 224
and rock formation 267
underwater 229
Volta, Alessandro **104**, 274
Vortigern, king of Britain 16
voting 87, 142, 144, 158, 326, 349
Voyager spacecraft 245

Wailing Wall 257
Wake Island 235
Wales 144, 321, **323**, 325, 327, 328, **341**
Wales, Prince of 323, 341
Wallace, William 327
walnuts 138
wars
Africa 8, 10, 12
British Empire 337
Europe 117, 118, 119, 152, 159, 217, 256
Korea 75
USA 334
Vietnam 334, **338**
see also armies; battles; civil wars; World War I; World War II
Warsaw Pact 75
warthogs 308
Washington, D.C., USA 332
Washington, George 332, 333
wasps 168
waste dumping 250
watches 189
water 39, 133, 234, 342-343
and light 180
seed dispersal 139
Water Babies 337
water boatman 174
water cycle 255
waterfalls 108, 265, 290
water lilies 139, 174
water pressure 343
watershed 265
water snakes 174
water solutions 343
waterspouts 302
water treatment 343
water vapour 38, 342
waterweeds 173
Watt, James 110, 273
waves (oceans) 229
waves (physics) 35, 108, 179
sound 48, 108, **287**
weaning 192
weapons 239, 295, 306, 307
prehistoric 56, 172, 301
Viking 339
see also nuclear weapons
weather 38, **344-345**
forecasting 344, 345, 348
mountains 209, 210
rain and snow 255
satellites 271
storms 302
wind 348
see also climate
weather stations 344
weaving 160, 202
webs 298
Wedgwood, Josiah 285
weeds 247
weever fish 276
Wegener, Alfred 83
weight 147
weightlessness 33
weightlifting 108
welding 200, 234
welfare state 326
Wellington, New Zealand 218
West Africa 8
West Indies **61-62**, 107, 284-285
Westminster Abbey 16
Westminster government 143
weta crickets 81
wetlands 100, **193**
whales 21, 230, 248, 249, **346-347**
whale sharks 279
wheat 125, 139, 332
wheelbarrows 189
wheels 47, 56, 273, 306
axles 189
whelks 277
whirlwinds *see* tornadoes
whiskers 95
whisky 275
white blood cells 151
Whitman, Walt 184
Whittle, Frank 110
Wi-Fi technology 80
Wilberforce, William 285
wildebeest 145
wildlife
Africa 10
deserts 88-89, 153, 223
forests 134-135
grasslands 145-146

lakes and rivers 173-174
marshes and swamps **193**, 222
mountains 210
North America 221, 222, 223, 224
oceans and seas 85-86, 230-231
polar regions 248-249
seashore 276-277
William the Conqueror (Willam I) 16, 220, 325
William of Orange (William III) 303, 328
willow trees 174
willows, dwarf 249
Wills, William 45
winches 189
Winchester, England 198
wind 139, 302, 344, **348**
monsoons 161, 348
windmills 198, 306, 348
windsocks 348
wind turbines 348
Windward Islands 62
wisdom teeth 308
woad 53
Wolfe, James 54
wolverines 134
women
medieval 199
Muslim 233
pirates 243
and reproduction 261-262
rights of 137, 158, 294, **349**
Spartan 148
Viking 339
workers 336, 349, 352
women's liberation movement 349
Wonders of the Ancient World 47, **350**
wood *see* timber
woodwind instruments 215
work 108
workers
Soviet 294
women 336, 349, 352
World Cup, FIFA 215, 289
World War I 55, 119, 329, 334, 349, **324-325**
World War II 75, 107, 117, 119, 329, **353-354**
battle of Midway 235, 354
Germany 353-354
Holocaust 354
Japan 31
Soviet Union 294, 295
USA 334
World Wide Web 169
worm lizards 263
worms 19, 282, 283
Wounded Knee, USA 158
Wren, Sir Christopher 128
Wright, Frank Lloyd 22
Wright, Orville and Wilbur **14**, 274
writing 15, 47, 56, 72, 102, 194, 304

X · Y · Z

Xochimilco, Lake 174
X-rays 35, 308, **355**
yachts 37, **281**
Yangtze, River 27, 29, 73
Yeager, Chuck 14
years 313
Xochimilco, Lake 174
X-rays 35, 308, 355
yachts 37, 281
Yangtze, River 27, 29, 73
Yeager, Chuck 14
years 313
Ypres, Belgium 324
Yucatan, Mexico 194, 223
yucca plant 89
Yugoslavia 75, 116, 119, 129
yurts 205
zebras 145, **154-155**
Zeus, statue of 350
ziggurats 47, 304
Zimbabwe 11
zodiac 300
zoology 272
see also animals
zoos 356
Zoroastrianism 240
Zulus 12
Zworykin, Vladimir 312

ACKNOWLEDGEMENTS

Contributors Simon Adams, Neil Ardley, Norman Barrett, Gerard Cheshire, Judy Clark, Chris Cooper, Margaret Crowther, John Farndon, Will Fowler, Adrian Gilbert, Barbara Gilgallon, Peter Lafferty, Margaret Lincoln, Caroline Lucas, Antony Mason, Rupert Matthews, Dan McCausland, Steve Parker, Steve Peak, Theodore Rowland-Entwistle, Sue Seddon, Marilyn Tolhurst, Marcus Weeks, Philip Wilkinson, Frances Williams, Tim Wood, Elizabeth Wyse.
Additional editorial assistance from Helen Abramson, Sam Atkinson, Jane Birdsell, Lynn Bresler, Azza Brown, Liza Bruml, Caroline Chapman, Claire Gillard, Matilda Gollon, Carl Gombrich, Samantha Gray, Sudhanshu Gupta, Prita Maitra, Caroline Murrell, Pallavi Narain, Connie Novis, Louise Pritchard, Ranjana Saklani, Jill Somerscales.

Additional design assistance from Sukanto Bhattacharjya, Tina Borg, Duncan Brown, Darren Holt, Spencer Holbrook, Shuka Jain, Ruth Jones, Sabyasachi Kundu, Johnny Pau, Clare Watson, Simon Yeomans.
Illustration Coordinator Ted Kinsey
Picture Research Maureen Cowdroy, Diane LeGrand, Samantha Nunn, Deborah Pownall, Louise Thomas, Bridget Tily, Emma Wood.

Cartographers Pam Alford, Tony Chambers, Ed Merritt, Rob Stokes, Peter Winfield.
DTP Harish Aggarwal, Georgia Bryer, Siu Chan, Nomazwe Madonko, Pankaj Sharma, Claudia Shill.
Photography Stephen Oliver
Index Jackie Brind
Proofreader Lee Wilson
Additional Production Chris Avgherinos

ADVISORS AND CONSULTANTS

Chemistry and Physics: Ian M. Kennedy BSc; Jeff Odell BSc, MSc, PhD; David Glover; Dr. Jon Woodcock. **Culture and Society:** Iris Barry; Peter Chrisp MA; Margaret Cowan; John Denny B.Mus. Hons; Dr. Peter Drewett BSc, PhD, FSA, MIFA; Dr. Jamal, Islamic Cultural Centre; Miles Smith-Morris; Brian Williams BA; The Buddhist Society. **Earth Resources:** April Arden Dip.M; Hedda Bird BSc; Conservation Papers Ltd.; Peter Nolan, British Gas Plc; Stephen Webster BSc, M. Phil; Earth

Conservation Data Centre. **Earth Sciences:** Erica Brissenden; Alan Heward PhD; Keith Lye BA, FRGS; Rodney Miskin MIPR, MAIE; Shell UK Ltd.; Christine Woodward; The Geological Museum, London; Meteorological Office. **Engineering:** Karen Barratt; Jim Lloyd, Otis Plc; Alban Wincott; Mark Woodward MSc, DICC.Eng. **History:** Reg Grant; Dr. Anne Millard BA, Dip Ed, PhD; Philip Parker MA; Ray Smith; The Indian High Commission; Campaign for Nuclear

Disarmament. **Medicine and the Human Body:** Dr. Sue Davidson; Dr. T. Kramer MB, BS, MRCS, LRCP; Richard Walker; Dr. Frances Williams MB, BChir, MRCP. **Music:** Simon Wales BA, MBA, London Symphony Orchestra. **Natural History:** Kim Bryan; Wendy Ladd and the staff of the Natural History Museum; London Zoo. **Space Science:** NASA; Neil MacIntyre MA, PhD, FRGS; Dr. Jacqueline Mitton; John Randall BSc, PGCE; Christian Ripley BSc, MSc; Carole Stott BA, FRAS. **Sport:** Brian

Aldred; David Barber; Lance Cone; John Jelley BA; International Olympic Committee.**Technology:** Alan Buckingham; Jeremy Hazzard BISC; Paul Macarthy BSc, MSc; Cosson Electronics Ltd.; Robert Stone BSc, MSc; C. Psychol, AFBsF, M.ErgS; Advanced Robotic Research Ltd.; Stuart Wickes B. Eng. **Transport:** Ian Graham; Doug Lloyd; Westland Helicopters; John Pimlott BA, PhD; Tony Robinson; Wing Commander Spilsbury, RAF; M. J. Whitty GI Sore.E.

In addition, Dorling Kindersley would like to thank the following people and organizations for their assistance in the production of this book:

Liz Abrahams, BBC; Alan Baker; All England Tennis Club; Alvis Ltd.; Amateur Swimming Assoc.; Apple UK Ltd.; Ariane Space Ltd.; David Atwill, Hampshire Constabulary; Pamela Barron; Beech Aircraft Corp.; Beaufort Air Sea Equipment; Bike UK Ltd.; BMW; Boeing Aircraft Corporation; BP Ltd.; British Amateur Athletics Assoc.; British Amateur Gymnastics Assoc.; British Antarctic Survey; British Canoe Union; British Coal Ltd.; British Forging Industry Assoc.; British Foundry Assoc.; British Gas Ltd.; British Museum; British Paper and Board Federation; British Parachuting Assoc.; British Post Office; British Ski Federation; British Steel; British Sub-Aqua Club; British Telecom International Ltd.; Paul Bush; Michelle Byam; Karen Caftledine, Courtauld Fibres; Martin Christopher, VAG Group; Citroen; CNHMS; Colourscan, Singapore; "Coca-Cola" and "Coke" are registered trade marks, which identify the same products of

The Coca-Cola Company; Commander Richard Compton-Hall; Lyn Constable-Maxwell; Cottrell & Co Ltd.; Geoffrey Court; Sarah Crouch, Black & Decker Ltd.; F. Darton and Co. Ltd.; Department of Energy, Energy Conservation Support Unit; Adrian Dixon; DRG Paper Ltd.; Patrick Duffy, IBA Museum; Earth Observation Data Centre; Electronic Arts; Embassy of Japan, Transport Department; Esso Plc; Eurotunnel Ltd.; Ford UK Ltd.; Sub Officer Jack Goble, London Fire Brigade; Julia Golding; Brian Gordon; Paul Greenwood, Pentax Cameras Ltd.; Patrick and Betty Gunzi; Hamleys, Regent Street, London; Helmets Ltd.; Jim Henson Productions Ltd.; Alan Heward, Shell UK Ltd.; cartoon frames taken from "Spider in the Bath", reproduced by permission from HIBBERT RALPH ENTERTAINMENT © and SILVEYJEX PARTNERSHIP ©; Hoover Ltd.; Horniman Museum; House of Vanheems Ltd.; IAL security products; ICI Ltd.; Ilford Ltd.; Imperial War Museum; Institute of Metals; Institution of Civil Engineers; Janes Publications Ltd.; Nina Kara; Jonathan Kettle; Haymarket Publishing; Julia Kisch, Thorn EMI

Ltd.; Kite Shop, London; Sarah Kramer; Krauss-Maffei GMBH; Lambda Photometrics Ltd.; Sandy Law; Richard Lawson Ltd.; Leica GmbH; Leyland Daf Ltd.; London Transport Museum; London Weather Centre; The Lord Mayor of Westminster's New Year Parade; Lyndon-Dykes of London; Joan MacDonnell, Sovereign Oil and Gas Ltd.; Neil MacIntyre; Marconi Electronic Devices Ltd., Lincoln; Paul McCarthy, Cosser Electronics Ltd.; McDonnell Douglas Aircraft Corporation; Philip Mead; Mercedes; The Meteorological Office, London; Ruth Milner, Comark Ltd.; A. Mondadori Editore, Verona; Mysteries New Age Centre, London; National Army Museum; National Grid Company Ltd.; National Physical Laboratory; National Remote Sensing Centre, Farnborough; Nautilus Ltd.; Newcastle Hindu Temple; Helene Oakley; Olympus Ltd.; The Ordnance Survey; Osel Ltd.; Otis PLC; Gary Palmer, Marantz Ltd.; Personal Protection Products; Pilkington Glass Ltd.; Pioneer Ltd.; Philips Ltd.; Porter Nash Medical; Powell Cotton Museum; John Reedman Associates; Renaissance Musée du Louvre; Robertson

Research Ltd.; Tony Robinson; Rockware Glass Ltd.; Rod Argent Music; Rolls Royce Ltd.; Liz Rosney; Royal Aircraft Establishment; Royal Astronomical Society, London; Royal Military Academy, Sandhurst; SNCF; Andrew Saphir; Malcolm Saunders, Simon Gloucester Saro Ltd.; Seagate Ltd.; Sedgewick Museum; Shell UK Ltd.; Skyship International Ltd.; Dennis Slay, Wessex Consultants Ltd.; Amanda Smith, Zanussi Ltd.; Ross Smith, Winchcombe Folk Police Museum; Sony Ltd.; Rachael Spaulding, McDonald's Restaurant Ltd.; Stanfords Map Shop, London; Steelcasting Research and Trade Assoc.; Stollmont Theatres Ltd.; Swatch Watches Ltd.; Tallahassee Car Museum; Texaco Ltd.; The Theatre Museum, Covent Garden, London; Toyota; Trafalgar House, Building and Civil Engineering; Trevor Hyde; Wastewatch; Jim Webb; Westland Helicopters Ltd.; Westminster Cathedral; Malcolm Willingale, V Ships, Monaco; Wiggins Teape Ltd.; Howard Wong, Covent Garden Records, London; Woods Hole Oceanographic Institute; Yarrow Shipbuilders Ltd.; The YHA Shop, London.

PICTURE SOURCES

The publisher would like to thank the following for their kind permission to reproduce their photographs: Abbreviations: a = above, b = below, c = centre, f = far, l = left, r = right, t = top.

A
Action Plus: Glyn Kirk 341bl. **Courtesy of Akai Professional:** 216br. **AKG London:** 259bl. **Alamy Images:** Helene Rogers 204crb; Keith Dannemiller 204bl; Michael Gilday 169c; Oleksiy Maksymenko 169cb; Simon Kotowicz 127cb. **Album:** 127t. **Bryan And Cherry Alexander Photography:** 191bc. **Max Alexander:** 219br. **Alvis Ltd:** 266br. **Allsport:** Ben Bradford 61cl; Howard Boylan 323cl; Shaun Botterill 218bl. **Amtrak:** 109br. **Ancient Art & Architecture Collection:** 53bl, 177tl, 177bc; Charles Tait 53tr; N.P.Stevens 102tr; Ronald Sheridan 53cr, 90tl, 148cla, 260ca, 304tl, 327tl, 327bl. **Animal Photography:** Sally Anne Thompson 240bl. **Animals Unlimited:** Patty Cutts 240cr. **Courtesy of Apple:** 79b; 312tr. **Ardea London Ltd:** Francies Gohier 83bc; Chateau Malmaison 119cla. **The Art Archive:** 118cl, 118bl; Chateau Malmaison 119cla. **Ashmolean Museum, Oxford:** 101bc. **Associated Press Ap:** 116cr, 295crb. **Australian Tourist Commission:** 40bl. **National Archaeological Museum:** 56cl. **Neil Audley:** 35bl. **Australian Overseas Information Services, London:** 45bl. **Axiom:** Chris Caldicott 258br.

B
Barnaby's Picture Library: 313bl. **Belkin. com:** 80fcrb. **Bite Communications Ltd.:** 169cl, 169c. **BMW:** 109cb. **The Boeing**

Company: 13ca. **D. C. Brandt, Joyce and Partners:** 22cb, 23clb. **Bridgeman Art Library, London / New York:** *Greeks under Siege* by Eugene Delacroix 106tr; *King James I of England* by Paul Van Somer 150cla, 152clb, 186br; *William Morris*, photographic portrait by Hollyer, 1884 238bc; *Henry Wrothesley 3rd Earl Southampton* 278cl; *Sir Francis Bacon* bust by Roubillac 278cr, 285tr, 303br, 356tr; *Belvoir Castle Henry VIII* by Hans Holbein younger 152tr; Bibliotheque Nationale, Paris 237c; Bonhams *Samuel Pepys* portait by John Riley 128r; Bristol City Museum Art Gallery *Bristol Harbour* 1785, by Nicholas Pocock 285tl; British Library 16bc, St. Cuthbert from Bede 8th century 17clb, Queen Mary Psalter, bailiff berating peasants 239bc; British Museum 15cb; British Museum London, *Nineveh Epic of Gilgaresh* (clay tablet 7th Century BC) 304tl; British Museum, London 39cb, 195cl, 237tl; Christies, London 252tr; Eton College, Windsor 195cr; Forbes Magazine Collection 217crb; Galleria Degli Uffizi 328tl; Galleria dell Accademia Firenze 260bl; Hever Castle 152crb; Lambeth Palace Library collection, burning of Thomas Cranmer from the *Foxe's Book of Martyrs* 1563 (woodcut), 320bl; Lauros Girandon Musée de la Ville de Paris; *Leeds Museum and Gallery Kirkstall Abbey* by George Alexander 152bl; Louvre, Paris 148cc, 256bc; Musée d'Orsay, Paris (© DACS) 238cr; National Portrait Gallery 106tl; New Zealand High Commission,

London 219cl; *Henry VIII*, portait, Philip Mould 152tl; Phillips Fine Art Auctioneers 320tl; Sherlock Holmes 186br, 333cr; Richard Philip 16br; Royal Albert Memorial Museum *Olandah Equiano* portrait 1780's 285bc; Staaliche Museen zu Berlin 67bc; T.U.C. London 164cb; Tate Gallery, London 47bc; Wilberforce House Museum, Hull *The Kneeling Slave* 13th century, England (painting) 285cl. **British Film Institute:** Stills, Posters and Designs 127tr. **British Library, London:** 17tl, 51cra, 51crb, 56bl, 198bl, 198bc; Stuart 303tr. **British Museum, London:** 46cl, 56br; British Museum 17bc. **Britstock-ifa:** 150bc. **British Tourist Authority:** 321bl.

C
Casio: 312tr. **Bruce Coleman Ltd:** 52crb, 68cr, 70cr, 72tl, 95bl, 96tl, 139bc, 154tr, 214cr, 235bc, 235bcr, 247crb, 319br, 331bl, 334bc; Jack Dermid 277tl; Bernol Thies 277cla; Brian Coates 50bl, 235bcl; C.B. Frith 94tl, 94tl, 155tr; Charles Henneghein 74bc, 174tr; Chris Hollerbeck 331tl; David Davies 265bc; David Hughes 276tl; Dieter & Mary Plage 348crb, 214cl; Dr. Echart Pott 180bc, 250bl; Dr. Frieder Sanct 203c; Eric Crichton 131cb; Fitz Prenzel 38bl; G. D. Plage 154cl, 181cl, 155cc; Gene A. Ahrens 330tl; Gerald Cubitt 26bc, 82cr, 161c, 190bl; Hans Reinhardt 115bl; 190cb; Hans Richard 104tr; Inigo Everson 249tc, 249cr; Jane Burton 100bc, 146cl, 202bc, 212crb; Jaroslav Poncar 343cla; Jeff Simon 174clb; Joe Van Wormer 249bl; John Markhom 51cb; John Shaw 97c, 255br; Jonathan Wright 228tl, 281tr; Keith Gunner 209cl; Kim Taylor 105bc, 121cl, 212cra, 350tl; Leonard Lee Rue III 308cr; M. Timothy

O' Keefe 264tr; Michael Freeman 216bc; Michel Viard 212tl; N.A.S.A. 96cr, 99tl, 208bl; Norbert Rosig 115tr; Norbert Schwertz 340crb; Norman Myers 207bl, 250tr; Norman Owen Tomalin 206crb, 265cra, 329cra; Norman Plyers 181tr; R. Campbell 136crb; Rod Williams 207cl; Udo Hirsch 160cl; Vatican Museums and Galleries, Rome 237clb; Walter Lankinen 174cl, 153cb, 153bl, 38bc; Werner Stoy 96c, 340clb. **Collections:** Bill Wells 138bc; Brian Keen 323cr; Brian Shuel 170cr, 171bl, 176crb; Gena Davies 341cla; Geoff Howard 176crb; John Miller 176bl; Nigel Hawkins 111bl; Sandra Lousada 323br; Select 225bc; Yuri Lewinski 17cr. **Corbis UK Ltd.:** Adrian Wilson / Beateworks 311c; Andy Rain / EPA 143bl; Car Culture 63cb; E.M. Pasieka / Science Photo Library 52crb; Karen Kasmauski 256bl; Keith Hunter / Arcaid 144cr; John Noble 24b; Moodboard 179tc; Murat Taner 326cb; Peter Beck 195crb; Reuters 244br; Rolf Vennebernd / EPA 64c; Frederic Larson / San Francisco Chronicle 98clb; Ariel Skelley 169crb; Tom Wagner 166tl.

D, E
James Davis Travel Photography: 36cr. **Dickens House Museum:** 90tr, 90bl. **DK Images:** NASA 290tr. **Dominic Photography:** Zoe Dominic 278bl. **Empics Ltd.:** 232tr. **T. Malcolm English:** 255bc. **Environmental Images:** Steve Morgan 144ca; Toby Adamson 141bl. **European Space Agency:** 35cra. **European Parliament Photolibrary:** 117cl, 117bl. **Mary Evans Picture Library:** 12tl, 12tr, 14br, 39tr, 39bl, 45tl, 45cl, 57clb, 67tl, 84cr, 84bl, 84bl, 87tr, 87cl, 97bv, 104bl, 110cb, 112tr, 112cb, 112bl,